DUMBARTON OAKS
MEDIEVAL LIBRARY

Daniel Donoghue, General Editor

THE OLD ENGLISH
CATHOLIC HOMILIES

ÆLFRIC

DOML 86

The Old English Catholic Homilies

The First Series

ÆLFRIC

Edited and Translated by

ROY M. LIUZZA

DUMBARTON OAKS
MEDIEVAL LIBRARY

HARVARD UNIVERSITY PRESS
CAMBRIDGE, MASSACHUSETTS
LONDON, ENGLAND
2024

Library of Congress Cataloging-in-Publication Data

Names: Aelfric, Abbot of Eynsham, author. | Liuzza, R. M., editor, translator. |
    Aelfric, Abbot of Eynsham. Catholic homilies. 1st series. | Aelfric, Abbot of
    Eynsham. Catholic homilies. 1st series. English.

Title: The Old English Catholic homilies / Ælfric, edited and translated by Roy M.
    Liuzza.

Other titles: Dumbarton Oaks medieval library ; 86.

Description: Cambridge : Harvard University Press, 2024– | Series: Dumbarton
    Oaks medieval library ; DOML 86 | Includes bibliographical references and
    index. | Contents: [vol. 1]. The First Series—Introduction—Latin preface—
    English preface—On the Origin of the created world—The nativity of the
    Lord—Saint Stephen—Assumption of John the Evangelist—The Feast of the
    Holy Innocents—Circumcision—Epiphany—Third Sunday after Epiphany—
    Purification—Quinquagesima—(Sunday before Ash Wednesday)—First Sunday
    in Lent—Mid-Lent Sunday—Annunciation—Palm Sunday—Easter Sunday—
    First Sunday after Easter—Second Sunday after Easter—On the greater Litany—
    (Rogationtide)—Tuesday, on the Lord's Prayer—Wednesday, on the Catholic
    faith—Ascension—Pentecost—Second Sunday after Pentecost—Fourth Sunday
    after Pentecost—The nativity of John the Baptist—The Passion of the apostles—
    Peter and Paul—Saint Paul—Eleventh Sunday after Pentecost—Saint
    Lawrence—Assumption of Mary—Saint Bartholomew—The beheading of John
    the Baptist—Seventeenth Sunday after Pentecost—Dedication of the Church of
    Saint Michael the Archangel—Twenty-first Sunday after Pentecost—All Saints—
    Saint Clement—Saint Andrew—First Sunday in Advent—Second Sunday in
    Advent—Abbreviations—Notes on the text—Notes to the text—Notes to the
    translation. | Old English with English translation on facing pages; Latin preface
    with English translation on facing pages; introduction in English.

Identifiers: LCCN 2024002698 | ISBN 9780674297685 (cloth)

Subjects: LCSH: Catholic Church—Sermons—Early works to 1800. | Christian
    literature, English (Old)—Early works to 1800. | Sermons, English (Old)—Early
    works to 1800. | Sermons, Medieval—England—Early works to 1800.

Classification: LCC BX1756.A447 A38 2024 | DDC 252—dc23/eng/20240513

LC record available at https://lccn.loc.gov/2024002698

Contents

Introduction   ix

LATIN PREFACE   2

ENGLISH PREFACE   6

1. ON THE ORIGIN OF THE CREATED
WORLD   14

2. THE NATIVITY OF THE LORD   38

3. SAINT STEPHEN   56

4. ASSUMPTION OF JOHN THE EVANGELIST   72

5. THE FEAST OF THE HOLY INNOCENTS   94

6. CIRCUMCISION   110

7. EPIPHANY   126

8. THIRD SUNDAY AFTER EPIPHANY   146

9. PURIFICATION   162

CONTENTS

10. Quinquagesima
(Sunday before Ash Wednesday) 182

11. First Sunday in Lent 198

12. Mid-Lent Sunday 216

13. Annunciation 230

14. Palm Sunday 248

15. Easter Sunday 264

16. First Sunday after Easter 280

17. Second Sunday after Easter 292

18. On the Greater Litany
(Rogationtide) 300

19. Tuesday, On the Lord's Prayer 316

20. Wednesday, On the
Catholic Faith 336

21. Ascension 358

22. Pentecost 378

23. Second Sunday after Pentecost 398

24. Fourth Sunday after Pentecost 410

CONTENTS

25. THE NATIVITY OF
JOHN THE BAPTIST   428

26. THE PASSION OF THE
APOSTLES PETER AND PAUL   446

27. SAINT PAUL   470

28. ELEVENTH SUNDAY
AFTER PENTECOST   490

29. SAINT LAWRENCE   508

30. ASSUMPTION OF MARY   530

31. SAINT BARTHOLOMEW   552

32. THE BEHEADING OF
JOHN THE BAPTIST   578

33. SEVENTEENTH SUNDAY
AFTER PENTECOST   596

34. DEDICATION OF THE CHURCH OF
SAINT MICHAEL THE ARCHANGEL   608

35. TWENTY-FIRST SUNDAY
AFTER PENTECOST   630

36. ALL SAINTS   652

37. SAINT CLEMENT   676

CONTENTS

38. Saint Andrew 698

39. First Sunday in Advent 726

40. Second Sunday in Advent 734

Abbreviations 751
Note on the Text 753
Notes to the Text 771
Notes to the Translation 805
Bibliography 869
Index 871

Introduction

This volume is the first of two containing a series of homilies and sermons written between 987 and 995 CE by the English monk and abbot Ælfric of Eynsham, collected by him into two sets now known as the *Catholic Homilies,* First Series, and *Catholic Homilies,* Second Series (CH 1 and CH 2). In the English Preface to the First Series, Ælfric says that he was moved to write them "because I saw and heard great error in many English books, which unlearned people in their simplicity have taken for great wisdom, and I regretted that they did not know or did not have the gospel teaching among their writings" (CH 1.0.5). He describes his work as a "translation," though it is quite a bit more than that, and he presumes that it will be used for preaching by the clergy to lay people. Like much else in Ælfric's substantial and diverse body of work, the *Catholic Homilies* are written with distinctive clarity and care and reveal a breadth of learning and accomplishment that is almost unrivaled in English in the early medieval period. They were widely copied and circulated long after the Norman Conquest and stand as one of the monuments of Old English literary and religious culture.

ÆLFRIC'S LIFE AND TIMES

Though Ælfric's work was widely read, and he was presumably known and well regarded, what little we know of his life comes not from external records but from statements in his own writings.[1] He was born, probably in Wessex, around 950 or 955; after an early miseducation at the hands of a half-learned secular priest,[2] he entered the cathedral monastery of the Old Minster, Winchester. There he became a monk and priest, and was educated by Æthelwold (ca. 904–989; bishop of Winchester 963–984), a fact in which he took life-long pride. Around 987 he was sent to the small and newly reformed monastery of Cerne Abbas in modern Dorset. There he entered a prolific period of composition, in which he wrote or completed CH 1 and 2—though he appears to have continued to revisit and revise these for many years afterward—as well as a Latin *Grammar,* a work on cosmology called *De temporibus anni (On the Seasons of the Year),* books of Old Testament translation, pastoral letters, other homilies, a collection of saints' lives, and other works.[3] Ælfric enjoyed the patronage of Æthelweard, ealdorman[4] of the Western Provinces, and his son Æthelmær, pious and well-educated noblemen who commissioned works in English from him; they were responsible for his move to Cerne Abbas, which they had founded.[5] Around 1005 Ælfric became abbot of the monastery of Eynsham in present-day Oxfordshire, the same year the monastery was refounded by Æthelmær.[6] There he continued to write and revise until his death, around 1010.[7]

Ælfric's work should be understood in the context of

the tenth-century monastic reform, a movement that sought to impose more rigorous observance of monastic rules on clergy in monasteries and cathedrals.[8] The reform, inspired by developments in monastic life on the continent, was championed by Dunstan, archbishop of Canterbury, and Æthelwold, bishop of Winchester and Ælfric's teacher, and had the support of King Edgar (r. 959–975). Under their leadership monasteries were founded or refounded along stricter lines and organized to follow the *Rule* of Saint Benedict; in some places cathedral canons, who were not monks, were replaced by reformed monks. Reformed monasteries were home to a remarkable renewal of literary and artistic culture in both English and Latin.

Ælfric was active in the second generation of the reform, when some resistance among regional landowners, the less enthusiastic support of King Æthelred (who ruled from 978 to 1016), and the renewal of Viking attacks after 991 all contributed to a loss of momentum in the movement. But as a reformer by training and temperament, Ælfric felt there was still much to do to improve English religious life and observance; he appears to have felt a pressing responsibility for writing and teaching sound doctrine, and to have recognized an opportunity to impose monastic authority and orthodoxy over the preaching and teaching of the secular clergy, priests who were not monastics and lived in their parishes among lay people.[9] He was a strong advocate for monastic discipline and adherence to the Benedictine *Rule* among cloistered monks, but equally engaged in pastoral care for the laity. His homilies attest to his concern for educating both lay people and clerics in orthodox belief and right conduct.

The Homily

Throughout this introduction and elsewhere in this book, I have adopted the popular usage that treats "homily" and "sermon" as synonyms for any short text intended for preaching, but strictly speaking the two terms refer to two different kinds of texts. A "homily" is an explanation of a biblical passage, usually the gospel passage read at Mass on a given day (called a *pericope*), while a "sermon" is a more general address or explanation of doctrine not tied to a specific day or occasion.[10] Ælfric's homilies in CH 1 and 2 are of both kinds, though predominately the former. The general outline of a homily, whether in Latin or English, almost always consisted of an opening quotation of the biblical pericope; an address to the congregation, an historical, doctrinal, or moral exposition of the biblical passage; and a concluding formulaic doxology (statement of faith).[11] Homilies were preached on various occasions throughout the Church year, which unfolded in two interlocking cycles. The *sanctorale* was the celebration of the saints on fixed days in the calendar year; the *temporale* was the cycle of movable feasts (feasts that occur on different dates in different years), from Lent to Easter to Pentecost to Advent, along with a few feasts of Christ and Mary on fixed days (such as the Epiphany, on January 6; the Annunciation, on March 25; and Christmas, on December 25). The *Catholic Homilies,* each organized around the course of a year, supply readings for Sundays and major feasts in both the *temporale* and the *sanctorale*. In some cases Ælfric recounts the life *(vita)* and/or martyrdom *(passio)* of a saint, which could be read on the saint's feast day; in a few cases, such as the feast of Saint Andrew (CH 1.38), he includes both an explanation of the gospel reading and a vivid account of the saint's death.[12]

Ælfric's manner of reading the Bible may require some explanation. Commentators in the late classical and early medieval periods saw the Bible as a multivalent text that could be understood on many levels; as Ælfric puts it, "the miracles that Christ performed revealed one thing by power, and signified another thing by mystery" (CH 1.10.3). The *literal,* or *historical,* level was concerned with events as they happened in their historical context. The *typological* level connects the Old Testament and the New Testament, showing how events in the former were a prefiguration of events in the latter. The *moral,* or *tropological,* level offers instruction on how one should live. The *anagogical* level reads events as foreshadowings of future events, such as the Last Judgment, or as descriptions of the nature of heaven or hell. These four levels were not always strictly distinguished, and any or all might be brought forward as the "meaning" of a passage at any time; Ælfric, generally following his sources, often moves from one level of interpretation to another within the same homily. Thus in CH 1.5, a homily for the feast of the Holy Innocents, Ælfric spends some time identifying Herod historically and explaining his background; in CH 1.7, on the Epiphany, he identifies the shepherds who heard news of Christ's birth with the apostles, and sees the Magi as foreshadowing the heathen people who would be converted to Christianity. The star that led the Magi but disappeared when they visited Herod he reads morally, as a warning that "he who turns from God to the devil loses God's grace—that is, his mind's enlightenment" (CH 1.7.9). The three gifts of the Magi (gold, frankincense, and myrrh) are said to signify typologically the threefold nature of Christ as king, God, and mortal human being, and the fact that the Magi returned to their homeland by a different way teaches us that "our country is Paradise, to which we cannot return by the way we came" (CH 1.7.19). For most of these interpretations Ælfric is following his source, a homily of Gregory the Great, but in his explanation of the Star of Bethlehem he also finds time for a long discussion of fate, free will, and predestination that is mostly his own composition. Ælfric's purpose as an author seems always to have been instructional—teaching Church history and doctrine or explicating the Bible to lay people as well as to priests and monks. He was equally careful about the orthodoxy of his sources and the clarity of his prose; the *Catholic Homilies* are written in a self-consciously clear style that Ælfric took pains to regularize and correct, and with a distinctive precision in vocabulary that reflected his training in Winchester.[13] In CH 2 he develops a more ornamented prose style characterized by alliterating rhythmical phrases much in the manner of Old English verse.

The *Catholic Homilies*

The *Catholic Homilies* (the work is titled *Sermones Catholici* in its manuscripts, with "catholic" used in its original sense of "universal") comprises two sets of forty homilies each to be delivered over the course of the liturgical year. CH 1 was probably completed in 989, CH 2 in the period between 991 and 992.[14] Both sets contain reworkings of sermons by the Church fathers, exegesis of gospel readings, lives of saints, sermons of moral instruction, and explanations of Church doctrines, such as the Trinity, the nature of angels, and the resurrection of the dead at the Last Judgment. Every text except the first (CH 1.1, "On the Origin of the Created World") was written to be read on a specific occasion, whether a Sunday Mass, the feast of a saint, or the special Masses before the Ascension, called "Litanies" or Rogationtide. Each series was regarded by Ælfric as sufficient for an entire year of preaching (Latin Preface, CH 1.0.2).

Cerne Abbas, where Ælfric composed the *Catholic Homilies,* was a much smaller establishment than Winchester, where he was trained. If it was not furnished with an adequate library during its refoundation, Ælfric could have visited nearby Sherborne (in whose diocese Cerne Abbas lay) or more distant Winchester to consult the cathedral libraries there, or borrowed books from these establishments to compose his homilies. The range of sources used in the homilies indicates fairly wide reading in a good library, and the number of surviving copies implies a large and well-staffed scriptorium to publish his work. Copies were also sent to Canterbury—the Latin Preface to CH 1 indicates that it was sent to Archbishop Sigeric there some time between 990 and 994—and Canterbury became a center for the dissemination of copies of the work. The wide circulation of Ælfric's homilies attests to their popularity and to the success of his project.

The homilies were not simply completed, sent off to copyists, and forgotten; the evidence of surviving manuscripts suggests that Ælfric worked and reworked these texts several times.[15] As Aaron J. Kleist puts it, "The *Catholic Homilies* were a passion for Ælfric that occupied him, as best we can tell, from his early years of training to the end of his days."[16] Some manuscripts contain material that is certainly by Ælfric but is not in other manuscripts, while others have canceled passages and corrections that appear to be authorial rather than scribal. Peter Clemoes discerned six stages of composition for CH 1, and while some have questioned the details of his conclusions, the evidence clearly indicates that the homilies were revised and reworked in several stages. Even manuscript A (London, British Library, Royal 7 c.xii), generally taken as representing Ælfric's earliest full draft of CH 1, has material that is not found in any other copy of the text, suggesting that it is in fact an even earlier draft than his first "published" version from which other copies were made.[17] Ælfric appears to have made numerous small corrections to the language of this copy, regularizing grammar and usage. He continued to tinker with and revise the text after copies had begun to circulate; Kleist aptly describes Ælfric's editorial work on CH 1 and 2: "It was extensive. It touched every single homily. It revisited individual homilies again and again. It involves periods of intensive activity. It pursued multiple programmes of revision simultaneously. It continued concurrently with other authorial activity. And it spanned nearly the whole of Ælfric's career."[18]

SOURCES

As mentioned earlier, Ælfric states that he wrote the *Catholic Homilies* because he was concerned with the "great error" he saw in other English writing, presumably other collections of homilies.[19] To avoid this he was careful to base his own homilies on the writings of the most orthodox and widely regarded writers of the early Church. Like most Old English homilies, almost all of Ælfric's homilies are translations, often very close ones, of a Latin source.[20] Even where he is not translating closely but is "weaving and interweaving" citations, allusions, images, associations, and remembered texts from several authorities and his own favorite themes, Ælfric is often careful to appear to be relying on an authoritative source.[21] In the Latin Preface to CH 1 he notes that he has followed authors whose authority is most freely accepted by all orthodox Christians; he names Augustine of Hippo, Jerome, Bede, Gregory, Smaragdus, and Haymo.[22] By invoking these names Ælfric is evoking the authority of the universal Church and its greatest teachers and writers. His actual use of sources, however, is somewhat more complicated than this straightforward list of authorities might suggest.[23]

The writings of the Church fathers feature prominently in Ælfric's homilies, and of these Gregory the Great is by far the source cited most commonly; Bede is another frequent source.[24] Augustine and Jerome are drawn on less frequently, and not all the works Ælfric attributes to them are regarded as genuine by modern scholars.[25] Even when Ælfric cites an authority such as Gregory or Augustine by name, however, he is usually not drawing on that author directly, but rather on an excerpt found in a secondary source. Ælfric undoubtedly encountered most of the works of the Church fathers not in separate volumes by individual authors but in homiliaries, compiled collections of homilies by various authors arranged in a sequence for reading during the Church year.[26] Foremost among these was the homiliary of Paul the Deacon. This work, commissioned by Charlemagne at the end

of the eighth century, is a large anthology, carefully orthodox, organized according to the liturgical year usually with
multiple homilies for each occasion, and giving source at-
tributions for each homily. Nearly all of Ælfric's patristic
sources can be found in Paul the Deacon's homiliary; the
collection offered Ælfric a sturdy foundation for his own
work and the confidence that he was basing his work on the
most authoritative sources available.[27]

Another homiliary available to Ælfric was that of Smaragdus, a ninth-century Frankish monk of Saint-Mihiel and
prolific author of commentaries on the *Rule* of Benedict
and the gospels and epistles read at Mass.[28] Unlike Paul the
Deacon, whose homiliary contained whole texts by patristic
authors, Smaragdus strung together shorter extracts from
different authorities into composite homilies, and provided
marginal abbreviations citing the authorities for the extracts he included. Yet another source was the homiliary of
Haymo of Auxerre, a ninth-century monk of Saint-Germain
d'Auxerre whose homilies offer "a concatenation of patristic
texts, embellished with occasional quotations from Scripture and illustrated with incidents from Church history."[29]
Being texts compiled from collected excerpts, homiliaries
were naturally subject to alteration and expansion as they
were copied and circulated, and there is a certain amount of
repetition and overlap between one collection and another.
The Latin tradition of biblical exegesis is "profoundly inter-
textual," as Joyce Hill writes, "with shared liturgical order,
common biblical lections, and often some measure of agreement in text and attribution."[30] So when Ælfric cites a patristic source such as Bede or Gregory, it is not always easy
to tell whether he read their work directly, in an anthol-

ogy such as the homiliary of Paul the Deacon, or as an excerpt in Smaragdus's *Expositio libri comitis* or the homiliary of Haymo.[31] But what does seem clear is that Ælfric took pains to compose his works using the most reliably orthodox sources he could find.

AUDIENCE

Ælfric's Latin Preface to CH 1 states that he has translated his homilies "for the edification . . . of simple people who know only this language" (CH 1.0.1); in the English Preface he stresses the need for good teaching and pastoral care "especially at this time which is the ending of this world" (CH 1.0.6). In several places it is clear that the homilies were intended to be read after the reading of the gospel in Latin at Mass; CH 1.10.1 mentions "this gospel, which we have just heard from the deacon's mouth," and CH 1.11.2 refers to "this gospel . . . which has just now been read before you." In his pastoral letter to Wulfsige, Ælfric stresses the need for priests to explain the meaning of the gospel to the people in English on Sundays and Mass-days.[32] So we may assume that his primary intention was to provide material to fulfill this pastoral duty, and his first audience was the congregation at Mass before whom these homilies were read. But what sort of congregation was it?

Though the tenth-century monastic reform worked to encourage monks to focus on their cloistered liturgical observance rather than public ministry, it was also true that in many places monasteries had an outward-facing role of providing pastoral care for the surrounding lay community, beginning with the presence of laypeople at Mass on Sundays and feast days. Mass in Ælfric's own church at Cerne Abbas would most likely have been attended by both monks and lay people, who might have ranged from those who worked the fields of the monastery to the local gentry who supported it financially. In Ælfric's day a system of smaller churches with secular priests and lay congregations was developing alongside the existing network of minsters, monasteries, and cathedrals.[33] These parish priests would also have needed materials for preaching and teaching, and they may have relied on the larger monastic and cathedral communities, with better libraries and resources, for access to copies of Ælfric's works. Most copies of CH 1 and 2 survive from larger cathedral centers such as Canterbury, Rochester, Exeter, and Worcester, and the surviving manuscripts "look like clean, relatively high-status copies"; these could have been kept as exemplars from which other, more utilitarian copies were produced.[34] As always, this evidence may reflect the accident of survival rather than a pattern of distribution—larger libraries were more likely to be preserved than smaller ones, and small, plain books were more likely to be discarded once their language was no longer comprehensible. Because of this the surviving manuscripts may not tell the full story of the use and circulation of Ælfric's homilies.

The homilies were written for broad distribution, and some ambiguity in the intended audience may have been deliberate. One of their functions may have been the education of the secular clergy, who could then in turn read them to a lay congregation.[35] In this way Ælfric could not only supply reliably orthodox material for preaching but also assert some measure of control over what the secular clergy were preaching. Apart from their delivery at Mass, the homilies could have served as reading for monks during the night office,[36] or for priests whose Latin was not as good as it should be, or for literate laypeople such as Ælfric's patrons Æthelweard and Æthelmær—at the end of the English Preface to CH 1, a Latin note in one manuscript says that Æthelweard has requested a bespoke copy with forty-four homilies rather than the standard forty. Monks, nuns, secular clerics, lay congregations, patrons, readers, and listeners may all have been in Ælfric's mind as he composed CH 1 and 2.

Once out of Ælfric's hands, the homilies were separated and recombined, abridged and excerpted; some two dozen manuscripts and fragments contain some of the homilies, but only four manuscripts have the whole of CH 1, and only one has the whole of CH 2. Most later manuscripts contain selected homilies, and sometimes parts of homilies, copied alongside other works by Ælfric and other authors. Some manuscripts combine homilies from CH 1 and CH 2 with other homilies to create a full *temporale* sequence. Ælfric authorized the combination of his two series of homilies into one set in the Latin Preface to CH 1, and it is clear that many copyists and compilers of his work took him at his word.[37]

Special thanks are due to Dan Donoghue for his support and encouragement, to Nicole Eddy for her editorial guidance and patience with a long-delayed project, and to the various readers of early drafts of this book who have saved me from many errors and infelicities. This book, which hopes to bring Ælfric to a broader and more general audience, would not have been possible without the monumental work of the many scholars who have made Ælfric their life's work; I have admired their insight and eye for detail, and relied on their guidance and expertise. Of these my most obvious debt is to the work of Peter Clemoes and Malcolm Godden, particularly Godden's *Ælfric's Catholic Homilies: Introduction, Commentary, and Glossary*. Readers should consult this volume for a much fuller study of Ælfric's sources, including quotations from Latin homilies.

NOTES

1 See Joyce Hill, "Ælfric: His Life and Works," in *A Companion to Ælfric,* ed. Hugh Magennis and Mary Swan (Leiden, 2009), 35–65; and Jonathan Wilcox, *Ælfric's Prefaces* (Durham, 1994), 2–15, for what is known about Ælfric's life. A good brief introduction is found in Mary Clayton and Juliet Mullins, eds. and trans., *Old English Lives of Saints,* by Ælfric, Dumbarton Oaks Medieval Library 58–60 (Cambridge, MA, 2019), vol. 1, pp. vii–xxxii.

2 He discusses this in the preface to his translation of *Genesis.*

3 Peter Clemoes, "The Chronology of Ælfric's Works," in *The Anglo-Saxons: Studies in Some Aspects of Their History and Culture Presented to Bruce Dickins,* ed. Peter Clemoes (London, 1959), 212–47, remains foundational for defining the canon and order of Ælfric's works, though much work has been done since then that adds nuance to his findings.

4 An ealdorman was a high-ranking royal official who ruled a shire or region; the rank of ealdorman was just below that of the king.

5 For more details see Catherine Cubitt, "Ælfric's Lay Patrons," in Magennis and Swan, *A Companion to Ælfric,* 165–92; and Barbara Yorke, "Æthelmær: The Foundation of the Abbey at Cerne and the Politics of the Tenth Century," in *The Cerne Abbey Millennium Lectures,* ed. Katherine Barker (Cerne Abbas, 1988), 15–25.

6 See Christopher A. Jones, ed. and trans., *Ælfric's Letter to the Monks of Eynsham* (Cambridge, 1998), 5–12.

7 Aaron J. Kleist in *The Chronology and Canon of Ælfric of Eynsham,* Anglo-Saxon Studies 37 (Cambridge, 2019), proposes some revisions to this chronology; among these he places Ælfric's move to Eynsham a few years earlier, between approximately 1002 and 1005.

8 See Christopher A. Jones, "Ælfric and the Limits of 'Benedictine Reform,'" in Magennis and Swan, *A Companion to Ælfric*, 67–108. Some of the best introductions to the reform are still the essays in David Parsons, ed., *Tenth-Century Studies: Essays in Commemoration of the Millennium of the Council of Winchester and "Regularis concordia"* (London, 1975). For a more recent survey of scholarship on the reform, see Nicola Robertson, "The Benedictine Reform: Current and Future Scholarship," *Literature Compass* 3 (2006): 282–99.

9 Rebecca Stephenson, *The Politics of Language: Byrhtferth, Ælfric, and the Multilingual Identity of the Benedictine Reform* (Toronto, 2015), 153.

10 Thomas N. Hall, "The Early Medieval Sermon," in *The Sermon*, ed. Beverly Mayne Kienzle, Typologie des sources du moyen âge occidental 81–83 (Turnhout, 2000), 203–69.

11 D. R. Letson, "The Form of the Old English Homily," *American Benedictine Review* 30 (1979): 399–431. See also Thomas L. Amos, "Early Medieval Sermons and Their Audience," in *De l'homélie au sermon: Histoire de la prédication médiévale, actes du colloque international de Louvain-la-Neuve,* ed. Jacqueline Hamesse and Xavier Hermand (Louvain-la-Neuve, 1993), 1–14 (at 6–7).

12 Other examples include CH 1.26 (The Passion of the Apostles Peter and Paul), CH 1.27 (Saint Paul), and CH 1.34 (Dedication of the Church of Saint Michael the Archangel).

13 See Helmut Gneuss, "The Origin of Standard Old English and Æthelwold's School at Winchester," *ASE* 1 (1972): 63–83; reprinted and updated as the first article in Helmut Gneuss, *Language and History in Early England* (Aldershot, 1996). See also Mechthild Gretsch, "Ælfric, Language, and Winchester," in Magennis and Swan, *A Companion to Ælfric,* 109–37.

14 These dates, particularly the date for the composition of CH 2, are controversial. See Kleist, *Chronology and Canon,* 7–14.

15 See the Note on the Text for descriptions of the manuscripts of CH 1 and 2, including a list of the abbreviations assigned to those manuscripts.

16 Kleist, *Chronology and Canon,* 21. On Ælfric's revisions to CH 1 and 2, see Peter Clemoes, ed., *Ælfric's Catholic Homilies: The First Series,* EETS s.s. 17 (Oxford, 1997), 64–97; and Malcolm Godden, ed., *Ælfric's Catholic Homilies: The Second Series,* EETS s.s. 5 (Oxford, 1979), lxxvii–lxxxvi. A useful survey of manuscripts, and a plausible reconstruction of Ælfric's writing habits, can be found in Aaron J. Kleist, "A Fourth Ælfrician Commonplace

Book? Vestiges in Cambridge, Corpus Christi College 190," *JEGP* 118 (2019): 31–72.

17 Clemoes, *First Series,* 135.

18 See Kleist, *Chronology and Canon,* 39.

19 See Malcolm Godden, "Ælfric and the Vernacular Prose Tradition," in *The Old English Homily and Its Backgrounds,* ed. Paul E. Szarmach and Bernard F. Huppé (Albany, 1978), 99–117; for a survey of texts, see Donald G. Scragg, "The Corpus of Vernacular Homilies and Prose Saints' Lives before Ælfric," *ASE* 8 (1979): 223–77. Ælfric's careful orthodoxy is discussed in Lynne Grundy, *Books and Grace: Ælfric's Theology* (London, 1991).

20 Charles D. Wright, "Old English Homilies and Latin Sources," in *The Old English Homily: Precedent, Practice, and Appropriation,* ed. Aaron J. Kleist, Studies in the Early Middle Ages 17 (Turnhout, 2007), 15–66 (at 15), notes that "relatively few Old English homilies are entirely independent of Latin sources, and many are direct translations of a Latin source or of multiple Latin sources."

21 Joyce Hill, "Weaving and Interweaving: The Textual Traditions of Two of Ælfric's *Supplementary Homilies,*" in *Textiles, Text, Intertext: Essays in Honour of Gale R. Owen-Crocker,* ed. Maren Clegg Hyer and Jill Frederick (Martlesham, 2016), 211–23.

22 See Godden, *Second Series,* xxxviii–lxii, on Ælfric's sources.

23 Work on Ælfric's sources has been ongoing for more than a century. The seminal studies are Max Förster, *Über die Quellen von Ælfrics "Homiliae Catholicae,"* part 1, *Legenden* (Berlin, 1892), and Max Förster, "Über die Quellen von Ælfrics exegetischen *Homiliae Catholicae,*" *Anglia* 16 (1894): 1–61. For more recent work, see Joyce Hill, "Ælfric's Sources Reconsidered: Some Case Studies from the *Catholic Homilies,*" in *Studies in English Language and Literature: "Doubt Wisely"; Papers in Honour of E. G. Stanley,* ed. M. J. Toswell and E. M. Tyler (London and New York, 1996), 362–86, and Joyce Hill, "Translating the Tradition: Manuscripts, Models and Methodologies in the Composition of Ælfric's *Catholic Homilies,*" *Bulletin of the John Rylands Library* 79 (1977): 43–65.

24 Gregory's homilies are edited by Raymond Étaix as *Homiliae in evangelia,* CCSL 141 (Turnhout, 1999); an English translation is David Hurst, trans., *Forty Gospel Homilies,* Cistercian Studies 123 (Kalamazoo, 1990). For the circulation of Gregory's writings in England, see Thomas N. Hall,

"The Early English Manuscripts of Gregory the Great's *Homilies on the Gospel* and *Homilies on Ezechiel:* A Preliminary Survey," in *Rome and the North: The Early Reception of Gregory the Great in Germanic Europe,* ed. Rolf H. Bremmer, Jr., Kees Dekker, and David F. Johnson, Mediaevalia Groningana 4 (Paris, 2001), 115–36. For Ælfric's use of Gregory, see Joyce Hill, "Defining and Redefining: Ælfric's Access to Gregory's *Homiliae in evangelia* in the Composition of the *Catholic Homilies,*" in *Old English Lexicology and Lexicography: Essays in Honor of Antonette DiPaolo Healey,* ed. Maren Clegg Hyer, Haruko Momma, and Samantha Zacher, Anglo-Saxon Studies 40 (Cambridge, 2020), 67–79. Bede's homilies on the gospels are edited by David Hurst, *Homiliarum evangelii libri II,* in *Opera homiletica; Opera rhythmica,* ed. David Hurst and J. Fraipont, CCSL 122 (Turnhout, 1955), pp. v–403; they are translated by Lawrence T. Martin and David Hurst, *Homilies on the Gospels,* 2 vols. (Collegeville, MN, 1991).

25 See CH 1.3 (for Augustine) and CH 1.30 (for Jerome).

26 Mary Clayton, "Homiliaries and Preaching in Anglo-Saxon England," *Peritia* 4 (1985): 207–42; reprinted with corrections in *Old English Prose: Basic Readings,* ed. Paul E. Szarmach (New York, 2000), 151–98.

27 See Cyril Smetana, "Ælfric and the Early Medieval Homiliary," *Traditio* 15 (1959): 163–204; Cyril Smetana, "Paul the Deacon's Patristic Anthology," in Szarmach and Huppé, *The Old English Homily and Its Backgrounds,* 75–97; Réginald Grégoire, *Homéliares liturgiques médiévaux: Analyse des manuscrits* (Spoleto, 1980), 423–79; and Joyce Hill, "Ælfric's Manuscript of Paul the Deacon's Homiliary: A Provisional Analysis," in Kleist, *The Old English Homily: Precedent, Practice, and Appropriation,* 67–96. See also J. E. Cross, "Ælfric and the Medieval Homiliary—Objection and Contribution," *Scripta minora Regiae societatis humaniorum litterarum Lundensis* 4 (1961–1962): 1–34. A version of Paul the Deacon's homiliary can be found in *Paulus Winfridi diaconi opera ascetica, sive operum ejus omnium pars secunda: Homiliarius,* PL 95 (Paris, 1851), cols. 1159–584, though this is very different from the version(s) that might have been available to Ælfric.

28 See Joyce Hill, "Ælfric and Smaragdus," *ASE* 21 (1992): 203–37. Smaragdus's work is edited in *Collectiones in epistolas et evangelia,* PL 102 (Paris, 1851), cols. 13–552.

29 See Cyril Smetana, "Ælfric and the Homiliary of Haymo of Halberstadt," *Traditio* 17 (1961): 457–69. Smetana's conflation of Haymo of Aux-

erre with Haymo of Halberstadt has no effect on his argument. Haymo's work is edited in *Homiliae de tempore,* PL 118 (Paris, 1852), 11–746. See Joyce Hill, "Ælfric and Haymo Revisited," in *Intertexts: Studies in Anglo-Saxon Culture Presented to Paul E. Szarmach,* ed. Virginia Blanton and Helene Scheck (Tempe, AZ, 2008), 331–47.

30 Hill, "Ælfric's Manuscript of Paul the Deacon's Homiliary," 72. See also Joyce Hill, "Authority and Intertextuality in the Works of Ælfric," *Proceedings of the British Academy* 131 (2005): 157–81.

31 Hill, "Ælfric and Smaragdus," 204. Sources for individual homilies can be found in the Notes to the Translation. Most of these are taken from Malcolm Godden, *Ælfric's Catholic Homilies: Introduction, Commentary, and Glossary,* EETS s.s. 18 (Oxford, 2000); readers should consult this volume for a much fuller study of Ælfric's sources, including quotations from Latin homilies.

32 See Bernhard Fehr, *Die Hirtenbriefe Ælfrics in altenglischer und lateinischer Fassung* (Hamburg, 1914; repr., 1966), letter 1.61.

33 On monastic pastoral care, see Jonathan Wilcox, "Ælfric in Dorset and the Landscape of Pastoral Care," in *Pastoral Care in Late Anglo-Saxon England,* ed. Francesca Tinti (Woodbridge, 2005), 52–62; Francesca Tinti, "Benedictine Reform and Pastoral Care in Late Anglo-Saxon England," *Early Medieval Europe* 23 (2015): 229–51; and more generally John Blair, *The Church in Anglo-Saxon England* (Oxford, 2005), 291–425.

34 Wilcox, "Ælfric in Dorset," 61. For other evidence for the circulation of booklets containing Ælfric's work, see Jonathan Wilcox, "The Use of Ælfric's Homilies: MSS Oxford, Bodleian Library, Junius 85 and 86 in the Field," in Magennis and Swan, *A Companion to Ælfric,* 345–68.

35 Malcolm Godden, "The Development of Ælfric's Second Series of *Catholic Homilies,*" *English Studies* 54 (1973): 209–16; and Helen Gittos, "The Audience for Old English Texts: Ælfric, Rhetoric, and 'The Edification of the Simple,'" *ASE* 43 (2014): 231–66.

36 See Clayton, "Homiliaries and Preaching," 207–12.

37 For more information, see the Note on the Text.

THE OLD ENGLISH
CATHOLIC HOMILIES

Ego, Ælfricus, alumnus Aðelwoldi, benevoli et venerabilis praesulis, salutem exopto domino archiepiscopo Sigerico in Domino. Licet temere vel praesumptiose, tamen transtulimus hunc codicem ex libris Latinorum, scilicet sanctae scripturae, in nostram consuetam sermocinationem ob aedificationem simplicium qui hanc norunt tantummodo locutionem, sive legendo sive audiendo; ideoque nec obscura posuimus verba, sed simplicem Anglicam, quo facilius possit ad cor pervenire legentium vel audientium ad utilitatem animarum suarum, quia alia lingua nesciunt erudiri quam in qua nati sunt. Nec ubique transtulimus verbum ex verbo, sed sensum ex sensu, cavendo tamen diligentissime deceptivos errores, ne inveniremur aliqua haeresi seducti seu fallacia fuscati. Hos namque auctores in hac explanatione sumus secuti, videlicet, Augustinum Hipponiensem, Hieronimum, Bedam, Gregorium, Smaragdum, et aliquando Haegmonem, horum denique auctoritas ab omnibus catholicis libentissime suscipitur. Nec solum evangeliorum tractatus in isto

Latin Preface

HERE BEGINS THE PREFACE OF THIS BOOK,
IN THE NAME OF THE LORD

I, Ælfric, student of the benevolent and venerable prelate Æthelwold, send salutations in the Lord to the lord archbishop Sigeric. We have translated, however rashly or presumptuously, this volume from Latin books, namely the holy scripture, into our accustomed language for the edification, whether by their reading or hearing, of simple people who know only this language; therefore we did not use obscure words, but simple English, by which it may more easily reach the heart of readers or listeners for the benefit of their souls, for they cannot be instructed in any language other than the one into which they were born. We have not translated word for word throughout, but sense by sense, yet guarding most diligently against deceptive errors, so that we might not be found to have been misled by any heresy or darkened by fallacy. For we have followed these authors in this exposition, namely, Augustine of Hippo, Jerome, Bede, Gregory, Smaragdus, and sometimes Haymo, because their authority is most freely accepted by all the orthodox. In this little book we have not only expounded

3

libello exposuimus, verum etiam sanctorum passiones vel vitas, ad utilitatem idiotarum istius gentis.

2   Quadraginta sententias in isto libro posuimus, credentes hoc sufficere posse per annum fidelibus, si integre eis a ministris Dei recitentur in ecclesia. Alterum vero librum modo dictando habemus in manibus, qui illos tractatus vel passiones continet quos iste amisit. Nec tamen omnia evangelia tangimus per circulum anni, sed illa tantummodo quibus speramus sufficere posse simplicibus ad animarum emendationem, quia saeculares omnia nequeunt capere, quamvis ex ore doctorum audiant. Duos libros in ista translatione facimus, persuadentes ut legatur unus per annum in ecclesia Dei et alter anno sequenti, ut non fiat taedium auscultantibus; tamen damus licentiam, si alicui melius placet, ad unum librum ambos ordinare. Ergo si alicui displicit, sive in interpretatione (quod non semper verbum ex verbo, aut quod breviorem explicationem quam tractatus auctorum habent) sive quod non per ordinem ecclesiastici ritus omnia evangelia tractando percurrimus, condat sibi altiore interpretatione librum, quomodo intellectui eius placet. Tantum obsecro ne pervertat nostram interpretationem, quam speramus, ex Dei gratia, non causa iactantiae, nos studiose sicuti valuimus interpretari.

3   Precor modo obnixe almitatem tuam, mitissime pater Sigerice, ut digneris corrigere per tuam industriam, si aliquos naevos malignae haeresis aut nebulosae fallaciae in nostra interpretatione reperies; et adscribatur dehinc hic codicellus tuae auctoritati, non vilitati nostrae despicabilis personae.

4   Vale in Deo omnipotenti iugiter. Amen.

gospel homilies, but also the passions or lives of the saints, for the benefit of the uneducated among this people.

We have placed forty discourses in this book, believing 2 this to be sufficient for the faithful for a year, if they are recited to them in church in their entirety by the ministers of God. But we now have in hand another book in composition, which contains those homilies and passions which this one omits. Yet we have not touched on all the gospels in the course of the year, but only those which we hope will be sufficient for the improvement of the souls of simple people, for secular people cannot take in everything they hear, even from the mouths of the learned. We have made this translation in two books, intending that one be read one year in the church of God and the other the following year, so it does not become tedious for the listeners; but we give permission, if it pleases anyone better, to organize both into one book. And so, if it displeases anyone, whether in the translation (because it is not always word for word, or is a shorter exposition than is in the writings of the authorities) or because we do not go through all the gospels in the order they are treated in ecclesiastical customs, let him make for himself a better-translated book, however it pleases his understanding. Yet I implore him not to distort our translation, which we hope, by the grace of God, and not through vainglory, we have translated as accurately as we are able.

Now I earnestly beg your kindness, most mild father 3 Sigeric, that if you find any flaws, malignant heresies, or murky fallacies in our translation, you would deign to correct them through your industry; and henceforth let this little book be ascribed to your authority, not to the worthlessness of our contemptible person.

Be forever well in the Lord almighty. Amen. 4

Praefatio

5 Ic, Ælfric, munuc and mæssepreost, swa ðeah waccre þonne swilcum hadum gebyrige, wearð asend on Æþelredes dæge cyninges fram Ælfeage biscope, Aðelwoldes æftergengan, to sumum mynstre ðe is Cernel gehaten, þurh Æðelmæres bene ðæs þegenes, his gebyrd and goodnys sind gehwær cuðe. Þa bearn me on mode—ic truwige ðurh Godes gife—þæt ic ðas boc of Ledenum gereorde to Engliscre spræce awende, na þurh gebylde micelre lare, ac forðan ðe ic geseah and gehyrde mycel gedwyld on manegum Engliscum bocum, ðe ungelærede menn ðurh heora bilewitnysse to micclum wisdome tealdon, and me ofhreow þæt hi ne cuðon ne næfdon ða godspellican lare on heora gewritum, buton ðam mannum anum ðe þæt Leden cuðon, and buton þam bocum ðe Ælfred cyning snoterlice awende of Ledene on Englisc, ða synd to hæbbene.

6 For ðisum antimbre ic gedyrstlæhte, on Gode truwiende, þæt ic ðas gesetnysse undergann, and eac forðam ðe menn behofiað godre lare, swiðost on þisum timan þe is geendung þyssere worulde, and beoð fela frecednyssa on mancynne ærðan þe se ende becume, swa swa ure Drihten on his godspelle cwæð to his leorningcnihtum: "Þonne beoð swilce gedreccednyssa swilce næron næfre ær fram frymðe middangeardes. Manega lease Cristas cumað on minum naman, cweðende 'Ic eom Crist,' and wyrcað fela tacna and wundra to bepæcenne mancynn, and eac swylce ða gecorenan men, gif hit gewurðan mæg. And butan se ælmihtiga God ða dagas

English Preface

Preface

I, Ælfric, monk and Mass priest, although weaker than is   5
fitting for such ranks, was sent in King Æthelred's day by
Bishop Ælfheah, Æthelwold's successor, to a monastery
which is called Cerne, at the request of Æthelmær the
thane, whose birth and goodness are known everywhere.
Then it came to my mind—I trust through God's grace—
that I should translate this book from the Latin language
into English speech, not from the presumption of great
learning, but because I saw and heard great error in many
English books, which unlearned people in their simplicity
have taken for great wisdom, and I regretted that they did
not know or did not have the gospel teaching among their
writings, except only for those who knew Latin, and except
for those books which King Alfred wisely translated from
Latin to English, which are available.

For this reason I presumed, trusting in God, to under-   6
take this task, and also because people need good instruction, especially at this time which is the ending of this world,
and there will be many perils among humanity before the
end comes, as our Lord said to his disciples in his gospel:
"Then there will be such tribulations as have never been
from the beginning of the world. Many false Christs will
come in my name, saying 'I am Christ,' and they will work
many signs and wonders to deceive humanity, and even the
chosen, if it may be. And unless almighty God should

7

gescyrte, eall mennisc forwurde; ac for his gecorenum he gescyrte ða dagas."

7   Gehwa mæg þe eaðelicor þa toweardan costnunge acumen, ðurh Godes fultum, gif he bið þurh boclice lare getrymmed, forðan ðe ða beoð gehealdene þe oð ende on geleafan þurhwuniað. Fela gedreccednyssa and earfoðnyssa becumað on ðissere worulde ær hire geendunge, and þa sind ða bydelas þæs ecan forwyrdes on yfelum mannum, þe for heora mandædum siððan ecelice ðrowiað on ðære sweartan helle. Þonne cymð se Antecrist, se bið mennisc mann and soð deofol, swa swa ure hælend is soðlice mann and God on anum hade. And se gesewenlica deofol þonne wyrcð ungerima wundra and cwyð þæt he sylf God beo, and wile neadian mancynn to his gedwylde; ac his tima ne bið na langsum, forðan ðe Godes grama hine fordeð, and ðeos weoruld bið siððan geendod.

8   Crist ure Drihten gehælde untrume and adlige, and þes deofol þe is gehaten Antecrist, þæt is gereht "ðwyrlic Crist," aleuað and geuntrumað þa halan, and nænne ne gehælð fram untrumnyssum buton þam anum þe he sylf ær awyrde. He and his gingran awyrdað manna lichaman digellice ðurh deofles cræft, and gehælað hi openlice on manna gesihðe, ac he ne mæg nænne gehælan þe God sylf ær geuntrumode. He neadað þurh yfelnysse þæt men sceolon bugan fram heora scyppendes geleafan to his leasungum, se ðe is ord ælcere leasunge and yfelnysse. Se ælmihtiga God geðafað þam arleasan Antecriste to wyrcenne tacna and wundra and ehtnysse to feorðan healfan geare; forðan ðe on ðam timan bið swa micel yfelnyss and þwyrnys betwux mancynne þæt hi wel wyrðe beoð þære deoflican ehtnysse, to ecum forwyrde þam ðe him onbugað, and to ecere myrhðe þam þe

8

shorten those days, all humanity will perish; but for his chosen ones he will shorten those days."

Everyone can withstand the coming temptation more   7
easily, through God's help, if he is strengthened by book
learning, for those who persist in their faith until the end
will be saved. Many tribulations and hardships will come
into this world before its end, and those are the heralds of
eternal damnation to evil persons, who for their crimes will
afterward suffer eternally in the darkness of hell. Then the
Antichrist will come, who will be a human being and true
devil, just as our savior is truly human and God in one person. And the visible devil will then work countless miracles
and say that he himself is God, and will compel humanity to
his heresy; but his time will not be long, for God's anger will
destroy him, and then this world will be ended.

Christ our Lord healed the weak and diseased, and this   8
devil who is called Antichrist, which is interpreted "against
Christ," weakens and enfeebles the healthy, and heals no one
from diseases except those whom he himself has previously
injured. He and his disciples injure people's bodies secretly
through the devil's power, and heal them openly in the sight
of people, but he cannot heal those whom God himself has
afflicted. Through wickedness he compels people to turn
away from the faith of their creator to his lies, for he is the
beginning of all lies and evil. Almighty God will allow the
impious Antichrist to work signs and wonders and persecution for three and a half years; in that time there will be so
much evil and perversity among humanity that they will be
well worthy of the devil's persecution, to the eternal damnation of those who bow down to him, and to the eternal joy

him þurh geleafan wiðcweðað. God geðafað eac þæt his gecorenan ðegenas beon aclænsade fram eallum synnum ðurh ða ormætan ehtnyssa, swa swa gold beð on fyre afandod. Þa ofslihð se deofol ðe him wiðstandað, and hi ðonne farað, mid halgum martyrdome, to heofenan rice. Þa ðe his leasungum gelyfað þam he arað, and hi habbað syððan þa ecan susle to edleane heora gedwyldes. Se arleasa deð þæt fyr cymð ufan, swilce of heofonum, on manna gesihðe, swilce he God ælmihtig sy, ðe ah geweald heofenas and eorðan; ac þa Cristenan sceolon beon þonne gemyndige hu se deofol dyde ða ða he bæd æt Gode þæt he moste fandian Iobes: he gemacode ða þæt fyr com ufan swilce of heofenum, and forbærnde ealle his scep ut on felda, and þa hyrdas samod, buton anum þe hit him cyðan sceolde. Ne sende se deofol ða fyr of heofenum, þeah ðe hit ufan come; forðan ðe he sylf næs on heofonum syððan he, for his modignysse, of aworpen wæs.

9   Ne eac se wælhreowa Antecrist næfð þa mihte þæt he heofenlic fyr asendan mæge, ðeah ðe he þurh deofles cræft hit swa gehiwige. Beð nu wislicor þæt gehwa ðis wite, and cunne his geleafan, weald hwa ða micclan yrmðe gebidan sceole. Ure Drihten bebead his discipulum þæt hi sceoldon læran and tæcan eallum þeodum ða ðing þe he sylf him tæhte; ac ðæra is nu to lyt ðe wile wel tæcan and wel bysnian. Se ylca Drihten clypode þurh his witegan Ezechiel, "Gif ðu ne gestentst þone unrihtwisan, and hine ne manast þæt he fram his arleasnysse gecyrre and lybbe, þonne swelt se arleasa on his unrihtwisnysse, and ic wylle ofgan æt ðe his blod," þæt is, his lyre. "Gif ðu ðonne þone arleasan gewarnast, and he nele fram his arleasnysse gecyrran, þu alysdest þine sawla mid þære mynegunge, and se arleasa swylt

of those who resist him through faith. God also allows his chosen servants to be cleansed from all sins through great persecutions, just as gold is tried in fire. Then the devil will kill those who resist him, and they will go with holy martyrdom to the kingdom of heaven. He will honor those who believe his lies, and they will afterward have eternal torment as a reward for their folly. The impious one will make fire come from above, as if from heaven, in human sight, as if he were almighty God, who has power over heaven and earth; but Christians must then remember what the devil did when he asked God if he might be allowed to tempt Job: he made fire come from above as if from heaven, and burned up all his sheep out in the field, and the shepherds with them, except for one who had to announce it to him. The devil did not send fire from heaven, though it came from above; for he himself was not in heaven after he had been cast out for his pride.

Nor does the cruel Antichrist have the power to send down heavenly fire, though he may pretend so through the devil's craft. It will now be wiser that everyone know this, and know his faith, in case anyone might have to endure that great misery. Our Lord commanded his disciples to instruct and teach all peoples the things which he himself had taught them; but there are now too few of those who will teach well and be a good example. The same Lord cried out through his prophet Ezekiel, "If you do not warn the unrighteous, and do not urge him to turn from his wickedness and live, then the wicked will die in his unrighteousness, and I will require from you his blood," that is, his damnation. "But if you warn the wicked, and he will not turn from his wickedness, you have redeemed your soul with that admonition,

on his unrihtwisnysse." Eft cwæð se ælmihtiga to þam witegan Isaiam, "Clypa and ne geswic ðu; ahefe ðine stemne swa
swa byme and cyð minum folce heora leahtras, and Iacobes
hirede heora synna."

10   For swylcum bebodum, wearð me geðuht þæt ic nære unscyldig wið God gif ic nolde oðrum mannum cyðan, oþþe
þurh tungan oððe þurh gewritu, ða godspellican soðfæstnysse þe he sylf gecwæð, and eft halgum lareowum onwreah.
Forwel fela ic wat on ðisum earde gelæredran þonne ic sy, ac
God geswutelað his wundra ðurh ðone ðe he wile; swa swa
ælmihtig wyrhta, he wyrcð his weorc þurh his gecorenan, na
swylce he behofige ures fultumes, ac þæt we geearnion þæt
ece lif þurh his weorces fremminge. Paulus se apostol cwæð,
"We sind Godes gefylstan," and swa ðeah ne do we nan ðing
to Gode buton Godes fultume.

11   Nu bydde ic and halsige, on Godes naman, gif hwa þas
boc awritan wylle, þæt he hi geornlice gerihte be ðære bysene, þy læs ðe we ðurh gymelease writeras geleahtrode
beon. Mycel yfel deð se ðe leas writ, buton he hit gerihte;
swylce he gebringe þa soðan lare to leasum gedwylde. Forði
sceal gehwa gerihtlæcan þæt þæt he ær to woge gebigde, gif
he on Godes dome unscyldig beon wile. *Quid necesse est in hoc
codice capitula ordinare, cum praediximus quod quadraginta sententias in se contineat, excepto quod Æþelwerdus dux vellet habere
xl quattuor in suo libro?*

and the wicked will die in his unrighteousness." Again the almighty said to the prophet Isaiah, "Cry out and do not cease; raise your voice like a trumpet and declare to my people their crimes, and to the household of Jacob their sins."

Because of such commands, it seemed to me that I would not be guiltless before God if I did not declare to others, either by tongue or by writings, the gospel truth which he himself spoke, and afterward revealed to holy teachers. I know a great many in this country more learned than I am, but God manifests his wonders through whomever he wishes; as an almighty worker, he works his work through his chosen, not because he needs our help, but so that we may merit eternal life by the performance of his work. Paul the apostle said, "We are God's assistants," and yet we do nothing for God without God's help. 10

Now I pray and beseech, in God's name, if anyone wants to transcribe this book, that he correct it carefully by the exemplar, lest we be blamed because of careless writers. He who writes falsely does great evil, unless he corrects it; it is as though he turns true doctrine to false error. Therefore everyone should correct what he has previously turned to error, if he wants to be guiltless at God's judgment. *What need is there to list a table of contents in this book, when we have said before that it contains forty pieces in it, except that Ealdorman Æthelweard wants to have forty-four in his book?* 11

I

INCIPIT LIBER
CATHOLICORUM SERMONUM ANGLICE,
IN ECCLESIA
PER ANNUM RECITANDORUM

Sermo de initio creaturae
ad populum, quando volueris

An angin is ealra ðinga, þæt is God ælmihtig. He is ordfruma and ende—he is ordfruma, forði þe he wæs æfre; he is
ende butan ælcere geendunge, forðan ðe he bið æfre ungeendod. He is ealra cyninga cyning and ealra hlaforda hlaford;
he hylt mid his mihte heofonas and eorðan, and ealle gesceafta butan geswince, and he besceawað þa niwelnyssa ðe
under þyssere eorðan sind. He awecð ealle duna mid anre
handa, and ealle eorðan he belicð on his handa, and ne mæg
nan ðing his willan wiðstandan. Ne mæg nan gesceaft fulfremedlice smeagan ne understandan ymbe God. Maran
cyððe habbað englas to Gode þonne men, and þeahhweðere
hi ne magon fulfremedlice understandan ymbe God. He gesceop gesceafta ða ða he wolde; þurh his wisdom he geworhte ealle ðing, and þurh his willan he hi ealle geliffæste.
Þeos Ðrynnys is an God, þæt is, se Fæder, and his Wisdom
of him sylfum æfre acenned, and heora begra willa, þæt is, se
Halga Gast. He nis na acenned, ac he gæð of ðam Fæder and
of ðam Suna gelice. Þas ðry hadas sindon an ælmihtig God,
se geworhte heofenas and eorðan and ealle gesceafta.

14

I

On the Origin of the Created World

HERE BEGINS THE BOOK OF
CATHOLIC HOMILIES IN ENGLISH,
FOR READING IN CHURCH
THROUGH THE YEAR

*Sermon on the Origin of the Created World
for the Public, Whenever You Wish*

There is one beginning of all things, which is God almighty. He is beginning and end—he is the beginning, because he always was; he is the end without any ending, because he is forever unended. He is king of all kings and lord of all lords; he holds heaven and earth with his might, and all creation without effort, and he looks upon the abyss which is under the earth. He weighs all the mountains with his hands, and he encloses all the earth in his hands, and nothing can withstand his will. No creature can completely imagine or understand God. The angels have greater kinship to God than men, and yet they cannot completely understand God. He created creation just as he wanted; through his wisdom he made all things, and through his will he gave them all life. This Trinity is one God, that is, the Father, and his Wisdom eternally begotten of himself, and the will of both of them, that is, the Holy Spirit. He is not born, but he goes equally from the Father and the Son. These three persons are one almighty God, who made the heavens and earth and all creation.

2   He gesceop tyn engla werod, þæt sind, englas and heahenglas, *throni, dominationes, principatus, potestates, virtutes,*
cherubim, seraphim. Her sindon nigon engla werod; hi nabbað
nænne lichaman, ac hi sindon ealle gastas, swiðe strange and
mihtige and wlitige, on micelre fægernysse gesceapene to
lofe and to wurðmynte heora scyppende. Þæt teoðe werod
abreað and awende on yfel. God hi gesceop ealle gode and
let hi habban agenne cyre, swa hi heora scyppend lufedon
and filigdon, swa hi hine forleton. Þa wæs ðæs teoðan
werodes ealdor swiðe fæger and wlitig gesceapen, swa þæt
he wæs gehaten "Leohtberend." Ða began he to modigenne
for ðære fægernysse þe he hæfde, and cwæð on his heortan
þæt he wolde and eaðe mihte beon his scyppende gelic, and
sittan on ðam norðdæle heofenan rices and habban andweald and rice ongean God ælmihtigne. Þa gefæstnode he
ðisne ræd wið þæt werod þe he bewiste, and hi ealle to ðam
ræde gebugon. Ða ða hi ealle hæfdon ðysne ræd betwux him
gefæstnod, þa becom Godes grama ofer hi ealle, and hi ealle
wurdon awende of þam fægeran hiwe þe hi on gesceapene
wæron to laðlicum deoflum. And swiðe rihtlice him swa getimode: ða ða he wolde mid modignysse beon betera þonne
he gesceapen wæs, and cwæð þæt he mihte beon þam ælmihtigum Gode gelic, þa wearð he and ealle his geferan
forcuþran and wyrsan þonne ænig oðer gesceaft. And ða
hwile ðe he smeade hu he mihte dælan rice wið God, þa
hwile gearcode se ælmihtiga scyppend him and his geferum
helle wite, and hi ealle adræfde of heofenan rices myrhðe
and let befeallan on þæt ece fyr ðe him gegearcod wæs for
heora ofermettum.

3   Þa sona ða nigon werod þe ðær to lafe wæron bugon to
heora scyppende mid ealre eaðmodnesse and betæhton

He made ten hosts of angels, that is, angels and archan- 2
gels, *thrones, dominions, principalities, powers, virtues, cherubim,*
seraphim. Here are nine hosts of angels; they have no body,
but they are all spirits, very strong and mighty and lovely,
created in great beauty for the praise and honor of their creator. The tenth host rebelled and turned to evil. God created them all good and let them have their own choice, either to love and follow their creator or forsake him. The
leader of this tenth host was created very fair and beautiful,
so that he was called "Lightbearer." Then because of his
beauty he began to be proud, and said in his heart that he
would and easily could be equal to his creator, and sit in the
north part of the kingdom of heaven and have power and
rule against God almighty. Then he confirmed this plan with
the host that he ruled, and they all agreed to that council.
When they had all confirmed this council among themselves, God's anger came over them all, and they were all
turned from the fair form in which they were created into
loathsome devils. And quite rightly this happened to them:
when in his pride he wanted to be better than he was created, and said that he might be equal to the almighty God,
then he and all his companions became more wicked and
worse than any other creature. And while he was scheming
how he might share the kingdom with God, the almighty
creator was preparing the torments of hell for him and his
companions, and drove them all from the joy of the kingdom of heaven and let them fall into the eternal fire that was
prepared for them because of their arrogance.

Then at once the nine hosts that remained bowed to their 3
creator with all humility and dedicated their counsel to his

heora ræd to his willan. Þa getrymde se ælmihtiga God þa nigon engla werod and gestaþelfæste swa þæt hi næfre ne mihton ne noldon syððan fram his willan gebugan; ne hi ne magon nu ne hi nellað nane synne gewyrcan, ac hi æfre beoð ymbe þæt an, hu hi magon Gode gehyrsumian and him gecweman. Swa mihton eac ða oðre þe ðær feollon don gif hi woldon, forði ðe God hi geworhte to wlitegum engla gecynde, and let hi habban agenne cyre, and hi næfre ne gebigde ne ne nydde mid nanum þingum to ðam yfelan ræde. Ne næfre se yfela ræd ne com of Godes geðance, ac com of ðæs deofles, swa swa we ær cwædon.

4 Nu ðencð menig man and smeað hwanon deofol come; þonne wite he þæt God gesceop to mæran engle ðone þe nu is deofol. Ac God ne gesceop hine na to deofle, ac ða ða he wæs mid ealle fordon and forscyldgod þurh þa micclan upahefednysse and wiðerweardnysse, þa wearð he to deofle awend se ðe ær wæs mære engel geworht.

5 Ða wolde God gefyllan and geinnian ðone lyre þe forloren wæs of þam heofenlicum werode, and cwæð þæt he wolde wyrcan mannan of eorðan, þæt se eorðlica man sceolde geðeon and geearnian mid eadmodnysse ða wununga on heofenan rice þe se deofol forwyrhte mid modignysse. And God þa geworhte ænne mannan of lame, and him on ableow gast and hine geliffæste, and he wearð þa mann gesceapen on sawle and on lichaman. And God him sette naman Adam, and he wæs þa sume hwile anstandende. God þa hine gebrohte on Neorxnawange and hine þær gelogode, and him to cwæð, "Ealra ðæra ðinga þe on Neorxnawange sindon ðu most brucan, and hi ealle beoð þe betæhte, buton anum treowe ðe stent on middan Neorxnawange: ne hrepa ðu ðæs treowes wæstm, forðan ðe þu bist deadlic gif þu ðæs treowes wæstm geetst."

will. Then almighty God confirmed the nine hosts of angels and established them so that they never afterward could nor would turn away from his will; now they cannot and will not commit any sin, but they are always concerned with one thing, how they might obey God and please him. So too the others who fell might have done if they had wanted, for God made them with the beautiful nature of angels, and let them have their own choice, and never bent them or forced them in any way to that evil counsel. The evil counsel never came from God's mind, but from the devil's, as we have said.

Now many will think and wonder where the devil came 4 from; they should know that God created the one who is now the devil as a great angel. God did not create him as a devil, but when he was completely ruined and damned through his great arrogance and enmity, he who had been created a great angel was turned into a devil.

Then God wanted to replace and make up the missing 5 portion that was lost from the heavenly host, and said that he would make a human of earth, that the earthly human should prosper and merit with humility the dwelling in the heavenly kingdom which the devil had lost through pride. And God made a human out of clay, and blew a spirit into him and gave him life, and he was then a human being formed in soul and in body. And God gave him the name Adam, and for some time he was alone. God brought him to Paradise and established him there, and said to him, "You may enjoy all the things that are in Paradise, and they are all entrusted to you, except one tree that stands in the middle of Paradise: do not touch the fruit of that tree, because you will be mortal if you eat that tree's fruit."

6   Hwi wolde God swa lytles ðinges him forwyrnan, ðe
him swa miccle oðre þing betæhte? Gyse, hu mihte Adam
tocnawan hwæt he wære, buton he wære gehyrsum on sumum þince his Hlaforde? Swylce God cwæde to him, "Nast
þu na þæt ic eom ðin Hlaford and þæt þu eart min ðeowa
buton ðu do þæt ic ðe hate, and forgang þæt ic ðe forbeode.
Hwæt mæg hit ðonne beon þæt þu forgan sceole? Ic ðe
secge, forgang ðu anes treowes wæstm, and mid þære eaðelican gehyrsumnysse þu geearnast heofenan rices myrhðu,
and þone stede þe se deofol of afeoll þurh ungehyrsumnesse.
Gif ðu þonne ðis lytle bebod tobrecst, þu scealt deaðe
sweltan."

7   And ða wæs Adam swa wis þæt God gelædde to him nytenu and deorcynn and fugelcynn, ða ða he hi gesceapene
hæfde, and Adam him eallum naman gesceop, and swa swa
he hi þa genamode, swa hi sindon gyt gehatene. Þa cwæð
God, "Nis na gedafenlic þæt þes man ana beo and næbbe
nænne fultum; ac uton gewyrcan him gemacan him to fultume and to frofre." And God þa geswefode þone Adam,
and þa þa he slep, ða genam he an rib of his sidan, and geworhte of ðam ribbe ænne wifman, and axode Adam hu heo
hatan sceolde. Þa cwæð Adam, "Heo is ban of minum banum and flæsc of minum flæsce; beo hire nama *virago,* þæt
is, 'fæmne,' forðan ðe heo is of hire were genumen." Ða sette
Adam eft hire oðerne naman, *Aeva,* þæt is, "lif," forðan ðe
heo is ealra lybbendra modor.

8   Ealle gesceafta—heofonas and englas, sunnan and monan, steorran and eorðan, ealle nytenu and fugelas, sæ and
ealle fixas, and ealle gesceafta—God gesceop and geworhte
on six dagum, and on ðam seofoðan dæge he geendode his
weorc and geswac ða, and gehalgode þone seofoðan dæg,

Why would God forbid him such a small thing, when he 6
entrusted him with other things so great? Indeed, how could
Adam know what he was, unless he were obedient to his
Lord in some thing? It is as if God had said to him, "You do
not know that I am your Lord and you are my servant unless
you do what I command, and forgo what I forbid. So what
should you forgo? I say to you, forgo the fruit of one tree,
and with that easy obedience you will merit the joy of the
heavenly kingdom, and the place from which the devil fell
through disobedience. If you break this little commandment, you will suffer death."

Adam was so wise that God led the beasts and wild ani- 7
mals and birds to him, when he had created them, and Adam
made names for them all, and just as he named them, so they
are still called. Then God said, "It is not fitting that this person should be alone and have no help; let us make him a
partner for his help and comfort." And God put Adam to
sleep, and while he slept, he took a rib from his side, and
from that rib made a woman, and asked Adam what she
should be called. Adam said, "She is bone of my bones and
flesh of my flesh; let her name be *virago,* that is, 'female,' because she is taken from her man." Later Adam gave her another name, *Eve,* that is, "life," because she is the mother of
all living.

God created and made all creation—heaven and angels, 8
sun and moon, stars and earth, all beasts and birds, the sea
and all fish, and all creatures—in six days, and on the seventh day he ended his work and stopped, and blessed the

forðan ðe he on ðam dæge his weorc geendode. And he beheold þa ealle his weorc ðe he geworhte, and hi wæron ealle
swiðe gode. Ealle ðing he geworhte buton ælcum antimbre.
He cwæð, "Geweorðe leoht," and ðærrihte wæs leoht geworden. He cwæð eft, "Geweorðe heofen," and þærrihte
wæs heofen geworht, swa swa he mid his wisdome and mid
his willan hit gedihte. He cwæð eft and het ða eorðan þæt
heo sceolde forð lædan cuce nytenu, and he ða gesceop of
ðære eorðan eall nytencynn and deorcynn, ealle ða ðe on
feower fotum gað; ealswa eft of wætere he gesceop fixas and
fugelas, and sealde ðam fixum sund, and ðam fugelum fliht.
Ac he ne sealde nanum nytene ne nanum fisce nane sawle, ac
heora blod is heora lif, and swa hraðe swa hi beoð deade, swa
beoð hi mid ealle geendode. Þa ða he worhte ðone mann
Adam, he ne cwæð na, "Geweorðe man geworht," ac he
cwæð, "Uton gewyrcan mannan to ure anlicnysse," and he
worhte ða þone man mid his handum, and him on ableow
sawle; forði is se man betera, gif he gode geðihð, þonne ealle
ða nytenu sindon, forðan ðe hi ealle gewurðað to nahte, and
se man is ece on anum dæle, þæt is on ðære sawle, heo
ne geendað næfre. Se lichama is deadlic þurh Adames gylt,
ac ðeah hwæðere God arærð eft ðone lichaman to ecum
ðingum on domes dæg.

9   Nu cwædon gedwolmen þæt deofol gesceope sume gesceafta, ac hi leogað; ne mæg he nane gesceafta gescyppan
forðan ðe he nis na scyppend, ac is atelic sceocca, ac mid
leasunge he wile beswican and fordon þone unwaran. Ac he
ne mæg nænne man to nanum leahtre geneadian buton se
mon his agenes willes to his lare gebuge. Swa hwæt swa is on
gesceaftum wiðerweardlic geþuht and mannum derige þæt
is eall for urum synnum and yfelum geearnungum.

seventh day, because on that day he ended his work. And he beheld all his works that he had made, and they were all very good. He made all things without any material. He said, "Let there be light," and at once light was made. Then he said, "Let there be heaven," and at once heaven was made, just as he had designed it with his wisdom and will. He spoke again and commanded the earth to bring forth living animals, and from the earth he made all types of beasts and wild animals, all those that go on four legs; likewise from the water he made fishes and birds, and gave to fish the power of swimming, and flight to the birds. He did not give any beast or any fish a soul, but their blood is their life, and as soon as they are dead, they are entirely ended. When he made the human Adam, he did not say "Let a human be made," but he said, "Let us make a human in our image," and then he made the human with his hands, and blew a soul into him; therefore a human, if he strives for good, is better than all the beasts, because they all turn to nothing, and a human is eternal in one part, namely the soul, which is never ended. The body is mortal through Adam's guilt, but nevertheless God will raise that body again to eternity on the day of judgment.

Heretics say that the devil made some creatures, but they 9 lie; he cannot make any creature because he is not the creator, but a horrible demon, and he seeks to deceive and destroy the unwary with his lies. But he cannot force anyone to sin unless someone bends to his teaching of his own will. Whatever in creation seems to be harmful and might hurt people, that is entirely because of our sins and evil merits.

10 Þa ongeat se deofol þæt Adam and Eva wæron to ðy gesceapene þæt hi sceoldon, mid eadmodnysse and mid gehyrsumnysse, geearnian ða wununge on heofenan rice ðe he of afeoll for his upahefednysse, þa nam he micelne graman and andan to þam mannum, and smeade hu he hi fordon mihte. He com ða on næddran hiwe to þam twam mannum, ærest to ðam wife, and hire to cwæð, "Hwi forbead God eow þæs treowes wæstm ðe stent onmiddan Neorxnawange?" Þa cwæð þæt wif, "God us forbead þæs treowes wæstm and cwæð þæt we sceoldon deaðe sweltan gif we his onbyrigdon." Ða cwæð se deofol, "Nis hit na swa ðu segst, ac God wat genoh geare gif ge of ðam treowe geetað þonne beoð eowere eagan geopenode, and ge magon geseon and tocnawan ægðer ge god ge yfel, and ge beoð englum gelice." Næron hi blinde gesceapene, ac God hi gesceop swa bilewite þæt hi ne cuðon nan ðing yfeles, naðor ne on gesihðe, ne on spræce, ne on weorce. Wearð þeah þæt wif ða forspanen þurh ðæs deofles lare, and genam of ðæs treowes wæstme and geæt, and sealde hire were, and he geæt. Ða wæron hi butu deadlice, and cuðon ægðer ge god ge yfel; and hi wæron ða nacode, and him ðæs sceamode. Þa com God and axode hwi he his bebod tobræce, and adræfde hi butu of Neorxnawange, and cwæð, "Forðan ðe ðu wære gehyrsum ðines wifes wordum and min bebod forsawe, þu scealt mid earfoðnyssum þe metes tilian, and seo eorðe, þe is awyriged on þinum weorce, sylð þe ðornas and bremblas. Þu eart of eorðan genumen, and þu awenst to eorðan; þu eart dust, and ðu awentst to duste."

11 God him worhte ða reaf of fellum, and hi wæron mid þam fellum gescrydde. Ða deadan fell getacnodon þæt hi wæron ða deadlice þe mihton beon undeadlice gif hi heoldon þæt

24

When the devil saw that Adam and Eve were created so   10
that they might, through humility and obedience, merit the
dwelling in the heavenly kingdom that he had fallen from
for his arrogance, he felt great anger and envy toward the
humans, and schemed how he might destroy them. He came
to the two humans in the form of a serpent, first to the
woman, and said to her, "Why has God forbidden you the
fruit of the tree that stands in the middle of Paradise?" The
woman said, "God forbade us that tree's fruit and said that
we would suffer death if we tasted it." The devil said, "It is
not as you say, but God knows well enough that if you eat of
that tree your eyes will be opened, and you will see and know
both good and evil, and you will be like angels." They were
not created blind, but God made them so innocent that
they knew nothing of evil, neither by sight nor speech nor
deed. And yet the woman was seduced by the devil's teaching, and took the tree's fruit and ate it, and gave it to her
man, and he ate. Then they were both mortal, and knew
both good and evil; and they were naked, and they were
ashamed of it. Then God came and asked why he had broken his commandment, and drove them both from Paradise,
and said, "Because you were obedient to your wife's words
and despised my commandment, you will toil for your food
with hardship, and the earth, which is cursed in your work,
will give you thorns and brambles. You were taken from the
earth, and you will to return to the earth; you are dust, and
you will return to dust."

Then God made them garments of skin, and they were   11
clothed with the skins. The dead skin signified that they
were then mortal who might have been immortal if they had

eaðelice Godes bebod. Ne þorfte Adam ne eal mancynn þe him siððan of acom næfre deaðes onbyrian, gif þæt treow moste standan ungehrepod and his nan man ne onbyrigde; ac sceolde Adam and his ofspring tyman on asettum tyman, swa swa nu doð clæne nytenu, and siððan ealle buton deaðe faran to ðan ecan life. Næs him gesceapen fram Gode, ne he næs genedd þæt he sceolde Godes bebod tobrecan, ac God hine let frigne and sealde him agenne cyre swa he wære gehyrsum swa he wære ungehyrsum. He wearð þa deofle gehyrsum and Gode ungehyrsum, and wearð betæht he and eal mancynn, æfter ðisum life, into hellewite mid þam deofle ðe hine forlærde. Þa wiste God hwæðere þæt he wæs forlæred, and smeade hu he mihte his and ealles mancynnes eft gemiltsian.

12   On twam þingum hæfde God þæs mannes sawle gegodod, þæt is, mid undeadlicnysse and mid gesælðe. Þa þurh deofles swicdom and Adames gylt we forluron þa gesælðæ ure sawle, ac we ne forluron na þa undeadlicnyssæ; heo is ece and næfre ne geendað, þeah se lichama geendige, þe sceal eft þurh Godes mihte arisan to ecere wununge. Adam ða wæs wunigende on ðisum life mid geswince, and he and his wif ða bearn gestryndon, ægðer ge suna ge dohtra; and he leofode nigon hund geara and þrittig geara and siððan swealt, swa swa him ær behaten wæs for þan gylte, and his sawul gewende to helle.

13   Nu smeagiað sume men hwanon him come sawul, hwæþer ðe of þam fæder þe of ðære meder? We cweðað, of heora naðrum, ac se ylca God þe gesceop Adam mid his handum he gescypð ælces mannes lichaman on his modor innoðe, and se ylca se ðe ableow on Adames lichaman and him forgeaf sawle, se ylca forgyfð cildum sawle and lif on heora

kept God's easy commandment. Neither Adam nor all the human race that came from him ever needed to have tasted death, if that tree could have stood untouched and no one had tasted it; but Adam and his offspring would have produced their young at set times, like clean beasts do, and later they all would have gone without death to eternal life. It was not ordained by God, nor was he compelled to break God's commandment, but God left him free and gave him his own choice whether to be obedient or disobedient. He was obedient to the devil and disobedient to God, and he and all humankind were consigned, after this life, to the torments of hell with the devil who misled him. But God knew that he had been misled, and planned how he might afterward have mercy on him and all humanity.

God had endowed the human soul with two things, that 12 is, with immortality and with happiness. Through the devil's deceit and Adam's guilt we lost the happiness of our soul, but we did not lose the immortality; that is eternal and never ends, even though the body ends, which will rise again through God's might to an eternal dwelling. Adam then was dwelling in this life with toil, and he and his wife produced children, both sons and daughters; and he lived nine hundred thirty years and then died, as had been promised him for that sin, and his soul went to hell.

Now some will wonder where their soul comes from, 13 from the father or from the mother? From neither of them, we say, but the same God who created Adam with his hands creates every person's body in his mother's womb, and the same one who blew into Adam's body and gave him a soul gives children a soul and life in their mother's womb when

modor innoðe þonne hi gesceapene beoð, and he lætt hi
habban agenne cyre þonne hi geweaxene beoð, swa swa
Adam hæfde.

14 Þa wearð þa hrædlice micel mennisc geweaxen, and
wæron swiðe manega on yfel awende, and gegremodon God
mid mislicum leahtrum, and swiðost mid forligere. Ða
wearð God to þan swiðe gegremod þurh manna mandæda
þæt he cwæð þæt him ofðuhte þæt he æfre mancynn gesceop. Þa wæs, hwæþere, an man rihtwis ætforan Gode, se
wæs Noe gehaten. Þa cwæð God to him, "Ic wylle fordon eal
mancynn mid wætere for heora synnum, ac ic wylle gehcal-
dan þe ænne, and ðin wif and þine þry suna, Sem, and Cham,
and Iafeth, and heora ðreo wif, forðan ðe ðu eart rihtwis and
me gecweme. Wyrc ðe nu ænne arc, þreo hund fæðma lang
and fiftig fæðma wid and þritig fæðma heah; gehref hit eall,
and geclæm ealle ða seamas mid tyrwan, and ga inn syððan
mid þinum hiwum. Ic gegaderige in to ðe of deorcynne and
of fugelcynne symble gemacan, þæt hi eft to fostre beon. Ic
wille sendan flod ofer ealne middangeard."

15 He dyde þa swa him God bebead, and God beleac hi binnon ðam arce, and asende ren of heofonum feowertig daga
togædere, and geopenode þær togeanes ealle wyllspringas
and wæterðeotan of ðære micclan niwelnysse. Þæt flod
weox ða and abær up ðone arc, and hit oferstah ealle duna.
Wearð þa ælc ðing cuces adrenct, buton ðam þe binnon ðam
arce wæron; of þam wearð eft geedstaðelod eall middangeard. Þa behet God þæt he nolde næfre eft eal mancynn
mid wætere acwellan, and cwæð to Noe and to his sunum,
"Ic wylle settan min wedd betwux me and eow to ðisum behate: þæt is, þonne ic oferteo heofenas mid wolcnum, þonne
bið æteowod min renboga betwux þam wolcnum, þonne

they are created, and he lets them have their own choice when they are grown, just as Adam had.

Then quickly a great mass of humanity grew, and very 14 many of them turned to evil, and angered God with various crimes, and most particularly with fornication. God was so greatly angered by humanity's sinful deeds that he said that he regretted that he had ever created human beings. There was, however, one person, called Noah, who was righteous before God. God said to him, "I will destroy all humanity with water for their sins, but I will save you alone, and your wife and three sons, Shem, and Ham, and Japheth, and their three wives, because you are righteous and acceptable to me. Build yourself an ark, three hundred fathoms long and fifty fathoms wide and thirty fathoms high; roof it all, and smear all the seams with tar, and then go in with your household. I will gather in to you pairs of every kind of beast and bird, so that they may later produce offspring. I will send a flood over the whole world."

He did as God commanded him, and God closed him in 15 the ark, and sent rain from heaven forty days altogether, and opened against it all the wellsprings and torrents of the great abyss. The flood grew and bore up the ark, and it rose up above all mountains. Every living thing was drowned, except those that were inside the ark; through them all the world was later reestablished. God then promised that he would never again destroy all humankind with water, and said to Noah and his sons, "I will set my covenant between me and you as a promise of this: that is, when I cover the heavens with clouds, then my rainbow will appear among

beo ic gemyndig mines weddes, þæt ic nelle heononforð mancynn mid wætere adrencan." Noe leofode on eallum his life, ær ðam Flode and æfter ðam Flode, nigon hund geara and fiftig geara, and he ða forðferde.

16 Ða wæs þa sume hwile Godes ege on mancynne æfter ðam Flode, and wæs an gereord on him eallum. Þa cwædon hi betwux him þæt hi woldon wyrcan ane burh, and ænne stypel binnon ðære byrig swa heahne þæt his hrof astige up to heofenum. And begunnon þa to wyrcenne. Ða com God þærto þa þa hi swiðost worhton, and sealde ælcum men þe ðær wæs synderlice spræce. Þa wæron ðær swa fela gereord swa ðær manna wæron, and heora nan nyste hwæt oðer cwæð. And hi ða geswicon þære getimbrunge, and toferdon geond ealne middangeard.

17 Ða siððan wearð mancynn þurh deofol beswicen, and ge-biged fram Godes geleafan, swa þæt hi worhton him anlic-nyssa, sume of golde, sume of seolfre, sume eac of stanum, sume of treowe, and sceopon him naman—ðæra manna na-man þe wæron entas and yfeldæde. Eft ðonne hi deade wæron, þonne cwædon ða cucan þæt hi wæron godas, and wurðodon hi and him lac offrodon; and comon þa deoflu to heora anlicnyssum and ðæron wunodon, and to mannum spræcon swilce hi godas wæron. And þæt beswicene men-nisc feoll on cneowum to þam anlicnyssum, and cwædon, "Ge sind ure godas, and we besettað urne geleafan and urne hiht on eow." Ða asprang þis gedwyld geond ealne middan-geard, and wæs se soða scyppend, se ðe ana is God, forsewen and geunwurþod.

18 Þa wæs, hwæðere, an mægð þe næfre ne abeah to nanum deofolgylde, ac æfre wurðode þone soðan God. Seo mægð asprang of Noes eltstan suna, se wæs gehaten Sem; he

the clouds, and I will be reminded of my covenant, that I will never again drown humankind with water." Noah lived all his life, before the Flood and after, nine hundred and fifty years, and then departed.

Then for some time after the Flood there was fear of God 16 among humanity, and there was one language among them all. Then they said among themselves that they would build a city, and a tower within that city so high that its roof would rise up to heaven. And they set to work. Then God came to them while they were most diligently working and gave a separate language to each person who was there. Then there were as many languages as there were people, and none of them knew what the other said. And so they stopped building, and traveled out over all the earth.

Then afterward humanity was deceived by the devil, and 17 turned away from faith in God, so that they made images for themselves, some of gold, some of silver, some also of stone, some of wood, and gave them names—the names of people who were giants and evildoers. Later when they were dead, the living said that they were gods, and worshiped them and offered sacrifices to them; and devils came to their images and dwelled in them, and spoke to people as if they were gods. And the deceived human race fell to its knees before those images, and said, "You are our gods, and we place our faith and our hope in you." This error sprang up throughout all the earth, and the true creator, who alone is God, was despised and dishonored.

There was, however, one family which never bowed down 18 to any idol, but always worshiped the true God. This family sprang from Noah's eldest son, who was called Shem; he

leofode six hund geara, and his sunu hatte Arfaxað, se leofode ðreo hund geara and ðreo and þrittig, and his sunu
hatte Sale, se leofode feower hund geara and xxxiii. Þa gestrynde he sunu se wæs gehaten Eber, of ðam asprang þæt
Ebreisce folc, þe God lufode; and of ðam cynne comon ealle
heahfæderas and witegan þa ðe cyðdon Cristes tocyme to
ðisum life, þæt he wolde man beon fornean on ende þyssere
worulde, for ure alysednesse, se ðe æfre wæs God mid þam
healican Fæder. And þyssere mægðe God sealde and gesette
æ, and he hi lædde ofer sæ mid drium fotum, and he hi
afedde feowertig wintra mid heofenlicum hlafe, and fela
wundra on ðam folce geworhte, forðan ðe he wolde of þyssere mægðe him modor geceosan.

19   Ða æt nextan, ða se tima com þe God foresceawode, þa
asende he his engel Gabrihel to anum mædene of þam
cynne, seo wæs Maria gehaten. Þa com se engel to hire and
hi gegrette mid Godes wordum, and cydde hire þæt Godes
sunu sceolde beon acenned of hire buton weres gemanan.
And heo ða gelyfde his wordum and wearð mid cilde. Ða þa
hire tima com, heo acende, and þurhwunode mæden. Þæt
cild is tuwa acenned: he is acenned of þam Fæder on heofonum buton ælcere meder, and eft ða, ða he man gewearð, þa
wæs he acenned of þam clænan mædene Marian buton ælcum eorðlicum fæder. God Fæder geworhte mancynn and
ealle gesceafta þurh ðone Sunu; and eft ða, ða we forwyrhte
wæron, þa asende he ðone ylcan Sunu to ure alysednesse.

20   Seo halige moder Maria þa afedde þæt cild mid micelre
arwurðnesse, and hit weox swa swa oðre cild doð, buton
synne anum. He wæs buton synnum acenned, and his lif wæs
eal buton synnum. Ne worhte he ðeah nane wundra openlice
ær ðan ðe he wæs þritig wintre on þære menniscnysse; þa

lived six hundred years, and his son was called Arphaxad, who lived three hundred thirty-three years, and his son was called Salah, who lived four hundred thirty-three years. Then he produced a son who was called Eber, from whom arose the Hebrew people, whom God loved; and from that tribe came all the patriarchs and prophets who announced Christ's coming to this life, that he who was eternally God with the exalted Father would be human almost at the end of this world, for our redemption. And to this tribe God gave and established a law, and he led them over the sea with dry feet, and fed them forty years with heavenly bread, and performed many miracles among the people, because he would choose his mother from this tribe.

Then at last, when the time came which God had fore- 19 seen, he sent his angel Gabriel to a virgin of that tribe, whose name was Mary. The angel came to her and greeted her with God's words, and revealed to her that God's son would be born of her without intercourse with a man. And she believed his words and became pregnant. When her time came, she gave birth, and remained a virgin. That child is twice born: he is born of the Father in heaven without any mother, and later, when he became a human, he was born of the pure virgin Mary without any earthly father. God the Father made humanity and all creation through the Son; and later, when we were condemned, he sent the same Son for our redemption.

The holy mother Mary nourished that child with great 20 devotion, and it grew just as other children do, except without sin. He was born without sins, and his life was entirely without sin. Yet he performed no miracles openly before he was thirty years in human form; then afterward he chose

siðþan geceas he him leorningcnihtas—ærest twelf, þa we hataõ *apostolas,* þæt sind, "ærendracan"; siþþan he geceas twa and hundseofontig, õa sind genemnede *discipuli,* þæt sind, "leorningcnihtas." Ða worhte he fela wundra þæt men mihton gelyfan þæt he wæs Godes bearn. He awende wæter to wine, and eode ofer sæ mid drium fotum, and he gestilde windas mid his hæse, and he forgeaf blindum mannum ge- sihõe, and healtum and lamum rihtne gang, and hreoflium smeõnysse and hælu heora lichaman; dumbum he forgeaf getingnysse, and deafum heorcnunge; deofolseocum and wodum he sealde gewitt and þa deoflu todræfde, and ælce untrumnysse he gehælde. Deade men he arærde of heora byrgenum to life, and lærde þæt folc þe he to com mid mic- clum wisdom, and cwæð þæt nan man ne mæg beon ge- healden buton he rihtlice on God gelyfe and he beo geful- lod, and his geleafan mid godum weorcum geglenge. He onscunode ælc unriht and ealle leasunga, and tæhte rihtwis- nysse and soõfæstnysse.

21 Þa nam þæt Iudeisce folc micelne andan ongean his lare and smeadon hu hi mihton hine to deaõe gedon. Þa wearõ an õæra twelfa Cristes geferena, se wæs Iudas gehaten, þurh deofles tihtinge beswicen, and he eode to õam Iudeiscum folce, and smeade wið hi hu he Crist him belæwan mihte. Þeah õe eal mennisc wære gegaderod, ne mihton hi ealle hine acwellan gif he sylf nolde, forõi he com to us þæt he wolde for us deað þrowian, and swa eal mancynn þa õe ge- lyfað mid his agenum deaõe alysan fram hellewite. He nolde geniman us neadunge of deofles anwealde buton he hit for- wyrhte; þa he hit forwyrhte genoh swiõe þa þa he gehwette and tihte õæra Iudeiscra manna heortan to Cristes slege.

disciples—first, twelve whom we call *apostles,* that is, "messengers"; later, he chose seventy-two who are called *disciples,* that is, "students." He performed many miracles so that people might believe that he was the son of God. He turned water to wine, and went over the sea with dry feet, and he calmed the winds by his command, and he gave sight to the blind, and proper gait to the crippled and lame, and to lepers smoothness and health to their bodies; to the mute he gave speech, and to the deaf hearing; to those possessed by devils and to the insane he gave sense and drove out the devils, and he healed every disease. He raised the dead from their graves to life, and taught the people he came to with great wisdom, and said that no one could be saved unless he should rightly believe in God and be baptized, and adorn his faith with good works. He rejected all injustice and all lies, and taught righteousness and truth.

Then the Jewish people felt great envy toward his teaching and plotted how they might put him to death. Then one of Christ's twelve companions, called Judas, was deceived through the urging of the devil, and he went to the Jewish people and plotted with them how he might betray Christ to them. Even if all humanity were gathered together, they all could not kill him if he himself did not wish it, because he came to us so that he would suffer death for us, and so through his own death he might rescue all believers from the torments of hell. He would not take us by force from the devil's power unless he had forfeited it; the devil forfeited it completely when he urged and tempted the hearts of the Jewish people to the killing of Christ. Then Christ

21

Crist ða geðafode þæt þa wælhreowan hine genamon and gebundon, and on rode hengene acwealdon.

22 Hwæt ða twegen gelyfede men hine arwurðlice bebyrigdon; and Crist, on ðære hwile, to helle gewende and þone deofol gewylde, and him of anam Adam and Evan and heora ofspring—þone dæl ðe him ær gecwemde—and gelædde hi to heora lichaman, and aras of deaðe mid þam micclum werede on þam þriddan dæge his þrowunge. Com þa to his apostolum and hi gefrefrode, and geond feowertigra daga fyrst him mid wunode, and ða ylcan lare þe he him ær tæhte eft geedlæhte, and het hi faran geond ealne middangeard bodigende fulluht and soðne geleafan. Drihten ða on ðam feowerteogoðan dæge his æristes astah to heofenum ætforan heora ealra gesihðe, mid þam ylcan lichaman þe he on ðrowode, and sitt on ða swiðran his Fæder and ealra gesceafta gewylt.

23 He hæfð gerymed rihtwisum mannum infær to his rice, and ða ðe his beboda eallunga forseoð beoð on helle besencte. Witodlice, he cymð on ende þyssere worulde mid micclum mægenðrymme on wolcnum, and ealle ða ðe æfre sawle underfengon arisað of deaðe him togeanes. And he ðonne ða manfullan deofle betæcð, into ðam ecan fyre helle susle; þa rihtwisan he læt mid him into heofonan rice, on þam hi rixiað a on ecnysse. Men ða leofestan, smeagað þysne cwyde, and mid micelre gymene forbugað unrihtwysnysse, and geearniað mid godum weorcum þæt ece lif mid Gode, se ðe ana on ecnysse rixað. Amen.

consented that those bloodthirsty ones should take him and bind him, and kill him by hanging on a cross.

At this, two faithful men buried him honorably; and during that time Christ went to hell and overcame the devil, and took from him Adam and Eve and their offspring—that portion which had been acceptable to him—and led them to their bodies, and arose from death with that great host on the third day after his passion. Then he came to his apostles and comforted them, and remained with them for a space of forty days, and repeated the same teaching he had taught them before, and commanded them to go throughout all the earth preaching baptism and true faith. Then on the fortieth day after his resurrection the Lord ascended into heaven in the sight of them all, with the same body in which he had suffered, and he sits at the right hand of his Father and rules all creation. 22

He has opened the entrance to his kingdom to righteous people, and those who completely despise his commandments will be cast down into hell. Indeed, he will come at the end of this world with great majesty in the heavens, and all those who have ever received a soul will arise from death toward him. He will then consign the wicked to the devil, into the eternal fire of hell's torment; the righteous he will lead with him into the kingdom of heaven, where they will rule for all eternity. Most beloved people, consider this discourse, and with great care turn away from unrighteousness, and merit with good works that eternal life with God, who alone rules for eternity. Amen. 23

VIII KALENDAS JANUARII

Sermo de Natale Domini

We wyllað, to trymminge eowres geleafan, eow gereccan þæs hælendes acennednysse be ðære godspellican ende-byrdnysse, hu he on ðysum dægðerlicum dæge on soðre menniscnysse acenned wæs, se ðe æfre buton angynne of ðam ælmightigan Fæder acennyd wæs on godcundnysse.

2   Lucas se godspellere awrat on Cristes bec þæt "On ðam timan se Romanisca casere Octavianus sette gebann þæt wære on gewritum asett eall ymbhwyrft. Þeos towritennys wearð aræred fram ðam ealdormen Cyrino of Sirian lande, þæt ælc man oferheafod sceolde cennan his gebyrde and his are on ðære byrig þe he to gehyrde. Þa ferde Ioseph, Cristes fosterfæder, fram Galileiscum earde, of ðære byrig Nazareð, to Iudeiscre byrig seo wæs Dauides and wæs geciged Beth-leem, forðan ðe he wæs of Dauides mægðe, and wolde an-dettan mid Marian hire gebyrde, þe wæs ða gyt bearneaca. Ða gelamp hit þa þa hi on þære byrig Bethleem wicodon þæt hire tima wæs gefylled þæt heo cennan sceolde, and acende ða hyre frumcennedan sunu and mid cildclaðum be-wand, and alede þæt cild on heora assena binne, forþan þe ðær næs nan rymet on þam gesthuse.

3   "Þa wæron hyrdas on þam earde waciende ofer heora eo-wede; and efne ða Godes engel stod onemn hi, and Godes

2

The Nativity of the Lord

DECEMBER 25

Homily on the Nativity of the Lord

For the confirmation of your faith, we want to tell you of the savior's birth according to the gospel narrative, how on this present day he was born in true humanity, he who was eternally begotten of the almighty Father in divinity.

Luke the Evangelist wrote in Christ's book that "At that time the Roman emperor Octavian established a decree that all the world should be set down in writing. This recording was instituted by the governor Quirinius of Syria, that every person generally should make known his birth and his property in the city to which he belonged. Then Joseph, Christ's foster father, went from the city of Nazareth in the land of Galilee to the city of David in Judea, which was called Bethlehem, because he was of David's tribe, and wanted to declare the birth with Mary, for she was then pregnant. Then it happened while they were in the city of Bethlehem that her time to give birth was fulfilled, and she brought forth her firstborn son and wrapped him in swaddling clothes, and laid the child in their asses' manger, because there was no room in the inn.

"There were shepherds in that country keeping watch over their flocks; and behold, the angel of God stood before

beorhtnys hi bescean, and hi wurdon micclum afyrhte. Ða cwæð se Godes engel to ðam hyrdum, 'Ne ondrædað eow; efne ic eow bodige micelne gefean þe becymð eallum folce, forðan þe nu todæg is eow acenned hælend, Crist, on Dauides ceastre. Ge geseoð þis tacen: ge gemetað þæt cild mid cildclaðum bewunden and on binne geled.' Þa færlice æfter þæs engles spræce wearð gesewen micel menigu heofenlices werodes, God herigendra and singendra, *'Gloria in excelsis Deo, et in terra pax hominibus bonae voluntatis,'* þæt is, on urum gereorde, 'Sy wuldor Gode on heannyssum, and on eorðan sibb mannum, þam þe beoð godes willan.' And ða englas ða gewiton of heora gesihðe to heofonum.

4   "Hwæt ða hyrdas þa him betweonan spræcon: 'Uton faran to Bethleem and geseon þæt word þe us God æteowde.' Hi comon ða hrædlice and gemetton Marian and Ioseph and þæt cild geled on anre binne, swa swa him se engel cydde. Þa hyrdas soðlice oncneowon be þam worde þe him gesæd wæs be ðam cilde, and ealle wundrodon þe þæt gehyrdon and eac be ðam ðe þa hyrdas him sædon. Maria soðlice heold ealle þas word, aræfniende on hire heortan. Ða gecyrdon þa hyrdas ongean wuldrigende and herigende God on eallum ðam ðingum þe hi gehyrdon and gesawon, swa swa him fram þam engle gesæd wæs."

5   Mine gebroðra þa leofostan, ure hælend, Godes Sunu, euenece and gelic his Fæder, se ðe mid him wæs æfre buton anginne, gemedemode hine sylfne þæt he wolde on ðisum dægðerlicum dæge for middangeardes alysednysse beon lichamlice acenned of þam mædene Marian. He is ealdor and scyppend ealra godnyssa and sibbe, and he foresende ær his acennednysse ungewunelice sibbe, forðan ðe næfre næs swilc sibb ær þam fyrste on middangearde swilc swa wæs on

them, and God's brightness shone on them, and they were very much afraid. Then God's angel said to the shepherds, 'Do not be afraid; behold, I announce great joy to you which will come to all people, for now today a savior, Christ, is born to you in the city of David. You will see this sign: you will find the child wrapped in swaddling clothes and laid in a manger.' Then suddenly after the angel's speech there was seen a great multitude of the heavenly host, praising God and singing, *'Glory to God in the highest, and on earth peace to people of good will,'* that is, in our language, 'Glory be to God in the heights, and on earth peace to people who are of good will.' And the angels then departed from their sight into heaven.

"At this the shepherds spoke among themselves: 'Let us 4 go to Bethlehem and see the word that God has revealed to us.' They came quickly and found Mary and Joseph and the child laid in a manger, just as the angel had revealed to them. The shepherds truly understood the word that had been said to them concerning the child, and all who heard it marveled, and also at what the shepherds said to them. But Mary held all these words, pondering them in her heart. Then the shepherds returned, glorifying and praising God for all the things they had heard and seen, just as had been told to them by the angel."

My dearest brothers, our savior, God's Son, coeternal and 5 equal to his Father, who with him was eternally without beginning, humbled himself on this present day to be physically born of the virgin Mary for the redemption of the world. He is the lord and creator of all goodness and peace, and he sent in advance of his birth uncommon peace, for there never was such peace before that time in the world as his gebyrdtide, swa þæt eall middangeard wæs anes mannes rice underðeod, and eal mennisc him anum cynelic gafol ageaf. Witodlice, on swa micelre sibbe wæs Crist acenned, se ðe is ure sib, forðan ðe he geðeodde englas and men to anum hirede þurh his menniscnysse.

6 He wæs acenned on þæs caseres dagum þe wæs Octavia-nus gehaten, se gerymde Romana rice to ðan swiðe þæt him eal middangeard tobeah, and he wæs forði *Augustus* geciged, þæt is, "geycende his rice." Se nama gedafenað þam heofon-lican cyninge Criste þe on his timan acenned wæs, se ðe his heofonlice rice geyhte, and ðone hryre þe se feallenda deo-fol on engla werode gewanode, mid menniscum gecynde eft gefylde. Na þæt an þæt he ðone lyre anfealdlice gefylde, ac eac swylce micclum geihte. Soðlice, swa micel getel man-cynnes becymð þurh Cristes menniscnysse to engla wero-dum swa micel swa on heofonum belaf haligra engla æfter ðæs deofles hryre.

7 Þæs caseres gebann, þe het ealne middangeard awritan, getacnode swutellice þæs heofonlican cyninges dæde, þe to ði com on middangeard þæt he of eallum ðeodum his gecorenan gegaderode and heora naman on ecere eadignysse awrite. Þeos towritennys asprang fram ðam ealdormen Cyrino: *Cyrinus* is gereht "yrfenuma," and he getacnode Crist, se ðe is soð yrfenuma þæs ecan Fæder, and he us for-gifð þæt we mid him beon yrfenuman and efenhlyttan his wuldres. Ealle ðeoda þa ferdon þæt ælc synderlice be him sylfum cennan sceolde on ðære byrig ðe he to hyrde. Swa swa on ðam timan, be ðæs caseres gebanne, gehwilce æn-lipige on heora burgum be him sylfum cendon, swa eac nu us cyðað lareowas Cristes gebann þæt we us gegadrian to his halgan gelaðunge, and on ðære ures geleafan gafol mid

there was at the time of his birth, so that all the world was subject to the rule of one person, and all humanity paid royal tribute to him alone. Indeed, Christ, who is our peace, was born in such peace, because he joined angels and men in one family through his incarnation.

He was born in the days of the emperor called Octavian, 6 who expanded the Roman empire so much that all the world bowed to him, and because of that he was called *Augustus,* that is, "increasing his kingdom." The name suits the heavenly king Christ, who was born in his time, who increased his heavenly kingdom, and with the human race replenished the loss by which the devil's fall had diminished the host of angels. Not only did he simply replenish that loss, but also greatly increased it. Indeed, as great a number of humankind will join to the hosts of angels through Christ's incarnation as there remained of holy angels in heaven after the devil's fall.

The emperor's decree, which commanded that all the 7 world be written down, clearly signified the heavenly king's deed, who came into the world so that he might gather his chosen ones from all nations and write their names in eternal blessedness. This enrollment sprang from the governor Quirinius: *Cyrinus* is interpreted "heir," and he signified Christ, who is the true heir of the eternal Father, and he grants us that we might be heirs with him and sharers in his glory. All people then went so that each might separately declare himself in the city to which he belonged. Just as at that time, according to the emperor's decree, everyone individually declared themselves in their cities, so now teachers make known to us Christ's decree that we should gather ourselves into his holy church, and there give him the trib-

estfullum mode him agifan, þæt ure naman beon awritene on lifes bec mid his gecorenum.

8 Drihten wæs acenned on þære byrig ðe is gehaten Bethleem, forðan ðe hit wæs swa ær gewitegod þisum wordum: "Þu, Bethleem, Iudeisc land, ne eart ðu wacost burga on Iudeiscum ealdrum: soðlice, of ðe cymð se latteow þe gewylt Israhela ðeoda." Crist wolde on ytinge beon acenned, to ði þæt he wurde his ehterum bedigelod. *Bethleem* is gereht "hlafhus," and on hire wæs Crist, se soða hlaf, acenned, ðe be him sylfum cwæð, "Ic eom se liflica hlaf, þe of heofenum astah, and se ðe of ðam hlafe geett ne swylt he on ecnysse." Þæs hlafes we onbyriað þonne we mid geleafan to husle gað, þe þæt halige husel is gastlice Cristes lichama, and þurh ðone we beoð alysede fram ðam ecan deaðe.

9 Maria acende ða hire frumcennedan sunu on ðisum andweardan dæge, and hine mid cildclaðum bewand, and for rymetleaste on anre binne gelede. Næs þæt cild forði gecweden hire frumcennede cild swilce heo oðer siððan acende, ac forði þe Crist is frumcenned of manegum gastlicum gebroðrum. Ealle Cristene men sind his gastlican gebroðra, and he is se frumcenneda on gife, and on godcundnysse ancenned of ðam ælmihtigan Fæder. He wæs mid wacum cildclaðum bewæfed þæt he us forgeafe ða undeadlican tunecan þe we forluron on ðæs frumsceapenan mannes forgægednysse. Se ælmihtiga Godes Sunu, ðe heofenas befon ne mihton, wæs geled on nearuwre binne, to ði þæt he us fram hellicum nyrwette alysde. Maria wæs ða Cuma ðær, swa swa þæt godspel us segð; and for ðæs folces geðryle wæs þæt gesthus ðearle genyrwed. Se Godes Sunu wæs on his gesthuse genyrwed þæt he us rume wununge on heofonan

ute of our faith with devout mind, so that our names might be written in the book of life with his chosen ones.

The Lord was born in the city called Bethlehem, because 8 it had been prophesied thus in these words: "You, Bethlehem, land of Judah, you are not the least of cities among the lords of Judah: indeed, from you will come the leader that will rule the people of Israel." Christ wished to be born on a journey, so that he might be hidden from his persecutors. *Bethlehem* is interpreted "house of bread," and in it was born Christ, the true bread, who said of himself, "I am the bread of life, which came down from heaven, and whoever eats of this bread will not die for all eternity." We taste this bread when we go with faith to the Eucharist, because the holy Eucharist is spiritually Christ's body, and through it we are rescued from eternal death.

Mary brought forth her firstborn son on this present day, 9 and wrapped him in swaddling clothes, and for lack of a room laid him in a manger. That child was not called her firstborn child because she later brought forth another, but because Christ is the firstborn of many spiritual brothers. All Christians are his spiritual brothers, and he is the firstborn in grace, and only-begotten in divinity of the almighty Father. He was wrapped in poor swaddling clothes so that he might give us the immortal garment which we lost by the transgression of the first-created person. The almighty Son of God, whom the heavens could not contain, was laid in a narrow manger, so that he might rescue us from the narrowness of hell. Mary was a stranger there, as the gospel tells us; and because of the press of people the inn was greatly crowded. The Son of God was crowded in his inn so that he might give us a spacious dwelling in the kingdom of heaven,

rice forgife, gif we his willan gehyrsumiað. Ne bitt he us nanes ðinges to edleane his geswinces buton ure sawle hælo, þæt we us sylfe clæne and ungewemmede him gegearcian to blisse and to ecere myrhðe.

10 Þa hyrdas ðe wacodon ofer heora eowode on Cristes acennednysse getacnodon ða halgan lareowas on Godes gelaðunge, þe sind gastlice hyrdas geleaffulra sawla. And se engel cydde Cristes acennednysse hyrdemannum, forðam ðe ðan gastlicum hyrdum, þæt sind, lareowas, is swiðost geopenod embe Cristes menniscnysse, þurh boclice lare; and hi sceolon gecneordlice heora underþeoddum bodian þæt þæt him geswutelod is, swa swa ða hyrdas þa heofenlican gesihðe gewidmærsodan. Þam lareowe gedafenað þæt he symle wacol sy ofer Godes eowode, þæt se ungesewenlica wulf Godes scep ne tostence.

11 Gelome wurdon englas mannum æteowode on ðære ealdan æ, ac hit nis awriten þæt hi mid leohte comon; ac se wurðmynt wæs þises dæges mærðe gehealden, þæt hi mid heofenlicum leohte hi geswutelodon ða ða þæt soðe leoht asprang on ðeostrum rihtgeþancodum, se mildheorta and se rihtwisa Drihten. Se engel cwæð to þam hyrdum, "Ne beo ge afyrhte. Efne, ic bodige eow micelne gefean ðe eallum folce becymð, forðan þe nu todæg is acenned hælend Crist on Dauides ceastre." Soðlice he bodade micelne gefean se ðe næfre ne geendað, forðan þe Cristes acennednys gegladode heofenwara, and eorðwara, and helwara. Se engel cwæð, "Nu todæg is eow acenned hælend Crist on Dauides ceastre"; rihtlice he cwæð "on dæge" and na "on nihte," forðan ðe Crist is se soða dæg se ðe todræfde mid his tocyme ealle nytennysse þære ealdan nihte and ealne middangeard mid

if we will obey his will. He asks nothing of us as a reward for his labor except the salvation of our soul, that we may prepare ourselves for him pure and unblemished for bliss and eternal joy.

The shepherds who kept watch over their flock at Christ's birth signified the holy teachers in God's Church, who are the spiritual shepherds of faithful souls. And the angel announced Christ's birth to the shepherds, because Christ's humanity is chiefly revealed to the spiritual shepherds, that is, teachers, through teaching in books; and they should diligently preach to those placed under them what has been revealed to them, just as the shepherds proclaimed the heavenly vision. It is appropriate for the teacher to be always watchful over God's flock, so that the invisible wolf might not scatter God's sheep. 10

Angels appeared to people frequently in the old law, but it is not written that they came with light; but that honor was reserved for the greatness of this day, that they should reveal themselves with heavenly light just when that true light, the merciful and righteous Lord, sprang up in darkness for right-minded people. The angel said to the shepherds, "Do not be afraid. Behold, I announce to you great joy which will come to all people, for today the savior Christ is born in the city of David." Truly he announced great joy which will never end, because Christ's nativity gladdened the inhabitants of heaven, and of earth, and of hell. The angel said, "Now today is born to you a savior Christ in the city of David"; rightly he said "in the day" and not "in the night," because Christ is the true day who with his coming drove away all the ignorance of the old night and enlightened the whole world with his grace. We should always hold in our 11

his gife onlihte. Þæt tacen ðe se engel ðam hyrdum sæde we sceolon symle on urum gemynde healdan, and þancian ðam hælende þæt he gemedemode hine sylfne to ðan þæt he dæl-nimend wære ure deadlicnysse, mid menniscum flæsce be-fangen and mid waclicum cildclaðum bewunden.

12   "Þa færlice, æfter ðæs engles spræce, wearð gesewen mi-cel menigu heofenlices werodes, God herigendra and sin-gendra, '*Gloria in excelsis Deo, et in terra pax hominibus bonae voluntatis*'; þæt is, on urum gereorde, 'Sy wuldor Gode on heannyssum, and on eorðan sibb þam mannum þe beoð godes willan.'" An engel bodade þam hyrdum þæs heofon-lican cyninges acennednysse, and ða færlice wurdon æteo-wode fela ðusend engla, þy læs ðe wære geþuht anes engles ealdordom to hwonlic to swa micelre bodunge. And hi ealle samod mid gedremum sange Godes wuldor hleoðrodon, and godum mannum sibbe bodedon, swutellice æteowiende þæt þurh his acennednysse men beoð gebigede to anes geleafan sibbe, and to wuldre godcundlicere herunge. Hi sungon, "Sy wuldor Gode on heannyssum, and on eorðan sibb mannum ðam ðe beoð godes willan." Ðas word geswuteliað þæt ðær wunað Godes sib, þær se goda willa bið. Eornostlice, man-cynn hæfde ungeþwærnysse to englum ær Drihtnes acen-nednysse; forðan ðe we wæron þurh synna ælfremede fram Gode, þa wurde we eac ælfremede fram his englum getealde. Ac siððan se heofenlica cyning urne eorðlican lichaman un-derfeng, siððan gecyrdon his englas to ure sibbe, and ða ðe hi ær ðan untrume forsawon, þa hi wurðiað nu him to ge-ferum.

13   Witodlice, on ðære ealdan æ Loð and Iosue and gehwilce oðre ðe englas gesawon hi luton wið heora and to him ge-bædon, and ða englas þæt geðafodon. Ac Iohannes se

48

memory the sign which the angel said to the shepherds, and thank the savior that he so humbled himself that he was a sharer in our mortality, clothed in human flesh and wrapped in lowly swaddling clothes.

"Then suddenly, after the angel's speech, a great multi- 12
tude of the heavenly host was seen, praising God and singing, '*Glory to God in the highest, and on earth peace to people of good will*'; that is, in our language, 'Glory be to God in the heights, and on earth peace to people who are of good will.'" One angel announced the heavenly king's birth to the shepherds, and then suddenly there appeared many thousands of angels, lest the authority of one angel might seem too small for so great an announcement. And they all together proclaimed God's glory with harmonious song, and announced peace to good people, showing clearly that through his birth people will be inclined to the peace of one faith, and to the glory of divine praise. They sang, "Glory be to God in the heights, and on earth peace to people who are of good will." These words reveal that where God's peace dwells, there will be good will. Indeed, humanity had discord with the angels before the Lord's incarnation; because we were alienated from God through sins, we were also considered alienated from his angels. But after the heavenly king took on our earthly body, then his angels turned to peace with us, and those they had once despised as infirm, they now honor as their companions.

Truly, in the old law Lot and Joshua and some others who 13
saw angels bowed before them and prayed to them, and the angels allowed that. But John the Evangelist in the New

godspellere on ðære Niwan Gecyðnysse wolde hine gebiddan to þam engle þe him to spræc, þa forwyrnde se engel
him ðæs and cwæð, "Beheald þæt þu þas dæde ne do. Ic eom
ðin efenðeowa and ðinra gebroðra; gebide þe to Gode
anum." Englas geðafodon ær Drihtnes tocyme þæt mennisce men him to feollon, and æfter his tocyme þæs for-
wyrndon, forðan ðe hi gesawon þæt heora scyppend þæt gecynd underfeng ðe hi ær ðan waclic tealdon, and ne dorston
hit forseon on us þonne hi hit wurðiað bufon him sylfum on
ðam heofonlican cyninge. Ne hi manna geferrædene ne
forhogiað þonne hi, feallende hi, to þam menniscum Gode
gebiddað. Nu we sind getealde Godes ceastergewaran and
englum gelice; uton forði hogian þæt leahtras us ne totwæmon fram ðisum micclum wurðmynte. Soðlice men syndon
godas gecigede; heald forði, ðu mann, þinne Godes wurðscipe wið leahtras, forðan þe God is geworden mann for ðe.

14   Þa hyrdas ða spræcon him betweonan æfter ðæra engla
framfærelde, "Uton gefaran to Bethleem and geseon þæt
word þe geworden is, and God us geswutelode." Eala hu
rihtlice hi andetton þone halgan geleafan mid þisum wordum! "On frymðe wæs word, and þæt word wæs mid Gode,
and þæt word wæs God." Word bið wisdomes geswutelung,
and þæt word, þæt is, se wisdom, is acenned of ðam ælmihtigum Fæder butan anginne, forðan ðe he wæs æfre God
of Gode, wisdom of ðam wisan Fæder. Nis he na geworht,
forðan ðe he is God and na gesceaft; ac se ælmihtiga Fæder
gesceop þurh ðone wisdom ealle gesceafta, and hi ealle ðurh
þone Halgan Gast geliffæste. Ne mihte ure mennisce gecynd Crist on ðære godcundlican acennednysse geseon, ac
þæt ylce word wæs geworden flæsc and wunode on us þæt
we hine geseon mihton. Næs þæt word to flæsce awend, ac

Testament wanted to pray to the angel who spoke to him, and the angel forbade him and said, "See that you do not do this deed. I am your fellow servant and one of your brothers; pray to God alone." Before the Lord's coming angels allowed humans to fall down before them, and after his coming forbade it, because they saw that their creator took on that nature which they had previously considered lowly, and they dared not despise it in us when they honor it above themselves in the heavenly king. Nor do they disdain the fellowship of humans when they, falling down, pray to the God made human. Now we are considered citizens of God and equal to the angels; let us therefore take care that sins do not separate us from this great dignity. Truly humans are called gods; therefore, human, protect your divine dignity against sins, since God has become human for you.

The shepherds then spoke among themselves after the 14 departure of the angels, "Let us go to Bethlehem and see the word which has come to pass, and that God revealed to us." Oh how rightly they confessed the holy faith with these words! "In the beginning was the word, and the word was with God, and the word was God." A word is the revelation of wisdom, and the word, that is, wisdom, is begotten of the almighty Father without beginning, for he was ever God of God, wisdom of the wise Father. He is not made, for he is God and not a creature; but the almighty Father created all creatures through that wisdom, and gave them all life through the Holy Spirit. Our human nature could not see Christ in that divine nativity, but that same word was made flesh and dwelled among us so that we might see him. The word was not turned to flesh, but it was clothed with human

hit wæs mid menniscum flæsce befangen. Swa swa anra gehwilc manna wunað on sawle and on lichaman an mann, swa
eac Crist wunað on godcundnysse and menniscnysse on
anum hade an Crist. Hi cwædon, "Uton geseon þæt word þe
geworden is," forðan ðe hi ne mihton hit geseon ær ðan ðe
hit geflæschamod wæs and to menn geworden. Nis þeah
hwæðre seo godcundnys gemenged to ðære menniscnysse,
ne ðær nan twæming nys. We mihton eow secgan ane lytle
bysne, gif hit to waclic nære: sceawa nu on anum æge, hu þæt
hwite ne bið gemenged to ðam geolcan, and bið hwæðere an
æg. Nis eac Cristes godcundnys gerunnen to ðære menniscnysse, ac he þurhwunað þeah a on ecnysse on anum hade
untotwæmed.

15   Hrædlice ða comon þa hyrdas and gemetton Marian and
Ioseph and þæt cild geled on ðære binne. Maria wæs, be
Godes dihte, þam rihtwisan Iosepe beweddod for micclum
gebeorge, forðan ðe hit wæs swa gewunelic on Iudeiscre ðeode, æfter Moyses æ, þæt gif ænig wimman cild hæfde butan
be rihte æwe, þæt hi man sceolde mid stanum oftorfian. Ac
God asende his engel to Iosepe ða Maria eacnigende wæs,
and bead þæt he hire gymene hæfde and þæs cildes fosterfæder wære. Þa wæs geðuht ðam Iudeiscum swilce Ioseph
þæs cildes fæder wære, ac he næs, þe hit næs nan neod þam
ælmihtigum scyppende þæt he of wife acenned wære, ac
he genam ða menniscnysse of Marian innoðe and forlet hi
mæden, na gewemmed ac gehalgod þurh his acennednysse.
Ne oncneow heo weres gemanan, and heo acende butan
sare, and þurhwunað on mægðhade. Þa hyrdas gesawon and
oncneowon be ðam cilde, swa swa him gesæd wæs. Nis nan
eadignys butan Godes oncnawennesse, swa swa Crist sylf

flesh. Just as every person remains in soul and in body one person, so also Christ remains in divine nature and human nature one Christ in one person. They said, "Let us see the word that has come to pass," because they could not see it before it was incarnate and had become human. Nevertheless the divine nature is not mingled with the human nature, nor is there any separation. We might give you a little example, if it were not too trivial: look at an egg, how the white is not mingled with the yolk, and yet it is one egg. Christ's divinity is not run together with his humanity, but he remains for all eternity in one person undivided.

The shepherds came quickly and found Mary and Joseph 15 and the child laid in the manger. Mary was betrothed, by God's direction, to the righteous Joseph for greater security, because it was the custom among the Jewish people, according to the law of Moses, that if any woman had a child except in lawful wedlock, she should be put to death with stones. But God sent his angel to Joseph when Mary was pregnant, and commanded that he should take care of her and be the child's foster father. Then it seemed to the Jews that Joseph was child's father, but he was not, because there was no need for the almighty creator to be born of woman, but he took human nature from Mary's womb and left her a virgin, not defiled but sanctified through his birth. She knew no intercourse with a man, and she gave birth without pain, and remains in virginity. The shepherds saw and recognized the child, just as it had been said to them. There is no happiness without acknowledgment of God, as Christ himself

cwæð ða ða he us his Fæder betæhte: "Þæt is ece lif, þæt hi
ðe oncnawon soðne God, and þone ðe ðu asendest hælend
Crist."

16   "Hwæt ða ealle ða ðe þæt gehyrdon micclum ðæs wundrodon, and be ðam ðe ða hyrdas sædon. Maria soðlice
heold ealle ðas word, aræfniende on hire heortan." Heo
nolde widmærsian Cristes digelnesse, ac anbidode oð þæt
he sylf þa ða he wolde hi geopenode. Heo cuðe Godes æ, and
on ðæra witegena gesetnysse rædde þæt mæden sceolde
God acennan. Þa blissode heo micclum þæt heo hit beon
moste. Hit wæs gewitegod þæt he on ðære byrig Bethleem
acenned wurde, and heo ðearle wundrode þæt heo, æfter
ðære witegunge, ðær acende. Heo gemunde hwæt sum
witega cwæð, "Se oxa oncneow his hlaford, and se assa his
hlafordes binne"; þa geseah heo þæt cild licgan on binne,
ðær se oxa and se assa gewunelice fodan secað. Godes heahengel Gabrihel bodode Marian ðæs hælendes tocyme on
hire innoðe, and heo geseah ða þæt his bodung unleaslice
gefylled wæs. Ðyllice word Maria heold, aræfnigende on
hire heortan. "And ða hyrdas gecyrdon ongean, wuldrigende
and herigende God on eallum ðam ðingum ðe hi gehyrdon
and gesawon, swa swa him gesæd wæs."

17   Þyssera ðreora hyrda gemynd is gehæfd be eastan Bethleem ane mile, on Godes cyrcan geswutelod þam ðe ða stowe
geneosiað. We sceolon geefenlæcan þysum hyrdum, and
wuldrian and herian urne Drihten on eallum ðam ðingum þe
he for ure lufe gefremode, us to alysednysse and to ecere
blisse. Ðam sy wuldor and lof mid þam ælmihtigum Fæder,
on annysse þæs Halgan Gastes, on ealra worulda woruld.
Amen.

said when he entrusted us to his Father: "That is eternal life, that they acknowledge you as true God, and the one you have sent as the savior Christ."

"Now all those who heard that wondered greatly at it, and 16 at what the shepherds said. But Mary held all these words, pondering them in her heart." She would not announce Christ's mystery, but waited until he himself revealed it when it pleased him. She knew God's law, and had read in the account of the prophets that a virgin should give birth to God. Then she greatly rejoiced that it might be she. It was prophesied that he would be born in the city of Bethlehem, and she wondered greatly that she had given birth there, according to that prophecy. She remembered what a certain prophet had said, "The ox knows his lord, and the ass his lord's manger"; then she saw the child lying in the manger, where the ox and the ass usually seek food. God's archangel Gabriel announced to Mary the savior's coming into her womb, and she saw then that his announcement was fulfilled without falsehood. Such words Mary held, pondering them in her heart. "And the shepherds returned, glorifying and praising God for all the things they had heard and seen, as had been said to them."

The memory of these three shepherds is preserved one 17 mile east of Bethlehem, displayed in God's church to those who seek out the place. We should imitate these shepherds, and glorify and praise our Lord for all those things which he has done for love of us, for our redemption and eternal joy. To him be glory and praise with the almighty Father, in the unity of the Holy Spirit, world without end. Amen.

3

VII KALENDAS JANUARII

Passio beati Stephani protomartyris

We rædað on ðære bec þe is gehaten *Actus apostolorum* þæt ða apostolas gehadodon seofon diaconas on ðære gelaðunge þe of Iudeiscum folce to Cristes geleafan beah æfter his ðrowunge and æriste of deaðe and upstige to heofenum. Þæra diacona wæs se forma Stephanus, þe we on ðisum dæge wurðiað. He wæs swiðe geleafful, and mid þam Halgum Gaste afylled. Þa oðre six wæron gecigede ðisum namum: Stephanus wæs se fyrmesta, oðer Philippus, þridda Procorus, feorða Nicanor, fifta Timotheus, sixta Parmenen, seofoða Nicolaus. Ðas seofon hi gecuron and gesetton on ðæra apostola gesihðe, and hi ða mid gebedum and bletsungum to diaconum gehadode wurdon. Weox ða dæghwomlice Godes bodung, and wæs gemenigfylld þæt getel Cristenra manna þearle on Hierusalem.

2 Þa wearð se eadiga Stephanus mid Godes gife and mid micelre strencðe afylled, and worhte forebeacena and micele tacna on ðam folce. Ða astodon sume ða ungeleaffullan Iudei and woldon mid heora gedwylde þæs eadigan martyres lare oferswiðan, ac hi ne mihton his wisdome wiðstandan, ne ðam Halgum Gaste ðe ðurh hine spræc. Þa setton hi lease gewitan ðe hine forlugon, and cwædon þæt hi tallice word spræce be Moyse and be Gode. Þæt folc wearð ða micclum

3

Saint Stephen

DECEMBER 26

The Passion of Blessed Stephen, Protomartyr

We read in the book called *Acts of the Apostles* that the apostles ordained seven deacons in the congregation which, from among the Jewish people, had turned to belief in Christ after his passion and resurrection from death and ascension into heaven. The first of these deacons was Stephen, whom we honor today. He was very faithful, and filled with the Holy Spirit. The other six were called by these names: Stephen was the first, the second Philip, the third Prochorus, the fourth Nicanor, the fifth Timothy, the sixth Parmenas, the seventh Nicolas. They chose these seven and set them in the presence of the apostles, and they were ordained as deacons with prayers and blessings. God's preaching grew daily, and the number of Christians was greatly multiplied in Jerusalem.

Then the blessed Stephen was filled with God's grace and with great strength, and he performed miracles and great signs among the people. Then some of the unbelieving Jews stood up and wanted to overpower the blessed martyr's teaching with their error, but they could not withstand his wisdom, nor the Holy Spirit who spoke through him. Then they brought out false witnesses who lied about him, and said that he spoke blasphemous words about Moses and

2

astyréd, and þa heafodmenn and þa Iudeiscan boceras, and gelæhton Stephanum and tugon to heora geþeahte, and ða leasan gewitan him on besædon: "Ne geswicð ðes man to sprecenne tallice word ongean þas halgan stowe and Godes æ. We gehyrdon hine secgan þæt Crist towyrpð þas stowe, and towent ða gesetnysse ðe us Moyses tæhte." Þa beheoldon ða hine ðe on þam geðeahte sæton, and gesawon his nebwlite swylce sumes engles ansyne.

3 Ða cwæð se ealdorbiscop to ðam eadigan cyðere, "Is hit swa hi secgað?" Ða wolde se halga wer Stephanus heora ungeleaffullan heortan gerihtlæcan mid heora forðfædera gebysnunge and gemynde, and to soðfæstnysse wege mid ealre lufe gebigan. Begann ða him to reccenne be ðam heahfædere Abrahame, hu se heofenlica God hine geceas him to geþoftan, and him behet þæt ealle ðeoda on his ofspringe gebletsode wurdon, for his gehyrsumnesse. Swa eac ðæra oðra heahfædera gemynd mid langsumere race ætforan him geniwode, and hu Moyses ðurh Godes mihte heora foregengan ofer ða Readan Sæ wundorlice gelædde, and hu hi siððan feowertig geara on westene wæron, mid heofenlicum bigleofan dæghwomlice gereordode; and hu God hi lædde to ðam Iudeiscan earde, and ða hæðenan ðeoda ætforan heora gesihðum eallunga adwæscte; and be Dauides mærðe þæs mæran cyninges, and Salomones wuldor, ðe Gode þæt mære tempel arærde. Cwæð þa æt nextan, "Ge wiðstandað þam Halgum Gaste mid stiðum swuran and ungeleaffulre heortan; ge sind meldan and manslagan, and ge ðone rihtwisan Crist niðfullice acwealdon. Ge underfengon æ on engla gesetnysse, and ge hit ne heoldon."

God. Then the people were greatly stirred up, along with the leaders and the Jewish scribes, and they seized Stephen and dragged him to their council, and the false witnesses accused him: "This man will not stop speaking blasphemous words against this holy place and God's law. We heard him say that Christ will destroy this place, and overthrow the laws which Moses taught us." Then those who sat in the council looked at him, and saw the beauty of his countenance like the face of an angel.

Then the chief priest said to the blessed martyr, "Is it as 3 they say?" The holy man Stephen wanted to correct their unbelieving hearts with the example and memory of their ancestors, and turn them to the way of righteousness with all love. He began to explain to them about the patriarch Abraham, how the God of heaven chose him for his associate, and promised him that, because of his obedience, all nations would be blessed in his offspring. Likewise, with a long narrative he reminded them of the memory of the other patriarchs, and how Moses miraculously led their ancestors over the Red Sea through God's might, and how afterward they were in the desert forty years, nourished daily with heavenly food; and how God led them to the land of Judea, and completely destroyed the heathen nations before their sight; and of the greatness of the famous king David, and the glory of Solomon, who raised the great temple to God. At the end he said, "You resist the Holy Spirit with a stiff neck and an unbelieving heart; you are traitors and murderers, and you violently put to death the righteous Christ. You received the law by the commands of angels, and you have not held it."

4   Hwæt ða Iudeiscan þa wurdon þearle on heora heortan astyrode, and biton heora teð him togeanes. Se halga Stephanus wearð þa afylled mid þam Halgum Gaste, and beheold wið heofonas weard, and geseah Godes wuldor, and þone hælend standende æt his Fæder swiðran; and he cwæð, "Efne! Ic geseo heofenas opene, and mannes Sunu standende æt Godes swiðran." Iudei ða, mid micelre stemne hrymende, heoldon heora earan, and anmodlice him to scuton and hi hine gelæhton, and of ðære byrig gelæddon to stænenne. Þa leasan gewitan ða ledon heora hacelan ætforan fotum sumes geonges cnihtes se wæs geciged Saulus. Ongunnon ða oftorfian mid heardum stanum ðone eadigan Stephanum; and he clypode and cwæð, "Drihten hælend, onfoh minne gast." And gebigde his cneowu, mid micelre stemne clypigende, "Min Drihten, ne sete ðu ðas dæda him to synne." And he mid þam worde ða gewat to ðan ælmihtigum hælende þe he on heofenan healicne standende geseah.

5   Se wisa Augustinus spræc ymbe ðas rædinge, and smeade hwi se halga cyðere Stephanus cwæde þæt he gesawe mannes Bearn standende æt Godes swyðran, and nolde cweðan Godes Bearn, þonne ðe is geðuht wurðlicor be Criste to cweðenne Godes Bearn ðonne mannes Bearn. Ac hit gedafenode þæt se hælend swa geswutelod wære on heofenum, and swa gebodod on middangearde. Eall ðæra Iudeiscra teona aras þurh þæt—hwi Drihten Crist, se ðe æfter flæsce soðlice is mannes Sunu, eac swilce wære gecweden Godes Sunu. Forði gemunde swiðe gedafenlice þæt godcunde gewrit mannes Sunu standan æt Godes swiðran, to gescyndenne ðæra Iudeiscra ungeleaffulnysse. Crist wæs æteowed his eadigan cyðere Stephane on heofenum, se ðe fram

60

At this the Jews were deeply troubled in their hearts, and 4 gnashed their teeth against him. The holy Stephen was then filled with the Holy Spirit, and looked up toward heaven, and saw the glory of God, and the savior standing at his Father's right hand; and he said, "Look! I see the heavens open, and the Son of man standing at God's right hand." Then the Jews, crying out with a loud voice, covered their ears, and with one accord rushed toward him and seized him, and led him out of the city to be stoned. The false witnesses laid their cloaks at the feet of a young man who was called Saul. They began to stone the blessed Stephen with hard stones; he called out and said, "Lord savior, receive my spirit." And he bent his knees, calling out with a loud voice, "My Lord, do not count these deeds against them as a sin." And with these words he departed to the almighty savior whom he had seen standing high in heaven.

The wise Augustine spoke about this reading, and won- 5 dered why the holy martyr Stephen said that he saw the Son of man standing at God's right hand, and would not say the Son of God, when it seems more honorable for Christ to be called the Son of God than the Son of man. But it was fitting that the savior should be revealed this way in heaven, and so announced on earth. All the anger of the Jews arose because of this—why the Lord Christ, who is truly the Son of man after the flesh, should also be called the Son of God. For this reason the divine scripture very appropriately remembers the Son of man standing at God's right hand, to shame the unbelief of the Jews. Christ was shown in the heavens to his blessed martyr Stephen, who was killed by unbelievers on

ungeleaffullum on middangearde acweald wæs, and seo heofenlice soðfæstnys be ðam cydde gecyðnysse þone ðe seo
eorðlice arleasnyss huxlice tælde. Hwa mæg beon rihtlice
geciged mannes Bearn buton Criste anum, þonne ælc man is
twegra manna bearn buton him anum? Se eadiga Stephanus
geseah Crist standan forþan þe he wæs his gefylsta on ðam
gastlicum gefeohte his martyrdomes. Witodlice we andettað on urum credan þæt Drihten sitt æt his Fæder swiðran.
Setl gedafenað deman, and steall fylstendum oððe feohten-
dum. Nu andet ure geleafa Cristes setl, forðan ðe he is se
soða dema lybbendra and deadra; and se eadiga cyðere
Stephanus hine geseah standende, forðan ðe he wæs his gefylsta, swa swa we ær sædon.

6   Ealra gecorenra halgena deað is deorwurðe on Godes gesihðe, ac ðeah hwæðere is geþuht gif ænig todal beon mæg
betwux martyrum, þæt se is healicost se ðe ðone martyrdom
æfter Gode astealde. Witodlice Stephanus wæs to diacone
gehadod æt ðæra apostola handum, ac he hi forestop on
heofenan rice mid sigefæstum deaðe; and swa se ðe wæs
neoðor on endebyrdnysse wearð fyrmest on ðrowunge, and
se ðe wæs leorningcniht on hade ongann wesan lareow on
martyrdome. Ðone deað soðlice þe se hælend gemedemode
for mannum þrowian, ðone ageaf Stephanus fyrmest manna
þam hælende. He is gecweden *protomartyr,* þæt is, "se forma
cyðere," forðan ðe he æfter Cristes ðrowunge ærest martyrdom geðrowode. Stephanus is Grecisc nama, þæt is on
Leden *Coronatus,* þæt we cweðað on Englisc, "Gewuldorbeagod," forðan ðe he hæfð þone ecan wuldorbeah, swa swa his
nama him forewitegode.

7   Þa leasan gewitan ðe hine forsædon hine ongunnon ærest
to torfienne, forðan ðe Moyses æ tæhte þæt swa hwa swa

earth, and the heavenly truth bore witness to him whom earthly wickedness shamefully accused. Who can rightly be called the Son of man except Christ alone, when every person except him alone is the offspring of two persons? The blessed Stephen saw Christ standing because he was his support in the spiritual fight of his martyrdom. Truly we confess in our creed that the Lord sits at the right hand of his Father. A seat befits a judge, and standing suits one who helps or fights. Now our faith confesses Christ's seat, because he is the true judge of the living and the dead; and the blessed martyr Stephen saw him standing, because he was his help, as we have said.

The death of all the chosen saints is precious in God's 6 sight, yet it seems that if any distinction can be made between martyrs, then he is most exalted who suffered martyrdom next after God. Now Stephen was ordained deacon at the hands of the apostles, but he preceded them in the kingdom of heaven by a triumphant death; and so he who was lower in rank became first in suffering, and he who was in the role of a student began to be a teacher in martyrdom. Truly, Stephen was the first person to give back to the savior the same death that the savior humbled himself to suffer for humanity. He is called *protomartyr,* that is, "the first martyr," because he suffered martyrdom first after Christ's passion. Stephen is a Greek name, which is in Latin *Coronatus,* or as we say in English, "Crowned with Glory," because he has the eternal crown of glory, just as his name foretold to him.

The false witnesses who had falsely accused him began 7 to stone him first, because the law of Moses taught that

oðerne to deaðe forsæde sceolde wurpan ðone forman stan to ðam ðe he ær mid his tungan acwealde. Ða reðan Iudei, wedende, þone halgan stændon, and he clypode and cwæð, "Drihten, ne sete ðu ðas dæda him to synne." Understandað nu, mine gebroðra, þa micclan lufe þæs eadigan weres: on deaðe he wæs gesett, and ðeah he bæd mid soðre lufe for his cwelleras, and betwux ðæra stana hryre, ða ða gehwa mihte his leofostan frynd forgytan, ða betæhte he his fynd Gode, þus cweðende, "Drihten, ne sete þu ðas dæda him to synne." Swiðor he besorgade þa heora synna þonne his agene wunda, swiðor heora arleasnysse þonne his sylfes deað; and rihtlice swiðor, forðan ðe heora arleasnysse fyligde se eca deað, and þæt ece lif fyligde his deaðe.

8   Saulus heold ðæra leasra gewitena reaf, and heora mod to þære stæninge geornlice tihte. Stephanus soðlice gebigedum cneowum Drihten bæd þæt he Saulum alysde. Wearð ða Stephanes ben fram Gode gehyred, and Saulus wearð alysed; se arfæsta wæs gehyred, and se arleasa wearð gerihtwisod. On ðyssere dæde is geswutelod hu micclum fremige þære soðan lufe gebed. Witodlice, næfde Godes gelaðung Paulum to lareowe gif se halga martyr Stephanus swa ne bæde. Efne nu Paulus blissað mid Stephane on heofenan rice; mid Stephane he bricð Cristes beorhtnysse, and mid him he rixað. Þider ðe Stephanus forestop, mid Saules stanum oftorfod, ðider folgode Paulus, gefultumod þurh Stephanes gebedu. Þær nis Paulus gescynd þurh Stephanes slege, ac Stephanus gladað on Paules gefærrædene, forðan þe seo soðe lufu on heora ægðrum blissað. Seo soðe lufu oferwann ðæra Iudeiscra reðnysse on Stephane, and seo ylce lufu oferwreah synna micelnysse on Paule, and heo on heora ægðrum samod geearnode heofenan rice. Eornostlice seo

whoever accused another to death should throw the first stone at the one whom he had already slain with his tongue. The cruel Jews, raving, stoned the holy one, and he called out and said, "Lord, do not count these deeds against them as a sin." Understand now, my brothers, the great love of this blessed man: he was condemned to death, and yet he prayed for his killers with true love, and between the falling of the stones, when anyone might forget his dearest friends, he commended his enemies to God, saying, "Lord, do not count these deeds against them as a sin." He was more sorrowful for their sins than his own wounds, more for their wickedness than his own death; and rightly so, because eternal death followed their wickedness, and eternal life followed his death.

Saul held the garments of the false witnesses, and eagerly 8 incited their minds to the stoning. But with bended knees Stephen asked the Lord to redeem Saul. Stephen's request was heard by God, and Saul was redeemed; the pious one was heard, and the wicked one was justified. In this deed is revealed the great effect of a prayer of true love. Indeed, God's Church would not have had Paul as a teacher if the holy martyr Stephen had not prayed for him. And now Paul rejoices with Stephen in the kingdom of heaven; with Stephen he enjoys Christ's radiance, and rules with him. Where Stephen preceded, stoned to death with Saul's stones, there Paul followed, assisted by Stephen's prayers. Paul is not put to shame by Stephen's death, but Stephen rejoices in Paul's fellowship, because true love delights in them both. True love overcame the cruelty of the Jews to Stephen, and the same love covered over the greatness of sin in Paul, and in both of them together it merited the kingdom of heaven.

soðe lufu is wylspring and ordfruma ealra godnyssa and
æðele trumnys, and se weg ðe læt to heofonum. Se ðe færð
on soðre lufe ne mæg he dwelian ne forhtian; heo gewissað
and gescylt and gelæt. Þurh ða soðan lufe wæs þes halga
martyr swa gebyld þæt he bealdlice ðæra Iudeiscra ungeleaffulnysse ðreade, and he orsorh betwux ðam greatum hagol-
stanum þurhwunode, and he for ðam stænendum welwil-
lende gebæd, and þærtoeacan ða heofenlican healle cucu
and gewuldorbeagod innferde.

9   Mine gebroðra, uton geefenlæcan, be sumum dæle; swa
miccles lareowes geleafan and swa mæres cyðeres lufe; uton
lufian ure gebroðra on Godes gelaðunge mid swilcum mode
swa swa ðes cyðere þa lufode his fynd. Beoð gemyndige
hwæt seo sylfe soðfæstnys on ðam halgum godspelle behet,
and hwilc wedd us gesealde. Se hælend cwæð, "Gif ge forgyfað þam mannum ðe wið eow agyltað, þonne forgifð eow
eower Fæder eowere synna; gif ge ðonne nellað forgyfan,
nele eac eower Fæder eow forgifan eowere gyltas." Ge gehyrað nu, mine gebroðra, þæt hit stent þurh Godes gyfe on
urum agenum dihte hu us bið æt Gode gedemed. He cwæð,
"Gif ge forgyfað, eow bið forgyfen." Ne bepæce nan man
hine sylfne: witodlice gif hwa furðon ænne man hatað on
ðisum middangearde, swa hwæt swa he to gode gedeð, eal he
hit forlyst. Forðan ðe se apostol Paulus ne bið geligenod þe
cwæð, "Þeah ðe ic aspende ealle mine æhta on ðearfena
bigleofan, and ðeah ðe ic minne agenne lichaman to cwale
gesylle swa þæt ic forbyrne on martyrdome, gif ic næbbe ða
soðan lufe, ne fremað hit me nan ðing." Be ðan ylcan cwæð
se godspellere Iohannes, "Se ðe his broðor ne lufað, he wunað on deaðe." Eft he cwæð, "Ælc ðæra ðe his broðor hatað
is manslaga." Ealle we sind gebroðra þe on God gelyfað, and

Indeed, true love is the wellspring and origin of all goodness and noble fortitude, and the way that leads to heaven. He who journeys in true love can neither err nor fear; it guides and protects and leads. Through true love the holy martyr was so emboldened that he boldly rebuked the unbelief of the Jews, and remained free from care amid the great hail of stones, and benevolently prayed for those stoning him, and moreover entered the heavenly hall living and crowned with glory.

My brothers, let us imitate, in some part, the faith of so 9 great a teacher and the love of so great a martyr; let us love our brothers in God's Church with the same spirit as this martyr loved his enemies. Remember what the truth itself promises in the holy gospel, and what assurance it has given us. The savior said, "If you forgive those who sin against you, then your Father will forgive your sins; if you will not forgive, your Father will not forgive your sins." You hear now, my brothers, that through God's grace it remains within our own control how we will be judged before God. He said, "If you forgive, you will be forgiven." Let no one deceive himself: truly if anyone hates even one person in this world, whatever good he may do, he will lose it all. For the apostle Paul is not a liar when he says, "Though I spend all my wealth on food for the poor, and though I give my own body to death so that I burn in martyrdom, if I do not have true love, it is of no benefit to me." Concerning the same thing John the Evangelist said, "He who does not love his brother remains in death." Again he said, "Anyone who hates his brother is a murderer." We who believe in God are all

we ealle cweðað "*Pater noster qui es in caelis,*" þæt is, "Ure
Fæder þe eart on heofonum." Ne gedyrstlæce nan man be
mægðhade butan soðre lufe; ne truwige nan man be ælmes-
dædum oððe on gebedum butan ðære foresædan lufe.
Forðan ðe swa lange swa he hylt ðone sweartan nið on his
heortan, ne mæg he mid nanum ðinge þone mildheortan
God gegladian. Ac gif he wille þæt him God milde sy, þonne
hlyste he godes rædes, na of minum muðe ac of Cristes sylfes. He cwæð, "Gif ðu offrast ðine lac to Godes weofode,
and þu þær gemyndig bist þæt ðin broðor hæfð sum ðing
ongean ðe, forlæt ðærrihte ða lac ætforan ðam weofode, and
gang ærest to þinum breðer and þe to him gesibsuma, and
ðonne ðu eft cymst to ðam weofode, geoffra ðonne ðine
lac." Gif ðu ðonne þinum Cristenum breðer deredest, þonne
hæfð he sum ðing ongean ðe, and þu scealt, be Godes tæcunge, hine gegladian ær ðu ðine lac geoffrige. Gif ðonne se
Cristena mann þe ðin broðor is ðe ahwar geyfelode, þæt ðu
scealt miltsigende forgifan. Ure gastlican lac sind ure gebedu
and lofsang and huselhalgung, and gehwilce oðre lac ðe we
Gode offriað, þa we sceolon mid gesibsumere heortan and
broðerlicere lufe Gode betæcan.

10   Nu cwyð sum man ongean ðas rædinge, "Ne mæg ic
minne feond lufian, ðone ðe ic dæghwomlice wælhreowne
togeanes me geseo." Eala ðu mann, þu sceawast hwæt ðin
broðor ðe dyde, and þu ne sceawast hwæt ðu Gode gedydest
þonne þu micele swærran synna wið God gefremodest! Hwi
nelt ðu forgyfan ða lytlan gyltas anum menn, þæt se ælmihtiga God þe ða micclan synna forgyfe? Nu cwyst ðu eft, "Micel gedeorf bið me þæt ic minne feond lufige, and for ðone
gebidde þe me hearmes cepð." Ne wiðcweðe we þæt hit micel gedeorf ne sy; ac gif hit is hefigtyme on ðyssere worulde,

brothers, and we all say "*Our Father, who are in heaven,*" that is, "Our Father who is in heaven." Let no one presume on kinship without true love; let no one trust in almsgiving or in prayers without the aforesaid love. For as long as he holds black malice in his heart, he cannot in any way please the merciful God. But if he wants God to be merciful to him, let him listen to good counsel, not from my mouth but from that of Christ himself. He said, "If you offer your gift at God's altar, and there you remember that your brother has something against you, immediately leave the gift before the altar, and go first to your brother and be reconciled to him, and when you come back to the altar, then offer your gift." If you have injured your Christian brother, then he has something against you, and you should, according to God's teaching, please him before you offer your gift. But if the Christian who is your brother has done any evil to you, you should mercifully forgive that. Our spiritual gifts are our prayers and hymns and consecration of the Eucharist, and every other gift that we offer to God, which we should give to God with peaceful heart and brotherly love.

Now someone will say against this reading, "I cannot love 10 my enemy, whom I see bloodthirsty against me every day." O human, you see what your brother has done to you, but you do not see what you have done to God when you have committed much heavier sins against God! Why will you not forgive the little offenses of one person, so that the almighty God might forgive your great sins? Now you will say in reply, "It is a great hardship for me to love my enemy, and to pray for the one who intends harm against me." We will not deny that it is a great hardship; but if it is difficult in this

hit becymð to micelre mede on ðære toweardan. Witodlice,
þurh ðines feondes lufe þu bist Godes freond; and na þæt an
þæt ðu his freond sy, ac eac swilce þu bist Godes bearn þurh
ða rædene þæt þu þinne feond lufige, swa swa Crist sylf
cwæð, "Lufiað eowere fynd, doð þam tela þe eow hatiað, þæt
ge beon eoweres Fæder cild se ðe on heofenum is." Menigfealde earfoðnyssa and hospas wolde gehwa eaðelice forberan wið þan þæt he moste sumum rican men to bearne
geteald beon, and his yrfenuma to gewitendlicum æhtum;
forberað nu geðyldelice, for ðam ecan wurðmynte þæt ge
Godes bearn getealde beon and his yrfenuman on heofenlicum spedum, þæt þæt se oðer forðyldigan wolde for ateori-
gendlicere edwiste.

11   We secgað eow Godes riht; healdað gif ge willon. Gif we
hit forsuwiað, ne bið us geborgen. Cristes lufu us neadað
þæt we simle þa godan tihton þæt hi on godnysse þurhwun-
ion; and ða yfelan we mynegiað þæt hi fram heora yfelnes-
sum hrædlice gecyrron. Ne beo se rihtwisa gymeleas on his
anginne, ne se yfela ne ortruwige ðurh his unrihtwisnysse.
Ondræde se goda þæt he fealle; hogige se yfela þæt he
astande. Se ðe yfel sy, geefenlæce he Paules gecyrrednysse; se
ðe god sy, þurhwunige he on godnysse mid Stephane, forðan
ðe ne bið nan anginn herigendlic butan godre geendunge.
Ælc lof bið on ende gesungen.

12   Mine gebroðra, gyrstandæg gemedemode ure Drihten
hine sylfne þæt he ðysne middangeard þurh soðe menniscnysse geneosode; nu todæg se æðela cempa Stephanus, fram
lichamlicere wununge gewitende, sigefæst to heofenum
ferde. Crist niðerastah mid flæsce bewæfed; Stephanus
upastah þurh his blod gewuldorbeagod. Gyrstandæg sungon

world, it will lead to a great reward in the next. Indeed, by loving your enemy you will be God's friend; and not only will you be his friend, but you will also be a child of God through the counsel that you love your enemy, as Christ himself said, "Love your enemies, do good to those who hate you, that you may be children of your Father who is in heaven." Anyone would easily endure many hardships and insults so that he might be accounted the child of some rich person and heir to his transitory possessions; what another would undergo for fleeting material wealth, bear now patiently for the eternal honor of being accounted children of God and his heirs in heavenly riches.

We are telling you God's law; hold it if you will. If we kept 11 it quiet, we would not be spared. Love of Christ compels us always to exhort good people to continue in goodness; and we admonish the wicked to quickly turn away from their wickedness. Let the righteous not be heedless at his beginning, nor the wicked despair through his unrighteousness. Let the good person dread lest he fall; let the wicked take care that he stand back up. He who is wicked, let him imitate the conversion of Paul; he who is good, let him persist in goodness with Stephen, for no beginning is praiseworthy without a good ending. All praise will be sung at the end.

My brothers, yesterday our Lord humbled himself to visit 12 this world in true human nature; now today the noble champion Stephen, departing his bodily dwelling, went triumphant to heaven. Christ descended clothed with flesh; Stephen ascended crowned with glory through his blood.

englas "Gode wuldor on heannyssum"; nu todæg hi underfengon Stephanum blissigende on heora geferrædene, mid
þam he wuldrað and blissað a on ecnysse. Amen.

4

VI KALENDAS JANUARII

Assumptio sancti Iohannis apostoli

Iohannes se godspellere, Cristes dyrling, wearð on ðysum
dæge to heofenan rices myrhðe, þurh Godes neosunge, genumen. He wæs Cristes moddrian sunu, and he hine lufode
synderlice, na swa micclum for ðære mæglican sibbe swa for
ðære clænnysse his ansundan mægðhades. He wæs on
mægðhade Gode gecoren, and he on ecnysse on ungewem-
medum mægðhade þurhwunode. Hit is geræd on gewyrde-
licum racum þæt he wolde wifian, and Crist wearð to his
gyftum gelaðod. Þa gelamp hit þæt æt ðam gyftum win
wearð ateorod. Se hælend ða het þa ðenigmen afyllan six
stænene fatu mid hluttrum wætere, and he mid his bletsunge þæt wæter to æðelum wine awende; þis is þæt forme
tacn ðe he on his menniscnysse openlice geworhte. Þa wearð
Iohannes swa onbryrd þurh þæt tacn þæt he ðærrihte his
bryde on mægðhade forlet and symle syððan Drihtne

Yesterday the angels sang "Glory to God in the highest";
now today they received Stephen rejoicing into their fellowship, with whom he glories and rejoices forever in eternity.
Amen.

4

Assumption of John the Evangelist

DECEMBER 27

The Assumption of Saint John the Apostle

John the Evangelist, Christ's beloved, was taken on this
day to the joy of the kingdom of heaven, through God's visitation. He was the son of Christ's maternal aunt, and he particularly loved him, not so much for their kinship as for the
purity of his unblemished virginity. He was chosen by God
in virginity, and he remained forever in undefiled virginity. It
is read in historical accounts that he wanted to marry, and
Christ was invited to his wedding. Then it happened that
the wine at the wedding ran out. The savior then ordered
the servants to fill six stone vessels with pure water, and with
his blessing he turned the water to fine wine; this is the first
miracle that he openly worked in his human state. John was
so inspired by that miracle that he immediately left his bride
in virginity and ever afterward followed the Lord, and was

folgode, and wearð ða him inweardlice gelufod forðan ðe he hine ætbræd þam flæsclicum lustum. Witodlice, ðisum leofan leorningcnihte befæste se hælend his modor þa þa he, on rode hengene, mancynn alysde, þæt his clæne lif ðæs clænan mædenes Marian gymde; and heo ða on hyre swyster suna ðenungum wunode.

2   Eft on fyrste, æfter Cristes upstige to heofonum, rixode sum wælhreow casere on Romana rice æfter Nerone; se wæs Domicianus gehaten, Cristenra manna ehtere. Se het afyllan ane cyfe mid weallendum ele, and þone mæran godspellere þæron het bescufan; ac he ðurh Godes gescyldnysse ungewemmed of ðam hatum bæðe eode. Eft ða, ða se wælreowa ne mihte ðæs eadigan apostoles bodunge alecgan, þa asende he hine on wræcsið to anum igeoðe þe is Paðmas geciged, þæt he ðær þurh hungres scearpnysse acwæle. Ac se ælmihtiga hælend ne forlet to gymeleaste his gelufedan apostol, ac geswutelode him on ðam wræcsiðe þa toweardan onwrigenysse, be ðære he awrat ða boc ðe is gehaten *Apocalipsis*. And se wælhreowa Domicianus on ðam ylcan geare wearð acweald æt his witena handum, and hi ealle anmodlice ræddon þæt ealle his gesetnyssa aydlode wæron. Þa wearð Nerua, swiðe arfæst man, to casere gecoren. Be his geðafunge gecyrde se apostol ongean mid micclum wurðmynte, se ðe mid hospe to wræcsiðe asend wæs. Him urnon ongean weras and wif, fægnigende and cweðende, "Gebletsod is se ðe com on Godes naman."

3   Mid þam ðe se apostol Iohannes stop into ðære byrig Ephesum, þa bær man him togeanes anre wydewan lic to byrigenne, hire nama wæs Drusiana. Heo wæs swiðe gelyfed and ælmesgeorn, and þa ðearfan, ðe heo mid cystigum mode eallunga afedde, dreorige mid wope ðam lice folgodon. Ða

deeply loved by him because he had withdrawn himself from fleshly lusts. Indeed, the savior entrusted his mother to this beloved disciple when he redeemed mankind by hanging on the cross, so that his pure life might look after the pure virgin Mary; and she dwelled in the household of her sister's son.

Some time later, after Christ's ascension into heaven, a cruel emperor ruled the kingdom of Rome after Nero; he was called Domitian, a persecutor of Christians. He commanded that a tub be filled with boiling oil, and ordered the great Evangelist to be thrown into it; but with God's protection he emerged from that hot bath unharmed. Then, when the cruel one could not suppress the blessed apostle's preaching, he sent him into exile to an island called Patmos, so that he might die from the ravages of hunger. The almighty savior did not abandon his beloved apostle to neglect, but revealed to him in his exile the revelations of future things, about which he wrote in the book called *Apocalypse*. That same year, the cruel Domitian was killed by the hands of his council, and they all unanimously agreed that his decrees should be annulled. Then Nerva, a very honorable man, was chosen as emperor. With his consent the apostle who had been sent away to exile in great disgrace returned with great honor. Men and women ran to meet him, rejoicing and saying, "Blessed is he who comes in God's name."

As the apostle John arrived in the city of Ephesus, people carried out toward him the body of a widow to be buried, whose name was Drusiana. She was very faithful and generous with alms, and the poor, whom she had bountifully fed with a charitable spirit, followed the corpse, sad with

het se apostol ða bære settan, and cwæð, "Min Drihten, hælend Crist, arære ðe, Drusiana! Aris and gecyrr ham, and gearca us gereordunge on þinum huse." Drusiana þa aras swilce of slæpe awreht and, carfull be ðæs apostoles hæse, ham gewende.

4   On ðam oðrum dæge eode se apostol be ðære stræt, þa ofseah he hwær sum uðwita lædde twegen gebroðru, þe hæfdon behwyrfed eall heora yldrena gestreon on deorwurðum gymstanum, and woldon ða tocwysan on ealles þæs folces gesihðe to wæfersyne, swylce to forsewennysse woruldlicra æhta. Hit wæs gewunelic on ðam timan þæt ða ðe woldon woruldwisdom gecneordlice leornian þæt hi behwyrfdon heora are on gymstanum, and ða tobræcon; oððe on sumum gyldenum wecge, and ðone on sæ awurpan, þi læs ðe seo smeaung þæra æhta hi æt ðære lare hremde. Þa clypode se apostol ðone uðwitan Graton him to and cwæð, "Dyslic bið þæt hwa woruldlice speda forhogige for manna herunge, and beo on Godes dome geniðerod. Ydel bið se læcedom þe ne mæg ðone untruman gehælan; swa bið eac ydel seo lar ðe ne gehælð ðære sawle leahtras and unðeawas. Soðlice min lareow Crist sumne cniht þe gewilnode þæs ecan lifes þysum wordum lærde, þæt he sceolde ealle his welan beceapian, and þæt wurð ðearfum dælan, gif he wolde fulfremed beon, and he syððan hæfde his goldhord on heofenum, and ðærtoeacan þæt ece lif." Graton ða se uðwita him andwyrde, "Þas gymstanas synd tocwysede for ydelum gylpe, ac gif ðin lareow is soð God, gefeg ðas bricas to ansundnysse, þæt heora wurð mæge þearfum fremian." Iohannes þa gegaderode ðæra gymstana bricas, and beseah to heofonum, þus cweðende, "Drihten hælend, nis ðe nan ðing earfoðe. Þu geedstaðelodest ðisne tobrocenan middangeard on þinum

weeping. The apostle ordered the bier to be set down, and said, "May my Lord, the savior Christ, raise you up, Drusiana! Rise and go home, and prepare us a meal in your house." Drusiana then rose as if awakened from sleep, and mindful of the apostle's command, returned home.

The next day the apostle went along the street, and saw 4 where a certain philosopher led two brothers, who had exchanged all their ancestral wealth for precious stones, and wanted to crush them in front of all the people as a spectacle, as if in contempt of worldly possessions. It was a custom of that time for those who diligently wanted to learn philosophy that they would convert their possessions into gemstones, and then smash them; or into a chunk of gold, and throw it in the sea, lest the contemplation of those possessions should hinder their studies. Then the apostle called the philosopher Graton to him and said, "It is foolish that anyone should despise worldly riches for human praise, and be condemned in God's judgment. The medicine that cannot heal the sick is worthless; likewise that teaching is worthless that does not heal the sins and vices of the soul. Truly my teacher Christ taught a young man who desired eternal life in these words, that if he wanted to be perfect he should sell all his wealth, and distribute its value to the poor, and he afterward would have his treasure in heaven, and eternal life as well." Graton the philosopher answered him, "These gemstones are crushed for an idle boast, but if your teacher is the true God, join the fragments to wholeness, that their value may benefit the poor." John then gathered the fragments of the gemstones, and looked up to heaven, saying, "Lord savior, nothing is difficult for you. You restored this broken world for your faithful through the sign

77

geleaffullum þurh tacen þære halgan rode; geedstaðela nu þas deorwurðan gymstanas ðurh ðinra engla handa, þæt ðas nytenan menn ðine mihta oncnawon and on þe gelyfon." Hwæt, ða færlice wurdon ða gymstanas swa ansunde þæt furðon nan tacen ðære ærran tocwysednysse næs gesewen. Þa se uðwita Graton, samod mid þam cnihtum, feoll to Iohannes fotum, gelyfende on God. Se apostol hine fullode mid eallum his hirede, and he ongann Godes geleafan open-lice bodian. Þa twegen gebroðra, Atticus and Eugenius, seal-don heora gymstanas and ealle heora æhta dældon wædlum, and filigdon þam apostole, and micel menigu geleaffulra him eac to geðeodde.

5   Þa becom se apostol æt sumum sæle to þære byrig Per-gamum, þær ða foresædan cnihtas iu ær eardodon, and ge-sawon heora ðeowan mid godewebbe gefreatewode and on woruldlicum wuldre scinende. Ða wurdon hi mid deofles flan þurhscotene, and dreorige on mode þæt hi wædligende on anum waclicum wæfelse ferdon and heora ðeowan on woruldlicum wuldre scinende wæron. Þa undergeat se apostol ðas deoflican facn, and cwæð, "Ic geseo þæt eower mod is awend and eower andwlita, forðan ðe ge eowre speda þearfum dældon and mines Drihtnes lare fyligdon. Gað nu forði to wuda and heawað incre byrðene gyrda, and gebrin-gað to me." Hi dydon be his hæse, and he on Godes naman ða grenan gyrda gebletsode, and hi wurdon to readum golde awende. Eft cwæð se apostol Iohannes, "Gað to ðære sæstrande, and feccað me papolstanas." Hi dydon swa, and Iohannes þa on Godes mægenðrymme hi gebletsode, and hi wurdon gehwyrfede to deorwurðum gymmum. Þa cwæð se apostol, "Gað to smiððan, and fandiað þises goldes and ðissera gymstana." Hi ða eodon, and eft comon, þus

of the holy cross; restore now these precious stones by the hands of your angels, that these ignorant people might recognize your power and believe in you." At this, suddenly the gemstones were so whole that no sign at all of their former brokenness was visible. Then the philosopher Graton, together with the youths, fell at John's feet, believing in God. The apostle baptized him with all his household, and he began openly to preach God's faith. The two brothers, Atticus and Eugenius, sold their gemstones and distributed all their wealth to the poor, and followed the apostle, and a great multitude of believers also joined him.

At a certain time the apostle came to the city of Pergamon, where the aforementioned young men had lived, and saw their servants dressed in fine clothes and gleaming with worldly splendor. Then they were pierced with the devil's arrows, and were sad that they went begging in a meager cloak while their servants were gleaming with worldly splendor. The apostle saw the devil's deceit, and said, "I see that your heart and your countenance are changed, because you have given your possessions to the poor and followed my Lord's teaching. So go now to the woods and cut down a bundle of sticks, and bring them to me." They did as he commanded, and he blessed the green sticks in God's name, and they were turned to red gold. Then the apostle John said, "Go to the seashore, and fetch me some pebbles." They did so, and John then blessed them by God's majesty, and they were turned into precious gems. Then the apostle said, "Go to the smith, and test this gold and these gems." They

5

cweðende, "Ealle ðas goldsmiðas secgað þæt hi næfre ær swa clæne gold ne swa read ne gesawon. Eac ðas gymwyrhtan secgað þæt hi næfre swa deorwurðe gymstanas ne gemetton." Þa cwæð se apostol him to, "Nimað þis gold and ðas gymstanas, and farað and bicgað eow landare, forðan þe ge forluron ða heofenlican speda. Bicgað eow pællene cyrtlas, þæt ge to lytelre hwile scinon swa swa rose, þæt ge hrædlice forweornion. Beoð blowende and welige hwilwendlice, þæt ge ecelice wædlion. Hwæt la, ne mæg se ælmihtiga wealdend þurhteon þæt he do his ðeowan rice for worulde, genihtsume on welan and unwiðmetenlice scinan? Ac he sette gecamp geleaffullum sawlum, þæt hi gelyfon to geagenne þa ecan welan, ða ðe for his naman þa hwilwendan speda forhogiað. Ge gehældon untruman on þæs hælendes naman, ge afligdon deoflu, ge forgeafon blindum gesihðe and gehwilce uncoðe gehældon. Efne nu is ðeos gifu eow ætbroden, and ge sind earmingas gewordene, ge ðe wæron mære and strange. Swa micel ege stod deoflum fram eow þæt hi be eowere hæse þa ofsettan deofolseocan forleton; nu ge ondrædað eow deoflu. Þa heofenlican æhta sind us eallum gemæne. Nacode we wæron acennede, and nacode we gewitað. Þære sunnan beorhtnys and þæs monan leoht and ealra tungla sind gemæne þam rican and ðam heanan. Renscuras and cyrcan duru, fulluht and synna forgyfennys, huselgang and Godes neosung, sind eallum gemæne, earmum and eadigum. Ac se ungesæliga gytsere wile mare habban þonne him genihtsumað, þonne he furðon orsorh ne bricð his genihtsumnysse. Se gytsere hæfð ænne lichaman, and menigfealde scrud; he hæfð ane wambe and þusend manna bigleofan; witodlice þæt he for gytsunge uncyste nanum oðrum syllan ne mæg, þæt he hordað and nat hwam,

went, and came back, saying, "All the goldsmiths say that they have never before seen such pure and such red gold. Likewise the jewelers say that they have never encountered such precious gems." Then the apostle said to them, "Take this gold and these gems, and go and buy land, because you have lost heavenly possessions. Buy yourselves purple tunics, so you can shine like a rose for a little while, that you may quickly fade. Be flourishing and rich for a time, that you may be eternally poor. Lo, may not the almighty ruler bring it about that he makes his servants rich in the world, abounding in wealth and shining peerlessly? But he has placed a struggle in faithful souls, that those who despise transitory possessions for his name may believe in order to possess eternal riches. You healed the sick in the savior's name, you drove out devils, you gave sight to the blind and cured every disease. And now this gift is taken away from you, and you who were great and strong have become poor wretches. The devils stood in such great terror of you that at your command they abandoned those possessed by demons; now you will fear devils. Heavenly possessions are common to us all. Naked we were born, and naked we depart. The sun's brightness and the moon's light, and all the stars, are common to the rich and the lowly. Showers of rain and the church door, baptism and forgiveness of sins, going to Communion and God's visitation, are common to all, the wretched and the wealthy. But the unhappy miser wants to have more than he needs, though he does not enjoy even his abundance free from care. The miser has one body, and many garments; he has one belly and food for a thousand; truly what he cannot give to others because of the vice of avarice, he hoards and does not know for whom, as the

swa swa se witega cwæð, 'On idel bið ælc man gedrefed se ðe hordað, and nat hwam he hit gegaderað.' Witodlice, ne bið he ðæra æhta hlaford ðonne he hi dælan ne mæg, ac he bið þæra æhta ðeowa þonne he him eallunga þeowað; and þær-toeacan, him weaxað untrumnyssa on his lichaman, þæt he ne mæg ætes oððe wætes brucan. He carað dæges and nihtes þæt his feoh gehealden sy; he gymð grædelice his teolunge, his gafoles, his gebytlu; he berypð þa wannspedigan, he fulgæð his lustum and his plegan; þonne færlice gewitt he of ðissere worulde, nacod and forscyldigod, synna ana mid him ferigende; þe he sceal ece wite ðrowian."

6   Efne ða ða se apostol þas lare sprecende wæs, ða bær sum wuduwe hire suna lic to bebyrgenne; se hæfde gewifod þri-tigum nihtum ær. Seo dreorige modor þa, samod mid þam licmannum, rarigende hi astrehte æt þæs halgan apostoles fotum, biddende þæt he hire sunu on Godes naman arærde, swa swa he dyde þa wydewan Drusianam. Iohannes ða ofhreow þære meder and ðæra licmanna dreorignysse, and astrehte his lichaman to eorðan on langsumum gebede, and ða æt nextan aras, and eft upahafenum handum langlice bæd. Þa ða he ðus ðriwa gedon hæfde, ða het he unwindan þæs cnihtes lic, and cwæð, "Eala ðu cniht, ðe þurh ðines flæsces lust hrædlice ðine sawle forlure; eala þu cniht, þu ne cuðest ðinne scyppend: þu ne cuðest manna hælend; þu ne cuðest ðone soðan freond, and forði þu beurne on þone wyrstan feond. Nu ic ageat mine tearas, and for ðinre nyten-nysse geornlice bæd, þæt þu of deaðe arise and þisum twam gebroðrum, Attico and Eugenio, cyðe hu micel wuldor hi forluron, and hwilc wite hi geearnodon." Mid ðam þa aras se cniht Stacteus and feoll to Iohannes fotum, and begann to

prophet said, 'In vain every person who hoards is troubled, and does not know for whom he gathers.' Truly, he is not lord of those possessions when he cannot distribute them, but he is the slave of those possessions when he completely serves them; and moreover, diseases grow in his body, so that he may not enjoy food or drink. He worries day and night that his money is safe; he greedily cares for his gain, his rent, his buildings; he robs the poor, he follows his lusts and his pleasure; then suddenly he departs from this world, naked and guilty, taking only his sins with him; therefore he will suffer eternal punishment."

While the apostle was speaking this teaching, a certain 6 widow bore her son's body to be buried; he had been married thirty days earlier. The grieving mother, together with the mourners, prostrated herself wailing at the feet of the holy apostle, praying that he would raise up her son in God's name, as he had done to the widow Drusiana. John then pitied the grief of the mother and the mourners, and stretched out his body on the earth in lengthy prayer, and finally rose up, and then with upraised hands prayed a long time. When he had done this three times, he commanded them to unwrap the young man's body, and said, "O young man, you who have suddenly lost your soul through the lust of your flesh; O young man, you who did not know your creator: you did not know the savior of humanity; you did not know the true friend, and therefore you have run to the worst enemy. Now I have shed my tears, and prayed earnestly for your ignorance, that you may rise from death and declare to these two brothers, Atticus and Eugenius, what great glory they have lost, and what punishment they have earned." With this the youth Stacteus arose and fell at John's feet, and be-

ðreagenne þa gebroðru þe miswende wæron, þus cweðende, "Ic geseah þa englas þe eower gymdon dreorige wepan, and ða awyrigedan sceoccan blissigende on eowerum forwyrde. Eow wæs heofenan rice gearo, and scinende gebytlu mid wistum afyllede and mid ecum leohte; þa ge forluron þurh unwærscipe, and ge begeaton eow ðeosterfulle wununga mid dracum afyllede and mid brastligendum ligum, mid unasecgendlicum witum afyllede and mid anðræcum stencum, on ðam ne ablinð granung and þoterung dæges oþþe nihtes. Biddað forði mid inweardre heortan ðysne Godes apostol, eowerne lareow, þæt he eow fram ðam ecum forwyrde arære, swa swa he me fram deaðe aærde, and he eowre saula, þe nu synd adylegode of þære liflican bec, gelæde eft to Godes gife and miltsunge."

7   Se cniht þa Stacteus, ðe of deaðe aras, samod mid þam gebroðrum astrehte hine to Iohannes fotswaðum, and þæt folc forð mid ealle, anmodlice biddende þæt he him to Gode geþingode. Se apostol þa bebead ðam twam gebroðrum þæt hi ðritig daga behreowsunge dædbetende Gode geofrodon, and on fæce geornlice bædon þæt þa gyldenan gyrda eft to þan ærran gecynde awendon, and þa gymstanas to heora wacnysse. Æfter ðritigra daga fæce, þa þa hi ne mihton mid heora benum þæt gold and þa gymstanas to heora gecynde awendan, ða comon hi mid wope to þam apostole, þus cweðende, "Symle ðu tæhtest mildheortnysse, and þæt man oðrum miltsode; and gif man oðrum miltsað, hu micele swiðor wile God miltsian and arian mannum his handgeweorce? Þæt þæt we mid gitsigendum eagum agylton, þæt we nu mid wependum eagum bereowsiað." Ða andwyrde se apostol, "Berað ða gyrda to wuda, and þa stanas to sæstrande: hi synd gecyrrede to heora gecynde." Þa ða hi þis gedon

gan to reproach the brothers who had gone astray, saying, "I saw the angels who had charge of you sadly weeping, and the cursed demons rejoicing in your destruction. The kingdom of heaven was ready for you, and shining buildings filled with feasts and with eternal light; you have lost these through carelessness, and have earned for yourselves gloomy dwellings filled with serpents and with crackling flames, full of unspeakable torments and horrible stenches, in which groaning and howling never cease day or night. Therefore ask with sincere heart this apostle of God, your teacher, that he raise you from eternal damnation, as he has raised me from death, and that he lead your souls, which are now erased from the book of life, back to God's grace and mercy."

Then the youth Stacteus, who had risen from death, together with the brothers prostrated himself in John's footsteps, and the people with them, all praying with one mind that he would intercede for them with God. The apostle then ordered the two brothers to offer penance to God, atoning for thirty days, and in that time earnestly pray that the golden sticks might be returned to their former nature, and the gemstones to their worthlessness. After thirty days' time, when they could not return the gold and the gemstones to their nature by their prayers, they came with weeping to the apostle, saying, "You have always taught mercy, and that one should have mercy on others; and if one has mercy on another, how much more will God show mercy and spare his handiwork, humanity? What we have committed with covetous eyes, we now repent with weeping eyes." Then the apostle replied, "Bear the sticks to the woods, and the stones to the seashore; they will be returned to their nature." When they had done this, they again received

7

hæfdon, ða underfengon hi eft Godes gife, swa þæt hi adræfdon deoflu, and blinde and untrume gehældon, and feala
tacna on Drihtnes naman gefremedon, swa swa hi ær dydon.

8   Se apostol þa gebigde to Gode ealne þone eard Asiam, se
is geteald to healfum dæle middaneardes, and awrat ða
feorðan Cristes boc, seo hrepað swyðost ymbe Cristes godcundnysse; ða oðre þry godspelleras, Matheus, Marcus, Lucas, awriton æror be Cristes menniscnysse. Þa asprungon
gedwolmenn on Godes gelaðunge, and cwædon þæt Crist
nære ær he acenned wæs of Marian. Þa bædon ealle þa leod-
bisceopas ðone halgan apostol þæt he þa feorðan boc gesette and þæra gedwolmanna dyrstignesse adwæscte. Iohannes þa bead ðreora daga fæsten gemænelice, and he æfter
ðam fæstene wearð swa miclum mid Godes gaste afylled þæt
he ealle Godes englas and ealle gesceafta mid heahlicum
mode oferstah, and mid ðysum wordum þa godspellican gesetnysse ongan: *In principio erat verbum, et verbum erat apud
Deum, et Deus erat verbum, et reliqua,* þæt is on Englisc, "On
frymðe wæs word, and þæt word wæs mid Gode, and þæt
word wæs God; þis wæs on frymðe mid Gode. Ealle ðing
sind þurh hine geworhte, and nis nan þing buton him
gesceapen," and swa forð. On ealre þære godspellican gesetnysse, he cydde fela be Cristes godcundnysse, hu he ecelice
butan angynne of his Fæder acenned is, and mid him rixað
on annysse þæs Halgan Gastes, a butan ende. Feawa he
awrat be his menniscnysse, forðan þe þa ðry oðre godspelleras genihtsumlice be þam heora bec setton.

9   Hit gelamp æt sumum sæle þæt þa deofolgyldan þe þa gyt
ungeleaffulle wæron gecwædon þæt hi woldon þone apostol
to heora hæðenscipe geneadian. Þa cwæð se apostol to ðam
hæðengyldum, "Gað ealle endemes to Godes cyrcan, and

86

God's grace, so that they drove out devils, and healed the blind and the sick, and performed many miracles in the Lord's name, as they had done before.

The apostle then converted to God all the land of Asia, 8 which is accounted half the world, and wrote the fourth book of Christ, which deals chiefly with Christ's divinity; the other three Evangelists, Matthew, Mark, and Luke, had already written of Christ's humanity. Heretics had sprung up in God's Church, and said that Christ did not exist before he was born of Mary. All the diocesan bishops asked the holy apostle to compose the fourth book and extinguish the audacity of the heretics. John then ordered a general fast of three days, and after the fast he was so greatly filled with the spirit of God that he excelled all God's angels and all creatures with his elevated mind, and began the gospel narrative with these words: *In the beginning was the word, and the word was with God, and God was the word, etc.,* that is in English, "In the beginning was the word, and the word was with God, and the word was God; this was in the beginning with God. All things are made through him, and without him nothing is created," and so forth. In all the gospel's account he made known many things concerning Christ's divinity, how he is eternally begotten of his Father without beginning, and rules with him in the unity of the Holy Spirit, forever without end. He wrote few things about his human nature, because the three other Evangelists had composed their books abundantly about that.

It happened at a certain time that the idolaters who were 9 still unbelievers said that they would force the apostle to their heathenship. Then the apostle said to the idolaters, "Go all together to God's church, and call to your gods that

clypiað ealle to eowerum godum þæt seo cyrce afealle ðurh
heora mihte; ðonne buge ic to eowerum hæðenscipe. Gif
ðonne eower godes miht þa halgan cyrcan towurpan ne
mæg, ic towurpe eower tempel þurh ðæs ælmihtigan Godes
mihte, and ic tocwyse eower deofolgyld; and bið þonne riht-
lic geðuht þæt ge geswycon eoweres gedwyldes and gelyfon
on ðone soðan God, se ðe ana is ælmihtig." Þa hæðengyldan
ðisum cwyde geðwærlæhton, and Iohannes mid geswæsum
wordum þæt folc tihte þæt hi ufor eodon fram þam deofles
temple, and mid beorhtre stemne ætforan him eallum clypode, "On Godes naman ahreose þis tempel mid eallum
þam deofolgyldum þe him on eardiað, þæt þeos menigu
tocnawe þæt ðis hæðengyld deofles biggeng is." Hwæt, ða
færlice ahreas þæt tempel grundlunga, mid eallum his
anlicnyssum to duste awende. On ðam ylcan dæge wurdon
gebigede twelf ðusend hæðenra manna to Cristes geleafan,
and mid fulluhte gehalgode.

10   Þa sceorede ða gyt se yldesta hæðengylda mid mycelre
þwyrnysse, and cwæð þæt he nolde gelyfan buton Iohannes
attor drunce, and þurh Godes mihte ðone cwelmbæran
drenc oferswiðde. Þa cwæð se apostol, "Þeah þu me attor
sylle, þurh Godes naman hit me ne derað." Ða cwæð se
hæðengylda Aristodemus, "Þu scealt ærest oðerne geseon
drincan and ðærrihte cwelan, þæt huru ðin heorte swa
forhtige for ðam deadbærum drence." Iohannes him andwyrde, "Gif ðu on God gelyfan wylt, ic unforhtmod ðæs
drences onfo." Þa getengde se Aristodemus to ðam heahgerefan, and genam on his cwearterne twegen ðeofas, and
sealde him ðone unlybban ætforan eallum ðam folce, on Iohannes gesihðe; and hi ðærrihte æfter þam drence gewiton.
Syððan se hæðengylda eac sealde ðone attorbæran drenc

88

the church might fall down through their power; then I will submit to your heathenship. If the power of your god cannot cast down the holy church, then I will cast down your temple through the power of the almighty God, and I will crush your idol; and then it will seem right that you cease your error and believe in the true God, who alone is almighty." The idolaters agreed to this proposal, and John with kind words urged the people to go out of the devil's temple, and with a clear voice cried before them all, "In God's name let this temple fall down with all the idols that dwell within it, that this multitude may know that this idolatry is the worship of the devil." At once the temple fell suddenly to the ground, with all its images turned to dust. On that same day twelve thousand heathens were converted to belief in Christ, and sanctified with baptism.

The chief idolater still refused with great perverseness, and said that he would not believe unless John drank poison and overcame the deadly drink through God's might. Then the apostle said, "Even if you give me poison, through God's name it will not harm me." Then the idolater Aristodemus said, "First you will see another drink it and instantly die, so that at least your heart might be afraid of the deadly drink." John answered him, "If you will believe in God, I will take this drink without fear." Then Aristodemus went to the high reeve, and took two thieves from his prison, and gave them the deadly poison before all the people, in John's presence; they died immediately after drinking it. Then the idolater gave the poisonous drink to the apostle, and he armed his

þam apostole, and he mid rodetacne his muð and ealne his lichaman gewæpnode, and ðone unlybban on Godes naman halsode, and siððan mid gebildum mode hine ealne gedranc. Aristodemus ða and þæt folc beheoldon þone apostol ðreo tida dæges, and gesawon hine habban glædne andwlitan buton blacunge and forhtunge; and hi ealle clypodon, "An soð God is, se ðe Iohannes wurðað." Þa cwæð se hæðengylda to ðam apostole, "Gyt me tweonað, ac gif ðu ðas deadan sceaðan on ðines Godes naman aræst, þonne bið min heorte geclænsod fram ælcere twynunge." Ða cwæð Iohannes, "Aristodeme, nim mine tunecan, and lege bufon ðæra deadra manna lic, and cweð, 'Þæs hælendes Cristes apostol me asende to eow, þæt ge on his naman of deaðe arison, and ælc man oncnawe þæt dead and lif ðeowiað minum hælende.'" He ða, be ðæs apostoles hæse, bær his tunecan and alede uppon ðam twam deadum, and hi ðærrihte ansunde arison. Þa ða se hæðengylda þæt geseah, ða astrehte he hine to Iohannes fotum, and syððan ferde to ðam heahgerefan and him ða wundra mid hluddre stemne cydde. Hi ða begen þone apostol gesohton, his miltsunge biddende. Þa bead se apostol him seofon nihta fæsten, and hi siððan gefullode; and hi æfter ðam fulluhte towurpon eall heora deofolgyld, and mid heora maga fultume and mid eallum cræfte arærdon Gode mære cyrcan on ðæs apostoles wurðmynte.

II   Þa ða se apostol wæs nigon and hundnigontig geara þa æteowode him Drihten Crist mid þam oðrum apostolum þe he of ðisum life genumen hæfde, and cwæð, "Iohannes, cum to me; tima is þæt þu mid ðinum gebroðrum wistfullige on minum gebeorscipe." Iohannes þa aras and eode wið þæs hælendes, ac he him to cwæð, "Nu on Sunnandæg, mines æristes dæge, þu cymst to me." And æfter ðam worde

mouth and his whole body with the sign of the cross, and exorcised the deadly poison in God's name, and then with a bold heart drank it all. Then Aristodemus and the people watched the apostle for three hours, and saw that he had a glad expression without pallor or fear; and they all cried, "There is one true God, whom John worships." Then the idolater said to the apostle, "I still doubt, but if you raise up these dead thieves in the name of your God, then my heart will be cleansed from every doubt." Then John said, "Aristodemus, take my tunic, and lay it over the bodies of the dead men, and say, 'The apostle of the savior Christ has sent me to you, that in his name you may rise from death, and everyone may know that death and life serve my savior.'" Then, at the apostle's command, he took his tunic and laid it on the two dead ones, and they immediately rose up unharmed. When the idolater saw that, he prostrated himself at John's feet, and then went to the high reeve and announced those miracles to him with a loud voice. Then they both sought out the apostle, asking for his mercy. The apostle ordered them to fast for seven days, and afterward baptized them; and after their baptism they cast down all their idols, and with the help of their relatives and with all skill they raised a great church to God in honor of the apostle.

When the apostle was ninety-nine years old, the Lord 11 Christ appeared to him with the other apostles whom he had taken from this life, and said, "John, come to me; it is time that you should feast with your brothers at my banquet." John arose and went toward the savior, but he said to him, "On Sunday, the day of my resurrection, you will come to me." And after those words the Lord returned to heaven.

Drihten gewende to heofenum. Se apostol micclum blissode
on ðam behate and on þam sunnanuhtan ærwacol to ðære
cyrcan com, and þam folce fram hancrede oð undern Godes
gerihta lærde, and him mæssan gesang, and cwæð þæt se
hælend hine on ðam dæge to heofonum gelaðod hæfde. Het
ða delfan his byrgene wið þæt weofod, and þæt greot ut
awegan; and he eode cucu and gesund into his byrgene,
and astrehtum handum to Gode clypode, "Drihten Crist, ic
þancige ðe þæt þu me gelaðodest to þinum wistum; þu wast
þæt ic mid ealre heortan þe gewilnode. Oft ic ðe bæd þæt ic
moste to ðe faran, ac þu cwæde þæt ic anbidode, þæt ic ðe
mare folc gestrynde. Þu heolde minne lichaman wið ælce
besmittennysse, and þu simle mine sawle onlihtest, and me
nahwar ne forlete. Þu settest on minum muðe þinre soðfæstnysse word, and ic awrat ða lare ðe ic of ðinum muðe gehyrde, and ða wundra ðe ic ðe wyrcan geseah. Nu ic ðe
betæce, Drihten, þine bearn, ða ðe þin gelaðung, mæden
and moder, þurh wæter and þone Halgan Gast ðe gestrynde.
Onfoh me to minum gebroðrum mid ðam ðe ðu come and
me gelaðodest. Geopena ongean me lifes geat, þæt ðæra
ðeostra ealdras me ne gemeton. Þu eart Crist, ðæs lifigendan
Godes Sunu, þu þe be ðines Fæder hæse middangeard
gehældest, and us ðone Halgan Gast asendest. Þe we heriað
and þanciað þinra menigfealdra goda geond ungeendode
worulde. Amen."

12 Æfter ðysum gebede æteowode heofenlic leoht bufon
ðam apostole, binnon ðære byrgene, ane tid swa beorhte
scinende þæt nanes mannes gesihð þæs leohtes leoman
sceawian ne mihte; and he mid þam leohte his gast ageaf
þam Drihtne, þe hine to his rice gelaðode. He gewat swa
freoh fram deaðes sarnysse of ðisum andweardan life swa

The apostle rejoiced greatly in that promise and, rising early at dawn, he came to the church, and from cockcrow until midmorning taught the people God's law, sang Mass for them, and said that the savior had invited him to heaven on that day. He then ordered his grave to be dug opposite the altar, and the soil to be removed; then he went alive and whole into his grave, and with outstretched hands cried to God, "Lord Christ, I thank you that you have invited me to your banquet; you know that I have desired you with all my heart. I have often prayed that I might go to you, but you said that I should wait, so that I might win more people to you. You have preserved my body against every uncleanness, and you have always enlightened my soul, and have nowhere forsaken me. You have put the word of your truth in my mouth, and I have written down the teaching which I heard from your mouth, and the wonders I saw you work. Now, Lord, I commit to you those children which your Church, virgin and mother, has gained for you through water and the Holy Spirit. Receive me among my brothers with whom you came and invited me. Open the gate of life to me, that the princes of darkness might not find me. You are Christ, Son of the living God, who saved the world at your Father's request, and sent us the Holy Spirit. We praise and thank you for your manifold benefits throughout the eternal world. Amen."

After this prayer a heavenly light appeared above the [12] apostle, inside the grave, shining so brightly for an hour that no one's sight could look upon the beams of light; and with that light he gave his spirit to the Lord, who had invited him to his kingdom. He departed from this present life just as

swa he wæs ælfremed fram lichamlicere gewemmednysse. Soðlice syððan wæs his byrgen gemet mid mannan afylled— manna wæs gehaten se heofenlica mete þe feowertig geara afedde Israhela folc on westene. Nu wæs se bigleofa gemett on Iohannes byrgene, and nan ðing elles; and se mete is weaxende on hire oð ðisne andweardan dæg. Þær beoð fela tacna æteowode, and untrume gehælde and fram eallum frecednyssum alysede þurh ðæs apostoles ðingunge. Þæs him getiðað Drihten Crist, þam is wuldor and wurðmynt mid Fæder and Halgum Gaste, a butan ende. Amen.

5

V KALENDAS JANUARII

Natale innocentium infantum

Nu todæg Godes gelaðung geond ealne ymbhwyrft mær-saõ þæra eadigra cildra freolstide þe se wælhreowa Herodes, for Cristes acennednysse, mid arleasre ehtnysse acwealde, swa swa us seo godspellice racu swutellice cyð.

2   Matheus awrat on þære forman Cristes bec ðysum wordum be ðæs hælendes gebyrdtide, and cwæð: "Þa ða se hælend acenned wæs on þære Iudeiscan Bethleem, on Herodes dagum cyninges, efne ða comon fram eastdæle

free from the pain of death as he had been exempt from bodily defilement. Later his grave was found filled with manna—manna was the name of the heavenly food which fed the people of Israel for forty years in the wilderness. Now this food was found in John's grave, and nothing else; and that food is increasing in it to the present day. Many miracles have been revealed there, and the sick healed and released from all dangers through the apostle's intercession. The Lord Christ grants this to him, to whom is honor and glory with the Father and the Holy Spirit, forever without end. Amen.

5

The Feast of the Holy Innocents

DECEMBER 28

The Feast of the Innocent Infants

Today God's Church throughout the world celebrates the feast day of the blessed children whom the cruel Herod, because of Christ's birth, killed with wicked persecution, as the gospel narrative clearly tells us.

Matthew wrote in the first book of Christ in these words [2] concerning the time of the savior's birth, and said, "When the savior was born in Bethlehem of Judea, in the days of King Herod, three astrologers came from the eastern part

95

middangeardes þry tungelwitegan to ðære byrig Hierusalem, þus befrinende, 'Hwær is Iudeiscra leoda cyning se ðe
acenned is? We gesawon soðlice his steorran on eastdæle,
and we comon to ði þæt we us to him gebiddon.' Hwæt ða
Herodes cyning þis gehyrende wearð micclum astyred, and
eal seo burhwaru samod mid him. He ða gesamnode ealle þa
ealdorbiscopas and ðæs folces boceras, and befran hwær
Cristes cenningstow wære. Hi sædon, 'On ðære Iudeiscan
Bethleem. Þus soðlice is awriten þurh ðone witegan Micheam, "Eala þu Bethleem, Iudeisc land, ne eart ðu nateshwon wacost burga on Iudeiscum ealdrum; of ðe cymð se
heretoga se ðe gewylt and gewissað Israhela folc."' Ða
clypode Herodes þa ðry tungelwitegan on sunderspræce,
and geornlice hi befran to hwilces timan se steorra him ærst
æteowode, and asende hi to Bethleem, ðus cweðende, 'Farað
ardlice, and befrinað be ðam cilde, and þonne ge hit gemetað
cyðað me, þæt ic mage me to him gebiddan.'

3   "Þa tungelwitegan ferdon æfter þæs cyninges spræce, and
efne ða, se steorra þe hi on eastdæle gesawon glad him beforan, oð þæt he gestod bufon ðam gesthuse þær þæt cild on
wunode. Hi gesawon ðone steorran and þearle blissodon.
Eodon ða inn and þæt cild gemetton mid Marian his meder,
and niðerfeallende hi to him gebædon. Hi geopenodon
heora hordfatu and him lac geoffrodon, gold, and recels, and
myrran. Hwæt, ða God on swefne hi gewarnode and bebead
þæt hi eft ne gecyrdon to ðan reðan cyninge Herode, ac þurh
oðerne weg hine forcyrdon, and swa to heora eðele becomon.

4   "Efne ða Godes engel æteowode Iosepe, ðæs cildes fosterfæder, on swefnum, cweðende, 'Aris, and nim þis cild mid
þære meder, and fleoh to Egypta lande, and beo þær oð þæt

of the world to the city of Jerusalem, asking, 'Where is the king of the Jewish people who is born? Truly we saw his star in the east, and we have come so that we may worship him.' Lo, on hearing this, King Herod was greatly troubled, and all the citizens together with him. He then gathered all the high priests and scribes of the people, and inquired where the birthplace of Christ would be. They said, 'In Bethlehem of Judea. Truly it is written in the prophet Micah: "O Bethlehem, land of Judah, you are by no means least of cities among the princes of Judea; from you will come the leader who will rule and govern the people of Israel."' Then Herod called the three astrologers aside privately, and eagerly questioned them about what time the star had first appeared to them, and sent them to Bethlehem, saying, 'Go quickly, and inquire about the child, and when you find it let me know, that I may worship him.'

"The astrologers left after the king's speech, and lo, the 3 star which they had seen in the east glided before them, until it stood over the inn where the child was staying. They saw the star and greatly rejoiced. Then they went in and found the child with Mary his mother, and falling down they worshiped him. They opened their coffers and offered him gifts, gold, and frankincense, and myrrh. And then God warned them in a dream and commanded that they should not return to the cruel king Herod, but should avoid him by another way, and so come to their own country.

"And then God's angel appeared in a dream to Joseph, the 4 child's foster father, saying, 'Arise, and take this child with the mother, and flee to the land of Egypt, and stay there

ic þe eft secge; soðlice toweard is þæt Herodes smeað hu he
þæt cild fordo.' Ioseph ða aras nihtes, and þæt cild mid þære
meder samod to Egypta lande ferede, and þær wunode oð
þæt Herodes gewat, þæt seo witegung wære gefylled þe be
ðære fare ær ðus cwæð, 'Of Egypta lande ic geclypode minne
sunu.'"

5   Nu secgað wyrdwriteras þæt Herodes betwux ðisum
wearð gewreged to þam Romaniscan casere, þe ealne middangeard on þam timan geweold. Þa gewende he to Rome
be ðæs caseres hæse þæt he hine betealde, gif he mihte. Þa
betealde he hine swiðe geaplice, swa swa he wæs snotor-
wyrde to ðan swiðe þæt se casere hine mid maran wurðmynte ongean to Iudeiscum rice asende. Þa þa he ham com,
þa gemunde he hwæt he ær be ðan cilde gemynte, and geseah þæt he wæs bepæht fram ðam tungelwitegum, and
wearð þa ðearle gegremod. Sende ða his cwelleras, and ofsloh ealle ða hysecild þe wæron on þære byrig Bethleem, and
on eallum hyre gemærum, fram twywintrum cilde to anre
nihte, be ðære tide þe he geaxode æt ðam tungelwitegum.
Þa wæs gefylled Hieremias witegung, þe ðus witegode,
"Stemn is gehyred on heannysse, micel wop and ðoterung;
Rachel beweop hire cildru, and nolde beon gefrefrod, forðan
ðe hi ne sind."

6   On ðam twelftan dæge Cristes acennednysse comon ða
ðry tungelwitegan to Herode, and hine axodon be ðam
acennedan cilde; and þa þa hi his cenningstowe geaxodon þa
gewendon hi wið þæs cildes, and noldon ðone reðan cwellere
eft gecyrran swa swa he het. Þa ne mihte he forbugan þæs
caseres hæse, and wæs ða þurh his langsume fær þæra cildra
slege geuferod swiðor þonne he gemynt hæfde; and hi

until I speak to you again; for it will come to pass that Herod will scheme how he might destroy the child.' Joseph then arose at night, and took the child together with the mother to the land of Egypt, and dwelled there until Herod departed, that the prophecy might be fulfilled which had spoken of that journey, 'From the land of Egypt I have called my son.'"

Now historians say that in the midst of all this Herod was denounced to the Roman emperor, who ruled the whole world at that time. He went to Rome at the emperor's command to defend himself, if he could. He defended himself very cleverly, because he was so wise of speech that the emperor sent him back to the kingdom of Judea with more honor. When he came home, he remembered what he had intended to do about the child, and saw that he was deceived by the astrologers, and was greatly angered. Then he sent his executioners, and killed all the male children who were in the city of Bethlehem, and in all its borderlands, from a child of two years old to that of one day, according to the time which he had learned from the astrologers. Then the prophecy of Jeremiah was fulfilled, who thus prophesied, "A voice is heard on high, great weeping and wailing; Rachel wept for her children, and would not be comforted, because they are no more."

On the twelfth day after Christ's birth the three astrologers came to Herod, and asked him about the child that was born; and when they had discovered his birthplace they went to the child, and would not return to the cruel murderer as he had commanded. He could not avoid the emperor's command, and because of his long journey the slaughter of the children was delayed longer than he had intended;

wurdon ða on ðysum dægþerlicum dæge wuldorfullice ge-
martyrode—na swaþeah þæs geares þe Crist acenned wæs
ac æfter twegra geara ymbryne, æfter ðæs wælhreowan
hamcyme.

7 Næs he æðelboren, ne him naht to þam cynecynne ne ge-
byrode; ac mid syrewungum and swicdome he becom to
ðære cynelican geðincðe, swa swa Moyses be ðam awrat, þæt
ne sceolde ateorian þæt Iudeisce cynecynn oþ þæt Crist sylf
come. Ða com Crist on ðam timan þe seo cynelice mæigð
ateorode, and se ælfremeda Herodes þæs rices geweold. Þa
wearð he micclum afyrht and anðracode þæt his rice feallan
sceolde þurh tocyme þæs soðan cyninges. Þa clypode he ða
tungelwitegan on sunderspræce and geornlice hi befran on
hwilcne timan hi ærest þone steorran gesawon, forðan ðe he
ondred—swa swa hit gelamp—þæt hi eft hine ne gecyrdon.
Þa het he forðy acwellan ealle ða hysecild þære burhscire,
fram twywintrum cilde oð anre nihte; ðohte gif he hi ealle
ofsloge, þæt se an ne ætburste þe he sohte. Ac he wæs unge-
myndig þæs halgan gewrites ðe cwyð, "Nis nan wisdom ne
nan ræd naht ongean God."

8 Se swicola Herodes cwæð to ðam tungelwitegum, "Farað,
and geornlice befrinað be ðam cilde, and cyðað me þæt ic
eac mage me to him gebiddan." Ac he cydde syððan his fa-
cenfullan syrewunge, hu he ymbe wolde gif he hine gemette,
ða ða he ealle his efenealdan adylegode for his anes ehtnysse.
Þearflæs he syrwde ymbe Crist; ne com he forðy þæt he
wolde his eorðlice rice, oþþe æniges oðres cyninges, mid riccetere him to geteon, ac to ði he com þæt he wolde his heofenlice rice geleaffullum mannum forgyfan. Ne com he to ðy
þæt he wære on mærlicum cynesetle ahafen, ac þæt he wære
mid hospe on rode hengene genæglod. He wolde ðeah þæs

and they were gloriously martyred on this present day—not in the year Christ was born but two years later, after the return of the bloodthirsty king.

Herod was not of noble birth, nor did he belong to the 7 royal line; but by scheming and deception he rose to royal rank, because as Moses wrote concerning this, the royal line of the Jews would not decay until Christ himself came. Christ came at the time that the royal family was decayed, and the foreigner Herod ruled the kingdom. Then he was very much afraid and terrified that his kingdom would fall through the coming of the true king. He called the astrologers aside privately and eagerly asked them at what time they first saw the star, for he feared—as it happened—that they would not return to him. For this reason he commanded that all the male children of that district be killed, from two years old to one day; he thought that if he killed them all, the one he sought would not escape. But he was not mindful of the holy scripture that says, "No wisdom or counsel is of any value against God."

The treacherous Herod said to the astrologers, "Go, and 8 diligently inquire about the child, and let me know so that I too may worship him." But he later revealed his deceitful scheming, how he would have acted if he had found him, when he destroyed all those of the same age in order to persecute one of them. He schemed against Christ needlessly; he did not come to take for himself his or any other king's earthly kingdom by violence, but so that he might give his heavenly kingdom to faithful people. He did not come to be exalted on a grand throne, but that he might with contempt be nailed on a cross. Yet he wanted to escape the scheming

wælhreowan syrewunge mid fleame forbugan, na forði þæt
he deað forfluge—se ðe sylfwilles to ðrowienne middangearde genealæhte—ac hit wære to hrædlic, gif he ða on cildcradole acweald wurde, swilce ðonne his tocyme mancynne
bediglod wære. Þi forhradode Godes engel þæs arleasan
geþeaht, and bebead þæt se fosterfæder þone heofenlican
æþeling of ðam earde ardlice ferede.

9   Ne forseah Crist his geongan cempan, ðeah ðe he lichamlice on heora slege andwerd nære; ac he asende hi fram
þisum wræcfullum life to his ecan rice. Gesælige hi wurdon
geborene þæt hi moston for his intingan deað þrowian.
Eadig is heora yld, seo ðe þa gyt ne mihte Crist andettan,
and moste for Criste þrowian. Hi wæron þæs hælendes gewitan, ðeah ðe hi hine ða gyt ne cuðon. Næron hi geripode
to slege, ac hi gesæliglice þeah swulton to life. Gesælig wæs
heora acennednys, forðan ðe hi gemetton þæt ece lif on
instæpe þæs andweardan lifes. Hi wurdon gegripene fram
moderlicum breostum, ac hi wurdon betæhte þærrihte en-
gellicum bosmum. Ne mihte se manfulla ehtere mid nanre
ðenunge þam lytlingum swa micclum fremian swa micclum
swa he him fremode mid ðære reðan ehtnysse hatunge. Hi
sind gehatene martyra blostman, forðan ðe hi wæron swa
swa upaspringende blostman on middeweardan cyle ungeleaffulnysse, swilce mid sumere ehtnysse forste forsodene.
Eadige sind þa innoðas þe hi gebæron, and ða breost þe
swylce gesihton. Witodlice ða moddru on heora cildra martyrdome þrowodon; þæt swurd ðe þæra cildra lima þurharn
becom to ðæra moddra heortan, and neod is þæt hi beon
efenhlyttan þæs ecan edleanes, þonne hi wæron geferan
ðære ðrowunge. Hi wæron gehwæde and ungewittige
acwealde, ac hi arisað on þam gemænelicum dome mid

of the bloodthirsty king by flight, not because he would flee from death—he who willingly came to the world in order to suffer—but it would have been too soon if he had been killed in the cradle, because his coming would then have been hidden from humanity. God's angel therefore prevented the shameful plan, and commanded the foster father to bear the heavenly prince out of the country quickly.

Christ did not despise his young warriors, though he was not physically present at their slaughter; but he sent them from this life of misery to his eternal kingdom. They were born blessed to suffer death for his sake. Happy is their age, which could not yet confess Christ, and yet might suffer for Christ. They were the savior's witnesses, though they did not yet know him. They were not ripened for slaughter, yet they blessedly died to life. Blessed was their birth, because they found eternal life at the entrance of this present life. They were snatched from their mothers' breasts, but they were immediately entrusted to the bosoms of angels. The wicked persecutor could not benefit these little ones by any service as greatly as he benefitted them by the fierce hate of persecution. They are called blossoms of martyrs, because they were like blossoms springing up in the midst of the chill of unfaithfulness, as it were consumed by the frost of persecution. Blessed are the wombs which bore them, and the breasts that suckled them. Indeed the mothers suffered through their children's martyrdom; the sword that pierced their children's limbs entered their mothers' hearts, and they must be sharers in the eternal reward, when they were companions in suffering. They were killed while small and without reason, but they will arise at the Last Judgment in

9

fullum wæstme and heofenlicere snoternysse. Ealle we cumað to anre ylde on þam gemænelicum æriste, þeah ðe we
nu on myslicere ylde of þyssere worulde gewiton.

10 Þæt godspel cweð þæt "Rachel beweop hire cildra, and
nolde beon gefrefrod, þe hi ne sind." Rachel hatte Iacobes
wif ðæs heahfæderes, and heo getacnode Godes gelaðunge,
þe bewypð hire gastlican cild; ac heo nele swa beon gefrefrod þæt hi eft to woruldlicum gecampe gehwyrfon, þa þe
æne mid sygefæstum deaðe middangeard oferswiðdon, and
his yrmða ætwundon to wuldorbeagienne mid Criste.

11 Eornostlice ne breac se arleasa Herodes his cynerices mid
langsumere gesundfulnysse, ac buton yldinge him becom
seo godcundlice wracu, þe hine mid menigfealdre yrmðe
fordyde, and eac geswutelode on hwilcum suslum he moste
æfter forðsiðe ecelice cwylmian. Hine gelæhte unasecgendlic adl; his lichama barn wiðutan mid langsumere hætan, and
he eal innan samod forswæled wæs and toborsten. Him wæs
metes micel lust, ac ðeah mid nanum ætum his gyfernysse
gefyllan ne mihte; he hriðode and egeslice hweos, and
angsumlice siccetunga teah, swa þæt he earfoðlice orðian
mihte. Wæterseocnyss hine ofereode beneoðan þam gyrdle,
to ðan swiðe þæt his gesceapu maðan weollon, and stincende attor singallice of ðam toswollenum fotum fleow.
Unaberendlic gyhða ofereode ealne ðone lichaman, and
ungelyfendlic toblawennys his innoð geswencte. Him stod
stincende steam of ðam muðe, swa þæt earfoðlice ænig læce
him mihte genealæcan. Fela ðæra læca he acwealde, cwæð
þæt hi hine gehælan mihton and noldon. Hine gedrehte
singal slæpleast swa þæt he þurhwacole niht buton slæpe
adreah; and gif he hwon hnappode, ðærrihte hine drehton
nihtlice gedwimor, swa þæt him ðæs slæpes ofþuhte. Þa ða

full growth and with heavenly wisdom. We will all come to the same age at the universal resurrection, although we now leave this world at various ages.

The gospel says that "Rachel wept for her children, and 10 would not be comforted, because they are no more." Rachel was the wife of the patriarch Jacob, and she signified God's Church, which weeps for its spiritual children; but it will not be so comforted that they should return again to worldly strife, once they have overcome the world by a triumphant death and escaped from its miseries to be crowned with glory with Christ.

In fact the impious Herod did not enjoy his kingdom in 11 long good health, for without delay divine vengeance came upon him, which afflicted him with many miseries, and also revealed what torments he must suffer eternally after death. An unspeakable disease took hold of him; his body burned on the outside with a prolonged heat, and inside he was all inflamed and torn apart. He had a great desire for food, but could not satisfy his cravings with any nourishment; he convulsed and wheezed terribly, and painfully drew sighs, so that he could scarcely breathe. Swelling and edema came upon him below the waist, so much so that his genitals swarmed with maggots, and stinking poison constantly flowed from his swollen feet. Unbearable itching spread over his whole body, and incredible swelling afflicted his entrails. Stinking vapor came out of his mouth, so that any doctor could hardly approach him. He killed many of the doctors, saying that they could heal him but would not. Chronic insomnia afflicted him so that he suffered the whole night without sleep; and if he dozed at all, nightmares immediately tormented him, so that he regretted his sleep.

he mid swiðlicum luste his lifes gewilnode, þa het he hine
ferigan ofer ða ea Iordanen, ðær þær wæron gehæfde hate
baðu þe wæron halwende gecwedene adligendum lichaman.
Wearð þa eac his læcum geðuht þæt hi on wlacum ele hine
gebeðedon. Ac ða ða he wæs on ðissere beðunge geled, þa
wearð se lichama eal toslopen, swa þæt his eagan wendon on
gelicnysse sweltendra manna, and he læg cwydeleas, butan
andgite. Eft ða ða he com, þa het he hine ferigan to ðære
byrig Hiericho.

12   Þa þa he wearð his lifes orwene, þa gelaðode he him to
ealle ða Iudeiscan ealdras of gehwilcum burgum, and het hi
on cwearterne beclysan, and gelangode him to his swustur
Salome and hire wer Alexandrum, and cwæð, "Ic wat þæt ðis
Iudeisce folc micclum blissigan wile mines deaðes, ac ic
mæg habban arwurðfulle licðenunge of heofigendre menigu
gif ge willað minum bebodum gehyrsumian. Swa ricene swa
ic gewite, ofsleað ealle ðas Iudeiscan ealdras ðe ic on cwearterne beclysde; þonne beoð heora siblingas to heofunge ge-
neadode, þa ðe wyllað mines forðsiðes fagnian." He ða his
cempan to ðam slege genamode, and het heora ælcum fiftig
scyllinga to sceatte syllan, þæt hi heora handa fram ðam
blodes gyte ne wiðbrudon. Þa ða he mid ormætre angsumnysse wæs gecwylmed þa het he his agenne sunu Antipatrem
arleaslice acwellan, toeacan þam twam þe he ær acwealde.
Æt nextan, ða ða he gefredde his deaðes nealæcunge, þa
het he him his seax aræcan to screadigenne ænne æppel,
and hine sylfne hetelice ðyde þæt him on acwehte. Þyllic
wæs Herodes forðsið, þe manfullice ymbe þæs heofenlican
æþelinges tocyme syrwde, and his efenealdan lytlingas unscæððige arleaslice acwealde.

13   "Efne ða Godes engel æfter Herodes deaðe æteowode

Because he had a very great desire to live, he commanded that he be carried over the river Jordan, where there were hot baths which were said to be healthy for diseased bodies. It was also thought by his doctors that they should bathe him in warm oil. But when he was laid in this bath, his body became all limp, so that his eyes became like dead men's eyes, and he lay speechless and senseless. When he came to, he commanded to be carried to the city of Jericho.

When he despaired of life, he called all the Jewish elders 12 from every city to him, and ordered them to be confined in prison, and sent for his sister Salome and her husband Alexander, and said, "I know that this Jewish people will greatly rejoice at my death, but I can have an honorable funeral service from the grieving multitude if you will obey my commands. As soon as I am gone, kill all the Jewish elders whom I have confined in prison; then their families, who will rejoice at my departure, will be forced to mourn." He then named soldiers for that slaughter, and commanded that each of them be given payment of fifty shillings, so that they would not withdraw their hands from that bloodshed. When he was tormented with intense agony he commanded his own son Antipater to be wickedly killed, in addition to the two sons he had killed already. Finally, when he felt his death approaching, he commanded them to hand him his knife to peel an apple, and violently stabbed himself so that it quivered in him. Such was Herod's death, who wickedly schemed at the coming of the heavenly prince, and shamefully killed the innocent little ones of the same age.

"Just after Herod's death God's angel appeared to Joseph 13

Iosepe on swefnum on Egypta lande, þus cweðende, 'Aris,
and nim þæt cild and his moder samod, and gewend ongean
to Israhela lande; soðlice hi sind forðfarene ða ðe ymbe þæs
cildes feorh syrwdon.' He ða aras, swa swa se engel him bebead, and ferode þæt cild mid þære meder to Israhela lande.
Þa gefran Ioseph þæt Archelaus rixode on Iudea lande æfter
his fæder Herode, and ne dorste his neawiste genealæcan.
Þa wearð he eft on swefne gemynegod þæt he to Galilea
gewende, forðan ðe se eard næs ealles swa gehende þam
cyninge, þeah ðe hit his rice wære. Þæt cild ða eardode on
þære byrig þe is gehaten Nazareth, þæt seo witegung wære
gefylled þe cwæð þæt he sceolde beon Nazarenisc geciged."
Se engel cwæð to Iosepe, "Þa sind forðfarene þe embe ðæs
cildes feorh syrwdon." Mid þam worde he geswutelode
þæt ma ðæra Iudeiscra ealdra embe Cristes cwale smeadon;
ac him getimode swiðe rihtlice þæt hi mid heora arleasan
hlaforde ealle forwurdon.

14   Nelle we ðas race na leng teon, þy læs ðe hit eow æðryt
þince; ac biddað eow þingunge æt þysum unscæððigum
martyrum. Hi sind ða ðe Criste folgiað on hwitum gyrlum
swa hwider swa he gæð; and hi standað ætforan his ðrym-
setle butan ælcere gewemmednysse, hæbbende heora palmtwigu on handa, and singað þone niwan lofsang þam ælmihtigum to wurðmynte, se þe leofað and rixað a butan ende.
Amen.

in a dream in the land of Egypt, saying, 'Arise, and take the child and his mother, and return to the land of Israel; for those who schemed against the child's life are dead.' He then arose, as the angel had commanded him, and brought the child and his mother to the land of Israel. Then Joseph learned that Archelaus reigned in the land of Judea after his father Herod, and he dared not approach near to him. Then he was again reminded in a dream that he should go to Galilee, because the country there was not quite so near to the king, although it was in his kingdom. The child then lived in the city called Nazareth, so that the prophecy, which said that he should be called a Nazarene, might be fulfilled." The angel said to Joseph, "Those who schemed against the child's life are dead." With that word he revealed that more of the Jewish elders plotted Christ's killing; but it quite rightly befell them that they all perished with their wicked lord.

We will not draw out this narrative any longer, lest it 14 might seem tedious to you; but pray for the intercession of these innocent martyrs. They are the ones who follow Christ in white garments wherever he goes; and they stand before his victorious throne without any impurity, having their palm branches in hand, singing the new hymn of praise in honor of the almighty, who lives and reigns forever without end. Amen.

6

KALENDAS JANUARII

Octabas et circumcisio Domini nostri

Se godspellere Lucas beleac þis dægþerlice godspel mid feawum wordum, ac hit is mid menigfealdre mihte þære heofenlican gerynu afylled. He cwæð, "*Postquam consummati sunt dies octo ut circumcideretur puer, vocatum est nomen eius Iesus, quod vocatum est ab angelo priusquam in utero conciperetur.*" Þæt is on ure geðeode, "Æfter þan ðe wæron gefyllede ehta dagas Drihtnes acennednysse þæt he ymbsniden wære, þa wæs his nama geciged Iesus, þæt is 'hælend,' ðam naman he wæs gehaten fram ðam engle ær ðam þe he on innoðe geeacnod wære."

2 Abraham se heahfæder wæs ærest manna ymbsniden, be Godes hæse. Abraham wæs Godes gespreca, and God to him genam geþoftrædene æfter Noes Flode swiðost, and him to cwæð, "Ic eom ælmihtig Drihten; gang beforan me and beo fulfremed, and ic sette min wed betwux me and ðe and ic ðe þearle gemenigfylde, and þu bist manegra þeoda fæder. Cyningas aspringað of ðe, and ic sette min wed betwux me and ðe, and þinum ofspringe æfter ðe, þæt ic beo ðin God and ðines ofspringes." Abraham hine astrehte eallum limum to eorðan, and God him to cwæð, "Heald þu min wed, and þin ofspring æfter ðe on heora mægðum. Ðis is min wed þæt ge healdan sceolon betwux me and eow: þæt

6

Circumcision

The Octave and Circumcision of Our Lord

The Evangelist Luke concluded this day's gospel in few words, but it is filled with the manifold power of the heavenly mysteries. He said, "*After eight days were fulfilled that the child should be circumcised, his name was called Jesus, which he was called by the angel before he was conceived in the womb.*" That is in our language, "After the eight days were fulfilled from the Lord's birth when he should be circumcised, his name was called Jesus, that is, 'savior,' by which name he was called by the angel before he was conceived in the womb."

The patriarch Abraham was the first man circumcised, by   2 God's command. Abraham was God's confidant, and God held conversation very frequently with him after Noah's Flood, and said to him, "I am the Lord almighty; walk before me and be perfect, and I will set my covenant between me and you and I will greatly multiply you, and you will be the father of many nations. Kings shall spring from you, and I will set my covenant between me and you, and your offspring after you, that I will be the God of you and your offspring." Abraham stretched out all his limbs on the earth, and God said to him, "Hold my covenant, and your offspring after you in their tribes. This is my covenant, which you shall hold between me and you: that every male child in your

ælc hysecild on eowrum cynrene beo ymbsniden. Þæt tacn sy betwux me and eow: ælc hysecild, þonne hit eahta nihta eald bið, sy ymbsniden, ægðer ge æþelboren ge þeowetling; and se ðe þis forgæið, his sawul losað, forðan þe he min wed aydlode. Ne beo ðu geciged heononforð Abram ac Abraham, forðan þe ic gesette ðe manegra þeoda fæder. Ne ðin wif ne beo gehaten Sarai, ac beo gehaten Sarra; and ic hi gebletsige, and of hire ic ðe sylle sunu þone ðu gecigest Isaac; and ic sette min wed to him and to his ofspringe on ecere fæstnunge." And æfter ðære spræce se ælmihtiga up gewende. On þam ylcan dæge wæs Abraham ymbsniden, and eal his hyred, and syððan his sunu Isaac, on ðam eahtoðan dæge his acennednysse.

3   Abrahames nama wæs æt fruman mid fif stafum gecweden, *Abram,* þæt is, "healic fæder"; ac God geyhte his naman mid twam stafum and gehet hine *Abraham,* þæt is, "manegra ðeoda fæder," forðan þe God cwæð þæt he hine gesette manegum ðeodum to fæder. *Sarai* wæs his wif gehaten, þæt is gereht "min ealdor," ac God hi het syððan *Sarra,* þæt is, "ealdor," þæt heo nære synderlice hire hiredes ealdor geciged, ac forðrihte "ealdor," þæt is to understandenne ealra gelyfedra wifa moder. Hundteontig geara wæs Abraham, and his gebedda hundnigontig, ær ðan ðe him cild gemæne wære. Þa ða him cild com, þa com hit mid Godes foresceawunge and bletsunge, to þan swiðe þæt God behet eallum mancynne bletsunge þurh his cynn. Ða heold Abrahames cynn symle syððan Godes wed; and se heretoga Moyses, and eal Israhela mægð, ealle hi ymbsnidon heora cild on þam eahtoðan dæge and him naman gesceopon, oð þæt Crist on menniscnysse acenned wearð, se ðe fulluht astealde

family should be circumcised. Let that be that a sign between me and you: let every male child, both the nobly born
and the slave, be circumcised when it is eight days old;
and whoever neglects this, his soul shall perish, because he
has disregarded my covenant. Now henceforth you will not
be called Abram but Abraham, because I will establish you
as the father of many nations. Your wife will not be called
Sarai, but she will be called Sarah; and I will bless her, and
from her I will give you a son whom you will call Isaac; and I
will set my covenant with him and his offspring for an everlasting bond." And after this speech the almighty went up.
On the same day Abraham was circumcised, and all his
household, and later his son Isaac, on the eighth day after
his birth.

At first Abraham's name was spelled with five letters, 3
Abram, that is, "high father"; but God increased his name by
two letters and called him *Abraham,* that is, "father of many
nations," because God said that he would make him the father of many nations. His wife was called *Sarai,* that is, "my
chief," but God later called her *Sarah,* that is, "chief," so that
she was not exclusively called chief of her family, but simply
"chief," which is to be understood as mother of all believing
women. Abraham was a hundred years old, and his partner
ninety, before they had a child between them. When a child
came, it came with God's providence and blessing, so much
so that God promised blessing to all humanity through his
family. Abraham's family kept God's covenant ever afterward; the leader Moses, and all the tribes of Israel, all circumcised their children on the eighth day and gave them
names, until Christ was born in human form, who estab-

and ðære ealdan æ getacnunge to gastlicere soðfæstnysse awende.

4 Wen is þæt eower sum nyte hwæt sy ymbsnidennys. God bebead Abrahame þæt he sceolde and his ofspring his wed healdan, þæt sum tacn wære on heora lichaman to geswutelunge þæt hi on God belyfdon, and het þæt he name scearpecgedne flint and forcurfe sumne dæl þæs felles æt foreweardan his gesceape. And þæt tacn wæs ða swa micel on geleaffullum mannum swa micel swa nu is þæt halige fulluht, buton ðam anum þæt nan man ne mihte Godes rice gefaran ær ðan þe se come þe ða ealdan æ sette, and eft on his andwerdnysse hi to gastlicum þingum awende; ac gehwylce halgan andbidodon on Abrahames wununge buton tintregum, þeah on hellewite, oð þæt se alysend com þe ðone ealdan deofol gewylde and his gecorenan to heofenan rice gelædde.

5 Se ylca hælend þe nu egefullice and halwendlice clypað on his godspelle, "Buton gehwa beo geedcenned of wætere and of þam Halgum Gaste, ne mæg he faran into heofenan rice," se ylca clypode gefyrn þurh ða ealdan æ, "Swa hwylc hysecild swa ne bið ymbsniden on þam fylmene his flæsces, his sawul losað, forðan þe he aydlode min wed." Þis tacen stod on Godes folce oð þæt Crist sylf com, and he sylf wæs þære halgan æ underþeod þe he gesette, þæt he ða alysde þe neadwislice ðære æ underþeodde wæron. He cwæð þæt he ne come to ðy þæt he wolde þa ealdan æ towurpan ac gefyllan. Þa wearð he on þam eahtoðan dæge his gebyrdtide lichamlice ymbsniden, swa swa he sylf ær tæhte, and mid þam geswutelode þæt seo ealde æ wæs halig and god on hire timan þam ðe hire gehyrsume wæron. Hit wæs gewunelic þæt þa magas sceoldon þam cilde naman gescyppan on ðam eahtoðan dæge mid þære ymbsnidennysse, ac hi ne dorston

lished baptism and changed the significance of the old law to spiritual truth.

I expect that some of you do not know what circumci- 4 sion is. God commanded Abraham that he and his offspring should keep his covenant, that there would be some sign on their bodies to show that they believed in God, and commanded him to take a sharp-edged flint and cut off a part of the skin at the tip of his penis. That was as great a sign among believers then as holy baptism is now, except that no one could go to God's kingdom before the one came who would confirm the old law and then by his presence turn it to spiritual meanings; but every holy person waited in Abraham's dwelling without torments, although in the pains of hell, until the redeemer came who overcame the old devil and led his chosen ones to the kingdom of heaven.

The same savior who now fearfully and wholesomely 5 cries in his gospel, "Unless someone is born again of water and the Holy Spirit, he cannot enter the kingdom of heaven," the same long ago cried through the old law, "Whatever male child is not circumcised in the foreskin of his flesh, his soul shall perish, because he has disregarded my covenant." This sign remained among God's people until Christ himself came, and he himself was subject to the holy law that he had established, that he might release those who had been subject by necessity to the law. He said that he did not come to overthrow the old law but to fulfill it. On the eighth day after his birth he was circumcised in his body, as he himself had taught, and with that he made clear that the old law was holy and good in its time for those who were obedient to it. It was customary that the parents should give the child a name on the eighth day along with the circumci-

nænne oðerne naman Criste gescyppan þonne se heahengel him gesette ær ðan þe he on his modor innoðe geeacnod wære, þæt is, *Iesus,* and on urum gereorde, "hælend," forðan ðe he gehælð his folc fram heora synnum.

6   Nis nu alyfed Cristenum mannum þæt hi ðas ymbsnide-nysse lichamlice healdan, ac þeah hwæðere nan man ne bið soðlice Cristen buton he ða ymbsnidenysse on gastlicum ðeawum gehealde. Hwæt getacnað þæs fylmenes ofcyrf on ðam gesceape buton galnysse wanunge? Eaðe mihte þes cwyde beon læwedum mannum bediglod, nære seo gastlice getacnung. Hit ðincð ungelæredum mannum dyselic to ge-hyrenne, ac gif hit him dyslic þince, þonne cide he wið God þe hit gesette, na wið us þe hit secgað. Ac wite gehwa to gewissan: buton he his flæsclican lustas and galnysse ge-wanige, þæt he ne hylt his Cristendom mid rihtum biggenge. Be ðysum ðinge ge habbað oft gehyred, ac us is acumend-licore eower gebelh þonne þæs ælmihtigan Godes grama, gif we his bebodu forsuwiað. Gif ge willað æfter menniscum gesceade lybban, þonne sind ge gastlice ymbsnidene; gif ge þonne eowere galnysse underþeodde beoð, þonne beo ge swa se witega cwæð, "Se mann ða ða he on wurðmynte wæs he hit ne understod; he is forðy wiðmeten stuntum nyte-num, and is him gelic geworden."

7   Forðy sealde God mannum gescead þæt hi sceoldon on-cnawan heora scyppend, and mid biggenge his beboda þæt ece lif geearnian. Witodlice se fyrenfulla bið earmra ðonne ænig nyten, forðan þe þæt nyten næfð nane sawle, ne næfre ne geedcucað ne þa toweardan wita ne ðrowað. Ac we ðe sind to Godes anlicnysse gesceapene and habbað unateori-gendlice saule, we sceolon of deaðe arisan, and agyldan Gode gescead ealra ura geðohta, and worda, and weorca. Ne

sion, but they dared not give any other name to Christ than the one the archangel had set for him before he was conceived in his mother's womb, that is, *Jesus,* and in our language, "savior," because he saves his people from their sins.

It is not now permitted that Christians observe circum- 6 cision bodily, but nevertheless no one is truly a Christian unless he observes circumcision in spiritual conduct. What does the cutting off of the foreskin of the penis signify but a decrease of lust? This discussion might easily be hidden from lay people, were it not for its spiritual significance. To an unlearned person it seems foolish to hear, but if it seems foolish to him, let him complain to God who established it, not to us who say it. But let everyone know for certain: unless he diminishes his fleshly desires and lusts, he does not hold his Christianity with proper observance. You have often heard of this matter, but to us your anger is more tolerable than the wrath of almighty God, if we were to keep silent about his commandments. If you will live according to human reason, then you are spiritually circumcised; but if you are a slave to your lust, then you will be as the prophet said, "The person did not understand it when he was in his dignity; therefore he is compared to the foolish beasts, and has become like them."

God gave humans reason so that they might recognize 7 their creator, and merit eternal life by observing his commandments. Truly the wicked is more wretched than any beast, because the beast has no soul, and will never come to life again or suffer future punishments. But we who are created in God's likeness and have an imperishable soul will arise from death, and render to God an account of all our thoughts, words, and deeds. Therefore we should not merely

sceole we forðy sinderlice on anum lime beon ymbsnidene, ac we sceolon ða fulan galnysse symle wanian, and ure eagan fram yfelre gesihðe awendan, and earan from yfelre heorcnunge, urne muð fram leasum spræcum, handa fram mandædum, ure fotwylmas fram deadbærum siðfæte, ure heortan fram facne. Gif we swa fram leahtrum ymbsnidene beoð, þonne bið us geset niwe nama, swa swa se witega Isaias cwæð, "God gecigð his ðeowan oðrum naman." Eft se ylca witega cwæð, "Þu bist geciged niwum naman, þone ðe Godes muð genemnode." Se niwa nama is *Cristianus,* þæt is, "Cristen." Ealle we sind of Criste Cristene gehatene, ac we sceolon ðone arwurðfullan naman mid æðelum þeawum geglengan, þæt we ne beon lease Cristene. Gif we ðas gastlican ymbsnidennysse on urum ðeawum healdað, þonne sind we Abrahames cynnes æfter soðum geleafan; swa swa se þeoda lareow, Paulus, cwæð to geleaffullum, "Gif ge sind Cristes, þonne sind ge Abrahames sæd, and æfter behate yrfenuman." Petrus eac se apostol tihte geleaffulle wif to eadmodnysse and gemetfæstnysse, ðus cweðende, "Swa swa Sarra gehyrsumode Abrahame and hine hlaford het, ðære dohtra ge sind, wel donde and na ondrædende ænige gedrefednysse."

8   Se eahtoða dæg, þe þæt cild on ymbsniden wæs, getacnode ða eahtoðan ylde ðyssere worulde, on þære we arisað of deaðe, ascyrede fram ælcere brosnunge and gewemmednysse ures lichaman. Þæt stænene sex þe þæt cild ymbsnað getacnode ðone stan ðe se apostol cwæð, "Se stan soðlice wæs Crist." He cwæð "wæs" for ðære getacnunge, na for edwiste. Þurh Cristes geleafan, and hiht, and soðe lufe, beoð singallice estfulle heortan mid dæghwomlicere ymbsnidenysse afeormode fram leahtrum, and ðurh his gife onlihte.

be circumcised in one member, but we should always diminish foul lust, and turn our eyes from evil seeing, and our ears from evil hearing, our mouth from lying speeches, our hands from wicked deeds, our footsteps from the deadly path, our hearts from deceit. If we are thus circumcised from sins, then a new name will be given to us, as the prophet Isaiah said, "God will call his servants by another name." Again the same prophet said, "You will be called by a new name, which the mouth of God has named." That new name is *Christianus,* that is, "Christian." We are all called Christians from Christ, but we should adorn that honorable name with noble behavior, lest we be false Christians. If we observe this spiritual circumcision in our behavior, then are we of Abraham's family in true faith; as the teacher of the nations, Paul, said to the faithful, "If you are Christ's, then you are Abraham's seed, and heirs according to the promise." Peter the apostle also exhorted faithful women to humility and modesty, saying, "As Sarah obeyed Abraham, whose daughters you are, and called him lord, doing well and not fearing any affliction."

The eighth day, on which the child was circumcised, signified the eighth age of this world, in which we will arise from death, cut off from every corruption and stain of our body. The stone knife which circumcises the child signified the stone of which the apostle said, "The stone truly was Christ." He said "was" in a figural meaning, not a literal one. Through faith in Christ, and hope, and true love, devout hearts are continually cleansed from their sins by daily circumcision, and enlightened through his grace. 8

9   We habbað oft gehyred þæt men hatað þysne dæg "geares
dæg," swylce þes dæg fyrmest sy on geares ymbryne; ac we
ne gemetað nane geswutelunge on Cristenum bocum hwi
þes dæg to geares anginne geteald sy. Þa ealdan Romani, on
hæðenum dagum, ongunnon þæs geares ymbryne on ðysum
dæge, and ða Ebreiscan leoda on lengctenlicere emnihte, ða
Greciscan on sumerlicum sunstede, and þa Egyptiscan
ðeoda ongunnon heora geares getel on hærfeste. Nu onginð
ure gerim æfter Romaniscre gesetnysse on ðysum dæge, for
nanum godcundlicum gesceade, ac for ðam ealdan gewunan.
Sume ure ðeningbec onginnað on *Adventum Domini,* nis
ðeah þær forðy ðæs geares ord, ne eac on ðisum dæge nis
mid nanum gesceade, þeah ðe ure gerimbec on þissere stowe
geedlæcon. Rihtlicost bið geðuht þæt þæs geares anginn on
ðam dæge sy gehæfd þe se ælmihtiga scyppend sunnan and
monan and steorran, and ealra tida anginn gesette; þæt is, on
þam dæge þe þæt Ebreisce folc heora geares getel onginnað,
swa swa se heretoga Moyses on ðam ælicum bocum awrat.
Witodlice God cwæð to Moysen be ðam monðe, "Þes
monað is monða anginn, and he bið fyrmest on geares
monðum." Nu heold þæt Ebreisce folc ðone forman geares
dæg on lenctenlicere emnihte, forðan ðe on ðam dæge wurdon gearlice tida gesette.

10   Se eahteteoða dæg þæs monðes þe we hatað *Martius,*
ðone ge hatað "Hlyda," wæs se forma dæg ðyssere worulde.
On ðam dæge worhte God leoht, and merigen and æfen. Ða
eodon þry dagas forð buton tida gemetum, forðan þe tunglan næron gesceapene ær on þam feorðan dæge. On ðam
feorðan dæge gesette se ælmihtiga ealle tungla and gearlice
tida, and het þæt hi wæron to tacne dagum and gearum. Nu

We have often heard that people call this day "year's day," 9 as if this day were first in the course of the year; but we find no explanation in Christian books why this day should be considered the beginning of the year. The old Romans, in heathen days, began the course of the year on this day, and the Hebrew people on the spring equinox, the Greeks on the summer solstice, and the Egyptian people began the reckoning of their year in the fall. Now our calendar begins on this day according to the Roman reckoning, not for any religious reason, but because of ancient custom. Some of our service books begin on the *Advent of the Lord,* but that is not therefore the beginning of the year, nor is there any reason why it should be today, though our calendars repeat it in this place. It seems most proper that the beginning of the year should be observed on the day on which the almighty creator established the sun and the moon and the stars, and the beginning of all the seasons; that is, on the day on which the Hebrew people begin the reckoning of their year, as the leader Moses wrote in the books of the law. Indeed, God said to Moses concerning that month, "This month is the beginning of months, and it is first of the months of the year." Now the Hebrew people observed the first day of the year on the spring equinox, because on that day the yearly seasons were set.

The eighteenth day of the month that we call *March,* 10 which you call "Hlyda," was the first day of this world. On that day God made light, and morning and evening. Then three days went by without measurement of time, because the heavenly bodies were not created until the fourth day. On the fourth day the almighty established all the heavenly bodies and the seasons of the year, and commanded that

ongynnað þa Ebreiscan heora geares anginn on þam dæge þe
ealle tida gesette wæron, þæt is on ðam feorðan dæge woruldlicere gesceapenysse, and se lareow Beda telð mid micclum gesceade þæt se dæg is XII *Kalendas Aprilis,* ðone dæg
we freolsiað þam halgum were Benedicte to wurðmynte, for
his micclum geðincðum. Hwæt eac seo eorðe cyð mid hire
ciðum, þe ðonne geedcuciað, þæt se tima is þæt rihtlicoste
geares anginn ðe hi on gesceapene wæron.

II   Nu wigliað stunte men menigfealde wigelunga on ðisum
dæge mid micclum gedwylde, æfter hæðenum gewunan, ongean heora Cristendom, swylce hi magon heora lif gelengan
oþþe heora gesundfulnysse mid þam ðe hi gremiað þone
ælmihtigan scyppend. Sind eac manega mid swa micclum
gedwylde befangene þæt hi cepað be ðam monan heora fær,
and heora dæda be dagum, and nellað heora ðing wanian on
Monandæg for anginne ðære wucan; ac se Monandæg nis na
fyrmest daga on þære wucan ac is se oðer. Se Sunnandæg is
fyrmest on gesceapenysse and on endebyrdnysse and on
wurðmynte. Secgað eac sume gedwæsmenn þæt sum orfcyn
sy þe man bletsigan ne sceole, and cweðað þæt hi þurh bletsunge misfarað, and ðurh wyrigunge geðeoð, and brucað
þonne Godes gife him on teonan buton bletsunge, mid deofles awyrigednysse. Ælc bletsung is of Gode, and wyrigung
of deofle. God gesceop ealle gesceafta, and deofol nane
gesceafta scyppan ne mæg, ac he is yfel tihtend and leas wyr-
cend, synna ordfruma and sawla bepæcend. Þa gesceafta ðe
sind þwyrlice geðuhte, hi sind to wrace gesceapene yfeldædum. Oft halige men wunedon on westene betwux reðum
wulfum and leonum, betwux eallum deorcynne and wurm-
cynne, and him nan ðing derian ne mihte; ac hi totæron þa
hyrnedan næddran mid heora nacedum handum, and þa

they should be as a sign for days and for years. Now the Hebrews begin their year on the day when all times were established, that is, on the fourth day of the world's creation, and
the teacher Bede reckons with great understanding that
that day is *March 21,* the day we celebrate in honor of the
holy man Benedict, for his great virtues. Indeed, the earth
also makes known by her young plants, which return to life
then, that the time at which they were created is the most
correct beginning of the year.

Now foolish people practice various divinations on this 11
day with great error, after heathen custom, against their
Christianity, as if they could prolong their life or their health
while they provoke the almighty creator. Many are also possessed with such great error that they regulate their journeys by the moon, and their deeds according to days, and
will not let their blood on Monday because of the beginning
of the week; but Monday is not the first day of the week but
the second. Sunday is the first in creation and in order and
in dignity. Some foolish people also say that there are some
kinds of animals which one should not bless, and say that
they fare badly by blessing, but thrive by cursing, and so use
God's gift to their injury without blessing, with the devil's
cursing. Every blessing is from God, and cursing from the
devil. God created all creatures, and the devil cannot create
any creatures, for he is an inciter to evil and maker of lies,
origin of sins and deceiver of souls. The creatures that are
thought to be monstrous have been created for the punishment of evil deeds. Holy men often dwelt in the desert
among fierce wolves and lions, among all kinds of beasts and
serpents, and nothing could harm them; but they tore apart
the horned adders with their bare hands, and they easily

micclan dracan eaðelice acwealdon buton ælcere dare, þurh Godes mihte.

12 Wa ðam men þe bricð Godes gesceafta buton his bletsunge, mid deofellicum wiglungum, þonne se ðeoda lareow cwæð, Paulus, "Swa hwæt swa ge doð on worde oððe on weorce, doð symle on Drihtnes naman, þancigende þam ælmihtigan Fæder þurh his Bearn." Nis þæs mannes Cristendom naht þe mid deoflicum wiglungum his lif adrihð; he is gehiwod to Cristenum men, and is earm hæðengylda, swa swa se ylca apostol be swylcum cwæð, "Ic wene þæt ic swunce on ydel ða ða ic eow to Gode gebigde, nu ge cepað dagas and monðas mid ydelum wiglungum."

13 Is hwæðere æfter gecynde on gesceapennysse ælc lichamlic gesceaft ðe eorðe acenð fulre and mægenfæstre on fullum monan þonne on gewanedum. Swa eac treowa, gif hi beoð on fullum monan geheawene, hi beoð heardran and langfærran to getimbrunge, and swiðost gif hi beoð unsæpige geworhte. Nis ðis nan wiglung, ac is gecyndelic ðincg þurh gesceapenysse. Hwæt eac seo sæ wunderlice geþwærlæcð þæs monan ymbrene; symle hi beoð geferan on wæstme and on wanunge. And swa swa se mona dæghwomlice feower pricon lator arist, swa eac seo sæ symle feower pricum lator fleowð.

14 Uton besettan urne hiht and ure gesælða on þæs ælmihtigan scyppendes foresceawunge, se ðe ealle gesceafta on ðrim ðingum gesette, þæt is on gemete, and on getele, and on hefe. Sy him wuldor and lof a on ecnysse. Amen.

killed great dragons without any injury, through God's might.

Woe to the one who uses God's creation without his 12 blessing, with devilish divination, for the teacher of the nations, Paul, has said, "Whatever you do in word or in deed, do always in the name of the Lord, thanking the almighty Father through his Son." If a person directs his life with devilish divination, his Christianity is nothing; he is a Christian only in appearance, and is a wretched idol worshipper, just as the same apostle said of such people, "I believe that I labored in vain when I inclined you to God, now that you observe days and months with vain divinations."

Yet it is according to the nature of creation that every 13 bodily creature which the earth produces is fuller and stronger in the full moon than in the waning moon. Likewise trees, if they are cut down during the full moon, are harder and more lasting for building, especially if they are worked when sapless. This is not divination, but is a natural thing from their creation. Likewise the sea agrees wonderfully with the course of the moon; they are always companions in their increase and waning. And just as the moon every day rises four points later, so also the sea always flows four points later.

Let us place our hope and our happiness in the provi- 14 dence of the almighty creator, who has established all creation in three things, that is in measure, and in number, and in weight. To him be glory and praise forever to eternity. Amen.

VIII IDUS JANUARII

Epiphania Domini

Men ða leofostan, nu for feawum dagum we oferræddon þis godspel ætforan eow þe belimpð to ðysses dæges ðenunge, for gereccednysse ðære godspellican endebyrdnysse; ac we ne hrepodon þone traht na swiðor þonne to ðæs dæges wurðmynte belamp. Nu wille we eft oferyrnan þa ylcan godspellican endebyrdnysse, and be ðyssere andweardan freolstide trahtnian.

2   Matheus se Godspellere cwæð: *Cum natus esset Iesus in Bethleem Iudae, in diebus Herodis regis, ecce Magi ab oriente venerunt Hierosolimam, dicentes, "Ubi est qui natus est rex Iudeorum?" et reliqua.* "Þa ða se hælend acenned wæs on þære Iudeiscan Bethleem, on Herodes dagum cyninges, efne ða comon fram eastdæle middangeardes ðry tungelwitegan to ðære byrig Hierusalem, þus befrinende, 'Hwær is Iudeiscra leoda cyning, se ðe acenned is? We gesawon soðlice his steorran on eastdæle, and we comon to ði þæt we us to him gebiddan.' Hwæt ða Herodes cyning þis gehyrende wearð micclum astyred, and eal seo burhwaru samod mid him. He ða gesamnode ealle ða ealdorbiscopas and þæs folces boceras, and befran hwær Cristes cenningstow wære. Hi sædon, 'On ðære Iudeiscan Bethleem; ðus soðlice is awriten þurh ðone witegan Micheam, "Eala ðu Bethleem, Iudeisc land, ne eart

7

Epiphany

JANUARY 6

The Epiphany of the Lord

Most beloved people, a few days ago we read through in your presence the gospel that belongs to this day's service, for an account of the gospel narrative; but we did not touch on the exposition any further than was proper for the dignity of that day. Now we will run through the same gospel narrative again, and explain it according to the present feast day.

Matthew the Evangelist said: *When Jesus was born in Bethlehem of Judea, in the days of King Herod, behold, Magi from the east came to Jerusalem, saying, "Where is he who has been born king of the Jews?" etc.* "When the savior was born in Bethlehem of Judea, in the days of king Herod, three astrologers came from the eastern part of the world to the city of Jerusalem, asking, 'Where is the king of the Jewish people, who is born? Truly we saw his star in the east, and we have come so that we may worship him.' Lo, on hearing this, King Herod was greatly troubled, and all the citizens together with him. He then gathered all the high priests and scribes of the people, and inquired where the birthplace of Christ would be. They said, 'In Bethlehem of Judea; truly it is written through the prophet Micah, "O Bethlehem, land of

2

ðu nateshwon wacost burga on Iudiscrum ealdrum; of ðe cumð se heretoga se ðe gewylt and gewissað Israhela folc."' Þa clypode Herodes þa ðry tungelwitegan on sundersprǣce, and geornlice hi befran to hwilces timan se steorra him ǣrest ǣteowode, and sende hi to Bethleem, þus cweðende, 'Farað ardlice, and befrinað be ðam cilde, and þonne ge hit gemetað cyðað me, þæt ic mage me to him gebiddan.'

3 "Þa tungelwitegan ferdon æfter þæs cyninges sprǣce, and efne ða se steorra þe hi on eastdæle gesawon glad him beforan, oð þæt he gestod bufon ðam gesthuse þær þæt cild on wunode. Hi gesawon ðone steorran and ðearle blissodon. Eodon ða inn and þæt cild gemetton mid Marian his meder, and niðerfeallende hi to him gebædon. Hi geopenodon heora hordfatu and him lac geoffrodon, gold, and recels, and myrran. Hwæt, ða God on swefne hi gewarnode and bebead þæt hi eft ne gecyrdon to ðam reðan cyninge Herode, ac þurh oðerne weg hine forcyrdon, and swa to heora eðele becomon."

4 Ðes dæg is gehaten *Epiphania Domini,* þæt is, "Godes geswutelungdæg." On þysum dæge Crist wæs geswutelod þam ðrym cyningum ðe fram eastdæle middangeardes hine mid þrimfealdum lacum gesohton. Eft embe geara ymbrynum, he wearð on his fulluhte on þysum dæge middangearde geswutelod, ða ða se Halga Gast on culfran hiwe uppon him gereste and þæs Fæder stemn of heofenum hlude swegde, þus cweðende, "Þes is min leofa Sunu þe me wel licað; gehyrað him." Eac on ðisum dæge he awende wæter to æðelum wine, and mid þam geswutelode þæt he is se soða scyppend þe ða gesceafta awendan mihte. For ðisum þrym ðingum is ðes freolsdæg "Godes swutelung" gecweden. On ðam forman dæge his gebyrdtide he wearð æteowed þrym hyrdum

Judah, you are by no means least of cities among the princes of Judea; from you will come the leader who will rule and govern the people of Israel.'" Then Herod called the three astrologers aside privately, and eagerly questioned them about what time the star had first appeared to them, and sent them to Bethlehem, saying, 'Go quickly, and inquire about the child, and when you find it let me know, that I may worship him.'

"The astrologers left after the king's speech, and lo, the 3 star which they had seen in the east glided before them, until it stood over the inn where the child was staying. They saw the star and greatly rejoiced. Then they went in and found the child with Mary his mother, and falling down, they worshiped him. They opened their coffers and offered him gifts, gold, and frankincense, and myrrh. And then God warned them in a dream and commanded that they should not return to the cruel king Herod, but should avoid him by another way, and so come to their own country."

This day is called *Epiphany of the Lord,* that is, "God's rev- 4 elation day." On this day Christ was revealed to the three kings who sought him out from the eastern part of the world with threefold gifts. Later, after the course of some years, he was revealed to the world on this day at his baptism, when the Holy Spirit in the form of a dove rested on him and the Father's voice sounded loudly from heaven, saying, "This is my beloved Son who is well pleasing to me; obey him." Also on this day he turned water into fine wine, and with that revealed that he is the true creator, who is able to transform his creation. For these three reasons this feast day is called "God's revelation." On the day of his birth he was shown to

on Iudeiscum earde, þurh ðæs engles bodunge. On ðam ylcum dæge he wearð gecydd þam ðrym tungelwitegum on eastdæle, þurh ðone beorhtan steorran; ac on þysum dæge hi comon mid heora lacum.

5   Hit wæs gedafenlic þæt se gesceadwisa engel hine cydde þam gesceadwisum Iudeiscum ðe Godes æ cuðon, and ðam haðenum þe ðæs godcundan gesceades nyston na ðurh stemne, ac ðurh tacn wære geswutelod. Þa Iudeiscan hyrdas getacnodon ða gastlican hyrdas, þæt sind ða apostolas, þe Crist geceas of Iudeiscum folce, us to hyrdum and to lareowum. Ða tungelwitegan, ðe wæron on hæðenscipe wunigende, hæfdon getacnunge ealles hæðenes folces ðe wurdon to Gode gebigede þurh ðæra apostola lare, þe wæron Iudeiscre ðeode. Soðlice se sealmsceop awrat be Criste, þæt he is se hyrnstan þe gefegð þa twegen weallas togædere, forðan ðe he geþeodde his gecorenan of Iudeiscum folce and þa geleaffullan of hæðenum, swilce twegen wagas to anre gelaðunge. Be ðam cwæð Paulus se apostol, "Se hælend bodade on his tocyme sibbe us ðe feorran wæron, and sibbe þam ðe gehende wæron. He is ure sibb, se ðe dyde ægðer to anum, towurpende ða ærran feondscipas on him sylfum." Þa Iudeiscan ðe on Crist gelyfdon wæron him gehendor stowlice, and eac ðurh cyððe þære ealdan æ. We wæron swiðe fyrlyne, ægðer ge stowlice ge ðurh uncyððe; ac he us gegaderode mid anum geleafan to ðam healicum hyrnstane, þæt is to annysse his gelaðunge.

6   Ða easternan tungelwitegan gesawon niwne steorran beorhtne, na on heofenum betwux oðrum tunglum, ac wæs angenga betwux heofenum and eorðan. Ða undergeaton hi þæt se seldcuða tungel gebicnode þæs soðan cyninges acennednysse on ðam earde ðe he oferglad. And forði comon

three shepherds in the land of the Jews, through the angel's announcement. On the same day he was made known to the three astrologers from the east, through the bright star, but on this day they came with their gifts.

It was fitting that the rational angel should make him 5 known to those rational Jews who knew God's law, and to the heathens who did not know divine reason he should be revealed not through a voice, but through a sign. The Jewish shepherds signified the spiritual shepherds, that is, the apostles, whom Christ chose from the Jewish people to be our shepherds and teachers. The astrologers, who were dwelling in heathenism, signified all heathen people who would be turned to God through the teaching of the apostles, who were of the Jewish nation. Truly the psalmist wrote that Christ is the cornerstone which joins the two walls together, because he united his chosen ones of the Jewish people and the faithful of the heathens, like two walls to one church. Concerning this Paul the apostle said, "At his coming the savior announced peace to us who were far off, and peace to those who were close at hand. He is our peace, he who has made both one, abolishing the former enmity in himself." The Jews who believed in Christ were nearer to him in place, and also through knowledge of the old law. We were very remote, both in place and through ignorance; but he gathered us with one faith to the high cornerstone, that is, to the unity of his Church.

The eastern astrologers saw a bright new star, not in the 6 heavens among other heavenly bodies, but solitary between heaven and earth. Then they understood that the unusual star indicated the birth of the true king in the country over which it passed. And for that reason they came to the

to Iudea rice, and þone arleasan cyning Herodem mid heora
bodunge ðearle afærdon; forðan ðe buton tweon seo eorðlice arleasnys wearð gescynd þa ða seo heofenlice healicnyss
wearð geopenod.

7   Swutol is þæt ða tungelwitegan tocneowon Crist soðne
mann ða ða hi befrunon, "Hwær is se ðe acenned is?" Hi
oncneowon hine soðne cyning þa ða hi cwædon, "Iudea cyning." Hi hine wurðodon soðne God þa ða hi cwædon, "We
comon to ðy þæt we us to him gebiddan." Eaðe mihte God
hi gewissian þurh ðone steorran to ðære byrig þe þæt cild on
wæs, swa swa he his acennednysse þurh ðæs steorran upspring geswutelode. Ac he wolde þæt ða Iudeiscan boceras
ða witegunge be ðam ræddon, and swa his cenningstowe
geswutelodon, þæt hi gehealdene wæron gif hi woldon mid
þan tungelwitegum hi to Criste gebiddan; gif hi þonne
noldon, þæt hi wurdon mid þære geswutelunge geniðerode.
Þa tungelwitegan ferdon and hi gebædon, and ða Iudeiscan
boceras bæftan belifon, þe þa cenningstowe þurh boclic gescead gebicnodon.

8   Ealle gesceafta oncneowon heora scyppendes tocyme,
buton ðam arleasum Iudeiscum anum. Heofonas oncneowon heora scyppend ða ða hi on his acennednysse niwne
steorran æteowdon. Sæ oncneow ða ða Crist mid drium
fotwylmum ofer hyre yða mihtelice eode. Sunne oncneow
þa þa heo on his ðrowunge hire leoman fram middæge oð
non behydde. Stanas oncneowon ða ða hi on his forðsiðe
sticmælum toburston. Seo eorðe oncneow ða ða heo on his
æriste eall byfode. Hell oncneow ða ða heo hire hæftlingas
unðances forlet. And ðeah þa heardheortan Iudei noldon
for eallum ðam tacnum þone soðan scyppend tocnawan
þe þa dumban gesceafta undergeaton and mid gebicnungum

kingdom of Judea, and greatly frightened the wicked king Herod by their announcement; for without a doubt earthly wickedness was put to shame when the heavenly greatness was disclosed.

It is clear that the astrologers knew Christ to be a true 7 human when they asked, "Where is he who is born?" They acknowledged him as a true king when they said, "king of Judea." They honored him as true God when they said, "We come that we may worship him." God might easily have directed them by the star to the city in which the child was, just as he had revealed his birth by the rising of that star. But he wanted the Jewish scholars to read the prophecy about him, and so reveal his birthplace, so that they might be saved if they would worship Christ with the astrologers; if they would not, that they would be condemned by that revelation. The astrologers went and worshiped, and the Jewish scholars, who had pointed out that birthplace through their knowledge of books, remained behind.

All creatures acknowledged the coming of their creator, 8 except for the faithless Jews alone. The heavens acknowledged their creator when they displayed a new star at his birth. The sea acknowledged him when Christ passed mightily over its waves with dry footsteps. The sun acknowledged him when at his passion it hid its beams from midday until the ninth hour. The stones acknowledged him when they shattered into pieces at his departure. The earth acknowledged him when it all trembled at his resurrection. Hell acknowledged him when it unwillingly released its captives. And yet for all those signs the hard-hearted Jews would not acknowledge the true creator whom the mute

geswutolodon. Næron hi swaðeah ealle endemes ungeleaffulle, ac of heora cynne wæron ægðer ge witegan ge apostolas, and fela ðusenda gelyfedra manna.

9   Þa þa ða tungelwitegan þone cyning gecyrdon, þa wearð
se steorra him ungesewen; and eft ða ða hi to ðam cilde gecyrdon, þa gesawon hi eft ðone steorran, and he ða hi
gelædde to þam huse þær he inne wunode. Ne glad he ealne
weig him ætforan, ac syððan hi comon to Iudeiscum earde
syððan he wæs heora latteow oð þæt he bufan Cristes gesthuse ætstod. Herodes hæfde deofles getacnunge; and se ðe
fram Gode bichð to deofle he forlyst Godes gife—þæt is his
modes onlihtinge—swa swa ða tungelwitegan ðone steorran
forluron ða ða hi ðone reðan cyning gecyrdon. Gif he ðonne
eft þone deofol anrædlice forlæt, ðonne gemet he eft þæs
halgan Gastes gife, þe his heortan onliht and to Criste gelæt.

10   Us is eac to witenne þæt wæron sume gedwolmen ðe
cwædon þæt ælc man beo acenned be steorrena gesetnys-
sum, and þurh heora ymbryna him wyrd gelimpe; and namon to fultume heora gedwylde þæt niwe steorra asprang þa
þa Drihten lichamlice acenned wearð, and cwædon þæt se
steorra his gewyrd wære. Gewite ðis gedwyld fram geleaffullum
heortum, þæt ænig gewyrd sy buton se ælmihtiga scyppend, se ðe ælcum men foresceawað lif be his geearnungum.
Nis se man for steorrum gesceapen, ac ða steorran sint mannum to nihtlicere lihtinge gesceapene. Þa ða se steorra glad
and þa tungelwitegan gelædde, and him ðæs cildes inn gebicnode, ða geswutelode he þæt he wæs Cristes gesceaft,
and rihtlice his scyppende þenode; ac he næs his gewyrd. Eft
we biddað þæt nan geleafful man his geleafan mid þisum
gedwylde ne befyle. Witodlice Rebecca, Isaaces wif, acende
twegen getwysan, Iacob and Esau, on anre tide, swa þæt

creation knew and revealed by signs. Yet they were not all equally unbelieving, and in their race were both prophets and apostles, and many thousands of believers.

When the astrologers went to the king, the star became 9 invisible to them; afterward, when they went to the child, they saw the star again, and it led them to the house in which he was staying. It did not glide before them all the way, but once they came to the Jewish country it was their guide until it stopped above Christ's inn. Herod signifies the devil; and he who turns from God to the devil loses God's grace— that is, his mind's enlightenment—just as the astrologers lost the star when they turned to the cruel king. If he later resolutely forsakes the devil, then he will find again the grace of the Holy Spirit, which enlightens his heart and leads to Christ.

We should also know that there were some heretics who 10 said that every person is born according to the position of the stars, and that his destiny befalls him through their course; in support of their error they took the fact that a new star sprang up when the Lord was physically born, and said that that star was his destiny. Let this error depart from faithful hearts, that there is any destiny except the almighty creator, who provides life for every person according to his merits. People are not created for the stars, but the stars are created for people as a light by night. When the star glided and led the astrologers, and pointed out to them the child's inn, it revealed that it was Christ's creature, and rightly served its creator; but it was not his destiny. Again we pray that no faithful person defile his faith with this error. Indeed Rebekah, Isaac's wife, brought forth twins, Jacob and Esau, at one time, so that Jacob held his elder brother Esau

Iacob heold þone yldran broðer Esau be ðam fet on ðære cenninge; and hi næron ðeah gelice on ðeawum, ne on lifes geearnungum. Witodlice þæt halige gewrit cwyð þæt God lufode Iacob and hatode Esau—na for gewyrde, ac for mislicum geearnungum. Hit gelimpð forwel oft þæt on anre tide acenð seo cwen and seo wyln, and ðeah geðicð se æðeling be his gebyrdum to healicum cynesetle, and ðære wylne sunu wunað eal his lif on ðeowte.

11 Nu cweðað oft stunte men þæt hi be gewyrde lybban sceolon, swylce God hi neadige to yfeldædum. Ac we wyllað þyssera stuntra manna ydele leasunge adwæscan mid deopnysse godcundra gewrita. Se ælmihtiga scyppend gesceop englas þurh his godcundan mihte, and for his micclan rihtwisnysse forgeaf him agenne cyre, þæt hi moston ðurhwunian on ecere gesælðe ðurh gehyrsumnysse, and mihton eac ða gesælða forleosan, na for gewyrde ac for ungehyrsumnysse. His deope rihtwisnys nolde hi neadian to naðrum, ac forgeaf him agenne cyre; forðan ðe þæt is rihtwisnys þæt gehwylcum sy his agen geðafod. Þonne wære seo rihtwisnys awæged gif he hi neadunge to his ðeowte gebigde, oððe gif he hi to yfelnysse bescufe. Ða miswendon sume þa englas heora agenne cyre, and þurh modignysse hy sylfe to awyrigedum deoflum geworhton.

12 Eft ða, ða se ðrimwealdenda scyppend mancyn geworhte, þa forgeaf he Adame and Euan agenne cyre, swa hi ðurh gehyrsumnysse a on ecnysse butan deaðe on gesælðe wunodon mid eallum heora ofspringe, swa hi ðurh ungehyrsumnysse deadlice wurdon. Ac ða þa hi Godes bebod forgægdon and þæs awyrigedan deofles lare gehyrsumodon, þa wurdon hi deadlice, and forscyldegode þurh agenne cyre, hi and eall heora offspring. And ðeah ðe næfre ne wurde syððan man-

by the foot at his birth; yet they were not alike in character, nor in the merits of their lives. Indeed holy scripture says that God loved Jacob and hated Esau—not by destiny, but for their different merits. It happens very often that a queen and a slave give birth at the same time, and yet by his birth the prince grows up to a lofty throne, and the son of the slave remains in slavery all his life.

Now foolish people often say that they must live accord- 11 ing to destiny, as if God compels them to evil deeds. But we will extinguish the idle lies of these foolish people with the deepness of divine scriptures. The almighty creator made angels through his divine might, and in his great righteousness gave them their own choice, that they might remain in eternal happiness through obedience, and might also lose that happiness, not by destiny but by disobedience. His great righteousness would not compel them to either, but gave them their own choice; because it is righteousness that everyone be allowed his own choice. Righteousness would be empty if he bent them to his service by necessity, or if he compelled them to evil. Some angels abused their own choice, and through pride transformed themselves to cursed devils.

Later, when the glorious creator made human beings, 12 he gave Adam and Eve their own choice, whether through obedience they would always in eternity dwell in happiness without death with all their offspring, or through disobedience they would become mortal. So when they transgressed God's command and obeyed the teaching of the cursed devil, they and all their offspring became mortal, and guilty through their own choice. And even if mercy were never

cynne gemiltsod ðe ma ðe ðam deoflum is, ðeah wære Godes rihtwisnys eallunga untæle. Ac eft seo miccle mildheortnys ures Drihtnes us alysde þurh his menniscnysse, gif we his bebodum mid ealre heortan gehyrsumiað. Witodlice ða ðe nu, þurh agenne cyre and deofles tihtinge, God forlætað, God forlæt hi eac to ðam ecan forwyrde.

13   Georne wiste se ælmihtiga scyppend, ær ðan þe he þa gesceafta gesceope, hwæt toweard wæs. He cuðe gewislice getel ægðer ge gecorenra engla ge gecorenra manna, and eac ðæra modigra gasta and arleasra manna þe ðurh heora ar-leasnysse forwurðað. Ac he ne forestihte nænne to yfelnysse, forðan þe he sylf is eall godnyss; ne he nænne to forwyrde ne gestihte, forðan ðe he is soð lif. He forestihte ða gecorenan to ðam ecan life forðan ðe he wiste hi swilce towearde, þurh his gife and agene gehyrsumnysse. He nolde forestihtan þa arleasan to his rice, forðan ðe he wiste hi swilce towearde, þurh heora agene forgægednysse and ðwyrnysse.

14   Healdað þis fæste on eowerum heortum, þæt se ælmih-tiga and se rihtwisa God nænne mann ne neadað to syngi-genne, ac he wat swa ðeah on ær hwilce þurh agenne willan syngian willað. Hwi ne sceal he ðonne rihtlice wrecan þæt yfel þæt he onscunað? He lufað ælc god and rihtwisnysse, forðan ðe he is gecyndelice god and rihtwis; and he hatað ealle ða ðe unrihtwisnysse wyrcað, and þa fordeð þe leasunge sprecað. Witodlice þa þe on God belyfað hi sind þurh ðone Halgan Gast gewissode. Nis seo gecyrrednys to Gode of us sylfum, ac of Godes gife, swa swa se apostol cwyð, "Þurh Godes gife ge sind gehealdene on geleafan." Þa ðe ne gelyfað ðurh agenne cyre hi scoriað, na ðurh gewyrd, forðan ðe gewyrd nis nan ðing buton leas wena; ne nan ðing soðlice be

again shown to humankind any more than to devils, nevertheless God's righteousness would be entirely infinite. But later the great mercy of our Lord redeemed us through his humanity, if we obey his commandments with all our heart. Truly, God will abandon to eternal damnation those who now abandon God through their own choice and the devil's instigation.

The almighty creator well knew what was to come before 13 he created his creatures. He knew with certainty the number of both the chosen angels and chosen people, and also of the proud spirits and wicked people who perish through their wickedness. He did not preordain anyone to evil, because he himself is all goodness; nor did he ordain anyone for damnation, because he is true life. He preordained the chosen for eternal life because he knew that they would be such, through his grace and their own obedience. He would not preordain the wicked to his kingdom, because he knew in advance that they would be such, through their own transgression and perversity.

Hold this fast in your hearts, that the almighty and righteous God does not compel any person to sin, yet he knows 14 beforehand who will sin through their own will. Why then should he not rightly avenge the evil which he hates? He loves every good and righteousness, for he is by nature good and righteous; and he hates all those who do unrighteousness, and destroys those who speak lies. Indeed those who believe in God are led by the Holy Spirit. This turning to God is not from ourselves, but by God's grace, as the apostle says, "Through God's grace we are held in faith." Those who do not believe perish through their own choice, not through destiny, because destiny is nothing but a false idea; truly

gewyrde ne gewyrð, ac ealle ðing þurh Godes dom beoð
geendebyrde, se ðe cwæð þurh his witegan, "Ic afandige
manna heortan and heora lendena, and ælcum sylle æfter his
færelde and æfter his agenre afundennysse." Ne talige nan
man his yfelan dæda to Gode, ac talige ærest to þam deofle
þe mancyn beswac, and to Adames forgægednysse; ac ðeah
swiðost to him sylfum, þæt him yfel gelicað and ne licað god.

15   Bið þeah gelome ofsprincg forscyldegod þurh forðfædera
mandæda, gif he mid yfele him geefenlæhð. Gif ðonne se
ofspring rihtwis bið, þonne leofað he on his rihtwisnysse,
and nateshwon his yldrena synna ne aberð. Ne sy nan man to
ðan arleas þæt he Adam wyrige oððe Euan, ðe nu on heofenum mid Gode rixiað, ac geearnige swiðor Godes mildheortnysse, swa þæt he wende his agenne cyre to his scyppendes gehyrsumnysse and bebodum. Forðan þe nan man ne
bið gehealden buton þurh gife hælendes Cristes, þa gife he
gearcode and forestihte on ecum ræde ær middangeardes
gesetnysse.

16   Mine gebroðra, ge habbað nu gehyred be ðan leasan
wenan þe ydele men gewyrd hatað; uton nu fon on þæs godspelles trahtnunge þær we hit ær forleton. Þa tungelwitegan
eodon into ðæs cildes gesthuse, and hine gemetton mid
þære meder. Hi ða mid astrehtum lichaman hi to Criste gebædon, and geopenodon heora hordfatu and him geoffrodon þryfealde lac, gold, and recels, and myrran. Gold
gedafenað cyninge; stor gebyrað to Godes ðenunge; mid
myrran man behwyrfð deaddra manna lic þæt hi late rotian.
Ðas ðry tungelwitegan hi to Criste gebædon, and him ge-
tacnigendlice lac offrodon. Þæt gold getacnode þæt he is
soð cyning, se stor þæt he is soð God, seo myrre þæt he wæs
ða deadlic, ac he þurhwunað nu undeadlic on ecnysse.

nothing happens by destiny, but all things are arranged by the judgment of God, who said through his prophet, "I test people's hearts and their loins, and give to everyone according to his way of life and according to his own behavior." Let no one ascribe his evil deeds to God, but ascribe them first to the devil who deceived humanity, and to Adam's transgression; but above all to himself, that evil pleases him and good does not.

Yet frequently someone's offspring is condemned 15 through the wicked deeds of his ancestors, if he imitates them in evil. But if the offspring is righteous, then he will live in his righteousness, and will not bear the sins of his parents at all. Let no one be so wicked that he curse Adam or Eve, who now reign with God in heaven, but let him rather merit God's mercy, so that he might turn by his own choice to his creator's obedience and commandments. For no one will be saved except through the grace of the savior Christ, the grace he prepared and preordained by eternal decree before the foundation of the world.

My brothers, you have now heard about the false idea 16 which vain people call destiny; let us now take up the exposition of the gospel where we left off. The astrologers went into the child's lodging, and found him with his mother. Then, prostrate, they worshiped Christ, and opened their coffers and offered to him threefold gifts of gold, and frankincense, and myrrh. Gold befits a king; frankincense belongs to God's service; with myrrh the bodies of the dead are prepared so that they might decay slowly. These three astrologers worshiped Christ, and offered him gifts with significance. The gold signified that he is a true king, the frankincense that he is true God, the myrrh that he was then mortal, though he now remains immortal in eternity.

17 Sume gedwolmen wæron þe gelyfdon þæt he God wære,
ac hi nateshwon ne gelyfdon þæt he æghwær rixode: hi offrodon Criste gastlice recels, and noldon him gold offrian.
Eft wæron oðre gedwolmen ðe gelyfdon þæt he soð cyning
wære, ac hi wiðsocon þæt he God wære: ðas, buton twyn,
him offrodon gold, and noldon offrian recels. Sume gedwolan andetton þæt he soð God wære and soð cyning, and wið-
socon þæt he deadlic flæsc underfenge; þas witodlice him
brohton gold and stor, and noldon bringan myrran þære on-
fangenre deadlicnysse. Mine gebroðra, uton we geoffrian
urum Drihtne gold, þæt we andettan þæt he soð cyning sy
and æghwær rixige. Uton him offrian stor, þæt we gelyfon
þæt he æfre God wæs, se ðe on þære tide man æteowde.
Uton him bringan myrran, þæt we gelyfan þæt he wæs deadlic on urum flæsce, se ðe is unðrowigendlic on his godcundnysse. He wæs deadlic on menniscnysse ær his ðrowunge, ac
he bið heononforð undeadlic, swa swa we ealle beoð æfter
ðam gemænelicum æriste.

18 We habbað gesæd, embe ðas þryfealdan lac, hu hi to
Criste belimpað; we willað eac secgan hu hi to us belimpað,
æfter ðeawlicum andgite. Mid golde witodlice bið wisdom
getacnod, swa swa Salomon cwæð, "Gewilnigendlic goldhord lið on ðæs witan muðe." Mid store bið geswutelod halig
gebed, be ðam sang se sealmscop, "Drihten, sy min gebed
asend swa swa byrnende stor on ðinre gesihðe." Þurh myrran is gehiwod cwelmbærnys ures flæsces, be ðam cweð
seo halige gelaðung, "Mine handa drypton myrran." Þam
acennedan cyninge we bringað gold gif we on his gesihðe
mid beorhtnysse þæs upplican wisdomes scinende beoð.
Stor we him bringað gif we ure geðohtas, ðurh gecnyrdnysse
haligra gebeda, on weofode ure heortan onælað, þæt we

142

There were some heretics who believed that he was God, 17
but they did not believe at all that he reigned everywhere:
they offered frankincense to Christ spiritually, and would
not offer him gold. There were also other heretics who believed that he was a true king, but they denied that he was
God: these, without doubt, offered him gold, and would not
offer frankincense. Some heretics confessed that he was
true God and true king, but denied that he assumed mortal
flesh; these indeed brought him gold and frankincense, but
would not bring the myrrh of the mortality he assumed. My
brothers, let us offer our Lord gold, that we might confess
that he is a true king and reigns everywhere. Let us offer
him frankincense, that we might believe that he was always
God, who at that time revealed himself as a human. Let us
bring him myrrh, that we believe that he who is incapable of
suffering in his divine nature was mortal in our flesh. He was
mortal in human nature before his passion, but he is henceforth immortal, just as we all will be after the universal
resurrection.

We have said how these threefold gifts pertain to Christ; 18
we also want to say how they pertain to us, in a moral sense.
Truly, by gold wisdom is signified, as Solomon said, "A desirable treasure lies in the mouth of the wise." With frankincense holy prayer is indicated, of which the psalmist sang,
"Lord, let my prayer be sent forth like burning incense in
your sight." By myrrh is figured the mortality of our flesh,
concerning which the holy Church says, "My hands dripped
myrrh." To the king who was born we bring gold if we are
shining in his sight with the brightness of heavenly wisdom.
We bring him frankincense if, by the diligence of holy
prayers, we kindle our thoughts on the altar of our heart, so

magon hwæthwega wynsumlice ðurh heofenlice gewilnunge stincan. Myrran we him offriað gif we ða flæsclican lustas þurh forhæfednysse cwylmiað. Myrra deð, swa we ær cwædon, þæt þæt deade flæsc eaðelice ne rotað. Witodlice þæt deade flæsc rotað leahtorlice þonne se deadlica lichama ðeowað þære flowendan galnysse, swa swa se witega be sumum cwæð, "Ða nytenu forrotedon on heora meoxe." Þonne forrotiað þa nytenu on heora meoxe þonne flæsclice men on stence heora galnysse geendiað heora dagas. Ac gif we ða myrran Gode gastlice geoffriað, þonne bið ure deadlica lichama fram galnysse stencum ðurh forhæfednysse gehealden.

19   Sum ðing miccles gebicnodon þa tungelwitegan us mid þam þæt hi ðurh oðerne weg to heora earde gecyrdon. Ure eard soðlice is Neorxnawang, to ðam we ne magon gecyrran þæs weges ðe we comon. Se frumsceapena man and eall his ofspring wearð adræfed of Neorxenawanges myrhðe þurh ungehyrsumnysse, and for ðigene þæs forbodenan bigleofan, and ðurh modignysse, ða ða he wolde beon betera ðonne hine se ælmihtiga scyppend gesceop. Ac us is micel neod þæt we ðurh oðerne weg þone swicolan deofol forbugan, þæt we moton gesæliglice to urum eðele becuman, þe we to gesceapene wæron. We sceolon þurh gehyrsumnysse, and forhæfednysse, and eadmodnysse, anmodlice to urum eðele stæppan, and mid halgum mægnum ðone eard ofgan þe we ðurh leahtras forluron. Rihtlice wæs se swicola Herodes fram þam tungelwitegum bepæht, and he to Criste ne becom forðan ðe he mid facenfullum mode hine sohte. He getacnode þa leasan licceteras ðe mid hiwunge God secað and næfre ne gemetað. He is to secenne mid soðfæstre heortan and anrædum mode, se ðe leofað and rixað mid Fæder and Halgum Gaste, on ealra worulda woruld. Amen.

that we may smell somewhat sweetly through heavenly desire. We offer him myrrh if we calm the lusts of the flesh through continence. Myrrh, as we have said, acts so that dead flesh does not easily rot. Indeed the dead flesh rots viciously when the mortal body serves wanton lust, as the prophet said concerning some people, "The beasts rotted in their dung." The beasts rot in their dung when fleshly people end their days in the stench of their lust. But if we offer myrrh to God spiritually, then our mortal body will be preserved through continence from the stenches of lust.

The astrologers pointed out a great thing to us when they returned to their land by another way. For our country is Paradise, to which we cannot return by the way we came. The first-created human and all his offspring were driven from the joy of Paradise through disobedience, for tasting the forbidden food, and through pride, when he wanted to be better than the almighty creator had made him. But we greatly need to avoid the treacherous devil by another way, that we may happily come to the homeland for which we were created. By obedience, and continence, and humility, we should resolutely proceed to our homeland, and with holy virtues claim the country that we lost through sin. The treacherous Herod was rightly deceived by the astrologers, and he did not come to Christ because he sought him with a deceitful mind. He signified the false hypocrites who seek God with outward show and never find him. He should be sought with a true heart and a steadfast mind, he who lives and reigns with the Father and the Holy Spirit, for ever and ever. Amen.

19

8

Dominica III post
Epiphania Domini

Cum descendisset Iesus de monte secutae sunt eum turbae multae,
et reliqua.

2   Matheus se eadiga godspellere awrat on þissere godspellican rædinge þæt "Se hælend niðereode of anre dune, and
him filigde micel menigu. Efne ða com sum hreoflig mann,
and aleat wið þæs hælendes, þus cweðende, 'Drihten, gif þu
wilt, þu miht me geclænsian.' Se hælend astrehte his hand
and hine hrepode, and cwæð, 'Ic wylle; and sy ðu geclænsod.'
Þa sona wearð his hreofla eal geclænsod, and he wæs gehæled. Ða cwæð se hælend him to, 'Warna þæt þu hit nanum menn ne secge, ac far to Godes temple and geswutela
ðe sylfne ðam sacerde, and geoffra ðine lac, swa swa Moyses
bebead, him on gewitnysse.'"

3   Se lareow Hægmon cweð on ðissere trahtnunge þæt seo
dun þe se hælend ofastah getacnode heofenan rice, of ðam
niðerastah se ælmihtiga Godes Sunu ða ða he underfeng ure
gecynd and to menniscum men geflæschamod wearð to ðy
þæt he mancynn fram deofles anwealde alysde. He wæs ungesewenlic and unðrowigendlic on his gecynde; þa wearð he
gesewenlic on urum gecynde, and þrowigendlic. Seo micele
menigu ðe him filigde getacnode ða geleaffullan Cristenan,
þe mid heora þeawa stæpum Drihtne filiað. Witodlice, we

8

Third Sunday after Epiphany

The Third Sunday after the
Epiphany of the Lord

When *Jesus descended from the mountain, a great multitude followed him, etc.*

The blessed Evangelist Matthew wrote in this gospel   2
reading that "The savior came down from a mountain, and a
great crowd followed him. Then there came a leper, and fell
down before the savior, saying, 'Lord, if you will it, you can
cleanse me.' The savior stretched out his hand and touched
him, and said, 'I will it; be cleansed.' At once his leprosy was
completely cleansed, and he was healed. The savior said to
him, 'Beware that you tell this to no one, but go to God's
temple and show yourself to the priest, and offer your gift,
as Moses commanded, as a testimony.'"

The teacher Haymo says in his commentary that the   3
mountain that the savior came down from signified the
kingdom of heaven, from which the almighty Son of God
descended when he took on our nature and became incarnate like human beings so he might rescue humanity from
the devil's power. He was invisible in his nature and incapable of suffering; then he became visible in our nature, and
capable of suffering. The great crowd that followed him signified the faithful Christians, who follow the Lord with the

folgiað Cristes fotswaðum gif we his gebisnungum mid godum weorcum geefenlæcað.

4   "Efne ða com sum hreoflig man, and aleat wið þæs
hælendes, þus cweðende, 'Drihten, gif þu wilt, ðu miht me
geclænsian.' Se hælend astrehte his hand and hine hrepode,
and cwæð, 'Ic wille; and sy ðu geclænsod.' Þa sona wearð his
hreofla eal geclænsod, and he wæs gehæled." On ðissere
dæde is geswutelod Godes miht and his eadmodnys. Moyses
æ forbead to hrepenne ænigne hreoflan, ac se eadmoda
Crist nolde hine forseon, þeah ðe he atelic wære; and eac
geswutelode þæt he wæs hlaford þære ealdan æ and na ðeow.
Mihtiglice he mihte mid his worde hine gehælan, buton hrepunge; ac he geswutelode þæt his hrepung is swiðe halwende
geleaffullum. Geleafful wæs se hreoflia ða ða he cwæð,
"Drihten, gif þu wilt, ðu miht me geclænsian." Se hælend
andwyrde, "Ic wylle; and þu beo geclænsod." Godes hæs
soðlice is weorc, swa swa se sealmwyrhta cwæð, "He hit gecwæð, and þa gesceafta wæron geworhte. He bebead, and hi
wæron gesceapene."

5   On gastlicum andgite getacnode þes hreoflia man eal
mancyn, þe wæs atelice hreoflig mid mislicum leahtrum on
þam inran menn; ac hit gebeah to Cristes geleafan, and
gleawlice undergeat þæt hit ne mihte þære sawle clænsunge
onfon buton þurh Drihten, þe nane synne ne worhte, ne nan
facn næs on his muðe gemet. Laðlic bið þæs hreoflian lic
mid menigfealdum springum and geswelle and mid mislicum fagnyssum; ac se inra mann, þæt is seo sawul, bið micele
atelicor gif heo mid mislicum leahtrum begripen bið. We
sceolon rihtlice gelyfan on Crist þæt he ure sawle fram synna
fagnyssum gehælan mæge; and we sceolon anrædlice his willan to ðære fremminge biddan. His hand getacnað his mihte

steps of their virtues. Indeed, we follow Christ's footsteps if
we imitate his examples with good works.

"Then a certain leper came and fell down before the sav-   4
ior, saying, 'Lord, if you will it, you can cleanse me.' The savior stretched out his hand and touched him, and said, 'I will
it; be cleansed.' At once his leprosy was completely cleansed,
and he was healed." God's power and humility are revealed
in this act. The law of Moses forbade the touching of any
leper, but the humble Christ would not despise him, though
he was loathsome; he also revealed that he was the lord of
the old law and not its servant. In his power he could have
healed him with his word, without touching; but he revealed
that his touch is very healing to believers. The leper was a
believer when he said, "Lord, if you will it, you can cleanse
me." The savior answered, "I will it; be cleansed." God's
command is truly his deed, as the psalmist said, "He spoke,
and creation was made. He commanded, and they were created."

In a spiritual sense the leper signified all humanity, which   5
was foully leprous in the inward person with various sins;
but it turned to faith in Christ, and wisely understood that
it could not receive the soul's cleansing except through the
Lord, who committed no sin, and no deceit was found in his
mouth. A leper's body is loathsome with many ulcers and
blisters and various blemishes; but the inner person, that is,
the soul, is much more loathsome if it is seized by various
sins. We should rightly believe that Christ can heal our soul
from the blemishes of sin; we should steadfastly ask his will
to do that. His hand signifies his power and his incarnation.

and his flæsclicnysse. Swa swa Crist mid his handa hrepunge þone hreoflian gehælde, swa eac he alysde us fram ure sawla synnum ðurh anfenge ures flæsces; swa swa se witega Isaias cwæð, "Soðlice, he sylf ætbræd ure adlunga, and ure sarnyssa he sylf abær."

6   Mid þam ðe he forbead þam gehæledum hreoflian þæt he hit nanum men ne cydde, mid þam he sealde us bysne þæt we ne sceolon na widmærsian ure weldæda, ac we sceolon onscunian mid inweardre heortan þone ydelan gylp gif we hwæt lytles to gode gedoð. Witodlice, ne bið us mid nanum oðrum edleane forgolden, gif we good for gylpe doð, buton mid helle susle, forðan ðe gilp is an heofodleahter.

7   Seo ealde æ bebead þæt gehwilc hreoflig man gecome to þam sacerde, and se sacerd sceolde hine fram mannum ascirian gif he soðlice hreoflig wære. Gif he nære swutelice hreoflig, wære ðonne be his dome clæne geteald. Gif se sacerd hine hreofligne tealde, and Godes miht hine syððan gehælde, þonne sceolde he mid lace his clænsunge Gode ðancian. Swa sceal eac se ðe mid heafodleahtrum wiðinnan hreoflig bið cuman to Godes sacerde, and geopenian his digelnysse ðam gastlican læce, and be his ræde and fultume his sawle wunda dædbetende gelacnian. Sume men wenað þæt him genihtsumige to fulfremedum læcedome gif hi heora synna mid onbryrdre heortan Gode anum andettað, and ne ðurfon nanum sacerde geandettan, gif hi yfeles ge-swicað; ac gif heora wena soð wære, ðonne nolde Drihten asendan þone ðe he sylf gehælde to þam sacerde mid ænigre lace. For ðære ylcan gebisnunge eac he asende Paulum, þone ðe he sylf of heofenum gespræc, to ðam sacerde Annanian, þus cweðende, "Ga inn to ðære ceastre, and ðær þe bið gesæd hwæt þe gedafenað to donne."

Just as Christ healed the leper with the touch of his hand, so too he redeemed us from the sins of our souls by taking on our flesh; as the prophet Isaiah said, "Truly, he himself took away our sickness, and he himself bore our pains."

When he forbade the healed leper to reveal it to anyone, 6 he gave us an example that we should not publicize our good deeds, but we should shun empty pride with our inward heart if we are to accomplish anything good. Indeed, if we do good deeds for pride, no other reward will be given to us than the pains of hell, because pride is a deadly sin.

The old law commanded that every leper should come to 7 the priest, and the priest should separate him from people if he really was leprous. If he clearly was not leprous, he would then by his judgment be considered clean. If the priest considered him leprous, and the power of God later healed him, then he should thank God for his cleansing with an offering. So too anyone who is leprous within with deadly sins should come to God's priest, and open his secrets to the spiritual physician, and by his counsel and aid heal the wounds of his soul with penance. Some people think that it is enough for them to have a complete cure if they confess their sins with compunction of heart to God alone, and they do not need to reveal it to any priest, if they refrain from evil; but if their opinion were true, then the Lord would not have sent the one whom he himself had healed to the priest with any offering. For the same example he sent Paul, whom he himself had spoken to from heaven, to the priest Ananias, saying, "Go into the city, and there you will be told what you ought to do."

8 Ne gedyde se sacerd þone man hreofligne oððe unhreof-
ligne, ac he demde þæt he sceolde beon ascyred fram manna
neawiste gif his hreofla wyrsigende wære, oððe betwux mannum wunian gif his hreofla godigende wære. Swa sceal don
se gastlica sacerd: he sceal gerihtlæcan Godes folc, and ðone
ascyrian and amansumian fram Cristenum mannum þe swa
hreoflig bið on manfullum ðeawum þæt he oðre mid his yfelnysse besmit; be ðam cwæð se apostol Paulus, "Afyrsiað
þone yfelan fram eow, ðy læs ðe an wannhal scep ealle ða
eowde besmite." Gif his hreofla bið godigende, þæt is, gif he
yfeles geswicð and his unðeawas ðurh Godes ege gerihtlæcð,
he hæbbe wununge betwux Cristenum mannum, oð þæt he
full hal sy on his drohtnungum.

9 Se godspellere cwæð þæt "Drihten ferde æfter ðisum to
anre byrig þe is gehaten Capharnaum; þa genealæhte him to
sum hundredes ealdor, biddende and cweðende, 'Drihten,
min cniht lið æt ham bedreda, and is yfele geðreatod.'
Drihten him andwyrde, 'Ic cume and hine gehæle.' Þa andwyrde se hundredes ealdor and cwæð, 'Drihten, ne eom ic
wyrðe þæt þu innfare under minum hrofe; ac cweð þin word,
and min cniht bið gehæled. Ic eom an man geset under anwealde, hæbbende under me cempan; and ic cweðe to
ðisum, "Far ðu," and he færð; to oðrum, "Cum ðu," and he
cymð; to minum ðeowan, "Do ðis," and he deð.' Þa wundrode se hælend ða ða he ðis gehyrde, and cwæð to ðære
fyligendan menigu, 'Soð ic eow secge, ne gemette ic swa
micelne geleafan on Israhela ðeode. Ic secge eow to soðum
þæt manega cumað fram eastdæle and westdæle, and gerestað hi mid Abrahame ðam heahfædere, and Isaace, and
Iacobe, on heofenan rice. Þa rican bearn beoð aworpene
into ðam yttrum þeostrum, þær bið wop and toða gebitt.'

The priest did not make the person leprous or unleprous, 8
but he judged that he should be separated from the company of others if his leprosy was getting worse, or remain
among people if his leprosy was getting better. The spiritual
priest should do the same: he should correct God's people,
and separate and excommunicate from Christian people the
one who is so leprous in sinful practices that he defiles others with his evil; of this the apostle Paul said, "Remove the
evil one from among you, lest one unhealthy sheep infect
the whole flock." If his leprosy is getting better, that is, if he
ceases his evil and corrects his bad ways through fear of
God, he should have a dwelling among Christians, until he is
completely healed in his conduct.

The Evangelist said that "After this the Lord went to a 9
city called Capernaum; there a certain centurion approached him, praying and saying, 'Lord, my servant lies at
home bedridden, and is greatly tormented.' The Lord answered him, 'I will come and heal him.' The centurion answered and said, 'Lord, I am not worthy that you should enter under my roof; but say your word, and my servant will be
healed. I am a person placed in a position of authority, having soldiers under me; and I say to this one, "Go," and he
goes; to another, "Come," and he comes; to my servant, "Do
this," and he does it.' When he heard this the savior marveled, and said to the crowd following, 'Truly I say to you, I
have not found so great faith in the people of Israel. I tell
you truly that many will come from the east and the west,
and rest with the patriarch Abraham, and Isaac, and Jacob,
in the kingdom of heaven. The rich children will be cast into
outer darkness, where there will be weeping and gnashing of

Ða cwæð eft se hælend to þam hundredes ealdre, 'Far ðe ham, and getimige ðe swa swa ðu gelyfdest.' And se cniht wearð gehæled of ðære tide."

10 Þes hundredes ealdor genealæhte ðam hælende na healfunga, ac fulfremedlice. He genealæhte mid micclum geleafan and mid soðre eadmodnysse, and snotornysse, and soðre lufe. Micelne geleafan he hæfde þa þa he cwæð, "Drihten, cweð þin word, and min cniht bið hal." Soðlice he geswutelode micele eadmodnysse mid þam ðe he cwæð, "Drihten, ne eom ic wyrðe þæt þu innfare under mine ðecene." He hæfde micele snotornysse þa þa he understod þæt Crist is æghwær andweard þurh godcundnysse, se ðe lichamlice betwux mannum gesewenlic eode. Næs he bedæled þære soðan lufe ða ða he bæd Drihten for his ðeowan hæle. Manega oðre men bædon Drihten, sume for heora agenre hæle, sume for heora bearna, sume for leofra freonda; ac ðes ðegen bæd for his þeowan hælðe mid soðre lufe, forðan ðe heo ne toscæt nænne be mæglicere sibbe. Drihten geseah ðises ðegenes menigfealdan godnysse and cwæð, "Ic cume and ðinne cniht gehæle."

11 Iohannes se godspellere awrat þæt "Sum undercyning com to Criste, and hine bæd þæt he ham mid him siðode and his sunu gehælde, forðan þe he læig æt forðsiðe. Þa cwæð se hælend to ðam undercyninge, 'Gewend þe ham, þin sunu leofað.' He gelyfde þæs hælendes spræce, and ham siðode. Ða comon his ðegnas him togeanes and cyddon þæt his sunu gesund wære. He ða befran on hwilcere tide he gewyrpte; hi sædon, 'Gyrstandæg ofer midne dæg hine forlet se fefor.' Þa oncneow se fæder þæt hit wæs seo tid on ðære ðe se hælend him to cwæð, 'Far ðe ham, þin sunu leofað.' Se cyning gelyfde ða on God, and eal his hired."

teeth.' Then the savior replied to the centurion, 'Go home, and let it be for you as you have believed.' And the servant was healed from that hour."

The centurion approached the savior not halfway, but 10 fully. He approached with great faith and with true humility, and wisdom, and true love. He had great faith when he said, "Lord, say your word, and my servant will be healed." Truly he revealed great humility when he said, "Lord, I am not worthy that you should enter under my roof." He had great wisdom when he understood that Christ, who went about physically visible among people, is everywhere present through his divine nature. He was not deprived of true love when he asked the Lord for the healing of his servant. Many others beseeched the Lord, some for their own health, some for their children's, some for their dear friends'; but this officer asked for the health of his servant with true love, because that makes no distinction with regard to family relationship. The Lord saw the manifold goodness of this officer and said, "I will come and heal your servant."

John the Evangelist wrote that "A certain underking came 11 to Christ, and asked him to travel home with him and heal his son, for he lay at the point of death. The savior said to the underking, 'Return home, your son lives.' He believed the savior's speech, and went home. Then his servants came toward him and declared that his son was well. He asked at what hour he recovered; they said, 'Yesterday, after midday, the fever left him.' Then the father knew that it was the hour at which the savior said to him, 'Go home, your son lives.' The king then believed in God, and all his household."

12   Drihten nolde gelaðod lichamlice siðian to þæs cyninges untruman bearne, ac unandweard mid his worde hine gehælde; and he wæs gearo, ungelaðod, to siðigenne lichamlice mid þam hundredes ealdre. Wel wat gehwa þæt cyning hæfð maran mihte þonne ænig hundredes ealdor, ac se ælmihtiga Godes Sunu geswutelode mid þære dæde þæt we ne sceolon ða rican for heora riccetere wurðian, ac for menniscum gecynde; ne we ne sceolon ða wannspedigan for heora hafenleaste forseon, ac we sceolon Godes anlicnysse on him wurðian. Se eadmoda Godes Sunu wæs gearo to geneosigenne þone ðeowan mid his andwerdnysse, and he gehælde þone æðeling mid hæse; be ðam cwæð se witega, "Se healica Drihten sceawað þa eadmodan, and þa modigan feorran oncnæwð."

13   Drihten wundrode þæs hundredes ealdres geleafan, na swilce he hine ær ne cuðe, se ðe ealle ðing wat, ac he geswutelode mannum his geleafan mid herunge þam þe he wundorlic wæs. Hwanon com se geleafa þam þegene buton of Cristes gife, se ðe hine syððan þisum wordum herede? "Soð ic eow secge, na gemette ic swa micelne geleafan on Israhela ðeode." Næs ðis gecweden be ðam heahfæderum oððe witegum, ac be ðam andwerdan folce, ðe ða gyt næron swa miccles geleafan.

14   Maria and Martha wæron twa geswystru swiðe on God belyfede. Hi cwædon to Criste, "Drihten, gif ðu her andwerd wære, nære ure broðer forðfaren." Þes ðegen cwæð to Criste, "Cweð þin word, and min cniht bið hal. Ic eom man under anwealde gesett, hæbbende under me cempan; and ic secge ðisum, 'Far ðu,' and he færð; to oðrum, 'Cum ðu,' and he cymð; to minum þeowan, 'Do þis,' and he deð. Hu miccle swiðor miht ðu, þe ælmihtig God eart, þurh ðine hæse

The Lord would not travel physically to the king's sick 12
son when invited but, absent, healed him with his word; and
he was ready, uninvited, to travel physically with the centurion. Everyone well knows that a king has greater power
than any centurion, but the almighty Son of God revealed
by that deed that we should not honor the rich for their
riches, but for human nature; nor should we despise the
poor for their poverty, but we should honor God's likeness
in them. The humble Son of God was ready to approach the
servant by his presence, and he healed the prince with his
command; of this the prophet said, "The exalted Lord looks
on the humble, and the proud he knows from afar."

The Lord marveled at the centurion's faith, not because 13
he did not know it before, he who knows all things, but he
revealed his faith to the people with praise of him who was
wondrous. Where did the faith of this officer come from
but from Christ's grace, who afterward praised him in these
words? "Truly I say to you, I have not found so great faith in
the people of Israel." This was not said of the patriarchs or
prophets, but of the people present, who were not yet of
such great faith.

Mary and Martha were two sisters who greatly believed 14
in God. They said to Christ, "Lord, if you had been present
here, our brother would not have died." This officer said to
Christ, "Say your word, and my servant shall be healed. I am
a person placed in a position of authority, having soldiers
under me; and I say to this one, 'Go,' and he goes; to another, 'Come,' and he comes; to my servant, 'Do this,' and he
does it. How much more can you, who are almighty God,

gefremman swa hwæt swa ðu wilt." Drihten cwæð, "Ic secge
eow to soðan þæt manega cumað fram eastdæle and westdæle, and gerestað hi mid Abrahame þam heahfædere, and
Isaace, and Iacobe, on heofenan rice." Þas word sind lustbære to gehyrenne, and hi micclum ure mod gladiað, þæt
manega cumað fram eastdæle middangeardes, and fram
westdæle, to heofenan rice, and mid þam heahfæderum on
ecere myrhðe rixiað.

15   Þurh ða twegen dælas, eastdæl and westdæl, sind getacnode ða feower hwemmas ealles middangeardes, of þam
beoð gegaderode Godes gecorenan of ælcere mægðe to þæra
heahfædera wununge and ealra halgena. Þurh eastdæl magon beon getacnode þa ðe on geogoðe to Gode bugað,
forðan ðe on eastdæle is þæs dæges angin. Þurh westdæl
sind getacnode þa ðe on ylde to Godes ðeowdome gecyrrað,
forðan ðe on westdæle geendað se dæg.

16   Ðes æfterfiligenda cwyde is swiðe egefull: "Þa rican bearn
beoð aworpene into ðam yttrum ðeostrum, þær bið wop
and toða gebitt." Ða rican bearn sind þa Iudeiscan, on ðam
rixode God ðurh ða ealdan æ; ac hi awurpon Crist and his
lare forsawon, and he awyrpð hi on ða yttran þeostru, ðær
bið wop and toða gebitt. Fela riccra manna geðeoð Gode,
swaþeah, gif hi rihtwise beoð and mildheorte. Rice man wæs
se heahfæder Abraham, and Dauid se mæra cyning, and
Zacheus, se ðe healfe his æhta þearfum dælde, and mid healfum dæle forgeald be feowerfealdum swa hwæt swa he ær on
unriht be anfealdum reafode. Þas rican and heora gelican
becumað þurh gode gecyrrednysse to ðam ecan rice, ðe him
næfre ne ateorað.

17   Ða sind Godes bearn gecigede þe hine lufiað swiðor
þonne þisne middangeard, and ða sind ða rican bearn

perform whatever you wish through your command." The
Lord said, "I say to you in truth that many will come from
the east part and the west part, and rest with the patriarch
Abraham, and Isaac, and Jacob, in the kingdom of heaven."
These words are pleasant to hear, and they greatly gladden
our minds, that many will come from the eastern part of the
world, and from the western part, to the kingdom of heaven,
and reign with the patriarchs in eternal joy.

By the two parts, the east and the west, are signified the 15
four corners of the whole world, from which God's chosen
will be gathered from every people into the dwelling of the
patriarchs and all the saints. By the eastern part may be signified those who turn to God in their youth, because in the
eastern part is the day's beginning. By the western part is
signified those who turn to God's service in old age, because
in the western part the day ends.

The following sentence is very terrifying: "The rich chil- 16
dren will be cast into the outer darkness, where there will be
weeping and gnashing of teeth." The rich children are the
Jews, over whom God ruled by the old law; but they rejected
Christ and despised his teaching, and he casts them into
the outer darkness, where there is weeping and gnashing of
teeth. Many rich people, however, thrive in God, if they are
righteous and merciful. The patriarch Abraham was rich,
and David the great king, and Zacchaeus, who gave half his
possessions to the poor, and with the other half repaid fourfold whatever he had wrongfully gained onefold. These rich
people and those like them come by good conversion to the
eternal kingdom, which will never fail them.

They are called children of God who love him more than 17
this world, and those are called rich children who plant the

gecwedene ðe heora heortan wyrtruman on ðisum andwer-
dum life plantiað swiðor þonne on Criste; swylce beoð
on þeostru aworpene. Þæt godspel cwyð, "on þa yttran
þeostru." Ða yttran þeostru sind þæs lichaman blindnyssa
wiðutan; ða inran þeostru sind þæs modes blindnyssa wiðinnan. Se ðe on ðisum andweardum life is wiðinnan ablend,
swa þæt he næfð nan andgit ne hoga embe Godes beboda,
he bið þonne eft wiðutan ablend and ælces leohtes bedæled,
forðan ðe he ær his lif aspende butan Godes gemynde. Þa
earman forscyldegodan cwylmiað on ecum fyre, and swaðeah
þæt swearte fyr him nane lihtinge ne deð. Wurmas toslitað
heora lichaman mid fyrenum toðum, swa swa Crist on his
godspelle cwæð, "Þær næfre heora wyrm ne swylt, ne heora
fyr ne bið adwæsced." Þær beoð þonne geferlæhte on anre
susle þa þe on life on mandædum geðeodde wæron, swa þæt
þa manslagan togædere ecelice on tintregum cwylmiað, and
forligras mid forligrum; gitseras mid gytserum, sceaðan mid
sceaðum, ða forsworenan mid forsworenum, on ðam bradan
fire butan ælcere geendunge forwurðað. Þær bið wop and
toða gebitt, forðan ðe ða eagan tyrað on ðam micclum bryne,
and ða teð cwaciað eft on swiðlicum cyle. Gif hwam twynige
be ðam gemænelicum æriste, þonne understande he þisne
drihtenlican cwyde, þæt þær bið soð ærist, ðær ðær beoð
wepende eagan and cearcigende teð.

18   Drihten cwæð to þam hundredes ealdre, "Far ðe ham, and
getimige ðe swa swa ðu gelyfdest"; and his cniht wearð gehæled of ðære tide. Be ðisum is to understandenne hu micclum þam Cristenum men his agen geleafa fremige, þonne
oðres mannes swa micclum fremode. Witodlice, for ðæs
hundredes ealdres geleafan wearð se bedreda gehæled. Geleafa is ealra mægena fyrmest; buton þam ne mæg nan man

root of their hearts in this present life more than in Christ; such will be cast into darkness. The gospel says, "into outer darkness." The outer darkness is the outer blindness of the body; the inner darkness is the mind's blindness within. He who is blinded within in this present life, so that he has no understanding nor care of God's commandments, will then be blinded without and deprived of every light, because he had spent his life without remembrance of God. The miserable guilty ones will be tormented in everlasting fire, and yet that dark fire will give them no light. Worms will tear their bodies with fiery teeth, as Christ said in his gospel, "There their worm will never die, nor their fire be quenched." There will be brought together in one torment those who were united in evil deeds in life, so that murderers will eternally be tortured together, and adulterers with adulterers; the greedy with the greedy, robbers with robbers, perjurers with perjurers, will perish in the broad flame without ending. There will be weeping and gnashing of teeth, for their eyes will shed tears in the great burning, and their teeth will chatter in the intense cold. If anyone doubts the universal resurrection, let him understand this divine saying, that where there will be weeping eyes and gnashing teeth, there will be a true resurrection.

The Lord said to the centurion, "Go home, and let it be 18 for you as you have believed"; and his servant was healed in that hour. By this we should understand how much a Christian's own faith can accomplish, when that of another person accomplished so much. Truly, the bedridden was healed for the centurion's faith. Faith is first of all virtues; without

Gode lician, and se rihtwisa leofað be his geleafan. Uton gelyfan on þa Halgan Ðrynnysse and on soðe Annysse, þæt se
ælmihtiga Fæder, and his Sunu þæt is his wisdom, and se
Halga Gast se ðe is heora begra lufu and willa, þæt hi sind
þry on hadum and on namum, and an God on anre godcundnysse æfre wunigende, butan angynne and ende. Amen.

9

IIII NONA FEBRUARII

In Purificatione sanctae Mariae

P̶ostquam impleti sunt dies purificationis Mariae, et reliqua.

2   God bebead on þære ealdan æ, and het Moyses þone
heretogan þæt he hit awrite betwux oðrum bebodum, þæt
ælc wif ðe cild gebære sceolde gebidan feowertig daga æfter
þære cennynge, swa þæt heo ne come into Godes temple, ne
on anum bedde mid hire were, ær ðam fyrste þe we ær cwædon, þæt is feowertig daga, gif hit hysecild wære. Gif hit
þonne mædencild wære, þonne sceolde heo forhabban fram
ingange Godes huses hundehtatig daga, and eac fram hire
gebeddan; and æfter ðam fyrste gan mid lace to Godes huse,
and beran þæt cild forð mid þære lace, and syððan mid
Godes bletsunge genealæcan hyre gemacan. Þis wæs geset
be wifum.

it no one can be pleasing to God, and the righteous lives by his faith. Let us believe in the Holy Trinity and in true Unity, that the almighty Father, and his Son that is his wisdom, and the Holy Spirit who is the love and will of them both, that they are three in person and in name, and one God in one divine nature ever continuing, without beginning and end. Amen.

9

Purification

FEBRUARY 2

The Purification of Saint Mary

When the days of the purification of Mary were fulfilled, etc.

God commanded in the old law, and ordered the leader 2 Moses to write among other commandments, that every woman who bore a child should wait forty days after the birth, so that she should not come into God's temple, nor into bed with her husband, before the time which we said, that is, forty days, if it was a male child. If it was a female child, then she should refrain from going into God's house, and also from her husband, for eighty days; and after that time she should go with an offering to God's house and bear forth the child with the offering, and afterward approach her spouse with God's blessing. This was decreed for women.

3   Nu wæs ðeah hwæðere þæt halige mæden Maria, Cristes
moder, Godes beboda gemyndig, and eode on ðysum dæge
to Godes huse mid lace, and gebrohte þæt cild þe heo
acende, hælend Crist, gelacod to þam Godes temple swa
swa hit on Godes æ geset wæs. Ða wæs þær binnan þære
byrig Hierusalem sum Godes mann, and his nama wæs
Symeon; he wæs swyðe rihtwis, and hæfde micelne Godes
ege, and he geandbidode ðone frofer ðe behaten wæs þam
folce Israhel, þæt is, Cristes tocyme. Se Halga Gast wæs wunigende on ðæm Symeone, and he wiste genoh georne þæt
se ælmihtiga Godes Sunu wolde to mannum cuman and
menniscnysse underfon. Þa wæs ðes man swiðe oflyst ðæs
hælendes tocymes, and bæd æt Gode dæighwamlice on his
gebedum þæt he moste Crist geseon ær he deaðes onbyrigde. Þa, forðy þe he swa micele gewilnunge hæfde Cristes
tocymes, ða com him andswaru fram þam Halgan Gaste,
þæt he ne sceolde deaðes onbyrigan ær þam ðe he Crist gesawe. And he wæs þa bliðe þæs behates, and com to Godes
temple þurh myngunge ðæs Halgan Gastes. And seo halige
Maria com ða to ðam temple mid þam cilde, and se ealda
man Symeon eode togeanes þam cilde, and geseah þone
hælend, and hine georne gecneow þæt he wæs Godes Sunu,
alysend ealles middaneardes. He hine genam ða on his
earmas mid micelre onbryrdnesse and hine gebær into þam
temple, and þancode georne Gode þæt he hine geseon
moste. He cwæð þa, "Min Drihten, ðu forlætst me nu mid
sibbe of þisum life, after þinum worde; forðon þe mine eagan gesawon þinne halwendan, ðone ðu gearcodest ætforan
ansyne ealles folces; leoht to onwrigennysse þeoda, and wuldor þinum folce Israhele."

Now the holy virgin Mary, Christ's mother, was neverthe- 3
less mindful of God's commandments, and went on this day
to God's house with an offering, and brought the child that
she had given birth to, the savior Christ, to be presented to
God's temple just as it was established in God's law. In the
city of Jerusalem there was a certain man of God whose
name was Simeon; he was very righteous and had great fear
of God, and he awaited the consolation that was promised
to the people of Israel, that is, Christ's coming. The Holy
Spirit was dwelling in Simeon, and he knew very well that
the almighty Son of God would come to humanity and assume human form. This man was very eager for the savior's
coming, and daily asked God in his prayers that he might see
Christ before he tasted death. And then, because he had
such great desire for Christ's coming, an answer came to
him from the Holy Spirit, that he should not taste death before he had seen Christ. He was glad for that promise, and
came to God's temple through the urging of the Holy Spirit.
And the holy Mary came to the temple with the child, and
the old man Simeon went toward that child, and saw the
savior, and knew well that he was God's Son, redeemer of all
the earth. He took him in his arms with great zeal and carried him into the temple, and eagerly thanked God that he
was allowed to see him. He said then, "My Lord, you let me
now leave this life in peace, according to your word; for my
eyes have seen your salvation, which you have prepared in
the sight of all people; a light for the revelation of the nations, and the glory of your people Israel."

4   Hit is awriten on Cristes bec, and gehwær on oþrum
bocum, þæt fela witegan and rihtwise men woldan geseon
Cristes tocyme, ac hit næs na him getiðod; ac wæs getiðod
þisum ealdan men, forðam þe hit is be him awriten þæt he
cwæde dæghwamlice on his gebedum, "Ela, hwænne cymð
se hælend? Hwænne við he acenned? Hwænne mot ic hine
geseon? Hwæðer ic mote lybban oð þæt ic hine geseo?" And
þa for ðysre gewilnunge him com andswaru, þæt he ne gesawe deað ær ðam ðe he Crist gesawe.

5   Maria, Cristes moder, bær þæt cild, and se ealda Symeon
eode hire togeanes, and gecneow þæt cild ðurh Godes onwrigenysse, and hit beclypte and bær into ðam temple. He
bær þæt cild, and þæt cild bær hine. Hu bær þæt cild hine?
Þone bær se ealda Symeon on his earmum þe ealle ðing hylt
and gewylt. Lytel he wæs ðær gesewen, ac ðeah hwæðere he
wæs swiðe micel and ormæte. Lytel he wæs gesewen, forðan
ðe he wolde gefeccan þa lytlan and gebringan up to his rice.
Hwæt synd ða lytlan ðe he wolde habban up to his rice? Þæt
synd ða eaðmodan. Ne sohte Crist na ða modigan, þa þa
micele beoð on hyra geþance; ac ða ðe beoð lytle and eað-
mode on heora heortan, þa cumað to Godes rice, ac ðider ne
mæg astigan nan modignys. Þær wæs se deofol ðe modegode, ac his modignes hine awearp into helle grunde; forðy
ne mæg ure tyddernes ðyder astigan gif heo modig bið, þa þa
se engel ðær beon ne mihte þa þa he modegode.

6   God bebead, on þære ealdan æ, his folce þæt hi sceoldon
him offrian ælc frumcenned hysecild, oþþe alysan hit ut mid
fif scyllingum. Eac on heora orfe, swa hwæt swa frumcenned
wære bringan þæt to Godes huse, and hit ðær Gode offrian.
Gif hit þonne unclæne nyten wære, þonne sceolde se hlaford hit acwellan, oþþe syllan Gode oþer clæne nyten. We ne

It is written in Christ's book, and elsewhere in other 4
books, that many prophets and righteous people wanted to
see Christ's coming, but it was not granted to them; it was
granted to this old man, because it is written of him that he
said daily in his prayers, "Alas! When will the savior come?
When will he be born? When can I see him? Shall I be allowed to live until I see him?" And because of this desire an
answer came to him, that he would not see death before he
had seen Christ.

Mary, Christ's mother, carried that child, and the old 5
Simeon went toward her, recognized that child by God's
revelation, embraced it, and carried it into the temple. He
carried that child, and the child carried him. How did the
child carry him? The old Simeon carried in his arms the one
who holds and controls all things. He appeared little there,
but yet he was very great and immense. He appeared little,
because he would gather the little ones and bring them up to
his kingdom. Who are the little ones he would raise up to
his kingdom? They are the humble. Christ did not seek the
proud, those who are great in their thoughts; those who are
little and humble in their hearts will come to God's kingdom, but no pride may ascend there. The devil who became
proud was there, but his pride cast him into the depths of
hell; therefore our weakness, if it is proud, cannot ascend
there to where the angel could not be when he grew proud.

In the old law, God commanded his people to offer every 6
firstborn male child to him, or redeem it with five shillings.
They should also bring whatever was firstborn of their cattle
to God's house, and there offer it to God. If it was an unclean
beast, then the lord should kill it, or give God another clean

167

þurfon þas bebodu healdan nu lichamlice, ac gastlice. Þonne on urum mode bið acenned sum ðing godes and we þæt to weorce awendað, þonne sceole we þæt tellan to Godes gyfe and þæt Gode betæcan. Ure yfelan geðohtas oððe weorc we sceolan alysan mid fif scyllingum; þæt is, we sceolon ure yfelnysse behreowsian mid urum fif andgitum, þæt synd gesihþ, and hlyst, and swæc, and stenc, and hrepung. Eac swa þa un-clænan nytenu getacniað ure unclænan geðohtas and weorc, ða we sceolon symle acwellan oððe behwyrfan mid clænum; þæt is, þæt we sceolon ure unclænnysse and ure yfelnesse symle adwæscan, and forlætan yfel and don god.

7   Seo eadige Maria ða geoffrode hire lac Gode mid þam cilde, swa hit on Godes æ geset wæs. Hit wæs swa geset on þære ealdan æ þurh Godes hæse þæt ða þe mihton ðurhteon sceoldon bringan anes geares lamb mid heora cylde Gode to lace, and ane culfran oþþe ane turtlan. Gif þonne hwylc wif to ðam unspedig wære þæt heo ðas ðing begytan ne mihte, þonne sceolde heo bringan twegen culfran briddas, oððe twa turtlan. Þas læssan lac, þæt sind þa fugelas, þe wæron wannspedigra manna lac, wæron for Criste geoffrode. Se æl-mihtiga Godes Sunu wæs swiðe gemyndig ure neoda on eal-lum ðingum; na þæt an þæt he wolde mann beon for us ða ða he God wæs, ac eac swylce he wolde beon þearfa for us ða ða he rice wæs, to ðy þæt he us forgeafe dæl on his rice and mænsumunge on his godcundnysse. Lamb getacnað un-scæððinysse and þa maran godnysse; gif we þonne swa earme beoð þæt we ne magon þa maran godnysse Gode offrian, þonne sceole we him bringan twa turtlan oþþe twegen cul-fran briddas, þæt is twyfealdlic onbryrdnes eges and lufe. On twa wisan bið se man onbryrd: ærest he him ondræt helle wite and bewepð his synna; syððan he nimð eft lufe to

beast. We do not need to keep these commands physically, but spiritually. When some good thing is brought forth in our mind and we turn it to action, then we should account that to God's grace and offer it to God. We should redeem our evil thoughts or actions with five shillings; that is, we should repent of our wickedness with our five senses, which are sight, and hearing, and taste, and smell, and touch. Likewise, the unclean beasts signify our unclean thoughts and actions, which we should always kill or exchange for pure ones; that is, we should always destroy our impurity and our wickedness, and forsake evil and do good.

The blessed Mary offered her gift to God with the child, as it was established in God's law. It was established in the old law by God's command that those who could manage it should bring a yearling lamb with their child as an offering to God, and a pigeon or a turtledove. If any woman were so poor that she could not obtain those things, then she should bring two young pigeons, or two turtledoves. These lesser gifts, that is, the birds, which were the gifts of poor persons, were offered for Christ. The almighty Son of God was very mindful of our needs in all things; not only would he become human for us when he was God, but he would also be poor for us when he was rich, so that he might give us a share in his kingdom and participation in his divinity. A lamb signifies innocence and greater goodness; if we are so poor that we cannot offer the greater goodness to God, then we should bring him two turtledoves or two pigeons, that is a twofold affection of fear and love. In two ways a person is brought to compunction: first, he dreads the torment of hell and weeps for his sins; later he feels love for God, then he

7

Gode, þonne onginð he to murcnienne, and ðincð him to lang hwænne he beo genumen of ðyses lifes earfoðnyssum and gebroht to ecere reste.

8   Lytel wæs an lamb, oððe twa turtlan, Gode to bringenne; ac he ne sceawað na þæs mannes lac swa swiðe swa he sceawað his heortan. Nis Gode nan neod ure æhta; ealle ðing sindon his: ægðer ge heofen, ge eorðe, and sæ, and ealle ða ðing ðe on him wuniað. Ac he forgeaf eorðlice ðing mannum to brice, and bebead him þæt hi sceoldon mid þam eorðlicum ðingum hine oncnawan þe hi ær forgeaf, na for his neode, ac for mancynnes neode. Gif ðu oncnæwst ðinne Drihten mid ðinum æhtum, be ðinre mæðe, hit fremeð þe sylfum to ðam ecan life; gif ðu hine forgitst hit hearmað þe sylfum and na Gode, and þu ðolast ðære ecan mede. God gyrnð þa godnysse ðines modes, and na ðinra æhta. Gif ðu hwæt dest Gode to lofe mid cystigum mode, þonne geswutelast ðu þa godnysse þines modes mid þære dæde; gif þu ðonne nan god don nelt Gode to wurðmynte, ðonne geswutelast ðu mid þære uncyste ðine yfelnysse, and seo yfelnys þe fordeð wið God.

9   On ðære ealdan æ is gehwær gesett þæt God het gelomlice þas fugelas offrian on his lace, for ðære getacnunge þe hi getacniað. Nis nu nanum men alyfed þæt he healde þa ealdan æ lichomlice, ac healde gehwa hi gastlice. Culfran sind swiðe unscæððige fugelas and bilewite, and hi lufiað annysse and fleoð him floccmælum. Do eac swa se Cristena man: beo him unsceaðþig and bilewite, and lufige annysse and broðorrædene betwux Cristenum mannum; þonne geoffrað he gastlice Gode þa culfran briddas. Þa turtlan getacniað clænnysse: hi sind swa geworhte gif hyra oðer oþerne forlyst, þonne ne secð seo cucu næfre hire oðerne gemacan. Gif

begins to murmur, and it seems to him too long until he is taken from the troubles of this life and brought to eternal rest.

Little was a lamb, or two turtledoves, to bring to God; 8 but he does not look on a person's offering so much as he looks into his heart. God does not need our possessions; all things are his: heaven, earth, sea, and all the things which dwell in them. But he gave earthly things to human beings for their use, and commanded them that with those earthly things they should acknowledge him who first gave them, not for his need, but for humanity's need. If you acknowledge your Lord with your possessions, according to your ability, it prepares you for eternal life; if you forget him, you harm yourself and not God, and you lose the eternal reward. God desires the goodness of your mind, not of your possessions. If you do anything for the praise of God with a devout mind, then you show the goodness of your mind by that deed; if you do not want to do any good for the honor of God, then you show your wickedness by that offense, and that wickedness will condemn you with God.

It is recorded in several places in the old law that God 9 frequently commanded birds to be offered as a gift to him, for the meaning which they signify. It is not now allowed for anyone to hold the old law physically, but everyone should hold it spiritually. Pigeons are very innocent and gentle birds, and they love unity and fly in flocks. Let the Christian do likewise: let him be innocent and gentle, and love unity and fellowship among Christians; then he offers pigeons to God spiritually. Turtledoves signifies purity: they are so created that if one of them loses the other, the living one never

ðonne se Cristena man swa deð for Godes lufon, þonne geoffrað he ða turtlan on þa betstan wisan. Ðas twa fugelcyn ne singað na swa swa oðre fugelas, ac hi geomeriað, forðan ðe hi getacniað haligra manna geomerunge on ðisum life, swa swa Crist cwæð to his apostolum, "Ge beoð geunrot-sode on þisum life, ac eower unrotnys bið awend to ecere blisse." And eft he cwæð, "Eadige beoð þa þe heora synna bewepað, forðan ðe hi beoð gefrefrode."

10   Se ealda man Symeon, þe we ær embe spræcon, ne gyrnde na þæt he moste Crist gehyran sprecan, forðan ðe he hine gecneow þæt he God wæs, ðeah ðe he ða gyt on þære men-niscnysse unsprecende wære. Sprecan he mihte gif he wolde, and ealswa wis he wæs ða, þa þa he wæs anre nihte, swa swa he wæs þa þa he wæs ðrittig geara; ac he wolde abidan his wæstma timan on ðære menniscnysse, swa swa hit gecyn-delic is on mancynne. Symeon cwæð þa, "Drihten, þu for-lætst me nu on sibbe of ðysum life, forðon þe mine eagan habbað gesewen ðinne halwendan." Se halwenda þe he embe spræc is ure hælend Crist, se ðe com to gehælenne ure wunda, þæt sindon ure synna. He cwæð þa Symeon, "ðone þu gearcodest ætforan gesihðe ealles folces." Hine ne ge-sawon na ealle men lichomlice, ac he is gebodod eallum mannum: gelyfe se ðe wylle. Se þe on hine gelyfð he gesihð hine nu mid his geleafan, and on þan ecan life mid his eagum. Symeon cwæð þa gyt, "He is leoht to onwrigennysse ðeoda, and wuldor þinum folce Israhel." Ealle ðas word spræc se Symeon be ðam cilde to þam heofenlican Fæder, þe hine to mannum sende. He is soð leoht þe todræfde þa þeostra ðises lifes, swa swa he sylf cwæð on his godspelle, "Ic eom leoht ealles middangeardes; se ðe me fyligð ne cymð he na on þystrum, ac he hæfð lifes leoht." Swa swa leoht todræfð

seeks another mate for itself. If a Christian does this for God's love, then he offers the turtledoves in the best way. These two types of birds do not sing like other birds, but they murmur, because they signify the groaning of holy people in this life, as Christ said to his apostles, "You will be sad in this life, but your sadness will be turned to eternal joy." Again he said, "Blessed are those who weep for their sins, for they will be comforted."

The old man Simeon, whom we spoke of earlier, did not 10 yearn to hear Christ speak, because he knew that he was God, though in his humanity he was yet without speech. He could have spoken if he had wanted to, and he was as wise then at one day old as he was when he was thirty years old; but he would await the time of his growth in human nature, as is natural in human beings. Simeon said, "Lord, now you let me go in peace from this life, because my eyes have seen your salvation." The salvation he spoke of is our savior Christ, who came to heal our wounds, that is, our sins. Simeon then said, "which you have prepared in the sight of all peoples." All people did not see him physically, but he is preached to all people: let those who will, believe. He who believes in God sees him now with his faith, and in the eternal life with his eyes. Simeon then said, "He is a light for the revelation of the nations, and the glory of your people Israel." Simeon spoke all these words concerning the child to the heavenly Father, who sent him to humanity. He is the true light that drove out the darkness of this life, as he himself said in his gospel, "I am the light of all the world; he who follows me will not come into darkness, but he will have the light of life." As light drives away darkness, so too the love

þeostra, swa eac todræfð Cristes lufu and his geleafa ealle leahtras and synna fram ure heortan; and he is wuldor and bliss ealles gelyfedes folces.

11 Þa Maria þæt halige mæden, and þæs cildes fostorfæder Ioseph, wæron ofwundrode þæra worda þe se ealda Symeon clypode be ðam cilde. And se Symeon him ða sealde bletsunge, and witegode gyt mare be þam cilde, and cwæð, "Þis cild is gesett manegum mannum to hryre, and manegum to æriste, and to tacne, and þam bið wiðcweden." Swa swa ða men þe on Crist gelyfað beoð gehealdene þurh his tocyme, swa eac þa þe nellað gelyfan on Crist beoð twyfealdlice fordemde. Anfealdlice hi sind scyldige ðurh Adames synne, and twyfealdlice hi beoð fordemde þonne hi wiðsacað Cristes tocymes, and nellað gelyfan on ðone soðan hælend. Ðam ungeleaffullum mannum com Crist to hryre and þam geleaffullum to æriste; and eac anum gehwilcum gelyfedum men wæs Cristes tocyme ægðer ge hryre ge ærist. Hu ðonne? He com to ðy þæt he wolde ælc yfel towurpan, and ælc good aræran. Nu towyrpð he on us leahtras, and arærð mihta. He towyrpð modignysse, and arærð eadmodnysse. He towyrpð galnysse, and arærð clænnysse. And ealle unðeawas he towyrpð on his gecorenum mannum, and arærð on him ealle godnysse. Ne mæg þæt god beon getymbrod buton þæt yfel beo ær toworpen. "To tacne com Crist, and þam is wiðcweden." His acennednys is wundorlic tacn, forðan ðe he wæs of mædene acenned, swa swa nan oðer nis; and þæt wiðcwædon þa ungeleaffullan men, and noldon gelyfan. And eac his æriste of deaðe, and his upstige to heofenum, and ealle ða wundra þe he worhte—ealle hit wæron tacna, and ðam wiðcwædon þa ungeleaffullan, and þa geleaffullan gelyfdon.

12 Þa cwæð se ealda Symeon to ðære eadigan Marian, "His

and faith of Christ drives out all vices and sins from our hearts; he is the glory and joy of all believing people.

Then the holy virgin Mary and Joseph, the child's foster 11 father, were filled with wonder at the words which the old Simeon spoke concerning the child. Simeon gave him his blessing, and prophesied further about the child, and said, "This child is set for the fall of many, and the rise of many, and for a sign, and it will be contradicted." Just as those who believe in Christ are saved by his coming, so also those who will not believe in Christ are doubly condemned. They are guilty once through the Adam's sin, and they will be doubly condemned when they deny Christ's coming, and will not believe in the true savior. Christ came for the fall of unbelievers and the rise of the faithful; likewise, to every believer Christ's coming was both a fall and a rising. How so? He came so that he would cast down all evil, and raise up all good. Now he casts down our vices, and raises up virtues. He casts down pride, and raises up humility. He casts down lust, and raises up chastity. And he casts down all wickedness in his chosen ones, and raises up in them all goodness. Good cannot be built unless evil is first cast down. "Christ came as a sign, and it will be contradicted." His birth is a wonderful sign, because he was born of a virgin, as none other is; and unbelievers contradicted that, and would not believe. Likewise his resurrection from death, and his ascension into heaven, and all the wonders which he performed—they were all signs, and unbelievers contradicted them, and the faithful believed.

Then the old Simeon said to the blessed Mary, "His sword 12

swurd sceal ðurhgan ðine sawle." Þæt swurd getacnode
Cristes ðrowunge. Næs seo eadige Maria na ofslegen ne
gemartyrod lichomlice, ac gastlice. Ða ða heo geseh niman
hyre cild, and adrifan isene næglas þurh þa handa and þurh
ða fet, and syððan mid spere gewundigan on ða siðan, þa
wæs Cristes ðrowung hire ðrowung; and heo wæs mare
ðonne martyr, forðon þe mare wæs hyre modes þrowung
þonne wære hire lichaman, gif heo gemartyrod wære. Ne
cwæð na se Symeon þæt Cristes swurd sceolde þurhgan
Marian lichaman, ac hyre sawle. Cristes swurd is her gesett,
swa swa we cwædon, for his ðrowunge. Þeah ðe Maria gelyfde þæt Crist arisan wolde of deaðe, þeah hwæðere eode
hyre cildes þrowung swiðe þearle into hire heortan.

13   Þa ða se Symeon hæfde gewitegod þas witegunge be
Criste, þa com þær sum wuduwe, seo wæs Anna gehaten.
"Seo leofode mid hire were seofon gear, and syððan heo wæs
wuduwe feower and hundeahtatig geara, and þeowode Gode
on fæstenum, and on gebedum, and on clænnysse, and wæs
on eallum þam fyrste wunigende binnan þam Godes temple.
And com ða to þam cilde and witegode be him, and andette
Gode." Rihtlice swa halig wif wæs þæs wyrðe þæt heo moste
witigian embe Crist, ða ða heo swa lange on clænnesse Gode
þeowode. Behealde, ge wif, and understandað hu be hire
awriten is. Seofon gear heo leofode mid hire were, and
siððan heo wæs wunigende on wudewan hade oð feower and
hundeahtatig geara, swa lybbende swa se apostol tæhte. He
cwæð, se apostol Paulus, "Seo wuduwe þe lyfað on estmet-
tum, heo ne lyfað na, ac heo is dead." Þeos Anna ðe we embe
sprecað ne lufude heo na estmettas, ac lufude fæstenu. Ne
lufude heo ydele spellunge, ac beeode hire gebedu. Ne ferde
heo worigende geond land, ac wæs wunigende geþyldelice

will pierce your soul." The sword signified Christ's passion. The blessed Mary was not slain or martyred physically, but spiritually. When she saw her child taken, and iron nails driven through his hands and his feet, and then wounded in the side with a spear, then Christ's suffering was her suffering; and she was more than a martyr, for her mind's suffering was greater than her body's would have been if she had been martyred. Simeon did not say that Christ's sword should pierce Mary's body, but her soul. Christ's sword is here intended, as we said, for his suffering. Though Mary believed that Christ would rise from death, nevertheless her child's suffering went very deeply into her heart.

When Simeon had prophesied this prophecy concerning 13 Christ, there came a certain widow named Anna. "She had lived with her husband seven years, and afterward was a widow eighty-four years, and served God with fasting, and prayers, and chastity, and in all that time was dwelling within God's temple. And she came to the child and prophesied about him, and confessed to God." Rightly was so holy a woman worthy to prophesy about Christ, since she had served God so long in chastity. Pay heed to this, you women, and understand what is written about her. Seven years she lived with her husband, and was afterward remaining in widowhood eighty-four years, living as the apostle taught. The apostle Paul said, "The widow who lives in luxuries does not live, but is dead." This Anna we are speaking of did not love luxuries, but loved fasts. She did not love idle talk, but busied herself in prayer. She did not go wandering through the land, but dwelled patiently within God's

binnan Godes temple. Gif wife getimige þæt heo hire wer forleose, ðonne nime heo bysne be ðisre wudewan.

14 Ðry hadas sindon þe cyðdon gecyðnysse be Criste: þæt is mæigðhad, and wudewanhad, and riht sinscype. Mæden is Cristes modor, and on mægðhade wunude Iohannes se Fulluhtere, þe embe Crist cydde, and manega oðre toeacan him. Widewe wæs ðeos Anna, þe we gefyrn ær embe spræcon. Zacharias, Iohannes fæder, wæs wer; ægðer ge he ge his wif witegodon embe Crist. Þas ðry hadas syndon Gode gecweme, gif hi rihtlice lybbað. Mægðhad is ægþer ge on wæpmannum ge on wifmannum; þa habbað rihtne mægðhad þa þe fram cildhade wuniað on clænnysse, and ealle galnysse on him sylfum forseoð, ægðer ge modes ge lichoman, ðurh Godes fultum. Þonne habbað hi æt Gode hundfealde mede on ðam ecan life. Widewan beoð þa þe, æfter heora gemacan, on clænnysse wuniað for Godes lufon; hi habbað þonne syxtigfealde mede æt Gode hyra geswinces. Þa ðe rihtlice healdað hyra æwe, and on alyfedum timan, for bearnes gestreone, hæmed begað, hi habbað þrittigfealde mede for hyra gesceadwisnysse. Se ðe wile his galnysse gefyllan swa oft swa hine lyst, þonne bið he wiðmeten nytenum and na mannum. Be þysum tæhte se apostol Paulus, "Þa ðe wif habbað beon hi swilce hi nan nabbon." Forðan ealle hyra unlustas hi sceolon gebetan sylfwylles on þyssum life, oððe unþances æfter ðyssum life; and hi cumað siððan to ðam ecan life mid maran earfoðnysse. Þa men þe beoð butan rihtre æwe, and yrnað fram anum to oðrum, nabbað hi nænne dæl ne nane bletsunge mid Criste buton hi ðæs geswicon and hit gebeton.

15 Uton fon nu on þæt godspel ðær we hit ær forleton. Seo eadige Maria, and Ioseph, ðæs cildes fostorfæder, gecyrdon

temple. If it should happen that a woman should lose her husband, let her take example by this widow.

There are three states which bore witness to Christ: that is, virginity, widowhood, and lawful matrimony. Christ's mother is a virgin, and John the Baptist, who testified about Christ, remained in virginity, and many others besides them. This Anna, of whom we spoke before, was a widow. Zechariah, the father of John, was a married man; both he and his wife prophesied concerning Christ. These three states are pleasing to God, if people live in them rightly. There is virginity both among men and women; they have true virginity who dwell in chastity from childhood, and despise all lust of mind and body in themselves, through God's help. They will have a hundredfold reward from God in eternal life. Widows are those who, after the death of their spouse, live in chastity for love of God; they will have a sixtyfold reward from God for their labor. Those who rightly hold their marriage vow, and undertake sexual intercourse at permitted times for the procreation of children, will have a thirtyfold reward for their discretion. He who will satisfy his lust as often as he likes will be compared to the beasts and not to humans. Concerning this the apostle Paul taught, "Let those who have wives be as though they had none." For they should atone for all their evil lusts, either voluntarily in this life or involuntarily after this life; and they will come afterward to the eternal life with greater difficulty. Those who are without a lawful spouse, and run from one to another, have no part and no blessing with Christ unless they cease and make atonement.

Let us now pick up the gospel where we previously left it. The blessed Mary, and Joseph, the child's foster father,

to þære byrig Nazareth mid þam cilde; "and þæt cild weox, and wæs gestrangod, and mid wisdome afylled, and Godes gifu wæs on him wunigende." He weox and wæs gestrangod on þære menniscnysse, and he ne behofode nanes wæstmes ne nanre strangunge on þære godcundnysse. He æt, and dranc, and slep, and weox on gearum, and wæs þeah hwæðere eal his lif butan synnum. He nære na man geðuht gif he mannes life ne lyfode. He wæs mid wisdome afylled forþan ðe he is himsylf wisdom, and on him wunað eal gefyllednys þære godcundnysse; lichomlice Godes gifu wunude on him. Micel gifu wæs þæt ðære menniscnysse, þæt he wæs Godes Sunu and God sylf swa hraðe swa he ongann man to beonne. He wæs æfre God of þam Fæder acenned, and wunigende mid þam Fæder and mid þam Halgan Gaste: hi ðry, an God untodæledlic—þry on hadum, and an God on anre godcundnysse, and on anum gecynde æfre wunigende. Se Sunu ana underfeng þa menniscnysse, and hæfde anginn, se ðe æfre wæs. He wæs cild, and weox on þære menniscnysse, and þrowode deað sylfwilles, and aras of deaðe mid þam lichaman þe he ær on þrowode, and astah to heofenum, and wunað nu æfre on godcundnysse and on menniscnysse, an Crist, ægðer ge God ge mann, undeadlic, se ðe ær his ðrowunge wæs deadlic. He þrowade, ac he ne ðrowað heononforð næfre eft, ac bið æfre butan ende, eallswa ece on þære menniscnysse swa he is on þære god-cundnysse.

16   Wite gehwa eac þæt geset is on cyrclicum þeawum þæt we sceolon on ðisum dæge beran ure leoht to cyrcan and lætan hi ðær bletsian, and we sceolon gan siððan mid þam leohte betwux Godes husum, and singan ðone lofsang ðe þærto geset is. Þeah ðe sume men singan ne cunnon, hi

returned to the city of Nazareth with the child; "and the child grew, and was strengthened, and filled with wisdom, and God's grace was dwelling in him." He grew and was strengthened in human nature, and he needed no growth and no strengthening in his divine nature. He ate, and drank, and slept, and grew in years, and was nevertheless without sin all his life. He would not have seemed human if he had not lived a human life. He was filled with wisdom because he himself is wisdom, and in him dwells all fullness of divinity; God's grace dwelt bodily within him. Great grace was in his human nature, that he was the Son of God and God himself as soon as he began to be human. He was always God begotten of the Father, and dwelling with the Father and with the Holy Spirit: these three, one God indivisible—three in persons, and one God in one divinity, and continuing eternally in one nature. The Son alone assumed human nature, and had a beginning, he who always was. He was a child, and grew in human nature, and voluntarily suffered death, and arose from death with the body in which he had suffered, and ascended to heaven, and he dwells now forever in divine nature and in human nature, one Christ, both God and human, immortal, who before his passion was mortal. He suffered, but henceforth he will never suffer again, but will be forever without end, as eternal in his human nature as he is in his divine nature.

Everyone should also know that it is decreed in the ecclesiastical customs that on this day we should bear our lights to church and let them be blessed there, and then we should go with the light among God's houses, and sing the hymn that is set for that. Though some people do not know how

16

beron þeah hwæðere þæt leoht on heora handum; forðy on
ðissum dæge wæs þæt soðe leoht Crist geboren to þam temple, se ðe us alysde fram þystrum and us gebrincð to þam
ecan leohte, se ðe leofað and rixað a butan ende. Amen.

10

Dominica in Quinquagesima

*A*dsumpsit Iesus XII *discipulos suos, et reliqua.*

2   Her is geræd on þissum godspelle, þe we nu gehyrdon of
ðæs diacones muðe, þæt "Se hælend gename onsundron his
twelf leorningcnihtas and cwæð to him, 'Efne, we sceolon
faran to ðære byrig Hierusalem, and þonne beoð gefyllede
ealle ða ðing þe wæron be me awritene þurh witegan. Ic sceal
beon belæwed ðeodum, and hi doð me to bysmore and
beswingað, and syððan ofsleað, and ic arise of deaðe on þam
ðriddan dæge.' Þa nyston his leorningcnihtas nan andgit
þyssera worda. Ða gelamp hit þæt hi genealæhton anre byrig
þe is gehaten Hiericho, and ða sæt þær sum blind man be
ðam wege; and þa þa he gehyrde þæs folces fær mid þam
hælende, ða acsode he hwa þær ferde. Hi cwædon him to
þæt þæt wære ðæs hælendes fær. Þa begann he to hrymenne,

to sing, they should nevertheless bear the light in their hands; for on this day Christ the true light was borne to the temple, who released us from darkness and brings us to the eternal light, who lives and reigns forever without end. Amen.

10

Quinquagesima (Sunday before Ash Wednesday)

Quinquagesima Sunday

Jesus took his twelve disciples, etc.

It is here read in this gospel, which we have just heard from the deacon's mouth, that "The savior took his twelve disciples aside and said to them, 'Behold, we will travel to the city of Jerusalem, and then all the things that were written about me in the prophets will be fulfilled. I will be betrayed to the nations, and they will mock me and scourge me, and then kill me, and I will arise from death on the third day.' His disciples did not know the meaning of these words at all. Then it happened that they approached a city called Jericho, and there sat a blind person along the way; when he heard the people passing with the savior, he asked who was passing there. They said to him that the savior was passing. 2

and cwæð, 'Hælend, Dauides bearn, gemiltsa min.' Ða men
þe beforan þam hælende ferdon ciddon ongean ðone blindan þæt he suwian sceolde. He clypode þa miccle swiðor,
'Hælend, Dauides bearn, gemiltsa min.' Þa stod se hælend,
and het lædan þone blindan to him. Þa ða he genealæhte, þa
acsode se hælend hine, 'Hwæt wylt ðu þæt ic þe do?' He
cwæð, 'Drihten, þæt ic mage geseon.' And se hælend him
cwæð to, 'Loca nu: þin geleafa hæfð ðe gehæled.' And he
ðærrihte geseah, and fyligde þam hælende and hine mær-
sode. Þa eal þæt folc þe þæt wundor geseh herede God mid
micelre onbryrdnysse."

3   Ðyses godspelles anginn hrepode ures hælendes þrowunge, þeah hwæðere ne ðrowade he na on ðysne timan; ac
he wolde feorran and lange ær cyðan his ðrowunge his leorningcnihtum, þæt hi ne sceoldon beon to swiðe afyrhte þurh
ða þrowunge þonne se tima come þæt he ðrowian wolde.
Heora mod wearð afyrht þurh Cristes segene, ac he hi eft
gehyrte mid þam worde þe he cwæð, "Ic arise of deaðe on
þam ðriddan dæge." Þa wolde he heora geleafan gestrangian
and getrymman mid wundrum. And hi ða comon to ðære
stowe þær se blinda man sæt be ðam wege, and Crist hine
gehælde ætforan gesihðe ealles þæs werodes, to ði þæt he
wolde mid þam wundre hi to geleafan gebringan. Þeah
hwæðere þa wundra þe Crist worhte oðer ðing hi æteowdon
þurh mihte, and oðre ðing hi getacnodon þurh geryno. He
worhte þa wundra soðlice þurh godcunde mihte, and mid
þam wundrum þæs folces geleafan getrymde; ac hwæðre
þær wæs oðer ðing digle on ðam wundrum, æfter gastlicum
andgite. Þes an blinda man getacnode eall mancynn, þe
wearð ablend þurh Adames gylt, and asceofen of myrhðe
Neoxenawanges and gebroht to ðisum life, þe is wiðmeten

He began to cry out, and said, 'Savior, son of David, have mercy on me.' The people who went before the savior scolded the blind man to be quiet. He then called out much louder, 'Savior, son of David, have mercy on me.' The savior stopped, and asked that the blind man be led to him. When he came near, the savior asked him, 'What do you want me to do for you?' He said, 'Lord, that I might see.' And the savior said to him, 'Look now: your faith has healed you.' And at once he saw, and followed the savior and glorified him. And all the people who saw that miracle praised God with great zeal."

The beginning of this gospel touched on our savior's pas- 3 sion, though he did not suffer at this time; but he wanted to make his passion known to his disciples from afar and long before, so they would not be too much afraid of that passion when the time came that he had to suffer. Their minds were frightened by Christ's speech, but he cheered them afterward with his words when he said, "I will arise from death on the third day." Then he wanted to strengthen and confirm their faith with miracles. So they came to the place where the blind person sat by the way, and Christ healed him in the sight of all the multitude, because he wanted to bring them to faith with that miracle. And yet the miracles that Christ performed revealed one thing by power, and signified another thing by mystery. He performed miracles truly through divine power, and with those miracles confirmed the people's faith; yet there was another hidden thing in those miracles, in a spiritual sense. This one blind person signified all humanity, who were blinded through Adam's sin, and driven from the joy of Paradise and brought to this life, which is compared to a prison. Now we are shut

cwearterne. Nu sind we ute belocene fram ðam heofenlican leohte, and we ne magon on ðissum life þæs ecan leohtes brucan; ne we his na mare ne cunnon buton swa micel swa we ðurh Cristes lare on bocum rædað. Þeos woruld, þeah ðe heo myrige hwiltidum geðuht sy, nis heo hwæðere ðe geliccre ðære ecan worulde þe is sum cweartern leohtum dæge. Eal mancyn wæs, swa we ær cwædon, ablend mid geleaflæste and gedwylde; ac þurh Cristes tocyme we wurdon abrodene of urum gedwyldum and onlihte þurh geleafan. Nu hæbbe we þæt leoht on urum mode, þæt is Cristes geleafa; and we habbað þone hiht þæs ecan lifes myrhðe, þeah ðe we gyt lichamlice on urum cwearterne wunian.

4   Se blinda man sæt æt þære byrig þe is gehaten Hiericho. *Hiericho* is gereht and gehaten "mona." Se mona deð ægðer ge wycxð ge wanað: healfum monðe he bið weaxende, healfum he bið wanigende. Nu getacnað se mona ure deadlice lif and ateorunge ure deadlicnysse. On oðerne ende men beoð acennede, on oþerne ende hi forðfarað. Þa ða Crist com to ðære byrig Hiericho, þe ðone monan getacnað, þa underfeng se blinda man gesihðe. Þæt is, ða ða Crist com to ure deadlicnysse and ure menniscnysse underfeng, þa wearð mancyn onliht and gesihðe underfeng. He sæt wið ðone weig; and Crist cwæð on his godspelle, "Ic eom weig, and soðfæstnys, and lif." Se man þe nan ðing ne cann ðæs ecan leohtes he is blind; ac gif he gelyfð on þone hælend, þonne sitt he wið þone weig. Gif he nele biddan þæs ecan leohtes, he sitt ðonne blind be ðam wege, unbiddende. Se ðe rihtlice gelyfð on Crist, and geornlice bitt his sawle onlihtinge, he sitt be ðam wege biddende. Swa hwa swa oncnæwð þa blindnyssæ his modes, clypige he mid inweardre heortan swa swa se blinda cleopode, "Hælend, Dauides bearn, gemiltsa min."

out from the heavenly light, and we cannot enjoy the eternal light in this life; nor can we know any more of it than as much as we read in books through Christ's teaching. This world, though it might sometimes seem pleasant, is no more like the eternal world than a prison is like the light of day. All humanity, as we have said, was blinded with lack of faith and error; but through Christ's coming we were led out of our errors and enlightened by faith. Now we have that light, that is faith in Christ, in our minds; and we have the hope of the joy of eternal life, though we still dwell physically in our prison.

The blind person sat near the city which is called Jericho. *Jericho* is interpreted and called "moon." The moon both waxes and wanes: for half a month it is waxing, for half it is waning. Now the moon signifies our mortal life and the decay of our mortality. At one end people are born, at the other they depart. When Christ came to the city of Jericho, which signifies the moon, the blind person received sight. That is, when Christ came to our mortality and assumed our human nature, humanity was enlightened and received sight. He sat by the way; and Christ said in his gospel, "I am the way, and truth, and life." The person who knows nothing of the eternal light is blind; but if he believes in the savior, then he sits by the way. If he will not pray for the eternal light, then he sits by the way blind, not praying. He who rightly believes in Christ, and fervently prays for the enlightenment of his soul, he sits by the way praying. Whoever recognizes the blindness of his mind, let him cry with inward heart as the blind person cried, "Savior, son of David, have mercy on me."

4

5   Seo menigu þe eode beforan ðam hælende ciddon ðam blindan and heton þæt he stille wære. Seo menigu getacnað ure unlustas and leahtras, þe us hremað and ure heortan ofsittað þæt we ne magon us swa geornlice gebiddan swa we behofedon. Hit gelimpð gelomlice, þonne se man wile yfeles geswican and his synna gebetan and mid eallum mode to Gode gecyrran, ðonne cumað þa ealdan leahtras þe he ær geworhte and hi gedrefað his mod, and willað gestillan his stemne þæt he to Gode ne clypige. Ac hwæt dyde se blinda þa þa þæt folc hine wolde gestyllan? He hrymde ðæs ðe swiðor, oð þæt se hælend his stemne gehyrde and hine ge-hælde. Swa we sceolon eac don, gif us deofol drecce mid me-nigfealdum geðohtum and costnungum: we sceolon hryman swiðor and swiðor to ðam hælende, þæt he todræfe ða yfelan costnunga fram ure heortan, and þæt he onlihte ure mod mid his gife. Gif we ðonne þurhwuniað on urum gebedum, þonne mage we gedon mid urum hreame þæt se hælend stent, se ðe ær eode, and wile gehyran ure clypunge, and ure heortan onlihtan mid godum and mid clænum geðohtum. Ne magon ða yfelan geðohtas us derian gif hi us ne liciað; ac swa us swiðor deofol bregð mid yfelum geðohtum, swa we beteran beoð, and Gode leofran, gif we ðone deofol forseoð and ealle his costnunga ðurh Godes fultum.

6   Hwæt is þæs hælendes stede, oððe hwæt is his fær? He ferde ðurh his menniscnysse, and he stod þurh þa godcund-nysse. He ferde ðurh ða menniscnysse, swa þæt he wæs acenned, and ferde fram stowe to stowe, and dead þrowade, and of deaðe aras, and astah to heofenum. Þis is his fær. He stent ðurh ða godcundnysse, forðon ðe he is ðurh his mihte æghwær andweard, and ne ðearf na faran fram stowe to

The multitude that went before the savior scolded the 5
blind person and ordered him to be still. The multitude signifies our evil desires and vices, which call to us and occupy
our hearts so that we cannot pray as fervently as we ought. It
happens frequently, when a person wants to cease doing evil
and atone for his sins and turn to God with his whole mind,
then the old vices which he had previously practiced will
come and afflict his mind, and will silence his voice so that
he might not call out to God. But what did the blind person
do when the people wanted to silence him? He called out
even louder, until the savior heard his voice and healed him.
So should we also do, if the devil troubles us with manifold
thoughts and temptations: we should call out louder and
louder to the savior, that he might drive the evil temptations
from our hearts, and that he might enlighten our mind with
his grace. If we persist in our prayers, then with our cries we
might make the savior, who was passing by, stop and want to
hear our calling, and enlighten our hearts with good and
pure thoughts. Evil thoughts cannot harm us if they are not
pleasing to us; but the more the devil terrifies us with evil
thoughts, so much the better will we be, and dearer to God,
if with God's help we despise the devil and all his temptations.

What is the savior's staying, or what is his passing? He 6
passed through his human nature, and he stayed through
the divine nature. He passed through human nature, so that
he was born, and went from place to place, and suffered
death, and arose from death, and ascended to heaven. This
is his passing. He stays through his divine nature, because by
his power he is everywhere present, and does not need to go

stowe, forðon ðe he is on ælcere stowe þurh his godcundnysse. Þa ða he ferde þa gehyrde he þæs blindan clypunge,
and þa þa he stod þa forgeaf he him gesihðe, forðan þurh ða
menniscnysse he besargað ures modes blindnysse, and ðurh
ða godcundnysse he forgifð us leoht and ure blindnysse onliht. He cwæð to ðam blindan men, "Hwæt wilt ðu þæt ic ðe
do?" Wenst ðu þæt he nyste hwæt se blinda wolde, se ðe hine
gehælan mihte? Ac he wolde þæt se blinda bæde, forðon þe
he tiht ælcne swiðe gemaglice to gebedum; ac hwæðere he
cwyð on oðre stowe, "Eower heofenlica Fæder wat hwæs ge
behofiað ær ðan ðe ge hine æniges ðinges biddan," þeah
hwæðere wile se goda God þæt we hine georne biddon,
forðan þurh ða gebedu bið ure heorte onbryrd and gewend
to Gode.

7   Ða cwæð se blinda, "La leof, do þæt ic mæge geseon." Ne
bæd se blinda naðor ne goldes ne seolfres, ne nane woruldlice ðing, ac bæd his gesihðe. For nahte he tealde ænig ðing
to biddenne buton gesihðe; forðan ðeah se blinda sum ðing
hæbbe, he ne mæg butan leohte geseon þæt he hæfð. Uton
forði geefenlæcan þisum men þe wæs gehæled fram Criste,
ægðer ge on lichaman ge on sawle: ne bidde we na lease
welan, ne gewitenlice wurðmyntas, ac uton biddan leoht æt
urum Drihtne—na þæt leoht ðe bið geendod, þe bið mid
þære nihte todræfed, þæt ðe is gemæne us and nytenum; ac
uton biddan þæs leohtes þe we magon mid englum anum
geseon, þæt ðe næfre ne bið geendod. To ðam leohte soðlice
ure geleafa us sceal gebringan, swa swa Crist cwæð to ðam
blindan menn, "Loca nu, þin geleafa ðe gehælde."

8   Nu smeað sum ungeleafful man, hu mæg ic gewilnian ðæs
gastlican leohtes þæt þæt ic geseon ne mæg? Nu cweðe ic to

from place to place, because he is in every place through his divine nature. When he was passing, he heard the blind person's cry, and when he stopped, he gave him sight, because through his human nature he laments the blindness of our minds, and through his divine nature he gives us light and enlightens our blindness. He said to the blind person, "What do you want me to do for you?" Do you think that he who could heal him did not know what the blind person wanted? But he wanted the blind person to ask, because he exhorts everyone very urgently to prayers; for though he says in another place, "Your heavenly Father knows what you need before you ask him for anything," yet the good God wants us to pray fervently to him, because by prayer our heart is stimulated and turned to God.

Then the blind person said, "Sir, make me see." The blind 7 person did not ask for gold or silver, or any worldly thing, but asked for his sight. He thought that praying for anything but sight was nothing; because though a blind person may have something, without light he cannot see what he has. And so let us imitate this person who was healed by Christ both in body and soul: let us not pray for false riches, nor fleeting honors, but let us pray to our Lord for light—not for that light which will be ended, which is driven away with the night, that which is common to us and to beasts; but let us pray for that light which will never be ended, which only we and the angels can see. Truly our faith will bring us to that light, as Christ said to the blind person, "Look now, your faith has healed you."

Now some unbelieving person will wonder, how can I de- 8 sire the spiritual light which I cannot see? Now I say to that

ðam menn þæt ða ðing þe he understynt and undergytan mæg, ne undergyt he na ða ðing þurh his lichaman ac þurh his sawle; þeah hwæðere ne gesihð nan man his sawle on ðisum life. Heo is ungesewenlic, ac ðeah hwæðere heo wissað þone gesewenlican lichaman. Se lichama, ðe is gesewenlic, hæfð lif of ðære sawle, þe is ungesewenlic. Gewite þæt ungesewenlice ut, þonne fylð adune þæt gesewenlice, þe hit ne stod na ær ðurh hit sylf. Þæs lichoman lif is seo sawul, and þære sawle lif is God. Gewite seo sawul ut, ne mæg se muð clypian, þeah ðe he gynige; ne eage geseon, þeah ðe hit open sy; ne nan limn ne deð nan ðing, gif se lichama bið sawulleas. Swa eac seo sawul, gif God hi forlæt for synnum, ne deð heo nan ðing to gode. Ne mæg nan man nan ðing to gode gedon butan Godes fultume. Ne bið seo synfulle sawul na mid ealle to nahte awend, ðeah ðe heo gode adeadod sy; ac heo bið dead ælcere duguðe and gesælðe and bið gehealden to ðam ecan deaðe, þær þær heo æfre bið on pinungum wunigende, and þeah hwæðere næfre ne ateorað.

9   Hu mæg þe nu twynian þæs ecan leohtes, ðeah hit ungesewenlic sy, þonne þu hæfst lif of ungesewenlicre sawle, and þe ne twynað nan ðing þæt þu sawle hæbbe, ðeah ðu hi geseon ne mage? Se blinda, ða ða he geseon mihte, þa fyligde he ðam hælende. Se man gesihð and fylið Gode se ðe cann understandan God and god weorc wyrcð. Se man gesihð and nele Gode fylian, se ðe understent God and nele god wyrcan. Ac uton understandan God and god weorc wyrcean: uton behealdan hwider Crist gange and him fylian; þæt is, þæt we sceolon smeagan hwæt he tæce and hwæt him licige, and þæt mid weorcum gefyllan, swa swa he sylf cwæð, "Se ðe me þenige, fylige he me"; þæt is, geefenlæce he me, and onscunige ælc yfel, and lufige ælc god, swa swa ic do. Ne

person that the things he understands and may comprehend, he understands not through his body but through his soul; yet no one in this life sees his soul. It is invisible, yet it guides the visible body. The body, which is visible, has life from the soul, which is invisible. Let the invisible depart, and the visible will fall down, because it did not stand by itself at all. The life of the body is the soul, and the life of the soul is God. If the soul departs, the mouth cannot call out, though it might gape; the eye cannot see, though it might be open; nor will any limb do anything, if the body is soulless. So also the soul, if God abandons it for sin, will do nothing good. No one can do anything good without God's support. The sinful soul will not be turned entirely to nothing, though it might be dead to good; it will be dead to every virtue and happiness and will be preserved for eternal death, where it will be forever dwelling in torments, and yet will never perish.

How can you now doubt the eternal light, though it is invisible, when you have life from an invisible soul, and you do not doubt at all that you have a soul, though you cannot see it? The blind person, when he could see, followed the savior. That person who can understand God sees and follows God and does good works. That person who understands God and will not do good works, sees and will not follow God. But let us understand God and do good works: let us watch where Christ goes and follow him; that is, we should meditate on what he teaches and what is pleasing to him, and fulfill that with works, as he himself said, "He who will serve me, let him follow me"; that is, let him imitate me, and shun every evil, and love every good, as I do. Christ did

9

teah Crist him na to on ðisum life land ne welan, swa swa he
be him sylfum cwæð, "Deor habbað hola, and fugelas habbað nest hwær hi restað, and ic næbbe hwider ic ahylde min
heafod." Swa micel he hæfde swa he rohte, and leofode be
oðra manna æhtum, se ðe ealle ðing ah.

10   We rædað on Cristes bec þæt þæt folc rædde be him þæt
hi woldon hine gelæccan and ahebban to cyninge, þæt he
wære heora heafod for worulde, swa swa he wæs godcundlice. Þa þa Crist ongeat ðæs folces willan ða fleah he
anstandende to anre dune, and his geferan gewendon to sæ,
and se hælend wæs up on lande. Ða on niht eode se hælend
up on ðam wætere mid drium fotum, oð þæt he com to his
leorningcnihtum, ðær ðær hi wæron on rewute. He forfleah
þone woruldlican wurðmynt þa þa he wæs to cyninge
gecoren; ac he ne forfleah na þæt edwit and ðone hosp þa þa
ða Iudeiscan hine woldon on rode ahon. He nolde his heafod befon mid gyldenum cynehelme, ac mid þyrnenum, swa
swa hit gedon wæs on his þrowunge. He nolde on ðissum life
rixian hwilwendlice, se ðe ecelice rixað on heofonum. Nis
ðeos woruld na ure eðel ac is ure wræcsið; forði ne sceole we
na besettan urne hiht on þissum swicelum life, ac sceolon
efstan mid godum geearnungum to urum eðele þær we to
gesceapene wæron, þæt is, to heofenan rice. Soðlice hit is
awriten, "Swa hwa swa wile beon freond þisre worulde, se
bið geteald Godes feond."

11   Crist cwæð on sumere stowe þæt "Se weig is swiðe nearu
and sticol se ðe læt to heofonan rice; and se is swiðe rum and
smeðe se ðe læt to hellewite." Se weig se ðe læt to heofenan
rice is forði nearu and sticol forði þæt we sceolon mid earfoðnysse geearnian urne eðel. Gif we hine habban willað, we
sceolon lufian mildheortnysse, and clænnysse, and soðfæstnysse, and rihtwisnysse, and eadmodnysse, and habban soðe

not gain land or riches for himself in this life, as he said of himself, "The beasts have holes, and the birds have nests where they rest, and I do not have anywhere I can lay down my head." He who owned all things had as much as he cared to have, and lived on the possessions of others.

We read in Christ's book that the people agreed that they 10 would seize him and raise him up as king, that he might be their worldly head, just as he was divinely. When Christ saw the people's will, he fled alone to a mountain, and his companions went to the sea, and the savior was up on land. Then in the night the savior went on the water with dry feet, until he came to his disciples, where they were in a ship. When he was chosen king, he fled from worldly honor; but he did not flee from reproach and scorn when the Jews wanted to hang him on a cross. He would not encircle his head with a golden crown, but with one of thorns, as was done at his passion. He would not reign temporarily in this life, he who reigns eternally in heaven. This world is not our home but our place of exile; therefore we should not set our hope in this deceitful life, but should hasten with good merits to our home for which we were created, that is, to the kingdom of heaven. Truly it is written, "Whoever will be a friend of this world will be considered an enemy of God."

Christ said in some place that "The way is very narrow 11 and steep which leads to the kingdom of heaven; and it is very wide and smooth which leads to the torment of hell." The way which leads to the kingdom of heaven is narrow and steep so that we should achieve our home with difficulty. If we want to have it, we should love mercy, and chastity, and truth, and righteousness, and humility, and have

lufe to Gode and to mannum, and don ælmessan be ure
mæðe, and habban gemet on urum bigleofan, and gehwilce
oðere halige ðing began. Þas ðing we ne magon don butan
earfoðnyssum, ac gif we hi doð, þonne mage we mid þam
geswincum, ðurh Godes fultum, astigan ðone sticolan weg
þe us gelæt to ðam ecan life. Se weg se ðe læt to forwyrde is
forði brad and smeðe, forði þe unlustas gebringað þone man
to forwyrde. Him bið swiðe softe and nan geswinc þæt he
fylle his galnysse and druncennysse, and gytsunge begange
and modignysse, and ða unstrangan berype, and don swa
hwæt swa hine lyst; ac ðas unðeawas and oðre swilce gelædað
hine butan geswince to ecum tintregum, buton he ær his
ende yfeles geswice and god wyrce. Dysig bið se wegferenda
man se ðe nimð þone smeðan weg þe hine mislæt, and forlæt
ðone sticolan þe hine gebrincð to ðære byrig. Swa eac we
beoð soðlice ungerade gif we lufiað þa sceortan softnysse
and ða hwilwendlican lustas to ðan swiðe þæt hi us gebringan to ðam ecan pinungum. Ac uton niman þone earfoðran
weg, þæt we her sume hwile swincon to ðy þæt we ecelice
beon butan geswince. Eaðe mihte Crist, gif he wolde, on
þisum life wunian butan earfoðnyssum, and faran to his ecan
rice butan ðrowunge and butan deaðe; ac he nolde. Be ðam
cwæð Petrus se apostol, "Crist ðrowode for us, and sealde us
bysne þæt we sceolon fyligan his fotswaðum"; þæt is, þæt we
sceolon sum ðing þrowian for Cristes lufon and for urum
synnum. Wel ðrowað se man and Gode gecwemlice se ðe
winð ongean leahtras, and godnysse gefremað swa swa he
fyrmest mæg. Se ðe nan ðing nele on ðissum life ðrowian he
sceal ðrowian unþances wyrsan ðrowunga on þam toweardan life.

true love for God and for humanity, and give alms according to our means, and be moderate in our food, and observe all other holy things. We cannot do these things without difficulties, but if we do them, then with those labors we may, through God's help, ascend the steep way which leads to eternal life. The way which leads to destruction is broad and smooth, because wicked desires bring a person to destruction. It is very easy and no labor to satisfy one's lust and drunkenness, and to practice greed and pride, to rob the weak, and to do whatever one desires; but those vices, and others like them, lead without labor to eternal torments, unless one ceases from evil before the end and does good. Foolish is the traveler who takes the smooth path that leads him astray, and forsakes the steep way that brings him to the city. So too we will be truly ignorant if we love brief comforts and transitory pleasures so much that they bring us to eternal torments. But let us take the more difficult way, that we may labor here for some time so that we might be eternally without labor. If he had wanted, Christ could easily have dwelled in this life without hardships, and gone to his everlasting kingdom without suffering and without death; but he did not want to. Concerning this the apostle Peter said, "Christ suffered for us, and gave us an example that we should follow his footsteps"; that is, that we should suffer some things for love of Christ and for our sins. The person who strives against sin suffers well and acceptably to God, and promotes goodness as completely as he can. He who will suffer nothing in this life will suffer worse suffering against his will in the life to come.

12   Nu genealæcð clæne tid and halig, on þære we sceolon
ure gimeleaste gebetan: cume forði gehwa Cristenra manna
to his scrifte and his diglan gyltas geandette, and be his lareowes tæcunge gebete; and tihte ælc oðerne to gode mid
godre gebysnunge, þæt eal folc cweðe be us swa swa be ðam
blindan gecweden wæs ða ða his eagan wæron onlihte; þæt
is, eall folc þe þæt wundor geseah herede God, se ðe leofað
and rixað a butan ende. Amen.

II

Dominica prima in Quadragesima

*D*uctus est Iesus in desertum a Spiritu, et reliqua.

2   Ic wolde eow trahtnian þis godspel ðe mann nu beforan
eow rædde, ac ic ondræde þæt ge ne magon ða micelan
deopnysse þæs godspelles swa understandan swa hit gedafenlic sy. Nu bidde ic eow þæt ge beon geðyldige on
eowerum geðance, oð þæt we ðone traht mid Godes fylste
oferrædan magon.

3   "Se hælend wæs gelæd fram þam Halgan Gaste to anum
westene, to ðy þæt he wære gecostnod fram deofle; and he
ða fæste feowertig daga and feowertig nihta, swa þæt he ne
onbyrigde ætes ne wætes on eallum þam fyrste, ac siððan
him hingrode. Þa genealæhte se costnere and him to cwæð,

Now a pure and holy time is approaching, in which we   12
should atone for our failures: so let every Christian come to
confession and confess his secret sins, and amend by the instruction of his teacher; and let everyone encourage each
other to do good by good example, that all people might say
of us what was said of the blind person when his eyes were
enlightened; that is, all people who saw that miracle praised
God, who lives and reigns forever without end. Amen.

II

First Sunday in Lent

First Sunday in Lent

J̶esus was led by the Spirit into the desert, etc.

I would like to explain this gospel to you which has just   2
now been read before you, but I fear that you cannot understand the great depth of the gospel as much as it is fitting.
Now I ask you to be patient in your thoughts, until with
God's assistance we can read through the explanation.

"The savior was led by the Holy Spirit to a desert, so that   3
he might be tempted by the devil; and there he fasted forty
days and forty nights, so that he did not taste either food
or drink in all that time, but afterward he was hungry.
Then the tempter approached and said to him, 'If you are

'Gif ðu sy Godes Sunu, cweð to ðisum stanum þæt hi beon awende to hlafum.' Ða andwearde se hælend and cwæð, 'Hit is awriten, ne leofað se mann na be hlafe anum, ac lyfað be eallum ðam wordum þe gað of Godes muðe.' Þa genam se deofol hine and gesette hine uppan ðam scylfe þæs heagan temples, and cwæð, 'Gif ðu Godes Sunu sy, feall nu adun; hit is awriten þæt englum is beboden be ðe þæt hi ðe on hira handum ahebbon, þæt þu furðon ne ðurfe ðinne fot æt stane ætspurnan.' Þa cwæð se hælend eft him to, 'Hit is awriten, "Ne fanda þines Drihtnes."' Þa genam se deofol hine eft, and gesette hine uppan anre swiðe heahre dune, and æteowde him ealles middangeardes welan and his wuldor, and cwæð him to, 'Ealle ðas ðing ic forgife ðe, gif ðu wilt feallan to minum fotum and gebiddan þe to me.' Ða cwæð se hælend him to, 'Ga ðu underbæcc, Sceocca! Hit is awriten, "Gehwa sceal hine gebiddan to his Drihtne anum, and him anum ðeowian."' Þa forlet se deofol hine, and him comon englas to and him ðenodon."

4   Se Halga Gast lædde þone hælend to þam westene to ðy þæt he wære þær gecostnod. Nu wundrað gehwa hu se deofol dorste genealæcan to ðam hælende þæt he hine costnode; ac he ne dorste Cristes fandian gif him alyfed nære. Se hælend com to mancynne for ði þæt he wolde ealle ure costnunga oferswiðan mid his costnungum, and oferswiðan urne ðone ecan dead mid his hwilwendlicum deaðe. Nu wæs he swa eadmod þæt he geðafode ðam deofle þæt he his fandode, and he geðafode lyðrum mannum þæt hi hine ofslogon. Deofol is ealra unrihtwisra manna heafod, and þa yfelan men sind his lima; nu geðafode God þæt þæt heafod hine costnode, and þæt ða limu hine ahengon.

5   Þam deofle wæs micel twynung hwæt Crist wære. His lif

the Son of God, tell these stones to turn to bread.' The savior answered and said, 'It is written, one does not live by bread alone, but by all the words which proceed from the mouth of God.' Then the devil took him and set him on the summit of the high temple, and said, 'If you are the Son of God, fall down now; it is written that the angels are commanded to lift you up in their hands, that you may not even strike your foot on a stone.' Then the savior replied to him, 'It is written, "Do not test your Lord."' Then the devil took him again, and set him upon a very high mountain, and showed him all the wealth of the world and its glory, and said to him, 'All these things I will give you, if you will fall at my feet and worship me.' Then the savior said to him, 'Go behind, Satan! It is written, "Everyone shall worship only his Lord, and serve only him."' Then the devil left him, and angels came to him and served him."

The Holy Spirit led the savior to the desert so that he 4 would be tempted there. Now someone might wonder how the devil dared to approach the savior to tempt him; but he would not dare test Christ if he had not been allowed to. The savior came to humanity in order to overcome all our temptations by his temptations, and overcome our eternal death with his temporary death. Now he was so humble that he allowed the devil to test him, and he allowed the wicked to slay him. The devil is the head of all unrighteous people, and evil people are his limbs; God permitted the head to tempt him, and the limbs to crucify him.

The devil had great doubt as to what Christ was. His life 5

næs na gelogod swa swa oðra manna lif; Crist ne æt mid
gyfernysse, ne he ne dranc mid oferflowendnysse, ne his
eagan ne ferdon worigende geond mislice lustas. Þa smeade
se deofol hwæt he wære—hwæðer he wære Godes Sunu se
ðe manncynne behaten wæs. Cwæð þa on his geðance þæt
he fandian wolde hwæt he wære. Ða fæste Crist feowertig
daga and feowertig nihta on an, ða on eallum þam fyrste ne
cwæð se deofol to him þæt he etan sceolde, þe he geseh þæt
him nan ðing ne hingrode. Eft ða, ða Crist hingrode æfter
swa langum fyrste, ða wende se deofol soðlice þæt he God
nære, and cwæð to him, "Hwi hingrað þe? Gif ðu Godes
Sunu sy, wend þas stanas to hlafum, and et." Eaðe mihte
God—se ðe awende wæter to wine, and se ðe ealle gesceafta
of nahte geworhte—eaðelice he mihte awendan ða stanas to
hlafum, ac he nolde nan ðing don be ðæs deofles tæcunge, ac
cwæð him to andsware, "Ne lifað na se man be hlafe anum,
ac lifað be ðam wordum ðe gað of Godes muðe." Swa swa
þæs mannes lichama leofað be hlafe, swa sceal his sawul
lybban be Godes wordum, þæt is, be Godes lare, þe he þurh
wise menn on bocum gesette. Gif se lichama næfð mete,
oþþe ne mæg mete ðicgean, þonne forweornað he and
adeadað. Swa eac seo sawul, gif heo næfð þa halgan lare, heo
bið þonne weornigende and mægenleas; þurh ða halgan lare
heo bið strang and onbryrd to Godes willan. Þa wæs se deofol æne oferswiðed fram Criste.

6   "And he ða hine genam and bær upp on þæt templ, and
hine sette æt ðam scylfe, and cwæð to him, 'Gif ðu Godes
Sunu sy, sceot adun; þe englum is beboden be ðe, þæt hi ðe
on handum ahebban, þæt þu ne ðurfe ðinne fot æt stane
ætspurnan.'" Her begann se deofol to reccanne halige gewritu, and he leah mid þære race, forðan ðe he is leas, and

was not ordered like the lives of others; Christ did not eat with gluttony or drink to excess, nor did his eyes go wandering among various pleasures. Then the devil considered what he might be—whether he might be the Son of God who had been promised to humanity. He said to himself that he would test what he was. When Christ fasted forty days and forty nights together, in all that time the devil did not say to him that he should eat, because he saw that he did not hunger for anything. Afterward, when Christ hungered after so long a time, then the devil assumed that he was not God, and said to him, "Why do you hunger? If you are the Son of God, turn these stones to bread, and eat." God might easily—he who turned water to wine, and made all creatures from nothing—he might easily turn the stones to bread, but he would do nothing by the devil's instruction, but said to him in answer, "One does not live by bread alone, but by the words which proceed from the mouth of God." Just as one's body lives by bread, so shall the soul live by God's words, that is, by God's teaching, which he has set in books through wise ones. If the body has no food, or cannot eat food, then it decays and dies. So too the soul will be perishing and powerless if it does not have the holy teaching; by the holy teaching it will be strong and inspired to God's will. And so the devil was overcome once by Christ.

"And then he took him and carried him up on the temple, and set him on the summit, and said to him, 'If you are the Son of God, jump down; for it is commanded to the angels that they will lift you up in their hands, that you may not strike your foot against a stone.'" Here the devil began to recount holy scripture, and he lied in his account, because 6

nan soðfæstnys nis on him; ac he is fæder ælcere leasunge. Næs þæt na awriten be Criste þæt he ða sæde, ac wæs awriten be halgum mannum: hi behofiað engla fultumes on þissum life þæt se deofol hi costnian ne mote swa swiðe swa he wolde. Swa hold is God mancynne þæt he hæfð geset his englas us to hyrdum, þæt hi ne sceolon na geðafian þam reðum deoflum þæt hi us fordon magon. Hi moton ure afandian, ac hi ne moton us nydan to nanum yfle, buton we hit sylfe agenes willan don, þurh ða yfelan tihtinge ðæs deofles. We ne beoð na fulfremede buton we beon afandode. Þurh ða fandunge we sceolon geðeon, gif we æfre wiðsacað deofle and eallum his larum, and gif we genealæcað urum Drihtne mid geleafan, and lufe, and godum weorcum; gif we hwær aslidon, arisan eft þærrihte, and betan georne þæt ðær tobrocen bið.

7   Crist cwæð þa to ðam deofle, "Ne sceal man fandigan his Drihtnes." Þæt wære swiðe gilplic dæd gif Crist scute ða adun, þeah ðe he eaðe mihte butan awyrdnysse his lima nyðer asceotan, se ðe gebigde þone heagan heofenlican bigels; ac he nolde nan ðing don mid gylpe, forðon þe se gylp is an heafodleahter. Þa nolde he adun asceotan, forðon ðe he onscunode þone gylp, ac cwæð, "Ne sceal man his Drihtnes fandian." Se man fandiað his Drihtnes se ðe, mid dyslicum truwan and mid gylpe, sum wundorlic ðing on Godes naman don wile, oððe se ðe sumes wundres dyslice and butan neode æt Gode abiddan wile. Þa wæs se deofol oðere siðe þurh Cristes geðyld oferswiðed.

8   "Þa genam he hine eft, and abær hine upp on ane dune, and ætywde him ealles middangeardes welan and his wuldor, and cwæð to him, 'Ealle ðas ðing ic forgife ðe, gif ðu wilt afeallan to minum fotum and þe to me gebiddan.'" Dyrstelice spræc se deofol her, swa swa he ær spræc þa þa he on

he is false, and there is no truth in him; he is the father of every lie. What he said there was not written of Christ, but of holy persons: they need the support of angels in this life so that the devil may not tempt them as much as he would like. God is so kind to humanity that he has set his angels over us as guardians, that they should not allow the fierce devils to destroy us. They may test us, but they cannot force us to any evil, unless we do it ourselves of our own will, through the evil urging of the devil. We will not be perfect unless we are tested. Through testing we will thrive, if we always reject the devil and all his teachings, and if we draw near to our Lord with faith, and love, and good works; if we slip anywhere, arise at once, and earnestly mend what is broken.

Christ said to the devil, "No one should test his Lord." It 7 would have been a very prideful deed if Christ had thrown himself down, though he who bowed the high arch of heaven might easily have cast himself down without injury to his limbs; but he would do nothing in pride, because pride is a deadly sin. So he would not throw himself down, because he avoided pride, but said, "No one should test his Lord." That person tests his Lord who, with foolish confidence and with pride, wants to do some miraculous thing in God's name, or who will foolishly and without need pray to God for some miracle. Then the devil was overcome by Christ's patience a second time.

"Then he took him again, and carried him up on a moun- 8 tain, and showed him all the riches of the world and its glory, and said to him, 'All these things I will give you, if you will fall at my feet and worship me.'" The devil spoke boldly here, as he had before when he was in heaven, when he

heofenum wæs, þa þa he wolde dælan heofonan rice wið his scyppend and beon Gode gelic; ac his dyrstignys hine awearp ða into helle. And eac nu his dyrstignys hine geniðerode, þa ða he, ðurh Cristes þrowunge, forlet mancynn of his anwealde. He cwæð, "Þas ðing ic forgife ðe." Him ðuhte þæt he ahte ealne middangeard, forðon ðe him ne wiðstod nan man ær ðam þe Crist com þe hine gewylde. Hit is awriten on halgum bocum, "Eorðe and eall hire gefyllednys, and eal ymbhwyrft and þa ðing ðe on ðam wuniað, ealle hit syndon Godes æhta," and na deofles. Þeah hwæðere Crist cwæð on his godspelle be ðam deofle, þæt he wære middangeardes ealdor, and he sceolde beon utadræfed. He is ðæra manna ealdor þe lufiað þisne middangeard and ealne heora hiht on þissum life besettað, and heora scyppend forseoð. Ealle gesceafta—sunne and mona and ealle tunglan, land and sæ, and nytenu—ealle hi ðeowiað hyra scyppende, forðon þe hi farað æfter Godes dihte. Se lyðra man ana, þonne he forsihð Godes beboda and fullgæð deofles willan, oððe þurh gytsunge, oþþe ðurh leasunge, oððe ðurh graman, oððe ðurh oðre leahtras, þonne bið he deofles ðeowa þonne he deofle gecwemð, and þone forsihð þe hine geworhte.

9 "Crist cwæð ða to ðam deofle, 'Ga ðu underbæcc, Sceocca! Hit is awriten, man sceal hine gebiddan to his Drihtne, and him anum ðeowian.'" *Quidam dicunt non dixisse salvatorem, "Satane, vade retro," sed tantum "Vade"; sed tamen in rectioribus et vetustioribus exemplaribus habetur, "Vade retro, Satanas," sicut interpretatio ipsius nominis declarat; nam diabolus "deorsum ruens" interpretatur. Apostolo igitur Petro dicitur a Christo, "Vade retro me," id est, "Sequere me." Diabolo non dicitur "Vade retro me," sed "Vade retro," sicut jam diximus, et sic scripsit beatus Hieronimus in una epistola.* He cwæð to ðam deofle, "Ga

FIRST SUNDAY IN LENT

would divide up the kingdom of heaven with his creator and
be equal to God; but his boldness cast him down into hell.
And now too his boldness brought him down, when through
Christ's passion he let humanity go out of his power. The
devil said, "These things I will give you." It seemed to him
that he possessed all the world, because no one had opposed
him before Christ who subdued him came. It is written in
holy books, "The earth and all its fullness, and all the globe
and those things that dwell on it, all are God's possessions,"
and not the devil's. Nevertheless, Christ said in his gospel
that the devil was the prince of the world, and he should be
driven out. He is the prince of those people who love this
world and set all their hope in this life, and despise their creator. All creatures—sun and moon and all stars, land and sea,
and beasts—all serve their creator, because they proceed according to God's direction. The wicked alone, when he despises God's commandments and fulfills the devil's will,
whether through covetousness, or lying, or anger, or other
sins, is the devil's servant when he pleases the devil, and despises the one who created him.

"Christ then said to the devil, 'Go behind, Satan! It is   9
written, one shall worship his Lord, and serve him alone.'"
*Some say that the savior did not say "Satan, go behind," but only
"go"; but in the older and more correct manuscripts it is "Go behind,
Satan," as the interpretation of his name declares; for "devil" means
"falling downward." To the apostle Peter Christ said, "Go behind
me," that is, "Follow me." He did not say to the devil "Go behind
me," but "Go behind," as we have just said, and as the blessed
Jerome writes in a letter. He said to the devil, "Go behind."*

ðu underbæc." Deofles nama is gereht "Nyðerhreosende."
Nyðer he ahreas, and underbæc he eode fram frimðe his an-
ginnes, þa ða he wæs ascyred fram ðære heofonlican blisse.
On hinder he eode eft þurh Cristes tocyme; on hinder he
sceal gan on domes dæge, þonne he bið belocen on hellewite
on ecum fyre, he and ealle his geferan, and hi næfre siððan
utbrecan ne magon.

10   Hit is awriten on ðære ealdan æ þæt nan man ne sceal
hine gebiddan to nanum deofelgylde, ne to nanum ðinge buton to Gode anum, forðon ðe nan gesceaft nys wyrðe þæs
wurðmyntes buton se ana se ðe scyppend is ealra ðinga. To
him anum we sceolon us gebiddan; he ana is soð Hlaford and
soð God. We biddað þingunga æt halgum mannum, þæt hi
sceolon us ðingian to heora Drihtne and to urum Drihtne;
ne gebidde we na ðeah hwæðere us to him swa swa we to
Gode doð, ne hi þæt geðafian nellað. Swa swa se engel cwæð
to Iohanne þam apostole ða ða he wolde feallan to his fotum, he cwæð, "Ne do þu hit na, þæt þu to me abuge. Ic eom
Godes þeowa, swa swa ðu and þine gebroðra: gebide ðe to
Gode anum."

11   "Þa forlet se deofol Crist, and him comon englas to and
him ðenodon." He wæs gecostnod swa swa mann, and æfter
ðære costnunge him comon halige englas to and him
ðenodon swa swa heora scyppende. Buton se deofol gesawe
þæt Crist man wære, ne gecostnode he hine; and buton he
soð God wære, noldon ða englas him ðenian. Mycel wæs
ures hælendes eaðmodnys and his geþyld on ðisre dæde.
He mihte mid anum worde besencan ðone deofol on þære
deopan nywelnysse; ac he ne æteowde his mihte, ac mid halgum gewritum he andwyrde ðam deofle, and sealde us bysne
mid his geðylde þæt swa oft swa we fram ðwyrum mannum

The devil's name is interpreted as "falling down." Down he fell, and backward he went from his very beginning, when he was cut off from heavenly bliss. He went behind again through Christ's advent; he will go behind on the day of judgment, when he and all his companions will be locked up in the torments of hell in eternal fire, and never afterward will they be able to break out.

It is written in the old law that no one shall worship any 10 idol, nor anything but God alone, because no creature is worthy of that honor but him alone who is the creator of all things. Him alone we should worship; he alone is true Lord and true God. We ask intercessions from holy men, that they might intercede for us with their Lord and our Lord; yet we do not worship them as we do God, nor will they permit it. As the angel said to John the apostle when he would fall at his feet, "Do not do it, that you should bow to me. I am God's servant, just like you and your brothers: you should pray to God alone."

"Then the devil left Christ, and angels came to him and 11 served him." He was tempted just like a human, and after the temptation holy angels came to him and served him as their creator. Unless the devil had seen that Christ was a human, he would not have tempted him; and unless he were true God, the angels would not have served him. Great was our savior's humility and his patience in this act. With one word he might have sunk the devil into the deep abyss; but he did not manifest his might, but answered the devil with holy scriptures, and gave us an example by his patience that as often as we suffer anything from perverse people, we

ænig ðing þrowiað, þæt we sceolon wendan ure mod to
Godes lare swiðor þonne to ænigre wrace.

12   On ðreo wisan bið deofles costnung: þæt is on tihtinge,
on lustfullunge, on geðafunge. Deofol tiht us to yfele, ac we
sceolon hit onscunian and ne geniman nane lustfullunge to
ðære tihtinge; gif ðonne ure mod nimð gelustfullunge,
þonne sceole we huru wiðstandan, þæt ðær ne beo nan geðafung to ðam yfelan weorce. Seo yfele tihting is of deofle;
ðonne bið oft þæs mannes mod gebiged to ðære lustfullunge, hwilon eac aslit to ðære geðafunge, forðon þe we sind
of synfullum flæsce acennede. Næs na se hælend on ða wisan
gecostnod, forðon ðe he wæs of mædene acenned buton
synne, and næs nan ðing ðwyrlices on him. He mihte beon
gecostnod þurh tihtinge, ac nan lustfullung ne hrepede his
mod. Þær næs eac nan geðafung, forðon ðe ðær næs nan
lustfullung; ac wæs ðæs deofles costnung forðy eall wiðutan,
and nan ðing wiðinnan. Ungewiss com se deofol to Criste,
and ungewiss he eode aweig, þe se hælend ne geswutulode
na him his mihte, ac oferdraf hine geðyldelice mid halgum
gewritum.

13   Se ealda deofol gecostnode urne fæder Adam on ðreo
wisan: þæt is mid gyfernysse, and mid idelum wuldre, and
mid gitsunge; and þa wearð he oferswiðed forðon þe he
geðafode þam deofle on eallum þam ðrim costnungum. Þurh
gyfernysse he wæs oferswiðed þa þa he, ðurh deofles lare, æt
ðone forbodenan æppel. Þurh idel wuldor he wæs oferswiðed ða ða he gelyfde ðæs deofles wordum ða ða he cwæð,
"Swa mære ge beoð swa swa englas gif ge of þam treowe
etað." And hi ða gelyfdon his leasunge, and woldon mid
idelum gylpe beon beteran þonne hi gesceapene wæron; ða
wurdon hi wyrsan. Mid gytsunge he wæs oferswiðed þa þa se

should turn our mind to God's teaching rather than to any vengeance.

The devil's temptation comes in three ways: in entice- 12 ment, in pleasure, and in consent. The devil entices us to evil, but we should shun it and take no pleasure in the enticement; but if our mind takes pleasure, then we should at least resist, so that there is no consent to the evil deed. Enticement to evil is from the devil; but a person's mind is often bent to pleasure, and sometimes it slips into consent, because we are born of sinful flesh. The savior was not tempted in this way, because he was born of a virgin without sin, and there was nothing perverse in him. He might have been tempted by enticement, but no pleasure touched his mind. There was also no consent, because there was no pleasure there; the devil's temptation was all exterior, and nothing interior. The devil came to Christ uncertain, and he went away uncertain, because the savior did not reveal his power to him, but overcame him patiently by the holy scriptures.

The old devil tempted our father Adam in three ways: 13 that is, with gluttony, and with vainglory, and with covetousness; and then he was overcome because he consented to the devil in all three of those temptations. He was overcome through gluttony when, by the devil's instruction, he ate the forbidden apple. He was overcome through vainglory when he believed the devil's words when he said, "You will be as great as angels if you eat of that tree." And they believed his lies, and would in their vainglory be better than they had been created; then they became worse. He was overcome with covetousness when the devil said to him,

deofol cwæð to him, "And ge habbað gescead ægðer ge godes ge yfeles." Nis na gytsung on feo anum, ac is eac on gewilnunge micelre geðincðe.

14   Mid þam ylcum ðrim ðingum þe se deofol ðone frumsceapenan mann oferswiðde, mid þam ylcan Crist oferswiðde hine and astrehte. Þurh gyfernysse fandode se deofol Cristes ða ða he cwæð, "Cweð to ðysum stanum þæt hi beon to hlafum awende, and et." Þurh idel wuldor he fandode his þa þa he hine tihte þæt he sceolde sceotan nyðer of ðæs temples scylfe. Þurh gitsunge he fandode his ða ða he, mid leasunge, him behet ealles middangeardes welan gif he wolde feallan to his fotum. Ac se deofol wæs þa oferswiðed ðurh Crist on þam ylcum gemetum þe he ær Adam oferswiðde, þæt he gewite fram urum heortum, mid þam innfære gehæft mid þam þe he inn afaren wæs and us gehæfte.

15   We gehyrdon on ðisum godspelle þæt ure Drihten fæste feowertig daga and feowertig nihta on an. Ða ða he swa lange fæste, þa geswutelode he þa micelan mihte his godcundnysse, þurh ða he mihte on eallum ðisum andweardum life butan eorðlicum mettum lybban, gif he wolde. Eft, ða ða him hingrode, þa geswutelode he þæt he wæs soð man, and forði metes behofode. Moyses se heretoga fæste eac feowertig daga and feowertig nihta to ði þæt he moste underfon Godes æ; ac he ne fæste na þurh his agene mihte, ac þurh Godes. Eac se witega Elias fæste ealswa lange, eac þurh Godes mihte, and siððan wæs genumen butan deaðe of ðisum life.

16   Nu is ðis fæsten eallum Cristenum mannum geset to healdenne on ælces geares ymbryne; ac we moton ælce dæg ures metes brucan mid forhæfednysse, ðæra metta þe alyfede sind. Hwi is ðis fæsten þus geteald þurh feowertig daga?

"And you will have knowledge of good and evil." Covetousness is not only for money, but is also in the desire for high status.

With the same three things by which the devil overcame the first-created human, with the same three things Christ overcame him and prostrated him. The devil tested Christ through gluttony when he said, "Say to these stones that they be turned to bread, and eat." He tested him through vainglory when he urged him to throw himself down from the temple's summit. He tested him through covetousness when, with his lies, he promised him all the world's wealth if he would fall at his feet. But the devil was overcome by Christ by the same means with which he had overcome Adam, so that he should depart from our hearts, made captive by the same entrance through which he had entered and made us captives. 14

We have heard in this gospel that our Lord fasted forty days and forty nights together. When he fasted so long, he revealed the great power of his divinity, by which he might have lived all this present life without earthly food, if he had wanted. Afterward, when he was hungry, he revealed that he was a true human, and therefore required food. Moses the leader also fasted forty days and forty nights so that he might receive God's law; but he did not fast through his own power, but through God's. The prophet Elijah also fasted just as long, also through God's power, and was later taken from this life without death. 15

Now this fast is established for all Christians in the course of every year; but every day we must eat in moderation those foods which are permitted. Why is this fast 16

On eallum geare sind getealde ðreo hund daga and fif and sixtig daga. Þonne gif we teoðiað þas gearlican dagas, þonne beoð þær six and ðritig teoðingdagas; and fram ðisum dæge oð þone halgan Easterdæg sind twa and feowertig daga—do þonne ða six Sunnandagas of ðam getele, þonne beoð þa six and ðritig þæs geares teoðingdagas us to forhæfednysse getealde.

17   Swa swa Godes æ us bebyt þæt we sceolon ealle ða ðing þe us gesceotað of ures geares teolunge Gode þa teoðunge syllan, swa we sceolon eac on ðisum teoðingdagum urne lichaman mid forhæfednysse Gode to lofe teoðian. We sceolon us gearcian on eallum ðingum swa swa Godes þenas, æfter þæs apostoles tæcunge, on micclum geðylde, and on halgum wæccum, on fæstenum, and on clænnysse modes and lichaman; forði læsse pleoh bið þam Cristenum men þæt he flæsces bruce þonne he on ðissere halgan tide wifes bruce. Lætað aweg ealle saca and ælc geflitt, and gehealdað þas tid mid sibbe and mid soðre lufe; forðon ne bið nan fæsten Gode andfenge butan sibbe. And doð swa swa God tæhte: tobrec ðinne hlaf and syle ðone oþerne dæl hungrium men, and læd into þinum huse wædlan and ða earman ælfremedan men, and gefrefra hi mid þinum godum. Þonne ðu nacodne geseo, scryd hine, and ne forseoh ðin agen flæsc. Se mann þe fæst buton ælmyssan he deð swilce he sparige his mete, and eft ett þæt he ær mid forhæfednysse foreode; ac þæt fæsten tælð God. Ac gif ðu fæstan wille Gode to gecwemednysse, þonne gehelp ðu earmra manna mid þam dæle ðe ðu þe sylfum oftihst—and eac mid maran, gif ðe to onhagige. Forbugað idele spellunge and dyselice blissa, and bewepað eowre synna; forðon ðe Crist cwæð, "Wa eow þe nu hlihgað,

counted as forty days? In every year there are three hundred sixty-five days. If we tithe these yearly days, then will there be thirty-six tithing days; and from this day to the holy Easter day are forty-two days—take away the six Sundays from that number, then there will be thirty-six days of the year's tithing days reckoned for our abstinence.

Just as God's law commands us to give a tithe to God of all the things which are allotted to us from our yearly labor, so should we likewise on these tithing days tithe our body with abstinence to the praise of God. We should prepare ourselves in all things as God's servants, according to the apostle's teaching, with great patience, and with holy vigils, with fasts, and with chastity of mind and body; for it is less dangerous for a Christian to eat flesh than to have intercourse with a woman at this holy time. Set aside all quarrels and every dispute, and hold this time with peace and true love; for no fast is acceptable to God without peace. And do as God taught: break your bread and give the other portion to the hungry, lead the poor and wretched strangers into your house, and comfort them with your possessions. When you see someone naked, clothe him, and do not despise your own flesh. The person who fasts without alms acts as if he spares his food, and afterward eats what he had previously forgone in his abstinence; but God condemns such fasting. If you would fast to please God, then help the poor with the portion which you withhold from yourself—and also with more, if you are so inclined. Avoid idle talk and foolish pleasures, and weep for your sins; for Christ said, "Woe to you

ge sceolon heofian and wepan." Eft he cwæð, "Eadige beoð
ða ðe nu wepað, forðon þe hi sceolon beon gefrefrode."

18   We lybbað mislice on twelf monðum; nu sceole we ure
gymeleaste on þysne timan geinnian, and lybban Gode, we
ðe oðrum timan us sylfum leofodon. And swa hwæt swa we
doð to gode, uton don þæt butan gylpe and idelre herunge.
Se mann þe for gylpe hwæt to gode deð, him sylfum to
herunge, næfð he ðæs nane mede æt Gode, ac hæfð his wite.
Ac uton don swa swa God tæhte, þæt ure godan weorc beon
on ða wisan mannum cuðe þæt hi magon geseon ure godnysse, and þæt hi wuldrian and herigan urne heofenlican
Fæder, God ælmihtigne, se ðe forgilt mid hundfealdum
swa hwæt swa we doð earmum mannum for his lufon, se ðe
leofað and rixað a butan ende on ecnysse. Amen.

12

Dominica in media Quadragesima

Abiit Iesus trans Mare Galileae, et reliqua.

2   "Se hælend ferde ofer ða Galileiscan Sæ, þe is gehaten
Tyberiadis, and him filigde micel menigu, forðon þe hi beheoldon ða tacna þe he worhte ofer ða untruman men. Þa
astah se hælend up on ane dune and þær sæt mid his leorningcnihtum, and wæs ða swiðe gehende seo halige Easter-

who now laugh, you will mourn and weep." Again he said, "Blessed are they who now weep, for they shall be comforted."

For twelve months we live variously; now in this time we 18 should repair our heedlessness, and live for God, we who at other times have lived for ourselves. And whatever good we do, let us do it without pride and vain praise. The person who does any good for pride, to his own praise, will have not reward with God, but punishment. Let us do as God has taught, that our good works may be known to people in such a way that they may see our goodness, and glorify and praise our heavenly Father, God almighty, who repays a hundredfold whatever we do for the poor for love of him, who lives and reigns forever without end to eternity. Amen.

12

Mid-Lent Sunday

Mid-Lent Sunday

Jesus went across the Sea of Galilee, etc.

"The savior went over the Sea of Galilee, which is called 2 *Tiberias,* and a great crowd followed him, because they had seen the signs which he performed for the sick. The savior went up on a mountain and sat with his disciples, and it was very near to the holy time of Easter. The savior looked up

tid. Þa beseah se hælend up and geseah þæt ðær wæs mycel
mennisc toweard, and cwæð to anum his leorningcnihta, se
wæs gehaten Philippus, 'Mid hwam mage we bicgan hlaf
ðisum folce?' Þis he cwæð to fandunge þæs leorningcnihtes;
he sylf wiste hwæt he don wolde. Ða andwyrde Philippus,
'Þeah her wæron gebohte twa hund peningwurð hlafes, ne
mihte furðon hyra ælc anne bitan of ðam gelæccan.' Þa
cwæð an his leorningcnihta, se hatte Andreas, Petres broðor,
'Her byrð an cnapa fif berene hlafas and twegen fixas, ac to
hwan mæg þæt to swa micclum werode?' Þa cwæð se hælend,
'Doð þæt þæt folc sitte.' And þær wæs micel gærs on ðære
stowe, myrige on to sittenne, and hi ða ealle sæton, swa swa
mihte beon fif ðusend wera. Ða genam se hælend þa fif
hlafas and bletsode, and tobræc, and todælde betwux ðam
sittendum. Swa gelice eac þa fixas todælde; and hi ealle
genoh hæfdon. Þa ða hi ealle fulle wæron, ða cwæð se
hælend to his leorningcnihtum, 'Gaderiað þa lafe, and hi ne
losion.' And hi ða gegaderodon ða bricas, and gefyldon twelf
wilian mid ðære lafe. Þæt folc ða ðe ðis tacen geseah cwæð
þæt Crist wære soð witega se ðe wæs toweard to ðisum
middangearde."

3   Seo sæ þe se hælend oferferde getacnað þas andweardan
woruld, to ðære com Crist and oferferde. Þæt is, he com to
ðisre worulde on menniscnysse and ðis lif oferferde; he com
to deaðe, and of deaðe aras. And astah up on ane dune and
þær sæt mid his leorningcnihtum, forðon ðe he astah up to
heofenum and þær sitt nu ða mid his halgum. Rihtlice is seo
sæ wiðmeten þisre worulde, forðon ðe heo is hwiltidum
smylte and myrige on to rowenne, hwilon eac swiðe hreoh
and egeful on to beonne. Swa is þeos woruld; hwiltidum heo
is gesundful and myrige on to wunigenne, hwilon heo is eac

and saw that there was a great crowd coming, and said to one of his disciples, who was called Philip, 'How can we buy bread for these people?' He said this to test his disciple; he himself knew what he would do. Philip answered, 'Even if we bought two hundred pennies' worth of bread here, each of them would hardly get a bite.' One of his disciples named Andrew, brother of Peter, said, 'A boy here has five barley loaves and two fish, but what is that among so many?' The savior said, 'Make the people sit down.' There was much grass in that place, pleasant to sit on, and they all sat, about five thousand people. The savior took the five loaves and blessed them, broke them, and distributed them to those sitting. Likewise he distributed the two fish; and they all had enough. When they were all full, the savior said to his disciples, 'Gather up the remainder, and do not let it be lost.' And they gathered up the fragments, and filled twelve baskets with the remainder. The people who saw this sign said that Christ was the true prophet who was to come to this world."

The sea which the savior passed over signifies this present world, to which Christ came and passed over. That is, he came to this world in human nature and passed over this life; he came to death, and arose from death. And he went up on a mountain and sat there with his disciples, because he ascended to heaven and now sits there with his saints. The sea is rightly compared to this world, for it is sometimes smooth and pleasant to navigate on, sometimes also very rough and terrifying to be on. So is this world; sometimes it is wholesome and pleasant to dwell in, sometimes it

swiðe styrnlic and mid mislicum þingum gemenged, swa þæt
heo foroft bið swiðe unwynsum on to eardigenne. Hwilon
we beoð hale, hwilon untrume; nu bliðe, and eft on micelre
unblisse; forðy is þis lif, swa swa we ær cwædon, þære sæ
wiðmeten.

4   Þa se hælend gesæt up on ðære dune, ða ahof he up his
eagan and geseh þæt ðær wæs micel mennisc toweard. Ealle
þa ðe him to cumað—þæt is ða ðe bugað to rihtum geleafan—þa gesihð se hælend, and þam he gemiltsað, and
hyra mod onliht mid his gife, þæt hi magon him to cuman
butan gedwylde; and ðam he forgifð ðone gastlican fodan,
þæt hi ne ateorian be wege. Þa ða he axode Philippum
hwanon hi mihton hlaf ðam folce gebicgan, ða geswutelode
he Philippes nytennysse. Wel wiste Crist hwæt he don
wolde, and he wiste þæt Philippus þæt nyste. Ða cwæð Andreas þæt an cnapa þær bære fif berene hlafas and twegen
fixas; þa cwæð se hælend, "Doð þæt þæt folc sitte," and swa
forðon, swa we eow ær rehton. Se hælend geseh þæt
hungrige folc and he hi mildheortlice fedde, ægðer ge þurh
his godnysse ge ðurh his mihte. Hwæt mihte seo godnys ana,
buton ðær wære miht mid þære godnysse? His discipuli
woldon eac þæt folc fedan, ac hi næfdon mid hwam. Se
hælend hæfde þone godan willan to ðam fostre, and þa
mihte to ðære fremminge.

5   Fela wundra worhte God, and dæghwamlice wyrcð; ac ða
wundra sind swiðe awacode on manna gesihðe forðon ðe hi
sind swiðe gewunelice. Mare wundor is þæt God ælmihtig
ælce dæg fet ealne middangeard, and gewissað þa godan,
þonne þæt wundor wære þæt he ða gefylde fif ðusend manna
mid fif hlafum; ac ðæs wundredon men, na forði þæt hit
mare wundor wære, ac forði þæt hit wæs ungewunelic. Hwa

is very harsh and mingled with various things, so that too often it is very unpleasant to live in. Sometimes we are healthy, sometimes sick; now happy, and then in great sadness; so this life, as we have said, is compared to the sea.

When the savior was sitting on the mountain, he lifted his eyes and saw a great crowd coming. The savior sees all who come to him—that is, those who turn to him with right faith—and he has mercy on them, and enlightens their mind with his grace, so that they may come to him without error; and he gives them spiritual food, so that they might not grow weak along the way. When he asked Philip where they might buy bread for the people, he revealed Philip's ignorance. Christ well knew what he would do, and he knew that Philip did not know. Then Andrew said that a boy there had five barley loaves and two fish; the savior said, "Make the people sit," and so forth, as we told you before. The savior saw the hungry people and he compassionately fed them, both through his goodness and through his power. What could goodness alone do, unless there were power in that goodness? His disciples also wanted to feed the people, but they did not have the means. The savior had the good will to nourish them, and the power to bring it about. 4

God has worked many miracles, and works them every day; but those miracles are very meager in people's sight because they are so common. It is a greater miracle that almighty God feeds the whole world every day, and directs its goods, than the miracle when he filled five thousand people with five loaves; but people wondered at that, not because it was a greater miracle, but because it was unusual. Who gives 5

sylð nu wæstm urum æcerum, and gemenigfylt þæt gerip of feawum cornum, buton se ðe ða gemænigfilde ða fif hlafas? Seo miht wæs ða on Cristes handum, and þa fif hlafas wæron swylce hit sæd wære, na on eorðan besawen ac gemenigfyld fram ðam ðe eorðan geworhte.

6 Þis wundor is swiðe micel, and deop on getacnungum. Oft gehwa gesihð fægre stafas awritene; þonne heraðhe ðone writere and þa stafas, and nat hwæt hi mænað. Se ðe cann ðæra stafa gescead, he heraðheora fægernysse and ræd þa stafas, and understent hwæt hi gemænað. On oðre wisan we sceawiað metinge, and on oðre wisan stafas. Ne gæð na mare to metinge buton þæt þu hit geseo and herige; nis na genoh þæt þu stafas sceawige buton ðu hi eac ræde and þæt andgit understande. Swa is eac on ðam wundre þe God worhte mid þam fif hlafum—ne bið na genoh þæt we þæs tacnes wundrian, oþþe þurh þæt God herian, buton we eac þæt gastlice andgit understandon.

7 Þa fif hlafas ðe se cnapa bær getacniað þa fif bec ðe Moyses se heretoga sette on ðære ealdan æ. Se cnapa ðe hi bær and heora ne onbyrigde wæs þæt Iudeisce folc, ðe ða fif bec ræddon, and ne cuðe þæron nan gastlic andgit ær ðan ðe Crist com and þa bec geopenode and hyra gastlice andgit onwreah his leorningcnihtum, and hi siððan eallum Cristenum folce. We ne magon nu ealle þa fif bec areccan, ac we secgað eow þæt God sylf hi dihte, and Moyses hi awrat, to steore and to lare ðam ealdan folce Israhel, and eac us on gastlicum andgite. Þa bec wæron awritene be Criste, ac þæt gastlice andgit wæs þam folce digle oð þæt Crist sylf com to mannum and geopenede þæra boca digelnysse æfter gastlicum andgite.

fruit to our fields, and multiplies the harvest from a few grains, but he who multiplied the five loaves? The power was in Christ's hands, and the five loaves were like a seed, not sown in the earth but multiplied by the one who made the earth.

This miracle is very great, and deep in its significance. 6 Often someone sees fair letters written; then he praises the writer and the letters, and does not know what they mean. He who understands the meaning of the letters praises their beauty and reads the letters, and understands what they mean. We look at a picture one way, and at letters another. For a picture you need do no more than see it and praise it; it is not enough to look at letters unless you also read them and understand their meaning. So it is with the miracle which God worked with the five loaves—it is not enough that we wonder at the sign, or praise God for it, without also understanding its spiritual sense.

The five loaves which the child carried signify the five 7 books which the leader Moses set down in the old law. The child who carried them and did not taste them was the Jewish people, who read the five books, and did not know the spiritual meaning in them before Christ came and opened the books and revealed their spiritual meaning to his disciples, and they afterward to all Christian people. We cannot explain all the five books now, but we will tell you that God himself dictated them, and Moses wrote them, for the guidance and instruction of the ancient people of Israel, and also for us in a spiritual sense. These books were written about Christ, but the spiritual sense was hidden from the people until Christ himself came to humanity and opened the secrets of the books according to the spiritual sense.

8   *Alii evangelistae ferunt quia panes et pisces Dominus discipulis
distribuisset, discipuli autem ministraverunt turbis.* He tobræc
ða fif hlafas and sealde his leorningcnihtum, and het beran
ðam folce; forðon þe he tæhte him ða gastlican lare, and hi
ferdon geond ealne middangeard and bodedon swa swa him
Crist sylf tæhte. Mid þam ðe he tobræc ða hlafas, þa wæron
hi gemenigfylde and weoxon him on handum; forðon ðe
ða fif bec wurdon gastlice asmeade, and wise lareowas hi
trahtnodon and setton of ðam bocum manega oðre bec; and
we mid þæra boca lare beoð dæghwomlice gastlice gereordode.

9   Þa hlafas wæron berene. Bere is swiðe earfoðe to gearci-
genne, and þeah hwæðere fet ðone mann þonne he gearo
bið. Swa wæs seo ealde æ swiðe earfoðe and digle to understandenne, ac ðeah hwæðere þonne we cumað to ðam smed-
man, þæt is to ðære getacnunge, þonne gereordað heo ure
mod and gestrangað mid þære diglan lare. Fif hlafas ðær
wæron, and fif ðusend manna þær wæron gereordode;
forðan ðe þæt Iudeisce folc wæs underðeodd Godes æ, ðe
stod on fif bocum awriten. Þa ða Crist axode Philippum and
he his afandode, swa swa we ær ræddon, þa getacnode he
mid þære acsunge þæs folces nytennysse þe wæs under ðære
æ and ne cuðe þæt gastlice andgit ðe on ðære æ bediglod
wæs.

10   Ða twegen fixas getacnodon sealmsang and ðæra witegena cwydas. An ðæra gecydde and bodode Cristes tocyme
mid sealmsange, and oðer mid witegunge. Nu sind þa twa
gesetnyssa, þæt is, sealmsang and witegung, swylce hi syf-
linge wæron to ðam fif berenum hlafum, þæt is, to ðam fif
ælicum bocum. Þæt folc þe ðær gereordode sæt up on ðam
gærse; þæt gærs getacnode flæsclice gewilnunge, swa swa se

Other Evangelists report that the Lord distributed the bread   8
and fish to his disciples, and the disciples served the crowd. He
broke the five loaves and gave them to his disciples, and
commanded them to bear them to the people; for he taught
them the spiritual teaching, and they went throughout all
the world and preached as Christ himself had taught. When
he broke the loaves, they were multiplied and grew in his
hands; for the five books were spiritually interpreted, and
wise teachers explicated them and from these books set
forth many other books; and with the teaching of those
books we are spiritually fed every day.

The loaves were of barley. Barley is very difficult to pre-   9
pare, and yet once it is prepared, it feeds a person. So was
the old law very difficult and obscure to understand, but
when we come to the flour, that is, to the significance, it
nourishes and strengthens our mind with its hidden teaching. There were five loaves, and five thousand people were
fed there; because the Jewish people were subject to God's
law, which stood written in five books. When Christ asked
Philip and tested him, as we read before, he indicated by
that question the ignorance of the people who were under
the law and who did not know the spiritual sense hidden in
that law.

The two fish signified the psalms and the sayings of the   10
prophets. One of these announced and proclaimed Christ's
coming with psalms, and the other with prophecy. Now
these two compositions, that is, the psalms and the prophets, are like relish to the five barley loaves, that is, to the five
books of the law. The people who ate there sat on the grass;
the grass signified fleshly desire, as the prophet said, "All

witega cwæð, "Ælc flæsc is gærs, and þæs flæsces wuldor is swilce wyrta blostm." Nu sceal gehwa se ðe wile sittan æt Godes gereorde and brucan þære gastlican lare oftredan þæt gærs and ofsittan, þæt is, þæt he sceal ða flæsclican lustas gewyldan, and his lichaman to Godes þeowdome symle gebigan.

11 Þær wæron getealde æt ðam gereorde fif ðusend wera, forðon þe ða menn þe to ðam gastlican gereorde belimpað sceolon beon werlice geworhte, swa swa se apostol cwæð— he cwæð, "Beoð wacole, and standað on geleafan, and onginnað werlice, and beoð gehyrte." Ðeah gif wifmann bið werlice geworht, and strang to Godes willan, heo bið þonne geteald to ðam werum þe æt Godes mysan sittað. "Þusend" getel bið fulfremed, and ne astihð nan getel ofer þæt. Mid þam getele bið getacnod seo fulfremednys ðæra manna ðe gereordiað heora sawla mid Godes lare.

12 "Se hælend het þa gegadrian þa lafe, þæt hi losian ne sceoldon; and hi ða gefyldon twelf wilion mid þam bricum." Ða lafe ðæs gereordes, þæt sind ða deopnyssa ðære lare þe woroldmen understandan ne magon, þa sceolon ða lareowas gegaderian, þæt hi ne losian, and healdan on heora fætelsum, þæt is on heora heortan, and habban æfre gearo to teonne forð þone wisdom and ða lare ægðer ge ðære ealdan æ ge ðære niwan. Hi ða gegaderodon twelf wilian fulle mid þam bricum. Þæt twelffealde getel getacnode þa twelf apostolas, þe hi underfengon þa digelnyssa þære lare ðe þæt læwede folc undergitan ne mihte.

13 "Þæt folc ða þe þæt wundor geseah cwædon be Criste þæt he wære soð witega ðe toweard wæs." Soð hi sædon, sumera ðinga: witega he wæs, forðan ðe he wiste ealle towearde þing, and eac fela ðing witegode ðe beoð gefyllede

flesh is grass, and the glory of the flesh is like the blooming of plants." Now anyone who wants to sit at God's meal and partake of spiritual teaching should tread on the grass and press it down, that is, he should overcome fleshly lusts, and always incline his body to God's service.

At that feast there were counted five thousand men, be- 11
cause those who belong to the spiritual meal should be manfully made, as the apostle said—he said, "Be watchful, and stand on faith, and undertake manfully, and be bold." If a woman is manfully made, however, and strong to God's will, she will be counted among the men who sit at God's table. "Thousand" signifies a perfect number, and no number extends beyond it. With that number is signified the perfection of those who nourish their souls with God's teaching.

"The savior commanded them to gather the remainder, 12
so that it would not be lost; and they filled twelve baskets with the fragments." Our teachers should gather the remainder of the feast, that is, the depth of the teaching which people in the world may not understand, so that it may not be lost, and keep it in their pouches, that is, in their hearts, and always be ready to draw forth the wisdom and teaching of both the old law and the new. They gathered twelve baskets full of the fragments. The twelvefold number signified the twelve apostles, because they received the mysteries of the teaching which lay people could not understand.

"The people who saw that miracle said of Christ that he 13
was the true prophet who was to come." They spoke the truth, in some ways: he was a prophet, because he knew all future things, and also prophesied many things which will

butan twyn. He is witega, and he is ealra witegena witegung, forðan ðe ealle witegan be him witegodon, and Crist gefylde heora ealra witegunga. Þæt folc geseah ða þæt wundor and hi ðæs swiðe wundredon. Þæt wundor is awriten, and we hit gehyrdon. Þæt ðe on him heora eagan gedydon, þæt deð ure geleafa on us. Hi hit gesawon, and we his gelyfað þe hit ne gesawon; and we sind forði beteran getealde, swa swa se hælend be us on oðre stowe cwæð, "Eadige beoð þa þe me ne geseoð, and hi hwæðere gelyfað on me, and mine wundra mærsiað."

14   Þæt folc cwæð ða be Criste þæt he wære soð witega. Nu cweðe we be Criste þæt he is ðæs lifigendan Godes Sunu, se ðe wæs toweard to alysenne ealne middangeard fram deofles anwealde and fram hellewite. Þæt folc ne cuðe ðæra goda þæt hi cwædon þæt he God wære, ac sædon þæt he witega wære. We cweðað nu, mid fullum geleafan, þæt Crist is soð witega, and ealra witegena witega, and þæt he is soðlice ðæs ælmihtigan Godes Sunu, ealswa mihtig swa his Fæder, mid ðam he leofað and rixað on annysse ðæs Halgan Gastes, a butan ende on ecnysse. Amen.

undoubtedly be fulfilled. He is a prophet, and he is the prophecy of all prophets, for all the prophets have prophesied of him, and Christ has fulfilled the prophecies of them all. The people saw the miracle and they greatly wondered at it. That miracle is recorded, and we have heard it. What their eyes did for them, our faith does for us. They saw it, and we who did not see it believe it; we are therefore considered better, as the savior said of us in another place, "Blessed are they who do not see me, and yet believe in me, and proclaim my miracles."

The people said then that Christ was a true prophet. 14 Now we say of Christ that he is the Son of the living God, who was to come to redeem the whole world from the power of the devil and the torment of hell. The people did not know the benefits of being able to say that he was God, but they said that he was a prophet. With full faith, we say now that Christ is a true prophet, and prophet of all prophets, and that he is truly Son of the almighty God, as mighty as his Father, with whom he lives and reigns in the unity of the Holy Spirit, forever without end to eternity. Amen.

13

VIII KALENDAS APRILIS

Annunciatio sanctae Mariae

M issus est Gabrihel angelus, et reliqua.

2   Ure se ælmihtiga scyppend, se ðe ealle gesceafta buton
ælcon antimbre þurh his wisdom gesceop, and þurh his willan geliffæste, he gesceop mancynn to ði þæt hi sceoldon
mid gehyrsumnysse and eadmodnysse ða heofenlican geðincðe geearnigan þe se deofol mid ofermettum forwyrhte.
Þa wearð eac se mann mid deofles lotwrencum bepæht, swa
þæt he tobræc his scyppendes bebod and wearð deofle
betæht and eal his ofspring into hellewite. Ða ðeah hwæðere
ofðuhte ðam ælmihtigum Gode ealles mancynnes yrmða,
and smeade hu he mihte his handgeweorc of deofles anwealde alysan; forði him ofhreow þæs mannes, forðon ðe
he wæs bepæht mid þæs deofles searocræftum. Ac him ne
ofhreow na ðæs deofles hryre, forðan ðe he næs þurh nane
tihtinge forlæred, ac he sylf asmeade ða upahefednysse þe
he ðurh ahreas; and he forði a on ecnysse wunað on forwyrde
wælræw deofol.

3   Þa fram frymðe mancynnes cydde se ælmihtiga God,
hwilon ðurh getacnunga, hwilon ðurh witegunga, þæt he
wolde mancynn ahreddan þurh ðone þe he ealle gesceafta
mid geworhte, ðurh his agen Bearn. Nu wæron ða witegunga
swiðe menigfealdlice gesette on halgum gewritum ær ðam

13

Annunciation

MARCH 25

The Annunciation of Saint Mary

The angel Gabriel was sent, etc.

Our almighty creator, who made all creatures through his   2
wisdom without any material, and gave them life through
his will, made humanity so that they should merit through
obedience and humility the heavenly honors that the devil
lost through arrogance. Then the human too was deceived
by the devil's tricks, so that he broke the creator's commandment and was delivered with all his offspring to the
devil in the torments of hell. But the almighty God regretted the miseries of all humankind, and considered how he
might redeem his handiwork from the power of the devil;
and so he took pity on humanity, because they had been deceived by the devil's deception. He did not regret the devil's
fall, because he had not been misled through any enticement, but he himself devised the presumption by which he
fell; and so he remains a bloodthirsty devil in damnation for
all eternity.

From the beginning of humanity, almighty God made   3
known, sometimes by signs, sometimes by prophecies, that
he would redeem humanity through the one with whom he
had made all creation, his own Son. Now, there were very
many prophecies recorded in the holy scriptures before the

ðe se Godes Sunu menniscnysse underfenge. Sume wæron eac be ðære eadigan Marian gewitegode. An ðæra witegunga is Isaiae, se awrat betwux his witegungum, þus cweðende, "Efne sceal mæden geeacnian on hire innoðe and acennan sunu, and his nama bið geciged *Emmanuhel,*" þæt is gereht on urum geðeode, "God is mid us." Eft Ezechihel se witega geseah on his witegunge an belocen geat on Godes huse, and him cwæð to sum engel, "Þis geat ne bið nanum menn geopenod, ac se hlaford ana færð inn þurh þæt geat, and eft ut færð, and hit bið belocen on ecnysse." Þæt beclysede geat on Godes huse getacnode þone halgan mæigðhad þære eadigan Marian. Se Hlaford, ealra hlaforda Hlaford, þæt is Crist, becom on hire innoð, and ðurh hi on menniscnysse wearð acenned, and þæt geat bið belocen on ecnysse; þæt is, þæt Maria wæs mæden ær ðære cenninge, and mæden on ðære cenninge, and mæden æfter ðære cenninge.

4   Þa witegunga be Cristes acennednysse and be ðære eadigan Marian mægðhade sindon swiðe menigfealdlice on ðære ealdan æ gesette, and se ðe hi asmeagan wile þær he hi afint mid micelre genihtsumnysse. Eac se apostol Paulus cwæð, "Þa þa ðæra tida gefyllednys com, ða sende God Fæder his Sunu to mancynnes alysednysse." Seo wurðfulle sand wearð on ðisum dæge gefylled, swa swa Cristes boc us gewissað, þus cweðende, "Godes heahengel Gabrihel wæs asend fram Gode to ðære Galileiscan byrig Nazareth to ðam mædene þe wæs Maria gehaten; and heo asprang of Dauides cynne, þæs maran cyninges, and heo wæs beweddod þam rihtwisan Iosepe." Þa stop se engel Gabrihel to ðam mædene and cwæð hire to, "*Ave,*" þæt is on urum gereorde greting word. "'*Ave, gratia plena, dominus tecum; benedicta tu in mulieribus.* Beo þu gesund. Ðu eart afylled mid Godes gife and God is

Son of God assumed human nature. Some of these were also prophesied of the blessed Mary. One of these prophecies is by Isaiah, who wrote among his prophecies, "Behold, a virgin shall conceive in her womb and bring forth a son, and his name shall be called *Emmanuel*," that is interpreted in our language, "God is with us." Also Ezekiel the prophet saw in his prophecy a locked gate in God's house, and an angel said to him, "This gate shall not be opened to anyone, for the Lord alone will go in by that gate, and go out again, and it will be shut for eternity." That closed gate in God's house signified the holy virginity of the blessed Mary. The Lord, Lord of all lords, that is, Christ, entered her womb, and through her was brought forth in human nature, and that gate is shut for eternity; that is, Mary was a virgin before the birth, a virgin at the birth, and a virgin after the birth.

The prophecies of the birth of Christ and the virginity of 4 the blessed Mary are recorded very frequently in the old law, and he who wishes to search for them will find them there in great abundance. Also the apostle Paul said, "When the fullness of time came, then God the Father sent his Son for the redemption of humankind." The glorious mission was fulfilled on this day, as Christ's book shows us, saying, "God's archangel Gabriel was sent from God to the city of Nazareth in Galilee to the virgin who was called Mary; she descended from the tribe of the great king David, and she was betrothed to the righteous Joseph." The angel Gabriel went to the virgin and said to her, "*Ave*," that is in our language a word of greeting. "*Hail, full of grace, the Lord is with you; blessed are you among women*. Be well. You are filled with God's

mid ðe. And þu eart gebletsod betwux wimmanum.' Þa ða þæt mæden ðas word gehyrde, ða wearð heo astyred and smeade þæt seo greting wære. Ða cwæð se engel to hyre, 'Ne beo ðu na afyrht, Maria. Ðu hæfst micele gife mid Gode. Efne ðu scealt geeacnian on ðinum innoðe and þu acenst sunu, and ðu hætst his naman Hiesus. Þes bið mære and micel and he bið geciged Sunu þæs hehstan, and him bið forgifen Dauides cynesetl. And he rixað on ecnysse ofer Iacobes hired, and ne bið nan ende his rices.' Ða andwyrde Maria ðam engle, 'Hu mæg ðis geworðan, forðan ðe ic ne bruce nanes weres?' Þa andwyrde se engel, 'Se Halga Gast becymð on ðe, and miht ðæs hehstan ofersceadwað þe, forði eac þæt halige þe of ðe bið acenned bið geciged Godes Sunu. And efne ðin mage Elisabeth geeacnode and sceal acennan cild on hire ylde þe ær on geogoðe ne mihte ac wæs gehaten unwæstmbære, þe ne bið nan ðing Gode unarefnigendlic. Þes monoð is se sixta monað siððan heo mid cilde wæs.' Þa cwæð seo eadige Maria to ðam engle, 'Ic eom Godes ðinen; getimige me æfter ðinum worde.' Ða gewat se engel of hyre gesihðe."

5 Ure alysednysse anginn we gehyrdon on ðisre dægþer-lican rædinge, þurh ða we awurpon þa derigendlican eald-nysse, and we sind getealde betwux Godes bearnum þurh Cristes flæsclicnysse. Swiðe þæslic anginn menniscre alysed-nysse wæs þæt þa se engel wearð asend fram Gode to ðam mædene, to cyðenne Godes acennednysse þurh hi; forðan ðe se forma intinga mennisces forwyrdes wæs þa þa se deo-fol asende oðerne deofol on næddran anlicnysse to ðam frumsceapenan wife Euan, hi to beswicenne. Us becom ða dead and forwyrd þurh wif, and us becom eft lif and hred-ding þurh wimman. Se heahengel ðe cydde þæs hælendes

grace and God is with you. And you are blessed among women.' When the virgin heard these words, she was moved and wondered what that greeting might be. The angel said to her, 'Do not be afraid, Mary. You have great favor with God. Behold, you will conceive in your womb and bear a son, and you will call his name Jesus. He will be famous and mighty, and he will be called the Son of the most high, and to him will be given the throne of David. And he will rule in eternity over the tribe of Jacob, and of his kingdom there will be no end.' Then Mary answered the angel, 'How can this be, because I do not have sexual relations with any man?' The angel answered, 'The Holy Spirit will come over you, and the power of the most high will overshadow you, and so the holy one that will be born of you will be called the Son of God. And look, your kinswoman Elizabeth has conceived and will bear a child in her old age, who could not in her youth and was called barren, because nothing is impossible for God. This is the sixth month since she has been with child.' Then the blessed Mary said to the angel, 'I am God's handmaid; let it be done to me according to your word.' Then the angel departed from her sight."

In this day's reading we have heard the beginning of our 5 redemption, through which we have cast off harmful old age, and are counted among God's children through Christ's incarnation. It was a very fitting beginning to human redemption when the angel was sent from God to the virgin, to announce the birth of God through her; because the first cause of human destruction was when the devil sent another devil in the likeness of a serpent to the first-created woman Eve, in order to deceive her. Death and destruction came to us through a woman, and later, life and salvation came to us through a woman. The archangel who announced the

acennednysse wæs gehaten *Gabrihel,* þæt is gereht "Godes
strengð"; þone he bodode toweardne, þe se sealmsceop mid
þisum wordum herede: "Drihten is strang and mihtig on
gefeohte"—on ðam gefeohte, butan tweon, þe se hælend
deofol oferwann, and middangeard him ætbræd.

6   "Maria wæs beweddod Iosepe ðam rihtwisan." Hwi wolde
God beon acenned of beweddodan mædene? For micclum
gesceade, and eac for neode. Þæt Iudeisce folc heold Godes
æ on þam timan; seo æ tæhte þæt man sceolde ælcne wimman þe cild hæfde butan rihtre æwe stænan. Nu ðonne, gif
Maria unbeweddod wære and cild hæfde, þonne wolde þæt
Iudeisce folc, æfter Godes æ, mid stanum hi oftorfian. Ða
wæs heo, ðurh Godes foresceawunge, þam rihtwisan were
beweddod, and gehwa wende þæt he ðæs cildes fæder wære,
ac he næs. Ac ða ða Ioseph undergeat þæt Maria mid cilde
wæs þa wearð he dreorig, and nolde hire genealæcan, ac
ðohte þæt he wolde hi diglice forlætan. Þa ða Ioseph þis
smeade, þa com him to Godes engel and bebead him þæt he
sceolde habban gymene ægðer ge ðære meder ge þæs cildes,
and cwæð þæt þæt cild nære of nanum men gestryned, ac
wære of þam Halgan Gaste. Nis na hwæðere se Halga Gast
Cristes fæder, ac he is genemned to ðære fremminge Cristes
menniscnysse forðan ðe he is willa and lufu þæs Fæder and
þæs Suna. Nu wearð seo menniscnys þurh ðone micclan
willan gefremed, and is ðeah hwæðere heora ðreora weorc
untodæledlic. Hi sind þry on hadum, Fæder, and Sunu, and
Halig Gast, and an God untodæledlic on anre godcundnysse. Ioseph ða, swa swa him se engel bebead, hæfde gymene ægðer ge Marian ge ðæs cildes, and wæs hyre gewita
þæt heo mæden wæs, and wæs Cristes fostorfæder, and mid
his fultume and frofre on gehwilcum ðingum him ðenode on
ðære menniscnysse.

savior's birth was called *Gabriel*, which is interpreted as "God's strength"; he announced what was to come, which the psalmist praised in these words: "The Lord is strong and mighty in battle"—no doubt in the battle in which the savior overcame the devil, and took the world from him.

"Mary was betrothed to the righteous Joseph." Why 6 would God be born of a betrothed virgin? For a great reason, and also of necessity. The Jewish people held God's law at that time; the law directed that any woman who had a child out of lawful wedlock should be stoned. Now, therefore, if Mary had been unmarried and had a child, the Jewish people, according to God's law, would have killed her with stones. And so she was, by God's providence, betrothed to that righteous man, and everyone thought that he was the child's father, but he was not. When Joseph understood that Mary was with child he became sad, and would not approach her, but thought that he would privately abandon her. While Joseph was considering this, God's angel came to him and commanded him to take care of both the mother and the child, and said that the child was not begotten by a man, but by the Holy Spirit. Yet the Holy Spirit is not Christ's father, but he is named as the maker of Christ's humanity because he is the will and love of the Father and the Son. Now his humanity was made through the great will, and yet it is the indivisible work of the three of them. They are three in persons, Father, and Son, and Holy Spirit, and one indivisible God in one divine nature. Joseph then, as the angel had commanded him, took care of both Mary and the child, and was her witness that she was a virgin, and was Christ's foster father and, with his support and comfort in all things, served him in his human state.

7   Se engel grette Marian, and cwæð þæt heo wære mid
Godes gife afylled, and þæt hyre wæs God mid, and heo wæs
gebletsod betwux wifum. Soðlice heo wæs mid Godes gife
afylled, forðon ðe hire wæs getiðod þæt heo ðone abær þe
astealde ealle gifa and ealle soðfæstnyssa. God wæs mid hire,
forðan ðe he wæs on hire innoðe belocen se ðe belicð ealne
middangeard on his anre handa. And heo wæs gebletsod
betwux wifum, forðan ðe heo, butan wiflicre bysnunge, mid
wlite hyre mægðhades, wæs modor þæs ælmihtigan Godes.

8   Se engel gehyrte hi mid his wordum, and cwæð hire to,
"Efne ðu scealt geeacnian on þinum innoðe, and þu acenst
sunu." Oncnawað nu, þurh ðas word, soðne mannan acen-
nedne of mædenlicum lichaman. His nama wæs *Hiesus,* þæt
is, "hælend," forðan ðe he gehælð ealle ða þe on hine rihtlice
gelyfað. "Þes bið mære, and he bið geciged Sunu þæs hex-
stan." Gelyfað nu, þurh ðas word, þæt he is soð God of
soðum Gode, and efenece his Fæder, of ðam he wæs æfre
acenned butan anginne. Crist heold Dauides cynesetl, na
lichamlice ac gastlice, forðan ðe he is ealra cyninga cyning,
and rixað ofer his gecorenan menn, ægðer ge ofer Israhela
folc ge ofer ealle oðre leodscipas ða ðe on rihtum geleafan
wuniað; and Crist hi ealle gebrincð to his ecan rice. Israhel is
gecweden "God geseonde," and Iacob is gecweden "forscrencend." Nu ða men ðe God geseoð mid heora mode
þurh geleafan, and þa ðe leahtras forscrencað, hi belimpað
to Godes rice, þe næfre ne ateorað.

9   Þa cwæð Maria to ðam engle, "Hu mæg þæt beon þæt ic
cild hæbbe, forðan ðe ic nanes weres ne bruce? Ic geteohode
min lif on mægðhade to geendigenne; hu mæg hit ðonne
gewurðan þæt ic, butan weres gemanan, cennan scyle?" Þa
andwyrde se engel ðam mædene, "Se Halga Gast cymð ufen

The angel greeted Mary, and said that she was filled with 7
God's grace, and that God was with her, and she was blessed
among women. Truly she was filled with God's grace, for it
was granted to her that she should bear the one who established all grace and all truth. God was with her, because he
who encloses the whole earth with one hand was enclosed in
her womb. And she was blessed among women, for she,
without female example, with the beauty of her virginity,
was mother of almighty God.

The angel encouraged her with his words, and said to her, 8
"Behold, you will conceive in your womb, and you will bear a
son." Recognize now, through these words, a true man born
of a virgin's body. His name was *Jesus,* that is "savior," because he saves all those who rightly believe in him. "He will
be great, and he will be called the Son of the most high."
Believe now, through these words, that he is true God of
true God, and coeternal with his Father, of whom he was
eternally begotten without beginning. Christ held David's
throne, not physically but spiritually, because he is king of
all kings, and rules over his chosen people, both the people
of Israel and all other nations who abide in the right faith;
and Christ will bring them all to his eternal kingdom. Israel
is interpreted "seeing God," and Jacob is interpreted "supplanter." Now those who see God in their mind through
faith, and those who root out sins, belong to God's kingdom, which will never fail.

Then Mary said to the angel, "How can it be that I should 9
have a child, for I have no sexual relations with any man? I
have resolved to end my life in virginity; how can it then be
that I, without the company of a man, should bear a child?"
The angel answered the virgin, "The Holy Spirit will come

on ðe, and miht ðæs hyhstan ofersceadewað ðe." Þurh ðæs
Halgan Gastes fremminge, swa swa we ær cwædon, wearð
Crist acenned on ðære menniscnysse; and Maria his modor
wæs ofersceadewed ðurh mihte þæs Halgan Gastes. Hu wæs
heo ofersceadewod? Heo wæs swa ofersceadewod þæt heo
wæs geclænsod and gescyld wið ealle leahtras þurh mihte
ðæs Halgan Gastes, and mid heofenlicum gifum gefylled and
gehalgod.

10   Se engel cwæð, "Þæt halige þe of ðe bið acenned bið geciged Godes Sunu." Witodlice ealle menn beoð, swa swa se
witega cwæð, mid unrihtwisnysse geeacnode and mid synnum acennede, ac ure hælend ana wæs geeacnod butan unrihtwisnysse and butan synnum acenned; and he wæs halig
þærrihte swa hraðe swa he mann wæs, and fulfremed God,
þæs ælmihtigan Godes Sunu, on anum hade mann and God.
Ða cwæð Maria to ðam engle, "Ic eom Godes ðinen; getimige me æfter ðinum worde." Micel eadmodnys wunode
on hyre mode þa þa heo ðus cleopode. Ne cwæð heo na, ic
eom Godes modor, oððe, ic eom cwen ealles middangeardes,
ac cwæð, "Ic eom Godes þinen"; swa swa us mynegað þæt
halige gewrit, þus cweðende, "Þonne ðu mære sy, geeadmed
þe sylfne on eallum ðingum, and ðu gemetst gife and lean
mid Gode." Heo cwæð to ðam engle, "Getimige me æfter
ðinum worde," þæt is, gewurðe hit swa ðu segst, þæt ðæs
ælmihtigan Godes Sunu becume on minne innoð, and
mennisce edwiste of me genime, and to alysednysse middangeardes forðstæppe of me, swa swa brydguma of his bryd-
bedde.

11   Þus becom ure hælend on Marian innoð on þissum dæge,
ðe is gehaten *Annuntiatio sanctae Mariae,* þæt is, Marian
Bodungdæg gecweden; on þam dæge bodode se heahengel

over you, and the power of the most high will overshadow you." Through the working of the Holy Spirit, as we said earlier, Christ was born in human nature; and Mary his mother was overshadowed by the power of the Holy Spirit. How was she overshadowed? She was so overshadowed that she was purified and shielded from all sins by the power of the Holy Spirit, and filled and sanctified with heavenly grace.

The angel said, "The holy one that will be born of you will be called the Son of God." Truly all people, as the prophet said, are conceived in unrighteousness and born in sins, but our savior alone was conceived without unrighteousness and born without sins; and he was holy as soon as he became human, and perfect God, the Son of the almighty God, human and God in one person. Then Mary said to the angel, "I am God's handmaid; let it be done to me according to your word." Great humility dwelled in her mind when she said this. She did not say, I am the mother of God, or, I am queen of the whole world, but said, "I am God's handmaid"; as the holy scripture warns us, saying, "When you are great, humble yourself in all things, and you will find grace and reward with God." She said to the angel, "Let it be done to me according to your word," that is, let it be as you say, that the Son of the almighty God should enter my womb, receive human substance from me, and proceed from me like a bridegroom from his bridal bed, for the redemption of the world.

Thus our savior entered the womb of Mary on this day, which is called the *Annunciation of Saint Mary,* that is, the Annunciation Day of Mary; on that day the archangel

Gabrihel ðam clænum mædene Godes tocyme to mannum ðurh hi, and heo gelyfde þæs engles bodunge, and swa mid geleafan onfeng God on hyre innoð, and hine bær oð mid-dewintres mæssedæg, and hine ða acende mid soðre men-niscnysse se ðe æfre wæs wunigende on godcundnysse mid his Fæder and mid þam Halgan Gaste, hi ðry an God un-todæledlic.

12   Nu seigð se godspellere þæt Maria ferde, æfter þæs engles bodunge, to hire magan Elisabeth, seo wæs Zacharian wif. Hi butu wæron rihtwise, and heoldon Godes beboda untæl-lice. Ða wæron hi butan cilde oð þæt hi wæron forwerede menn. Ða com se ylca engel Gabrihel to Zacharian syx monðum ær ðan ðe he come to Marian, and cydde þæt he sceolde be his ealdan wife sunu habban, Iohannem ðone Ful-luhtere. Þa wearð he ungeleafful þæs engles bodungum. Se engel ða him cwæð to, "Nu ðu nylt gelyfan minum wordum, beo ðu dumb oð þæt þæt cild beo acenned." And he ða adumbode on eallum ðam fyrste for his ungeleaffulnysse. "Nu com ða seo eadige Maria to his huse, and grette his wif, hyre magan Elisabeth. Ða mid þam þe þæt wif gehyrde þæs mædenes gretinge, ða blissode þæt cild Iohannes on his mo-dor innoðe, and seo moder wearð afylled mid þam Halgan Gaste, and heo clypode to Marian mid micelre stemne, and cwæð, 'Þu eart gebletsod betwux wifum, and gebletsod is se wæstm þines innoðes. Hu getimode me þæt mines Drihtnes moder wolde cuman to me? Efne mid þam þe seo stefn ðinre gretinge swegde on minum earum, ða blissode min cild on minum innoðe, and hoppode ongean his Drihten, þe þu berst on ðinum innoðe.'"

13   Þæt cild ne mihte na ða gyt mid wordum his hælend ge-gretan, ac he gegrette hine mid blissigendum mode. Heo

Gabriel announced to the pure virgin God's advent to humanity through her, and she believed the angel's announcement, and so with faith received God into her womb, and bore him until midwinter's Mass day, and then brought him forth in true human nature who was ever dwelling in divine nature with his Father and the Holy Spirit, those three one indivisible God.

Now the Evangelist says that after the angel's announcement, Mary went to her cousin Elizabeth, who was the wife of Zechariah. They were both righteous, and held God's commandments blamelessly. They were childless until they were old and feeble. Then the same angel Gabriel came to Zechariah six months before he came to Mary, and announced that he should have a son, John the Baptist, by his aged wife. He did not believe the angel's announcement. The angel then said to him, "Since you will not believe my words, you will be mute until the child is born." And he was mute during all that time for his disbelief. "Now the blessed Mary came to his house, and greeted his wife, her cousin Elizabeth. When the woman heard the virgin's greeting, the child John rejoiced in his mother's womb, and the mother was filled with the Holy Spirit, and she cried to Mary with a loud voice, and said, 'Blessed are you among women, and blessed is the fruit of your womb. How can it be that the mother of my Lord should come to me? As soon as the voice of your greeting sounded in my ears, my child rejoiced in my womb, and leaped toward his Lord, whom you bear in your womb."

The child could not yet greet his savior with words, but he greeted him with a rejoicing mind. She said, "Blessed are

cwæð, "Eadig eart ðu, Maria, forðon ðe þu gelyfdest þam wordum ðe þe fram Gode gebodode wæron, and hit bið gefremmed swa swa hit ðe gecydd wæs." Ða sang Maria þærrihte ðone lofsang þe we singað on Godes cyrcan æt ælcum æfensange, "*Magnificat anima mea Dominum,*" and forð oð ende, þæt is, "Min sawul mærsað Drihten, and min gast blissað on minum halwendum Gode, forðan ðe he geseh þa eadmodnysse his ðinene. Efne nu forði ealle mægða mancynnes hatad me eadige and gesælige; and Godes mildheortnys is fram mægðe to mægðe, ofer ða þe hine ondrædað. He gefremede micelle mihte on his strencðe, and tostencte ða modigan. He awearp ða rican of setle, and he ahof ða eadmodan. He gefylde ða hungrian mid his godum, and he forlet ða rican idele. He underfeng his cnapan Israhel, gemyndig his mildheortnysse, swa swa he spræc to urum fæderum, Abrahame and his ofspringe on worulda."

14   Langsum hit bið þæt we ealne þisne lofsang ofertrahtnian, ac we wyllað scortlice oferyrnan ða digelystan word. "God awearp ða rican of setle" — þæt sind ða modigan, ðe hi onhebbað ofer heora mæðe. "And he ahof ða eadmodan," swa swa Crist sylf cwæð on his godspelle, "Ælc ðæra þe hine onhefð, he sceal beon geeadmet, and se ðe hine geeadmet, he sceal beon ahafen."

15   "God gefylð þa hingrigendan mid his godum," swa swa he sylf cwæð, "Eadige beoð þa þe sind ofhingrode and oflyste rihtwisnysse, forðan ðe hi sceolon beon gefyllede mid rihtwisnysse." "He forlet ða rican idele" — þæt sind ða rican þa ðe mid modignysse þa eorðlican welan lufiað swiðor þonne ða heofonlican. Fela riccra manna geðeoð Gode, þæra ðe swa doð swa swa hit awriten is, "Þæs rican mannes welan

you, Mary, because you have believed the words that were announced to you from God, and it will be accomplished as it has been declared to you." Then at once Mary sang the hymn of praise which we sing in God's church at every Vespers, *My soul magnifies the Lord,* and so forth to the end, that is, "My soul magnifies the Lord, and my spirit rejoices in my saving God, for he has seen the humility of his handmaid. Behold, now all nations of humankind will call me blessed and fortunate; and God's mercy is from nation to nation, over those who fear him. He has worked great power in his strength, and scattered the proud. He has cast down the mighty from their thrones, and has lifted up the lowly. He has filled the hungry with his good things, and the rich he has sent away empty. He has received his servant Israel, mindful of his mercy, as he said to our fathers, to Abraham and his offspring forever."

It would be tedious for us to explain all this hymn, but we 14 will shortly run through its most obscure words. "God has cast down the mighty from their thrones"—these are the proud, who lift themselves up above their station. "And he has lifted up the lowly," as Christ himself said in his gospel, "Everyone who exalts himself will be humbled, and he who humbles himself will be exalted."

"God fills the hungry with his good things," as he himself 15 said, "Blessed are those who are hungry and longing for righteousness, for they shall be filled with righteousness." "He has sent the rich away empty"—those are the rich who in their pride love earthly riches more than heavenly. Many rich men prosper in God, those who do as it is written, "The

sind his sawle alysendnyss." His welan beoð his sawle alysednyss gif he mid þam gewitendlicum gestreonum beceapað
him þæt ece lif, and ða heofonlican welan mid Gode. Gif he
ðis forgymeleasað, and besett his hiht on ðam eorðlicum
welan, þonne forlæt God hine idelne and æmtigne fram ðam
ecum godnyssum.

16   "God underfeng his cnapan Israhel." Mid þam naman
syndon getacnode ealle ða þe Gode gehyrsumiað mid soðre
eadmodnysse, þa he underfechð to his werode. "Swa swa he
spræc to urum fæderum, Abrahame and his ofspringe on
worulda." God behet ðam heahfædere Abrahame þæt on his
cynne sceolde beon gebletsod eal mancynn. Of Abrahames
cynne asprang seo gesælige Maria, and of Marian com Crist,
æfter ðære menniscnysse, and þurh Crist beoð ealle ða geleaffullan gebletsode. Ne synd we na Abrahames cynnes
flæsclice, ac gastlice, swa swa se apostol Paulus cwæð,
"Witodlice, gif ge Cristene synd, þonne beo ge Abrahames
ofspring, and yrfenuman æfter behate." Þæt æftemyste
word is ðises lofsanges "on worulda," forðan ðe ure behat, þe
us God behet, ðurhwunað a on worulda woruld butan ende.

17   Uton biddan nu þæt eadige and þæt gesælige mæden
Marian þæt heo us geðingige to hyre agenum Suna and to
hire scyppende, hælende Criste, se ðe gewylt ealra ðinga mid
Fæder and mid þam Halgum Gaste, a on ecnysse. Amen.

rich man's wealth is his soul's redemption." His wealth is his soul's redemption if he buys eternal life for himself with those transitory treasures, and heavenly wealth with God. If he neglects this, and sets his hope on earthly wealth, then God will send him away idle and empty from eternal goodness.

"God has received his servant Israel." By that name are 16 signified all those who obey God with true humility, whom he receives into his company. "As he said to our fathers, to Abraham and his offspring forever." God promised the patriarch Abraham that in his tribe all humanity should be blessed. From the tribe of Abraham sprang the blessed Mary, and from Mary came Christ, according to his human nature, and through Christ all the faithful will be blessed. We are not of Abraham's tribe physically, but spiritually, as the apostle Paul said, "Truly, if you are Christians, then you are Abraham's offspring, and heirs according to the promise." The last word of this hymn is "forever," because our promise, which God has promised us, endures for ever and ever without end.

Let us now ask the blessed and fortunate virgin Mary to 17 intercede for us with her own Son and creator, the savior Christ, who rules all things with the Father and the Holy Spirit, forever in eternity. Amen.

14

In Dominica palmarum

Cum adpropinquasset Iesus Hierosolimis, et venisset Bethfage ad Montem Oliveti, et reliqua.

2   Cristes ðrowung wæs gerædd nu beforan us, ac we willað eow secgan nu ærest hu he com to ðære byrig Hierusalem and genealæhte his agenum deaðe, and nolde ða þrowunge mid fleame forbugan.

3   Se hælend ferde to ðære byrig Hierusalem, and ða ða he genealæhte ðære dune Oliueti, þa sende he his twegen leorningcnihtas, þus cweðende, "Gað to ðære byrig þe eow ongean is, and ge gemetað þærrihte getigedne assan and his folan samod. Untygað hi, and lædað to me. Gif eow hwa wiðstande, secgað þonne þæt se Hlaford heora behofað, and he hi sent eft ongean." Hi ða eodon and gemetton þone assan and his folan, and woldon lædan to ðam hælende. Þa cwæð þæs assan hlaford, "To hwi untige gyt ðone assan?" Hi cwædon swa swa him Crist bebead, and gebrohton ðone assan and his folan to ðam hælende, and wurpon heora reaf uppan ðone folan þe nan man ær ne bestrad, and se hælend rad uppan ðam folan to ðære byrig Hierusalem. Þis gewitegode ær Isaias se witega, ðus cweðende, "Secgað Siones dehter, efne ðin cyning cymð to ðe, swiðe geþwære, on assan ridende." Þa geaxode þæt geleaffulle folc binnan þære byrig þæt se hælend him wæs toweard, ða eodon hi togeanes him,

14

Palm Sunday

Palm Sunday

When Jesus was nearing Jerusalem, and he came to Bethphage at the Mount of Olives, etc.*

Christ's passion has just been read before us, but we first 2 want to tell you how he came to the city of Jerusalem and approached his own death, and would not avoid his passion by fleeing.

The savior went to the city of Jerusalem, and when he ap- 3 proached the Mount of Olives, he sent two of his disciples, saying, "Go to the city that is before you, and you will immediately find there an ass tied up together with its foal. Untie them, and lead them to me. If anyone stands in your way, say that the Lord has need of them, and he will send you away again." They went and found the ass and his foal, and wanted to lead them to the savior. Then the ass's master said, "Why do you two untie this ass?" They said as Christ commanded them, and brought the ass and its foal to the savior, and threw their garments over the foal, which no one had ever ridden before, and the savior rode on the foal to the city of Jerusalem. The prophet Isaiah had prophesied this, saying, "Say to Sion's daughter, behold your king is coming to you, very meek, riding on an ass." When the faithful people in the city learned that the savior was coming to

and wurpon hira reaf under þæs assan fet, and bricgodon
ðam hælende. Sume heawon bogas of treowum and ða wurpon under þæs assan fet, and eodon ða sume beforan, sume
bæftan, and hi ealle sungon, "Sy hælu Dauides bearne; sy gebletsod Israhela cyning, se ðe come on Godes naman. Beo
sibb on heofenum and wuldor on heannysse." Þam folce
wearð cuð þæt se hælend arærde lytle ær Lazarum of deaðe,
se þe læg stincende feower niht on byrgene. Þa comon þa
togeanes Criste þe geleaffulle wæron mid þam wurðmynte
swa we ær cwædon. Comon eac sume ða ungeleaffullan,
mid nanum wurðmynte ac mid micclum graman. Swa swa
Iohannes se godspellere cwæð þæt ða heafodmenn þæs
folces smeadon betwux him þæt hi woldon ofslean þone
Lazarum þe Crist of deaðe awrehte, forðan ðe manega ðæs
folces men gelyfdon on þone hælend þurh ðæs deadan
mannes ærist.

4   We wyllað nu fon on þone traht þissere rædinge. Þa
twegen leorningcnihtas þe Crist sende æfter þam assan
hi getacnodon þa lareowas þe God sende mancynne to
lærenne. Twegen hi wæron, for ðære getacnunge þe lareow
habban sceal. He sceal habban lare, þæt he mage Godes folc
mid wisdome læran to rihtum geleafan, and he sceal mid
godum weorcum ðam folce wel bysnian, and swa mid þam
twam ðingum, þæt is mid lare and godre gebysnunge, þæt
læwede folc gebige symle to Godes willan. Se getigeda assa
and his fola getacniað twa folc, þæt is Iudeisc and hæðen: ic
cweðe "hæðen" forði þe eal mennisc wæs ða gyt wunigende
on hæðenscipe, buton þam anum Iudeiscan folce, þe heold
þa ealdan æ on ðam timan. Hi wæron getigede, forðan ðe eal
mancyn wæs mid synnum bebunden, swa swa se witega
cwæð, "Anra gehwilc manna is gewriðen mid rapum his

them, they went out before him, and threw their garments under the ass's feet, and laid a path for the savior. Some cut branches from the trees and threw them under the ass's feet, and some went before, some behind, and they all sang, "Hail, son of David; blessed be the king of Israel, who comes in the name of God. Peace in the heavens and glory on high." The people knew that a short time before the savior had raised Lazarus from the dead, who lay stinking in the grave four nights. The believers came toward Christ with the honors we have mentioned. Some unbelievers also came, not with honors but with great anger. John the Evangelist said that the leaders of the people considered among themselves how they might kill Lazarus whom Christ raised from death, because many people believed in the savior because of the dead man's resurrection.

We will now take up the exposition of this reading. The 4 two disciples whom Christ sent after the ass signified the teachers God sent to instruct humanity. They were two, to signify what a teacher should have. He should have learning, that he may teach God's people with wisdom in true belief, and he should set a good example for the people by good works, and so with those two things, that is, with learning and good example, always draw the lay people to God's will. The tied ass and its foal signify two people, that is, the Jewish people and the heathens: I say "heathen" because all humanity was still dwelling in heathenism, except only for the Jewish people, who observed the old law at that time. They were tied, because all humanity was bound with sins, as the prophet said, "Every person is bound with the ropes of his

synna." Þa sende God his apostolas and heora æftergengan
to gebundenum mancynne, and het hi untigan and to him
lædan. Hu untigdon hi ðone assan and þone folan? Hi bodedon ðam folce rihtne geleafan and Godes beboda, and eac
mid micclum wundrum heora bodunge getrymdon. Þa
abeah þæt folc fram deofles þeowdome to Cristes biggen-
cum, and wæron alysede fram eallum synnum þurh þæt
halige fulluht, and to Criste gelædde.

5   Assa is stunt nyten and unclæne, and toforan oðrum nytenum ungesceadwis, and byrðenstrang. Swa wæron men, ær
Cristes tocyme, stunte and unclæne ða ða hi ðeowedon deofolgyldum and mislicum leahtrum, and bugon to þam anlicnyssum þe hi sylfe worhton, and him cwædon to, "Þu eart
min god." And swa hwilce byrðene swa him deofol on besette, þa hi bæron. Ac ða ða Crist com to mancynne, þa
awende he ure stuntnysse to gerade, and ure unclænnysse to
clænum ðeawum. Se getemeda assa hæfde getacnunge þæs
Iudeiscan folces, þe wæs getemed under þære ealdan æ. Se
wilda fola hæfde getacnunge ealles oðres folces, þe wæs þa
gyt hæðen and ungetemed; ac hi wurdon getemede and geleaffulle þa þa Crist sende his leorningcnihtas geond ealne
middangeard, þus cweðende, "Farað geond ealne middangeard, and lærað ealle ðeoda, and fulliað hi on naman þæs
Fæder, and þæs Suna, and þæs Halgan Gastes; and beodað
þæt hi healdon ealle ða beboda þe ic eow tæhte."

6   Þæra assena hlaford axode hwi hi untigdon his assan; swa
eac ða heafodmen gehwilces leodscipes woldon þwyrlice
wiðcweðan Godes bodunge. Ac ða ða hi gesawon þæt þa
bydelas gehældon, þurh Godes mihte, healte and blinde,
and dumbum spræce forgeafon, and eac ða deadan to life
arærdon, þa ne mihton hi wiðstandan þam wundrum, ac

sins." Then God sent his apostles and their successors to that bound humanity, and ordered them untied and led to him. How did they untie the ass and the foal? They preached right belief and God's commandments to the people, and also confirmed their preaching by many miracles. Then the people turned away from the service of the devil to the worship of Christ, and were freed from all sins through holy baptism, and thus led to Christ.

An ass is a foolish and unclean beast, more unreasoning 5 than other beasts, and strong for burdens. Likewise people, before Christ's coming, were foolish and unclean when they served idols and various sins, and bowed to the images they themselves had made, and said to them, "You are my god." And they bore whatever burdens the devil set on them. But when Christ came to humanity, he turned our foolishness to reason, and our uncleanness to pure conduct. The tamed ass signified the Jewish people, who were tamed under the old law. The wild foal signified all other people, who were still heathen and untamed; but they became tamed and believing when Christ sent his disciples over the whole earth, saying, "Go out over all the earth, and teach all nations, and baptize them in the name of the Father, and of the Son, and of the Holy Spirit; and command that they hold all the commandments which I have taught you."

The master of the asses asked why they untied his asses; 6 likewise the leaders of every people would perversely oppose God's preaching. But when they saw that the messengers, through God's might, healed the lame and the blind, and gave speech to the mute, and also raised the dead to life, then could they not oppose those miracles, but all finally

bugon ealle endemes to Gode. Cristes leorningcnihtas
cwædon, "Se Hlaford behofað þæra assena, and sent hi eft
ongean." Ne cwædon hi na "ure Hlaford," ne "ðin Hlaford,"
ac forðrihte, "Hlaford"; forðon ðe Crist is ealra hlaforda
Hlaford, ægðer ge manna ge ealra gesceafta. Hi cwædon,
"He sent hi eft ongean." We sind gemanode and gelaðode
to Godes rice, ac we ne sind na genedde. Þonne we sind
gelaðode, þonne sind we untigede; and ðonne we beoð forlætene to urum agenum cyre, þonne bið hit swilce we beon
ongean asende. Godes myldheortnys is þæt we untigede
syndon; ac gif we rihtlice lybbað þæt bið ægðer ge Godes
gifu ge eac ure agen geornfulnyss. We sceolon symle biddan
Drihtnes fultum, forðan ðe ure agen cyre næfð nænne forð-
gang buton he beo gefyrðrod þurh þone ælmihtigan.

7   Ne het Crist him to lædan modigne stedan mid gyldenum
gerædum gefreatewodne; ac þone wacan assan he geceas
him to byrðre, forðon þe he tæhte symle eadmodnysse, and
ðurh hine sylfne þa bysne sealde, and ðus cwæð, "Leorniað
æt me þæt ic eom liðe and swiðe eadmod, and ge gemetað
reste eowrum sawlum." Þis wæs gewitegod be Criste, and
ealle ða ðing þe he dyde, ær ðan þe he to men geboren wære.

8   *Sion* is an dun, and heo is gecweden "sceawungstow"; and
Hierusalem, "sibbe gesihð." Siones dohtor is seo gelaðung
geleaffulra manna, þe belimpð to ðære heofenlican Hierusalem, on þære is symle sibbe gesihð butan ælcere sace, to
ðære us gebrincð se hælend gif we him gelæstað.

9   Cristes leorningcnihtas ledon hyra reaf uppan þan assan,
þe he nolde on nacedum assan ridan. Reaf getacniað rihtwisnysse weorc, swa swa se witega cwæð, "Drihten, þine sacerdas sind ymbscrydde mid rihtwisnysse." Se nacoda assa bið
mid reafum gesadelod ðonne se idela man bið mid wisra

turned to God. Christ's disciples said, "The Lord needs the asses, and sends for them." They did not say "our Lord," or "your Lord," but simply, "the Lord"; for Christ is Lord of all lords, both of people and of all creatures. They said, "He sends for them." We are called and invited to God's kingdom, but we are not compelled. When we are invited, then are we untied; and when we are left to our own choice, then is it as though we are sent for. It is God's mercy that we are untied; but if we live rightly that is because of both God's grace and our own zeal. We should always pray for the Lord's support, because our own choice will have no success unless it is supported by the almighty.

Christ did not command them to lead to him a proud 7 steed adorned with golden harness; instead he chose a lowly ass to bear him, because he always taught humility, giving an example in himself, and said, "Learn from me that I am meek and very humble, and you will find rest for your souls." This and all the things Christ did were prophesied of him before he was born as a human being.

Sion is a hill, and it is interpreted "place of observation"; 8 and *Jerusalem,* "vision of peace." The daughter of Sion is the congregation of the faithful, who belong to the heavenly Jerusalem, in which there is always the vision of peace without any strife, to which the savior will bring us if we follow him.

Christ's disciples laid their garments upon the ass, so 9 he would not ride on a naked ass. Garments signify works of righteousness, as the prophet said, "Lord, your priests are clothed with righteousness." The naked ass is saddled with garments when the simple person is adorned for God's

lareowa mynegungum and gebisnungum to Godes handa gefrætwod; and he ðonne byrð Crist, swa swa se apostol cwæð,
"Ge sind gebohte mid micclum wurðe; wuldriað forði and
berað God on eowrum lichaman." God we berað on urum
lichaman forðan ðe we beoð tempel and fætels þæs Halgan
Gastes gif we us wið fule leahtras gescyldað, be ðam cwæð se
ylca apostol swiðe egeslice, "Se þe gewemð Godes tempel,
God hine fordeð." Se ðe ne bið Godes tempel he bið deofles
tempel, and byrð swiðe swære byrðene on his bæce.

10   We wyllað secgan eow sum bigspell. Ne mæg nan man
hine sylfne to cynge gedon, ac þæt folc hæfð cyre to ceo-
senne þone to cyninge þe him sylfum licað: ac siððan he to
cyninge gehalgod bið, þonne hæfð he anweald ofer þæt
folc, and hi ne magon his geoc of heora swuran asceacan.
Swa eac gehwilc man hæfð agenne cyre, ær ðam þe he syn-
gige, hweðer he wille filian deofles willan oððe wiðsacan.
Þonne gif he mid deofles weorcum hine sylfne bebint, ðonne
ne mæg he mid his agenre mihte hine unbindan buton se ælmihtiga God mid strangre handa his mildheortnysse hine
unbinde. Agenes willan and agenre gymeleaste he bið gebunden, ac þurh Godes mildheortnysse he bið unbunden,
gif he ða alysednysse eft æt Gode geearnað.

11   Þæt folc ðe heora reaf wurpon under þæs assan fet þæt
sind þa martyras, þe for Cristes geleafan sealdon heora
agenne lichaman to tintregum. Sume hi wæron on fyre forbærnde, sume on sæ adrencte, and mid mislicum pinungum
acwealde; and sealdon us bysne þæt we ne sceolon, for nanum ehtnyssum oððe earfoðnyssum, urne geleafan forlætan
and fram Criste bugan, ðe ma ðe hi dydon. Menig man is
Cristen geteald on sibbe þe wolde swiðe hraðe wiðsacan
Criste gif him man bude þæt man bead þam martyrum; ac

hands with the exhortations and examples of wise instructors; then he bears Christ, as the apostle said, "You are bought with a great price; therefore glorify and bear God in your bodies." We bear God in our bodies because we are a temple and vessel of the Holy Spirit if we guard ourselves against foul sins, of which the same apostle said very terribly, "He who defiles God's temple, God will destroy him." He who is not a temple of God is a temple of the devil, and bears a very heavy burden on his back.

We will tell you a parable. No one can make himself a 10 king, but the people have the choice to choose someone for king who is agreeable to them: but after he has been consecrated as king, he has power over the people, and they cannot shake his yoke from their necks. Likewise every person has his own choice, before he sins, whether he will follow the devil's will or reject it. Then if he binds himself with the works of the devil, he cannot unbind himself by his own might unless the almighty God unbinds him with the strong hand of his mercy. By his own will and carelessness he is bound, but through God's mercy he will be unbound, if he has merited his redemption from God.

The people who cast their garments under the ass's feet 11 are the martyrs, who for Christ's faith gave their own bodies to torment. Some were burned in fire, some drowned in the sea, and killed with various tortures; and they gave us an example that we should not, for any persecutions or hardships, forsake our faith and turn away from Christ, any more than they did. Many a person is considered a Christian in peace who would very quickly deny Christ if someone demanded of him what was demanded of the martyrs; but his

his Cristendom nis na herigendlic. Ac ðæs mannes Cristendom is herigendlic se ðe nele, for nanre ehtnysse, bugan
fram Criste, ne for swurde, ne for fyre, ne for wætere, ne for
hungre, ne for bendum, ac æfre hylt his geleafan mid Godes
herungum oð his lifes ende.

12   Þa ðe ðæra treowa bogas heowon and mid þam Cristes
weig gedæfton þæt sind þa lareowas on Godes cyrcan, þe
plucciað þa cwydas ðæra apostola and heora æftergengena,
and mid þam Godes folce gewisiað to Cristes geleafan þæt
hi beon gearwe to his færelde. Þæt folc ðe Criste beforan
stop, and þæt ðe him fyligde, ealle hi sungon, "*Osanna filio
David*," þæt is on urum geðeode, "Sy hælo Dauides bearne."
Þa ðe Criste beforan stopon þa sind ða heahfæderas and þa
witegan ðe wæron ær Cristes flæsclicnysse; and ða ðe him
bæftan eodon þæt sind ða ðe æfter Cristes acennednysse to
him gebugon, and dæghwamlice bugað. And ealle hi singað
ænne lofsang; forðan ðe we and hi ealle healdað ænne geleafan, swa swa Petrus se apostol cwæð ða ða he spræc be
ðam heahfæderum, "We gelyfað þæt we beon gehealdene
þurh Cristes gife, swa swa hi."

13   Hi cwædon "Dauides bearn," þe Crist is þæs mæran cyne-
cynnes Dauides æfter þære menniscnysse. Of ðam cynne
wæs seo eadige Maria his modor. Hi sungon, "Gebletsod is
se ðe com on Godes naman." Se hælend com on Godes naman, þe se heofenlica Fæder hine asende us to alysednysse;
and ealle ða wundra þe he worhte, on eallum he herede and
wuldrode his Fæder naman. "Sy hælo, Dauides bearne, on
heahnyssum." Þæs hælendes tocyme and his ðrowung wæs
halwendlic ægðer ge mannum ge englum, forðan ðe we ge-
eacniað heora werod þe se feallenda deofol gewanode; be
ðam cwæð se apostol Paulus, "Þæt sceoldon ealle heofenlice
ðing and eorðlice beon geedstaðelode on Criste."

Christianity is not praiseworthy. But that person's Christianity is praiseworthy who will not turn away from Christ for any persecution, neither for sword, nor for fire, nor for water, nor for hunger, nor for bonds, but always holds to his faith with the praises of God until the end of his life.

Those who cut the branches of the trees and prepared 12 Christ's way with them are the teachers in God's Church, who pluck the sayings of the apostles and their successors, and with them direct God's people to the faith of Christ so that they might be prepared for his way. The people who walked before Christ, and those who followed him, all sang "*Hosanna, son of David,*" that is, in our language, "Hail, son of David." Those who walked before Christ are the patriarchs and prophets who were before Christ's incarnation; and those who went after him are those who turned to Christ after his birth, and daily turn to him. All these sing one hymn of praise; because we and they all hold one faith, as Peter the apostle said when he spoke of the patriarchs, "We believe that we shall be saved by Christ's grace, just as they are."

They said "son of David," because Christ is of the great 13 royal lineage of David according to his human nature. The blessed Mary his mother was of that lineage. They sang, "Blessed is he who has come in God's name." The savior came in God's name, for the heavenly Father sent him for our redemption; and in all the miracles he performed, he praised and glorified his Father's name. "Hail, son of David, on high." The savior's advent and his passion were saving both to humans and angels, because we increase their host which the fallen devil diminished; of this the apostle Paul said, "That all heavenly and earthly things should be re-established in Christ."

14 Se hælend wæs wunigende binnan ðam temple of ðisum
dæge oð nu on Ðunresdæg, and ægðer ge mid lare ge mid
wundrum þæt folc tihte to soðfæstnysse and to rihtum geleafan. Þa namon ða heafodmen andan ongean his lare, and
syrwedon mid micelre smeaunge hu hi mihton hine to deaðe
gebringan. Ne mihte se deað him genealæcan gif he sylf
nolde, ac he com to mannum to ði þæt he wolde beon gehyrsum his Fæder oð dead, and mancynn alysan fram ðam ecan
deaðe mid his hwilwendlicum deaðe. Þeah hwæðere ne
nydde he na þæt Iudeisce folc to his cwale, ac deofol hi tihte
to ðam weorce, and God þæt geðafode to alysednysse ealles
geleaffulles mancynnes.

15 We habbað oft gesæd, and git secgað, þæt Cristes rihtwisnys is swa micel þæt he nolde niman mancyn neadunga of
ðam deofle buton he hit forwyrhte. He hit forwyrhte ða ða
he tihte þæt folc to Cristes cwale, þæs ælmihtigan Godes;
and ða þurh his unscæððigan dead wurdon we alysede fram
ðam ecan deaðe, gif we us sylfe ne forpærað. Þa getimode
ðam reðan deofle swa swa deð þam grædigan fisce, þe gesihð
þæt æs and ne gesihð ðone angel ðe on ðam æse sticað; bið
þonne grædig þæs æses, and forswylcð þone angel forð mid
þam æse. Swa wæs þam deofle: he geseh ða menniscnysse on
Criste, and na ða godcundnysse; ða sprytte he þæt Iudeisce
folc to his slege, and gefredde ða þone angel Cristes godcundnysse, þurh ða he wæs to deaðe aceocod, and benæmed
ealles mancynnes þara ðe on God belyfað.

16 Næs na Cristes ðrowung gefremmed on þisum dæge, ac
ða feower godspelleras awriton his ðrowunga on feower ge-
setnyssum; þa ane we rædað nu todæg, and ða oðre on ðisre
wucan. Þa Iudei genamon hine on Frige æfen and heoldon
hine ða niht, and ðæs on merigen hi hine gefæstnodon on

260

The savior was staying in the temple from this day until 14 Thursday, and both with teaching and with miracles inspired the people to truth and to the right faith. Then the leaders became envious of his teaching, and schemed with great cunning how they might lead him to death. Death could not have approached him if he himself had not willed it, but he came to humanity because he would be obedient to his Father unto death, and redeem humanity from eternal death by his temporary death. Yet he did not compel the Jewish people to kill him, but the devil enticed them to the work, and God allowed it for the redemption of all believing humanity.

We have often said, and still say, that the righteousness of 15 Christ is so great that he would not have taken humanity from the devil by force unless he had forfeited them. He forfeited them when he enticed the people to the killing of Christ, the almighty God; and then through his innocent death we were redeemed from eternal death, if we do not destroy ourselves. Then it happened to the cruel devil as it does to a greedy fish, which sees the bait and does not see the hook sticking in the bait; it is greedy for the bait, and swallows up the hook along with the bait. So it was with the devil: he saw the humanity in Christ, and not the divinity; he then incited the Jewish people to kill him, and then felt the hook of Christ's divinity, by which he was choked to death, and deprived of all people who believe in God.

Christ's passion was not completed on this day, but the 16 four Evangelists recorded his sufferings in four narratives: one we read now today, and the others during this week. The Jews took him on Thursday evening and held him that night, and in the morning fastened him on a cross with four nails,

rode mid feower nægelum, and mid spere gewundedon. And
ða embe nontid, þa þa he forðferde, þa comon twegen gelyfede men, Ioseph and Nichodemus, and bebyrigdon his
lic ær æfene on niwere ðryh, mid deorwyrðum reafum bewunden. And his lic læg on byrgene þa Sæterniht and Sun-
nanniht; and seo godcundnys wæs on ðære hwile on helle,
and gewrað þone ealdan deofol, and him of anam Adam,
þone frumsceapenan man, and his wif Euan, and ealle ða ðe
of heora cynne Gode ær gecwemdon. Þa gefredde se deofol
þone angel þe he ær grædelice forswealh. And Crist aras of
deaðe on þone Easterlican Sunnandæg, þe nu bið on seofon
nihtum; be ðam is gelimplicor þonne mare to reccenne
þonne nu sy, ac uton nu sprecan be ðyses dæges wurðmynte.

17   Se gewuna stent on Godes cyrcan, þurh lareowas geset,
þæt gehwær on Godes geladunge se sacerd bletsian sceole
palmtwigu on ðisum dæge, and hi swa gebletsode ðam folce
dælan; and sceolon ða Godes þeowas singan ðone lofsang þe
þæt Iudeisce folc sang togeanes Criste, þa þa he genealæhte
his ðrowunge. We geeuenlæcað þam geleaffullum of ðam
folce mid þisre dæde, forðan ðe hi bæron palmtwigu mid
lofsange togeanes þam hælende. Nu sceole we healdan urne
palm oð þæt se sangere onginne ðone offringsang, and geoffrian þonne Gode ðone palm for ðære getacnunge: palm
getacnað syge. Sygefæst wæs Crist ða ða he ðone micclan
deofol oferwann and us generede, and we sceolon beon eac
sygefæste þurh Godes mihte swa þæt we ure unðeawas, and
ealle leahtras, and ðone deofol oferwinnan, and us mid godum weorcum geglencgan, and on ende ures lifes betæcan
Gode ðone palm, þæt is, ure sige, and ðancian him georne
þæt we, ðurh his fultum, deoful oferwunnon, þæt he us
beswican ne mihte.

and wounded him with a spear. Then about the ninth hour, when he died, there came two believers, Joseph and Nicodemus, and buried his body before evening in a new sepulcher, wrapped in precious garments. And his body lay in the tomb Friday night and Saturday night; his divinity was in hell during that time, and tied up the old devil, and took Adam, the first-created human, from him, and his wife Eve, and all those of their race who had been pleasing to God. Then the devil felt the hook which he had greedily swallowed. And Christ arose from death on Easter Sunday, which will be in seven days; it is more fitting to say more about that then than it is now, but let us now speak of the dignity of this day.

The custom exists in God's Church, established by its teachers, that everywhere in God's congregation the priest should bless palm branches on this day, and after blessing them, distribute them to the people; God's servants should then sing the hymn of praise which the Jewish people sang before Christ, when he was approaching his passion. We imitate the faithful of that people with this deed, because they bore palm branches with a hymn of praise before the savior. Now we should hold our palm until the cantor begins the offertory, and then offer the palm to God because a palm signifies victory. Christ was victorious when he overcame the great devil and rescued us, and we should also be victorious through God's might so that we overcome our evil practices, and all sins, and the devil, and adorn ourselves with good works, and at the end of our life deliver to God the palm, that is, our victory, thanking him fervently that we, through his help, have overcome the devil, so that he could not deceive us.

18   Synfulra manna deað is yfel and earmlic, forðan ðe hi farað of ðisum scortan life to ecum pinungum, and rihtwisra manna deað is deorwyrðe, forði ðonne hi geendiað ðis geswincfulle lif þonne beoð hi gebrohte to ðam ecan life, and bið þonne swylce heora ende beo anginn, forðan ðe hi ne beoð na deade, ac beoð awende of deaðe to life. Se lichama, ðe is þære sawle reaf, anbidað þæs micclan domes; and ðeah he beo to duste formolsnod, God hine arærð, and gebrincð togædere sawle and lichaman to ðam ecan life, and bið þonne gefylled Cristes behat, ðe ðus cwæð, "Þonne scinað ða rihtwisan swa swa sunne on heora Fæder rice," se ðe leofað and rixað a butan ende on ecnysse. Amen.

19   Circlice ðeawas forbeodað to secgenne ænig spel on þam þrym swigdagum.

15

Dominica sanctae Pascae

Maria Magdalene et Maria Iacobi, et reliqua

2   Oft ge gehyrdon embe ðæs hælendes ærist, hu he on ðisum dæge of deaðe aras; ac we willað eow myngian, þæt hit ne gange eow of gemynde. "Þa ða Crist bebyrged wæs, ða cwædon þa Iudeiscan to heora ealdormenn Pilate, 'La leof, se swica ðe her ofslegen is cwæð gelomlice, þa þa he on life

The death of the sinful is evil and miserable, because they ₁₈ pass from this short life to eternal torments, but the death of the righteous is precious, because when they end this life of toil they will be brought to the eternal life, and then their end will be like a beginning, for they will not be dead, but will be turned from death to life. The body, which is the garment of the soul, will await the great judgment; and even if it is rotted to dust, God will raise it, and bring soul and body together to eternal life, and then Christ's promise will be fulfilled, who said, "Then the righteous will shine like the sun in their Father's kingdom," who lives and reigns forever without end to eternity. Amen.

Church customs forbid any sermon to be said on the ₁₉ three silent days.

15

Easter Sunday

Easter Sunday

M ary Magdalene and Mary the mother of James, etc.

You have often heard of the savior's resurrection, how he ₂ arose from death on this day; but we will remind you, so that it might not pass from your mind. "When Christ was buried, the Jews said to their governor Pilate, 'Lo, sir, the deceiver who has been slain here often said, when he was alive,

wæs, þæt he wolde arisan of deaðe on þam ðriddan dæge. Bebeod nu forði besittan his byrgene oð þone ðriddan dæg, þe læs þe his leorningcnihtas cumon and forstelon his lic, and secgan ðam folce þæt he of dead arise. Þonne bið þæt gedwyld wyrse þonne þæt oðer wære.' Þa andwyrde se ealdormann Pilatus, 'Ge habbað weardas; farað to and healdað.' Hi ða ferdon to and mearcodon ða þruh mid insegle, and besæton ða byrgenne.

3   "Þa beheold Maria þæs hælendes modor and ða wimmen ðe hyre mid wæron hwær he bebyrged wæs and eodon ða ongean to ðære byrig, and seo magdalenisce Maria and Maria Iacobes modor bohton deorwurðe sealfe þe bið geworht to smyrigenne deaddra manna lic mid þæt hi sceolon late rotian. And eodon ða þa wimmen on ðisum dæge on ærnemerigen, and woldon his lic behwurfan swa hit ðær gewunelic wæs on ðære ðeode. Þa cwædon ða wife betwux him, 'Hwa sceal us awilian ðone stan of ðære þrih? Se stan is ormætlice micel.' Þa ða hi ðis spræcon, ða wearð færlice micel eorðstyrung, and Godes engel fleah of heofenum to ðære byrgene and awylte ðone stan aweg, and gesæt him uppan ðam stane. Þa wæs ðæs engles wlite swilce liget, and his reaf swa hwit swa snaw. Ða wurdon ða weardmen afyrhte, and feollon adune swilce hi deade wæron. Ða cwæð se engel to ðam wifum, 'Ne bio ge ofdrædde: Ic wat þæt ge secað þone hælend þe wæs on rode gefæstnod. Nis he her; he aras of deaðe, swa swa he eow ær sæde. Cumað and sceawiað his byrgene þær he on læg, þe nu is æmtig. Gað nu ongean to his leorningcnihtum and secgað him þæt Crist aras of deaðe, and he cymð to him on þam earde þe is gehaten Galilea. Secgað þæt hi cumon him ðær togeanes, þær hi hine geseoð swa swa he him behet ær ðam þe he þrowade.'" Þa lagon ða scytan innon þære byrgene ðe he mid bewunden wæs.

that he would rise from death on the third day. Order his
tomb to be surrounded until the third day, lest his disciples
come and steal his body, and tell the people that he has risen
from death. Then that error will be worse than the former
one.' The governor Pilate answered, 'You have guards; go
and hold it.' They went and marked the sepulcher with a
seal, and surrounded the tomb.

"Then Mary, the savior's mother, and the women who 3
were with her saw where he was buried and went out to the
tomb, and Mary Magdalene and Mary the mother of James
bought expensive ointments that are made for anointing
the bodies of the dead so that they should decay more
slowly. The women went on this day early in the morning,
and wanted to tend to his body as was the custom among
that people. Then the women said between themselves,
'Who will roll away the stone at the tomb for us? The stone
is immensely big.' When they said this, there was suddenly a
great earthquake, and God's angel flew from heaven to the
tomb and rolled the stone away, and sat upon the stone. The
angel's countenance was like lightning, and his garments
white as snow. Then the guards were afraid, and fell down as
if they were dead. The angel said to the women, 'Do not be
afraid: I know that you seek the savior who was fastened to
the cross. He is not here; he has risen from death as he had
said to you. Come and look at the tomb where he lay, which
is now empty. Go back to his disciples and tell them that
Christ has risen from death, and he will come to them in the
land called Galilee. Say that they should come there to meet
him, where they will see him just as he promised before he
suffered.'" The sheets in which he had been wrapped lay inside the tomb.

4   And ða wif gecyrdon ða to Cristes leorningcnihtum mid
micclum ege and mid micelre blisse, and woldon him cyðan
Cristes ærist. Þa mid þam þa gemetton hi Crist, and he hi
gegrette, and hi feollon to his fotum. "Ða cwæð se hælend
him to, 'Farað and cyðað minum gebroðrum þæt hi cumon
togeanes me on þam lande Galilea, þær hi geseoð me.' Þa
mid ðam ðe ða wif eodon, þa comon ða weardmen and
cyddon þæt Crist aras of deaðe. Ða namon ða heafodmen ða
weardas on sundorspræce and sealdon him micelne sceatt to
ði þæt hi scoldon secgan þæt Cristes lic him wære forstolen
þa hwile ðe hi slæp fornam. And ða wearð þæt cuð geond
eal Iudea land, þæt ða weardas ðone sceat namon æt ðam
heafodmannum, and þæt Crist aras of deaðe." We cweðað
nu, gif hwa his lic forstæle, nolde he hine unscrydan, forðan
ðe stalu ne lufað nane yldinge.

5   Crist wearð æteowed on ðam ylcan dæge Petre and
oðrum twam his leorningcnihtum, and hi gefrefrode. "Þa æt
nextan com se hælend to his leorningcnihtum þær hi gegaderode wæron, and cwæð him to, 'Sy sib betwux eow. Ic
hit eom, ne beo ge na afyrhte.' Þa wurdon hi afærede, and
wendon þæt hit sum gast wære. Ða cwæð he him to, 'Hwi
synd ge afærede, and mislice ðencað be me? Sceawiað mine
handa and mine fet, þe wæron mid næglum þurhdrifene.
Grapiað and sceawiað—gif ic gast wære, ðonne næfde ic
flæsc and ban swa swa ge geseoð þæt ic hæbbe.' Þa ða he ðis
cwæð, þa ætiwde he him ægðer ge handa ge fet ge sidan ðe
he on gewundod wæs. Ða wæs heora mod mid micelre wun-
drunge and blisse ofernumen. Þa cwæð se hælend him eft
to, 'Hæbbe ge her ænig ðing þe to etene is?' Þa brohton hi
him gebrædne fisc and sumne dæl huniges, and he æt ða beforan him and sealde him his lafe, ðus cweðende, 'Ðis ic

And the women returned to Christ's disciples with great 4
fear and with great joy, and wanted to announce Christ's resurrection. In the midst of that they met Christ, and he
greeted them, and they fell to his feet. "The savior said to
them, 'Go and tell my brothers that they should come to me
in the land of Galilee, where they will see me.' As the women
went, the guards came and announced that Christ had risen
from death. The leaders held a secret conversation with the
guards and gave them a great deal of money if they would say
that Christ's body had been stolen from them while sleep
had overcome them. And that became known throughout
all the land of Judea, that the guards took the money from
their leaders, and that Christ arose from death." We say that
if someone had stolen his body, he would not have removed
his shroud, for theft does not like any delay.

Christ appeared on the same day to Peter and two other 5
of his disciples, and comforted them. "Then finally the savior came to his disciples where they were gathered, and said
to them, 'Peace be with you. It is I, do not be afraid.' And
they were frightened, and thought it was some spirit. And
he said to them, 'Why are you frightened, and thinking various things about me? Look at my hands and my feet, which
were pierced with nails. Grasp and see—if I were a spirit, I
would not have flesh and bones as you see that I have.' As he
said this, he showed them both his hands and his feet and
the side where he had been wounded. Then their minds
were overcome with great wonder and joy. Then the savior
said to them, 'Do you have anything here to eat?' They
brought him broiled fish and a portion of honey, and he ate
before them and gave them his leftovers, saying, 'What I

sæde eow ær minre ðrowunge hit is nu gefylled be me, swa
swa seo ealde æ and witegan be me awriton.' And he ða
him forgeaf andgit þæt hi mihton ða gewritu tocnawan, and
cwæð þa gyt, 'Þus wæs gewriten be me, þæt ic ðrowian
sceolde, and arisan of deaðe on þam ðriddan dæge, and sceal
beon gebodod on minum naman dædbot and synna forgife-
nyss on eallum ðeodum.'" Se hælend wearð þa gelomlice æti-
wed his leorningcnihtum, and hi gewissode to ðære lare and
to ðam geleafan hu hi eallum mancynne tæcan sceoldon; and
on ðam feowertigoðan dæge his æristes he astah lichamlice
to heofonum to his Fæder.

6   Ac we habbað nu micele maran endebyrdnysse þære Cristes bec gesæd þonne ðis dægðerlice godspel behæfð, for
trymminge eowres geleafan. Nu wylle we eow gereccan þæs
dægþerlican godspelles traht æfter ðæs halgan papan Gregories trahtnunge.

7   Mine gebroðra þa leofostan, ge gehyrdon þæt þa halgan
wif þe Drihtne on life filigdon comon to his byrgene mid
þære deorwyrðan sealfe, and þone ðe hi lufedon on life þam
hi woldon deadum mid menniscre gecneordnysse ðenian. Ac
ðeos dæd getacnað sum ðing to donne on Godes gelaðunge.
We ðe gelyfað Cristes æristes, we cumað gewislice to his
byrgene mid deorwyrðre sealfe gif we beoð gefyllede mid
bræðe haligra mihta, and gif we mid hlysan godra weorca
urne Drihten secað. Þa wif ðe ða sealfe brohton hi gesawon
englas, forðan ðe ða geseoð þa heofonlican englas þa þe mid
bræðum godra weorca gewilniað þæs upplican færeldes. Se
engel awylte þæt hlid of ðære ðryh, na þæt he Criste utgan-
ges rymde, ac he geswutelode mannum þæt he arisen wæs.
Se ðe com deaðlic to ðisum middangearde, acenned þurh

said to you before my suffering is now fulfilled in me, just as the old law and the prophets have written about me.' And then he gave them insight so that they could understand the scriptures, and said further, 'It was written about me that I should suffer, and arise from death on the third day, and in my name shall be preached repentance and the forgiveness of sins among all nations.'" The savior frequently appeared to his disciples, and directed them in doctrine and in faith how they should teach all humanity; and in the fortieth day of his resurrection he ascended bodily to his Father in heaven.

But we have now said much more of the narrative of $\quad$ 6 Christ's book than this present day's gospel contains, for the confirmation of your faith. We will now tell you the exposition of this day's gospel according to the commentary of the holy pope Gregory.

My dearest brothers, you have heard that the holy women $\quad$ 7 who followed the Lord in life came to his tomb with precious ointment, and they wanted to serve the one whom they had loved in life with human devotion when he was dead. But this deed signifies something to be done in God's Church. We who believe in Christ's resurrection, we come confidently to his tomb with precious ointment if we are filled with the breath of holy virtues, and if we seek our Lord with the reputation of good works. The women who brought the ointment saw angels, for those who desire the upward journey with the breath of good works see the heavenly angels. The angel rolled the lid from the sepulcher, not that he would make way for Christ's departure, but so he would reveal to people that he was risen. He who came mortal to this world, born from the closed womb of the virgin,

beclysedne innoð þæs mædenes, se ylca, butan tweon, ða ða
he aras undeaðlic, mihte belocenre ðrih faran of middangearde. Se engel sæt on ða swiðran healfe ðære byrgenne;
seo swiðre hand getacnað þæt ece lif, and seo wynstre ðis
andwearde lif. Rihtlice sæt se engel on ða swiðran hand,
forðon þe he cydde þæt se hælend hæfde ða oferfaren ða
brosnunga ðises andweardan lifes and wæs ða wunigende
on ecum ðingum undeaðlic. Se bydel wæs ymbscryd mid
scinendum reafe, forðan ðe he bodade þa blisse þisre freolstide, and ure mærða. Hwæðer cweðe we, ðe ure ðe ðæra
engla? We cweðað soðlice, ægðer ge ure ge heora. Þæs
hælendes ærist is ure freolstid and bliss, forðan ðe he
gelædde us mid his æriste to ðære undeadlicnysse þe we to
gesceapene wæron. His ærist wæs þæra engla bliss, forðon
ðe God gefylð heora getel þonne he us to heofonum gebrincð.

8   Se engel gehyrte ða wif, þus cweðende, "Ne beo ge
afyrhte"—swilce he swa cwæde, forhtian ða ðe ne lufiað
engla tocyme; beon ða ofdrædde þa þe sint ofsette mid
flæsclicum lustum, and nabbað nænne hiht to engla werode.
Hwi forhtige ge, ge ðe geseoð eowre geferan? "His wlite wæs
swilce liget, and his reaf swa hwit swa snaw." Soðlice on
ligette is oga, and on snawe liðnys þære beorhtnysse. Rihtlice wæs se bydel Cristes æristes swa gehiwod, forþan þonne
he sylf cymð to ðam micclan dome, þonne bið he swiðe egeful ðam synfullum, and swiðe liðe þam rihtwisum. He cwæð,
"Ge secað þone hælend; he aras, nis he her." He næs ða
lichamlice on ðære byrgene, se ðe æghwær bið þurh his godcundan mihte. Þær læig þæt reaf bæftan þe he mid bewunden wæs, forðon ðe he ne rohte þæs eorðlican reafes
syððan he of deaðe aras. Þeah man deadne mannan mid

the same one could, without doubt, depart from the world from an enclosed sepulcher when he arose immortal. The angel sat on the right side of the tomb; the right hand signifies eternal life, and the left this present life. Rightly the angel sat on the right hand, for he revealed that the savior had surmounted the corruptions of this present life and was then dwelling immortal in eternity. The messenger was clothed in a shining garment, because he announced the happiness of this feast day, and our glories. But we ask, ours or the angels'? We say truly, both ours and theirs. The savior's resurrection is our feast day and joy, for by his resurrection he led us to the immortality for which we were created. His resurrection was bliss to the angels, because God fills up their ranks when he brings us to heaven.

The angel encouraged the women, saying, "Do not be afraid"—as if he had said, let those fear who do not love the coming of angels; let those be terrified who are beset by fleshly lusts, and have no hope of the host of angels. Why are you afraid, you who see one like yourself? "His countenance was like lightning, and his garment white as snow." Truly there is terror in lightning, and in snow the mildness of brightness. The messenger of Christ's resurrection rightly appeared this way, for when he himself will come in the great judgment, he will be very terrible to the sinful, and very mild to the righteous. He said, "You seek the savior; he is risen, he is not here." He was not physically in the tomb, he who is everywhere through his divine power. The garment in which he had been wrapped lay behind, for he did not care about an earthly garment after he had risen from death. Though a dead person may be wrapped in a garment,

8

reafe bewinde, ne arist þæt reaf na ðe hraðor eft mid þam men, ac he bið mid þam heofenlicum reafe gescryd æfter his æriste.

9 Wel is gecweden be ðam hælende þæt he wolde cuman togeanes his geferon on Galilea. Galilea is gecweden "ofer-færeld." Se hælend wæs ða afaren fram ðrowunge to æriste, fram deaðe to life, fram wite to wuldre. And gif we farað fram leahtrum to halgum mægnum, þonne mote we geseon ðone hælend æfter urum færelde of ðisum life. Twa lif sind soðlice: þæt an we cunnon, þæt oðer us wæs uncuð ær Cristes tocyme. Þæt an lif is deadlic, þæt oðer undeadlic. Ac se hælend com and underfeng þæt an lif, and geswutelode þæt oðer. Þæt an lif he æteowde mid his deaðe, and þæt oðer mid his æriste. Gif he us deadlicum mannum ærist and þæt ece lif behete and þeah hwæðere nolde hit þurh hine sylfne geswutelian, hwa wolde þonne his behatum gelyfan? Ac ða ða he man beon wolde, ða gemedemode he hine sylfne eac to deaðe agenes willan, and he aras of deaðe þurh his godcundan mihte, and geswutelode þurh hine sylfne þæt þæt he us behet.

10 Nu cwyð sum man on his geðance, "Eaðe mihte he arisan of deaðe, forðan ðe he is God: ne mihte se deað hine gehæf-tan." Gehyre se mann þe þis smeað andsware his smeagunge. Crist forðferde ana on ðam timan, ac he ne aras na ana of deaðe, ac aras mid micclum werede. Se godspellere Matheus awrat on Cristes bec þæt manega halige menn ðe wæron on ðære ealdan æ forðfarene þæt hi arison mid Criste; and þæt sædon gehwilce wise lareowas þæt hi habbað gefremod heora ærist to ðam ecan life, swa swa we ealle don sceolon on ende þisre worulde. Þa lareowas cwædon þæt ða aræredan menn næron soðlice gewitan Cristes æristes gif hi

274

that garment does not rise again with him any sooner, but he will be clothed in a heavenly garment after his resurrection.

It is well said of the savior that he would meet his companions in Galilee. *Galilee* is interpreted "passing over." The savior had passed over from passion to resurrection, from death to life, from torment to glory. And if we pass from sins to holy virtues, then we may see the savior after our passage from this life. Truly there are two lives: the one we know, but the other was unknown to us before Christ's coming. The one life is mortal, the other immortal. But the savior came and took on the one life, and revealed the other. The one life he manifested by his death, and the other by his resurrection. If he had promised resurrection and eternal life to us mortals and yet had not been willing to reveal them in himself, who would believe in his promises? But when he would become human, then he also humbled himself to death by his own will, and he arose from death through his divine power, revealing in himself what he had promised to us. 9

Now someone might say in his thoughts, "He could easily arise from death, because he is God: death could not hold him captive." Let the one who so speculates hear an answer to his speculation. Christ departed alone at that time, but he did not arise alone from death, but arose with a great host. The Evangelist Matthew wrote in Christ's book that many holy people who had died in the old law arose with Christ; and all wise teachers have said that they have completed their resurrection to eternal life, as we all will do at the end of this world. Those teachers have said that the people raised up would not truly have been witnesses to Christ's 10

næron ecelice arærde. Nu sind adwæscede ealle geleaflystu, þæt nan man ne sceal ortruwian be his agenum æriste, þonne se godspellere awrat þæt fela arison mid Criste ðe wæron anfealde men, ðeah ðe Crist God sy.

11   Nu cwæð Gregorius se trahtnere þæt him come to ge-mynde hu ða Iudeiscan clypodon be Criste þa ða he wæs on ðære rode gefæstnod. Hi cwædon, "Gif he sy Israhela cyn-ing, þonne astige he nu of ðære rode, and we gelyfað on hine." Gif he ða of ðære rode astige, and nolde heora hosp forberan, þonne butan tweon ne sealde he us nane bysne his geðyldes. Ac he abad hwon and forbær heora hosp, and hæfde geðyld. Ac se ðe nolde of ðære rode abrecan se aras of ðære byrgene. Mare wundor wæs þæt he of deaðe aras þonne he cucu of ðære rode abræce. Mare miht wæs þæt he ðone deað mid his æriste tobræc þonne he his lif geheolde of ðære rode astigende. Ac ða ða hi gesawon þæt he ne astah of ðære rode for heora hospum, ac ðæron deaðes gebad, þa gelyfdon hi þæt he oferswiðed wære and his nama adwæsced; ac hit gelamp swa þæt of ðam deaðe asprang his nama geond ealne middangeard. Þa wearð hyra bliss awend to ðam mæstan sare, forðan ðe heora sorh bið endeleas.

12   Þas ðing getacnode se stranga Samson, se hæfde fæhðe to ðam folce ðe is gehaten Philistei. Ða getimode hit þæt he becom to heora byrig þe wæs Gaza gehaten; þa wæron ða Philistei swiðe bliðe, and ymbsæton ða burh. Ac se stranga Samson aras on midre nihte and gelæhte ða burhgeatu, and abær hi uppon ane dune, to bismere his gefaan. Se stranga

resurrection if they had not been raised eternally. Now all lack of faith is extinguished, so that no one should despair of his own resurrection, when the Evangelist wrote that many rose with Christ who were only human, even though Christ is God.

Now Gregory the commentator said that it came to 11 his mind how the Jews cried out about Christ when he was fastened on the cross. They said, "If he is the king of Israel, let him come down now from the cross, and we will believe in him." If he had come down from the cross then, and had not wished to endure their mockery, then without doubt he would not have given us any example of his patience. But he remained awhile and endured their mockery, and had patience. But he who would not break free from the cross arose from the grave. It was a greater miracle that he arose from death than that he should have broken free from the cross while living. It was a greater feat that he shattered death with his resurrection than that he should have preserved his life by coming down from the cross. When they saw that he did not come down from the cross because of their mockery, but awaited death on it, they believed that he was overcome and his name wiped out; but it turned out that from that death his name sprang forth over the whole earth. Then their joy was turned to the greatest pain, because their sorrow will be endless.

The strong Samson, who was the enemy of the people 12 called Philistines, signified these things. It happened that he came to their city called Gaza; then the Philistines were very joyful, and surrounded the city. But the strong Samson arose in the middle of the night and took the city gates, and carried them up on a hill, to humiliate his enemies. The

Samson getacnode Crist, seo burh Gaza getacnode helle,
and ða Philistei hæfdon Iudeisces folces getacnunge þe
besæton Cristes byrgene. Ac se Samson nolde gan ydel of
ðære byrig, ac he abær ða gatu up to ðære dune; forðon þe
ure hælend Crist tobræc helle gatu, and generode Adam,
and Euan, and his gecorenan of heora cynne, and freolice of
deaðe aras, and hi samod, and astah to heofonum. Þa manfullan he let bæftan to ðam ecum witum. And is nu helle geat
belocen rihtwisum mannum, and æfre open unrihtwisum.

13   Ungesælig wæs þæt Iudeisce folc þæt hi swa ungeleaffulle
wæron. Ealle gesceafta oncneowon heora scyppend buton
ðam Iudeiscum anum. Heofonas oncneowon Cristes acennednysse, ða ða he acenned wæs þa wearð gesewen niwe
steorra. Sæ oncneow Crist ða ða he eode mid drium fotum
uppon hire yðum. Eorðe oncneow þa þa heo eal bifode on
Cristes æriste. Seo sunne oncneow þa þa heo wearð aðystrod
on Cristes ðrowunge fram middæge oð non. Stanas oncneowon þa þa hi toburston on heora scyppendes forðsiðe. Hell
oncneow Crist ða ða heo forlet hyre hæftlingas ut þurh ðæs
hælendes hergunge. And ða heardheortan Iudei ðeah, þurh
ealle ða tacna, noldon gebugan mid geleafan to ðam mildheortan hælende, se ðe wile eallum mannum gehelpan on
hine gelyfendum. Ac uton we gelyfan þæt God Fæder wæs
æfre butan anginne, and æfre wæs se Sunu of ðam Fæder
acenned, forðan ðe he is se wisdom and miht ðe se Fæder
ealle gesceafta þurh gesceop; and hi ealle wurdon geliffæste
ðurh ðone Halgan Gast, se ðe is willa and lufu þæs Fæder
and þæs Suna, hi ðry an God untodæledlic, on anre godcundnysse wunigende, hi ealle gelice mihtige, swa hwæt swa
læsse bið and unmihtigre, þæt ne bið na God. Ac se Fæder

strong Samson signified Christ, the city of Gaza signified hell, and the Philistines were a sign of the Jewish people who surrounded Christ's tomb. Samson would not go empty-handed from the city, but carried the gates up to the hill; for our savior Christ broke the gates of hell, and delivered Adam, and Eve, and his chosen of their people, and freely arose from death, and they with him, and ascended to heaven. He left the wicked behind to eternal torments. And now the gate of hell is shut to righteous people, and always open to the unrighteous.

The Jewish people were unfortunate that they were so unbelieving. All creatures acknowledged their creator except the Jews alone. Heaven acknowledged the birth of Christ, for when he was born a new star was seen. The sea acknowledged Christ when he went with dry feet over its waves. Earth acknowledged him when it all trembled at Christ's resurrection. The sun acknowledged him when it was darkened at Christ's passion from midday until the ninth hour. The stones acknowledged him when they burst apart at their creator's departure. Hell acknowledged Christ when it released its captives through the savior's harrowing. And yet the hard-hearted Jews, through all these signs, would not turn with faith to the merciful savior, who will help all who believe in him. But let us believe that God the Father was forever without beginning, and that the Son was forever begotten of the Father, for he is the wisdom and power through which the Father made all creatures; and they were all brought to life by the Holy Spirit, who is the will and love of the Father and of the Son, these three one God, indivisible, dwelling in one divinity, all equally powerful, for whatsoever is lesser and less powerful, that is not

13

279

sende ðone Sunu to ure alisednysse, and he ana underfeng ða menniscnysse, and þrowode deað be his agenum willan, and aras of deaðe on ðisum dæge, and astah to heofonum on ðam feowertigeðan dæge his æristes ætforan manegra manna gesihðe, and rixað mid þam ælmihtigan Fæder and ðam Halgum Gaste, nu and a on ecnysse. Amen.

16

Dominica prima post Pasca

Cum esset sero die illo una sabbatorum, et reliqua.

2   "Æfter ðæs hælendes æriste wæron his discipuli belocene on anum huse for ðæs Iudeiscan folces ogan. Ða on anum restendæge com se hælend into him and cwæð him to, 'Sy sibb betwux eow.' Þa ða he ðis cwæð, þa æteowde he him his handa and his sidan, and hi wæron swiðe bliðe þurh his ærist and his tocyme. He cwæð þa eft, 'Sy sibb betwux eow. Swa swa min fæder asende me, swa wille ic eac sendan eow.' Ða ableow he him on upon and cwæð, 'Underfoð Haligne Gast. Þæra manna synna þe ge forgifað, þæra beoð forgifene, and ðam ðe ge ofteoð þa forgyfenysse, þam bið oftogen.'

3   "Þa næs Thomas þær, an ðæra twelf apostola. Eft þa þa Thomas com, ða cwædon his geferan him to, 'We gesawon þone hælend.' He andwyrde, 'Ne gelyfe ic þæt he of deaðe

God. The Father sent the Son for our redemption, and he alone assumed human nature, suffered death of his own will, arose from death on this day, and ascended to heaven on the fortieth day after his resurrection before the sight of many, and rules with the almighty Father and the Holy Spirit, now and forever to eternity. Amen.

16

First Sunday after Easter

The First Sunday after Easter

W*hen it was evening of that day, the first of the week, etc.*

"After the savior's resurrection his disciples were locked 2 in a house for fear of the Jewish people. Then on the sabbath the savior came in to them and said, 'Peace be among you.' As he said this, he showed them his hands and his side, and they were very happy because of his resurrection and his coming. He then said, 'Peace be among you. As my father has sent me, so I will send you.' Then he blew on them and said, 'Receive the Holy Spirit. The sins of those you forgive will be forgiven, and those from whom you withhold forgiveness, it will be withheld from them.'

"Thomas, one of the twelve apostles, was not there. 3 Later, when Thomas came, his companions said to him, 'We have seen the savior.' He answered, 'I will not believe that

281

arise buton ic geseo ða dolhswaðu on his handum and on fotum and on sidan.' Þa eft embe seofan niht com se hælend
into him þær hi beclysede wæron, and cwæð, 'Sy sibb betwux
eow.' Þa cwæð he to Thoman, 'Sete ðine hand on minum
dolhswaðum, and grapa mine handa and mine sidan; and ne
beo ðu na ungeleafful þæt ic of deaðe arise, ac gelyf.' Thomas
ða sceawode and grapode, and cwæð him to, 'Þu eart min
Drihten and min God.' Him andwyrde se hælend, 'Ðu gelyfst forðan ðe ðu me gesawe; ac ða beoð gesælige þe hit ne
gesawon and hwæðere gelyfað.'"

4 Nu cwyð se godspellere Iohannes þæt "Se hælend worhte
fela oðre tacna on gesihðe his leorningcnihta, þe næron
gesette on Cristes bec. Þas wundra sind awritene to ði þæt
ge sceolon gelyfan þæt se hælend is Godes Sunu, and ge
sceolon habban þæt ece lif ðurh ðone geleafan."

5 Nu trahtnað se papa Gregorius ðis godspel, and cwyð þæt
gehwa wundrað hu se hælend become in to his apostolum,
and wæron ðeah hwæðere þa dura belocene. Nu cwyð eft se
halga Gregorius þæt Cristes lichama com inn beclysedum
durum, se ðe wearð acenned of ðam mædene Marian beclysedum innoðe. Hwilc wundor is þæt se hælend mid ecum
lichaman come inn belocenum durum, se ðe mid deadlicum lichaman wearð acenned of beclysedum innoðe þæs
mædenes?

6 We rædað on ðære bec ðe is gehaten *Actus apostolorum*
þæt þa heafodmen Iudeisces folces gebrohton Cristes apostolas on cwearterne. Þa on niht com him to Godes engel,
and lædde hi ut of ðam cwearterne, and stod on merigen þæt
cweartern fæste belocen. God mæig don ealle ðing; nu
sceole we wundrian his mihte and eac gelyfan. Þone lichaman he æteowde to grapigenne, þone ðe he inn brohte

he has risen from death unless I see the wounds on his hands and feet and side.' Then seven nights later the savior came to them where they were locked in, and said, 'Peace be among you.' Then he said to Thomas, 'Put your hand in my wounds, and probe my hands and side, and do not be unbelieving that I have risen from death, but believe.' Thomas then examined and probed, and said to him, 'You are my Lord and my God.' The savior answered, 'You believe because you have seen me; blessed are those who have not seen and yet believe.'"

Now John the Evangelist says that "The savior performed 4 many other signs in the sight of his disciples, which were not recorded in Christ's book. These miracles are written so that you may believe that the savior is the Son of God, and you may have eternal life through that belief."

The pope Gregory comments on this gospel, and says 5 that some people wonder how the savior came in to his apostles even though the doors were locked. The holy Gregory replies that the body of Christ, who was born of the virgin Mary's closed womb, came in through the closed doors. What wonder is it that the savior with an eternal body came in through locked doors, he who with a mortal body was born of the closed womb of the virgin?

We read in the book called *Acts of the Apostles* that the 6 leaders of the Jewish people put Christ's apostles in prison. Then God's angel came to them by night and led them out of the prison, and in the morning the prison stood locked up fast. God can do all things; we should now wonder at his might and also believe. He brought in through closed doors

beclysedum durum. His lichama wæs grapigendlic, and ðeah hwæðere unbrosnigendlic; he æteowde hine grapigendlicne and unbrosnigendlicne, forðan ðe his lichama wæs þæs ylcan gecyndes ðe he ær wæs, ac wæs hwæðere þeah oðres wuldres.

7 Se hælend cwæð to him, "Beo sibb betwux eow." For sibbe com Crist to mannum, and sibbe he bead and tæhte, and nis nan ðing him gecweme þe bið butan sibbe gedon. "Swa swa min Fæder sende me, swa sende ic eow." Se Fæder lufað þone Sunu, ac ðeah hwæðere he sende hine to ðrowunge for manna alysednysse. Crist lufode eac his apostolas, and ðeah hwæðere ne sette he hi to cynegum ne to ealdormannum, ne to woruldlicere blisse; ac tosende hi geond ealne middangeard to bodigenne fulluht and ðone geleafan ðe he sylf tæhte. Þa bododon hi swa lange oð þæt þa ðweoran hi ofslogon, and hi ferdon sigefæste to heora Drihtne.

8 Crist bleow on ða apostolas, and cwæð, "Onfoð Haligne Gast." Tuwa com se Halga Gast ofer ða apostolas—nu æne, and eft oðre siðe æfter Cristes upstige. Crist ableow þone Halgan Gast ofer ða apostolas ða gyt wunigende on eorðan, for ðære getacnunge þæt ælc Cristen mann sceal lufian his nextan swa swa hine sylfne. Eft siððan he to heofenum astah, he sende þone ylcan Gast on fyres hiwe ofer ða apostolas, to ði þæt we sceolon lufian God ofer ealle oðre ðing. An is se Halga Gast, þeah ðe he tuwa become ofer ða apostolas. Swa is eac an lufu, and twa bebodu, þæt we sceolon lufian God and men. Ac we sceolon geleornian on mannum hu we magon becuman to Godes lufe, swa swa Iohannes se apostol cwæð, "Se ðe ne lufað his broðor þone ðe he gesihð, hu mæg he lufian God þone ðe he ne gesihð lichamlice?" Ær ðam fyrste wæs se Halga Gast wunigende on ðam apostolum, ac

the body he displayed to be touched. His body was tangible, and yet incorruptible; he showed himself tangible and incorruptible, because his body was of the same nature that it was before, but yet was of another glory.

The savior said to them, "Peace be among you." Christ 7 came to humanity for peace, and peace he commanded and taught, and nothing is acceptable to him which is done without peace. "As my Father has sent me, so I send you." The Father loves the Son, yet he sent him to suffer for the redemption of humanity. Christ also loved his apostles, and yet he did not set them up as kings or as leaders, or to worldly joy; he sent them throughout the world to preach baptism and the faith which he himself taught. They preached until the wicked killed them, and they went triumphant to their Lord.

Christ blew on the apostles, and said, "Receive the Holy 8 Spirit." The Holy Spirit came twice over the apostles—once here, and again another time after Christ's ascension. Christ blew the Holy Spirit over the apostles while yet dwelling on earth, to signify that every Christian should love his neighbor as himself. Then after he had ascended into heaven, he sent the same Spirit in the form of fire over the apostles, so that we should love God above all other things. The Holy Spirit is one, though he came twice over the apostles. So there is also one love, and two commandments, that we should love God and love humanity. But we should learn among people how we may come to the love of God, as John the apostle said, "He who does not love his brother, whom he sees, how can he love God, whom he does not see physically?" The Holy Spirit was dwelling in the apostles before

hi næron to ðan swiðe onbryrde þæt hi mihton swa bealdlice Godes geleafan bodian swa swa hi siððan mihton þurh gife ðæs Halgan Gastes. Hi sæton beclysede for ogan Iudeisces folces on anum huse; ac syððan hi wæron gefyllede mid þam Halgum Gaste, hi wurdon swa gehyrte and swa cene þæt hi bodedon freolice Godes naman reðum cynegum and wæl-reowum.

9   Crist cwæð to ðam apostolum, "Þæra manna synna þe ge forgyfað þæra beoð forgifene; and ðam ðe ge ofteoð þa for-gifenysse, ðam bið oftogen." Þisne anweald forgeaf Crist þam apostolum and eallum bisceopum, gif hi hit on riht healdað. Ac gif se bisceop deð be his agenum willan, and wile bindan þone unscyldigan and þone scyldigan alysan, þonne forlyst he ða mihte ðe him God forgeaf. Þam mannum he sceal don synna forgifenysse þe he gesihð þæt beoð on-bryrde ðurh Godes gife, and þam he sceal aheardian þe nane behreowsunge nabbað heora misdæda. Crist arærde of deaðe þone stincendan Lazarum, and þa þa he cucu wæs, þa cwæð he to his leorningcnihtum, "Tolysað his bendas, þæt he gan mæge." Þa alysdon hi þæs geedcucedan mannes bendas þe Crist arærde to life. For ði sceolon ða lareowas ða unbindan fram heora synnum þa ðe Crist geliffæst þurh onbryrdnysse. Ælc synful man þe his synna bediglað, he lið dead on byrgene. Ac gif he his synna geandett þurh onbryrd-nysse, þonne gæð he of þære byrgene, swa swa Lazarus dyde þa ða Crist hine arisan het; þonne sceal se lareow hine un-bindan fram ðam ecum wite, swa swa ða apostoli lichamlice Lazarum alysdon. Ac se læweda mann sceal him ondrædan þæs bisceopes cwyde, þeah he unscyldig sy, þy læs ðe he ðurh modignysse scyldig weorðe.

10   Ne getimode þam apostole Thome unforsceawodlice þæt

that time, but they were not so greatly inspired that they could preach God's faith as boldly as they could afterward through the grace of the Holy Spirit. They sat closed up in a house for fear of the Jewish people; but after they were filled with the Holy Spirit, they were so encouraged and so bold that they freely preached the name of God to fierce and bloodthirsty kings.

Christ said to the apostles, "The sins of those you forgive 9 will be forgiven; and those from whom you withhold forgiveness, it will be withheld from them." Christ gave this power to the apostles and to all bishops, if they hold it rightly. But if the bishop acts by his own will, and would bind the guiltless and release the guilty, then he loses the power which God gave him. He will give forgiveness of sins to those people whom he sees are inspired by God's grace, and he will be hardened to those who have no repentance of their misdeeds. Christ raised the stinking Lazarus from death, and when he was alive, he said to his disciples, "Release his bonds, that he may go." They loosened the bonds of the revived man whom Christ had raised to life. Therefore, teachers should unbind from their sins those to whom Christ gives life by inspiration. Every sinful person who conceals his sins lies dead in the grave. But if he confesses his sins through inspiration, then he goes from the grave, as Lazarus did when Christ commanded him to rise; then the teacher shall unbind him from eternal punishment, just as the apostles unbound Lazarus physically. The layman should fear the bishop's decree, even if he is innocent, lest he become guilty through pride.

It did not happen without providence that the apostle 10

he ungeleafful wæs Cristes æristes, ac hit getimode þurh Godes forsceawunge; forðan ðurh his grapunge we sind geleaffulle. Mare us fremode his tweonung þonne ðæra oðra apostola geleaffulnys; forðan ða ða he wæs gebroht to geleafan mid ðære grapunge, þa wearð seo twynung þurh þæt us ætbroden. Eaðe mihte Crist arisan of deaðe butan dolhswaðum, ac to ði he heold þa dolhswaðu þæt he wolde mid þam þa twynigendan getrymman. He cwæð to Thoman, "Þu gelyfst forðan ðe ðu me gesawe." He geseah ðone lichaman and þa dolhswaðu, and he gelyfde þæt he wæs God, se ðe arærde þone lichaman of deaðe. Swiðe blissiað þas word us þe her æfterfiliað, "Gesælige beoð þa þe me ne gesawon, and þeah on me gelyfað." Mid þam cwyde sind þa ealle getacnode þe Crist on lichaman ne gesawon, and ðeah hwæðere hine healdað on heora mode þurh geleafan. Se gelyfð soðlice on God se ðe mid weorcum begæð þæt þæt he gelyfð. Se ðe andet þæt he God cunne, and yfele weorc begæð, þonne wiðsæcð he God mid þam weorcum. "Se geleafa þe bið butan godum weorcum, se is dead." Þis sind ðæra apostola word; undernimað hi mid carfullum mode.

II   We sprecað embe ærist. Nu sind sume men þe habbað twynunge be æriste, and ðonne hi geseoð deadra manna ban þonne cweðað hi, "Hu magon ðas ban beon geedcucode?" swilce hi wislice sprecon. Ac we cweðað þær togeanes þæt God is ælmihtig, and mæg eal þæt he wile. He geworhte heofonas and eorðan and ealle gesceafta butan antimbre. Nu is geðuht þæt him sy sumera ðinga eaðelicor to arærenne ðone deadan of ðam duste þonne him wære to wyrcenne ealle gesceafta of nahte, ac soðlice him sind ealle ðing gelice eaðe, and nan ðing earfoðe. He worhte Adam of lame. Nu ne mage we asmeagan hu he of ðam lame flæsc worhte and

Thomas was unbelieving of Christ's resurrection, but it happened by the providence of God; for through his probing we are believers. His doubt accomplished more for us than the faith of the other apostles; for when he was brought to belief by that probing, then that doubt was taken from us by that. Christ might easily have arisen from death without wounds, but he kept the wounds so that by them he could reassure the doubtful. He said to Thomas, "You believe because you have seen me." He saw the body and the wounds, and he believed that he was God, who had raised the body from death. The words which follow here greatly gladden us, "Blessed are those who have not seen me, and yet believe in me." By that saying are signified all those who have not seen Christ in the body, and yet hold him in their mind through faith. He truly believes in God who practices by works what he believes. He who professes that he knows God, and performs evil works, denies God by those works. "Faith without good works is dead." These are the words of the apostles; receive them with an attentive mind.

We will speak about the resurrection. Now there are some people who have doubts about the resurrection, and when they see the bones of the dead they say, "How can these bones be brought back to life?" as if they spoke wisely. But against them we say that God is almighty, and can do all that he wants. He made heaven and earth and all creatures without matter. Now it seems that it would be somewhat easier for him to raise the dead from the dust than it was for him to make all creatures from nothing, but truly to him all things are equally easy, and nothing difficult. He made Adam from dirt. Now we cannot imagine how from that dirt he

blod, ban and fell, fex and næglas. Men geseoð oft þæt of anum lytlum cyrnele cymð micel treow, ac we ne magon geseon on þam cyrnele naðor ne wyrtruman, ne rinde, ne bogas, ne leaf: ac se God þe forðtihð of ðam cyrnle treow, and wæstmas, and leaf, se ylca mæg of duste aræran flæsc and ban, sina and fex, swa swa he cwæð on his godspelle, "Ne sceal eow beon forloren an hær of eowrum heafde."

12   Se apostol Paulus cwæð þæt we sceolon arisan of deaðe on ðære ylde þe Crist wæs þa ða he ðrowade, þæt is embe þreo and ðritig geara. Þeah cild forðfare, oððe forwerod man, þeah hwæþere hi cumað to þære ylde ðe we ær cwæ-don; hæfð þeah gehwa his agenne wæstm þe he on þissum life hæfde, oððe habban sceolde, gif he his gebide. Gif hwa alefed wære oððe limleas on þissum life, he bið þonne swa hit awriten is, þæt ealle ða þe to Godes rice gebyrigað nab-bað naðor ne womm ne awyrdnysse on heora lichaman. Hwæt sceole we smeagan embe ða oðre þe gewitað to ðam ecum forwyrde—hwæðer hi alefede beon oððe limlease þonne hi beoð on ecere susle wunigende?

13   Hit bið þonne swa swa Crist cwæð, þæt "Nan wer ne wi-fað, ne wif ne ceorlað, ne team ne bið getymed, ne hi deaðes ne abyrigað siððan, ac beoð englum gelice þonne hi mid en-glum wuniað." Ne him ne lyst nanre galnysse, ne hi næfre siððan synna ne gewyrceað. Ne bið þær sorh ne sar, ne nan gedreccednys, ac bið fulfremed sib and singal bliss, and beoð cuðe ge ða þe ær cuðe wæron ge ða þe uncuðe wæron, wunigende on broðorlicre lufe mid Gode a on ecnysse. Amen.

made flesh and blood, bone and skin, hair and nails. People often see that from one little kernel comes a great tree, but in the kernel we can see neither root, nor bark, nor branches, nor leaves: but the same God who draws forth from the kernel a tree, and fruits, and leaves, may from dust raise flesh and bones, sinews and hair, as he said in his gospel, "Not one hair of your head shall be lost to you."

The apostle Paul said that we should rise from death at the age that Christ was when he suffered, that is, about thirty-three years. Though a child should pass away, or a decrepit old person, yet they will come to the age we said before; yet everyone will have his own stature which he had in this life, or should have had, if he had lived to see it. If anyone is maimed or limbless in this life, he will be as it is written, that all those who belong to God's kingdom will have neither blemish nor hurt on their bodies. What should we imagine about those others who depart to eternal damnation—will they will be maimed or limbless when they are dwelling in eternal torment? 12

Then it will be as Christ said, that "No man will marry, nor woman take a husband, nor offspring will be conceived, nor will they taste death, but they will be like the angels when they dwell with angels." No lust will give them pleasure, nor will they ever afterward commit sins. There will be no sorrow or pain there, and no affliction, but there will be perfect peace and perpetual bliss, and there will be known both those who were known before and those who were unknown, dwelling in brotherly love with God forever in eternity. Amen. 13

17

Dominica 11 post Pasca

Dixit Iesus discipulis suis, "Ego sum pastor bonus," et reliqua.

2   Þis godspel þe nu geræd wæs cwyð þæt se hælend cwæde
be him sylfum, "Ic eom god hyrde. Se goda hyrde sylð his
agen lif for his sceapum. Se hyra, se ðe nis riht hyrde, he gesihð þone wulf cuman, and he forlæt ða scep and flyhð; and
se wulf sum gelæcð and ða oðre tostencð. Se hyra flyhð
forðan ðe his is hyra, and þa scep ne belimpað to him. Ic eom
god hyrde, and ic oncnawe mine scep and hi oncnawað me,
swa swa min fæder me oncnæwð and ic hine. And ic sylle
min agen lif for minum sceapum. Ic hæbbe eac oðre scep þe
ne sind na of ðisre eowde, and þa ic sceal lædan and hi gehyrað mine stemne, and bið an eowed and an hyrde."

3   Crist is good gecyndelice, and soðlice nis nan ðing god
butan Gode anum. Gif ænig gesceaft is god, þonne is seo
godnys of ðam scyppende, se ðe is healice god. He cwæð, "Se
goda hyrde sylð his agen lif for his sceapum." Ure alysend is
se goda hyrde, and we Cristene men sind his scep, and he
sealde his agen lif for ure alysednysse. He dyde swa swa he
manede, and mid þam he geswutelode hwæt he bebead.
God hyrde wæs Petrus, and god wæs Paulus, and gode
wæron ða apostoli, ðe hyra lif sealdon for Godes folce and
for rihtum geleafan; ac heora godnys wæs of ðam heafde,
þæt is Crist, ðe is heora heafod and hi sind his lima.

17

Second Sunday after Easter

The Second Sunday after Easter

J esus said to his disciples, "I am the good shepherd," etc.

This gospel which has just been read says that the savior 2
said of himself, "I am the good shepherd. A good shepherd
gives his own life for his sheep. The hireling, who is not the
rightful shepherd, sees the wolf coming, and he abandons
the sheep and flees; and the wolf seizes one and scatters the
others. The hireling flees because he is a hireling, and the
sheep do not belong to him. I am the good shepherd, and I
know my sheep and they know me, just as my father knows
me and I him. And I will give my own life for my sheep. I
also have other sheep which are not of this flock, and I will
lead these and they will hear my voice, and there will be one
flock and one shepherd."

Christ is good by nature, and truly there is nothing good 3
but God alone. If any creature is good, its goodness is from
the creator, who is supremely good. He said, "The good
shepherd gives his own life for his sheep." Our redeemer is
the good shepherd, and we Christians are his sheep, and he
gave his own life for our redemption. He did as he instructed, and with that he revealed what he commanded.
Peter was a good shepherd, and Paul was good, and the apostles were good, who gave their lives for God's people and for
the right faith; but their goodness came from the head, that
is, Christ, who is their head and they are his limbs.

4   Ælc bisceop and ælc lareow is to hyrde gesett Godes
folce, þæt hi sceolon þæt folc wið ðone wulf gescyldan. Se
wulf is deofol, þe syrwð ymbe Godes geladunge and cepð
hu he mage Cristenra manna sawla mid leahtrum fordon.
Þonne sceal se hyrde, þæt is se bisceop oððe oðer lareow,
wiðstandan þam reðan wulfe mid lare and mid gebedum.
Mid lare he sceal him tæcan, þæt hi cunnon hwæt deofol
tæchð mannum to forwyrde, and hwæt God bebyt to ge-
healdenne for begeate þæs ecan lifes. He sceal him fore
gebiddan, þæt God gehealde þa strangan and gehæle ða untruman. Se bið to strangum geteald se þe wiðstent deofles
lare; se bið untrum se ðe on leahtrum fylð. Ac se lareow bið
unscyldig gif he þæt folc mid lare gewissað, and him wið
God geðingað. Þa twa ðing he sceal ðam folce don, and eac
mid his agenum oðrum gehelpan, and gif hit swa getimað,
his agen lif syllan for ðæs folces hreddinge.

5   "Se hyra flihð þonne he ðone wulf gesihð." Se is hyra and
na hyrde, se ðe bið begripen on woruldðingum, and lufað
þone wurðmynt and ða ateorigendlican edlean, and næfð inweardlice lufe to Godes sceapum. He cepð þæra sceatta, and
blissað on ðam wurðmynte, and hæfð his mede for ðisum
life, and bið bescyred þære ecan mede. Nast ðu hwa bið
hyra, hwa hyrde, ær ðam ðe se wulf cume; ac se wulf
geswutelað mid hwilcum mode he gymde þæra sceapa. Se
wulf cymð to ðam sceapum, and sume he abitt, sume he
tostencð, þonne se reða deofol tihð þa Cristenan men—
sume to forligre, sume he ontent to gytsunge, sume he arærð
to modignysse, sume he þurh graman totwæmð, and mid
mislicum costnungum gastlice ofslihð. Ac se hyra ne bið
naðor ne mid ware ne mid lufe astyred, ac flyhð, þe he smeað
embe ða woruldlican hyðða and læt to gymeleaste þære

Every bishop and every teacher is placed as a shepherd 4
over God's people, so that they might protect the people
from the wolf. The wolf is the devil, who schemes around
God's Church and seeks how he might destroy Christian
souls with sins. Then the shepherd, that is, the bishop or
other teacher, should resist the fierce wolf with doctrine
and with prayers. He should teach them with doctrine, so
that they may know what the devil teaches for human destruction, and what God commands to be observed to attain eternal life. He should pray for them, that God may
preserve the strong and heal the weak. He is considered
strong who withstands the devil's teaching; he is weak who
falls into sins. But the teacher is guiltless if he directs the
people with doctrine, and intercedes for them with God.
He should do these two things for the people, and also help
others with his own goods, and if necessary, give his own life
to preserve the people.

"The hireling flees when he sees the wolf." He is a hireling 5
and not a shepherd, who is in the grip of worldly things, and
loves honors and perishable rewards, and has no inward love
for God's sheep. He seeks after money, rejoices in honors,
and has his reward in this life, but will be cut off from the
eternal reward. Before the wolf comes you do not know who
is a hireling, or who a shepherd; but the wolf reveals with
what mind he guards the sheep. The wolf comes to the
sheep, devouring some and scattering others, when the
fierce devil entices Christians—some to adultery, some he
inflames to greed, some he lifts up to pride, some he divides
through anger and slays spiritually with various temptations. The hireling is stirred neither by care nor love,
but flees, for he considers worldly advantages and leaves

sceapa lyre. Ne flyhð he na mid lichaman, ac mid mode. He flyhð þe he geseh unrihtwisnysse and suwade. He flyhð þe he is hyra and na hyrde; swilce hit swa gecweden sy, ne mæg se standan ongean fræcednyssa þæra sceapa, se ðe ne gymð þæra sceapa mid lufe, ac tylað his sylfes—þæt is, þæt he lufað þa eorðlican gestreon, and na Godes folc.

6   Wulf bið eac se unrihtwisa rica ðe bereafað þa Cristenan and ða eadmodan mid his riccetere ofsitt, ac se hyra oððe se medgylda ne gedyrstlæcð þæt he his unrihtwisnysse wiðstande þæt he ne forleose his wurðmynt, and ða woruldlican gestreon ðe he lufað swiðor ðonne þa Cristenan menn. Be ðisum awrat se witega Ezechiel, þus cweðende, "Ge hyrdas, gehyrað Godes word: Mine scep sint tostencte ðurh eowre gymeleaste, and sind abitene. Ge cariað embe eowerne bigleofan, and na embe þæra sceapa; forði ic wille ofgan ða scep æt eowrum handum, and ic do þæt ge geswicað þære wican, and ic wylle ahreddan mine eowde wið eow. Ic sylf wylle gadrian mine scep þe wæron tostencte, and ic wylle hi healdan on genihtsumre læse. Þæt þæt losode þæt ic wylle secan and ongean lædan; þæt þæt alefed wæs þæt ic gehæle; þæt untrume ic wylle getrymman, and þæt strange gehealdan, and ic hi læswige on dome and on rihtwisnysse."

7   Ðas word spræc God þurh ðone witegan Ezechiel be lareowum and be his folce. Ge sceolon beon geornfulle to eower agenre ðearfe, þeah hit swa getimige þæt se lareow gimeleas beo, and doð swa swa Crist tæhte: "Gif se lareow wel tæce and yfele bysnige, doð swa swa he tæcð, and na be ðam þe he bysnað." Se hælend cwæð be him, "Ic eom god hyrde, and ic oncnawe mine scep, and hi oncnawað me."

unheeded the loss of the sheep. He does not flee with his body, but with his mind. He flees because he saw iniquity and kept silent. He flees because he is a hireling and not a shepherd; it might be said that one cannot stand against the dangers of the sheep who does not guard the sheep with love, but provides for himself—that is, he loves worldly gain, and not God's people.

The wolf is also the unrighteous powerful person who robs Christians and oppresses the humble with his power, but the hireling or the mercenary does not dare oppose his unrighteousness lest he lose his honor, and the worldly gain which he loves more than Christian people. The prophet Ezekiel wrote about this, saying, "You shepherds, hear God's word: My sheep are scattered through your carelessness, and are devoured. You care for your own sustenance, and not for that of the sheep; therefore I will demand the sheep at your hands, and I will make you depart from the fold, and I will deliver my flock from you. I myself will gather my sheep that were scattered, and I will keep them in an abundant pasture. What was lost I will seek and lead back again; what was maimed I will heal; the sick I will strengthen, and keep watch over the strong, and I will pasture them in judgment and in righteousness." 6

God spoke these words through the prophet Ezekiel about teachers and about his people. You should be zealous for your own need, even if it so happens that the teacher is heedless, and do as Christ taught: "If the teacher teaches well and gives an evil example, do as he teaches, and not according to his example." The savior says of himself, "I am a good shepherd, and I know my sheep, and they know me." 7

Þæt is, ic lufige hi, and hi lufiað me. Se ðe ne lufað soðfæstnysse, ne oncneow he na gyt God. Ac behealde ge hwæðer ge
sind Godes scep, hwæðer ge hine gyt oncneowon, hwæðer
ge mid soðfæstnysse hine lufiað. He cwæð, "Swa swa min
Fæder oncnæwð me, and ic oncnawe hine, and ic sylle min
agen lif for minum sceapum." He oncnæwð his Fæder ðurh
hine sylfne, and we oncnawað þurh hine. Mid þære lufe þe
he wolde for mancynne sweltan, mid þære he cyðde hu micclan he lufað his Fæder. He cwæð, "Ic hæbbe oðre scep þe ne
sind na of ðisre eowde, and ða ic sceal lædan and hi gehyrað
mine stemne, and sceal beon an eowd, and an hyrde."

8   Þis he spræc on Iudea lande; ðær wæs an eowd of ðam
mannum þe on God belyfdon on ðam leodscipe. Þa oðre
scep syndon þa þe of eallum oðrum eardum to Gode bugað;
and Crist hi gebrincð ealle on anre eowde on ðam ecan life.
Manega sind hyrdas under Criste, and ðeah hwæðere he is
ana heora ealra hyrde, se ðe leofað and rixað mid Fæder and
mid Halgum Gaste, a on ecnysse. Amen.

That is, I love them, and they love me. He who does not love truth does not yet know God. Consider whether you are God's sheep, whether you know him yet, or whether you love him with truth. He said, "As my Father knows me, and I know him, and I give my own life for my sheep." He knows his Father through himself, and we know through him. He showed how much he loves his Father by that love with which he would die for humanity. He said, "I have other sheep which are not of this flock, and I will lead them and they will hear my voice, and there shall be one flock and one shepherd."

He spoke this in the land of Judea; there was a flock of 8 people who believed in God in that nation. The other sheep are those of all other lands who turn to God; and Christ will bring them all into one flock in eternal life. There are many shepherds under Christ, and yet he alone is shepherd of them all, who lives and reigns with the Father and with the Holy Spirit forever to eternity. Amen.

18

In Letania maiore

Ðas dagas synd gehatene *Letaniae,* þæt sint "gebeddagas."
On ðisum dagum we sceolon gebiddan ure eorðlicra wæstma
genihtsumnysse, and us sylfum gesundfulnysse and sibbe
and, þæt gyt mare is, ure synna forgyfenysse.

2   We rædað on bocum þæt ðeos gehealdsumnys wurde
aræred on ðone timan ðe gelamp on anre byrig ðe Uigenna is
gecweden micel eorðstyrung, and feollon cyrcan and hus,
and comon wilde beran and wulfas and abiton ðæs folces
micelne dæl, and þæs cynges botl wearð mid heofonlicum
fyre forbærned. Þa bead se biscop Mamertus ðreora daga
fæsten, and seo gedreccednys ða geswac; and se gewuna ðæs
fæstenes ðurhwunað gehwær on geleaffulre gelaðunge.

3   Hi namon þa bysne ðæs fæstenys æt ðam Niniueiscan
folce. Þæt folc wæs swiðe fyrenful; þa wolde God hi fordon,
ac hi gegladodon hine mid heora behreowsunge. God spræc
to anum witegan se wæs Ionas gehaten: "Far to ðære byrig
Niniuen, and boda ðær ða word þe ic ðe secge." Þa wearð se
witega afyrht, and wolde forfleon Godes gesihðe, ac he ne
mihte. Ferde ða to sæ and stah on scip. Ða ða þa scypmen
comon ut on sæ, þa sende him God to micelne wind and
hreohnysse, swa þæt þæt hi wæron orwene heora lifes. Hi ða

18

On the Greater Litany
(Rogationtide)

On the Greater Litany

These days are called *Litanies,* that is, "prayer days." On these days we should pray for an abundance of earthly fruits, and for our health and peace and, what is more, the forgiveness of our sins.

We read in books that this observance was established at 2 a time when there was a great earthquake in a city called Vienne, and churches and houses fell, and wild bears and wolves came and devoured a large portion of the people, and the king's palace was burned down with heavenly fire. Then the bishop Mamertus ordered a fast of three days, and the affliction stopped; and the custom of the fast continues everywhere in the faithful Church.

They took the example of the fast from the people of 3 Nineveh. Those people were very sinful; God would have destroyed them, but they appeased him with their penitence. God spoke to a prophet who was called Jonah: "Go to the city of Nineveh, and announce there the words which I will say to you." The prophet was afraid, and wanted to flee from God's presence, but he could not. He went to the sea and embarked on a ship. When the sailors went out on the sea, God sent them a great wind and storm, so that they

wurpon heora waru oforbord, and se witega læg slep. Hi
wurpon ða tan betweox him, and bædon þæt God sceolde
geswutulian hwanon him þæt ungelimp become; þa com
ðæs witegan ta upp. Hi axodon hine hwæt he wære oððe hu
he faran wolde; he cwæð þæt he wære Godes ðeow, se ðe gesceop sæ and land, and þæt he fleon wolde of Godes gesihðe.
Hi cwædon, "Hu do we ymbe ðe?" He andwyrde, "Weorpað
me oforbord; þonne geswicð þeos gedreccednys." Hi ða swa
dydon, and seo hreohnys wearð gestilled, and hi offrodon
Gode heora lac, and tugon forð.

4   God ða gegearcode ænne hwæl, and he forswealh þone
witegan and abær hine to ðam lande þe he to sceolde, and
hine ðær utaspaw. Þa com eft Godes word to ðam witegan,
and cwæð, "Aris nu, and ga to ðære mycelan byrig Niniuen,
and boda swa swa ic ðe ær sæde." He ferde and bodode þæt
him wæs Godes grama onsigende gif hi to Gode bugan
noldon. Ða aras se cyning of his cynesetle and awearp his
deorwyrðe reaf, and dyde hæran to his lice and axan uppan
his heafod, and bead þæt ælc man swa don sceolde, and
ægðer ge men ge ða sucendan cild and eac ða nytenu ne onbyrigdon nanes ðinges binnan ðrim dagum. Þa ðurh þa gecyrrednysse þæt hi yfeles geswicon, and ðurh þæt strange
fæsten, him gemildsode God and nolde hi fordon, swa swa
he ær þa twa burhwara Sodomam and Gomorram for heora
leahtrum, mid heofonlicum fyre forbærnde.

5   We sceolon eac on ðissum dagum began ure gebedu, and
fyligan urum haligdome ut and inn, and ðone ælmihtigan
God mid geornfulnysse herian. We wyllað nu þis godspel
eow gereccan þe her nu geræd wæs: *Quis vestrum habebit ami-*
cum, et reliqua. "Se hælend cwæð to his leorningcnihtum,

were despairing of their lives. They cast their cargo overboard, and the prophet lay asleep. They cast lots among
themselves, and prayed that God would reveal the source of
that affliction, and then the prophet's lot came up. They
asked him who he was or where he would go; he said that he
was a servant of God, who created sea and land, and that he
wanted to flee from God's presence. They said, "What will
we do about you?" He answered, "Throw me overboard;
then this affliction will stop." They did so, and the storm
was stilled, and they offered their gifts to God, and went on
their way.

God then prepared a whale, and it swallowed up the 4
prophet and carried him to the land he was supposed to go
to, and there vomited him out. Then God's word came again
to the prophet, and said, "Arise now, and go to the great city
Nineveh, and preach as I said to you before." He went and
preached that God's anger was coming upon them if they
would not turn to God. Then the king rose from his throne
and cast off his precious robes, and put sackcloth on his
body and ashes on his head, and commanded that every person should do the same, and that neither people nor nursing
children nor even cattle should taste anything for three
days. Then through that conversion in which they ceased
their evil, and through that strict fast, God had mercy on
them and would not destroy them, as he had once burned
the inhabitants of the two cities Sodom and Gomorrah with
heavenly fire, for their sins.

Also on these days we should recite our prayers, and fol- 5
low our relics out and in, and praise almighty God with eagerness. We will now explain to you this gospel which has
just been read: *Which of you has a friend, etc.* "The savior said

'Hwilc eower is þe hæfð sumne freond, and gæð him to on middere nihte, and cwyð, "Þu freond, alænne me ðry hlafas, forðan ðe me gesohte sum cuma, and ic næbbe nan ðing gearlices him to beodenne." Þonne andwyrt se hiredes ealdor of his bedde and cwyð, "Ne drece ðu me nu on ðisum timan; min duru is belocen and mine cild syndon on heora reste. Ic ne mæg nu arisan and ðe þæs tiðian." Þonne gif se oðer þurhwunað mid hreame and cnucunge, he arisð þonne for his onhrope and na for freondscype, and getiðað him þæs þe he bit.' Ða cwæð eft se hælend, 'Biddað and eow bið geseald; secað and ge gemetað; cnuciað and eow bið geopenod. Ælc mann ðe bitt he underfecð, and se ðe secð he gemet, and se ðe cnucað him bið geopenod. Hwilc eower bit his fæder hlafes, hu cwest ðu sylð he him stan for hlafe? Oððe gif he bitt fisces, sylð he him næddran? Oððe gif he bitt æges, sylð he him ðone wyrm ðe is gehaten ðrowend? Gif ge cunnon ða ðe yfele synd syllan ða godnysse eowrum bearnum, hu micele swyðor wyle eower heofenlica Fæder forgifan godne gast him biddendum?'"

6   Se halga Augustinus trahtnode þis godspel, and cwæð þæt seo niht getacnode þa nytennysse þisre worulde. Þeos woruld is afylled mid nytennysse. Nu sceal forði gehwa arisan of ðære nytennysse and gan to his frynd, þæt is, þæt he sceal gebugan to Criste mid ealre geornfulnysse, and biddan þæra ðreora hlafa, þæt is, geleafan þære halgan Ðrynnysse. Se ælmihtiga Fæder is God, and his Sunu is ælmihtig God, and se Halga Gast is ælmihtig God; na ðry godas, ac hi ealle an ælmihtig God untodæledlic. Þonne ðu becymst to ðisum ðrym hlafum, þæt is, to andgite ðære halgan Ðrynnysse, þonne hæfst ðu on ðam geleafan lif and fodan ðinre sawle, and miht oðerne cuman eac mid ðam fedan, þæt is, ðu miht

to his disciples, 'Who is there among you who has a friend, and goes to him at midnight, and says, "Friend, loan me three loaves, because a visitor has sought me out, and I have nothing prepared to offer him." The head of the household will then answer from his bed and say, "Do not disturb me at this time; my door is locked and my children are in their beds. I cannot rise now and give this to you." Then if the other continues with outcry and knocking, he will rise because of his clamor and not for friendship, and grant him what he asks for.' Then the savior said again, 'Ask, and it will be given to you; seek, and you will find; knock, and it will be opened for you. Everyone who asks will receive, and whoever seeks will find, and whoever knocks it will be opened for him. If one of you asks his father for bread, do you think he will give him a stone for bread? Or if he asks for fish, will he give him a snake? Or if he asks for an egg, will he give him the serpent that is called scorpion? If you who are evil know how to give good things to your children, how much more will your heavenly Father give a good spirit to those who ask him?'"

Saint Augustine commented on this gospel, and said that 6 the night signified the ignorance of this world. This world is filled with ignorance. So everyone should rise up from this ignorance and go to his friend, that is, he should turn to Christ with all zeal, and ask for the three loaves, that is, faith in the holy Trinity. The almighty Father is God, and his Son is almighty God, and the Holy Spirit is almighty God; not three gods, but they are all one almighty God, indivisible. When you come to these three loaves, that is, to an understanding of the holy Trinity, then you will have life in faith and food for your soul, and can also feed another visitor with

tæcan ðone geleafan oðrum frynd þe þe ðæs bitt. He cwæð "cuma," forðan ðe we ealle sind cuman on ðisum life, and ure eard nis na her; ac we sind her swilce wegferende men—an cymð, oðer færð; se bið acenned, se oðer forðfærð and rymð him setl. Nu sceal gehwa forði gewilnian þæs geleafan þære halgan Ðrynnysse, forðan ðe se geleafa hine gebrincð to ðam ecan life.

7   We wyllað eft embe ðone geleafan swiðor sprecan, forðan ðe ðises godspelles traht hæfð godne tige. Se hiredes ealdor þe wæs on his reste gebroht mid his cildum is Crist, þe sitt on heofonum mid his apostolum, and mid martyrum, and mid eallum þam halgum þe he on ðisum life gefette. We sceolon clypigan to Criste and biddan ðæra ðreora hlafa. Ðeah he us þærrihte ne getiðige, ne sceole we forði þære bene geswican. He elcað, and wyle hwæðere forgyfan. Þi he elcað þæt we sceolon beon oflyste, and deorwyrðlice healdan Godes gife. Swa hwæt swa man eaðelice begyt þæt ne bið na swa deorwyrðe swa þæt þæt earfoðlice bið begyten. Se hælend cwæð, "Gif he ðurhwunað cnucigende, þonne arist se hiredes ealdor for ðæs oðres onhrope, and him getiðað þæs ðe he bitt, na for freondrædene, ac for his unstilnysse." Þi he cwæð, "Na for freondrædene," forðan ðe nan man nære wyrðe ne þæs geleafan ne ðæs ecan lifes, gif Godes mildheortnys nære ðe mare ofer manncynne. Nu sceole we cnucian, and hryman to Criste, forðan ðe he wile us tiðian, swa swa he sylf cwæð, "Biddað, and eow bið forgifen; secað, and ge gemetað; cnuciað, and eow bið geopenod." Ælc ðæra ðe geornlice bitt and þære bene ne geswicð, þam getiðað God þæs ecan lifes.

8   He cwæð þa oðer bigspel. "Hwilc fæder wile syllan his cilde stan, gif hit hine hlafes bitt? Oþþe næddran, gif hit

it, that is, you can teach the faith to another friend who asks you. He said "visitor," because we are all visitors in this life, and our country is not here; but we are here like wayfarers — one comes, another goes; one is born, another departs and gives up his place to him. Therefore everyone should desire the faith in the Holy Trinity, for that faith will bring him to eternal life.

We will say more about faith, because the exposition of 7 this gospel has a good implication. The head of the household who had gone to rest with his children is Christ, who sits in heaven with his apostles, and with martyrs, and with all the saints whom he has fetched from this life. We should call to Christ and pray for the three loaves. Though he might not grant them to us right away, we should not cease our prayer because of that. He delays, and yet will give. He delays that we may be full of desire, and value the grace of God dearly. Whatever one gets easily is not as precious as that which is gotten with difficulty. The savior said, "If he continues knocking, the head of the household will arise because of the other's clamor, and grant him what he asks, not for friendship, but because of his noise." He said, "Not for friendship," because no one would be worthy either of faith or of eternal life, if God's mercy toward humanity were not greater. We should knock, and call to Christ, because he wants to give to us, as he himself said, "Ask, and it will be given to you; seek, and you will find; knock, and it will be opened to you." To everyone who fervently asks and does not cease from prayer, God will grant everlasting life.

He then said another parable. "What father will give his 8 child a stone, if he ask for bread? Or a snake, if he ask for a

fisces bitt? Oððe þone wyrm ðrowend, gif hit æges bitt?"
God is ure Fæder þurh his mildheortnysse, and se fisc getacnað geleafan, and þæt æig ðone halgan hiht, se hlaf ða
soðan lufe. Þas ðreo ðing forgifð God his gecorenum, forðan
ðe nan man ne mæg habban Godes rice butan he hæbbe ðas
ðreo ðing. He sceal rihtlice gelyfan, and habban hiht to
Gode, and soðe lufe to Gode and to mannum, gif he wile to
Godes rice becuman. Se fisc getacnað geleafan, forðan ðe his
gecynd is, swa hine swiðor ða yða wealcað, swa he strengra
bið, and swiðor batað. Swa eac se geleaffulla man, swa he
swiðor bið geswenct for his geleafan, swa se geleafa strengra
bið, þær ðær he æltæwe bið; gif he abryð on ðære ehtnysse,
he ne bið þonne geleafa ac bið hiwung. Þæt æig getacnað
hiht, forði ðe fugelas ne tymað swa swa oðre nytenu, ac ærest
hit bið æig, and seo modor siððan mid hihte bret þæt æig
to bridde. Swa eac ure hiht ne becom na gyt to ðam ðe
he hopað, ac is swilce he sy æig. Þonne he hæfð þæt him
behaten is, he bið fugel. Hlaf getacnað þa soðan lufe, seo
is ealra mægna mæst, swa swa se hlaf bið ealra metta fyrmest. Micel mægen is geleafa, and micel is se soða hiht,
þeah hwæðere seo lufu hi oferswið, forðan ðe heo bið a on
ecnysse, and ða oðre twa geendiað. We gelyfað nu on God,
and we hopiað to him; eft þonne we becumað to his rice, swa
swa he us behet, þonne bið se geleafa geendod, forðan ðe we
geseoð þonne þæt we nu gelyfað. Ure hiht bið eac geendod,
forþan ðe we beoð hæbbende ðæs ðe we ær hopedon. Ac seo
lufu ne ateorað næfre; nu is heo forði heora selest.

9   Seo næddre is geset on ðam godspelle ongean ðone fisc.
On næddran hiwe beswac se deofol Adam, and æfre he winð
nu ongean urne geleafan, ac seo gescyldnys is æt urum Fæder

fish? Or the serpent scorpion, if he ask for an egg?" God is our Father through his mercy, and the fish signifies faith, and the egg holy hope, the bread true love. God gives these three things to his chosen ones, for no one can have God's kingdom unless he has these three things. He must rightly believe, and have hope in God, and true love for God and for humanity, if he will come to God's kingdom. The fish signifies faith, because its nature is that the more the waves toss it and the more vigorously it strikes, the stronger it is. In the same way, the more a faithful person is afflicted for his faith, the stronger will his faith be, wherever it is perfectly sound; if it sinks under persecution, then it is not faith but hypocrisy. The egg signifies hope, because birds do not give birth like other animals, but first there is an egg, and afterward the mother nurtures the egg with hope into a young bird. Similarly our hope does not come yet to that which it hopes for, but is as it were an egg. When it has what it has been promised, it is a bird. Bread signifies true love, which is the greatest of all virtues, just as bread is the foremost of all foods. Faith is a great virtue, and great is true hope, yet love exceeds them, because it will be forever in eternity, and the other two will end. We now believe in God, and we hope in him; but after we come to his kingdom, as he has promised us, then faith will be ended, for we shall then see what we now believe. Our hope will also be ended, because we will be having what we had previously hoped for. But love will never decay; therefore is it the most excellent of them.

The serpent is placed in the gospel in opposition to the 9 fish. The devil deceived Adam in the form of a serpent, and now he always strives against our faith, but our protection is

gelang. Se wyrm ðrowend, þe is geset ongean þæt æig, is
ættren, and slihð mid þam tægle to deaðe. Þa ðing ðe we
geseoð on ðisum life ða sind ateorigendlice; þa ðe we ne geseoð, and us sind behatene, hi sind ece: strece ðærto þinne
hiht, and anbida oð þæt ðu hi hæbbe. Ne loca ðu underbæc;
ondræd þe ðone ðrowend þe geættrað mid þam tægle. Se
man locað underbæc þe geortruwað Godes mildheortnysse;
þonne bið his hiht geættrod mid þæs ðrowendes tægle. Ac
we nu sceolon, æigðer ge on earfoðnyssum ge on gelimpe
and on ungelimpe, cweðan swa swa se witega cwæð, "Ic
herige minne Drihten on ælcne timan." Getimige us tela
on lichaman, getimige us untela, symle we sceolon þæs
Gode ðancian and his naman bletsian; þonne bið ure hiht
gehealden wið þæs wyrmes slege.

10   Stan is gesett ongean ðone hlaf, þe heardmodnys is wiðer-
ræde soðre lufe. Heardheort bið se mann ðe nele þurh lufe
oðrum fremigan þær ðær he mæg. Þæt godspel cwæð, "Gif
ge cunnon, þa ðe yfele sind, syllan ða godnysse eowrum
bearnum, hu micele swiðor wile eower heofonlica Fæder
forgyfan godne gast him biddendum?" Hwæt sind ða god þe
men syllað heora cildum? Hwilwendlice godnyssa, swylce
swa þæt godspel hrepode—hlaf, and fisc, and æig. Gode sind
þas ðing be heora mæðe, forðan ðe se eorðlica lichama behofað þæs fodan. Nu ge, gleawe men, nellað syllan eowrum
cildum næddran for fisce; nele eac ure heofonlica Fæder us
syllan þæs deofles geleaflæste, gif we hine biddað þæt he
us sylle soðne geleafan. And ðu nelt syllan ðinum bearne
þrowend for æge; nele eac God us syllan orwenysse for
hihte. And ðu nelt ðinum bearne syllan stan for hlafe; nele
eac God us syllan heardheortnysse for soðre lufe. Ac se goda
heofonlica Fæder forgifð us geleafan, and hiht, and ða soðan

from our Father. The scorpion, which is placed in opposition to the egg, is poisonous, and stings to death with its tail. The things we see in this life are perishable; those we do not see, and which are promised to us, are eternal: stretch out your hope to them, and wait until you have them. Do not look behind; fear the scorpion, which poisons with its tail. The person who despairs of God's mercy looks behind; then his hope is poisoned by the scorpion's tail. We should, whether in difficulties or in chances or mischances, say as the prophet said, "I will praise my Lord at all times." Whether good or evil might befall us in our body, we should always thank God for it and bless his name; then our hope will be preserved from the serpent's sting.

A stone is set in opposition to bread, because hardness of mind is contrary to true love. Hard-hearted is the person who will not do good for others through love wherever he can. The gospel says, "If you who are evil know how to give what is good to your children, how much more will your heavenly Father give a good spirit to those who ask him?" What are the good things that people give to their children? Transitory goods, such as the gospel mentioned—bread, and fish, and eggs. These things are good in their way, because the earthly body requires food. Now you, prudent people, will not give your children a serpent for a fish; nor will our heavenly Father give us the devil's faithlessness, if we ask him to give us true faith. And you would not give your child a scorpion for an egg; nor will God give us despair for hope. And you would not give your child a stone for bread; nor too will God give us hard-heartedness for true love. The good heavenly Father will give us faith, and hope,

lufe, and deð þæt we habbað godne gast, þæt is, godne willan.

11   Us is to smeagenne þæt word þe he cwæð, "Ge ðe sind yfele." Yfele we sind, ac we habbað godne Fæder. We habbað gehyred urne naman, "Ge ðe synt yfele." Ac hwa is ure Fæder? Se ælmihtiga God. And hwilcera manna Fæder is he? Swutelice hit is gesæd, yfelra manna. And hwilc is se Fæder? Be ðam þe is gecweden for þæt, "Nis nan man god butan Gode anum." Se ðe æfre is god he gebrincð us yfele to godum mannum, gif we bugað fram yfele and doð god. God wæs se man gesceapen Adam, ac ðurh his agenne cyre and deofles tihtinge he wearð yfel and eal his ofspring. Se ðe synful bið he bið yfel, and nan man nis on life butan sumere synne. Ac ure goda Fæder us geclænsað and gehælð, swa swa se witega cwæð, "Drihten, gehæl me, and ic beo gehæled; geheald þu me, and ic beo gehealden."

12   Se ðe god beon wile clypige to ðam þe æfre is god, þæt he hine godne gewyrce. Se man hæfð gold, þæt is god be his mæðe; he hæfð land and welan, þa sint gode. Ac ne bið se man god þurh ðas ðing butan he mid þam god wyrce, swa swa se witega cwæð, "He aspende his ðing, and todælde ðearfum, and his rihtwisnys wunað a on worulde." He gewanode his feoh and geihte his rihtwisnysse. He gewanode þæt he forlætan sceal, and þæt bið geiht þæt þæt he habban sceal on ecnysse. Þu herast ðone mancgere ðe begytt gold mid leade, and nelt herigan ðone ðe begytt rihtwisnysse and heofonan rice mid brosnigendlicum his feo. Se rica and se ðearfa sind wegferende on ðisre worulde. Nu berð se rica swære byrðene his gestreona, and se ðearfa gæð æmtig. Se rica berð mare þonne he behofige to his formettum; se oðer

and true love, and cause us to have a good spirit, that is, good will.

We should consider the words he said, "You who are evil." 11
We are evil, but we have a good Father. We have heard our name, "You who are evil." But who is our Father? The almighty God. And whose Father is he? It is clearly said, of evil people. And what kind of Father is he? He of whom it is said, "No one is good but God alone." He who is always good will lead us evil ones to be good people, if we will turn away from evil and do good. The human Adam was created good, but by his own choice and the devil's enticement he and all his offspring became evil. He who is sinful is evil, and there is no one alive without some sin. But our good Father will cleanse and heal us, as the prophet said, "Lord, heal me, and I will be healed; save me, and I will be saved."

Let him who wants to be good call to the one who is ever 12
good, that he might make him good. A person has gold, which is good in its way; he has land and riches, which are good. But the person is not good through these things unless he does good with them, as the prophet said, "He distributed his things, and divided them among the poor, and his righteousness remains forever." He diminished his money and increased his righteousness. He diminished that which he must abandon, so that which he will have in eternity will be increased. You praise the merchant who acquires gold for lead, but will not praise the one who acquires righteousness and the kingdom of heaven with perishable wealth. The rich and the poor are wayfarers in this world. The rich person now bears the heavy burden of his treasures, and the poor one goes empty. The rich one bears more provisions for his journey than he needs; the other bears an

berð æmtigne pusan. Forði sceal se rica dælan his byrðene wið þone ðearfan; þonne wanað he ða byrðene his synna, and ðam þearfan gehelpð. Ealle we sind Godes þearfan; uton forði oncnawan þa ðearfan þe us biddað, þæt God oncnawe us þonne we hine biddað ure neoda. Hwæt sind þa ðe us biddað? Earme men, and tiddre, and deadlice. Æt hwam biddað hi? Æt earmum mannum, and tiddrum, and deadlicum. Butan þam æhtum, gelice sind þa þe ðær biddað and ða ðe hi ætbiddað. Hu mihtu for sceame æniges ðinges æt Gode biddan, gif ðu forwyrnst ðinum gelican þæs ðe ðu foreaðelice him getiðian miht? Ac se rica besihð on his pællenum gyrlum, and cwyð, "Nis se loddere mid his tættecon min gelica." Ac se apostol Paulus hine nebbað mid þisum wordum, "Ne brohte we nan ðing to ðisum middangearde, ne we nan ðing heonon mid us lædan ne magon."

13   Gif rice wif and earm acennað togædere, gangon hi aweig, nast ðu hwæðer bið þæs rican wifan cild, hwæðer þæs earman. Eft gif man openað deaddra manna byrgynu, nast ðu hwæðer beoð þæs rican mannes ban, hwæðer þæs ðearfan. Ac seo gytsung is ealra yfelra ðinga wyrtruma, and þa ðe fyligað þære gytsunge hi dweliað fram Godes geleafan, and hi befeallað on mislice costnunga and derigendlice lustas, ðe hi besencað on forwyrd. Oðer is þæt hwa rice beo, gif his yldran him æhta becwædon; oðer is gif hwa þurh gytsunge rice gewurðe. Þises mannes gytsung is gewreht wið God, na ðæs oðres æht, gif his heorte ne bið ontend mid þære gytsunge. Swilcum mannum bebead se apostol Paulus, "Bebeodað þam ricum þæt hi ne modigan, ne hi ne hopian on heora ungewissum welan; ac beon hi rice on godum weorcum, and syllan Godes ðearfum mid cystigum mode, and

empty purse. Therefore the rich person should share his burden with the poor one; then he will lessen the burden of his sins, and help the poor person. We are all God's poor; let us therefore acknowledge the poor who ask of us, that God might acknowledge us when we ask our needs of him. Who are those that ask of us? The poor, and weak, and mortal. Of whom do they ask? Of people who are poor, and weak, and mortal. Except for their possessions, those who ask and those whom they ask are equal. How can you for shame ask anything of God, if you refuse to your equal what you could most easily grant him? But the rich person looks on his purple garments and says, "The wretch with his rags is not my equal." But the apostle Paul retorts to him with these words, "We brought nothing into this world, nor can we take anything with us from it."

If a rich woman and a poor one give birth together and then go away, you will not know which is the rich woman's child, and which the poor one's. Or if you open the tombs of the dead, you do not know which are the rich person's bones, which the poor one's. Covetousness is the root of all evil things, and those who follow covetousness stray from God's faith and fall into various temptations and harmful desires, which sink them into damnation. It is one thing for someone to be rich, if his parents have bequeathed him possessions; it is another for someone to become rich through covetousness. That person's covetousness is accused before God, not the other's wealth, if his heart is not inflamed with covetousness. Of such people the apostle Paul warned, "Warn the rich that they should not be proud, nor hope in their uncertain wealth; but let them be rich in good works, and give to God's poor with a generous mind, and God will

13

God him forgylt mid hundfealdum swa hwæt swa he deð þam earman for his lufon."

14 Se rica and se þearfa sind him betwynan nydbehefe. Se welega is geworht forðan ðearfan, and se þearfa for ðan welegan. Þam spedigum gedafenað þæt he spende and dæle; ðam wædlan gedafenað þæt he gebidde for ðane dælere. Se earma is se weg þe læt us to Godes rice; mare sylð se ðearfa þam rican þonne he æt him nime. Se rica him sylð þone hlaf ðe bið to meoxe awend, and se ðearfa sylð þam rican þæt ece lif—na he swaðeah, ac Crist, se ðe þus cwæð, "Þæt þæt ge doð anum ðearfan on minum naman, þæt ge doð me sylfum," se ðe leofað and rixað mid Fæder and mid Halgum Gaste a butan ende. Amen.

19

Feria III, de Dominica oratione

Se hælend Crist, syððan he to ðisum life com and man wearð geweaxen, þa ða he wæs ðritig wintra eald on þære menniscnysse, þa begann he wundra to wyrcenne, and geceas ða twelf leorningcnihtas þa ðe we apostolas hatað. Þa wæron mid him æfre syððan, and he him tæhte ealne þone wisdom ðe on halgum bocum stent, and þurh hi ealne Cristendom astealde. Þa cwædon hi to ðam hælende, "Leof,

repay them a hundredfold whatever they do for the poor for love of him."

The rich and the poor are necessary to each other. The 14 wealthy person is made for the poor one, and the poor for the wealthy. The prosperous should spend and distribute; the beggar should pray for the distributor. The poor person is the way that leads us to God's kingdom; the poor person gives to the rich one more than he receives from him. The rich one gives him bread that will be turned to dung, and the poor gives to the rich eternal life—yet not he, but Christ, who said, "Whatever you do for one poor person in my name, you do for me," he who lives and reigns with the Father and the Holy Spirit forever without end. Amen.

19

Tuesday, On the Lord's Prayer

Tuesday, on the Lord's Prayer

The savior Christ, after he had come to this life and grown to adulthood, when he was thirty years old in human form, began to work miracles, and chose the twelve disciples whom we call apostles. These were afterward always with him, and he taught them all the wisdom contained in holy books, and through them established all Christianity. Then they said to the savior, "Sir, teach us how to pray." The savior

tæce us hu we magon us gebiddan." Ða andwyrde se hælend
and þus cwæð, "Gebiddað eow mid þisum wordum to minum Fæder and to eowrum Fæder, Gode ælmihtigum: *Pater
noster,* þæt is on Englisc, 'Þu ure Fæder þe eart on heofonum,
sy þin nama gehalgod. Cume ðin rice; sy ðin wylla on eorðan
swa swa on heofonum. Syle us todæg urne dæghwamlican
hlaf, and forgyf us ure gyltas swa swa we forgyfað ðam þe wið
us agyltað. And ne læd ðu na us on costnunge, ac alys us fram
yfele. Sy hit swa.'"

2   God Fæder ælmihtig hæfð ænne Sunu gecyndelice and
menige gewiscendlice. Crist is Godes Sunu, swa þæt se
Fæder hine gestrynde of him sylfum butan ælcere meder.
Næfð se Fæder nænne lichaman, ne he on ða wisan his bearn
ne gestrynde þe menn doð, ac his wisdom þe he mid ealle
gesceafta geworhte, se is his Sunu, se is æfre of ðam Fæder
and mid þam Fæder, God of Gode, ealswa mihtig swa se
Fæder. We men sind Godes bearn forðon þe he us geworhte;
and eft, ða ða we forwyrhte wæron, he sende his agen Bearn
us to alysednysse. Nu sind we Godes bearn, and Crist is ure
broðer, gif we ðam Fæder onriht gehyrsumiað, and mid eallum mode hine weorðiað. Crist is ure heafod and we sind his
lima: he is mid ure menniscnysse befangen, and he hæfð
urne lichaman, þone ðe he of ðam halgan mædene Marian
genam. Forði we magon cuðlice to him clypian swa swa to
urum breðer, gif we ða broðerrædene swa healdað swa swa
he us tæhte—þæt is, þæt we ne sceolon na geðafian þæt
deofol mid ænigum unðeawum us geweme fram Cristes
broðorrædene.

3   Witodlice se man þe deofle geefenlæcð se bið deofles
bearn, na þurh gecynd oððe þurh gesceapenysse, ac ðurh þa
geefenlæcunge and yfele geearnunga. And se man ðe Gode

answered and said, "Pray in these words to my father and to your father, God almighty: *Our Father,* that is in English, 'Our Father who are in heaven, may your name be sanctified. Let your kingdom come; let your will be done on earth as in heaven. Give us today our daily bread, and forgive us our offenses as we forgive those who offend against us. And do not lead us into temptation, but deliver us from evil. So be it.'"

God the almighty Father has one Son naturally and many by adoption. Christ is God's Son, because the Father produced him from himself without any mother. The Father has no body, nor did he produce his Son in the way that humans do, but his wisdom by which he made all creatures, that is his Son, is ever of the Father and with the Father, God of God, just as mighty as the Father. We humans are children of God because he made us; and afterward, when we were lost, he sent his own Son for our redemption. Now we are God's children, and Christ is our brother, if we will rightly obey the Father, and honor him with all our heart. Christ is our head and we are his limbs: he is clothed in our humanity, and he has our body, which he received from the holy virgin Mary. Therefore we may openly call to him as to our brother, if we hold our brotherhood as he has taught us—that is, that we should not allow the devil to seduce us away from the brotherhood of Christ with any evil practices. 2

Truly, the person who imitates the devil is a child of the devil, not by nature nor by creation, but by that imitation and evil merits. And the one who pleases God is a child of 3

gecwemð he bið Godes bearn, na gecyndelice, ac þurh
gesceapenysse and ðurh gode geearnunga, swa swa Crist
cwæð on his godspelle, "Se ðe wyrcð mines Fæder willan se
ðe is on heofonum, he bið min broðer and min moder and
min sweoster." Forði nu ealle Cristene men, ægðer ge rice ge
heane, ge æðelborene ge unæðelborene, and se hlaford and
se ðeowa, ealle hi sind gebroðra, and ealle hi habbað ænne
Fæder on heofonum. Nis se welega na betera on ðisum naman þonne se ðearfa. Eallswa bealdlice mot se ðeowa clypigan God him to Fæder ealswa se cyning. Ealle we sind gelice
ætforan Gode, buton hwa oðerne mid godum weorcum
forðeo. Ne sceal se rica for his welan þone earman forseon,
forðan oft bið se earma betera ætforan Gode þonne se rica.
God is ure Fæder, þi we sceolon ealle beon gebroðru on
Gode, and healdan þone broðerlican bend unforedne, þæt
is, ða soðan sibbe, swa þæt ure ælc oðerne lufige swa swa
hine sylfne, and nanum ne gebeode þæt þæt he nelle þæt
man him gebeode. Se ðe ðis hylt he bið Godes bearn and
Crist, and ealle halige men ðe Gode geðeoð beoð his gebroðru and his gesweostru.

4   We cweðað, *Pater noster qui es in celis,* þæt is, "Ure Fæder
ðe eart on heofonum," þe God Fæder is on heofonum, and
he is æghwar, swa swa he sylf cwæð, "Ic gefylle mid me sylfum heofonas and eorðan." And eft þæt halige godspel be
him þus cwyð, "Heofon is his þrymsetl, and eorðe is his
fotsceamul." We wendað us eastweard þonne we us gebiddað forðan ðe ðanon arist seo heofen: na swilce on eastdæle
synderlice sy his wunung and forlæte westdæl oððe oðre dælas, se þe æghwar is andweard, na ðurh rymyt þære stowe ac
þurh his mægenðrymmes andweardnysse. Þonne we wendað
ure neb to eastdæle þær seo heofen arist, seo ðe is ealra

God, not naturally, but by creation and by good merits, as Christ said in his gospel, "He who does the will of my Father in heaven, he is my brother and my mother and my sister." Now therefore all Christians, both high and low, noble and ignoble, the lord and the slave, are all brothers, and all have one Father in heaven. The wealthy person is not better in this name than the needy. The slave may call God his Father as boldly as the king. We all are alike before God, unless someone exceeds another in good works. The rich for his wealth should not despise the poor, for often the poor person is better before God than the rich. God is our Father, so we should all be brothers in God, and hold unbroken the brotherly bond, that is, true peace, so that each of us loves the other as himself, and commands no one to do that which he would not want someone to command him to do. Whoever observes this is a child of God and Christ, and all holy people who flourish in God are his brothers and his sisters.

We say, *"Our Father who are in heaven,"* that is, "Our Father who are in heaven," because God the Father is in heaven, and he is everywhere, as he himself said, "I fill heaven and earth with myself." And again, the holy gospel says of him, "Heaven is his throne, and the earth is his footstool." We turn eastward when we pray because heaven rises from there: not as if his dwelling were particularly in the eastern part and he would forsake the west or other parts, he who is everywhere present, not through his extension in space but by the presence of his majesty. When we turn our face to the east where heaven rises, which is rising over all bodily

lichomlicra ðinga oferstigende, þonne sceal ure mod beon mid þam gemyngod þæt hit beo gewend to ðam hehstan and þam fyrmestan gecynde, þæt is, God. We sceolon eac witan þæt se synfulla is eorðe gehaten, and se rihtwisa is heofen gehaten; þe on rihtwisum mannum is Godes wunung, and se goda man bið þæs Halgan Gastes templ. Swa eac ðær-togeanes se fordona man bið deofles templ, and deofles wunung: forði þonne swa micel is betwux godum mannum and yfelum swa micel swa bið betwux heofenan and eorðan.

5   Seofon gebedu sint on þam Paternoster. On þam twam formum wordum ne synd nane gebedu, ac sind herunga: þæt is, "Ure Fæder þe eart on heofonum." Þæt forme gebed is *"Sanctificetur nomen tuum,"* þæt is, "Sy ðin nama gehalgod." Nis þæt na swa to understandenne swylce Godes nama ne sy genoh halig, se ðe æfre wæs halig and æfre bið, and he us ealle gebletsað and gehalgað; ac þis word is swa to under-standenne, þæt his nama sy on us gehalgod, and he us þæs getiðige þæt we moton his naman mid urum muðe geblet-sian, and he us sylle þæt geðanc þæt we magon understan-dan þæt nan ðing nis swa halig swa his nama.

6   Þæt oðer gebed is *"Adveniat regnum tuum,"* þæt is on urum gereorde, "Cume ðin rice." Æfre wæs Godes rice and æfre bið; ac hit is swa to understandenne þæt his rice beo ofer us, and he on us rixige, and we him mid ealre gehyrsumnysse underþeodde syn, and þæt ure rice beo us gelæst and ge-fylled, swa swa Crist us behet þæt he wolde us ece rice for-gyfan, þus cweðende, "Cumað, ge gebletsode mines Fæder, and ge habbað þæt rice þæt eow gegearcod wæs fram an-ginne middangeardes." Þis bið ure rice, gif we hit nu geear-niað; and we beoð Godes rice þonne Crist us betæcð his

things, then our mind should be reminded thereby that it should be turned to the highest and first nature, that is, God. We should also know that the sinful person is called earth, and the righteous person is called heaven; for God's dwelling place is in righteous people, and the good person is a temple of the Holy Spirit. So also on the other hand the damned person is a temple of the devil, and the devil's dwelling place: therefore, there is as great a difference between good and evil people as there is between heaven and earth.

There are seven prayers in the Paternoster. There are no prayers in the first two phrases, but praises: that is, "Our Father who are in heaven." The first prayer is *"Hallowed be your name,"* that is, "May your name be sanctified." This is not to be understood as if the name of God, who was ever holy and ever will be, and who blesses and sanctifies us all, were not sufficiently holy; but this phrase is to be understood thus, that his name may be sanctified in us, and that he may grant us that we may bless his name with our mouth, and he may give us thought so that we may understand that nothing is as holy as his name. 5

The second prayer is *"May your kingdom come,"* that is in our language, "May your kingdom come." God's kingdom always was and always will be; but this is to be understood that his kingdom might be over us, and he might reign in us, and that we might be subject to him with all obedience, and that our kingdom might be realized and fulfilled for us, as Christ has promised us that he would give us an eternal kingdom, saying, "Come, you blessed of my Father, and you will have the kingdom that was prepared for you from the beginning of the world." This will be our kingdom, if we will merit it; and we will be God's kingdom when Christ delivers us to his 6

Fæder on domes dæge, swa swa þæt halige gewrit cwyð, *"Cum tradiderit regnum Patri suo,"* þæt is, "Þonne he betæcð rice his Fæder." Hwæt is þæt rice þæt he betæcð his Fæder buton ða halgan menn, ægðer ge weras ge wif, þa þe he alysde fram hellewite mid his agenum deaðe? Þa he betæcð his agenum Fæder on ende þisre worulde, and hi beoð þonne Godes rice, and mid Gode on ecnysse rixiað, ægðer ge mid sawle ge mid lichaman, and beoð þonne gelice englum.

7   Þæt ðridde gebed is *"Fiat voluntas tua sicut in caelo et in terra,"* þæt is, "Geweorðe þin willa on eorðan swa swa on heofonum." Þæt is, swa swa englas on heofonum þe gehyr-sumiað, and mid eallum gemete to ðe geðeodað, swa eac men, þe on eorðan sind and of eorðan geworhte, beon hi ðinum willan gehyrsume, and to ðe mid ealre geornfulnysse geðeodan. On þam mannum soðlice gewyrð Godes willa þe Godes willan gewyrceað. Ure sawul is heofonlic, and ure lichama is eorðlic. Nu bidde we eac mid þisum wordum þæt Godes willa geweorðe ægðer ge on ure sawle ge on urum lic-haman, þæt ægðer him gehyrsumige, and he ægðer gehealde and gescylde ge ure sawle ge urne lichaman fram deofles costnungum.

8   Þæt feorðe gebed is *"Panem nostrum cotidianum da nobis hodie,"* þæt is on urum gereorde, "Syle us nu todæg urne dæghwamlican hlaf." Þæt is on ðrim andgitum to understan-denne: þæt he us sylle fodan urum lichaman, and sylle eac ure sawle þone gastlican hlaf. Se gastlica hlaf is Godes be-bod, þæt we sceolon smeagan dæghwamlice and mid weorce gefyllan; forðan swa swa se lichama leofað be lichamlicum mettum, swa sceal seo sawul lybban be Godes lare and be gastlicum smeaungum. Hraðe se lichama aswint and for-weornað gif him bið oftogen his bigleofa; swa eac seo sawul

Father on judgment day, as the holy scripture says, *"When he delivers the kingdom to his Father,"* that is, "When he delivers the kingdom to his Father." What is the kingdom that he will deliver to his Father but those holy persons, both men and women, whom he redeemed from the torment of hell by his own death? He will deliver these to his own Father at the end of this world, and then they will be God's kingdom, and will reign with God for ever, both in soul and in body, and will be like angels.

The third prayer is *"Let your will be done on earth as in heaven,"* that is, "Let your will be done on earth as in heaven." That is, as the angels in heaven obey you, and in every way join themselves to you, so too may humans, who are on earth and formed of earth, be obedient to your will, and join themselves to you with all eagerness. Truly God's will is done in those people who do God's will. Our soul is heavenly, and our body is earthly. Now with these words we also pray that God's will be done both in our soul and in our body, that both may obey him, and that he may preserve and shield both our soul and our body from the temptations of the devil. 7

The fourth prayer is *"Give us today our daily bread,"* that is in our language, "Give us today our daily bread." This is to be understood in three senses: that he give us food for our body, and also give our soul spiritual bread. The spiritual bread is God's commandment, on which we should meditate daily and fulfill with works; for just as the body lives by bodily food, so shall the soul live by God's teaching and by spiritual meditations. The body quickly wastes away and decays if its sustenance is withdrawn from it; likewise the soul 8

forwyrð gif heo næfð þone gastlican bigleofan, þæt sind,
Godes beboda, on þam heo sceal geðeon and beon gegodad.
Eac se gastlica hlaf is þæt halige husel, mid þam we getrymmað urne geleafan; and ðurh ðæs halgan husles þygene us
beoð ure synna forgyfene, and we beoð gestrangode ongean
deofles costnunge. Þi we sceolon gelomlice mid þam gastlican gereorde ure sawle geclænsian and getrymman. Ne sceal
þeah se ðe bið mid healicum synnum fordon gedyrstlæcan
þæt he Godes husel þicge buton he his synna ær gebete; gif
he elles deð, hit bið him sylfum to bealowe geðyged. Se hlaf
getacnað ðreo ðing, swa swa we cwædon. An is þæs lichaman
bigleofa, oðer is ðære sawle; ðridde is þæs halgan husles ðy-
gen. Þyssera ðreora ðinga we sceolon dæghwamlice æt urum
Drihtne biddan.

9   Þæt fifte gebed is "*Et dimitte nobis debita nostra, sicut et nos
dimittimus debitoribus nostris*" þæt is, "Forgif us ure gyltas, swa
swa we forgifað þam mannum þe wið us agyltað." We sceolon don swa swa we on ðisum wordum behatað; þæt is, þæt
we beon mildheorte us betwynan, and, for ðære micclan lufe
Godes, forgyfan ðam mannum þe wið us agyltað, þæt God
ælmihtig forgyfe us ure synna. Gif we ðonne nellað forgyfan
þa lytlan gyltas ðæra manna þe us gegremedon, þone nele
eac God us forgyfan ure synna mycele and manega; swa swa
Crist sylf cwæð, "Þonne ge standað on eowrum gebedum,
forgyfað swa hwæt swa ge habbað on eowrum mode to ænigum men, and eower Fæder þe on heofonum is forgyfð eow
eowre synna. Gif ge þonne nellað forgyfan mid inweardre
heortan þam ðe eow gremiað, þonne eac eower Fæder ðe on
heofonum is nele eow forgyfan eowre synna; ac he hæt eow
gebindan and on cwearterne settan, þæt is on hellewite, and
eow ðær deofol getintregað oð þæt ge habban ealle eowre

perishes if it does not have spiritual sustenance, that is, God's commandments, on which it will thrive and be enriched. The spiritual bread is also the holy Eucharist, with which we confirm our faith; through partaking of the holy eucharist our sins will be forgiven, and we will be strengthened against the temptations of the devil. Therefore, we should frequently cleanse and confirm our soul with this spiritual refreshment. Yet one who is condemned with deadly sins should not dare to partake of God's Eucharist unless he should first atone for his sins; if he does otherwise, he will partake of it to his own harm. The bread, as we said, signifies three things. One is sustenance of the body; the second, of the soul; the third is the partaking of holy Eucharist. We should pray to our Lord for these three things every day.

The fifth prayer is *"And forgive us our debts, as we forgive* 9 *our debtors,"* that is, "Forgive us our offenses, as we forgive those people who offend against us." We should do as we promise in these words; that is, we should be merciful to each other, and, for the great love of God, forgive those who offend against us, so that God almighty may forgive our sins. But if we will not forgive the little offenses of those who have angered us, then God will not forgive us our great and many sins; as Christ himself said, "When you stand at your prayers, forgive whatever you have in your mind against anyone, and your Father who is in heaven will forgive you your sins. If you will not forgive in your inward heart those who anger you, then your Father who is in heaven will not forgive your sins; but he will command that you be bound and put in prison, that is, in the torments of hell, and there the devil will torture you until you shall have suffered for all your

gyltas geðrowade, oð þæt ge cumon to anum feorðlincge." Is
hwæðere getæht, æfter Godes gesetnysse, þæt wise men
sceolon settan steore dysigum mannum, swa þæt hi þæt
dysig and ða unðeawas alecgan, and þeah ðone man lufigan
swa swa agenne broðor.

10   Þæt sixte gebed is "Et ne nos inducas in temptationem," þæt
is, "Ne geðafa ðu God þæt we beon gelædde on costnunge."
Oðer is costnung, oðer is fandung. God ne costnað nænne
mannan, ac hwæðere nan man ne cymð to Godes rice buton
he sy afandod. Forði ne sceole we na biddan þæt God ure ne
afandige, ac we sceolon biddan þæt God us gescylde þæt we
ne abreoðon on ðære fandunge. Deofol mot ælces mannes
afandigan hwæðer he aht sy oððe naht—hwæðer he God
mid inweardlicre heortan lufige, oððe he mid hiwunge fare.
Swa swa man afandað gold on fyre, swa afandað God þæs
mannes mod on mislicum fandungum, hwæðer he anræde
sy. Genoh wel wat God hu hit getimað on þære fandunge, ac
hwæðere se man næfð na mycele geðincðe buton he afandod
sy. Þurh ða fandunge he sceal geðeon, gif he ðam costnungum wiðstent. Gif he fealle, he eft astande—þæt is, gif he
agylte, he hit georne gebete, and syððan geswice; forði ne
bið nan bot naht buton þær beo geswicenes. Se man þe gelomlice wile syngian and gelomlice betan he gremað God;
and swa he swiðor syngað swa he deofle gewyldra bið, and
hine þonne God forlæt, and he færð swa him deofol wissað,
swa swa tobrocen scip on sæ þe swa færð swa hit se wind
drifð. Se goda man, swa he swiðor afandod bið swa he rotra
bið, and near Gode, oð þæt he mid fulre geðincðe færð of
ðisum life to ðam ecan life. And se yfela, swa he oftor on
ðære fandunge abryð, swa he forcuðra bið, and deofle near,
oð þæt he færð of ðisum life to ðam ecan wite, gif he ær

offenses, until you come to the last farthing." It is taught, however, according to God's decrees, that the wise should give correction to the foolish, so that they lay aside their foolishness and their evil practices, and should nevertheless love the person as their own brother.

The sixth prayer is "*And do not lead us into temptation,*" that is, "Do not allow, God, that we be led into temptation." Temptation is one thing, trial is another. God does not tempt anyone, but nevertheless no one comes to the kingdom of God unless he has been tried. Therefore, we should not pray that God should not test us, but we should pray that God protect us so that we do not sink under trial. The devil may try everyone to see whether he is anything or nothing—whether he loves God with his inward heart, or acts with hypocrisy. As one tries gold in the fire, so God tries a person's mind in various trials, to see whether he is steadfast. God knows well enough how the trial will turn out, but yet one will have no great honor unless he has been tried. One will prosper by trial, if he withstands temptations. If he falls, let him stand up again—that is, if he sins, let him earnestly atone for it, and afterward cease; for atonement is nothing if there is not ceasing from evil. The person who will frequently sin and frequently atone angers God; and the more he sins the more he will be under the control of the devil, and then God will forsake him, and he will go as the devil guides him, like a broken ship at sea which goes as the wind drives it. The more a good person is tried the more cheerful he will be, and nearer to God, until he goes with full honor from this life to eternal life. The more often an evil person sinks under trial, the more wicked he will be, and the nearer to the devil, until he goes from this life to eternal

geswican nolde þa þa he mihte and moste. Forði anbidað
God oft þæs yfelan mannes, and læt him fyrst þæt he his
mandæda geswice and his mod to Gode gecyrre ær his ende,
gif he wile; gif he ðonne nele, þæt he beo, butan ælcere la-
dunge, swiðe rihtlice to deofles handa asceofen. Forði is nu
selre Cristenum mannum þæt hi mid earfoðnyssum and mid
geswince geearnian þæt ece rice and ða ecan blisse mid
Gode and mid eallum his halgum, ðonne hi mid softnysse
and mid yfelum lustum geearnian þa ecan tintrega mid eallum deoflum on hellewite.

11   Þæt seofoðe gebed is "*Set libera nos a malo,*" þæt is, "Ac alys
us fram yfele"—alys us fram deofle and fram eallum his
syrwungum. God lufað us, and deofol us hatað. God us fett
and gefrefrað, and deofol us wile ofslean gif he mot; ac him
bið forwyrned þurh Godes gescyldnysse, gif we us sylfe nellað fordon mid unðeawum. Forði we sceolon forbugan and
forseon þone lyðran deoful mid eallum his lotwrencum,
forðan ðe him ne gebyrað naht to us, and we sceolon lufian
and filigan urum Drihtne, se ðe us læt to ðam ecan life.

12   Seofon gebedu, swa swa we ær sædon, beoð on þam
Paternostre. Þa ðreo forman gebedu beoð us ongunnene on
ðysre worulde, ac hi beoð a ungeendode on þære toweardan
worulde. Seo halgung þæs mæran naman Godes ongann us
mannum þa þa Crist wearð geflæschamod mid ure menisc-
nysse; ac seo ylce halgung wunað on ecnysse, forðan ðe we
on ðam ecan life bletsiað and herigað æfre Godes naman.
And God rixað nu, and his rice stent æfre butan ende, and
Godes willa bið gefremod on ðisum life ðurh gode men; se
ylca willa wunað a on ecnysse. Þa oðre feower gebedu belimpað to ðisum life, and mid þisum life geendiað.

torment, if he has not ceased when he could and might. God therefore often waits for the evil person, and gives him time to stop his evil deeds and turn his mind to God before his end, if he will; if he will not, he should be very justly thrust into the hand of the devil without any excuse. It is better for Christians now to earn with hardships and toil the eternal kingdom and eternal bliss with God and all his saints, than that they earn with softness and evil lusts eternal tortures with all the devils in the torment of hell.

The seventh prayer is "*But deliver us from evil,*" that is, 11 "But deliver us from evil"—deliver us from the devil and from all his wiles. God loves us, and the devil hates us. God feeds and comforts us, and the devil will slay us if he can; but he will be prevented through God's protection, if we do not destroy ourselves with evil practices. Therefore we should turn away from and despise the vicious devil with all his schemes, for he is of no concern to us at all, and we should love and follow our Lord, who will lead us to everlasting life.

As we have said, there are seven prayers in the Paternos- 12 ter. The first three prayers are begun by us in this world, but they will be forever without ending in the world to come. The sanctification of the great name of God began with us when Christ became incarnate with our human form; but the same hallowing will continue to eternity, because in eternal life we will forever bless and praise the name of God. And God reigns now, and his kingdom stands forever without end, and God's will is fulfilled in this life by good people; the same will continues through all eternity. The other four prayers belong to this life, and end with this life.

13   On ðisum life we behofiað hlafes, and lare, and husel-
ganges. On þam toweardan life we ne behofiað nanes eorðlices bigleofan, forðan ðe we þonne mid þam heofonlicum
mettum beoð gereordode. Her we behofiað lare and wisdomes; on ðam heofonlican life beoð ealle ful wise, and on
gastlicre lare full gerade, þa ðe nu, þurh wisra manna lare,
beoð Godes bebodum underþeodde. And her we behofiað
ðæs halgan husles ðygene for ure beterunge; soðlice on ðære
heofonlican wununge we habbað mid us Cristes lichaman,
mid þam he rixað on ecnysse.

14   On þyssere worulde we biddað ure synna forgyfenysse,
and na on þære toweardan. Se man ðe nele his synna behreowsian on his life ne begyt he nane forgyfenysse on ðam
toweardan. And on ðisum life we biddað þæt God us
gescylde wið deofles costnunga, and us alyse fram yfele. On
ðam ecan life ne bið nan costnung ne nan yfel, forði ðær ne
cymð nan deofol ne nan yfel mann ðe us mæge dreccan oððe
derian. Þær beoð geþwære sawul and lichama, þe nu on
ðisum life him betweonan winnað. Ðær ne bið nan untrumnys ne geswinc, ne wana nanre godnysse, ac Crist bið mid us
eallum, and us ealle ðing deð butan edwite, mid ealre blisse.

15   Crist gesette þis gebed, and swa beleac mid feawum
wordum þæt ealle ure neoda, ægðer ge gastlice ge lichamlice, ðæron sind belocene; and þis gebed he gesette eallum
Cristenum mannum gemænelice. Ne cwyð na on ðam gebede, "Min Fæder, þu ðe eart on heofonum," ac cwyð, "Ure
Fæder," and swa forð—ealle ða word ðe þær æfterfyligað
sprecað gemænelice be eallum Cristenum mannum. On ðam
is geswutelod hu swiðe God lufað annysse and geþwærnysse
on his folce. Æfter Godes gesetnysse, ealle Cristene men
sceoldon beon swa geðwære swilce hit an man wære: forði

In this life we require bread, and instruction, and partak- 13
ing of the Eucharist. In the life to come we will require no
earthly sustenance, for we will be nourished with heavenly
food. Here we require instruction and wisdom; in the heavenly life all those who now, through the teaching of the wise,
are obedient to God's commandments will be completely
wise, and fully skilled in spiritual teaching. And here we require partaking in the Eucharist for our betterment; truly in
the heavenly dwelling we will have the body of Christ with
us, with which he reigns in eternity.

In this world, but not in the world to come, we pray for 14
forgiveness of our sins. The person who will not repent of
his sins in this life will obtain no forgiveness in the life to
come. And in this life we pray that God shield us against the
temptations of the devil, and deliver us from evil. In the
eternal life there will be no temptation and no evil, because
there will come no devil nor evil person to trouble or hurt
us. There soul and body, which now in this life struggle
against each other, will be in harmony. There will be no sickness or toil, nor lack of any goodness, but Christ will be with
us all, and will do all things for us without reproach, with all
joy.

Christ instituted this prayer, and confined it within few 15
words so that all our needs, both spiritual and physical, are
included in it; and he instituted this prayer for all Christians
in common. He does not say in that prayer, "My Father, who
are in heaven," but says, "Our Father," and so forth—all the
words which follow speak universally of all Christians. In
this is revealed how much God loves unity and harmony
among his people. According to God's decree, all Christians
should be as united as if they were one person: therefore

wa ðam men þe ða annysse tobrycð. Swa swa we habbað on anum lichaman manega lima, and hi ealle anum heafde ge-hyrsumiað, swa eac we sceolon manega Cristene men Criste on annysse gehyrsumian, forðon þe he is ure heafod, and we synd his lima. We magon geseon on urum agenum lichaman hu ælc lim oðrum þenað. Þa fet berað ealne ðone lichaman, and ða eagan lædað ða fet, and þa handa gearciað ðone bigleofan. Hraðe lið þæt heafod adune gif þa fet hit ne feriað; and hraðe ealle ða lima togædere forweorðað gif þa handa ne doð þone bigleofan þam muðe. Swa eac se rica man þe sitt on his heahsetle, hraðe geswicð he his gebeorscipes gif ða ðeowan geswicað ðæra teolunga. Beo se rica gemyndig þæt he sceal ealra ðæra goda þe him God alænde agyldan gescead hu he ða atuge.

16   Se bið ðin hand oððe ðin fot, se ðe þe ðine neoda deð. Se bið þin eage se ðe þe wisdom tæchð, and on rihtne weg þe gebrincð. Se ðe þe mundað swa swa fæder, he bið swylce he ðin heafod sy. Ealswa wel behofað þæt heafod þæra oðera lima, swa swa ða lima behofiað þæs heafdes. Gif an lim bið untrum, ealle ða oðre þrowiað mid þam anum. Swa we sceo-lon eac, gif bið an ure geferena on sumre earfoðnysse, ealle we sceolon his yfel besargian and hogian embe ða bote, gif we hit gebetan magon. And on eallum ðingum we sceolon healdan sibbe and annysse, gif we willað habban þa micclan geðincðe þæt we beon Godes bearn, se ðe on heofonum is, on ðære he rixað mid eallum his halgum on ealra worulda woruld on ecnysse. Amen.

woe to the person who breaks that unity. Just as in one body there are many limbs, and they all obey one head, so also we many Christians should obey Christ in unity, because he is our head, and we are his limbs. We may see in our own bodies how each limb serves another. The feet bear the whole body, and the eyes lead the feet, and the hands prepare nourishment. The head will lie down quickly if the feet do not bear it; and all the limbs will perish together quickly if the hands do not put nourishment in the mouth. Likewise, the rich man who sits on his high seat will soon stop his feasting if his servants cease their labor. Let the rich be mindful that he shall render an account how he employed all the good things which God has lent him.

Whoever meets your needs is your hand or your foot. He 16 is your eye who teaches you wisdom, and brings you into the right way. He who protects you like a father is, as it were, your head. As much as the head requires the other limbs, so these limbs require the head. If one limb is diseased, all the others suffer with that one. So also should we all, if one of our companions is in some distress, sorrow for his evil and strive toward its remedy, if we can repair it. And in all things we should hold peace and unity, if we will have the great honor of being children of God, who is in heaven, where he rules with all his saints through all ages to eternity. Amen.

20

Feria IIII, de fide catholica

ÆLc cristen man sceal æfter rihte cunnan ægðer ge his Paternoster ge his Credan. Mid þam Paternostre he sceal hine gebiddan, mid ðam Credan he sceal his geleafan getrymman. We habbað gesæd embe þæt Paternoster; nu we wyllað secgan eow þone geleafan þe on ðam Credan stent, swa swa se wisa Augustinus be ðære halgan Þrynnysse trahtnode.

2   An scyppend is ealra ðinga gesewenlicra and ungesewenlicra, and we sceolon on hine gelyfan, forðon ðe he is soð God and ana ælmihtig, se ðe næfre ne ongann ne anginn næfde; ac he sylf is anginn, and he eallum gesceaftum anginn and ordfruman forgeaf, þæt hi beon mihton, and þæt hi hæfdon agen gecynd, swa swa hit þære godcundlican fadunge gelicode. Englas he worhte, þa sind gastas and nabbað nænne lichaman. Menn he gesceop mid gaste and mid lichaman. Nytenu and deor, fixas and fugelas, he gesceop on flæsce butan sawle. Mannum he gesealde uprihtne gang; ða nytenu he let gan alotene. Mannum he forgeaf hlaf to bigleofan, and þam nytenum gærs.

3   Nu mage ge, gebroðru, understandan gif ge wyllað þæt twa ðing syndon: an is scyppend, oðer is gesceaft. He is scyppend se ðe gesceop and geworhte ealle ðing of nahte; þæt is gesceaft þæt se soða scyppend gesceop. Þæt sind ærest

20

Wednesday, On the Catholic Faith

Wednesday, on the Catholic Faith

Every Christian should rightly know both his Paternoster and his Creed. With the Paternoster he should pray, with the Creed he should confirm his faith. We have spoken about the Paternoster; we will now tell you about the faith which stands in the Creed, just as the wise Augustine commented on the holy Trinity.

There is one creator of all things visible and invisible, and we should believe in him, for he is true God and alone almighty, who never began or had a beginning; but he himself is the beginning, and he gave all creatures a beginning and origin, that they might exist and have their own nature, just as it pleased the divine dispensation. He made angels, which are spirits and have no body. He created human beings with spirit and with body. Beasts and wild animals, fishes and birds, he created in flesh without soul. To humans he gave an upright gait; he allowed the beasts to go bent down. To humans he gave bread for sustenance, and to the beasts grass. 2

Now brothers, you may understand if you will that there are two things: one is the creator, the other is creation. The creator is he who created and made all things from nothing; that which the true creator created is a creature. These are 3

heofonas, and englas þe on heofonum wuniað, and syððan
þeos eorðe mid eallum ðam ðe hire on eardiað, and sæ mid
eallum ðam þe hyre on swymmað. Nu ealle ðas ðing synd
mid anum naman genemnode, "gesceaft." Hi næron æfre
wunigende, ac God hi gesceop. Þa gesceafta sind fela; an is
se scyppend þe hi ealle gesceop, se ana is ælmihtig God. He
wæs æfre, and æfre he bið þurhwunigende on him sylfum
and ðurh hine sylfne. Gif he ongunne and anginn hæfde, butan tweon ne mihte he beon ælmihtig God; soðlice þæt
gesceaft ðe ongann and gesceapen is næfð nane godcundnysse. Forði ælc edwist þætte God nys þæt is gesceaft, and
þæt þe gesceaft nis, þæt is God.

4   Se God wunað on Ðrynnysse untodæledlic, and on annysse anre godcundnysse, soðlice oðer is se Fæder, oðer is se
Sunu, oðer is se Halga Gast; ac þeah hwæðere ðæra ðreora is
an godcundnys, and gelic wuldor, and efenece mægenðrym-
nys. Ælmihtig God is se Fæder, ælmihtig God is se Sunu,
ælmihtig God is se Halga Gast; ac þeah hwæðere ne sind ðry
ælmihtige Godas, ac an ælmihtig God. Ðry hi sind on hadum and on naman, and an on godcundnysse. Þry, forði þe se
Fæder bið æfre Fæder, and se Sunu bið æfre Sunu, and se
Halga Gast bið æfre Halig Gast; and hyra nan ne awent
næfre of ðam ðe he is. Nu habbað ge gehyred þa halgan
Þrynnysse; ge sceolon eac gehyran ða soðan Annysse.

5   Soðlice se Fæder, and se Sunu, and se Halga Gast habbað
ane godcundnysse, and an gecynd, and an weorc. Ne worhte
se Fæder nan ðing ne ne wyrcð butan ðam Suna, oððe butan
þam Halgan Gaste. Ne heora nan ne wyrcð nan ðing butan
oðrum, ac him eallum is an weorc, and an ræd, and an willa.
Æfre wæs se Fæder, and æfre wæs se Sunu, and æfre wæs se
Halga Gast an ælmihtig God. Se is Fæder, se ðe nis naðer ne

first the heavens, and the angels who dwell in heaven, and then this earth with all those that inhabit it, and the sea with all those that swim in it. Now all these things are called by one name, "creation." They were not always existing, but God created them. There are many creatures; the creator who created them all is one, who alone is almighty God. He always was, and he will always continue in himself and through himself. If he had begun and had origin, without doubt he could not be almighty God; truly the creature that began and is created has no divinity. Therefore, every substance that is not God is a creature, and what is not a creature is God.

God dwells in indivisible Trinity, and in unity of one divinity, for the Father is one, the Son is another, the Holy Spirit is another; and yet of these three there is one divinity, and the same glory, and coeternal majesty. The Father is almighty God, the Son is almighty God, the Holy Spirit is almighty God; but yet there are not three almighty Gods, but one almighty God. They are three in persons and in name, and one in divinity. Three, because the Father is always Father, and the Son is always Son, and the Holy Spirit is always Holy Spirit; and none of them will ever change from what he is. Now you have heard about the holy Trinity; you should also hear about the true Unity. 4

Truly the Father, and the Son, and the Holy Spirit have one divinity, and one nature, and one work. Without the Son, or without the Holy Spirit, the Father has not and does not make anything. Nor does any of them make anything without the others, but they have all one work, and one counsel, and one will. The Father always was, the Son always was, and the Holy Spirit always was one almighty God. He is 5

geboren ne gesceapen fram nanum oðrum. Se is Fæder gehaten forðan ðe he hæfð Sunu, ðone ðe he of him sylfum
gestrynde butan ælcre meder. Se Fæder is God of nanum
Gode, se Sunu is God of ðam Fæder Gode. Se Halga Gast is
God forðstæppende of þam Fæder and of ðam Suna. Þas
word sind sceortlice gesæde, and eow is neod þæt we hi
swutelicor eow onwreon.

6   Hwæt is se Fæder? Ælmihtig scyppend, na geworht ne
acenned, ac he sylf gestrynde bearn him sylfum efenece.
Hwæt is se Sunu? He is ðæs Fæder wisdom, and his word,
and his miht, þurh ðone se Fæder gesceop ealle ðing and ge-
fadode. Nis se Sunu na geworht ne gesceapen, ac he is
acenned. Acenned he is, and þeah hwæðere he is efeneald
and efenece his Fæder. Nis na swa on his acennednysse swa
swa bið on ure acennednysse. Þonne se mann sunu gestrynð,
and his cild acenned bið, þonne bið se fæder mara and se
sunu læssa. Hwi swa? Forði þonne se sunu wyxð, þonne
ealdað se fæder. Ne finst þu na gelice on mannum fæder and
sunu. Ac ic ðe sylle bysne hu ðu Godes acennednysse þy bet
understandan miht. Fyr acenð of him beorhtnysse, and seo
beorhtnys is efeneald þam fyre. Nis na þæt fyr of ðære
beorhtnysse, ac seo beorhtnys is of ðam fyre. Þæt fyr acenð
þa beorhtnysse, ac hit ne bið næfre butan ðære beorhtnysse.
Nu ðu gehyrst þæt seo beorhtnys is ealswa eald swa þæt fyr
ðe heo of cymð; geðafa nu forði þæt God mihte gestrynan
ealswa eald bearn and ealswa ece swa he sylf is. Se ðe mæg
understandan þæt ure hælend Crist is on ðære godcundnysse ealswa eald swa his Fæder, he ðancige þæs Gode and
blissige. Se ðe understandan ne mæg he hit sceal gelyfan,
þæt he hit understandan mæge; forðan þæs witegan word ne
mæg beon aidlod, ðe þus cwæð, "Buton ge hit gelyfan, ne

the Father, who was neither born nor created by any other. He is called Father because he has a Son, whom he brought forth of himself without any mother. The Father is God of no God; the Son is God of God the Father. The Holy Spirit is God proceeding from the Father and the Son. These words are quickly said, and you will need us to explain them more clearly.

What is the Father? The almighty creator, neither made nor born, but he himself produced a child coeternal with himself. What is the Son? He is the wisdom of the Father, and his word, and his might, through whom the Father created and arranged all things. The Son is neither made nor created, but he is begotten. He is begotten, and yet he is of the same age and coeternal with his Father. His birth is not the same as our birth. When a man produces a son, and his child is born, the father is greater and the son less. Why so? Because when the son grows up, the father grows old. You do not find among people a father and son who are equal. But I will give you an example so that you may better understand God's begetting. Fire produces brightness of itself, and the brightness is of the same age as the fire. The fire is not of the brightness, but the brightness is of the fire. The fire produces the brightness, but it is never without the brightness. Now you hear that the brightness is as old as the fire from which it comes; allow therefore that God might bring forth a child as old and as eternal as he himself is. He who can understand that our savior Christ in his divinity is as old as his Father, let him thank God for that and rejoice. He who cannot understand it should believe it, so that he may understand it; for the word of the prophet may not be in vain, who said, "Unless you believe it, you cannot under-

6

mage ge hit understandan." Nu habbað ge gehyred þæt se Sunu is of ðam Fæder butan ælcum anginne; forðan ðe he is ðæs Fæder wisdom, and he wæs æfre mid þam Fæder, and æfre bið.

7   Uton nu gehyran be ðan Halgan Gaste, hwæt he sy. He is se willa and seo soðe lufu þæs Fæder and þæs Suna, ðurh ðone sind ealle ðing geliffæste and gehealdene, be ðam is þus gecweden, "Godes Gast gefylð ealne ymbhwyrft middan-geardes, and he hylt ealle ðing, and he hæfð ingehyd ælces gereordes." Nis he geworht, ne gesceapen, ne acenned, ac he is forðstæppende—þæt is, ofgangende—of ðam Fæder and of ðam Suna, þam he is gelic and efenece. Nis se Halga Gast na sunu, forðan ðe he nis na acenned, ac he gæð of ðam Fæder and of ðam Suna gelice, forðan ðe he is heora beigra willa and lufu. Crist cwæð þus be him on his godspelle, "Se froforgast þe ic eow asendan wille, Gast ðære soðfæstnysse, ðe of minum Fæder gæð, he cyð gecyðnysse be me." Þæt is, he is min gewita þæt ic eom Godes Sunu. And eac se rihta geleafa us tæcð þæt we sceolon gelyfan on ðone Halgan Gast: he is se liffæstenda God, se gæð of ðam Fæder and of ðam Suna. Hu gæð he of him? Se Sunu is þæs Fæder wisdom, æfre of ðam Fæder; and se Halga Gast is heora beigra willa, æfre of him bam. Is forði þonne an Fæder, se ðe æfre is Fæder, and an Sunu, se ðe æfre bið Sunu, and an Halig Gast, se ðe æfre is Halig Gast.

8   Æfre wæs se Fæder, butan anginne; and æfre wæs se Sunu mid þam Fæder, forðan ðe he is þæs Fæder wisdom; æfre wæs se Halga Gast, se ðe is heora beigra willa and lufu. Nis se Fæder of nanum oðrum, ac he wæs æfre. Se Sunu is acenned of ðam Fæder, ac he wæs æfre on ðæs Fæder bosme, forðan ðe he is his wisdom, and he is of ðam Fæder eal þæt he is.

stand it." You have now heard that the Son is of the Father without any beginning; for he is the wisdom of the Father, and he was always with the Father, and ever will be.

Let us now hear about what the Holy Spirit is. He is the 7 will and the true love of the Father and of the Son, through whom all things are brought to life and preserved, about whom it is said, "The Spirit of God fills all the circumference of earth, and he holds all things, and he has knowledge of every speech." He is not made, nor created, nor begotten, but he is proceeding from—that is, going out from—the Father and the Son, with whom he is equal and coeternal. The Holy Spirit is not a son, for he is not begotten, but he proceeds from the Father and from the Son equally, for he is the will and love of both of them. Christ spoke of him thus in his gospel, "The Spirit of comfort whom I will send you, the Spirit of truth, which proceeds from my Father, will bear witness about me." That is, he is my witness that I am the Son of God. The right faith also teaches us that we should believe in the Holy Spirit: he is the life-giving God, who proceeds from the Father and the Son. How does he proceed from him? The Son is the wisdom of the Father, ever of the Father; and the Holy Spirit is the will of them both, ever of them both. There is therefore one Father, who is ever Father, and one Son, who is ever Son, and one Holy Spirit, who is ever Holy Spirit.

The Father always was, without beginning; and the Son 8 always was with the Father, for he is the wisdom of the Father; the Holy Spirit always was, who is the will and love of them both. The Father is of no other, for he always was. The Son is begotten of the Father, but he was always in the bosom of the Father, for he is his wisdom, and all that he is, is

Æfre wæs se Halga Gast, forðan ðe he is, swa we ær cwædon, willa and soð lufu þæs Fæder and ðæs Suna; soðlice
willa and lufu getacniað an ðing—þæt þæt þu wylt, þæt ðu
lufast, and þæt þæt ðu nelt, þæt ðu ne lufast.

9   Seo sunne ðe ofer us scinð is lichamlic gesceaft, and hæfð
swaðeah ðreo agennyssa on hire: an is seo lichamlice edwist,
þæt is ðære sunnan trendel; oðer is se leoma oððe beorhtnys
æfre of ðære sunnan, seo ðe onliht ealne middangeard;
þridde is seo hætu, þe mid þam leoman cymð to us. Se leoma
is æfre of ðære sunnan, and æfre mid hire; and ðæs ælmihtigan Godes Sunu is æfre of ðam Fæder acenned, and
æfre mid him wunigende, be ðam cwæð se apostol þæt he
wære his Fæder wuldres beorhtnys. Ðære sunnan hætu gæð
of hire and of hire leoman; and se Halga Gast gæð æfre of
ðam Fæder and of þam Suna gelice, be ðam is þus awriten,
"Nis nan þe hine behydan mæge fram his hætan."

10   Fæder and Sunu and Halig Gast ne magon beon togædere
genamode, ac hi ne beoð swaþeah nahwar totwæmede. Nis
se ælmihtiga God na ðryfeald, ac is Ðrynnys. God is se
Fæder, and se Sunu is God, and se Halga Gast is God: na ðry
Godas, ac hi ealle ðry an ælmihtig God. Se Fæder is eac wisdom of nanum oðrum wisdome. Se Sunu is wisdom of ðam
wisan Fæder. Se Halga Gast is wisdom, ac ðeah hwæðere hi
sind ealle ætgædere an wisdom. Eft se Fæder is soð lufu, and
se Sunu is soð lufu, and se Halga Gast is soð lufu; and hi ealle
ætgædere an God and an soð lufu. Eac swilce is se Fæder
gast and halig, and se Sunu is gast and halig untwylice; þeah
hwæðere se Halga Gast is synderlice gehaten Halig Gast,
þæt þæt hi ealle ðry sind gemænelice.

11   Swa micel gelicnys is on ðyssere halgan Ðrynnysse þæt se

of the Father. The Holy Spirit always was, for he is, as we said before, the will and true love of the Father and of the Son; indeed, will and love signify one thing—that which you will, you love, and that which you will not, you do not love.

The sun that shines over us is a physical creation, and yet 9 has three properties in itself: one is the physical substance, that is, the sun's orb; the second is the beams or brightness of the sun, which shine on all the earth; the third is the heat, which comes to us with the beams. The beams are always of the sun, and always with it; similarly the Son of almighty God is ever begotten of the Father, and ever existing with him, of whom the apostle said that he was the brightness of his Father's glory. The heat of the sun proceeds from it and from its beams; and the Holy Spirit ever proceeds from the Father and from the Son equally, of whom it is thus written, "There is no one who may hide from his heat."

Father and Son and Holy Spirit cannot be named to- 10 gether, but nevertheless they are nowhere separated. The almighty God is not threefold, but is a Trinity. The Father is God, and the Son is God, and the Holy Spirit is God: not three Gods, but they all three are one almighty God. The Father is also wisdom of no other wisdom. The Son is wisdom of the wise Father. The Holy Spirit is wisdom, but yet they are all together one wisdom. Again, the Father is true love, and the Son is true love, and the Holy Spirit is true love; and they are all together one God and one true love. Similarly the Father is a spirit and holy, and the Son is a spirit and undoubtedly holy; nevertheless the Holy Spirit is particularly called Holy Spirit, that which they all three are in common.

There is such great similarity in this holy Trinity that the 11

Fæder nis na mare þonne se Sunu on ðære godcundnysse, ne
se Sunu nis na mare þonne se Halgan Gast; ne nan heora an
nis na læsse þonne eall seo Ðrynnys. Swa hwær swa heora an
bið, þær hi beoð ealle ðry, æfre an God untodæledlic. Nis
heora nan mare þonne oðer, ne nan læssa ðonne oðer, ne nan
beforan oðrum, ne nan bæftan oðrum; forðan swa hwæt swa
læsse bið þonne God, þæt ne bið na God. Þæt þæt lator bið,
þæt hæfð anginn, ac God næfð nan anginn. Nis na se Fæder
ana Ðrynnys, oððe se Sunu Ðrynnys, oððe se Halga Gast
Ðrynnys, ac þas ðry hadas sindon an God on anre godcundnysse. Þonne ðu gehyrst nemnan þone Fæder, þonne understenst ðu þæt he hæfð Sunu. Eft, þonne þu cwyst Sunu, þu
wast, butan tweon, þæt he hæfð Fæder. Eft, we gelyfað þæt
se Halga Gast is ægðer ge ðæs Fæder ge ðæs Suna Gast.

12   Ne bepæce nan man hine sylfne swa þæt he secge oððe
gelyfe þæt ðry Godas syndon, oððe ænig had on þære halgan
Þrynnysse sy unmihtigra þonne oðer. Ælc ðæra þreora is
God, þeah hwæðere hi ealle an God; forðan ðe hi ealle habbað an gecynd, and ane godcundnysse, and ane edwiste, and
an geðeaht, and an weorc, and ane mægenðrynnysse, and
gelic wuldor, and efenece rice. Is hwæðere se Sunu ana geflæschamod and geboren to men of ðam halgan mædene
Marian. Ne wearð se Fæder mid menniscnysse befangen, ac
hwæðere he asende his Sunu to ure alysednysse, and him
æfre mid wæs, ægðer ge on life ge on ðrowunge, and on his
æriste and on his upstige. Eac eal Godes gelaðung andet, on
ðam rihtum geleafan, þæt Crist is acenned of ðam clænan
mædene Marian and of ðam Halgan Gaste. Nis se Halga
Gast þeah hwæðere Cristes Fæder—ne nan Cristen man
þæt næfre ne sceal gelyfan—ac se Halga Gast is willa þæs

Father is no greater than the Son in divinity, nor is the Son greater than the Holy Spirit; nor is one of them less than the whole Trinity. Wherever one of them is, there they are all three, ever one God indivisible. No one of them is greater than the other, nor one less than the other, nor one before the others, nor one after the others; for whatever is less than God is not God. That which is later has a beginning, but God has no beginning. The Father alone is not Trinity, nor the Son Trinity, nor the Holy Spirit Trinity, but these three persons are one God in one divinity. When you hear the Father named, then you understand that he has a Son. Again, when you say Son, you know, without doubt, that he has a Father. Again, we believe that the Holy Spirit is the Spirit both of the Father and of the Son.

Let no one deceive himself so as to say or to believe that there are three Gods, or that any person in the holy Trinity is less mighty than another. Each of the three is God, yet they are all one God; for they all have one nature, and one divinity, and one substance, and one counsel, and one work, and one majesty, and equal glory, and coeternal rule. But the Son alone was made flesh and born to humanity of the holy virgin Mary. The Father was not enclosed in human nature, but yet he sent his Son for our redemption, and was always with him, both in life and in suffering, and at his resurrection and at his ascension. Also all the Church of God confesses, according to true faith, that Christ was born of the pure virgin Mary and of the Holy Spirit. Yet the Holy Spirit is not Christ's Father—no Christian should ever believe that—but the Holy Spirit is the will of the Father and of the

Fæder and ðæs Suna; forði þonne swiðe rihtlice is awriten on urum geleafan þæt Cristes menniscnys wearð gefremmed þurh ðone Halgan willan.

13   Beheald þas sunnan mid gleawnysse, on ðære is, swa we ær cwædon, hætu and beorhtnys; ac seo hætu drygð, and seo beorhtnys onlyht. Oðer ðing deð seo hætu, and oðer seo beorhtnys; and ðeah ðe hi ne magon beon totwæmde, belimpð hwæðere ðeah seo hæðung to ðære hætan, and seo onlihting belimpð to ðære beorhtnysse. Swa eac Crist ana underfeng ða menniscnysse, and na se Fæder ne se Halga Gast; þeah hwæðere hi wæron æfre mid him on eallum his weorcum and on ealre his fare.

14   We sprecað ymbe God, deaðlice be undeaðlicum, tyddre be ælmihtigum, earmingas be mildheortum; ac hwa mæg weorðfullice sprecan be ðam ðe is unasecgendlic? He is butan gemete, forðy ðe he is æghwær. He is butan getele, forðon ðe he is æfre. He is butan hefe, forðon þe he hylt ealle gesceafta butan geswince; and he hi ealle gelogode on þam ðrim ðingum, þæt is on gemete, and on getele, and on hefe. Ac wite ge þæt nan man ne mæg fullice embe God sprecan, þonne we furðon þa gesceafta þe he gesceop ne magon asmeagan ne areccan. Hwa mæg mid wordum ðære heofenan freatewunge asecgan? Oððe hwa ðære eorðan wæstmbærnysse? Oððe hwa herað genihtsumlice ealra tida ymbhwyrft? Oððe hwa ealle oðre ðing, þonne we furðon þa lichomlican ðing þe we on lociað ne magon fullice befon mid ure gesihðe? Efne ðu gesihst ðone mannan beforan ðe, ac on ðære tide þe ðu his neb gesihst, þu ne gesihst na his hricg. Ealswa gif ðu sumne clað sceawast, ne miht ðu hine ealne togædere geseon, ac wenst abutan þæt ðu ealne hine

Son; therefore is it very rightly written in our faith that Christ's humanity was brought about by the Holy will.

Look with wisdom at the sun, in which there is, as we 13 have said, heat and brightness; but the heat dries, and the brightness gives light. The heat does one thing, and the brightness another; and though they cannot be separated, the heating nevertheless belongs to the heat, and the giving light belongs to the brightness. In the same way Christ alone assumed human nature, and not the Father or the Holy Spirit; nevertheless they were always with him in all his works and in all his journeys.

We speak of God, mortals of the immortal, the weak of 14 the almighty, the wretched of the merciful; but who may worthily speak of that which is ineffable? He is without measure, because he is everywhere. He is without number, for he ever is. He is without weight, because he holds all creatures without effort; and he disposed them all in three things, that is, in measure, and in number, and in weight. But know that no one can speak fully concerning God, when we cannot even imagine or recount the creation he has created. Who can tell with words the ornaments of heaven? Or who the fruitfulness of the earth? Or who adequately praises the circuit of all the seasons? Or who all other things, when we cannot even fully comprehend with our sight the physical things we look upon? For you see a person before you, but at the time that you see his face, you do not see his back. So also if you look at a cloth, you cannot see it all at once, but turn it around so that you might see it all. What wonder

geseo. Hwylc wundor is gif se ælmihtiga God is unasecgendlic and unbefangenlic, se ðe æghwær is eall and nahwar
todæled?

15   Nu smeað sum undeopðancol man hu God mæge beon
æghwær ætgædere, and nahwar todæled. Beheald þas sunnan, hu heage heo astihð, and hu heo asent hyre leoman
geond ealne middangeard, and hu heo onliht ealle ðas eorðan þe mancynn on eardað. Swa hraðe swa heo upasprincð
on ærne merigen, heo scinð on Hierusalem, and on Romebyrig, and on ðisum earde, and on eallum eardum ætgædere;
and hwæðere heo is gesceaft and gæð be Godes dihte. Hwæt
wenst ðu hu miccle swiðor is Godes andweardnys, and his
miht, and his neosung æghwær? Him ne wiðstent nan ðing,
naðer ne stænen weall ne bryden wah, swa swa hi wiðstandað þære sunnan. Him is nan ðing digle ne uncuð. Þu gescea-
wast ðæs mannes neb, and God sceawað his heortan. Godes
gast afandað ealra manna heortan; and ða ðe on hine gelyfað
and hine lufiað þa he clænsað and gegladað mid his neosunge, and ðæra ungeleaffulra manna heortan he forbyhð
and onscunað.

16   Wite eac gehwa þæt ælc man hæfð þreo ðing on him
sylfum untodæledlice and togædere wyrcende, swa swa God
cwæð þa þa he ærest mann gesceop. He cwæð, "Uton ge-
wyrcean mannan to ure gelicnysse." And he worhte ða Adam
to his anlicnysse. On hwilcum dæle hæfð se man Godes anlicnysse on him? On þære sawle, na on ðam lichaman. Þæs
mannes sawl hæfð on hire gecynde þære halgan Þrynnysse
anlicnysse, þe heo hæfð on hire ðreo ðing, þæt is gemynd,
and andgit, and willa. Þurh þæt gemynd se man geðencð þa
ðing ðe he gehyrde, oþþe geseah, oþþe geleornode. Þurh
þæt andgit he understent ealle ða ðing ðe he gehyrð oððe

is it if the almighty God is ineffable and incomprehensible, he who is everywhere all and nowhere divided?

Now some shallow-thinking person will inquire how God 15 can be everywhere together, and nowhere divided. Behold this sun, how high it ascends, and how its sends its beams over all the world, and how it enlightens all the earth on which humanity dwells. As soon as it rises up in the early morning, it shines on Jerusalem, on Rome, on this country, and on all countries at once; and yet it is a creation and goes by God's direction. How much greater do you think is God's presence, and his might, and his visitation everywhere? Nothing withstands him, neither stone wall nor broad barrier, as they withstand the sun. To him nothing is hidden or unknown. You see a person's face, and God sees his heart. The spirit of God tests the hearts of all people; and those who believe in him and love him he purifies and gladdens with his visitation, but the hearts of unbelievers he passes by and shuns.

Let everyone also know that every person has three 16 things in himself indivisible and working together, as God said when he first created humanity. He said, "Let us make a human in our own likeness." He then made Adam in his own likeness. In which part does a person have the likeness of God in him? In the soul, not in the body. The human soul has a likeness to the holy Trinity in its nature, because it has three things in it, that is, memory, and understanding, and will. By the memory a person thinks on the things he has heard, or seen, or learned. By the understanding he comprehends all the things which he hears or sees. From the will

gesihð. Of ðam willan cumað geðohtas, and word, and weorc, ægðer ge yfele ge gode. An sawul is, and an lif, and an edwist, seo ðe hæfð þas ðreo ðing on hire togædere wyrcende untodæledlice; forði þær þæt gemynd bið, þær bið þæt andgit and se willa, and æfre hi beoð togædere. Þeah hwæðere nis nan ðæra ðreora seo sawl, ac seo sawl þurh þæt gemynd gemanð, þurh þæt andgit heo understent, þurh ðone willan heo wile swa hwæt swa hire licað; and heo is hwæðere an sawl and an lif. Nu hæfð heo forði Godes anlicnysse on hire, forðan ðe heo hæfð þreo ðing on hire untodæledlice wyrcende. Is hwæðere se man an man, and na ðrynnys; God soðlice, Fæder and Sunu and Halig Gast, þurhwunað on Ðrynnysse hada and on annysse anre godcundnysse. Nis na se man on ðrynnysse wunigende swa swa God, ac he hæfð hwæðere Godes anlicnysse on his sawle þurh ða ðreo ðing þe we ær cwædon.

17   Arrius hatte an gedwolman, se flat wið ænne bisceop þe wæs genemned Alexander, wis and rihtgelyfed. Þa cwæð se gedwolman þæt Crist, Godes Sunu, ne mihte na beon his Fæder gelic, ne swa mihtig swa he; and cwæð þæt se Fæder wære ær se Sunu, and nam bysne be mannum, hu ælc sunu bið gingra þonne se fæder on ðisum life. Þa cwæð se halga bisceop Alexander him togeanes, "God wæs æfre, and æfre wæs his wisdom of him acenned, and se wisdom is his Sunu, ealswa mihtig swa se Fæder." Þa begeat se gedwola þæs caseres fultum to his gedwylde, and cwæð gemot ongean ðone bisceop, and wolde gebigan eal þæt folc to his gedwyldum. Þa wacode se bisceop ane niht on Godes cyrcan, and clypode to his Drihtne, and ðus cwæð, "Ðu ælmihtiga God, dem rihtne dom betwux me and Arrium." Hi comon ða þæs on mergen to ðam gemote. Þa cwæð se gedwola to his

come thoughts, and words, and works, both evil and good. There is one soul, and one life, and one substance, which has these three things in it working together inseparably; for where memory is, there is understanding and will, and they are always together. Yet none of these three is the soul, because the soul remembers through the memory, comprehends through the understanding, and wills whatever pleases it through the will; and yet it is one soul and one life. Now it therefore has God's likeness in itself, because it has three things working in it inseparably. Yet a person is one person, and not a trinity; but God, Father and Son and Holy Spirit, exists in a Trinity of persons and in the unity of one divinity. No person dwells in trinity like God, but nevertheless he has God's likeness in the soul because of the three things we have spoken of.

There was a heretic called Arius, who disputed with a bishop named Alexander, a wise and orthodox man. The heretic said that Christ, the Son of God, could not be equal to his Father, nor as mighty as he; and he said that the Father was before the Son, taking example from people, where every son is younger than his father in this life. Then the holy bishop Alexander said in opposition to him, "God ever was, and ever was his wisdom begotten of him, and the wisdom is his Son, as mighty as his Father." Then the heretic got the emperor's support for his heresy, and called a synod against the bishop, and wanted to bend all the people to his heresies. Then the bishop kept vigil one night in God's church, and cried to his Lord, saying, "Almighty God, judge right judgment between me and Arius." In the morning they came to the synod. The heretic said to his companions that he

17

geferum þæt he wolde gan embe his neode forð. Þa ða he to
gange com and he gesæt, þa gewand him ut eall his inne-
wearde æt his setle, and he sæt þær dead. Þa geswutulode
God þæt he wæs swa geæmtogod on his innoðe swa swa he
wæs ær on his geleafan. He wolde don Crist læssan þonne he
is, and his godcundnysse wurðmynt wanian; þa wearð him
swa bysmorlic deað geseald swa swa he wel wyrðe wæs.

18   Oðer gedwolman wæs se hatte Sabellius. He cwæð þæt se
Fæder wære, þa þa he wolde, Fæder; and eft, ða ða he wolde,
he wære Sunu; and eft, ða ða he wolde, wære Halig Gast; and
wære forði an God. Þa forwearð eac þes gedwola mid his
gedwylde.

19   Nu eft þæt Iudeisce folc, ðe Crist ofslogon swa swa he sylf
wolde and geðafode, secgað þæt hi willað gelyfan on þone
Fæder, and na on ðone Sunu ðe hyra magas ofslogon. Heora
geleafa is naht, and hi forði losiað. For ure alysednysse Crist
geðafode þæt hi hine ofslogon. Hit ne mihte eal mancynn
gedon, gif he sylf nolde; ac se halga Fæder gesceop and geworhte mancyn þurh his Sunu, and he wolde eft þurh ðone
ylcan us alysan fram hellewite ða ða we forwyrhte wæron.
Buton ælcere ðrowunge he mihte us habban, ac him ðuhte
þæt unrihtlic. Ac se deofol forwyrhte hine sylfne ða ða he
tihte þæt Iudeisce folc to ðæs hælendes slege, and we wurdon alysede þurh his unscyldigan deað fram ðam ecan deaðe.

20   We habbað þone geleafan ðe Crist sylf tæhte his apostolum, and hi eallum mancynne; and ðone geleafan God
hæfð mid manegum wundrum getrymmed and gefæstnod.
Ærest Crist ðurh hine sylfne dumbe and deafe, healte and
blinde, wode and hreoflige gehælde, and ða deadan to life
arærde; syððan, þurh his apostolas and oðre halige men, þas
ylcan wundra geworhte. Nu eac on urum timan, gehwær þær

would go out for his need. When he came to the privy and sat, all his entrails spilled out while he was sitting, and there he sat, dead. Thus God revealed that he was as empty in his inside as he had been in his belief. He wanted to make Christ less than he is, and diminish the dignity of his divinity; so he was given as shameful a death as he well deserved.

There was another heretic who was called Sabellius. He 18 said that the Father was, whenever he wanted, Father; and again, when he wanted, he was Son; and again, whenever he wanted, he was Holy Spirit; and was therefore one God. This heretic also perished with his heresy.

Now the Jewish people, who killed Christ as he himself 19 wanted and permitted, say that they will believe in the Father, but not in the Son whom their kinsmen killed. Their belief is nothing, and they will perish because of it. Christ permitted them to kill him for our redemption. All humankind could not have done it, if he himself had not willed it; but the holy Father created and made humankind through his Son, and through the same he would later redeem us from the torment of hell when we were condemned. He might have had us without any suffering, but that seemed unjust to him. But the devil condemned himself when he enticed the Jewish people to kill the savior, and by his innocent death we were redeemed from eternal death.

We have the faith that Christ himself taught to his apos- 20 tles, and they to all humanity; and God has confirmed and established that faith by many miracles. First Christ by himself healed mute and deaf, lame and blind, mad and leprous, and raised the dead to life; afterward, through his apostles and other holy ones, he performed the same miracles. Now

halige men hi restað, æt heora deadum banum God wyrcð
fela wundra, to ði þæt he wile folces geleafan mid þam wundrum getrymman. Ne wyrcð God na þas wundra æt nanes
Iudeisces mannes byrgene, ne æt nanes oðres gedwolan, ac
æt rihtgelyfedra manna byrgenum ða ðe gelyfdon on ða halgan Ðrynnysse and on soðe annysse anre godcundnysse.

21   Wite gehwa eac þæt nan man ne mot beon tuwa gefullod;
ac gif se man æfter his fulluhte aslide, we gelyfað þæt he
mæge beon gehealden gif he his synna mid wope behreowsað and be lareowa tæcunge hi gebet. We sceolon gelyfan
þæt ælces mannes sawul bið þurh God gesceapen, ac
hwæðere heo ne bið na of Godes agenum gecynde. Þæs
mannes lichaman antimber bið of ðam fæder and of ðære
meder, ac God gescypð þone lichaman of ðam antimbre,
and asent on þone lichaman sawle. Ne bið seo sawl nahwar
wunigende æror, ac God hi gescypð þærrihte and beset on
ðone lichaman, and læt hi habban agenne cyre swa heo syn-
gige swa heo synna forbuge. Þeah hwæðere heo behofað
æfre Godes fultumes þæt heo mæge synna forbugan and eft
to hyre scyppende gecuman þurh gode geearnunga; forðon
ðe nan man ne deð butan Gode nan ðing to gode.

22   Eac we sceolon gelyfan þæt ælc lichama ðe sawle underfeng sceal arisan on domes dæge mid þam ylcum lichaman
þe he nu hæfð, and sceal onfon edlean ealra his dæda; þonne
habbað ða godan ece lif mid Gode, and he sylð þa mede ælcum be his geearnungum. Þa synfullan beoð on hellewite a
ðrowigende, and heora wite bið eac gemetegod ælcum be his
geearnungum. Uton forði geearnian þæt ece lif mid Gode
þurh ðisne geleafan and ðurh gode geearnunga, se ðe þurhwunað on Ðrynnysse an ælmihtig God aa on ecnysse. Amen.

also in our time, wherever the saints rest, God works many miracles at their dead bones, so that he might confirm people's faith with those miracles. God does not work these miracles at any Jewish tombs, nor at any other heretic's, but at the tombs of orthodox people who believed in the holy Trinity and in the true unity of one divinity.

Let everyone also know that no one may be baptized 21 twice; but if a person should backslide after his baptism, we believe that he may be saved if he repents his sins with weeping and atones for them according to the teaching of his instructors. We should believe that the soul of every person is created by God, but it is not of God's own nature. The matter of a person's body is from the father and from the mother, but God creates the body from that matter, and sends a soul into the body. The soul previously did not exist anywhere, but God creates it at once and places it in the body, and lets it have its own choice either to sin or turn away from sins. Yet it always needs God's support to avoid sins and come back to its creator through good merits; for no one does anything good without God.

We should also believe that every body that has received 22 a soul will rise at judgment day with the same body that he now has, and will receive the reward of all his deeds; then the good will have eternal life with God, and he will give reward to each according to his merits. The sinful will be suffering forever in the torment of hell, and their torment will also be measured out to each one according to his merits. Let us therefore, through faith and good merits, merit eternal life with God, who dwells in Trinity, one almighty God forever to eternity. Amen.

21

Sermo in Ascensione Domini

Primum quidem sermonem feci, et reliqua.

2   Lucas se godspellere us manode on ðisre pistolrædinge, þus cweðende, "Se hælend, middangeardes alysend, æteowde hine sylfne cucenne his gingrum, æfter his þrowunge and his æriste, on manegum ðrafungum geond feowertig daga, and him to spræc ymbe Godes rice, samod mid him reordigende, and bebead him þæt hi of ðære byrig Hierusalem ne gewiton ac þæt hi ðær anbidedon his Fæder behates, he cwæð, 'þe ge of minum muðe gehyrdon. Forðan ðe Iohannes se Fulluhtere gefullode on wætere, and ge beoð gefullode on ðam Halgan Gaste nu æfter feawum dagum.' Eornostlice seo gegaderung his leorningcnihta cwæð ða anmodlice, 'Drihten leof, wilt ðu nu gesettan ende þysre worulde?' He him andwyrde, 'Nis na eow to gewitenne ða tid oððe ða handhwile þe min Fæder gesette þurh his mihte; ac ge underfoð þæs Halgan Gastes mihte, and ge beoð mine gewitan on Iudea lande and on eallum middangearde, oð þæt endenexte land.' And he lædde hi ða ut of ðære byrig up to anre dune ðe is gecweden *Mons Oliveti,* and hi gebletsode upahafenum handum. Þa mid þære bletsunge ferde he to heofonum him on locigendum; and þæt heofonlice wolcn leat wið his, and hine genam fram heora gesihðum.

3   "Ða ða hi up to heofonum starigende stodon, ða gesawon

21

Ascension

Sermon on the Lord's Ascension

The first discourse I made, etc.

Luke the Evangelist has admonished us in this epistle 2
reading, saying, "The savior, redeemer of the world, showed
himself alive to his disciples, after his passion and resurrection, by many reproofs for forty days, and spoke to them
about the kingdom of God, taking food with them, and
commanded that they not leave the city of Jerusalem but
wait there for his Father's promise, which, he said, 'you have
heard from my mouth. For John the Baptist baptized in water, but in a few days you will be baptized in the Holy Spirit.'
The gathering of his disciples said with one voice, 'Dear
Lord, will you now put an end to this world?' He answered
them, 'It is not for you to know the hour or the moment
which my father has appointed in his might; but you will receive the power of the Holy Spirit, and you will be my witnesses in the land of Judea and all the earth, to the most distant land.' And he led them out of the city to a hill called
Mount of Olives, and blessed them with raised hands. Then
with that blessing he went to heaven as they looked on, and
a heavenly cloud descended on him, and took him from
their sight.

"While they stood staring up into heaven, they saw two 3

THE OLD ENGLISH CATHOLIC HOMILIES

hi ðær twegen englas on hwitum gerelan, þus cweðende, 'Ge
Galileisce weras, hwi stande ge ðus starigende wið heofenas
weard? Se hælend þe is nu genumen of eowrum gesihðum to
heofonum swa he cymð eft swa swa ge gesawon þæt he to
heofonum astah.' Hi ða gecyrdon to ðære byrig Hierusalem
mid micelre blisse and astigon upp on ane upfleringe, and
þær wunedon oð Pentecosten on gebedum and on Godes
herungum, oð þæt se Halga Gast him to com, swa swa se
æðela cyning him ær behet. On ðyssere geferrædene wæron
Petrus and Iohannes, Iacob and Andreas, Philippus and
Thomas, Bartholomeus and Matheus, se oðer Iacob and
Simon, se oðer Iudas and Maria þæs hælendes modor,
and gehwilce oðre, ægðer ge weras ge wif. Eal seo menigu
wæs an hund manna and twentig, anmodlice on gebedum
wunigende."

4   Se hælend tæhte ða halgan lare his leorningcnihtum ær
his ðrowunge, and æfter his æriste he wæs wunigende betwux him þas feowertig daga, fram ðære halgan Eastertide
oð þisne dægðerlican dæg, and on manegum wisum ðrafode
and afandode his gingran, and geedlæhte þæt þæt he ær
tæhte to fulre lare and rihtum geleafan. He gereordode hine
æfter his æriste, na forði þæt he syððan eorðlices bigleofan
behofode, ac to ði þæt he geswutelode his soðan lichaman.
He æt þurh mihte, na for neode; swa swa fyr fornimð
wæteres dropan, swa fornam Cristes godcundlice miht ðone
geðigedan mete. Soðlice æfter ðam gemænelicum æriste ne
behofiað ure lichaman nanre strangunge eorðlicra metta, ac
se hælend us deð ealle ure neoda mid heofenlicum ðingum,
and we beoð mid wuldre gewelgode, and mihtige to gefremmenne swa hwæt swa us licað, and we beoð ful swyfte to
farenne geond ealle widgylnyssa Godes rices.

angels in white garments, saying, 'Men of Galilee, why do you stand here staring up toward heaven? The savior who is now taken from your sight into heaven will come again in the same way you have seen him ascend to heaven.' They returned to the city of Jerusalem with great joy and went to an upper room, and remained there until Pentecost in prayers and praises of God, until the Holy Spirit came to them, as the noble king had promised. In this company were Peter and John, James and Andrew, Philip and Thomas, Bartholomew and Matthew, the other James and Simon, the other Judas and Mary, the savior's mother, and several others, both men and women. The whole multitude was a hundred twenty persons, continuing in prayer with one mind."

The savior taught the holy doctrine to his disciples before his passion, and after his resurrection he was dwelling among them these forty days, from the holy time of Easter until this present day, and corrected and tested his disciples in many ways, and repeated what he had taught before to complete their instruction and right belief. He took food after his resurrection, not because he had need of earthly food then, but so that he might manifest his true body. He ate as an act of power, not for need; as fire consumes drops of water, so Christ's divine power consumed the meat he took. Truly after the universal resurrection our bodies will not need any strengthening from earthly food, but the savior will supply all our needs with heavenly things, and we will be enriched with glory, and strong enough to carry out whatever is pleasing to us, and swift enough to travel through all the vastness of the kingdom of God.

4

5   He behet his gingrum nu and gelome þæt he wolde him
sendan þone Halgan Gast, and þus cwæð, "Þonne he cymð
he eow tiht and gewissað to eallum ðam ðingum ðe ic eow
sæde." Þa com se Halga Gast on fyres hiwe to ðam halgum
hyrede on þam endleoftan dæge Cristes upstiges, and hi
ealle onælde mid undergendlicum fyre, and hi wurdon afyllede mid þære heofonlican lare, and cuðon ealle woruldlice
gereord, and bodedon unforhtlice geleafan and fulluht ricum and reðum.

6   Se halga heap befran Crist hwæðer he wolde on ðam
timan þisne middangeard geendian. He ða cwæð him to
andsware, "Nis na eower mæð to witenne þone timan þe
min Fæder þurh his mihte gesette." He cwæð eac on oðre
stowe, "Nat nan man ðone dæg ne ðone timan ðysre worulde
geendunge, ne englas ne nan halga, buton Gode anum."
Þeahhwæðere be ðam tacnum þe Crist sæde, we geseoð þæt
seo geendung is swiðe gehende, þeah ðe heo us uncuð sy.

7   Þa apostoli wæron gewitan Cristes weorca, forðan ðe
hi bodedon his ðrowunge, and his ærist, and upstige, ærst
Iudeiscre ðeode, and syððan becom heora stemn to ælcum
lande, and heora word to gemærum ealles ymbhwyrftes;
forðan ðe hi awriton Cristes wundra, and ða bec þurhwuniað
on Cristenre ðeode, ægðer ge ðær þær ða apostoli lichamlice
bodedon ge þær ðær hi na ne becomon.

8   Ealle gesceafta ðeniað heora scyppende. Þa þa Crist
acenned wæs, þa sende seo heofen niwne steorran, ðe bodade Godes acennednysse. Eft ða ða he to heofonum astah,
þa abeah þæt heofonlice wolcn wið his and hine underfeng—na þæt þæt wolcn hine ferede, forðan ðe he hylt heofona ðrymsetl, ac he siðode mid þam wolcne of manna gesihðum. Þær wæron ða gesewene twegen englas on hwitum

He promised his disciples at this time and frequently 5
that he would send them the Holy Spirit, saying, "When he
comes he will inspire and direct you to all the things I have
said to you." Then the Holy Spirit came in the form of fire to
the holy company on the eleventh day after Christ's ascension, and inflamed them all with harmless fire, and they were
filled with heavenly teaching, and knew all earthly languages, and fearlessly preached faith and baptism to the
powerful and cruel.

The holy company asked Christ whether he would put an 6
end to this world at that time. He said to them in answer, "It
is not your place to know the time which my Father has appointed through his power." He also said in another place,
"No one knows the day or the time of the ending of this
world, not the angels or any saint, save God alone." Yet by
the signs which Christ mentioned, we see that the ending is
very near at hand, though it is unknown to us.

The apostles were witnesses of Christ's works, for they 7
preached his passion, resurrection, and ascension, first to
the Jewish people, and afterward their voice came to every
land, and their words to the boundaries of the whole globe;
for they recorded Christ's miracles, and the books remain
among Christian people, both where the apostles physically
preached and where they did not come.

All created beings serve their creator. When Christ was 8
born, heaven sent a new star, which announced the birth of
God. Later when he ascended to heaven, the heavenly cloud
bowed down to him and received him—not that the cloud
carried him, for he holds the throne of heaven, but he passed
through the cloud out of human sight. Then two angels were
seen there in white garments. Similarly, at his birth angels

gyrelum. Eac swilce on his acennednysse wæron englas gesewene, ac þæt halige godspel ne ascyrde hu hi gefreatwode
wæron; forðan ðe God com to us swiðe eadmod. On his
upstige wæron gesewene englas mid hwitum gyrlum geglengede. Bliss is getacnod on hwitum reafe, forðon þe Crist
ferde heonon mid micelre blisse and mid micclum ðrymme.
On his acennednysse wæs geðuht swilce seo godcundnys
wære geeadmet, and on his upstige wæs seo menniscnys
ahafen and gemærsod. Mid his upstige is adylegod þæt cyrographum ure geniðerunge, and se cwyde ure brosnunge is
awend.

9 Þa ða Adam agylt hæfde, þa cwæð se ælmihtiga wealdend
him to, "Þu eart eorðe, and þu gewenst to eorðan; ðu eart
dust, and þu gewenst to duste." Nu todæg þæt ylce gecynd
ferde unbrosnigendlic into heofenan rice. Þa twegen englas
sædon þæt Crist cymð swa swa he upp ferde, forðan þe he
bið gesewen on ðam micclum dome on menniscum hiwe,
þæt his slagan hine magon oncnawan þe hine ær to deaðe
gedydon, and eac ða ðe his lare forsawon þæt hi ðonne rihtlice onfon þæt ece wite mid deofle. Þæt halige gewrit cwyð,
"*Tollatur impius ne videat gloriam Dei. Sy ðam arleasan ætbroden seo gesihð Godes wuldres.*" Ne geseoð þa arleasan
Cristes wuldor, ðe hine ær on life forsawon, ac hi geseoð
þonne egefulne þone ðe hi eadmodne forhygedon.

10 *Recumbentibus undecim discipulis, et reliqua.* We habbað nu
geræd Lucas gesetnysse embe Cristes upstige; nu wende we
ure smeagunge to ðam oðrum godspellere Marcum, þe cwæð
on ðisum dægðerlicum godspelle þæt se hælend æteowde
hine sylfne his apostolum and cidde him, forðan ðe hi
noldon æt fruman gelyfan his æristes of deaðe ða ða hit him
gecydd wæs. Þa cwæð se wealdend to his gingrum, "Farað

were seen, but the holy gospel does not describe how they were adorned; for God came to us very humble. At his ascension angels adorned with white garments were seen. Joy is signified by white garments, for Christ departed from here with great joy and with great majesty. At his birth it seemed as though the divine nature was humbled, and at his ascension humanity was exalted and magnified. With his ascension the writ of our condemnation is canceled, and the sentence of our destruction is reversed.

When Adam had sinned, the almighty ruler said to him, 9 "You are earth, and you will turn to earth; you are dust, and you will turn to dust." Now today that same nature went incorruptible into the kingdom of heaven. The two angels said that Christ will come just as he ascended, because at the great judgment he will be seen in human form, that his killers may recognize him whom they had put to death, and also that those who despised his teaching may then justly receive eternal punishment with the devil. Holy scripture says, "*Let the wicked be removed, so that he shall not see the glory of God. Let the sight of God's glory be taken away from the impious.*" The impious will not see the glory of Christ, whom they had despised in life, but they will then see him terrifying whom they had condemned when he was humble.

When the eleven disciples were sitting together, etc. We have 10 now read Luke's account of Christ's ascension; now let us turn our consideration to the other Evangelist, Mark, who said in this present day's gospel that the savior himself appeared to his apostles and reproached them, because at first they would not believe his resurrection from death when it was announced to them. Then the ruler said to his disciples,

geond ealne middangeard, and bodiað godspel eallum gesceafte. Se ðe gelyfð and bið gefullod se bið gehealden; se ðe
ne gelyfð, he bið genyðerod. Ðas tacnu fyligað þam mannum
þe gelyfað: hi adræfað deoflu on minum naman. Hi sprecað
mid niwum gereordum. Hi afyrriað næddran, and ðeah ðe hi
unlybban drincan, hit him ne derað. Hi settað heora handa
ofer adlige men, and him bið teala. Þa ða Drihten hæfde ðas
word gesprecen, þa wearð he genumen to heofonum, and
sitt on ða swiðran hand his Fæder. His apostolas ferdon ða
and bodedon gehwær, Gode samod wyrcendum and getrymmendum þa spræce mid æfterfylgendum tacnum."

II   Þis godspel is nu anfealdlice gesæd, ac we willað nu, æfter
Gregories trahtnunge, þa digelnysse eow onwreon. Ðæra
apostola tweonung be Cristes æriste næs na swa swiðe heora
ungeleaffulnys, ac wæs ure trumnys. Læs us fremodon þa ðe
hraðe gelyfdon ðonne ða þe twynigende wæron; forðan ðe hi
sceawedon and grapodon ða dolhswaðu Cristes wunda, and
swa adræfdon ealle twynunga fram ure heortan. Þa ðreade
se hælend his leorningcnihta twynunge ða ða he lichamlice
hi forlætan wolde, to ði þæt hi gemyndige wæron ðæra
worda þe he on his siðe him sæde. He cwæð þa, "Farað geond
ealne middangeard, and bodiað godspel eallum gesceafte."
Godspel is us to gehyrenne and ðearle lufigendlic, þæt we
moton forbugan hellewite and ða hreowlican tintrega þurh
ðæs hælendes menniscnysse, and becuman to engla werode
ðurh his eadmodnysse. He cwæð, "Bodiað eallum gesceafte,"
ac mid þam naman is se mann ana getacnod. Stanas sind
gesceafta, ac hi nabbað nan lif, ne hi ne gefredað. Gærs and
treowa lybbað butan felnysse; hi ne lybbað na ðurh sawle, ac
ðurh heora grennysse. Nytenu lybbað and habbað felnysse

"Travel through all the world, and preach the gospel to all creation. He who believes and is baptized will be saved; he who does not believe will be condemned. These signs will follow those who believe: they will drive out devils in my name. They will speak in new languages. They will drive away serpents, and even though they drink some deadly thing, it will not harm them. They will place their hands on the sick, and they will be well. When the Lord had said these words, he was taken into heaven, and sits at the right hand of his Father. His apostles then went and preached everywhere, God working with them and confirming their speech with subsequent signs."

This gospel is now simply said, but we will now unfold its 11 mysteries to you according to the exposition of Gregory. The apostles' doubt about Christ's resurrection was not so much their lack of faith, but was for our confirmation. Those who quickly believed accomplished less for us than those who were doubting; for they examined and touched the scars of Christ's wounds, and so drove out all doubts from our hearts. Then when he would bodily leave them, the savior reproached the doubts of his disciples, so that they might be mindful of the words which he said to them on his way. He said, "Travel through all the world, and preach the gospel to all creation." The gospel is for our hearing and exceedingly lovely, that we may avoid the torments of hell and cruel tortures through the incarnation of the savior, and come to the host of angels through his humility. He said, "Preach to all creation," but by that name humanity alone is signified. Stones are creatures, but they have neither life nor sense. Grass and trees live without feeling; they do not live by a soul, but by their greenness. Beasts live and have feeling

butan gesceade; hi nabbað nan gescead forðan ðe hi sind
sawullease. Englas lybbað, and gefredað, and tosceadað. Nu
hæfð se mann ealra gesceafta sum ðing. Him is gemæne mid
stanum þæt he beo wunigende; him is gemæne mid treowum þæt he lybbe, mid nytenum þæt he gefrede, mid englum þæt he understande. Nu is se mann gecweden "eall
gesceaft" forðan ðe he hæfð sum ðing gemæne mid eallum
gesceafte. Þæt godspel bið gebodad eallum gesceafte þonne
hit bið ðam menn anum gebodad, forðan þe ealle eorðlice
ðing sind gesceapene for ðam men anum, and hi ealle habbað sume gelicnysse to ðam men, swa swa we ær sædon.

12   "Se ðe gelyfð and bið gefullod he bið gehealden; and se
ðe ne gelyfð he bið geniðerod." Se geleafa bið soð se ðe ne
wiðcwyð mid þweorum ðeawum þæt þæt he gelyfð; be ðam
cwæð Iohannes se apostol, "Se ðe cwyð þæt he God cunne,
and his beboda ne hylt, he is leas." Eft cwyð se apostol Iacobus, "Se geleafa ðe bið butan godum weorcum se bið dead."
Eft he cwæð, "Hwæt fremað þe þæt ðu hæbbe geleafan, gif
ðu næfst ða godan weorc? Ne mæg se geleafa ðe gehealdan
butan ðam weorcum. Deoflu gelyfað, ac hi forhtiað." Þa
deoflu gesawon Crist on ðisum life on ðære menniscnysse,
ac hi feollon to his fotum and hrymdon, and cwædon, "Þu
eart Godes Sunu, forði ðu come þæt ðu woldest us fordon."
Se man ðe nele gelyfan on God, ne nænne Godes ege næfð,
he bið wyrsa þonne deofol. Se ðe gelyfð, and hæfð ege, and
nele ðeahhwæðere god wyrcan, se bið þonne deoflum gelic.
*In quodam tractu, qui estimatur sancti Hilarii fuisse, sic invenimus
scriptum, sicut Anglice hic interpretavimus, et ad testimonium
ipsam Latinitatem posuimus:* "Demones credunt et contremescunt;
qui autem non credit et non contremescit, demonibus deterior est;

without reason; they have no reason because they are soulless. Angels live, and feel, and reason. Now a human being has something of all creatures. He has in common with the stones that he is existing; he has in common with the trees that he lives, with the beasts that he has feeling, with angels that he understands. A human is called "all creation" because he has something in common with all creation. The gospel is preached to all creation when it is preached to humanity alone, for all earthly things are created for humans alone, and they all have some likeness to humans, as we have said.

"He who believes and is baptized will be saved; and he who does not believe will be condemned." That faith is true which does not contradict what it believes by wicked practices; of this John the apostle said, "He who says that he knows God, and does not hold his commandments, is a liar." Again, the apostle James says, "The faith which is without good works is dead." Later he said, "What does it profit you to have faith, if you do not have good works? Faith cannot save you without works. The devils believe, but they fear." The devils saw Christ in this life in his human state, but they fell at his feet and cried out, and said, "You are the Son of God, and so you have come to destroy us." The person who will not believe in God, nor has any fear of God, is worse than a devil. He who believes, and has fear, and yet will not do good, is like a devil. *In a certain tract, which is said to be by Saint Hilarius, we find written thus, as we have translated here in English, and supply the Latin as evidence of it: "Demons believe and are afraid; but whoever does not believe and is not afraid, is*

12

qui autem credit, et contremescit, et veritatem operibus non agit, demonibus similis est."

13   Se ðe rihtlice gelyfð and rihtlice his lif leofað, and mid Godes ege god weorc begæð oð ende his lifes, se bið gehealden, and he hæfð ece lif mid Gode and mid eallum his halgum. Drihten cwæð, þa ðe gelyfað, him fyligað þas tacnu: "On minum naman hi adræfað deoflu; hi sprecað mid niwum gereordum; hi afyrsiað næddran; and ðeah ðe hi unlybban drincan, hit him ne derað. Hi settað heora handa ofer adlige men, and him bið tela."

14   Þas wundra wæron nydbehefe on anginne Cristendomes, forðan ðurh ða tacna wearð þæt hæðene folc gebiged to geleafan. Se man ðe plantað treowa oððe wyrta, swa lange he hi wæterað oð þæt hi beoð ciðfæste; syððan hi growende beoð he geswycð þære wæterunge. Swa eac se ælmihtiga God swa lange he æteowde his wundra ðam hæðenum folce oð þæt hi geleaffulle wæron; syððan se geleafa sprang geond ealne middangeard, siððan geswicon ða wundra. Ac ðeahhwæðere Godes gelaðung wyrcð gyt dæghwamlice þa ylcan wundra gastlice þe ða apostoli ða worhton lichamlice. Þonne se preost cristnað þæt cild, þonne adræfð he ðone deofol of ðam cilde; forðan ðe ælc hæðen man bið deofles, ac þurh þæt halige fulluht he bið Godes, gif he hit gehylt. Se ðe forlæt bysmorlice spellunga, and talu, and derigendlice gaffetunga, and gebysegað his muð mid Godes herungum and gebedum, he sprecð þonne mid niwum gereordum. Se ðe ungeradum oððe ungeðyldigum styrð and þa biternysse his heortan gestilð, he afyrsað þa næddran, forðan ðe he adwæscð þa yfelnyssa his modes. Se ðe bið forspanen to forligre, and ðeahhwæðere ne bið gebiged to ðære fremminge, he drincð unlybban ac hit him ne derað, gif he mid gebedum to Gode

worse than demons; whoever believes, however, and has fear, and does not do works of truth, is like a demon."

He who rightly believes and lives his life rightly, and in fear of God practices good works until the end of his life, will be saved, and will have eternal life with God and all his saints. The Lord said these signs will follow those who believe: "In my name they will cast out devils; they will speak in new languages; they will drive away serpents; and though they drink some deadly thing, it will not harm them. They will set their hands over the sick, and they will be well." 13

These wonders were necessary at the beginning of Christianity, for by these signs the heathen people were inclined to faith. The person who plants trees or herbs waters them until they have taken root; after they are growing, he stops watering. Likewise the almighty God showed his miracles to the heathen people until they were believing; after faith had sprung up over all the world, miracles stopped. But yet God's Church still daily works the same miracles spiritually which the apostles then worked physically. When the priest christens a child, he casts out the devil from that child; for every heathen is the devil's, but through holy baptism he is God's, if he will observe it. He who forsakes shameful speech, slander, and harmful mockery, and busies his mouth with the praises of God and with prayers, speaks then in new languages. He who corrects thoughtlessness or impatience and stills the bitterness of his heart, drives away serpents, for he extinguishes the evils of his mind. He who is enticed to fornication, but yet is not induced to perform it, drinks a deadly drink but it does not harm him, if he flies to 14

flihð. Gif hwa bið geuntrumod on his anginne, and asolcen fram godre drohtnunge, gif hine hwa ðonne mid tihtinge and gebisnungum godra weorca getrymð and arærð, þonne bið hit swilce he sette his handa ofer untrumne and hine ge-hæle.

15   Þa gastlican wundra sind maran þonne þa lichamlican wæron, forðan ðe ðas wundra gehælað þæs mannes sawle, ðe is ece, and ða ærran tacna gehældon þone deadlican licha-man. Þa ærran wundra worhton ægðer ge gode men ge yfele. Yfel wæs Iudas, ðe Crist belæwde, þeah he worhte wundra æror ðurh Godes naman. Be swylcum mannum cwæð Crist on oðre stowe, "Ic secge eow, manega cweðað to me on ðam micclan dæge, 'Drihten, Drihten, la, hu ne witegode we on ðinum naman, and we adræfdon deoflo of wodum mannum, and we micele mihta on þinum naman gefremedon?' Þonne andette ic him, 'Ne can ic eow: gewitað fram me, ge unriht-wise wyrhtan.'" Mine gebroðru, ne lufige ge ða wundra þe magon beon gemæne godum and yfelum, ac lufiað þa tacna þe sind sinderlice godra manna, þæt synd soðre lufe and arfæstnysse tacna. Næfð se yfela ða soðan lufe, ne se goda nys hyre bedæled. Þas tacna sind digle and unpleolice, and hi habbað swa miccle maran edlean æt Gode, swa micclum swa heora wuldor is læsse mid mannum. Se wealdenda Drihten, æfter ðisum wordum, wæs genumen to heofonum, and sitt on ða swiðran hand his Fæder.

16   We rædað on ðære ealdan æ þæt twegen Godes men, Enoh and Helias, wæron ahafene to heofonum butan deaðe: ac hi elciað ongean ðone deað, and mid ealle ne forfleoð. Hi sind genumene to lyftenre heofenan, na to rodorlicere, and drohtniað on sumum diglan earde mid micelre strencðe lichaman and sawle oð þæt hi eft ongean cyrron on ende

God with prayers. If anyone is weakened in his intentions, and slothful for good living, then if someone with exhortation and examples of good works strengthens and raises him up, it is as though he sets his hand over the sick and heals him.

The spiritual miracles are greater than the bodily ones 15 were, for these miracles heal a person's soul, which is eternal, but the former signs healed the mortal body. Both good and evil persons performed the former miracles. Judas, who betrayed Christ, was evil, though he had performed miracles in the name of God. Of such people Christ said in another place, "I say to you, many will say to me on that great day, 'Lord, Lord, lo, did we not prophesy in your name, and we drove devils out of mad persons, and we performed great wonders in your name?' Then I will profess to them, 'I do not know you: depart from me, you unrighteous workers.'" My brothers, do not love those miracles which may be common to the good and the evil, but love those signs which are exclusively from good people, which are the signs of true love and piety. The evil person does not have true love, nor is the good person separated from it. These signs are secret and safe, and they have so much the greater reward with God as their glory is less among people. The ruling Lord, after these words, was taken to heaven, and sits at the right hand of his Father.

We read in the old law that two men of God, Enoch and 16 Elijah, were lifted up to heaven without death: but they put off death, and will not at all escape from it. They are taken to the heaven of the air, not to the celestial one, and remain in some secret place with great strength of body and soul until they will return again at the end of this world against

þisre worulde togeanes Antecriste, and deaðes onfoð. Ure
ælmihtiga alysend ne elcode na ongean þone deað, ac he
hine oferswiðde mid his æriste, and geswutulode his wuldor
þurh his upstige to ðam yfemystan þrymsetle.

17   We rædað be ðam witegan Heliam þæt englas hine feredon on heofonlicum cræte, forðan ðe seo untrumnys his gecyndes behofode sumes byrðres. Ure alysend Crist næs geferod mid cræte ne ðurh engla fultum; forðan se ðe ealle ðing
geworhte, he wæs geferod mid his agenre mihte ofer ealle
gesceafta. Se ærra man, Enoh, wæs geferod to lyftenre heofonan, and Helias wæs mid cræte up awegen; ac se ælmihtiga
hælend næs gefered ne awegen, ac he ðurhferde ða roder-
lican heofonan þurh his agene mihte.

18   Us is to smeagenne hu seo clænnys wæs ðeonde geond þa
geferedan ðenas, and þurh ðone astigendan hælend. Enoh
wæs geferod, se ðe wæs mid hæmede gestryned and mid
hæmede wæs strynende. Helias wæs on cræte geferod, se
ðe wæs þurh hæmed gestryned ac he ne strynde na þurh
hæmed, forðan ðe he wunade on his life butan wife. Se
hælend astah to heofonum, se ðe næs mid hæmede gestryned ne he sylf strynende næs; forðan þe he is ord and
anginn ealra clænnyssa, and him is seo clænnys swiðe lufigendlic mægen, þæt he geswutulode ða ða he geceas him
mædenmann to meder. And eall se halga heap ðe him fyligde
wæs on clænnysse wunigende, swa swa he cwæð sumum
godspelle, "Se ðe to me cymð ne mæg he beon min leorningcniht, buton he his wif hatige."

19   Se godspellere Marcus awrat on ðisum godspelle þæt ure
Drihten, æfter his upstige, sæte on his Fæder swiðran hand;
and se forma martyr Stephanus cwæð þæt he gesawe heofonas opene, and ðone hælend standan on his Fæder swiðran.

Antichrist, and will receive death. Our almighty redeemer did not put off his death, but he overcame it with his resurrection, and revealed his glory by his ascension to the highest throne.

We read of the prophet Elijah that angels carried him in a heavenly chariot, because the infirmity of his nature required some support. Our redeemer Christ was not carried in a chariot nor by the help of angels; for he who made all things was carried by his own power over all creation. The earlier man, Enoch, was carried to the heaven of the air, and Elijah was borne up in a chariot; but the almighty savior was neither carried nor borne, but he passed through the celestial heaven by his own might. 17

We should consider how chastity was cherished by the servants who were carried, and by the savior who ascended. Enoch was carried, who was begotten by sexual intercourse and who produced children by intercourse. Elijah was carried in a chariot, who was begotten by intercourse but did not produce children by intercourse, for he lived during his life without a wife. The savior ascended to heaven, who was not begotten by intercourse nor did he himself produce children; for he is the origin and beginning of all chastity, and to him chastity is a very admirable virtue, which he revealed when he chose a virgin for his mother. And all the holy company who followed him was living in chastity, as he says in a gospel, "He who comes to me cannot be my disciple, unless he hate his wife." 18

The Evangelist Mark wrote in this gospel that our Lord, after his ascension, sat at the right hand of his Father; and the first martyr Stephen said that he saw the heavens open, and the savior standing on his Father's right. Now the 19

Nu cwyð se trahtnere, "Þæt rihtlice is gecweden þæt he sæte æfter his upstige, forðan ðe deman gedafnað setl." Crist is se soða dema þe demð and toscæt ealle ðing, nu and eac on ðam endenextan dæge. Se martyr hine geseah standan, forðan ðe he wæs his gefylsta on ðære ðrowunge his martyrdomes, and ðurh his gife he wæs gebyld ongean ða reðan ehteras ðe hine wælhreowlice stændon.

20   Se ende is ðises godspelles þæt Cristes apostoli "ferdon and bodedon gehwær, Drihtne samod wyrcendum, and ða spræce getrymmendum mid æfterfyligendum tacnum." Þa apostoli, þæt sind Godes bydelas, toferdon geond ealne middangeard. Petrus bodade on Iudea lande, Paulus on hæðenum folce, Andreas on Scithia, Iohannes on Asia, Bartholomeus on India, Matheus on Ethiopia, and swa heora gehwilc on his dæle, and Godes miht him wæs mid, to gefremminge heora bodunga and ungerimra tacna; forðan ðe Crist cwæð, "Ne mage ge nan ðing don butan me." Eft he cwæð, "Ic beo mid eow eallum dagum, oð þisre worulde geendunge," se ðe lyfað and rixað mid þam ælmihtigan Fæder and ðam Halgum Gaste a on ecnysse. Amen.

commentator says, "That is rightly said that he sat after his ascension, because a seat is proper for a judge." Christ is the true judge who will judge and decide all things, now and also on the last day. The martyr saw him standing, because he was his supporter in the suffering of his martyrdom, and through his grace he was emboldened against the fierce persecutors who cruelly stoned him.

The end of this gospel is that Christ's apostles "went 20 and preached everywhere, the Lord working with them, and confirming their speech with subsequent signs." The apostles, that is, God's messengers, went over all the world. Peter preached in the land of Judea, Paul among the heathen peoples, Andrew in Scythia, John in Asia, Bartholomew in India, Matthew in Ethiopia, and so each of them in his part, and the power of God was with them, for the success of their preaching and of countless signs; for Christ said, "You can do nothing without me." Again he said, "I will be with you all days, until the end of this world," he who lives and reigns with the almighty Father and the Holy Spirit forever in eternity. Amen.

22

In die sancto Pentecosten

Fram ðam halgan Easterlican dæge sind getealde fiftig daga to þysum dæge, and þes dæg is gehaten Pentecostes, þæt is, se fifteogoða dæg ðære Easterlican tide. Þes dæg wæs on ðære ealdan æ gesett and gehalgod; God bebead Moyse on Egypta lande þæt he and eall Israhela folc sceoldon offrian, æt ælcum hiwisce, Gode an lamb anes geares, and mearcian mid þam blode rodetacn on heora gedyrum and oferslegum; ða on ðære nihte ferde Godes engel and acwealde, on ælcum huse ðæs Egyptiscan folces, þæt frum-cennyde cild and þæt leofoste. And Israhela folc ferde on ðære ylcan nihte of ðam leodscipe, and God hi lædde ofer ða Readan Sæ mid drium fotum. Þa tengde se Pharao æfter mid mycelre fyrde; ða ða he com on middan ðære sæ, þa wæs þæt Godes folc up agan, and God ða besencte ðone Pharao and eal his werod. Ða bebead God Moyse and þam folce þæt hi heoldon ða tid mid micelre arwurðnysse on ælces geares ymbrene. Þa wæs seo tid þam folce geset to Eastertide, forðan ðe God hi hredde wið heora fynd and heora ehteras fordyde. Þa þæs ymbe fiftig daga sette God þam folce æ, and wæs gesewen Godes wuldor upp on anre dune þe is gehaten Synay. Þær com micel leoht, and egeslic sweg, and blawende byman. Þa clypode God þone Moysen him to, and he wæs

22

Pentecost

For the Holy Day of Pentecost

Fifty days are counted from the holy day of Easter to today, and this day is called Pentecost, that is, the fiftieth day
of the Easter season. This day was established and consecrated in the old law; God commanded Moses in the land of
Egypt that he and all the people of Israel should offer a yearling lamb to God from every household, and with its blood
mark the sign of a cross on their doorposts and lintels; that
night God's angel went and killed the firstborn and dearest
child from every house of the Egyptians. The people of Israel went that same night from that nation, and God led
them over the Red Sea with dry feet. Then Pharaoh hurried
after them with a great army; when he came to the middle of
the sea, God's people had gone up, and God then drowned
Pharaoh and all his host. Then God commanded Moses and
the people to hold that time with great honor in the course
of every year. That time was established for the people as
Easter, because God had saved them from their enemies
and destroyed their persecutors. Then fifty days later God
established a law for the people, and the glory of God was
seen up on the mountain called Sinai. There came a great
light, and terrible noise, and blowing trumpets. God called

mid Gode feowertig daga, and awrat ða ealdan æ be Godes
dihte. Þa wæs se dæg Pentecostes gehaten on ðære Ealdan
Gesetnysse.

2   Þæt geoffrode lamb getacnode Cristes slege, se ðe unscæððig wæs his Fæder geoffrod for ure alysednysse. Nu is
his ðrowung and his ærist ure Eastertid, forðan ðe he us
alysde fram deofles þeowdome, and ure ehteras beoð besencte þurh þæt halige fulluht, swa swa wæs Pharao mid his
leode on ðære Readan Sæ. Þas fiftig daga fram ðam Easterlican dæge sind ealle gehalgode to anre mærsunge, and þes
dægðerlica dæg is ure Pentecostes, þæt is, se fifteogoða dæg
fram ðam Easterdæge. On ðam ealdan Pentecosten sette
God æ ðam Israhela folce, and on ðisum dæge com se Halga
Gast on fyres hiwe to Godes hirede; forðy ealswa þæt lamb
getacnode Cristes ðrowunge, swa eac seo ealde æ getacnode
godspelbodunge under Godes gife. Þreo tida sind on ðysre
worulde: an is seo ðe wæs butan æ; oðer is seo ðe wæs under
æ; seo ðridde is nu æfter Cristes tocyme. Þeos tid is gecweden "under Godes gife." We ne sind na butan æ, ne we ne
moton healdan Moyses æ lichamlice, ac Godes gifu us gewissað to his willan, gif we gemyndige beoð Cristes bebodum
and ðæra apostola lare.

3   Hit is gereht on ðyssere pistolrædinge hu se Halga Gast
on ðisum dæge com to ðam geleaffullan heape Cristes hyredes. Lucas se godspellere awrat on ðære bec *Actus apostolorum* þæt "se halga hyred wæs wunigende anmodlice on gebedum on anre upflora æfter Cristes upstige, anbidigende his
behates; þa on ðisum dæge þe is Pentecostes gecweden, com
færlice micel sweg of heofonum, and gefylde ealle ða upfleringe mid fyre, and wæs æteowed bufon heora ælcum swylce
fyrene tungan, and hi wurdon ða ealle gefyllede mid þam

Moses to him, and he was with God forty days, and wrote down the old law at God's direction. The day was called Pentecost in the Old Testament.

The lamb that was sacrificed signified Christ's death, who 2 was sacrificed innocent to his Father for our redemption. Now his passion and his resurrection are our Easter, because he redeemed us from the slavery of the devil, and our persecutors are drowned by holy baptism, just as Pharaoh was with his people in the Red Sea. These fifty days from the day of Easter are all consecrated to one celebration, and this present day is our Pentecost, that is, the fiftieth day from Easter day. On the old Pentecost God established a law for the people of Israel, and on this day the Holy Spirit came in form of fire to God's company; for just as the lamb signified Christ's passion, so also the old law signified the preaching of the gospel under God's grace. There are three ages in this world: one is that which was without law; the second is that which was under the law; the third is now after Christ's advent. This age is called "under God's grace." We are not without law, nor may we physically hold the law of Moses, but God's grace guides us to his will, if we are mindful of Christ's commandments and of the teaching of the apostles.

This epistle reading relates how the Holy Spirit came on 3 this day to the faithful group of Christ's company. Luke the Evangelist wrote in the book *Acts of the Apostles* that "the holy company was living united in prayers on an upper floor after Christ's ascension, awaiting his promise; then on this day which is called Pentecost, there came suddenly a great sound from heaven, and filled all the upper room with fire, and there appeared above each of them as it were tongues of

Halgum Gaste, and ongunnon to sprecenne mid mislicum gereordum, be ðam þe se Halga Gast him tæhte. Þa wæron gegaderode binnan ðære byrig Hierusalem eawfæste weras of ælcere ðeode ðe under heofonum eardiað; and þa apostoli spræcon to ðæs folces gegaderunge, and heora ælc oncneow his agen gereord.

4   "Ða wearð seo menigu swiðe ablicged, and mid wun-drunge cwædon, 'La hu, ne sind þas ðe her sprecað Gali-leisce? And ure ælc gehyrde hu hi spræcon urum gereordum on ðam ðe we acennede wæron. We gehyrdon hi sprecan Godes mærða mid urum gereordum. La, hwæt ðis beon sceole?' Þa cwædon ða Iudeiscan mid hospe, 'Þas men sin-don mid muste fordrencte.' Þa andwyrde Petrus, 'Hit is underntid; hu mihte we on ðysre tide beon fordrencte? Ac ðæs witegan cwyde Ioheles is nu gefylled. God cwæð þurh ðæs witegan muð þæt he wolde his Gast asendan ofer men-nisc flæsc; and manna bearn sceolon witigian, and ic sylle mine forebeacn ufan of heofonum, and mine tacna niðer on eorðan. Wite ge soðlice þæt Crist aras of deaðe, and on ure gewitnysse astah to heofonum, and sitt æt his Fæder swiðran, swa swa Dauid be him witegode, þus cweðende, "Drihten cwæð to minum Drihtne, site to minre swiðran, oðþæt ic alecge ðine fynd under þinum fotscamele."' Þa þæt folc ðis gehyrde, ða wurdon hi onbryrde, and cwædon to ðam apostolon, 'La leof, hwæt is us to donne?' Þa andwyrde Petrus, 'Behreowsiað eowre synna, and underfoð fulluht on Cristes naman, and eowre synna beoð adylegode, and ge underfoð þone Halgan Gast.' Þa underfengon hi his lare, and bugon to fulluhte on ðam dæge ðreo ðusend manna. Þa wæron ealle on annysse mid þam apostolum, and

fire, and they were all filled with the Holy Spirit, and began to speak with different languages, as the Holy Spirit taught them. Then in the city of Jerusalem pious men were gathered from every nation dwelling under heaven; and the apostles spoke to the gathering of people, and each of them recognized his own language.

"Then the multitude was greatly astonished, and said 4 with wonder, 'Lo, are not these who speak here Galileans? And each of us has heard how they speak in the language in which we were born. We have heard them speak of the glories of God in our languages. Lo, what could this be?' Then the Jews said in mockery, 'These people are drunk with new wine.' But Peter answered, 'It is midmorning; how could we be drunk at this time? But the words of the prophet Joel are now fulfilled. God spoke through the prophet's mouth that he would send his Spirit over human flesh, and the children of humans shall prophesy, and I will give my portents from heaven above, and my signs on earth below. Know truly that Christ arose from death, and in our sight ascended to heaven, and sits at his Father's right hand, just as David prophesied of him, saying, "The Lord said to my Lord, sit at my right hand, until I lay your enemies under your footstool."' When the people heard this, they were inspired and said to the apostles, 'Lo, sir, what should we do?' Peter answered, 'Repent your sins, and receive baptism in the name of Christ, and your sins will be blotted out, and you will receive the Holy Spirit.' They received his teaching, and on that day three thousand people submitted to baptism. And they were all in unity with the apostles, and sold their

beceapodon heora æhta, and þæt feoh betæhton ðam apostolum, and hi dældon ælcum be his neode.

5   "Eft on oðre bodunge gelyfdon fif ðusend wera on Crist, and wearð eall seo geleaffulle menigu swa anmod swilce hi ealle hæfdon ane heortan and ane sawle; ne heora nan næfde synderlice æhta, ac him eallum wæs gemæne heora ðing, ne ðær næs nan wædla betwux him. Þa ðe landare hæfdon hi hit beceapodon and þæt wurð brohton to ðæra apostola fotum; hi ða dældon ælcum be his neode."

6   Þa worhte God fela tacna on ðam folce ðurh ðæra apostola handa, swa þæt hi gelogodon ða untruman be ðære stræt þær Petrus forð eode, and swa hraðe swa his sceadu hi hreopode hi wurdon gehælede fram eallum untrumnyssum. Þa arn micel menigu to of gehendum burgum, and brohton heora untruman and ða deofolseocan, and hi ealle wurdon gehælede æt ðæra apostola handum. Hi setton heora handa ofer gelyfede men, and hi underfengon þone Halgan Gast. Þa wæs sum ðegen Annanias gehaten, and his wif Saphira; hi cwædon him betweonan þæt hi woldon bugan to ðæra apostola geferrædene. Namon ða to ræde þæt him wærlicor wære þæt hi sumne dæl heora landes wurðes æthæfdon, weald him getimode. Com ða se ðegen mid feo to ðam apostolum, þa cwæð Petrus, "Annania, deofol bepæhte ðine heortan, and ðu hæfst alogen þam Halgan Gaste. Hwi woldest ðu swician on ðinum agenum? Ne luge ðu na mannum, ac Gode." Þa he ðas word gehyrde, þa feol he adune and gewat. Þa ða he bebyrged wæs, þa com his wif Saphira, and nyste hu hire were gelumpen wæs. Ða cwæð Petrus, "Sege me, beceapode ge ðus micel landes?" Heo andwyrde, "Gea, leof, swa

possessions, and delivered the money to the apostles, and they distributed to each according to his need.

"Later at another preaching five thousand men believed 5 in Christ, and all the believing multitude was as unanimous as if they all had one heart and one soul; not one of them had separate possessions, but all their things were common to them all, and there was no poor person among them. Those who owned land sold it and brought the value to the feet of the apostles; they then distributed it to each according to his need."

Then God worked many signs among the people through 6 the hands of the apostles, so that they placed the sick along the street where Peter passed, and as soon as his shadow touched them they were healed of all sicknesses. Afterward a great multitude ran from the neighboring towns, bringing their sick and those possessed by devils, and they were all healed at the hands of the apostles. They set their hands over believers, and they received the Holy Spirit. There was an officer called Ananias, and his wife Sapphira; they said between themselves that they would turn to the fellowship of the apostles. They then decided that it would be more prudent for them to withhold some portion of the value of their land, in case anything should happen to them. When the officer came with the money to the apostles, Peter said, "Ananias, the devil has deceived your heart, and you have lied to the Holy Spirit. Why would you deceive with your own property? You have not lied to people, but to God." When he heard these words, he fell down and died. When he was buried, his wife Sapphira came, and did not know what had happened. Then Peter said, "Tell me, have you sold this much land?" She answered, "Yes, sir, that much." Peter

micel." Eft ða cwæð Petrus, "Hwi gewearð inc swa, þæt gyt dorston fandian Godes?" Heo feoll ðærrihte and gewat, and hi man bebyrigde to hyre were. Þa wearð micel ege on Godes gelaðunge and on eallum þe þæt geaxodon.

7   Þa apostoli siððan, ær ðam ðe hi toferdon, gesetton Iacobum, þe wæs gehaten Rihtwis, on Cristes setle, and eal seo geleaffulle gelaðung him gehyrsumode æfter Godes tæcunge. He ða gesæt þæt setl ðritig geara, and æfter him Symeon, þæs hælendes mæg. Æfter ðære gebysnunge wurdon arærede muneclif mid þære gehealdsumnysse, þæt hi drohtnian on mynstre be heora ealdres dihte, on clænnesse, and him beon heora æhta eallum gemæne, swa ða apostoli hit astealdon.

8   Ge gehyrdon lytle ær on ðisre rædinge þæt se Halga Gast com ofer ða apostolas on fyrenum tungum, and him forgeaf ingehyd ealra gereorda; forðan ðe se eadmoda heap geearnode æt Gode þæt iu ær þæt modige werod forleas. Hit getimode æfter Noes Flode þæt entas woldon aræran ane burh, and ænne stypel swa heahne þæt his hrof astige oð heofon. Þa wæs an gereord on eallum mancynne, and þæt weorc wæs begunnen ongean Godes willan. God eac forði hi tostencte, swa þæt he forgeaf ælcum ðæra wyrhtena seltcuð gereord, and heora nan ne cuðe oðres spræce tocnawan. Hi ða geswicon ðære getimbrunge, and toferdon geond ealne middangeard, and wæron siððan swa fela gereord swa ðæra wyrhtena wæs. Nu eft on ðisum dæge, þurh ðæs Halgan Gastes tocyme, wurdon ealle gereord geanlæhte and geðwære, forðan ðe eal se halga heap Cristes hyredes wæs sprecende mid eallum gereordum; and eac þæt wunderlicor wæs, ða ða heora an bodade mid anre spræce, ælcum wæs

said in return, "Why have you two done so, that you have dared test God?" She fell down right away and died, and they buried her by her husband. Then there was great fear in God's Church and in all those who heard of it.

Afterward the apostles, before they separated, set James, 7 who was called Just, on the seat of Christ, and all the faithful congregation obeyed him according to God's instruction. He sat on that seat thirty years, and after him Simeon, the kinsman of the savior. From that example monastic life arose with abstinence, so that they should live in chastity in a monastery according to the direction of their leader, and their possessions should be common to them all, as the apostles established it.

You have heard a little earlier in this reading that the 8 Holy Spirit came over the apostles in tongues of fire, and gave them knowledge of all languages; for the humble company merited from God what the proud host had lost long ago. It happened after Noah's Flood that giants wanted to raise up a city, and a tower so high that its roof should rise to heaven. There was then one language among all humanity, and the work was begun against God's will. So God scattered them, and he gave to each of the workmen an unknown language, and none of them could understand the speech of another. They then stopped their building and departed over all the world, and afterward there were as many languages as there were workmen. Now on this day, through the coming of the Holy Spirit, all languages once again became united and harmonious, for all the holy company of Christ's followers were speaking in all languages; and what was even more wonderful, when one of them preached in one language, it seemed to everyone who heard the

geðuht ðe ða bodunge gehyrde swilce he spræce mid his gereorde, wæron hi Ebreisce, oððe Grecisce, oððe Romanisce, oððe Egyptisce, oððe swa hwilcere ðeode swa hi wæron þe ða lare gehyrdon. On ðysre geferrædene geearnode heora eadmodnys þas mihte, and ðæra enta modignys geearnode gescyndnysse.

9   Se Halga Gast wæs æteowod ofer ða apostolas on fyres hiwe, and ofer Criste, on his fulluhte, on anre culfran anlicnysse. Hwi ofer Criste on culfran hiwe? Hwi ofer Cristes hirede on fyres gelicnysse? On bocum is gerædd be ðam fugelcynne, þæt his gecynd is swiðe bilewite and unscæððig and gesibsum. Se hælend is ealles mancynnes dema, ac he ne com na to demenne mancynn, swa swa he sylf cwæð, ac to gehælenne. Gif he ða wolde deman mancynn ða ða he ærest to middangearde com, hwa wurde þonne gehealden? Ac he nolde mid his tocyme ða synfullan fordeman, ac wolde to his rice gegaderian. Ærest he wolde us mid liðnysse styran, þæt he siððan mihte on his dome us gehealdan. Forði wæs se Halga Gast on culfran anlicnysse gesewen bufan Criste, forðan ðe he wæs drohtnigende on ðisre worulde mid bilewitnysse and unscæððignysse and gesibsumnysse. He ne hrymde, ne he biterwyrde næs, ne he sace ne astyrede, ac forbær manna yfelnysse þurh his liðnysse. Ac se ðe on ðam ærran tocyme liðegode þam synfullum to gecyrrednysse, se demð stiðne dom þam receleasum æt ðam æfteran tocyme.

10   Se Halga Gast wæs gesewen on fyrenum tungum bufon ðam apostolon forðan ðe he dyde þæt hi wæron byrnende on Godes willan, and bodigende ymbe Godes rice. Fyrene tungan hi hæfdon ða ða hi mid lufe Godes mærða bodedon þæt ðæra hæðenra manna heortan, ðe cealde wæron þurh geleaflæste and flæsclice gewilnunga, mihton beon ontende

preaching as though he spoke in his language, whether they were Hebrews, or Greeks, or Romans, or Egyptians, or of whatever nation they might be who heard that teaching. In this fellowship their humility earned them this power, as the pride of the giants earned them shame.

The Holy Spirit appeared over the apostles in the form of 9 fire, and over Christ, at his baptism, in the likeness of a dove. Why over Christ in the form of a dove? Why over Christ's followers in likeness of fire? We read about this type of bird in books, that its nature is very gentle and innocent and peaceful. The savior is the judge of all humanity, though he did not come to judge humanity, as he himself said, but to save it. If he would have judged humanity when he first came to earth, who would have been saved? He did not want to condemn the sinful by his coming, but wanted to gather them to his kingdom. He wanted first to direct us with gentleness, that he might afterward save us at his judgment. Therefore the Holy Spirit was seen in the likeness of a dove above Christ, because he was dwelling in this world in gentleness and innocence and peacefulness. He did not cry out, nor was he bitter in speech, nor did he stir up strife, but endured humanity's wickedness through his meekness. But he who was mild at his first coming for the conversion of the sinful will judge a stern judgment to the heedless at his second coming.

The Holy Spirit was seen as tongues of fire above the 10 apostles because he made it so that they were burning in God's will, and preaching about God's kingdom. They had fiery tongues when they preached the greatness of God with love so that the hearts of the heathens, which were cold through lack of faith and fleshly desires, might be kindled to

to ðam heofenlicum bebodum. Gif se Halga Gast ne lærð
þæs mannes mod wiðinnan, on idel beoð þæs bydeles word
wiðutan geclypode. Fyres gecynd is þæt hit fornimð swa
hwæt swa him gehende bið; swa sceal se lareow don se ðe bið
mid þam Halgan Gaste onbryrd ærest on him sylfum ælcne
leahter adwæscan, and siððan on his underðeoddum.

11   On culfran anlicnysse and on fyres hiwe wæs Godes Gast
æteowod; forðan ðe he deð þæt ða beoð bilewite on unscæððignysse and byrnende on Godes willan þe he mid his
gife gefylð. Ne bið seo bilewitnys Gode gecweme butan
snoternysse, ne seo snoternys butan bilewitnysse; swa swa
gecweden is be ðam eadigan Iob, þæt he wæs bilewite and
rihtwis. Hwæt bið rihtwisnys butan bilewitnysse? Oððe
hwæt bið bilewitnys butan rihtwisnysse? Ac se Halga Gast,
ðe tæhð rihtwisnysse and bilewitnysse, sceolde beon æteowod ægðer ge on fyre ge on culfran, forðan þe he deð þæra
manna heortan ðe he onliht mid his gife þæt hi beoð liðe
ðurh unscæððignysse, and onælede ðurh lufe and snoternysse. God is, swa swa Paulus cwæð, fornymende fyr. He is
unasecgendlic fyr and ungesewenlic; be ðam fyre cwæð se
hælend, "Ic com to ði þæt ic wolde sendan fyr on eorðan,
and ic wylle þæt hit byrne." He sende ðone Halgan Gast to
eorðan, and he mid his blæde onælde eorðlicra manna heortan. Þonne byrnð seo eorðe þonne ðæs eorðlican mannes
heorte bið ontend to Godes lufe, seo ðe ær wæs ceald þurh
flæsclice lustas.

12   Nis na se Halga Gast wunigende on his gecynde swa swa
he gesewen wæs, forðan ðe he is ungesewenlic; ac for ðære
getacnunge, swa we ær cwædon, he wæs æteowod on culfran
and on fyre. He is gehaten on Greciscum gereorde *Paraclitus,*
þæt is "froforgast," forði ðe he frefrað þa dreorian þe heora

the heavenly commands. If the Holy Spirit does not teach a person's mind within, in vain will the words of the messenger be proclaimed without. It is the nature of fire to consume whatever is near it; so should the teacher who is inspired by the Holy Spirit first extinguish every sin in himself, and afterward in those under his care.

God's spirit was manifested in the likeness of a dove and in the form of fire; for he causes those whom he fills with his grace to be gentle in innocence and burning in God's will. Gentleness is not pleasing to God without wisdom, nor wisdom without gentleness; as it is said of the blessed Job, that he was gentle and righteous. What is righteousness without gentleness? Or what is gentleness without righteousness? The Holy Spirit, who teaches righteousness and gentleness, should be manifested both as fire and as a dove, for he causes the hearts of those whom he enlightens with his grace to be gentle through innocence, and kindled by love and wisdom. God is, as Paul said, a consuming fire. He is a fire ineffable and invisible; of that fire the savior said, "I have come that I might send fire on earth, and I want it to burn." He sent the Holy Spirit to earth, and by his inspiration he kindled the hearts of earthly people. Then the earth burns when the earthly person's heart is kindled to love of God, which before was cold through fleshly desires.

The Holy Spirit does not exist in his nature as he was seen, for he is invisible; but for a sign, as we have said, he appeared as a dove and as fire. He is called in the Greek language *Paraclete,* that is, "spirit of comfort," because he comforts the mournful who repent of their sins, gives them

11

12

synna behreowsiað, and sylð him forgyfenysse hiht, and
heora unrotan mod geliðegað. He forgyfð synna, and he is se
weg to forgyfenysse ealra synna. He sylð his gife ðam ðe he
wile. Sumum men he forgifð wisdom and spræce, sumum
god ingehyd, sumum micelne geleafan, sumum mihte to
gehælenne untruman, sumum witegunge, sumum toscead
godra gasta and yfelra; sumum he forgifð mislice gereord,
sumum gereccednysse mislicra spræca. Ealle ðas ðing deð se
Halga Gast, todælende æghwilcum be ðam ðe him gewyrð;
forðam ðe he is ælmihtig wyrhta, and swa hraðe swa he þæs
mannes mod onliht, he hit awent fram yfele to gode. He onlihte Dauides heortan ða ða he on iugoðe hearpan lufode,
and worhte hine to psalmwyrhtan. Amos hatte sum hryðer-
hyrde, þone awende se Halga Gast to mærum witegan.
Petrus wæs fiscere, ðone awende se ylca Godes Gast to
apostole. Paulus ehte Cristenra manna; þone he geceas to
lareowe eallum ðeodum. Matheus wæs tollere, þone he
awende to godspellere. Þa apostoli ne dorston bodian þone
soðan geleafan for ogan Iudeisces folces; ac siððan hi wæron
onælede þurh ðone Halgan Gast, hi forsawon ealle lichamlice pinunga, and orsorhlice Godes mærða bodedon.

13   Þyses dæges wurðmynt is to mærsigenne forðan ðe se ælmihtiga God, þæt is se Halga Gast, gemedemode hine sylfne
þæt he wolde manna bearn on ðisre tide geneosian. On
Cristes acennednysse wearð se ælmihtiga Godes Sunu to
menniscum men gedon, and on ðisum dæge wurdon geleaffulle men godas, swa swa Crist cwæð: "Ic cwæð, 'Ge sind godas, and ge ealle sind bearn þæs Hehstan.'" Þa gecorenan
sind Godes bearn, and eac godas, na gecyndelice, ac ðurh
gife þæs Halgan Gastes. An God is gecyndelice on ðrim hadum: Fæder, and his Sunu, þæt is his Wisdom, and se Halga

hope of forgiveness, and gladdens their troubled minds. He forgives sins, and he is the way to forgiveness of all sins. He gives his grace to whomever he wishes. To one he gives wisdom and eloquence, to one good understanding, to one great faith, to one power to heal the sick, to one prophecy, to one discrimination of good and evil spirits; to one he gives various languages, to one interpretation of various speech. The Holy Spirit does all these things, distributing to each as it seems good to him; for he is the almighty worker, and as soon as he enlightens a person's mind, he turns it from evil to good. He enlightened David's heart when in his youth he loved the harp, and made him into a psalmist. There was a cowherd called Amos, whom the Holy Spirit turned to a great prophet. Peter was a fisherman, whom the same Spirit of God turned to an apostle. Paul persecuted Christians; he chose him for a teacher of all nations. Matthew was a tax collector, whom he turned to an Evangelist. The apostles did not dare preach the true faith for fear of the Jewish people; but after they were kindled by the Holy Spirit, they scorned all bodily tortures, and fearlessly preached the greatness of God.

This day's dignity should be celebrated because almighty 13 God, that is, the Holy Spirit, humbled himself to visit the children of humanity at this time. At the birth of Christ the almighty Son of God became a human being, and on this day believing people became gods, as Christ said: "I said, 'You are gods, and you are all children of the Most High.'" The chosen are God's children, and also gods, not naturally, but through grace of the Holy Spirit. There is one God naturally in three persons: the Father, and his Son, that is, his wisdom,

Gast, se ðe is heora begra lufu and willa. Heora gecynd is
untodæledlic, æfre wunigende on anre Godcundnysse. Se
ylca cwæð þeahhwæðere be his gecorenum, "Ge sint godas."
Þurh Cristes menniscnysse wurdon menn alisede fram
deofles ðeowte, and ðurh tocyme þæs Halgan Gastes mennisce men wurdon gedone to godum. Crist underfeng menniscnysse on his tocyme, and men underfengon God þurh
neosunge þæs Halgan Gastes. Se man ðe næfð Godes Gast
on him nis he Godes. Ælces mannes weorc cyðað hwilc gast
hine wissað. Godes Gast wissað symble to halignysse and
godnysse; deofles gast wissað to leahtrum and to mandædum.

14   Se Halga Gast becom tuwa ofer ða apostolas. Crist
ableow ðone Halgan Gast upon ða apostolas ær his upstige,
þus cweðende, "Onfoð Haligne Gast." Eft, on ðisum dæge,
asende se ælmihtiga Fæder and se Sunu heora begra Gast to
ðam geleaffullan heape on ðysre worulde wunigende. Se
hælend ableow his Gast on his gingran for ðære getacnunge
þæt hi and ealle Cristene men sceolon lufigan heora nehstan
swa swa hi sylfe. He sende eft, swa swa he ær behet, ðone
ylcan Gast of heofonum, to ði þæt we sceolon lufian God
ofer ealle oðre ðing. An is se Halga Gast, þeah ðe he tuwa
become ofer ða apostolas. Swa is eac an lufu and twa bebodu, þæt we sceolon lufian God and menn. Ac we sceolon
leornian on mannum hu we magon becuman to Godes lufe,
swa swa Iohannes se apostol cwæð, "Se ðe ne lufað his
broðor, ðone ðe he gesihð, hu mæg he lufian God, þone þe
he ne gesihð lichamlice?"

15   We wurðiað þæs Halgan Gastes tocyme mid lofsangum
seofon dagas, forðan ðe he onbryrt ure mod mid seofonfeal-
dre gife, þæt is, mid wisdome and andgyte, mid geðeahte

and the Holy Spirit, who is the love and will of them both. Their nature is indivisible, ever existing in one Godhead. Yet the same one has said of his chosen, "You are gods." Through Christ's incarnation people were redeemed from servitude to the devil, and through the coming of the Holy Spirit human people were made gods. Christ received human nature at his advent, and humans received God through the visitation of the Holy Spirit. The person who does not have the Spirit of God in him is not God's. Every person's works show what spirit directs him. The Spirit of God always directs to holiness and goodness; the spirit of the devil directs to sins and evil deeds.

The Holy Spirit came over the apostles on two occasions. 14 Christ blew the Holy Spirit on the apostles before his ascension, saying, "Receive the Holy Spirit." Later, on this day, the almighty Father and the Son sent the Spirit of both to the faithful company dwelling in this world. The savior blew his Spirit on his followers for a sign that they and all Christians should love their neighbors as themselves. Afterward he sent, as he had promised, the same Spirit from heaven, so that we should love God above all other things. The Holy Spirit is one, though he came twice over the apostles. So too there is one love and two commandments, that we should love God and love humankind. We should learn from humankind how we may come to the love of God, as John the apostle said, "He who does not love his brother, whom he sees, how can he love God, whom he does not physically see?"

We honor the coming of the Holy Spirit with hymns for 15 seven days, because he stimulates our mind with a sevenfold gift, that is, with wisdom and understanding, with counsel

and strenðe, mid ingehyde and arfæstnysse, and he us gefylð mid Godes ege. Se ðe þurh gode geearnunga becymð to ðissum seofonfealdum gifum þæs Halgan Gastes, he hæfð þonne ealle geðincðe. Ac se ðe wile to ðisre geðincðe becuman he sceal gelyfan on ða halgan Ðrynnysse and on soðe annysse, þæt se Fæder, and his Sunu, and heora begra Gast syndon ðry on hadum, and an God untodæledlic, on anre Godcundnysse wunigende. Þysne geleafan getacnodon ða ðreo ðusend þe ærest gebugon to geleafan æfter ðæs Halgan Gastes tocyme. Swa swa ða ðreo þusend wæron an werod, swa is seo halige Ðrynnys an God. And þæt werod wæs swa anmod swilce him eallum wære an heorte and an sawul; forðan ðe ðære halgan Þrynnysse is an Godcundnyss, and an gecynd, and an willa, and an weorc unascyrigendlice.

16   Þa geleaffullan brohton heora feoh and ledon hit æt ðæra apostola foton. Mid þam is geswutelod þæt Cristene men ne sceolon heora hiht besettan on woroldlice gestreon, ac on Gode anum. Se gitsere ðe beset his hiht on his goldhord, he bið swa swa se apostol cwæð, "þam gelic þe deofolgyld begæð." Hi heoldon þæt gold unwurðlice, forðan ðe seo gitsung næfde nænne stede on heora heortan; forði hi dydon heora ðing him gemæne, þæt hi on soðre sibbe butan gytsunge beon mihton. Hi setton heora handa ofer geleaffulle men, and him com to se Halga Gast ðurh heora biscepunge. Biscopas sind þæs ylcan hades on Godes gelaðunge, and healdað þa gesetnysse on heora biscepunge, swa þæt hi settað heora handa ofer gefullude menn and biddað þæt se ælmihtiga wealdend him sende ða seofonfealdan gife his Gastes, se ðe leofað and rixað a butan ende. Amen.

and strength, with knowledge and piety, and he fills us with fear of God. He who attains to these sevenfold gifts of the Holy Spirit through good merits, he will have all honor. But he who wishes to achieve this honor should believe in the holy Trinity and in true unity, that the Father, and his Son, and the Spirit of them both are three in persons, and one God indivisible, dwelling in one Godhead. This faith was signified by the three thousand who first inclined to belief after the coming of the Holy Spirit. Just as those three thousand were one company, so the holy Trinity is one God. And that company was as unanimous as if they all had one heart and one soul; for of the holy Trinity there is one Godhead, one nature, one will, and one work, inseparable.

The faithful brought their money and laid it at the feet of the apostles. By this is revealed that Christians should not set their hope in worldly riches, but in God alone. The covetous one who sets his hope in his treasure is, as the apostle said, "like one who practices idolatry." They regarded gold as worthless, because covetousness had no place in their hearts; and so they put their things in common, that they might be in true peace without covetousness. They laid their hands upon believers, and the Holy Spirit came to them through their confirmation. Bishops are of the same order in God's Church, and maintain that tradition by confirming, so that they lay their hands upon baptized people and pray that the almighty ruler send them the sevenfold gift of his Spirit, who lives and reigns forever without end. Amen.

23

Dominica secunda post Pentecosten

*H*omo quidam erat dives, et reliqua.

2 Se wealdenda Drihten sæde ðis bigspell his gingrum, þus cweðende, "Sum welig man wæs mid purpuran and gode-webbe geglenged, and dæghwamlice mærlice leofode. Þa læg sum wædla at his geate, and his nama wæs Lazarus. Se wæs licðrowere, and cepte ðæra crumena ðe man mid þam beodum ut abær, ac him wæs forwyrned. Þa comon hundas and his wunda liccodon. Ða gelamp hit þæt se ðearfa forðferde, and englas feredon his sawle to rest mid Abra-hame. Se rica eac gewat, and his sawul wearð besenct on helle deopnysse. Þa beseah he up of ðam tintregum, and gecneow ðone Lazarum on Abrahames wununge. He ða hrymde mid earmre stemne and cwæð, 'Þu fæder Abraham, gemiltsa min and send to me Lazarum, þæt he dyppe his finger on wætere and gecele mine tungan, forðam ðe ic eom on ðisum lige ðearle gecwylmed.' Him andwyrde Abraham, 'Ðu min bearn, beo ðe gemyndig þæt ðu underfenge welan on ðinum life, and Lazarus yrmðe. Nu is he gefrefrod, and þu eart getintregod. And betwux us is micel ðrosm gefæst-nod, þæt ure nan ne mæg to eow, ne ge to us.' He cwæð ða, 'Ic bidde þe, Fæder, þæt þu asende Lazarum ongean to minre mægðe, þæt he cyðe minum fif gebroðrum þæt hi warnigan geornlice þæt hi ne becuman to ðysre tintregunge.'

23

Second Sunday after Pentecost

Second Sunday after Pentecost

There was a certain rich man, etc.

The sovereign Lord told this parable to his disciples, say- 2
ing, "There was a certain wealthy man adorned with purple
and fine silk, and he lived grandly every day. A certain beggar
lay at his gate, and his name was Lazarus. He was a leper, and
longed for the crumbs that were thrown out from his table,
but these were denied him. Then dogs came and licked his
wounds. It happened then that the poor man died, and angels carried his soul to rest with Abraham. The rich man also
departed, and his soul was plunged into the depths of hell.
Then he looked up from his torments, and recognized Lazarus in Abraham's resting place. He called out with a pitiful
voice and said, 'Father Abraham, have mercy on me and send
Lazarus to me, that he might dip his finger in water and cool
my tongue, for I am cruelly tortured in this fire.' Abraham
answered him, 'My son, remember that you received good
things in your life, and Lazarus misery. Now he is comforted,
and you are tormented. And between us is fixed a great darkness, so that none of us may go to you, nor you to us.' He
then said, 'I ask you, Father, that you might send Lazarus
back to my relatives, that he might let my five brothers
know that they should diligently take care not to come to

399

Ða andwyrde Abraham, 'Hi habbað þone lareow Moysen and witegan þe him wissian sceolon; heorcnian hi heora lare gif hi willað.' Þa cwæð se rica, 'Nese, leof, nese; nellað hi heora synna behreowsian buton sum mann of deaðe arise and hi warnige.' Se heahfæder him andwyrde, 'Gif hi nellað gelyfan Moysen and ðam witegum, ne gecyrrað hi to dædbote ðurh nanes geedcucedes mannes mynegunge.'"

3   Þis godspel is nu anfealdlice gesæd; se halga papa Gregorius us onwreah ða digelnysse ðisre rædinge. He cwæð, "Ne sæde þæt halige godspel þæt se rica reafere wære, ac wæs uncystig and modegode on his welum." Be ðisum is to smeagenne hu se beo gewitnod þe oðerne berypð, þonne se bið to helle fordemed se his agen nolde for Godes lufon syllan. Ðises mannes uncyst and upahefednys hine besencte on cwycsusle forðan þe he næfde nane mildheortnysse, þæt he mid his gestreone his agene sawle alysde. Nu wenað sume menn þæt nan pleoh ne sy on deorwurðum gyrlum; ac gif hit gylt nære, þonne ne geswutulode þæt halige godspel swa gewislice be ðam rican þæt he wære mid purpuran and mid godewebbe geglencged. Ne cepð nan man deorwyrðra reafa buton for ydelum gylpe, soðlice þæt he sy toforan oðrum mannum þurh his glencge geteald. Drihten on oðre stowe herede Iohannem ðone Fulluhtere for ðære teartnysse his reafes, forðan ðe he wæs mid olfendes hærum gescryd, waclice and stiðlice.

4   Þa ða se hælend spræc be ðam rican þa cwæð he, "Sum rice man wæs"; eft be ðam wædlan, "Sum ðearfa wæs gehaten Lazarus." Cuð is eow þæt se rica bið namcuðre on his leode þonne se þearfa, þeahhwæðere ne nemde se hælend

this torment.' Abraham answered, 'They have the teacher Moses and the prophets, who should guide them; let them pay attention to their teaching if they will.' The rich man said, 'No, sir, no; they will not repent their sins unless someone should rise from the dead and warn them.' The patriarch answered him, 'If they will not believe Moses and the prophets, they will not turn to repentance because of any revived person's warning.'"

This gospel is now simply said; the holy pope Gregory has 3 revealed to us the mystery of this reading. He said, "The holy gospel did not say that the rich person was a robber, but he was stingy and took pride in his wealth." By this we should consider how someone will be punished who steals from another, when he is condemned to hell who would not give of his own possessions for love of God. This person's stinginess and arrogance plunged him into living torment because he had no compassion, so that with his treasure he might have redeemed his own soul. Now some will assume that there is no danger in precious garments; but if there were no sin, the holy gospel would not have so clearly revealed that the rich person was adorned with purple and with fine silk. No one cares about precious garments except for empty pride, truly so that through his splendor he might be considered above others. The Lord in another place praised John the Baptist for the crudeness of his dress, because he was clothed with camel's hair, poorly and roughly.

When the savior spoke of the rich person, he said, "There 4 was a certain rich man"; then of the poor person, "There was a certain poor man called Lazarus." You know that a rich person is better known among his people than a poor one, yet the savior did not name the wealthy one, but the needy

þone welegan, ac ðone wædlan; forðan ðe him is cuð þæra
eadmodra manna naman ðurh gecorennysse, ac he ne cann
ða modigan ðurh heora aworpennysse. Sume beladunge
mihte se rica habban his uncyste gif se reoflia wædla ne læge
ætforan his gesihðe; eac wære ðam earman leohtre on mode
gif he ðæs rican mannes welan ne gesawe. Mislice angsum-
nyssa he forbær ða ða he næfde ne bigleofan, ne hælðe, ne
hætera, and geseah ðone rican halne and deorweorðlice
geglencgedne brucan his estmettas. Genoh wære þam wædlan his untrumnys, þeah ðe he wiste hæfde; and eft him
wære genoh his hafenleast, ðeah ðe he gesundful wære. Ac
seo menigfealde earfoðnys wæs his sawle clænsung, and ðæs
rican uncyst and upahefednys wæs his geniðerung, forðon
ðe he geseah ðæs oðres yrmðe and hine mid toðundenum
mode forseah. Ac ða ða he wæs fram mannum forsewen, ða
genealæhton ða hundas and his wunda geliccedon; hundes
liccung gehælð wunda.

5   Þa gelamp hit þæt se wædla gewat, and englas ferodon his
sawle to ðæs heahfæderes wununge Abrahames, and ðæs
rican gast æfter forðsiðe wearð on helle besenct; and he
ða ðone wolde habban him to mundboran þam ðe he nolde
ær his cruman syllan. He bæd þa Abraham mid earmlicre
stemne þæt Lazarus moste his tungan drypan; ac him næs
getiðod ðære lytlan lisse, forðan ðe Lazarus ne moste ær on
life hedan ðæra crumena his mysan. His tungan he mænde
swiðost, forðan ðe hit is gewunelic þæt ða welegan on
heora gebeorscipe begað derigendlice gafetunge; þa wæs seo
tunge, ðurh rihtwisnysse edlean, teartlicor gewitnod for his
gegafspræce. Se heahfæder Abraham him cwæð to, "Ðu,
min bearn, beo ðe gemyndig þæt ðu underfenge welan on
ðinum life, and Lazarus yrmðe." Þes cwyde is swiðor to

one; because the names of the humble are known to him
through his choice, but he does not know the proud through
their rejection. The rich person might have had some excuse for his meanness if the leprous beggar had not lain before his sight; likewise the poor person's mind might have
been easier if he had not seen the rich person's wealth. He
endured various afflictions when he had neither nourishment, nor health, nor garments, and saw the rich person en-
joying his delicacies, healthy and expensively adorned. His
infirmity might have been enough for the beggar if he had
food; and again, his poverty might have been enough for
him if he were healthy. But the manifold hardship was the
cleansing of his soul, and the stinginess and pride of the rich
person were his condemnation, because he saw the other's
misery and with his puffed-up mind despised him. But when
he was despised by people, the dogs approached and licked
his wounds; the licking of a dog heals wounds.

It then happened that the beggar died, and angels carried 5
his soul to the dwelling of the patriarch Abraham, and the
rich person's spirit after his departure was plunged into hell;
and he then wanted to have for a protector the person to
whom he would not give his crumbs before. He then asked
Abraham with a pitiful voice that Lazarus might moisten his
tongue; but that little favor was not granted to him, because
Lazarus previously in his life could not gather the crumbs
from his table. He particularly lamented his tongue, because
it is common that the wealthy in their feasting practice
harmful mocking; so his tongue, through righteous retribu-
tion, was more harshly punished for his mocking speech.
The patriarch Abraham said to him, "My son, remember
that you received riches in your life, and Lazarus misery."

ondrædenne þonne to trahtnigenne. Ðam rican wæs forgolden mid ðam hwilwendlicum spedum, gif he hwæt to
gode gefremode; and ðam ðearfan wæs forgolden mid ðære
yrmðe, gif he hwæt to yfle gefremode. Þa underfeng se
welega his gesælðe to edleane to sceortum brice, and þæs
ðearfan hafenleast aclænsode his lytlan gyltas. Hine geswencte seo wædlung and afeormode; þone oðerne gewelgode his genihtsumnys and bepæhte.

6   Ic bidde eow, men ða leofostan, ne forseo ge Godes ðearfan ðeah ðe hi tallice hwæt gefremman, forðan ðe heora
yrmð afeormað þæt þæt seo gehwæde oferflowendnys gewemð. Hawiað be gehwilcum, forðan ðe oft getimað yfelum
teala for life. Se heahfæder cwæð to ðam welegan, "Betwux
us and eow is gefæstnod micel ðrosm; þeah hwa wille fram
us to eow, he ne mæg, ne eac fram eow to us." Mid micelre
geornfulnysse gewilniað þa wiðercoran þæt hi moton of
ðære susle ðe hi on cwylmiað, ac seo fæstnung ðære hellican
clysinge ne geðafað þæt hi æfre ut abrecon. Eac ða halgan
beoð mid heora scyppendes rihtwisnysse swa afyllede þæt hi
nateshwon ne besargiað ðæra wiðercorenra yrmðe, forðan
ðe hi geseoð þa fordonan swa micclum fram him geælfre-
mode swa micclum swa hi beoð fram heora leofan Drihtne
ascofene.

7   Siððan se rica wearð orwene his agenre alysednysse, ða
bearn him on mod his gebroðra gemynd; forðan ðe ðæra
wiðercorenra wite tiht forwel oft heora mod unnytwurðlice
to lufe, swilce hi þonne lufian heora siblingas, ðe ær on life
ne hi sylfe ne heora magas ne lufedon. Ne lufað se hine sylfne
se ðe hine mid synnum bebint. He oncneow Lazarum, ðone
ðe he ær forseah, and he gemunde his gebroðra, ða ðe he
bæftan forlet; forðan ðe se ðearfa nære fullice gewrecen on

This saying is rather to be feared than expounded. The rich person was rewarded with temporary prosperity, if he did anything good; and the poor person was rewarded with misery, if he had done anything evil. Then the wealthy man received his happiness as a reward to enjoy briefly enjoyment, and the poverty of the needy one cleansed his small sins. Poverty afflicted and purified him; his abundance enriched and deceived the other.

I pray you, most beloved people, do not despise God's 6 poor even if they do something blameworthy, because their misery cleanses that which a little excess corrupts. Observe each one, for good often befalls the evil for life. The patriarch said to the wealthy man, "Between us and you a great darkness is fixed; even if someone wanted to pass from us to you, he cannot, nor from you to us." With great eagerness the wicked wish that they might pass from the torment they suffer in, but the confinement of the hellish enclosure never allows them to break out. Moreover, the holy are so filled with their creator's righteousness that they in no way lament the misery of the wicked, because they see the damned are as much estranged from them as they are thrust away from their beloved Lord.

When the rich person despaired of his own deliverance, 7 the memory of his brothers came to his mind; for the punishment of the wicked very often uselessly stimulates their minds to love, so that they then love their relatives, who before in life loved neither themselves nor their kinsmen. He who binds himself up with sins does not love himself. He recognized Lazarus, whom he had scorned, and he remembered his brothers, whom he had left behind; for the needy one would not have been fully avenged on the rich if he had

ðam rican gif he on his wite hine ne oncneowe; and eft nære his wite fulfremed on ðam fyre, buton he ða ylcan pinunga his siblingum gewende.

8   Þa synfullan geseoð nu hwiltidum ða gecorenan on wuldre ðe hi forsawon on worulde, þæt seo angsumnys heora modes ðe mare sy; and ða rihtwisan symle geseoð ða unrihtwisan on heora tintregum cwylmigende, þæt heora bliss ðe mare sy and lufu to heora Drihtne, þe hi ahredde fram deofles anwealde and fram ðam manfullum heape. Ne astyrað þæra rihtwisra gesihð him nænne ogan, ne heora wuldor ne wanað; forðan ðe ðær ne bið nan besargung ðæra manfulra yrmðe, ac heora tintrega becymð þam gecorenum to maran blisse, swa swa on metinge bið forsewen seo blace anlicnys þæt seo hwite sy beorhtre gesewen. Þa gecorenan geseoð symle heora scyppendes beorhtnysse, and forði nis nan ðing on gesceaftum him bediglod.

9   Se welega nolde on lyfe gehyran ðone lareow Moysen, ne Godes witegan; ða wende he eac þæt his gebroðra hi woldon forseon swa swa he dyde, and gyrnde forði þæt Lazarus hi moste warnigan, þæt hi ne becomon to his susle. Se heahfæder him andwyrde, "Gif hi forseoð Moyses æ and ðæra witegena bodunga, nellað hi gelyfan, þeah hwa of deaðe arise." Þa ðe forgimeleasiað þa eaðelican beboda þære ealdan æ, hu willað hi ðonne gehyrsumian þam healicum bebodum Cristes lare, ðe of deaðe aras?

10   Ic bidde eow, mine gebroðra, þæt ge beon gemyndige ðæs Lazares reste and ðæs rican wite, and doð swa swa Crist sylf tæhte: "Tiliað eow freonda on Godes ðearfum, þæt hi on eowrum geendungum onfon eow into ecum eardungstowum." Manega Lazaras ge habbað nu licgende æt eowrum

not recognized him in his punishment; and again, his punishment would not have been complete in the fire, unless he had expected the same torments for his siblings.

From time to time the sinful see in glory the chosen ones 8 whom they had scorned in the world, so that the affliction of their minds might be the greater; and the righteous always see the unrighteous suffering in their torments, so that their bliss and love might be the greater for their Lord, who rescued them from the power of the devil and the company of the wicked. That sight strikes no terror in the righteous, nor diminishes their glory; for there will be no sorrowing for the misery of the wicked, but their torments will result in greater bliss for the chosen, just as in a picture a dark likeness is laid underneath so that the white might appear the brighter. The chosen always see their creator's brightness, and therefore nothing in creation is hidden from him.

Alive, the rich person would not hear the teacher Moses, 9 nor God's prophets; then he also assumed that his brothers would despise them as he did, and desired that Lazarus might warn them, so they might not end up in his torment. The patriarch answered him, "If they despise the law of Moses and the preaching of the prophets, they will not believe, even if someone should rise from death." Those who neglect the easy commandments of the old law, how will they obey the exalted commandments of the teaching of Christ, who arose from death?

I pray you, my brothers, that you be mindful of Lazarus's 10 rest and of the rich man's punishment, and do as Christ himself taught: "Gain friends for yourself among God's poor, that at your end they may receive you into eternal dwelling places." You have many Lazaruses now lying at your gates,

gatum, biddende eowre oferflowendnysse. Ðeah ðe hi syn
waclice geðuhte, þeahhwæðere hi beoð eft eowre ðingeras
wið ðone ælmihtigan. Soðlice we sceoldon beodan þam
ðearfum þæt hi us biddað, forðan ðe hi beoð ure mundboran, þa ðe nu wædligende æt us bigleofan wilniað. Ne sceole
we forseon heora wacnysse, forðan ðe Criste bið geðenod
þurh ðearfena anfenge, swa swa he sylf cwæð, "Me hingrode,
and ge me gereordodon; me ðyrste, and ge me scencton; ic
wæs nacod, and ge me scryddon."

II   Nu cweð se halga Gregorius þæt sum arwurðe munuc
wæs on ðam earde Licaonia, swiðe eawfæst, his nama wæs
Martirius. Se ferde be his abbudes hæse to sumum oðrum
mynstre on his ærende, ða gemette he be wege sumne
licðrowere licgende eal tocinen, and nahte his feðes geweald;
cwæð þæt he wolde genealæcan his hulce, gif he mihte. Þa
ofhreow ðam munece þæs hreoflian mægenleast, and be-
wand hine mid his cæppan and bær to mynstreweard. Þa
wearð his abbude geswutelod hwæne he bær, and hrymde
mid micelre stemne and cwæð, "Yrnað, yrnað, and undoð
þæs mynstres geat ardlice, forðan ðe ure broðor Martyrius
berð þone hælend on his bæce." Þa ða se munuc genealæhte
ðæs mynstres geate, þa wand se of his swuran þe wæs
hreoflig geðuht, and wearð gesewen on Cristes gelicnysse.
Ða beseah se munuc up and beheold hu he to heofonum
astah. Þa cwæð se hælend mid ðam upstige, "Martiri, ne
sceamode ðe min ofer eorðan, ne me ne sceamað þin on heofonum." Þa efste se abbud wið þæs muneces and neodlice
cwæð, "Broðor min, hwær is se ðe ðu feredest?" He cwæð,
"Gif ic wiste hwæt he wære, ic wolde licgan æt his fotum. Þa
ða ic hine bær, ne gefredde ic nanre byrðene swærnysse." Hu
mihte he gefredan æniges hefes swærnysse, ða ða he ðone

praying for your excess. Though they might seem lowly, nevertheless they will later be your intercessors with the almighty. Truly we ought to ask the poor to pray for us, because they will be our protectors, who now are begging for sustenance from us. We should not despise their poverty, for Christ is served by receiving the poor, as he himself said, "I was hungry, and you fed me; I was thirsty, and you gave me drink; I was naked, and you clothed me."

Now the holy Gregory says that there was a certain rever- 11 end monk in the country of Lycaonia, very pious, whose name was Martyrius. He was going by order of his abbot to some other monastery on his errand when he found a leper lying by the way, all chapped, and having no control of his feet; he said he wished to reach his hut, if he could. The monk took pity on the helplessness of the leper, and he wrapped him in his cloak and carried him toward his monastery. Then it was revealed to his abbot whom he was carrying, and he cried with a loud voice, saying, "Run, run, and open the gate of the monastery quickly, for our brother Martyrius bears the savior on his back." When the monk reached the gate of the monastery, the one who seemed like a leper let go of his neck, and appeared in the likeness of Christ. The monk then looked up and saw how he ascended to heaven. Then the savior said, while ascending, "Martyrius, you were not ashamed of me on earth, nor will I be ashamed of you in heaven." The abbot hurried to the monk and eagerly said, "My brother, where is the one you carried?" He said, "If I had known who he was, I would have lain at his feet. When I carried him, I felt no heaviness of any burden." How could he feel the heaviness of any weight, when he

ferode ðe hine bær? Nu cweð se halga Gregorius þæt se
hælend ða geseðde ðone cwyde þe he sylf cwæð, "Þæt þæt ge
doð þearfum on minum naman, þæt ge doð me sylfum."

12   Hwæt is on menniscum gecynde swa mærlic swa Cristes
menniscnys? And hwæt is atelicor geðuht on menniscum gecynde þonne is ðæs hreoflian lic, mid toðundennesse, and
springum, and reocendum stence? Ac se ðe is arwurðful ofer
ealle gesceafta he gemedemode hine sylfne þæt he wære gesewen on ðam atelican hiwe to ði þæt we sceolon besargian
menniscra manna yrmðe, and be ure mihte gefrefrian, for
lufe ðæs mildheortan and ðæs eadmodan hælendes, þæt he
us getiðige wununge on his rice to ecum life, se ðe us ahredde
fram deofles hæftnydum—se ðe rixað on ecnysse mid þam
ælmihtigan Fæder and þam Halgan Gaste, hi ðry on anre
Godcundnysse wunigende, butan anginne and ende, a on
worulde. Amen.

24

Dominica IIII post Pentecosten

Erant adpropinquantes ad Iesum, et reliqua.

2   Þæt halige godspel us segð þæt "gerefan and synfulle men
genealæhton ðam hælende and woldon his lare gehyran. Þa
ceorodon ða Sunderhalgan and ða boceras Iudeiscre ðeode,

carried the one who bore him? The holy Gregory says that the savior confirmed the saying which he himself said, "Whatever you do for the poor in my name, you do for me."

What is there in human nature so glorious as the human- 12 ity of Christ? And what is considered more hideous in humankind than the body of a leper, with tumors, and ulcers, and reeking stench? But he who is venerable above all creatures humbled himself to appear in that hideous form so that we might pity the misery of human beings, and comfort them according to our power, for love of the merciful and humble savior, so that he may grant us a dwelling in his kingdom to eternal life, he who rescued us from the captivity of the devil—he who reigns in eternity with the almighty Father and the Holy Spirit, those three dwelling in one Godhead, without beginning and end, forever to eternity. Amen.

24

Fourth Sunday after Pentecost

Fourth Sunday after Pentecost

T here were approaching Jesus, etc.

The holy gospel tells us that "overseers and sinners 2 approached the savior and wanted to hear his teaching. Then the Pharisees and the scribes of the Jewish people

forðan ðe se hælend underfeng ða synfullan and him mid gereordode. Ða sæde se hælend ðam Iudeiscum bocerum ðis
bigspel: 'Hwilc eower hæfð hundteontig sceapa, and gif he
forlyst an ðæra sceapa, la hu ne forlæt he ða nigon and hundnigontig on westene and gæð secende þæt an ðæt him
losode? Gif he hit ðonne gemet, he hit berð on his eaxlum to
ðære eowede blissigende; þonne he ham cymð he gelaðað
his frynd and nehgeburas him to and cwyð, "Blissiað mid
me, forðon ðe ic gemette min scep ðe me losede." Ic secge
eow þæt mare bliss bið on heofonum be anum synfullum
men, gif he his synna mid dædbote behreowsað, ðonne him
sy be nigon and hundnigontig rihtwisra ðe ne behofiað nanre
dædbote.'"

3   Þas word sind digle, ac se trahtnere Gregorius us geopenode þæt gastlice andgit. Mine gebroðra þa leofostan, ge gehyrdon on ðyssere godspellican rædinge þæt ða synfullan
genealæhton to ðæs hælendes spræce, and eac to his gereorde; and ða Iudeiscan boceras mid hete þæt tældon, ac
heora tal næs na of rihtwisnysse ac of niðe. Hi wæron untrume, ðeah ðe hi ðæs ne gymdon. Þa wolde se heofenlica
læce mid geswæsum bigspelle þæt geswell heora heortan
welwyllendlice gelacnian, and ðus cwæð, "Hwilc eower hæfð
hundteontig sceapa, and gif he forlysð an ðæra sceapa,
ðonne forlæt he ða nigon and hundnigontig on westene, and
gæð secende þæt an ðe him losode?" Hundfeald getel is fulfremed, and se ælmihtiga hæfde hundteontig sceapa ða ða
engla werod and mancynn wæron his æhta; ac him losode an
sceap ða ða se frumsceapena mann Adam syngigende forleas
Neorxenawanges bigwiste. Þa forlet se ælmihtiga Godes
Sunu eal engla werod on heofonum and ferde to eorðan, and
sohte þæt an sceap ðe him ætwunden wæs. Ða ða he hit

murmured, because the savior received sinful people and ate with them. Then the savior told this parable to the Jewish scribes: 'Which of you has a hundred sheep, and if he loses one of the sheep, lo, does he not abandon the ninety-nine in the wilderness and go looking for the one sheep that was lost to him? If he finds it, he bears it on his shoulders to the flock, rejoicing; when he comes home, he invites his friends and neighbors to him and says, "Rejoice with me, for I have found the sheep that was lost to me." I tell you there will be more joy in heaven over one sinner, if he repents his sins with penance, than there will be for the ninety-nine righteous ones who do not need penance.'"

These words are obscure, but the commentator Gregory has opened their spiritual meaning for us. My dearest brothers, you have heard in this gospel reading that the sinners drew near to the savior's speech, and also his table; the Jewish scribes reproached that with hate, but their reproach was not from righteousness but from envy. They were sick, though they did not notice it. Then the heavenly physician benevolently wanted to heal the swelling of their hearts with a pleasant parable, and said, "Which of you has a hundred sheep, and if he loses one of the sheep, then he leaves the ninety-nine in the wilderness, and goes seeking the one that was lost to him?" A hundredfold number is perfect, and the almighty had a hundred sheep when the hosts of angels and humankind were his possessions; but he lost one sheep when the first-created human Adam lost the sustenance of Paradise through sin. Then the almighty Son of God left all the hosts of angels in heaven and went to earth, seeking the one sheep that had escaped from him. When he found it, he

gemette, he hit bær on his exlum to ðære eowde blissigende.
Þa ða he underfeng ure mennisce gecynd and ure synna
abær, þa wæs þæt dweligende sceap ongean fered on his halgum exlum. Ðæra sceapa hlaford com ham, afundenum
sceape; forðan ðe Crist æfter ðære ðrowunge, ðe he mancyn
mid alysde, aras of deaðe, and astah to heofonum blissigende.

4   He gelaðode ða his frynd and his nehgeburas. His frynd
sind engla heapas, forðan ðe hi healdað on heora staðelfæst-
nysse singallice his willan. Hi sind eac his nehgeburas,
forðan ðe hi brucað þære wulderfullan beorhtnysse his gesihðe on heora andweardnysse. He cwæð, "Blissiað mid me,
forðan ðe ic gemette min forlorene sceap." Ne cwæð he,
"Blissiað mid þam sceape," ac "mid me," forðan ðe ure
alysednys soðlice is his bliss; and ðonne we beoð to ðære
heofonlican eardungstowe gelædde, þonne gefylle we ða
micclan mærsunge his gefean. He cwæð, "Ic secge eow, mare
bliss bið on heofonum be anum synfullan men, gif he his
synna mid dædbote behreowsað, ðonne sy be nigon and
hundnigontig rihtwisum ðe nanre behreowsunge ne behofiað." Þis is to smeagenne hwi sy mare bliss be gecyrredum synfullum þonne be unscyldigum rihtwisum.

5   We habbað gelomlice gesewen þæt gehwylce gebroðra ðe
ne befeollon on healice gyltas, þæt hi ne beoð ealles swa
carfulle to beganne ða earfoðlican drohtnunge, swilce hi
orsorge beon forðan ðe hi ða healican leahtras ne gefremedon; and gehwilce oðre ðe oncnawað þa swæran gyltas ðe hi
on geogoðe adrugon beoð mid micelre sarnysse onbryrde.
Hi forseoð alyfedlice ðing and gesewenlice, and mid wope
gewilniað þa ungesewenlican and ða heofonlican. Hi forseoð
hi sylfe and geeadmettað on eallum ðingum; and forði ðe hi

bore it on his shoulders to the flock, rejoicing. When he took on our human nature and bore our sins, then that wandering sheep was brought back on his holy shoulders. The master of the sheep came home, having found his sheep; for Christ after his passion, by which he redeemed humanity, arose from death, and ascended to heaven rejoicing.

He invited his friends and his neighbors. His friends are 4 companies of angels, because in their steadfastness they perpetually observe his will. They are also his neighbors, because they enjoy the glorious brightness of his sight in their presence. He said, "Rejoice with me, for I have found my lost sheep." He did not say, "Rejoice with the sheep," but "with me," because our redemption is truly his joy; and when we are led to the heavenly dwelling place, we will complete the great celebration of his gladness. He said, "I tell you, there will be more joy in heaven over one sinner, if he repents his sins with penance, than there is over ninety-nine righteous who do not need repentance." We should consider why there would be more joy over a converted sinner than over the guiltless righteous.

We have frequently seen that some brothers who have 5 not fallen into deadly sins are not quite so careful to practice a difficult course of life, as though they might be carefree because they have not committed deadly sins; and some others who acknowledge the grievous sins they have committed in youth are inspired with great grief. They despise permitted and visible things, and with weeping desire invisible and heavenly things. They despise themselves and are humble in all things; and because they departed from their

dweligende fram heora scyppende gewiton, hi willað geinnian ða æftran hinðe mid þam uferan gestreonum. Mare
bliss bið on heofonum be ðam gecyrredum synfullum, ðurh
swilce drohtnunga, þonne sy be ðam asolcenum þe truwað
be him sylfum þæt he lytle and feawa gyltas gefremode, and
eac hwonlice carað ymbe Godes beboda and his sawle
ðearfe. Maran lufe nimð se heretoga on gefeohte to ðam
cempan þe æfter fleame his wiðerwinnan ðegenlice ofer-
winð þonne to ðam þe mid fleame ne ætwand ne ðeah on
nanum gecampe naht ðegenlices ne gefremode. Ealswa se
yrðling lufað ðone æcer ðe æfter ðornum and bremelum
genihtsume wæstmas agifð swiðor þonne he lufige ðone ðe
ðornig næs ne wæstmbære ne bið. Sind ðeahhwæðere forwel
mænige rihtwise unscyldige wið heafodleahtras, and habbað
hwæðere ealswa stiðe drohtnunge swylce hi mid eallum synnum geancsumede wæron. Þam ne mæg nan dædbeta beon
geefenlæht, forðan ðe hi sind rihtwise and behreowsigende.
Be ðam is to smeagenne hu micclum se rihtwisa mid eadmodre heofunge God gegladige, gif se unrihtwisa mid soðre
dædbote hine gegladian mæg.

6   Drihten rehte ða gyt oðer bigspel be tyn scyllingum, and
ðæra an losode and wearð gemet. Þæt bigspel getacnað eft
nigon engla werod. To ðam teoðan werode wæs mancyn
gesceapen, forðan þe þæt teoðe wearð mid modignysse
forscyldigod, and hi ealle to awyrgedum deoflum wurdon
awende, and of ðære heofonlican blisse to helle suslum
bescofene. Nu sind ða nigon heapas, genemnede *angeli, archangeli, virtutes, potestates, principatus, dominationes, throni,
cherubin, seraphin.* Þæt teoðe forwearð; þa wæs mancynn gesceapen to geedstaðelunge ðæs forlorenan heapes.

7   *Angeli* sind gecwedene "Godes bodan"; *archangeli,* "healice

creator in error, they want to repair the injury that followed with higher gains. There will be greater joy in heaven over the converted sinner, through such practices, than there will be over the slothful one who is confident in himself that he has committed little and few sins, and at the same time cares little about God's commandments and the needs of his soul. A commander in battle feels greater love for the soldier who after flight boldly overcomes his adversary than for the one who never took to flight but did not perform any brave deed in any conflict. Similarly, the farmer loves the field which after thorns and brambles yields abundant fruits more than he loves the one that was not thorny but is not fruitful. Yet there are very many righteous who are guiltless of deadly sins, yet they keep a course of life as severe as though they were beset by all sins. No penitent can be compared with these, because they are righteous and repentant. By this we should consider how greatly the righteous person gladdens God with humble lamentation, if the unrighteous can gladden him with true penitence.

The Lord recounted another parable about ten shillings, 6 and one of them was lost and was found. That parable again signifies the nine hosts of angels. Humanity was created as the tenth host, because the tenth had been found guilty of pride, and they were turned into cursed devils, and thrust from heavenly bliss into the torments of hell. There are now nine companies, named *angels, archangels, virtues, powers, principalities, dominions, thrones, cherubim, seraphim.* The tenth perished; then humanity was created to supply the place of the lost company.

Angels are called "God's messengers"; *archangels,* "high 7

bodan"; *virtutes,* "mihta," ðurh ða wyrcð God fela wundra. *Potestates* sind "anwealdu" ðe habbað anweald ofer ða awyrge-dan gastas, þæt hi ne magon geleaffulra manna heortan swa micclum costnian swa hi willað. *Principatus* sind "ealdorsci-pas," ðe ðæra godra engla gymað, and hi be heora dihte ða godcundlican gerynu gefyllað. *Dominationes* sind "hlaford-scypas" gecwedene, forðan ðe him gehyrsumiað oðra engla werod mid micelre underðeodnysse. *Throni* sind "þrymsetl," þa beoð gefyllede mid swa micelre gife ðære ælmihtigan Godcundnysse þæt se eallwealdenda God on him wunað, and ðurh hi his domas tosceat. *Cherubin* is gecweden "ge-fyllednys ingehydes" oððe "gewittes"; hi sind afyllede mid gewitte swa miccle swiðor, swa hi gehendran beoð heora scyppende, ðurh wurðscipe heora geearnunga. *Seraphim* sind gecwedene "byrnende," oððe "onælende"; hi sind swa miccle swiðor byrnende on Godes lufe swa micclum swa hi sind to him geðeodde, forðan ðe nane oðre englas ne sind be-tweonan him and ðam ælmihtigan Gode. Hi sind byrnende na on fyres wisan, ac mid micelre lufe þæs wealdendan cy-ninges. Godes rice bið gelogod mid engla weredum and geðungenum mannum, and we gelyfað þæt of mancynne swa micel getel astige þæt uplice rice swa micel swa on heofo-num belaf haligra gasta æfter ðam hryre ðæra awyrgedra gasta.

8   Nigon engla werod þær wæron to lafe, and þæt teoðe for-ferde. Nu bið eft seo micelnys geðungenra manna swa micel swa ðæra staðelfæstra engla wæs, and we beoð geendebyrde to heora weredum æfter urum geearnungum. Menige geleaf-fulle men sind þe habbað lytel andgit to understandenne ða deopnysse Godes lare, and willað þeahhwæðere oðrum mannum mid arfæstnysse cyðan ymbe Godes mærða, be

messengers"; *virtues,* "strengths," through which God works many miracles. *Powers* are "powers," which have power over the accursed spirits, that they may not tempt the hearts of the faithful as much as they desire. *Principalities* are "authorities," which have charge of the good angels, and at their direction they fulfill the divine mysteries. *Dominions* are called "lordships," because the other hosts of angels obey them with great subjection. *Thrones* are "thrones," which are filled with such great grace of the almighty Godhead that the allpowerful God dwells in them, and through them decides his judgments. *Cherubim* is called "fullness of knowledge" or "understanding"; the nearer they are to their creator, the more they are filled with understanding, through the worthiness of their merits. *Seraphim* are called "burning" or "inflaming"; the more they are joined to God the more they are burning in love of him, for no other angels are between them and the almighty God. They are not burning in the manner of fire, but with great love of the powerful king. God's kingdom is composed of hosts of angels and of pious people, and we believe that as great a number of people will ascend to that exalted realm as there remained of holy spirits in heaven after the fall of the accursed spirits.

There were nine hosts of angels that remained, and the tenth perished. Now the multitude of pious people will again be as great as was that of the steadfast angels, and we shall be set in rank with their hosts according to our merits. There are many faithful who have little intellect to understand the deepness of God's teaching, and yet with piety will make known the glories of God to others, according to the

8

heora andgites mæðe: þas beoð geendebyrde to englum, þæt
is, to Godes bydelum. Þa gecorenan ðe magon asmeagan
Godes digelnysse, and oðrum bodian mid gastlicre lare, hi
beoð getealde to heahenglum, þæt is to healicum bodum. Þa
halgan ðe on life wundra wyrceað beoð geendebyrde betwux
ðam heofenlicum mihtum þe Godes tacna gefremmað. Sind
eac sume gecorene menn ðe aflyað þa awyrgedan gastas fram
ofsettum mannum ðurh mihte heora bena: hwærto beoð þas
geendebyrde buton to ðam heofenlicum anwealdum, þe
gewyldað þa feondlican costneras? Þa gecorenan ðe ðurh
healice geearnunga þa læssan gebroðru oferstigað mid eal-
dorscipe, þa habbað eac heora dæl betwux ðam heofenlicum
ealderdomum. Sume beoð swa geðungene þæt hi wealdað
mid heora hlafordscipe ealle uncysta and leahtras on him
sylfum, swa þæt hi beoð godas getealde ðurh ða healican
clænnysse; be ðam cwæð se ælmihtiga to Moysen, "Ic ðe gesette þæt þu wære Pharaones god." Þas Godes ðegnas, þe
beoð on swa micelre geðincðe on gesihðe þæs ælmihtigan
þæt hi sind godas getealde, hwider gescyt ðonne heora endebyrdnysse, buton to ðam werode ðe sind hlafordscipas gecwedene, forðan ðe him oðre englas underðeodde beoð?

9   On sumum gecorenum mannum ðe mid micelre gimene
on andweardum life drohtniað, bið Godes Gastes gifu swa
micel þæt he, on heora heortan swilce on ðrimsetle sittende,
toscæt and demð wundorlice oðra manna dæda. Hwæt
sind þas buton ðrymsetl heora scyppendes, on ðam ðe he
wunigende mannum demð? Seo soðe lufu is gefyllednys
Godes æ, and se ðe on his ðeawum hylt Godes lufe and
manna, he bið þonne cherubim rihtlice gehaten; forðan ðe
eal gewitt and ingehyd is belocen on twam wordum, þæt is
Godes lufu and manna. Sume Godes ðeowan sind onælede

measure of their intellect: these will be set in rank with the angels, that is, with God's messengers. The chosen who can investigate the mysteries of God, and preach to others with spiritual teaching, will be numbered with the archangels, that is, with the high messengers. The holy who work wonders in life will be ranked among the heavenly virtues who perform God's miracles. There are also some chosen ones who drive out accursed spirits from the possessed by the power of their prayers: where should these be ranked but with the heavenly powers, who control the demonic tempters? Those chosen ones who through high merit rise in authority above their lesser brethren, they too will have their portion among the heavenly princes. There are some so pious that they control with their authority all vices and sin in themselves, so that they are accounted gods through their exalted purity; of these the almighty said to Moses, "I will set you that you may be Pharaoh's god." These servants of God, who are in such great honor in the sight of the almighty that they are accounted gods, to what order are they assigned, if not to the host which is called dominions, because other angels are subordinate to them?

In some of the chosen who live with great vigilance in the present life, the grace of God's Spirit is so great that he, sitting in their hearts as if on a throne, decides and judges wondrously the deeds of others. What are these but thrones of their creator, abiding on which he judges people? True love is the fulfillment of God's law, and he who in his conduct holds love of God and of humanity, he will rightly be called cherubim; for all intelligence and inner thought is contained in two words, that is, love of God and of humanity. Some

9

mid swa micelre gewilnunge heora scyppendes neawiste þæt
hi forseoð ealle woruldlice ymbhydignysse, and mid byrnendum mode ealle ða ateorigendlican geðincðu oferstigað, and
mid ðam micclan bryne ðære heofenlican lufe oðre ontendað, and mid larlicre spræce getrymmað. Hu magon ðas
beon gecigede buton seraphim, þonne hi ðurh ðone micclan
bryne Godes lufe sind toforan oðrum eorðlicum his neawiste
gehendost?

10   Nu cweð se eadiga Gregorius, "Wa ðære sawle ðe orhlyte
hyre lif adrihð þæra haligra mihta," þe we nu sceortlice eow
gerehton. Ac seo ðe bedæled is þam godnyssum heo geom-
rige, and gewilnige þæt se cystiga wealdend þurh his gife hi
geðeode þam hlyte his gecorenra. Nabbað ealle menn gelice
gife æt Gode, forðan ðe he forgifð ða gastlican geðincðu ælcum be his gecneordnyssum. Se ðe læssan gife hæbbe ne an-
dige he on ðam foreðeondum, forðan ðe ða halgan ðreatas
ðæra eadigra engla sind swa geendebyrde þæt hi sume mid
underþeodnysse oðrum hyrsumiað, and sume mid ofersti-
gendre wurðfulnysse ðam oðrum sind foresette.

11   Micel getel is ðæra haligra gasta þe on Godes rice eardiað,
be ðam cwæð se witega Daniel, "Þusend ðusenda ðenodon
þam heofonlican wealdende, and ten ðusend siðan hundfealde ðusenda him mid wunodon." Oðer is ðenung, oðer is
mid wunung. Þa englas ðeniað Gode þe bodiað his willan
middangearde, and ða ðing gefyllað þe him liciað. Ða oðre
werod þe him mid wuniað brucað þære incundan embwla-
tunge his godcundnysse, swa þæt hi nateshwon fram his
andweardnysse asende ne gewitað. Soðlice ða ðe to us
asende becumað, swa hi gefremmað heora scyppendes hæse
wiðutan þæt hi ðeahhwæðere næfre ne gewitað fram his

servants of God are inflamed with so great a desire for the presence of their creator that they despise all worldly concerns, and with burning mind rise above all perishable honors, and kindle others with the great heat of heavenly love, and correct them with instructive speech. What should these be called but seraphim, when through the great heat of love of God they are nearest to his presence before other earthly ones?

Now the blessed Gregory says, "Woe to the soul that 10 passes its life devoid of the holy virtues," which we have just shortly explained to you. But the soul that is deprived of those excellences should mourn, and desire that the bountiful ruler will, through his grace, join it to the lot of his chosen ones. All people do not have the same grace from God, for he gives spiritual honors to each person according to his endeavors. Let the one who has less grace not envy those who are more excellent, because the holy companies of blessed angels are so ordered that some in subordination obey others, and some with surpassing honor are set before others.

Great is the number of holy spirits who dwell in God's 11 kingdom, of whom the prophet Daniel said, "A thousand thousand served the heavenly ruler, and ten thousand times hundredfold thousands dwelt with him." Serving is one thing, dwelling with is another. Those angels serve God who announce his will to the world, and perform the things which are pleasing to him. The other hosts that dwell with him enjoy the closest contemplation of his divinity, so that by no means do they depart from his presence when they are sent forth. Truly those who are sent to us perform their creator's command outside in such a way that they

godcundan myrhðe; forðam ðe God is æghwær, þeah ðe se
engel stowlic sy. Nis se ælmihtiga wealdend stowlic, forðan
ðe he is on ælcere stowe, and swa hwider swa se stowlica
engel flihð, he bið befangen mid his andwerdnysse.

12   Hi habbað sume synderlice gife fram heora scyppende,
and ðeahhwæðere heora wurðscipe him bið eallum gemæne,
and þæt þæt gehwilc on him sylfum be dæle hæfð, þæt
he hæfð on oðrum werode fulfremodlice. Be ðam cwæð se
sealmwyrhta, "Drihten, ðu ðe sitst ofer cherubin, geswutela
ðe sylfne."

13   We sædon litle ær on ðisre rædinge, þæt þæs ælmihtigan
ðrymsetl wære betwux ðam werode ðe sind *throni* gecigede:
ac hwa mæg beon eadig, buton he his scyppendes wununge
on him sylfum hæbbe? *Seraphim* sind ða gastas gecigede ðe
beoð on Drihtnes lufe byrnende, and ðeahhwæðere eal þæt
heofonlice mægen samod beoð onælede mid his lufe. *Cherubim* is gecweden "gefyllednys ingehydes oððe gewittes," and
ðeah hwilc engel is on Godes andwerdnysse ðe ealle ðing
nyte? Ac forði is gehwilc ðæra weroda þam naman geciged
ðe ða gife getacnað þe he fulfremedlicor underfeng.

14   Ac uton suwian hwæthwega be ðam digelnyssum ðæra
heofenlicra ceastergewarena, and smeagan be us sylfum, and
geomrian mid behreowsunge ure synna, þæt we, ðurh Drihtnes mildheortnysse, ða heofonlican wununge, swa swa he us
behet, habban moton. He cwæð on sumere stowe, "On
mines Fæder huse sind fela wununga"; forðan gif sume
beoð strengran on geearnungum, sume rihtwisran, sume
mid maran halignysse geglengede, þæt heora nan ne beo
geælfremod fram ðam micclan huse, þær ðær gehwilc
onfehð wununge be his geearnungum.

nevertheless never depart from his divine joy; for God is everywhere, though the angel might be in one place. The almighty ruler is not in one place, for he is in every place, and wherever the angel who has a place flies, he will be surrounded by his presence.

Some of them have special grace from their creator, and yet their dignity is common to all, and whatever each possesses in himself partially, he possesses perfectly in one of the other hosts. Of this the psalmist said, "Lord, you who sit above the cherubim, manifest yourself." 12

A little earlier in this reading, we said that the throne of the almighty was among the host which are called *thrones:* but who may be happy, unless he has his creator's dwelling in himself? The spirits are called *seraphim* who are burning with love of the Lord, and yet all the heavenly powers together are inflamed with his love. *Cherubim* is interpreted "fullness of inner knowledge or intelligence," and yet what angel is in God's presence who does not know all things? But each of those hosts is therefore called by the name which signifies the grace it has more perfectly received. 13

But let us stop speaking a little of the mysteries of the inhabitants of the city of heaven, and consider ourselves, and groan with repentance for our sins, so that we, through the Lord's mercy, may attain to the heavenly dwelling, as he has promised us. He said in a certain place, "In my Father's house are many dwellings"; for if some are stronger in merit, some more righteous, some adorned with greater holiness, none of them will be estranged from the great house, in which everyone will receive a dwelling according to his merits. 14

15   Se miltsienda Drihten cwæð þæt micel blis wære on heofonum be anum dædbetan; ac se ylca cwæð þurh his witegan,
"Gif se rihtwisa gecyrð fram his rihtwisnysse and begæð unrihtwisnysse arleaslice, ealle his rihtwisnysse ic forgyte; and
gif se arleasa behreowsað his arleasnysse and begæð rihtwisnysse, ne gemune ic nanra his synna." Behreowsigendum
mannum he miltsað, ac he ne behet þam elcigendum gewiss
lif oð merigen. Nis forði nanum synfullum to yldigenne
agenre gecyrrednysse, ðy læs ðe he mid sleacnysse forleose
ða tid Godes fyrstes. Smeage gehwilc man his ærran dæda,
and eac his andweardan drohtnunge, and fleo to ðam
mildheortan deman mid wope, ða hwile ðe he anbidað ure
betrunge se ðe is rihtwis and mildheort. Soðlice behreowsað
his gedwyld se ðe ne geedlæhð þa ærran dæda; be ðam cwæð
se hælend to ðam gehæledan bedredan, "Efne nu ðu eart gehæled; ne synga ðu heononforð, þy læs ðe ðe sum ðing wyrse
gelimpe."

16   Geleaffullum mannum mæg beon micel truwa and hopa
to ðam menniscum Gode Criste, se ðe is ure mundbora
and dema, se ðe leofað and rixað mid Fæder on annysse þæs
Halgan Gastes, on ealra worulda woruld. Amen.

The merciful Lord said that there was great joy in heaven 15
for one penitent; but the same said through his prophet, "If
the righteous turn from his righteousness and impiously
commits unrighteousness, I will forget all his righteousness;
and if the impious repents of his impiety and does righteousness, I will not remember any of his sins." To the repentant he is merciful, but to procrastinators he does not
promise certain life until tomorrow. No sinner ought therefore to delay his own repentance, lest he by slackness lose
the time of God's respite. Let every person consider his former deeds, and also his present way of life, and fly to the
merciful judge with weeping, while he who is righteous and
merciful awaits our improvement. He truly repents of his
error who does not repeat his former deeds; concerning this
the savior said to the healed invalid, "Behold, now you are
healed; do not sin henceforth, lest something worse befall
you."

The faithful may have great trust and hope in the incar- 16
nate God Christ, who is our protector and judge, who lives
and reigns with the Father in the unity of the Holy Spirit,
for ever and ever. Amen.

25

VIII KALENDAS IULII

Nativitate sancti Iohannes baptisti

Se godspellere Lucas awrat on Cristes bec be acennednysse Iohannes ðæs Fulluhteres, þus cweðende, "Sum
eawfæst Godes ðegen wæs gehaten Zacharias; his gebedda
wæs geciged Elisabeth. Hi butu wæron rihtwise ætforan
Gode, on his bebodum and rihtwisnyssum forðstæppende
butan tale. Næs him cild gemæne forðan þe Elisabeth wæs
untymende, and hi butu ða forwerode wæron. Hit gelamp
æt sumum sæle þæt Zacharias eode inn to Godes temple.
Ða mid ðam ðe he on his gebedum stod, him æteowde
Godes heahengel Gabrihel and him to cwæð, 'Ne beo ðu
afyrht, Zacharia; se ælmihtiga wealdend ðe het cyðan þæt he
gehyrde þine bene, and ðin wif sceal acennan sunu, and þu
gecigst his naman Iohannes. Hit bið þe micel bliss, and
manega on his acennednysse fægniað. He bið mære ætforan
Gode; ne abirigð he wines ne nan ðæra wætana þe men of
druncniað. He bið afylled mid þam Halgan Gaste on his modor innoðe. He gebigð fela þæs folces Israheles to Gode, and
he forestæpð his Drihtne on gaste and mihte þæs witegan
Helian, þæt he geðwærlæce fædera heortan to heora bearnum, and þæt he gebige ða ungeleaffullan to rihtwisra
snoternysse, and fulfremed folc Gode gearcige.' Zacharias
him andwyrde, 'Hu mæg ic ðinum wordum gelyfan, forðan

25

The Nativity of John the Baptist

The Nativity of Saint John the Baptist

The Evangelist Luke wrote in Christ's book about the birth of John the Baptist, saying, "There was a pious servant of God named Zechariah; his wife was called Elizabeth. They were both righteous before God, walking forth in his commandments and righteousness without blame. They had no child because Elizabeth was barren, and they were both very old. It happened at a certain time that Zechariah went into God's temple. As he stood at his prayers, God's archangel Gabriel appeared to him and said, 'Do not be afraid, Zechariah; the almighty ruler bids you know that he has heard your plea, and your wife will bear a son, and you will call his name John. It will be a great joy for you, and many will rejoice at his birth. He will be great before God; he will not taste wine or any of the liquors by which people become drunk. He will be filled with the Holy Spirit from his mother's womb. He will turn many of the people of Israel to God, and he will go before his Lord in the spirit and power of the prophet Elijah, that he might reconcile the hearts of fathers to their children, and turn the unbelievers to the wisdom of the righteous, and prepare a perfect people for God.' Zechariah answered him, 'How can I believe

ðe wit sind forwerede to bearnes gestreone?' Se engel cwæð, 'Ic eom Godes heahengel and dæghwamlice ic stande ætforan his gesihðe, and he me sende to ðe þis to cyðenne. Nu for ðinre geleaflæste, beo ðu dumb oð þæt min bodung gefylled sy.' He ða adumbode, and swa unsprecende ham gewende."

2   "Þa æfter feawum dagum geeacnode his wif Elisabeth, and on gefylledre tide sunu acende. Hire siblingas and nehgeburas þæs fægnodon, and woldon ðam cilde naman gescyppan Zacharias. Seo ealde cynnestre wiðcwæð þam magum: 'Ac beo he geciged Iohannes.' Hi andwyrdon, 'Hwi wiðcwest ðu urum geðeahtum? Nis nan man on ðinre mægðe Iohannes gehaten.' Hi þa bicnodon þam dumban fæder hwæt him be ðam ðuhte. Se fæder ða awrat, 'His nama is Iohannes.' Þa mid þam gewrite wearð his muð geopenod, and his tunge unbunden to rihtre spræce. Hwæt þa asprang micel oga ofer heora nehgeburas, and þæt wundor wearð swiðe gewidmærsod, and cwæð gehwa on his geðance, hwæt wenst ðu hwæt þis cild beon wylle? Godes miht soðlice wæs mid þam cilde, and se fæder wearð mid þan Halgan Gaste afylled and witiggende herode God, 'Sy gebletsod Drihten Israhela God, forðan ðe he geneosode his folc and alysde.'"

3   Þæt cild ðeah and wæs gestrangod mid Godes gaste. Þa ða he gewittig wæs, he forbeah ðæs folces neawiste and woruldlice unðeawas, and wunede on westene oð fullum wæstme. Eal his reaf wæs awefen of olfendes hærum; his bigleofa wæs stiðlic, ne dranc he wines drenc ne nanes gemencgedes wætan ne gebrowenes. Ofet hine fedde, and wudehunig, and oðre waclice ðigena.

4   "On ðam fifteoðan geare ðæs caseres rices Tyberii com Godes word ofer Iohannem on ðam westene, and he ferde

your words, because we are both too old to produce a child?' The angel said, 'I am the archangel of God and daily I stand before his sight, and he has sent me to reveal this to you. Now for your lack of faith, be mute until my announcement is fulfilled.' He then fell mute, and returned home unable to speak.

"Then after a few days his wife Elizabeth conceived, and when her time was fulfilled, she bore a son. Her relatives and neighbors rejoiced at that, and wanted to give the child the name Zechariah. The old mother contradicted her kinsmen: 'But he will be called John.' They answered, 'Why do you contradict our advice? There is no one in your family called John.' They then beckoned to the mute father to ask how it seemed to him. The father wrote, 'His name is John.' Then with that writing his mouth was opened, and his tongue unbound for proper speech. At this a great fear sprang up among their neighbors, and that wonder was made known very widely, and everyone said in his thoughts, what do you think this child will be? Truly God's power was with that child, and the father was filled with the Holy Spirit and praised God, prophesying, 'Blessed be the Lord, the God of Israel, for he has visited his people and set them free.'"

The child prospered and was strengthened with God's spirit. When he became capable of discretion, he turned away from human company and worldly vices, and lived in the desert until he was fully grown. All his garment was woven of camel's hair; his food was coarse, and he drank neither wine nor any mixed or brewed liquids. Fruit fed him, and wild honey, and other simple things.

"In the fifteenth year of the reign of the emperor Tiberius, the word of God came over John in the desert, and

to folces neawiste and bodade Iudeiscum folce fulluht on synna forgyfenysse, swa swa hit awriten is on Isaies wite-gunge." Cristes fulluht he bodade toweard eallum geleaffullum, on ðam is synna forgyfenys þurh ðone Halgan Gast. Io-hannes eac, be Godes dihte, fullode ða ðe him to comon ðæra Iudeiscra ðeoda, ac his fulluht ne dyde nanre synne for-gyfenysse, forðan ðe he wæs Godes bydel, and na God. He bodade mannum þæs hælendes tocyme mid wordum, and his halige fulluht mid his agenum fulluhte, on ðam he geful-lode ðone unsynnian Godes Sunu, ðe nanre synne forgyfe-nysse ne behofade.

5   Rihtlice weorðað Godes gelaðung ðisne dæg þæs mæran Fulluhteres gebyrdtide, for ðam manegum wundrum ðe ge-lumpon on his acennednysse. Godes heahengel Gabrihel bodade ðam fæder Zacharian his acennednysse, and his healican geðincðu and his mærlican drohtnunge. Þæt cild on his modor innoðe oncneow Marian stemne, Godes cyn-nestran; and on innoðe ða gyt beclysed, mid witigendlicre fægnunge getacnode þone halwendan tocyme ures aly-sendes. On his acennednysse he ætbræd þære meder hire unwæstmbærnysse, and þæs fæder tungan his nama unband, þe mid his agenre geleafleaste adumbod wæs.

6   Ðreora manna gebyrdtide freolsað seo halige gelaðung: ðæs hælendes, se ðe is God and mann, and Iohannes his bydeles, and ðære eadigan Marian his moder. Oðra gecorenra manna, ðe ðurh martyrdom oððe þurh oðre halige geear-nunga Godes rice geferdon, heora endenextan dæg, se ðe hi æfter gefyllednysse ealra earfoðnyssa sigefæste to ðam ecan life acende, we wurðiað him to gebyrdtide; and ðone dæg ðe hi to ðisum andweardan life acennede wæron we lætað to gymeleaste, forðan ðe hi comon hider to earfoðnyssum and

he went into the presence of people and preached baptism to the Jewish people for the forgiveness of sins, as it is written in the prophecy of Isaiah." To all believers he preached Christ's future baptism, in which is forgiveness of sins through the Holy Spirit. John also, at God's direction, baptized those of the Jewish nations who came to him, but his baptizing did not produce forgiveness of sin, for he was God's messenger, not God. He announced the coming of the savior to the people with words, and his holy baptism with his own baptism, with which he baptized the sinless Son of God, who needed no forgiveness of sin.

Rightly does God's Church honor on this day the birth- 5 day of the great Baptist, for the many wonders which happened at his birth. God's archangel Gabriel announced his birth to his father Zechariah, as well as his high honors and illustrious way of life. The child in his mother's womb knew the voice of Mary, the mother of God; and while still enclosed in the womb, he signified with prophetic rejoicing the saving advent of our redeemer. At his birth he removed his mother's barrenness, and his name unbound the tongue of his father, who had been made mute by his own lack of faith.

The holy Church celebrates the birthday of three per- 6 sons: the savior, who is God and human, John his messenger, and the blessed Mary his mother. With other chosen persons, who have gone to God's kingdom through martyrdom or other holy merits, we celebrate as their birthday their last day, which after the fulfillment of all their labors brought them forth victorious to eternal life; and the day on which they were born to this present life we leave unnoted, because they came here to hardships and temptations and various

costnungum and mislicum fræcednyssum. Se dæg bið gemyndig Godes ðeowum ðe ða halgan, æfter gewunnenum
sige, asende to ecere myrhðe fram eallum gedreccednyssum,
and se is heora soðe acennednys—na woplic swa swa seo
ærre, ac blissigendlic to ðam ecum life. Ac us is to wurði-
genne mid micelre gecnyrdnysse Cristes gebyrdtide, ðurh ða
us com alysednys.

7   Iohannes is geendung ðære ealdan æ and anginn ðære niwan, swa swa se hælend be him cwæð, "Seo ealde æ and witegan wæron oð Iohannes tocyme." Siððan ongann godspel-
bodung. Nu for his micclan halignysse is gewurðod his
acennednys, swa swa se heahengel behet his fæder mid
ðisum wordum: "Manega blissiað on his gebyrdtide." Maria,
Godes cynnestre, nis nanum oðrum gelic, forðan ðe heo is
mæden and modor, and ðone abær ðe hi and ealle gesceafta
gesceop; is heo forði wel wyrðe þæt hire acennednys arwurðlice gefreolsod sy.

8   Þa magas setton ðam cilde naman Zacharias, ac seo modor him wiðcwæð mid wordum, and se dumba fæder mid
gewrite; forðan ðe se engel ðe hine cydde toweardne him
gesceop naman be Godes dihte Iohannes. Ne mihte se
dumba fæder cyðan his wife hu se engel his cilde naman gesette, ac ðurh Godes Gastes onwrigenysse se nama hire
wearð cuð. *Zacharias* is gereht "gemindig Godes," and *Iohannes,* "Godes gifu," forðan ðe he bodade mannum Godes
gife, and Crist toweardne, þe ealne middangeard mid his
gife gewissað. He wæs asend toforan Drihtne swa swa se
dægsteorra gæð beforan ðære sunnan, swa swa bydel ætforan deman, swa swa seo Ealde Gecyðnys ætforan ðære
Niwan; forðan ðe seo ealde æ wæs swilce sceadu, and seo
Niwe Gecyðnys is soðfæstnys ðurh ðæs hælendes gife.

perils. The day that sends his saints, after winning the victory, to eternal joy from all afflictions, is memorable to the servants of God, and this is their true birth—not tearful like the first, but rejoicing in eternal life. But we ought to honor with great care the birthday of Christ, through which came our redemption.

John is the ending of the old law and the beginning of the new, as the savior said of him, "The old law and the prophets were until the coming of John." Afterward the preaching of the gospel began. Now his birth is honored because of his great holiness, just as the archangel promised his father with these words: "Many will rejoice in his birth." Mary, the mother of God, is like none other, for she is virgin and mother, and bore him who created her and all creatures; therefore she is well worthy that her birth should be honorably celebrated.

The relatives gave the child the name Zechariah, but the mother contradicted them by words, and the mute father by writing; because the angel who had announced that he was to come had given him the name John by God's direction. The mute father could not inform his wife how the angel had named his child, but by the revelation of God's Spirit the name was known to her. *Zechariah* is interpreted as "mindful of God," and *John,* "God's grace," because he preached the grace of God to humanity, and Christ to come, who guides all the earth with his grace. He was sent before the Lord as the daystar goes before the sun, as the herald before the judge, as the Old Testament before the New; for the old law was like a shadow, and the New Testament is truth through the savior's grace.

9   Anes geares cild hi wæron, Crist and Iohannes. On ðisum
dæge acende seo unwæstmbære moder ðone mæran witegan Iohannem, se is geherod mid þisum wordum ðurh
Cristes muð, "Betwux wifa bearnum ne aras nan mærra man
ðonne is Iohannes se Fulluhtere." On middes wintres mæs-
sedæge acende þæt halige mæden Maria þone heofenlican
æðeling, se nis geteald to wifa bearnum, forðon ðe he
is Godes Sunu on ðære godcundnysse, and Godes and
mædenes bearn ðurh menniscnysse.

10   Iohannes forfleah folces neawiste on geogoðe, and on
westene mid stiðre drohtnunge synna forbeah. Se hælend
betwux synfullum unwemme fram ælcere synne ðurhwunode. Se bydel gebigde on ðam timan micelne heap Israhela
ðeode to heora scyppende mid his bodunge. Drihten dæghwamlice of eallum ðeodum to his geleafan, ðurh onlihtinge
ðæs Halgan Gastes, ungerim sawla gebigð.

11   Þæt halige godspel cwyð be ðam Fulluhtere þæt he
forestope ðam hælende on gaste and on mihte þæs witegan
Helian; forðan ðe he wæs his forrynel æt ðam ærran tocyme,
swa swa Helias bið æt ðam æftran togeanes Antecriste. Nis
butan getacnunge þæt ðæs bydeles acennednys on ðære tide
wæs gefremod ðe se woruldlica dæg wanigende bið, and
on Drihtnes gebyrdtide weaxende bið. Þas getacnunge onwreah se ylca Iohannes mid ðisum wordum: "Criste gedafenað þæt he weaxe, and me þæt ic wanigende beo." Iohannes
wæs hraðor mannum cuð þurh his mærlican drohtnunga
þonne Crist wære, forðan ðe he ne æteowde his godcundan
mihte ærðam ðe he wæs ðritig geara on ðære menniscnysse.
Þa wæs he geðuht ðam folce þæt he witega wære, and Iohannes Crist. Hwæt ða Crist geswutelode hine sylfne ðurh
miccle tacna, and his hlisa weox geond ealne middangeard

436

They were children of the same year, Christ and John. On 9
this day the barren mother brought forth the great prophet
John, who is praised in these words from Christ's mouth,
"Among the children of women there has not arisen a greater
one than John the Baptist." On midwinter's Mass day the
holy virgin Mary brought forth the heavenly prince, who is
not numbered with the children of women, because he is
the Son of God in his divine nature, and the son of God and
a virgin by his human nature.

John fled from the company of people in his youth, and in 10
the desert avoided sin with a strict way of life. The savior
remained among the sinful, unstained by every sin. At that
time the messenger inclined a great company of the people
of Israel to their creator by his preaching. The Lord daily
inclines countless souls of all nations to his faith, through
the enlightenment of the Holy Spirit.

The holy gospel says of the Baptist that he preceded the 11
savior in the spirit and power of the prophet Elijah; because
he was his forerunner at his first coming, as Elijah will be at
the second against Antichrist. It is not without significance
that the birth of the messenger was completed on the day
when the worldly day is waning, and it is increasing on the
Lord's birthday. The same John revealed the significance of
this in these words: "It is fitting that Christ should increase,
and that I should be waning." John was known to people
through his famous way of life sooner than Christ was, for
he did not manifest his divine power before he had been
thirty years in human nature. Then it seemed to the people
that he was a prophet, and that John was Christ. But then
Christ revealed himself by great miracles, and his reputation

þæt he soð God wæs, se ðe wæs ærðan witega geðuht. Iohannes soðlice wæs wanigende on his hlisan, forðan ðe he wearð oncnawen witega, and bydel ðæs heofonlican æðelinges, se ðe wæs lytle ær Crist geteald mid ungewissum wenan. Þas wanunge getacnað se wanigenda dæg his gebyrdtide, and se ðeonda dæg ðæs hælendes acennednysse gebicnað his ðeondan mihte æfter ðære menniscnysse.

12 Fela witegan mid heora witegunge bodedon Drihten toweardne, sume feorran sume nean, ac Iohannes his tocyme mid wordum bodade, and eac mid fingre gebicnode, ðus cweðende, "Loca nu, efne her gæð Godes Lamb, se ðe ætbret middangeardes synna." Crist is manegum naman genemned. He is wisdom gehaten, forðan ðe se Fæder ealle gesceafta þurh hine geworhte. He is word gecweden, forðan þe word is wisdomes geswutelung. Be ðam worde ongann se godspellere Iohannes þa godspellican gesetnysse, ðus cweðende, "On frymðe wæs word, and þæt word wæs mid Gode, and þæt word wæs God." He is lamb gehaten, for ðære unscæððignysse lambes gecyndes; and wæs unscyldig, for ure alysednysse, his Fæder liflic onsægednys on lambes wisan geoffrod. He is leo geciged of Iudan mægðe, Dauides wyrtruma, forðan ðe he ðurh his godcundlican strencðe þone miclan deofol mid sige his ðrowunge oferswiðde.

13 Se halga Fulluhtere ðe we ymbe sprecað astealde stiðlice drohtnunge, ægðer ge on scrude ge on bigwiste, swa swa we hwene æror rehton; forðan ðe se wealdenda hælend þus be him cweðende wæs, "Fram Iohannes dagum Godes rice ðolað neadunge, and ða strecanmod hit gegripað." Cuð is gehwilcum snoterum mannum þæt seo ealde æ wæs eaðelicre þonne Cristes gesetnys sy, forðan ðe on ðære næs micel forhæfednys, ne ða gastlican drohtnunga þe Crist siððan

grew through all the world that he was true God, who before had seemed a prophet. Truly John was waning in his reputation, for he was acknowledged a prophet, and the messenger of the heavenly prince, who a little before had been accounted Christ by uncertain opinion. The waning day of his birthday signifies this waning, and the increasing day of the savior's birth signifies his increasing power according to his human nature.

Many prophets announced the Lord's coming in their 12 prophecies, some from afar and some near, but John announced his coming with words, and also signified it with his finger, saying, "Look now, behold here goes the Lamb of God, who takes away the sins of the world." Christ is named by many names. He is called wisdom, because the Father made all creation through him. He is called word, because a word is the manifestation of wisdom. The Evangelist John began the gospel account with the word, saying, "In the beginning was the word, and the word was with God, and the word was God." He is called lamb, from the innocence of the lamb's nature; and for our redemption he was guiltless offered as a living sacrifice to his Father in the manner of a lamb. He is called the lion of the tribe of Judah, the root of David, because through his divine strength he overcame the great devil by the victory of his passion.

The holy Baptist of whom we are speaking established a 13 strict way of life, both in clothing and in food, as we mentioned a little earlier; for the ruling savior was thus saying of him, "From the days of John the kingdom of God suffers force, and the violent seize it." It is known to every wise person that the old law was easier than Christ's decree is, for in it there was no great abstinence, nor the spiritual way of life

gesette and his apostoli. Oðer is seo gesetnys ðe se cyning bytt ðurh his ealdormenn oððe gerefan; oðer bið his agen gebann on his andweardnysse. Godes rice is gecweden on ðisre stowe seo halige gelaðung, þæt is eal Cristen folc, þe sceal mid neadunge and strecum mode þæt heofonlice rice geearnian. Hu mæg beon butan strece and neadunge þæt gehwa mid clænnysse þæt gale gecynd þurh Godes gife gewylde? Oððe hwa gestilð hatheortnysse his modes mid geðylde butan earfoðnysse? Oððe hwa awent modignysse mid soðre eadmodnysse, oððe hwa druncennysse mid syfernysse, oððe hwa gitsunge mid rumgifulnysse, butan strece? Ac se ðe his ðeawas mid anmodnysse, þurh Godes fultum, swa awent, he bið ðonne to oðrum menn geworht; oðer he bið þurh godnysse, and se ylca ðurh edwiste, and he gelæcð ðonne ðurh strece þæt heofenlice rice.

14   Twa forhæfednysse cynn syndon, an lichamlic, oðer gastlic. An is, þæt gehwa hine sylfne getemprige mid gemete on æte and on wæte, and werlice ða oferflowendlican ðygene him sylfum ætbrede. Oðer forhæfednysse cynn is deorwurðre and healicre, ðeah seo oðer god sy: styran his modes styrunge mid singalre gemetfæstnysse, and campian dæghwamlice wið leahtras, and hine sylfne ðreagian mid styrnysse ðære gastlican steore swa þæt he ða reðan deor eahta heafodleahtra swilce mid isenum midlum gewylde. Deorwyrðe is þeos forhæfednys and wulderfull ðrowung on Godes gesihðe, ða yfelan geðohtas and unlustas mid agenre cynegyrde gestyran, and fram derigendlicere spræce and pleolicum weorce hine sylfne forhabban swa swa fram cwylmbærum mettum. Se ðe ðas ðing gecneordlice begæð he gripð untweolice þæt behatene rice mid Gode and eallum his halgum. Micel strec bið þæt mennisce menn mid

which Christ and his apostles later established. The decree which the king ordains through his ealdormen or reeves is one thing; his own edict in his presence is another. In this place the holy Church is called God's kingdom, that is, all Christian people, who shall with force and a violent mind merit the heavenly kingdom. How can it be, without violence and force, that anyone could overcome a lecherous nature by chastity, through God's grace? Or who, without difficulty, stills the fury of his mind with patience? Or who exchanges pride for true humility, or drunkenness for sobriety, or covetousness for generosity, without violence? But he who, through God's support, so changes his ways with steadfastness, will then be made another person; he will be another in goodness, though the same in substance, and then he will seize the heavenly kingdom by violence.

There are two kinds of abstinence, one bodily, the other 14 spiritual. The one is when someone governs himself with moderation in food and in drink, and manfully puts away from himself superfluous partaking of food. The second kind of abstinence is more precious and exalted, though the other is good: to steer the agitation of his mind with constant moderation, and struggle daily against sins, and chastise himself with the sternness of spiritual correction so that he might control the fierce beast of the eight deadly sins as if with iron bonds. Precious in the sight of God is this abstinence and glorious suffering, to govern evil thoughts and sinful pleasures with one's own scepter, and to restrain himself from harmful speech and dangerous deeds as if from deadly foods. He who diligently undertakes these things undoubtedly seizes the promised kingdom with God and all his saints. It is great violence that human beings with hum-

eadmodum geearnungum ða heofenlican myrhðe begytan ðe
ða heofenlican englas ðurh modignysse forluron.

15   Us gelustfullað gyt furður to sprecenne be ðan halgan
were Iohanne, him to wurðmynte and us to beterunge. Be
him awrat se witega Isaias þæt he is "stemn clypigendes on
westene: 'Gearciað Godes weig, doð rihte his paðas. Ælc
dene bið gefylled, and ælc dun bið geeadmet, and ealle woh-
nyssa beoð gerihte, and scearpnyssa gesmeðode.'" Se witega
hine het stemn forðan ðe he forestop Criste, ðe is word gehaten: na swilc word swa menn sprecað, ac he is ðæs Fæder
wisdom, and word bið wisdomes geswutelung. Þæt word
is ælmihtig God, Sunu mid his Fæder. On ælcum worde
bið stemn gehyred ær þæt word fullice gecweden sy. Swa
swa stemn forestæpð worde, swa forestop Iohannes ðam
hælende on middangearde; forðan ðe God Fæder hine sende
ætforan gesihðe his bearnes, þæt he sceolde gearcian and
dæftan his weig. Hwæt ða Iohannes to mannum clypode þas
ylcan word, "Gearciað Godes weig." Se bydel ðe bodað
rihtne geleafan and gode weorc, he gearcað þone weig
cumendum Gode to ðæra heorcnigendra heortan.

16   Godes weg bið gegearcod on manna heortan þonne hi
ðære soðfæstnysse spræce eadmodlice gehyrað and gearuwe
beoð to lifes bebodum; be ðam cwæð se hælend, "Se ðe me
lufað, he hylt min bebod, and min Fæder hine lufað, and wit
cumað to him, and mid him wuniað." His paðas beoð gerihte
þonne, ðurh gode bodunge, aspringað clæne geðohtas on
mode ðæra hlystendra. Dena getacniað þa eadmodan, and
duna ða modigan. On Drihtnes tocyme wurdon dena afyllede, and duna geeadmette, swa swa he sylf cwæð, "Ælc ðæra
ðe hine onhefð bið geeadmet, and se ðe hine geeadmet bið
geuferod." Swa swa wæter scyt of ðære dune and ætstent on

ble merits should obtain that heavenly joy which the heavenly angels lost through pride.

It pleases us to speak further of the holy man John, for his 15 honor and our improvement. Of him the prophet Isaiah wrote that he is "the voice of one crying in the wilderness: 'Prepare the way of God, make right his paths. Every valley shall be filled, and every mountain shall be lowered, and all crookedness shall be made straight, and sharpness made smooth.'" The prophet called him a voice because he preceded Christ, who is called the word: not a word such as humans speak, but he is the wisdom of the Father, and a word is the manifestation of wisdom. The word is almighty God, the Son with his Father. In every word the voice is heard before the word is fully spoken. Just as the voice precedes the word, so John preceded the savior on earth; for God the Father sent him before the sight of his son, so he might prepare and make ready his way. Lo, John said these same words to people, "Prepare the way of God." The messenger who announces right belief and good works prepares the way for the coming of God to the heart of his hearers.

The way of God is prepared in people's hearts when they 16 humbly hear the speech of truth and are ready for the commandments of life; of this the savior said, "He who loves me keeps my commandment, and my Father loves him, and we two will come to him, and dwell with him." His paths will be straight when, through good preaching, pure thoughts spring up in the mind of the listeners. Valleys signify the humble, and mountains the proud. At the Lord's coming valleys were filled, and mountains lowered, as he himself said, "Everyone who exalts himself will be humbled, and he who humbles himself will be exalted." As water rushes from the

dene, swa forflihð se Halga Gast modigra manna heortan, and nimð wununge on ðam eadmodan, swa swa se witega cwæð, "On hwam gerest Godes Gast buton on ðam eadmodan?" Ðwyrnyssa beoð gerihte þonne ðwyrlicra manna heortan, þe beoð ðurh unrihtwisnysse hocas awegde, eft ðurh regolsticcan ðære soðan rihtwisnysse beoð geemnode. Scearpnyssa beoð awende to smeðum wegum ðonne ða yrsigendan mod and unliðe gecyrrað to manðwærnysse þurh ongyte ðære upplican gife.

17 Langsumlic bið us to gereccenne, and eow to gehyrenne, ealle ða deopnyssa ðæs mæran Fulluhteres bodunge: hu he ða heardheortan Iudeiscre ðeode mid stearcre ðreale and stiðre myngunge to lifes wege gebigde, and æfter his ðrowunge hellwarum Cristes tocyme cydde, swa swa he on life mancynne agene alysednysse mid hludre stemne bealdlice bodade.

18 Uton nu biddan ðone wealdendan hælend þæt he, ðurh his ðæs mæran forryneles and Fulluhteres ðingunge, us gemiltsige on andweardum life, and to ðam ecan gelæde, ðam sy wuldor and lof mid Fæder and Halgum Gaste a on ecnysse. Amen.

mountain and stands in the valley, so flees the Holy Spirit from the heart of the proud, and takes his dwelling in the humble, as the prophet said, "In whom does the Spirit of God rest but in the humble?" Crookedness will be straight when the hearts of perverse people, which are agitated by the snares of unrighteousness, are made even again by the ruling rods of true righteousness. Sharpness will be turned to smooth ways when angry and harsh minds turn to gentleness through the outpouring of heavenly grace.

It would be tedious for us to recount, and for you to hear, 17 all the depths of the great Baptist's preaching: how with harsh reproof and severe admonition he inclined the hardhearted Jewish people to the way of life, and after his suffering announced Christ's coming to the inhabitants of hell, just as in life he had boldly preached with a loud voice humanity's own redemption.

Let us now pray to the sovereign savior that he, through 18 the intercession of the great forerunner and Baptist, may be merciful to us in this present life, and lead us to eternal life, to whom be glory and praise with the Father and the Holy Spirit forever to eternity. Amen.

26

III KALENDAS IULII

Passio apostolorum Petri et Pauli

V*enit Iesus in partes Cesareae Philippi, et reliqua.*

2   Matheus se godspellere awrat on ðære godspellican gesetnysse, ðus cweðende, "Drihten com to anre burhscire ðe
is geciged Cesarea Philippi, and befran his gingran hu menn
be him cwyddedon. Hi andwyrdon, 'Sume menn cweðað
þæt ðu sy Iohannes se Fulluhtere, sume secgað þæt ðu sy
Helias, sume Hieremias, oððe sum oðer witega.' Se hælend
ða cwæð, 'Hwæt secge ge þæt ic sy?' Petrus him andwyrde,
'Þu eart Crist, ðæs lifigendan Godes Sunu.' Drihten him
cwæð to andsware, 'Eadig eart ðu, Simon culfran bearn,
forðan ðe flæsc and blod þe ne onwreah ðisne geleafan, ac
min Fæder se ðe on heofonum is. Ic ðe secge þæt þu eart
stænen, and ofer ðysne stan ic timbrige mine cyrcan, and
helle gatu naht ne magon ongean hi. Ic betæce ðe heofonan
rices cæge; and swa hwæt swa ðu bintst on eorðan, þæt bið
gebunden on heofonum, and swa hwæt swa ðu unbintst ofer
eorðan, þæt bið unbunden on heofonum.'"

3   Beda se trahtnere us onwrihð þa deopnysse ðysre
rædinge, and cwyð þæt Philippus se fyðerrica ða buruh Cesarea getimbrode, and on wurðmynte þæs caseres Tiberii, ðe

26

The Passion of the
Apostles Peter and Paul

JUNE 29

The Passion of the Apostles Peter and Paul

Jesus came into the district of Caesarea Philippi, etc.

Matthew the Evangelist wrote in the gospel account, say- 2
ing, "The Lord came to a township called Caesarea Philippi,
and asked his disciples how people spoke about him. They
answered, 'Some say that you are John the Baptist, some say
that you are Elijah, some Jeremiah, or some other prophet.'
The savior said, 'Who do you say that I am?' Peter answered
him, 'You are Christ, Son of the living God.' The Lord said
to him in reply, 'Blessed are you, Simon, son of a dove, for
flesh and blood has not revealed this belief to you, but my
Father who is in heaven. I say to you that you are made of
rock, and on this rock I will build my Church, and the gates
of hell can do nothing against it. I entrust you with the keys
to the kingdom of heaven; whatever you bind on earth will
be bound in heaven, and what you unbind on earth will be
unbound in heaven.'"

The commentator Bede unveils the mystery of this read- 3
ing for us, and says that Philip the tetrarch built the city of
Caesarea, and in honor of the emperor Tiberius, under

447

he under rixode, ðære byrig naman gesceop *Cesaream,* and
for his agenum gemynde to ðam naman geyhte *Philippi,* ðus
cweðende *Cesarea Philippi,* swilce seo burh him bam to wurðmynte swa genemned wære.

4   Þa ða se hælend to ðære burhscire genealæhte, þa befran
he hu woruldmenn be him cwyddedon—na swilce he nyste
manna cwyddunga be him, ac he wolde, mid soðre andetnysse ðæs rihtan geleafan, adwæscan ðone leasan wenan
dweligendra manna. His apostoli him andwyrdon, "Sume
men cwyddiað þæt ðu sy Iohannes se Fulluhtere, sume
secgað þæt ðu sy Helias, sume Hieremias, oððe an ðæra
witegena." Drihten ða befran, "Hwæt secge ge þæt ic sy?"
swylce he swa cwæde, "Nu woruldmenn ðus dwollice me
oncnawað, ge ðe godas sind, hu oncnawe ge me?" Se trahtnere cwæð "godas," forðan ðe se soða God, se ðe ana is ælmihtig, hæfð geunnen ðone wurðmynt his gecorenum, þæt
he hi godas gecigð. Him andwyrde se gehyrsuma Petrus,
"Ðu eart Crist, þæs lifigendan Godes Sunu." He cwæð "þæs
lifigendan Godes," for twæminge ðæra leasra goda ða ðe
hæðene ðeoda, mid mislicum gedwylde bepæhte, wurðodon.
Sume hi gelyfdon on deade entas, and him deorwurðlice anlicnyssa arærdon, and cwædon þæt hi godas wæron for ðære
micelan strencðe ðe hi hæfdon; wæs ðeah heora lif swiðe
manfullic and bysmurfull. Be ðam cwæð se witega, "Ðæra
hæðenra anlicnyssa sind gyldene and sylfrene, manna handgeweorc; hi habbað dumbne muð and blinde eagan, deafe
earan and ungrapigende handa, fet butan feðe, bodig butan
life." Sume hi gelyfdon on ða sunnan, sume on ðone monan,
sume on fyr, and on manega oðre gesceafta; cwædon þæt hi
for heora fægernysse godas wæron. Nu todælde Petrus
swutelice ðone soðan geleafan ða ða he cwæð, "Þu eart Crist,

whom he governed, gave the city the name *Caesarea,* and for his own remembrance added the name *Philippi,* saying *Caesarea Philippi,* as if the city were so named in honor of both of them.

When the savior approached that township, he asked 4 how the people of the world spoke about him—not as if he did not know people's reports about him, but he wanted, by the true confession of right faith, to destroy the false opinions of erring people. His apostles answered him, "Some people report that you are John the Baptist, some say that you are Elijah, some Jeremiah, or one of the prophets." The Lord then asked, "Who do you say that I am?" as if he would ask, "Now that the people of the world erroneously know me, you who are gods, how do you know me?" The commentator said "gods" because the true God, who alone is almighty, has granted this honor to his chosen ones, that he calls them gods. The obedient Peter answered him, "You are Christ, son of the living God." He said "the living God" to distinguish him from the false gods which the heathen people worshiped, deceived by various errors. Some of them believed in dead giants, and raised up precious idols to them, and said that they were gods because of their great strength; yet their lives were very sinful and shameful. Of them the prophet said, "The idols of the heathens are gold and silver, the work of human hands; they have a mute mouth and blind eyes, deaf ears and hands without grasping, feet without walking, body without life." Some believed in the sun, some in the moon, some in fire, and in many other creatures; they said that on account of their beauty they were gods. Now, Peter clearly distinguished the true faith when

ðæs lifigendan Godes Sunu." Se is lybbende God þe hæfð lif
and wununge ðurh hine sylfne, butan anginne, and se ðe
ealle gesceafta þurh his agen Bearn, þæt is his wisdom, gesceop, and him eallum lif forgeaf ðurh ðone Halgan Gast.
On ðissum ðrym hadum is an Godcundnys, and an gecynd,
and an weorc untodæledlice.

5   Drihten cwæð to Petre, "Eadig eart ðu, culfran sunu." Se
Halga Gast wæs gesewen ofer Criste on culfran anlicnysse.
Nu gecigde se hælend Petrum culfran bearn forðan ðe he
wæs afylled mid bilewitnysse and gife ðæs Halgan Gastes.
He cwæð, "Ne onwreah ðe flæsc ne blod þisne geleafan, ac
min Fæder se ðe on heofenum is." Flæsc and blod is gecweden his flæsclice mæið. Næfde he þæt andgit ðurh
mæglice lare, ac se heofenlica Fæder, ðurh ðone Halgan
Gast, ðisne geleafan on Petres heortan forgeaf.

6   Drihten cwæð to Petre, "Þu eart stænen." For ðære
strencðe his geleafan and for anrædnysse his andetnysse he
underfencg ðone naman, forðan ðe he geðeodde hine sylfne
mid fæstum mode to Criste, se ðe is "stan" gecweden fram
ðam apostole Paule: "And ic timbrige mine cyrcan uppon
ðisum stane," þæt is, ofer ðone geleafan ðe ðu andetst. Eal
Godes gelaðung is ofer ðam stane gebytlod, þæt is ofer
Criste; forðan ðe he is se grundweall ealra ðæra getimbrunga
his agenre cyrcan. Ealle Godes cyrcan sind getealde to anre
gelaðunge, and seo is mid gecorenum mannum getimbrod,
na mid deadum stanum, and eal seo bytlung ðæra liflicra
stana is ofer Criste gelogod; forðan ðe we beoð, þurh ðone
geleafan, his lima getealde, and he ure ealra heafod. Se ðe
bytlað of ðam grundwealle, his weorc hryst to micclum lyre.

7   Se Hælend cwæð, "Ne magon helle gatu naht togeanes
minre cyrcan." Leahtras and dwollic lar sindon helle gatu,

he said, "You are Christ, Son of the living God." He is a living God who has life and existence in himself, without beginning, and who made all creation through his own Son, that is, his wisdom, and gave them all life through the Holy Spirit. In these three persons is one Godhead, and one nature, and one work indivisibly.

The Lord said to Peter, "Blessed are you, son of a dove." 5 The Holy Spirit was seen over Christ in the likeness of a dove. Now, the savior called Peter the child of a dove because he was filled with meekness and with the grace of the Holy Spirit. He said, "Flesh and blood has not revealed this faith to you, but my Father who is in heaven." His fleshly condition is called flesh and blood. He did not have that understanding through parental teaching, but the heavenly Father put this belief in Peter's heart through the Holy Spirit.

The Lord said to Peter, "You are of stone." He received 6 that name for the strength of his faith and for the steadfastness of his profession, because he attached himself with firm mind to Christ, who is called "stone" by the apostle Paul: "And I will build my Church upon this stone," that is, on that faith which you profess. All God's Church is built on that stone, that is, upon Christ; for he is the foundation of all the buildings of his own Church. All God's churches are considered as one congregation, and that is constructed of chosen people, not of dead stones, and all the building of those living stones is founded on Christ; for through that faith we are considered his limbs, and he is the head of us all. Whoever builds away from that foundation, his work falls to great destruction.

The savior said, "The gates of hell can do nothing against 7 my Church." Sins and false doctrine are the gates of hell,

forðan ðe hi lædað þone synfullan swilce ðurh geat into helle
wite. Manega sind ða gatu, ac heora nan ne mæg ongean ða
halgan gelaðunge, ðe is getimbrod uppon ðam fæstan stane,
Criste; forðan ðe se gelyfeda, þurh Cristes gescyldnysse,
ætwint ðam frecednyssum ðæra deoflicra costnunga.

8   He cwæð, "Ic ðe betæce heofonan rices cæge." Nis seo
cæig gylden ne sylfren, ne of nanum antimbre gesmiðod, ac
is se anweald þe him Crist forgeaf, þæt nan man ne cymð
into Godes rice buton se halga Petrus him geopenige þæt
infær. "And swa hwæt swa ðu bintst ofer eorðan, þæt bið gebunden on heofonum; and swa hwæt swa ðu unbintst ofer
eorðan, þæt bið unbunden on heofenan." Þisne anweald he
forgeaf nu Petre, and eac syððan, ær his upstige, eallum his
apostolum ða ða he him on ableow, ðus cwæðende, "Onfoð
Haligne Gast: ðæra manna synna þe ge forgyfað beoð forgyfene; and ðam ðe ge forgifenysse ofunnon, him bið oftogen
seo forgyfenys."

9   Nellað ða apostoli nænne rihtwisne mid heora mansu-
munge gebindan, ne eac ðone manfullan miltsigende unbindan butan he mid soðre dædbote gecyrre to lifes wege. Þone
ylcan andweald hæfð se ælmihtiga getiðod biscopum and
halgum mæssepreostum, gif hi hit æfter ðære godspellican
gesetnysse carfullice healdað. Ac forði is seo cæig Petre
sinderlice betæht, þæt eal ðeodscipe gleawlice tocnawe þæt
swa hwa swa oðscyt fram annysse ðæs geleafan ðe Petrus ða
andette Criste, þæt him ne bið getiðod naðor ne synna forgyfenys ne infær þæs heofenlican rices.

because they lead the sinful as if through a gate into the torment of hell. The gates are many, but none of them can do anything against the holy Church, which is built upon that fast stone, Christ; for the faithful one, through Christ's protection, avoids the dangers of diabolical temptations.

He said, "I will entrust you with the key to the kingdom 8 of heaven." That key is not of gold nor of silver, nor forged of any material, but is the power which Christ gave him, that no one comes into God's kingdom unless the holy Peter opens the entrance for him. "And whatever you bind on earth will be bound in heaven; and whatever you unbind on earth will be unbound in heaven." He gave this power now to Peter, and also afterward, before his ascension, to all his apostles when he blew on them, saying, "Receive the Holy Spirit: the sins of those you forgive will be forgiven; and from those from whom you withhold forgiveness, forgiveness will be withdrawn."

The apostles will not bind any righteous person with 9 their excommunication, nor mercifully unbind the sinful unless he returns with true repentance to the way of life. The almighty has granted the same power to bishops and holy Mass priests, if they carefully hold it according to the gospel decree. But the key is especially entrusted to Peter, so that all peoples may certainly know that whoever deviates from the unity of the faith which Peter professed to Christ, to him will be granted neither forgiveness of sins nor entrance into the kingdom of heaven.

DE PASSIONE APOSTOLORUM

10 We wyllað æfter ðisum godspelle eow gereccan ðæra apostola drohtnunga and geendunge mid scortre race, forðan ðe heora ðrowung is gehwær on Engliscum gereorde fullice geendebyrd.

11 Æfter Drihtnes upstige wæs Petrus bodigende geleafan ðam leodscipum ðe sind gecwedene Galatia, Cappadocia, Bithinia, Asia, Italia. Syððan, ymbe tyn geara fyrst, he gewende to Romebyrig, bodigende godspel; and on ðære byrig he gesette his biscopsetl and ðær gesæt fif and twentig geara, lærende ða Romaniscan ceastregewaran Godes mærða mid micclum tacnum. His wiðerwinna wæs on eallum his færelde sum dry se wæs Simon gehaten. Þes dry wæs mid ðam awyrgedum gaste to ðam swyðe afylled þæt he cwæð þæt he wære Crist, Godes Sunu, and mid his drycræfte ðæs folces geleafan amyrde.

12 Þa gelamp hit þæt man ferede anre wuduwan suna lic ðær Petrus bodigende wæs. He ða cwæð to ðam folce and to ðam dry, "Genealæcað ðære bære, and gelyfað þæt ðæs bodung soð sy ðe ðone deadan to life arærð." Hwæt ða Simon wearð gebyld þurh deofles gast, and cwæð, "Swa hraðe swa ic þone deadan arære, acwellað minne wiðerwinnan Petrum." Þæt folc him andwyrde, "Cucenne we hine forbærnað." Simon ða mid deofles cræfte dyde þæt ðæs deadan lic styrigende wæs; þa wende þæt folc þæt he geedcucod wære. Petrus ða ofer eall clypode, "Gif he geedcucod sy, sprece to us, and astande; onbyrige metes, and ham gecyrre." Þæt folc ða hrymde hluddre stemne, "Gif Simon ðis ne deð, he sceal þæt wite ðolian ðe he ðe gemynte." Simon to ðisum wordum hine gebealh and fleonde wæs, ac þæt folc mid ormætum edwite hine gehæfte.

Of the Passion of the Apostles

After this gospel we will relate to you the lives and end of 10
those apostles in a short narrative, because their passion is
fully set forth in many places in the English language.

After the Lord's ascension Peter was preaching the faith 11
to the nations called Galatia, Cappadocia, Bithynia, Asia,
and Italy. Later, after a space of ten years, he went to Rome,
preaching the gospel; and in that city he established his
episcopal seat and sat there twenty-five years, teaching the
citizens of Rome the glories of God with many miracles. His
adversary in all his activity was a certain magician who was
called Simon. This magician was so filled with the accursed
spirit that he said he was Christ, the Son of God, and with
his magic corrupted the faith of the people.

Then it happened that the corpse of a widow's son was 12
brought to where Peter was preaching. He said to the people and to the magician, "Approach the bier, and believe that
his preaching is true who raises the dead to life." Lo, Simon
was made bold by the spirit of the devil, and said, "As soon as
I have raised the dead, kill my adversary Peter." The people
answered him, "We will burn him alive." Simon then through
the devil's craft made the corpse move; the people then
thought that he was restored to life. But Peter cried out over
everyone, "If he is restored to life, let him speak to us, and
stand up; let him taste food, and return home." The people
then cried out with loud voice, "If Simon does not do this,
he shall suffer the punishment that he intended for you." At
these words Simon grew angry and was fleeing away, but the
people with great reproach seized him.

13   Se Godes apostol ða genealæhte ðam lice mid aðenedum
earmum, ðus biddende, "Ðu, leofa Drihten, ðe us sendest to
bodigenne ðinne geleafan, and us behete þæt we mihton,
ðurh ðinne naman, deoflu todræfan, and untrume gehælan,
and ða deadan aræran: arær nu ðisne cnapan, þæt ðis folc
oncnawe þæt nan God nys buton ðu ana, mid ðinum Fæder
and ðam Halgan Gaste." Æfter ðisum gebede aras se deada,
and gebigedum cneowum to Petre cwæð, "Ic geseah hælend
Crist, and he sende his englas for ðinre bene, þæt hi me to
life gelæddon." Þæt folc ða mid anre stemne clypigende
cwæð, "An God is, ðe Petrus bodað," and woldon forbærnan
ðone dry, ac Petrus him forwyrnde; cwæð þæt se hælend
him tæhte ðone regol þæt hi sceoldon yfel mid gode forgyl-
dan.

14   Simon, ða ða he ðam folce ætwunden wæs, getigde ænne
ormætne ryððan innan ðam geate þær Petrus inn hæfde,
þæt he færlice hine abitan sceolde. Hwæt ða Petrus com and
ðone ryððan untigde mid ðisum bebode, "Yrn and sege
Simone þæt he leng mid his drycræfte Godes folc ne
bepæce, ðe he mid his agenum blode gebohte." And he sona
getengde wið þæs drys and hine on fleame gebrohte. Petrus
wearð æfterweard þus cweðende, "On Godes naman ic ðe
bebeode þæt ðu nænne toð on his lice ne gefæstnige." Se
hund, ða ða he ne moste his lichaman derian, totær his
hæteru sticmælum of his bæce, and hine draf geond ða weallas ðeotende swa swa wulf on ðæs folces gesihðe. He ða
ætbærst ðam hunde, and to langum fyrste siððan for ðære
sceame næs gesewen on Romanabyrig.

15   Syððan eft on fyrste he begeat sumne ðe hine bespræc to
ðam casere Nerone, and gelamp ða þæt se awyrgeda ehtere
þone deofles ðen his freondscipum geðeodde. Mid ðam ðe

The apostle of God then approached the corpse with 13
outstretched arms, thus praying, "Beloved Lord, you who
have sent us to preach your faith, and promised us that we
might drive away devils in your name, and heal the sick, and
raise the dead: raise now this boy, that this people may know
that there is no God but you alone, with your Father and the
Holy Spirit." After this prayer the dead one rose up, and on
bended knees said to Peter, "I saw the savior Christ, and at
your prayer he sent his angels to lead me to life." Then the
people, crying with one voice, said, "There is one God,
whom Peter preaches," and would burn the magician, but
Peter forbade them; he said that the savior had taught him
the rule that they should repay evil with good.

Simon, when he had escaped from the people, tied a huge 14
mastiff inside the gate where Peter had his dwelling, so that
he might suddenly tear him to pieces. But Peter came and
untied the mastiff with this command, "Run and tell Simon
that with his magic he may no longer deceive God's people,
whom he purchased with his own blood." And he immediately hastened toward the magician and put him to flight.
Afterward Peter was speaking, "In God's name I command
you that you do not sink a tooth in his body." The dog, when
he could not hurt his body, tore his garments piecemeal
from his back, and drove him beyond the walls howling like
a wolf in the sight of the people. He then escaped from the
dog, and for a long time after was not seen in the city of
Rome for shame.

Some time later he got someone to speak of him to the 15
emperor Nero, and it happened that the accursed persecutor united in friendship with the devil's servant. When this

hit ðus gedon wæs, ða æteowde Crist hine sylfne Petre on gastlicere gesihðe, and mid ðyssere tihtinge hine gehyrte: "Se dry Simon and se wælhreowa Nero sind mid deofles gaste afyllede, and syrwiað ongean ðe, ac ne beo ðu afyrht. Ic beo mid þe, and ic sende minne ðeowan Paulum ðe to frofre; se stæpð tomerigen into Romanabyrig, and gyt mid gastlicum gecampe winnað ongean ðone dry, and hine awurpað into helle grunde, and gyt siððan samod to minum rice becumað mid sige martyrdomes."

16   *Non passus est Paulus quando vinctus Romam perductus est, sed post aliquot annos, quando sponte illuc iterum reversus est.* Þis gelamp swa soðlice. On ðone oðerne dæg com Paulus into ðære byrig, and heora ægðer oðerne mid micelre blisse underfeng, and wæron togædere bodigende binnan ðære byrig seofon monðas þam folce lifes weig. Beah ða ungerim folces to Cristendome þurh Petres lare; and eac ðæs caseres gebedda Libia, and his heahgerefan wif Agripina, wurdon swa gelyfede þæt hi forbugon heora wera neawiste. Þurh Paules bodunge gelyfdon ðæs caseres ðegnas and hiredcnihtas, and æfter heora fulluhte noldon gecyrran to his hirede.

17   Simon se dry worhte ða ærene næddran, styrigende swylce heo cucu wære, and dyde þæt ða anlicnyssa ðæra hæðenra hlihhende wæron and styrigende; and he sylf wearð færlice upp on ðære lyfte gesewen. Þærtogeanes gehælde Petrus blinde, and healte, and deofolseoce, and ða deadan arærde, and cwæð to ðam folce þæt hi sceoldon forfleon þæs deofles drycræft, ðylæs ðe hi mid his lotwrencum bepæhte wurdon. Þa wearð ðis ðam casere gecydd, and he het ðone dry him to gefeccan, and eac ða apostolas. Simon bræd his

had taken place, Christ himself appeared to Peter in a spiritual vision, and heartened him with this encouragement: "The magician Simon and the cruel Nero are filled with the spirit of the devil, and scheme against you, but do not be afraid. I will be with you, and I will send my servant Paul to comfort you; he enters Rome tomorrow, and you two will fight in spiritual combat against the magician, and cast him into the abyss of hell, and you two will afterward come together to my kingdom with the triumph of martyrdom."

Paul did not suffer when he was led in chains to Rome, but a few 16 *years later, when he came back of his own accord.* Truly it happened like this. On the next day Paul came into the city, and they received one another with great joy, and they were together in the city seven months, preaching the way of life to the people. Countless people turned to Christianity through Peter's teaching; and the emperor's consort Livia, and Agrippina, the wife of his chief officer, were so full of faith that they turned away from the company of their husbands. Through Paul's preaching the servants and members of the emperor's retinue believed, and after their baptism would not return to his household.

Simon the magician then made a serpent of brass, moving 17 as if it were alive, and made the idols of the heathens appear to be laughing and moving; and he himself suddenly appeared up in the air. On the other hand, Peter healed the blind, and the lame, and those possessed by devils, and raised the dead, and said to the people that they should flee from the magic of the devil, lest they should be deceived by his wiles. This was made known to the emperor, and he commanded the magician to be brought to him, and also the apostles. Simon changed his appearance before the

hiw ætforan ðam casere, swa þæt he wearð færlice geðuht cnapa, and eft harwenge; hwiltidum on wimmannes hade, and eft ðærrihte on cnihthade.

18   Þa Nero þæt geseah, ða wende he þæt he Godes Sunu wære. Petrus cwæð þæt he Godes wiðersaca wære, and mid leasum drycræfte forscyldigod, and cwæð þæt he wære gewiss deofol on menniscre edwiste. Simon cwæð, "Nis na gedafenlic þæt ðu, cyning, hlyste anes leases fisceres wordum; ac ic ðisne hosp leng ne forbere: nu ic beode minum englum þæt hi me on ðisum fiscere gewrecon." Petrus cwæð, "Ne ondræde ic ðine awyrgedan gastas, ac hi weorðað afyrhte þurh mines Drihtnes geleafan." Nero cwæð, "Ne ondrætst ðu ðe, Petrus, Simones mihta, ðe mid wundrum his godcundnysse geswutelað?" Petrus cwæð, "Gif he godcundnysse hæbbe, ðonne secge he hwæt ic ðence, oððe hwæt ic don wylle." Nero cwæð, "Sege me, Petrus, on sundorspræce hwæt ðu ðence." He ða leat to ðæs caseres eare, and het him beran diglice berenne hlaf; and he bletsode ðone hlaf and tobræc, and bewand on his twam slyfum, ðus cweðende, "Sege nu, Simon, hwæt ic ðohte, oððe cwæde, oþþe gedyde." He ða gebealh hine, forðan þe he ne mihte geopenian Petres digelnysse, and dyde þa mid drycræfte þæt ðær comon micele hundas and ræsdon wið Petres weard; ac Petrus æteowde ðone gebletsodan hlaf ðam hundum, and hi ðærrihte of heora gesihðe fordwinon. He ða cwæð to ðam casere, "Simon me mid his englum geðiwde, nu sende he hundas to me, forðan ðe he næfð godcundlice englas, ac hæfð hundlice." Nero cwæð, "Hwæt is nu, Simon? Ic wene wit sind oferswiðde." Simon andwyrde, "Þu goda cyning, nat nan man manna geðohtas buton Gode anum." Petrus andwyrde, "Untwylice þu lihst þæt þu God sy, nu ðu nast manna geðohtas."

emperor, so that he suddenly seemed a boy, and afterward a gray-bearded man; sometimes in the form of a woman, and again suddenly in a child's shape.

When Nero saw that, he thought that he was the Son of God. Peter said that he was God's adversary, guilty of false magic, and said that he was certainly a devil in human substance. Simon said, "It is not fitting that you, king, should listen to the words of a lying fisherman; but I will no longer endure this shame: I will now command my angels to avenge me on this fisherman." Peter said, "I do not fear your cursed spirits, but they will become terrified through the faith of my Lord." Nero said, "Peter, do you not fear the powers of Simon, who shows you his divinity by miracles?" Peter said, "If he has divinity, then let him say what I am thinking, or what I will do." Nero said, "Tell me, Peter, in secret what you are thinking." He then bent down to the emperor's ear, and ordered a barley loaf to be brought to him secretly; he blessed the loaf, broke it, and wrapped it in his two sleeves, saying, "Say now, Simon, what I thought, or said, or did." Simon grew angry, for he could not reveal Peter's secret, and then by magic made large dogs come and rush toward Peter; but Peter showed the blessed bread to the dogs, and they immediately vanished from their sight. He then said to the emperor, "Simon threatened me with his angels, now he sends dogs to me, because his angels are not divine, but canine." Nero said, "What now, Simon? I think we are overcome." Simon answered, "Good king, no one knows human thoughts but God alone." Peter answered, "Undoubtedly you lie when you say you are God, since you do not know people's thoughts." 18

19 Þa bewende Nero hine to Paulum and cwæð, "Hwi ne cwest ðu nan word? Oððe hwa teah ðe? oððe hwæt lærdest ðu mid þinre bodunge?" Paulus him andwyrde, "La leof, hwæt wille ic ðisum forlorenum wiðersacan geandwyrdan? Gif ðu wilt his wordum gehyrsumian, þu amyrst ðine sawle and eac ðinne cynedom. Be minre lare, þe ðu axast, ic ðe andwyrde. Se hælend þe Petrum lærde on his andweardnysse, se ylca me lærde mid onwrigenysse; and ic gefylde mid Godes lare fram Hierusalem oðþæt ic com to Iliricum. Ic lærde þæt men him betweonan lufodon and gearwurðedon. Ic tæhte ðam rican þæt hi ne onhofon hi, ne heora hiht on leasum welan ne besetton, ac on Gode anum. Ic tæhte ðam medeman mannum þæt hi gehealdene wæron on heora bigwiste and scrude. Ic bebead þearfum þæt hi blissodon on heora hafenleaste. Fæderas ic manode þæt hi mid steore Godes eges heora cild geðeawodon; þam cildum ic bead þæt hi gehyrsume wæron fæder and meder to halwendum mynegungum. Ic lærde weras þæt hi heora æwe heoldon, forðan þæt se wer gewitnað on æwbræcum wife, þæt wrecð God on æwbræcum were. Ic manode æwfæste wif þæt hi heora weras inweardlice lufodon, and him mid ege gehyrsumodon swa swa hlafordum. Ic lærde hlafordas þæt hi heora ðeowum liðe wæron, forðan ðe hi sind gebroðru for Gode, se hlaford and se ðeowa. Ic bebead ðeowum mannum þæt hi getreowlice and swa swa Gode heora hlafordum þeowdon. Ic tæhte eallum geleaffullum mannum þæt hi wurðian ænne God ælmihtigne and ungesewenlicne. Ne leornode ic ðas lare æt nanum eorðlicum menn, ac hælend Crist of heofonum me spræc to, and sende me to bodigenne his lare eallum ðeodum, ðus cweðende, 'Far ðu geond þas woruld, and ic beo mid þe; and swa hwæt swa ðu cwyst oþþe dest, ic hit gerihtwisige.'" Se casere wearð þa ablicged mid þisum wordum.

Nero then turned to Paul and said, "Why do you not say a 19
word? Who has taught you? or what have you taught with
your preaching?" Paul answered him, "Oh sir, what will I answer this lost adversary? If you will obey his words, you will
injure your soul and also your kingdom. Since you ask about
my teaching, I will answer you. The same savior who taught
Peter while present, taught me by revelation; and I have fulfilled it with God's teaching from Jerusalem until I came to
Illyricum. I taught that people should love and honor each
other. I taught the rich not to exalt themselves, nor to place
their hope in false wealth, but in God alone. I taught people
of moderate means to be frugal in their food and clothing. I
commanded the poor to rejoice in their poverty. Fathers I
exhorted to bring up their children in the fear of God; children I commanded to be obedient to the salutary admonitions of father and mother. I taught husbands to hold their
spouse, because that which a man punishes in an adulterous
wife, God will avenge in an adulterous husband. I exhorted
pious wives inwardly to love their husbands, and with fear
obey them as masters. I taught masters to be kind to their
servants, because the master and the servant are brothers
before God. I commanded servants to serve their masters
faithfully and as God. I taught all believers to worship one
God almighty and invisible. I did not learn this doctrine
from any earthly person, but the savior Christ spoke to me
from heaven, and sent me to preach his doctrine to all nations, saying, 'Go throughout the world, and I will be with
you, and whatever you say or do, I will justify it.'" The emperor was astonished at these words.

20   Simon cwæð, "Ðu goda cyning, ne understenst ðu ðisra twegra manna gereonunge ongean me. Ic eom soðfæstnys, ac ðas ðweorigað wið me. Hat nu aræran ænne heahne torr, þæt ic ðone astige, forðan ðe mine englas nellað cuman to me on eorðan betwux synfullum mannum; and ic wylle astigan to minum fæder, and ic bebeode minum englum þæt hi ðe to minum rice gefeccan." Nero ða cwæð, "Ic wylle geseon gif ðu ðas behat mid weorcum gefylst," and het ða ðone torr mid micclum ofste on smeðum felda aræran, and bebead eallum his folce þæt hi to ðyssere wæfersyne samod comon. Se dry astah ðone torr ætforan eallum ðam folce, and astrehtum earmum ongann fleogan on ða lyft.

21   Paulus cwæð to Petre, "Broðer, þu wære Gode gecoren ær ic; ðe gedafnað þæt þu ðisne deofles ðen mid ðinum benum afylle, and ic eac mine cneowu gebige to ðære bene." Þa beseah Petrus to ðam fleondan dry, þus cweðende, "Ic halsige eow awirigede gastas, on Cristes naman, þæt ge forlæton ðone dry ðe ge betwux eow feriað," and ða deoflu þærrihte hine forleton, and he feallende tobærst on feower sticca. Þa feower sticca clifodon to feower stanum, ða sind to gewitnysse ðæs apostolican siges oð þisne andweardan dæg. Petres geðyld geðafode þæt ða hellican fynd hine up geond þa lyft sume hwile feredon, þæt he on his fylle þy hetelycor hreosan sceolde, and se ðe lytle ær beotlice mid deoflicum fiðerhaman fleon wolde þæt he ða færlice his feðe forlure. Him gedafenode þæt he on heannysse ahafen wurde, þæt he on gesihðe ealles folces hreosende ða eorðan gesohte.

22   Hwæt ða Nero bebead Petrum and Paulum on bendum gehealdan, and ða sticca Simones hreawes mid wearde besettan; wende þæt he of deaðe on ðam ðriddan dæge arisan

Simon said, "Good king, you do not understand the conspiracy of these two men against me. I am the truth, but these thwart me. Command now a high tower to be raised, that I may ascend it, for my angels will not come to me on earth among sinful people; and I will ascend to my father, and I will command my angels to fetch you to my kingdom." Nero then said, "I want to see if you fulfill these promises with deeds," and ordered that the tower be raised with great haste on the level field, and commanded all his people to come together to this spectacle. The magician then ascended the tower before all the people, and with outstretched arms began to fly in the air. 20

Paul said to Peter, "Brother, you were chosen by God before me; it is fitting that you cast down this servant of the devil with your prayers, and I will also bend my knees to that prayer." Peter then looked up at the flying magician, saying, "I command you, cursed spirits, in the name of Christ, to abandon the magician whom you bear between you," and the devils instantly abandoned him, and he, falling, broke into four pieces. The four pieces adhered to four stones, which are witness to the apostolic triumph up to this present day. Peter's patience allowed the hellish fiends to bear him up through the air for a while, so that in his fall he might descend more violently, and he who a little before would boastfully fly with devilish wings might suddenly lose his footing. It was fitting that he be raised up on high, so that, falling down in the sight of all the people, he might seek the earth. 21

At this Nero commanded Peter and Paul to be held in bonds, and the pieces of Simon's carcass to be guarded by a watch; he expected that he could rise from death on the 22

mihte. Petrus cwæð, "Ðes Simon ne geedcucað ær ðam gemænum æriste, ac he is to ecum witum geniðerod." Se Godes wiðerwinna ða, Nero, mid geðeahte his heahgerefan Agrippan, het Paulum beheafdian, and Petrum on rode ahon. Paulus ða, be ðæs cwelleres hæse, underbeah swurdes ecge, and Petrus rodehengene astah. Þa ða he to ðære rode gelæd wæs, he cwæð to ðam cwellerum, "Ic bidde eow, wendað min heafod adune, and astreccað mine fet wið heofonas weard; ne eom ic wyrðe þæt ic swa hangige swa min Drihten. He astah of heofonum for middangeardes alysednysse, and wæron forði his fet niðer awende. Me he clypað nu to his rice; awendað forði mine fotwelmas to ðan heofonlican wege." And ða cwelleras him ða þæs getiðodon.

23 Þa wolde þæt Cristene folc ðone casere acwellan, ac Petrus mid þisum wordum hi gestilde: "Min Drihten for feawum dagum me geswutelode þæt ic sceolde mid þysre ðrowunge his fotswaðum fylian; nu, mine bearn, ne gelette ge minne weg. Mine fet sind nu awende to ðam heofenlican life. Blyssiað mid me; nu todæg ic onfo minre earfoðnysse edlean." He wæs ða biddende his Drihten mid þisum wordum: "Hælend min, ic ðe betæce ðine scep, þe ðu me befæstest; ne beoð hi hyrdeleas þonne hi ðe habbað." And he mid þisum wordum ageaf his gast.

24 Samod hi ferdon, Petrus and Paulus, on ðisum dæge, sigefæste to ðære heofonlican wununge, on þam syx and þrittegoðan geare æfter Cristes ðrowunge, mid þam hi wuniað on ecnysse. *Igitur Hieronimus et quique alii auctores testantur quod in una die simul Petrus et Paulus martirizati sunt.* Æfter heora ðrowunge þærrihte comon wlitige weras, and uncuðe eallum folce; cwædon þæt hi comon fram Hierusalem to ðy

third day. Peter said, "This Simon will not be revived before the universal resurrection, but he is condemned to eternal torments." Then God's adversary, Nero, with the counsel of his chief officer Agrippa, commanded Paul to be beheaded, and Peter hanged on a cross. Paul then, at the executioner's command, bowed down to the sword's edge, and Peter ascended the cross. While he was being led to the cross, he said to the executioners, "I ask you, turn my head down, and stretch my feet toward heaven; I am not worthy to hang like my Lord. He descended from heaven for the redemption of the world, and therefore his feet were turned downward. He now calls me to his kingdom; therefore turn the soles of my feet to the heavenly way." And the executioners granted him this.

Then the Christian people would kill the emperor, but 23 Peter calmed them with these words: "A few days ago my Lord revealed to me that I should follow his footsteps with this suffering; now, my children, do not hinder my way. My feet are now turned to the heavenly life. Rejoice with me; now today I will receive the reward of my tribulation." He was then praying to his Lord with these words: "My savior, I entrust your sheep to you, which you committed to me; they will not lack a shepherd when they have you." And with these words he gave up his spirit.

Together they went, Peter and Paul, on this day, trium- 24 phant, to the heavenly dwelling, in the thirty-sixth year after Christ's passion, with whom they dwell in eternity. *Thus Jerome and a number of other authorities attest that Peter and Paul were martyred together on the same day.* Immediately after their passion there came beautiful men, unknown to all the people; they said that they came from Jerusalem in order to

þæt hi woldon ðæra apostola lic bebyrian. And swa dydon mid micelre arwurðnysse, and sædon þam folce þæt hi micclum blissian mihton forðan ðe hi swylce mundboran on heora neawiste habban moston.

25 Wite ge eac þæt ðes wyrresta cyning, Nero, rice æfter cwale þisra apostola healdan ne mot. Hit gelamp ða þæt eal ðæs wælhreowan caseres folc samod hine hatode, swa þæt hi ræddon anmodlice þæt man hine gebunde and oð deað swunge. Nero, ða ða he ðæs folces ðeaht geacsode, wearð to feore afyrht and mid fleame to wuda getengde. Þa sprang þæt word þæt he swa lange on ðam holte on cyle and on hungre dwelode, oðþæt hine wulfas totæron.

26 Þa gelamp hit æfter ðam þæt Grecas gelæhton ðæra apostola lichaman, and woldon east mid him lædan. Þa færinga gewearð micel eorðstyrung, and þæt Romanisce folc ðyder onette and ða lic ahreddan, on ðære stowe ðe is gehaten Catacumbas; and hi ðær heoldon oðer healf gear, oðþæt ða stowa getimbrode wæron ðe hi siððan on alede wæron mid wuldre and lofsangum. Cuð is geond ealle ðeodscipas þæt fela wundra gelumpon æt ðæra apostola byrgenum, ðurh ðæs hælendes tiðe, ðam sy wuldor and lof a on ecnysse. Amen.

bury the bodies of the apostles. And so they did with great honor, and said to the people that they could greatly rejoice because they should have such patrons in their proximity.

Know also that this worst of kings, Nero, could not hold his realm after the death of these apostles. It befell then that all the cruel emperor's people together hated him, so they resolved with one mind to bind him and scourge him to death. When he learned of the people's plan, Nero was afraid for his life and hastened in flight to the woods. Then the rumor sprang up that he remained so long in the woods, in cold and hunger, until wolves tore him to pieces.

It happened after this that Greeks seized the bodies of the apostles, and wanted to take them with them eastward. Suddenly there was a great earthquake, and the Roman people hurried there and rescued the bodies, in the place which is called the Catacombs; and they held them there for a year and a half, until the places were built in which they were afterward laid with glory and hymns. It is known among all nations that many wonders happened at the tombs of the apostles, by permission of the savior, to whom be glory and praise forever to eternity. Amen.

27

Natale sancti Pauli apostoli

Godes gelaðung wurðað þisne dæg ðam mæran apostole Paule to wurðmynte, forðam ðe he is gecweden ealra ðeoda lareow þurh soðfæste lare; wæs ðeahhwæðere his martyrdom samod mid ðam eadigan Petre gefremmed. He wæs fram cildhade on ðære ealdan æ getogen, and mid micelre gecnyrdnysse on ðære begriwen wæs. Æfter Cristes ðrowunge, ða ða se soða geleafa asprang þurh ðæra apostola bodunge, ða ehte he Cristenra manna þurh his nytennysse and sette on cwearterne, and eac wæs on geðafunge æt ðæs forman cyðeres Stephanes slege. Nis ðeahhwæðere be him geræd þæt he handlinga ænigne man acwealde.

2   He nam ða gewrit æt ðam ealdorbiscopum to ðære byrig Damascum þæt he moste gebindan ða Cristenan ðe he on ðære byrig gemette and gelædan to Hierusalem. Þa gelamp hit on þam siðe þæt him com færlice to micel leoht, and hine astrehte to eorðan, and he gehyrde stemne ufan þus cweðende, "Saule, Saule, hwi ehtst ðu min? Yfel bið ðe sylfum þæt ðu spurne ongean ða gade." He ða mid micelre fyrhte andwyrde þære stemne, "Hwæt eart ðu, leof Hlaford?" Him andwyrde seo clypung þære godcundan stemne, "Ic eom se hælend þe ðu ehtst: ac aris nu, and far forð to ðære byrig; þær ðe bið gesæd hwæt ðe gedafenige to donne."

27

Saint Paul

JUNE 30

The Feast of Saint Paul the Apostle

God's Church celebrates this day in honor of the great apostle Paul, because he is called the teacher of all nations through true doctrine; his martyrdom, however, was carried out along with the blessed Peter's. He was raised up in the old law from childhood, and nurtured in it with great diligence. After Christ's passion, when the true faith sprang up through the preaching of the apostles, he persecuted Christians in his ignorance and put them in prison, and also consented to the killing of the first martyr Stephen. It is not read of him, however, that he killed anyone with his own hands.

He then took a decree from the high priests to the city of Damascus, that he might bind any Christians he found in the city and lead them to Jerusalem. Then it happened on the journey that a great light suddenly came over him, and laid him out on the earth, and he heard a voice from above saying, "Saul, Saul, why do you persecute me? It will be evil for you to kick against the goad." With great fear he answered the voice, "Who are you, dear Lord?" The calling of the divine voice answered him, "I am the savior whom you persecute: arise now, and go forth to the city; there you will be told what you ought to do." He arose then with

He aras ða ablendum eagum, and his geferan hine swa blindne to ðære byrig gelæddon. And he ðær andbidigende ne onbyrigde ætes ne wætes binnan ðreora daga fæce.

3   Wæs ða sum Godes ðegen binnan ðære byrig, his nama wæs Annanias, to ðam spræc Drihten ðysum wordum, "Annania, aris, and gecum to minum ðeowan Saulum, se is biddende minre miltsunge mid eornistum mode." He and-wyrde ðære drihtenlican stemne, "Min hælend, hu mæg ic hine gesprecan se ðe is ehtere ðinra halgena, ðurh mihte ðæra ealdorbiscopa?" Drihten cwæð, "Far swa ic ðe sæde, forðan ðe he is me gecoren fætels þæt he tobere minne na-man ðeodum, and cynegum, and Israhela bearnum; and he sceal fela ðrowian for minum naman." Annanias ða becom to ðam gecorenan cempan and sette his handa him onuppan mid þisre gretinge, "Saule, min broðor, se hælend þe ðe be wege gespræc sende me wið ðin þæt þu geseo, and mid þam Halgan Gaste gefylled sy." Þa mid ðisum wordum feollon swylce fylmena of his eagum, and he ðærrihte gesihðe un-derfeng, and to fulluhte beah. Wunode ða sume feawa daga mid þam Godes ðeowum binnan ðære byrig, and mid micelre bylde þam Iudeiscum bodade þæt Crist, ðe hi wið-socon, is ðæs ælmihtigan Godes Sunu. Hi wurdon swiðlice ablicgede, and cwædon, "La hu, ne is ðes se wælhreowa ehtere Cristenra manna? Humeta bodað he Cristes ge-leafan?" Saulus soðlice micclum swyðrode, and ða Iudeiscan gescende, mid anrædnysse seðende þæt Crist is Godes Sunu.

4   Hwæt ða, æfter manegum dagum gereonodon ða Iudei-scan hu hi ðone Godes cempan acwellan sceoldon, and set-ton ða weardas to ælcum geate ðære ceastre. Paulus ongeat heora syrwunge, and ða Cristenan hine genamon and on anre wilian aleton ofer ðone weall. And he ferde ongean

blinded eyes, and his companions led him thus blind to the city. Waiting there, he tasted neither food nor drink for a space of three days.

There was a servant of God within the city whose name 3 was Ananias, to whom the Lord spoke in these words, "Ananias, arise, and go to my servant Saul, who is praying for my mercy with earnest mind." He answered the lordly voice, "My savior, how can I speak to him who is the persecutor of your holy ones, through the power of the high priests?" The Lord said, "Go as I have said to you, for he is a chosen vessel to me to bear my name to nations, and to kings, and to the children of Israel; and he shall suffer much for my name." Ananias went to the chosen champion and laid his hands upon him with this greeting, "Saul, my brother, the savior who spoke to you by the way has sent me to you that you might see, and be filled with the Holy Spirit." Then with these words something like films fell from his eyes, and he immediately received sight, and submitted to baptism. He remained a few days with the servants of God in the city, and with great boldness preached to the Jews that Christ, whom they denied, is the Son of the almighty God. They were greatly astonished, and said, "Lo, is this not the cruel persecutor of Christians? How is it that he preaches the faith of Christ?" But Saul grew much stronger, and put the Jews to shame, verifying with steadfastness that Christ is the Son of God.

Lo then, after many days the Jews conspired how they 4 might kill the champion of God, and they set guards at every gate of the city. Paul learned of their schemes, and the Christians took him and let him down over the wall in a

to Hierusalem and hine gecuðlæhte to ðam halgan heape
Cristes hiredes, and him cydde hu se hælend hine of heofenum gespræc. Syððan æfter sumum fyrste com clypung
of ðam Halgan Gaste to ðam geleaffullan werode, þus
cweðende, "Asendað Paulum and Barnaban to ðam weorce
ðe ic hi gecoren hæbbe." Se halga heap ða, be Godes hæse
and gecorennysse, hi asendon to lærenne eallum leodscipum
be Cristes tocyme for middangeardes alysednysse.

5   Barnabas wæs ða Paules gefera æt ðære bodunge to
langum fyrste. Ða æt nextan wearð him geðuht þæt hi on
twa ferdon, and swa dydon. Paulus wearð þa afylled and gefrefrod mid þæs Halgan Gastes gife, and ferde to manegum
leodscipum, sawende Godes sæd. On sumere byrig he wæs
twelf monað, on sumere twa gear, on sumere ðreo, and gesette biscopas and mæssepreostas and Godes ðeowas; ferde
siððan forð to oðrum leodscipe and dyde swa gelice. Asende
þonne eft ongean ærendgewritu to ðam geleaffullum ðe he
ær tæhte, and hi swa mid þam gewritum tihte and getrymde
to lifes wege.

6   We willað nu mid sumere scortre trahtnunge þas rædinge
oferyrnan, and geopenian gif heo hwæt digles on hyre hæbbende sy. Paulus ehte Cristenra manna, na mid niðe, swa swa
ða Iudeiscan dydon, ac he wæs midspreca and bewerigend
þære ealdan æ mid micelre anrædnysse. Wende þæt Cristes
geleafa wære wiðerwinna ðære ealdan gesetnysse; ac se hælend ðe gesette ða ealdan æ mid mislicum getacnungum, se
ylca eft on his andweardnysse hi awende to soðfæstnysse
æfter gastlicre getacnunge. Þa nyste Paulus ða gastlican getacnunge ðære æ, and wæs forði hyre foresprega, and ehtere
Cristes geleafan. God ælmihtig, þe ealle ðing wat, geseah his
geðanc, þæt he ne ehte geleaffulra manna ðurh andan ac

474

basket. He went back to Jerusalem and announced himself to the holy company of Christ's household, and made known to them how the savior had spoken to him from heaven. Some time later a call came from the Holy Spirit to the faithful company, saying, "Send Paul and Barnabas to the work for which I have chosen them." The holy company then, by God's command and election, sent them to teach all nations about the coming of Christ for the redemption of the world.

Barnabas was Paul's companion in preaching for a long time. Then at last it seemed to them that they should separate, and so they did. Paul was then filled and comforted with the grace of the Holy Spirit, and went to many countries, sowing God's seed. He was in one city for twelve months, in one two years, in one three, and appointed bishops and priests and servants of God; he went afterward to another country and did likewise. He sent back letters to the faithful whom he had taught, and so by those letters encouraged and confirmed them in the way of life.

We will now run through this reading with a short exposition, and explain it if it has any obscurity in it. Paul persecuted Christians, not with malice, as the Jews did, but because he was a very steadfast advocate and defender of the old law. He thought that the faith of Christ was contrary to the old covenant; but the same savior who established the old law by various miracles changed it afterward by his presence to truth according to its spiritual signification. Paul did not know the spiritual signification of that law, and was therefore its advocate, and a persecutor of the faith of Christ. Almighty God, who knows all things, saw his thoughts, that he did not persecute the faithful in anger but

ðurh ware ðære ealdan æ, and hine ða gespræc of heofonum
ðus cweðende, "Saule, hwi ehtst ðu min? Ic eom seo soðfæstnys ðe ðu werast. Geswic ðære ehtnysse—derigendlic bið ðe
þæt þu spurne ongean þa gade. Gif se oxa spyrnð ongean ða
gade, hit dereð him sylfum; swa eac hearmað þe ðin gewinn
togeanes me." He cwæð, "Hwi ehtst ðu min?" forðan ðe he is
Cristenra manna heafod, and besargað swa hwæt swa his
lima on eorðan ðrowiað, swa swa he ðurh his witegan cwæð,
"Se ðe eow hrepað, hit me bið swa egle swylce he hreppe ða
seo mines eagan." He wearð astreht, þus cweðende, "Hwæt
eart ðu, Hlaford?" His modignes wearð astreht, and seo soðe
eadmodnys wearð on him arǽred. He feoll unrihtwis, and
wearð arǽred rihtwis. Feallende he forleas lichamlice gesihðe; arisende he underfeng his modes onlihtinge. Þry dagas he wunode butan gesihðe, forðan ðe he wiðsoc Cristes
ærist on ðam ðriddan dæge.

7 *Annanias* is gereht on Hebreiscum gereorde "scep." Þæt
bilewite scep ða gefullode ðone arleasan Saulum, and worhte
hine arfæstne Paulum. He gefullode ðone wulf and geworhte
to lambe. He awende his naman mid ðeawum, and wæs ða
soðfæst bydel Godes gelaðunge, se ðe ær mid reðre ehtnysse
hi geswencte. He wolde forfleon syrewunge Iudeiscre ðeode,
and geðafode þæt hine man on anre wilian ofer ðone weall
nyðer alet, na þæt he nolde for Cristes geleafan deað
þrowian, ac forði he forfleah ðone ungeripedan deað; forðan
ðe he sceolde ærest menigne mann mid his micclum wisdome to Gode gestrynan, and syððan mid micelre geðincðe
to martyrdome his swuran astreccan. Micele maran witu he
ðrowode siððan for Cristes naman ðonne he ær his gecyrrednysse Cristenum mannum gebude. Saulus se arleasa beswang
ða Cristenan, ac æfter ðære gecyrrednysse wæs se arfæsta

for the defense of the old law, and spoke to him from heaven, saying, "Saul, why do you persecute me? I am the truth which you defend. Stop this persecution—it will be harmful to you to kick against the goad. If an ox kicks against the goad, it hurts itself; so too your struggle against me harms you." He said, "Why do you persecute me?" because he is the head of Christians, and laments whatever his limbs suffer on earth, as he said through his prophet, "He who touches you, it will be as painful to me as if he touched the pupil of my eye." He was prostrate, saying, "Who are you, Lord?" His pride was prostrated, and true humility was raised up in him. He fell unrighteous, and was raised up righteous. Falling he lost bodily sight; rising he received his mind's enlightenment. He remained without sight three days, because he had denied the resurrection of Christ on the third day.

In the Hebrew tongue *Ananias* is interpreted as 7 "sheep." The gentle sheep then baptized the impious Saul, and made him the pious Paul. He baptized the wolf and made him a lamb. He changed his name with his character, and he was then a true messenger of God's Church, who had before afflicted it with fierce persecution. He would flee from the schemes of the Jewish people, and consented to be let down in a basket over the wall, not because he did not want to suffer death for Christ's faith, but because he fled from premature death; for first he had to gain many for God by his great wisdom, and afterward with great honor to stretch out his neck to martyrdom. Later for Christ's name he suffered much greater torments than he had ordered for Christians before his conversion. Saul the impious scourged the Christians, but after his conversion the pious Paul was

Paulus for Cristes naman oft beswungen. Æne he wæs
gestæned oð dead swa þæt ða ehteras hine for deadne leton,
ac ðæs on merigen he aras and ferde ymbe his bodunge. He
wæs gelomlice on mycelre frecednysse ægðer ge on sæ ge
on lande, on westene, betwux sceaðum, on hungre and on
ðurste, and on manegum wæccum, on cyle, and on næcednysse, and on manegum cwearternum; swa he onette mid
þære bodunge, swylce he eal mennisc to Godes rice gebringan wolde. Ægðer ge mid lare ge mid gebedum ge mid gewritum, he symle tihte to Godes willan. He wæs gelæd to
heofonan oð ða ðriddan fleringe, and þær he geseh and gehyrde Godes digelnysse, ða he ne moste nanum men cyðan.
He besargode mid wope oðra manna synna, and eallum geleaffullum he æteowde fæderlice lufe. Mid his handcræfte
he teolode his and his geferena forðdæda, and ðærtoeacan
nis nan ðing tocnawen on soðre eawfæstnysse þæt his la-
reowdom ne gestaðelode. Þa oðre apostoli, be Godes hæse,
leofodon be heora lare unpleolice; ac ðeahhwæðere Paulus
ana, se ðe wæs on woruldcræfte teldwyrhta, nolde ða alyfdan
bigleofan onfon, ac mid agenre teolunge his and his geferena
neode foresceawode. His lara and his drohtnunga sind us
unasmeagendlice, ac se bið gesælig þe his mynegungum mid
gecneordnysse gehyrsumað.

Evangelium

8 *Dixit Simon Petrus ad Iesum, et reliqua.*

9 He forlet ealle woruldðing, and ðam hælende anum folgode, swa swa ðis godspel cwyð ðe ge nu æt ðisre ðenunge
gehyrdon. "On ðære tide cwæð Petrus se apostol to ðam
hælende, 'Efne we forleton ealle woruldðing, and ðe anum

478

often scourged for Christ's name. Once he was stoned to death so that his persecutors left him for dead, but in the morning he arose and went about his preaching. He was frequently in great danger both by sea and by land, in the desert, among thieves, from hunger and thirst, and from many vigils, from cold, from nakedness, and from many prisons; he so hastened with his preaching, as though he wanted to bring all humanity to God's kingdom. With teaching, with prayers and with letters, he always inspired to God's will. He was led to heaven as far as the third level, and there he saw and heard the secrets of God, which he might not make known to anyone. He lamented with weeping the sins of others, and he showed fatherly love to all the faithful. By his handicraft he toiled for his own and his companions' support, and in addition there was nothing known in true piety which his instruction did not confirm. The other apostles, by God's command, lived by their teaching, free from danger; yet Paul alone, who by worldly craft was a tentmaker, would not receive the sustenance he was allowed, but by his own toil provided for his own and his companions' needs. His teachings and his way of life are incomprehensible to us, but he will be happy who diligently obeys his admonitions.

Gospel

Simon Peter said to Jesus, etc. 8

He forsook all worldly things, and followed the savior 9
only, as this gospel says which you have just heard at this service. "At that time the apostle Peter said to the savior, 'Indeed, we have left all worldly things, and follow only you;

fyligað; hwæt dest ðu us þæs to leane?' Se hælend him andwyrde, 'Soð ic secge eow þæt ge ðe me fyligað sceolon sittan
ofer twelf domsetl on ðære edcynninge, ðonne ic sitte on
setle mines mægenðrymmes, and ge ðonne demað twelf
Israhela mæigðum. And ælc ðæra ðe forlæt for minum
naman fæder oððe moder, gebroðru oððe geswystru, wif
oððe bearn, land oððe gebytlu, be hundfealdum him bið forgolden, and he hæfð þærtoeacan þæt ece life.'"

10   Micel truwa hwearftlode on Petres heortan. He ana
spræc for ealne ðone heap, "We forleton ealle ðing." Hwæt
forlet Petrus? He wæs fiscere, and mid ðam cræfte his teolode, and ðeah he spræc mid micelre bylde: "We forleton
ealle ðing." Ac micel he forlet and his gebroðru ða ða hi forleton ðone willan to agenne. Þeah hwa forlæte micele æhta
and ne forlæt ða gitsunge, ne forlæt he ealle ðing. Petrus forlet lytle ðing, scipp and net, ac he forlet ealle ðing ða ða he,
for Godes lufon, nan ðing habban nolde. He cwæð, "We
fyligað ðe." Nis na fulfremedlic fela æhta to forlætenne
buton he Gode folgige. Soðlice ða hæðenan uðwitan fela
ðinga forleton, swa swa dyde Socrates, se ðe ealle his æhta
behwyrfde wið anum gyldenum wecge, and syððan awearp
ðone wecg on widre sæ, þæt seo gitsung ðæra æhta his willan
ne hremde and abrude fram ðære woruldlican lare ðe he
lufode. Ac hit ne fremede him swa gedon, forðan ðe he ne
fyligde Gode, ac his agenum willan, and forði næfde ða heofenlican edlean mid þam apostolum, þe ealle woruldðing
forsawon for Cristes lufon and mid gehyrsumnysse him
fyligdon.

11   Petrus ða befran, "Hwæt sceal us getimian? We dydon
swa swa ðu us hete, hwæt dest ðu us to edleane?" Se hælend
andwyrde, "Soð ic eow secge þæt ge ðe me fyligað sceolon

what will you give us as a reward for that?' The savior answered him, 'Truly I say to you that you who follow me will sit over twelve seats of judgment in the regeneration, when I will sit in the seat of my majesty, and you will judge the twelve tribes of Israel. And anyone who forsakes father or mother, brothers or sisters, wife or child, land or dwellings for my name, it will be repaid to him a hundredfold, and moreover he will have eternal life.'"

Great trust revolved in Peter's heart. He alone spoke for the whole company, "We have forsaken all things." What did Peter forsake? He was a fisherman, and provided for himself by that craft, and yet he spoke with great boldness: "We have forsaken all things." He and his brothers forsook much when they gave up the will to possess. If someone forsakes great possessions but does not forsake avarice, then he does not forsake all things. Peter forsook little things, a ship and net, but he forsook all things when, for love of God, he would have nothing. He said, "We follow you." It is not perfect to forsake many possessions unless one follows God. The heathen philosophers forsook many things, as Socrates did, who exchanged all his possessions for a wedge of gold, and then threw the wedge into the wide sea, so that greed for possessions might not obstruct his will and draw it from the worldly teaching that he loved. But it did him no good to do so, because he did not follow God, but his own will, and therefore did not have heavenly reward with the apostles, who scorned all worldly things for love of Christ and followed him with obedience.

Peter then asked, "What will become of us? We have done as you commanded us, what will you do for us as a reward?" The savior answered, "Truly I say to you that you

481

sittan ofer twelf domsetl on ðære edcynninge, ðonne ic sitte on setle mines mægenðrymmes; and ge ðonne demað twelf Israhela mægðum." "Edcynninge" he het þæt gemænelice ærist, on ðam beoð ure lichaman geedcynnede to unbrosnunge, þæt is to ecum ðingum. Tuwa we beoð on ðisum life acennede: seo forme acennednys is flæsclic, of fæder and of meder; seo oðer acennednys is gastlic, ðonne we beoð geedcennede on ðam halgan fulluhte, on ðam us beoð ealle synna forgyfene ðurh ðæs Halgan Gastes gife. Seo ðridde acennednys bið on ðam gemænelicum æriste, on ðam beoð ure lichaman geedcennede to unbrosnigendlicum lichaman.

12   On ðam æriste sittað þa twelf apostoli mid Criste on heora domsetlum and demað þam twelf mæigðum Israhela ðeode. Þis twelffealde getel hæfð micele getacnunge. Gif ða twelf mægða ana beoð gedemede æt ðam micclum dome, hwæt deð þonne seo ðreotteoðe mæigð, Leui? Hwæt doð ealle ðeoda middangeardes? Wenst ðu þæt hi beoð asyndrode fram ðam dome? Ac ðis twelffealde getel is geset for eallum mancynne ealles ymbhwyrftes, for ðære fulfremednysse his getacnunge. Twelf tida beoð on ðam dæge, and twelf monðas on geare; twelf heahfæderas sind, twelf witegan, twelf apostoli, and ðis getel hæfð maran getacnunge ðonne ða ungelæredan undergitan magon. Is nu forði mid ðisum twelffealdum getele ealles middangeardes ymbhwyrft getacnod.

13   Þa apostoli and ealle ða gecorenan ðe him geefenlæhton beoð deman on ðam micclum dæge mid Criste. Þær beoð feower werod æt ðam dome, twa gecorenra manna and twa wiðercorenra. Þæt forme werod bið þæra apostola and heora efenlæcendra, þa ðe ealle woruldðing for Godes naman forleton; hi beoð ða demeras, and him ne bið nan dom

who follow me will sit on twelve seats of judgment at the regeneration, when I will sit on the seat of my majesty; and then you will judge the twelve tribes of Israel." He called the universal resurrection "regeneration," at which our bodies will be regenerated to incorruption, that is, to eternity. We are born twice in this life: the first birth is fleshly, of father and of mother; the second birth is spiritual, when we are regenerated at holy baptism, in which all our sins are forgiven through the grace of the Holy Spirit. The third birth will be at the universal resurrection, at which our bodies will be regenerated to incorruptible bodies.

At the resurrection, the twelve apostles will sit with 12 Christ on their judgment seats and judge the twelve tribes of the people of Israel. This twelvefold number has great significance. If only the twelve tribes will be judged at the great judgment, what then will the thirteenth tribe, Levi, do? What will all the nations of the world do? Do you think that they will be cut off from the judgment? But this twelvefold number, for the completeness of its signification, stands for all humanity in all the world. There are twelve hours in the day, and twelve months in the year; there are twelve patriarchs, twelve prophets, twelve apostles, and this number has a greater significance than the unlearned can understand. And so by this twelvefold number is now signified the sphere of the whole world.

The apostles and all the chosen who imitated them will 13 be judges with Christ on the great day. There will be four hosts at the judgment, two of chosen ones and two of rejected. The first host will be of the apostles and their imitators, who forsook all worldly things for God's name; they will be the judges, and no judgment will be judged of them.

gedemed. Oðer endebyrdnys bið geleaffulra woruldmanna: him bið dom gesett, swa þæt hi beoð asyndrede fram gemanan ðæra wiðercorenra, þus cweðendum Drihtne, "Cumað to me, ge gebletsode mines Fæder, and onfoð þæt rice ðe eow is gegearcod fram frymðe middangeardes." An endebyrdnys bið þæra wiðercorenra þa þe ciððe hæfdon to Gode ac hi ne beeodon heora geleafan mid Godes bebodum; ðas beoð fordemede. Oðer endebyrdnys bið þæra hæðenra manna þe nane cyððe to Gode næfdon; þisum bið gelæst se apostolica cwyde, "Ða ðe butan Godes æ syngodon, hi eac losiað butan ælcere æ." To ðisum twam endebyrdnyssum cweð þonne se rihtwisa dema, "Gewitað fram me, ge awyrigedan, into ðam ecum fyre þe is gegearcod deofle and his awyrgedum gastum."

14   Þæt godspel cwyð forð gyt, "Ælc ðæra ðe forlæt for minum naman fæder oððe moder, gebroðru oððe geswystru, wif oððe bearn, land oððe gebytlu, be hundfealdum him bið forgolden, and he hæfð ðærtoeacan þæt ece lif." Hundfeald getel is fulfremed, and se ðe forlæt ða ateorigendlican ðing for Godes naman, he underfehð þa gastlican mede be hundfealdum æt Gode. Ðes cwyde belimpð swyðe to munuchades mannum, ða ðe for heofenan rices myrhðe forlætað fæder, and moder, and flæsclice siblingas. Hi underfoð manega gastlice fæderas and gastlice gebroðru, forðan ðe ealle þæs hades menn ðe regollice lybbað beoð him to fæderum and to gebroðrum getealde, and þærtoeacan hi beoð mid edleane þæs ecan lifes gewelgode. Þa ðe ealle woruldðing be Godes hæse forseoð, and on gemænum ðingum bigwiste habbað, hi beoð fulfremede and to ðam apostolum geendebyrde. Ða oðre, ðe ðas geðincðe nabbað þæt hi ealle heora æhta samod

The second rank will be of faithful people of this world: judgment will be set on them, so that they will be separated from the fellowship of the rejected, with the Lord saying, "Come to me, you blessed of my Father, and receive the kingdom which has been prepared for you from the beginning of the world." One rank of those rejected will be those who had knowledge of God but did not cultivate their faith with God's commandments; these will be condemned. The other rank will be those heathens who had no knowledge of God; on these will be fulfilled the apostolic sentence, "Those who have sinned without God's law, they shall also perish without any law." To these two ranks the righteous judge will then say, "Depart from me, you accursed, into the everlasting fire which is prepared for the devil and his accursed spirits."

The gospel says further, "Everyone who forsakes father or 14 mother, brothers or sisters, wife or child, land or dwellings for my name, it shall be repaid to him a hundredfold, and moreover he will have eternal life." A hundredfold number is perfect, and he who forsakes perishable things for the name of God will receive spiritual reward from God a hundredfold. This saying applies especially to people in the monastic order, who for the joy of the kingdom of heaven forsake father, mother, and fleshly relatives. They receive many spiritual fathers and spiritual brothers, for all people of that order who live according to the rule are considered their fathers and brothers, and moreover they will be enriched with the reward of eternal life. Those who despise all worldly things at God's command, and hold their provisions in common, are perfect and will be ranked with the apostles. Others, who do not have the privilege of being able to

forlætan magon, hi don þonne ðone dæl for Godes naman
ðe him to onhagige, and him bið be hundfealdum ecelice geleanod swa hwæt swa hi be anfealdum hwilwendlice dælað.

15   Micel todal is betwux þam gecyrredum mannum: sume hi
geefenlæcað þam apostolum, sume hi geefenlæcað Iudan,
Cristes belæwan, sume Annanian and Saphiran, sume Giezi.
Þa ðe ealle gewitendlice ðing to ðæra apostola efenlæcunge
forseoð for intingan þæs ecan lifes hi habbað lof and ða ecan
edlean mid Cristes apostolum. Se ðe betwux munecum
drohtnigende, on mynstres æhtum mid facne swicað, he bið
Iudan gefera, ðe Crist belæwde, and his wite mid hellwarum
underfehð. Se ðe mid twyfealdum geðance to mynsterlicre
drohtnunge gecyrð, and sumne dæl his æhta dælð, sumne
him sylfum gehylt, and næfð nænne truwan to ðam ælmihtigan þæt he him foresceawige andlyfene and gewæda and
oðere neoda, he underfehð þone awyrgedan cwyde mid Annanian and Saphiran, þe swicedon on heora agenum æhtum,
and mid færlicum deaðe ætforan ðam apostolum steorfende
afeollon. Se ðe on muneclicere drohtnunge earfoðhylde bið
and gyrnð ðæra ðinga ðe he on woruldlicere drohtnunge
næfde oððe begitan ne mihte, buton twyn him genealæhð se
hreofla Giezi, þæs witegan cnapan, and þæt þæt he on lichaman geðrowade, þæt ðrowað þes on his sawle. Se cnapa folgode ðam mæran witegan Eliseum; þa com him to sum rice
mann of þam leodscipe þe is Siria gehaten, his nama wæs
Naaman, and he wæs hreoflig. Þa becom he to ðam Godes
witegan Eliseum on Iudea lande, and he ðurh Godes mihte
fram ðære coðe hine gehælde. Þa bead he ðam Godes menn,
for his hælðe, deorwurðe sceattas. Se witega him andwyrde,
"Godes miht þe gehælde, na ic. Ne underfo ic ðin feoh;

forsake all their possessions together, let them then give in God's name what portion may please them, and they will be eternally rewarded a hundredfold for whatsoever they singly and temporarily distribute.

There is a great difference among converted people: some imitate the apostles, some imitate Judas, Christ's betrayer, some Ananias and Sapphira, some Gehazi. Those who in imitation of the apostles despise all transitory things for the sake of everlasting life will have praise and everlasting reward with Christ's apostles. He who, living among monks, treacherously commits fraud with the property of the monastery, he will be the companion of Judas, who betrayed Christ, and will receive his punishment with the inhabitants of hell. He who with divided thoughts turns to the monastic life, and bestows one part of his property but holds another for himself, and has no trust that the almighty will provide food and garments and other needs for him, he will receive the accursed sentence of Ananias and Sapphira, who committed fraud with their own property, and fell, perishing with sudden death before the apostles. He who is discontented in the monastic life and yearns for the things which he did not have or could not obtain in worldly life, without doubt resembles the leper Gehazi, the prophet's servant, and what he suffered in his body, this one suffers in his soul. The servant followed the great prophet Elisha; then there came to him a rich man of the nation called Syria, whose name was Naaman, and he was leprous. He came to God's prophet Elisha in the land of Judea, and through God's might he healed him from that disease. He then offered precious treasures to the man of God for his health. The prophet answered him, "God's might has healed you,

15

487

ðanca Gode ðinre gesundfulnysse, and bruc ðinra æhta."
Naaman ða gecyrde mid ealre his fare to his agenre leode.

16 Þa wæs ðæs witegan cnapa, Gyezi, mid gitsunge under-
cropen, and ofarn, ðone ðegen Naaman ðus mid wordum lic-
cetende, "Nu færlice comon tweigra witegena bearn to minum lareowe; asend him twa scrud and sum pund." Se ðegen
him andwyrde, "Waclic bið him swa lytel to sendenne; ac
genim feower scrud and twa pund." He ða gewende ongean
mid þam sceattum and bediglode his fær wið þone witegan.
Se witega hine befran, "Hwanon come ðu, Giezi?" He andwyrde, "Leof, næs ic on nanre fare." Se witega cwæð, "Ic geseah ðurh Godes Gast þa se ðegen alyhte of his cræte, and
eode togeanes ðe, and ðu name his sceattas on feo and on
reafe. Hafa ðu eac forð mid ðam sceattum his hreoflan, ðu
and eal ðin ofspring on ecnysse." And he gewende of his
gesihðe mid snawhwitum hreoflan beslagen.

17 Is nu forði munuchades mannum mid micelre gecnyrdnysse to forbugenne ðas yfelan gebysnunga, and geefenlæcan þam apostolum, þæt hi, mid him and mid Gode, þæt ece
lif habban moton. Amen.

not I. I will not take your money; thank God for your health, and enjoy your possessions." Naaman then returned with all his company to his own people.

Then the prophet's servant, Gehazi, was beguiled by ava- 16 rice, so he ran off, deceiving the officer Naaman in these words, "Now suddenly the sons of two prophets have come to my teacher; send him two garments and a pound." The officer answered him, "It will be poor to send him so little; but take four garments and two pounds." He then returned with the money and concealed his journey from the prophet. The prophet asked him, "Where are you coming from, Gehazi?" He answered, "Sir, I was not on any journey." The prophet said, "I saw through the Spirit of God that the officer got down from his chariot, and went toward you, and you took his payment in money and in garments. Have also henceforth his leprosy along with the payment, you and all your offspring forever." And he turned from his sight, stricken with snow-white leprosy.

Now, therefore, monastics ought to avoid these evil ex- 17 amples with great care, and imitate the apostles so that they, with them and with God, may have everlasting life. Amen.

28

Dominica xi post Pentecosten

Cum adpropinquaret Iesus Hierusalem, et reliqua.

2   "On sumere tide wæs se hælend farende to Hierusalem; ða ða he genealæhte þære ceastre and he hi geseah, ða weop he ofer hi, ðus cweðende, 'Gif ðu wistest hwæt ðe toweard is, þu weope mid me. Witodlice on ðisum dæge þu wunast on sibbe, ac seo towearde wracu is nu bediglod fram ðinum eagum. Se time cymð þæt ðine fynd ðe ymbsittað mid ymb-trymminge, and ðe on ælce healfe genyrwiað, and to eorðan þe astreccað and þine bearn samod þe on ðe synd. Ne for-lætað hi on ðe stan ofer stane, forðan ðe ðu ne oncneowe ðone timan ðinre geneosunge.' Se hælend ða eode into ðam temple, and adræfde ut ða cypmen ðe ðær binnan syllende and bicgende wæron, cweðende to him, 'Hit is awriten þæt min hus is gebedhus, ac ge hit habbað gedon sceaðum to scræfe.' Þa genealæhton him to blinde and healte and he hi gehælde, and wæs tæcende dæghwomlice binnan þam temple."

3   Gregorius se trahtnere cwæð þæt se hælend beweope ðære ceastre toworpennysse, ðe gelamp æfter his ðrowunge for ðære wrace heora mandæda þæt hi ðone heofenlican æðeling manfullice acwellan woldon. He spræc mid woplicre stemne, na to ðam weorcstanum oððe to ðære getimbrunge, ac spræc to ðam ceastergewarum, þa he mid fæderlicere lufe

28

Eleventh Sunday after Pentecost

Eleventh Sunday after Pentecost

Wh*en Jesus approached Jerusalem, etc.*

"At a certain time the savior was going to Jerusalem; when   2
he approached the city and saw it, he wept over it, saying, 'If
you knew what is ahead for you, you would weep with me.
Truly on this day you dwell in peace, but the coming vengeance is hidden from your eyes. The time is coming when
your enemies will surround you with fortifications, and oppress you on every side, and lay you out on the earth along
with your children who are in you. They will not leave one
stone on another in you, because you did not know the time
of your visitation.' The savior then went into the temple,
and drove out the merchants who were buying and selling
within, saying to them, 'It is written that my house is a house
of prayer, but you have made it a den of thieves.' Then the
blind and lame drew near to him and he healed them, and
was teaching every day within the temple."

The commentator Gregory said that the savior wept for   3
the overthrow of the city, which happened after his passion
in vengeance for their evil deeds because they sinfully
wanted to kill the heavenly prince. He spoke with weeping
voice, not to the worked stones or the building, but to the
inhabitants, whom he lamented with fatherly love, because

besargode, forðan ðe he wiste heora forwyrd hrædlice
toweard. Feowertig geara fyrst Godes mildheortnys forlet
ðam wælhreowum ceastergewarum to behreowsunge heora
mandæda, ac hi ne gymdon nanre dædbote, ac maran mandæda gefremedon, swa þæt hi oftorfodon mid stanum ðone
forman Godes cyðere Stephanum, and Iacobum, Iohannes
broðer, beheafdodon. Eac ðone Rihtwisan Iacobum hi ascu-
fon of ðam temple and acwealdon, and ehtnysse on ða oðre
apostolas setton. Seo Godes gelaðung þe on ðære byrig
æfter Cristes ðrowunge under þam Rihtwisan Iacobe drohtnigende wæs ferde eal samod of ðære byrig to anre wic wið
ða ea Iordanen; forðan ðe him com to Godes hæs þæt hi
sceoldon fram ðære manfullan stowe faran ærðam ðe seo
wracu come. God ða oncneow þæt ða Iudeiscan nanre dædbote ne gymdon, ac ma and ma heora mandæda geyhton;
sende him ða to Romanisc folc, and hi ealle fordyde.

4   Vespasianus hatte se casere ðe on ðam dagum geweold
ealles middangeardes cynedomes. Se asende his sunu Titum
to oferwinnenne ða earman Iudeiscan. Þa gelamp hit swa
þæt hi wæron gesamnode binnan ðære byrig Hierusalem,
six hund ðusend manna, swylce on anum cwearterne beclysede; and hi wurdon ða utan ymbsette mid Romanischum
here swa lange þæt ðær fela ðusenda mid hungre wurdon
acwealde, and for ðære menigu man ne mihte hi bebyrigan,
ac awurpon ða lic ofer ðone weall. Sume ðeah for mæiglicre
sibbe hi bebyrigan woldon, ac hi hrædlice for mægenleaste
swulton. Gif hwa hwæt lytles æniges bigwistes him sylfum
gearcode, him scuton sona to reaferas and ðone mete him of
ðam muðe abrudon. Sume hi cuwon heora gescy, sume heora
hætera, sume streaw, for ðære micclan angsumnysse ðæs
hatan hungres. Hit nis na gedafenlic þæt we, on ðisum

he knew that their destruction was soon coming. The mercy of God left a space of forty years for the cruel inhabitants to repent their crimes, but they did not care for penitence, but committed greater crimes, so that they killed with stones the first martyr of God, Stephen, and beheaded James, the brother of John. They also drove James the Just from the temple and killed him, and persecuted the other apostles. The congregation of God which was living in the city after Christ's passion under James the Just went all together from the city to a village on the river Jordan; for God's command had come to them that they should go from the wicked place before the vengeance came. God knew that the Jews did not care for any penitence, but increased their crimes more and more; he sent the Roman people to them, and they destroyed them all.

The emperor was called Vespasian, who in those days 4 ruled the kingdom of the whole world. He sent his son Titus to conquer the wretched Jews. It then so happened that they were assembled within the city of Jerusalem, six hundred thousand people, enclosed as if in a prison; and they were surrounded from without by the Roman army for so long that many thousands were killed by hunger, and because of the number they could not bury them, but threw the bodies over the wall. Some, however, wanted to bury them for the sake of kinship, but these soon died from weakness. If anyone had provided any little sustenance for himself, robbers would suddenly rush on him and pull the food from his mouth. Some gnawed their shoes, some their garments, some straw, for the great anguish of burning hunger. It is not fitting that we, in this holy gospel, recount all

halgan godspelle, ealle ða sceamlican yrmðu gereccan þe ge-
lumpon ðam ymbsettum Iudeiscum ærðan ðe hi on hand
gan woldon. Wearð ða se mæsta dæl ðæra arleasra mid þam
bysmerlicum hungre adyd, and þa lafe ðæs hungres ofsloh se
Romanisca here and ða burh grundlunga towurpon, swa þæt
ðær ne belaf stan ofer stane, swa swa se hælend ær mid wope
gewitegode. Þæra cnapena ðe binnan syxtyne geara ylde
wæron, hundnigontig ðusenda hi tosendon to gehwylcum
leodscipum to ðeowte, and on ðam earde ne belaf nan ðing
ðæs awyrgedan cynnes. Seo burh wearð syððan on oðre
stowe getimbrod and mid ðam Sarasceniscum gesett.

5   Se Hælend geswutelode for hwilcum intingan ðeos to-
stencednys þære byrig gelumpe ða ða he cwæð, "Forðan þe
ðu ne oncneowe ðone timan ðinre geneosunge." He geneosode ða buruhware ðurh his menniscnysse, ac hi næron his
gemyndige, naðor ne ðurh lufe ne þurh ege. Be ðære
gymeleaste spræc se witega mid ceorigendre stemne, ðus
cweðende, "Storc and swalewe heoldon ðone timan heora
tocymes, and þis folc ne oncneow Godes dom." Drihten
cwæð to ðære byrig, "Gif þu wistest hwæt þe toweard is,
þonne weope ðu mid me. Witodlice on ðisum dæge þu
wunast on sibbe, ac ða toweardan wraca sind nu bediglode
fram ðinum eagum." Seo buruhwaru wæs wunigende on
woruldlicere sibbe þa þa heo orsorhlice wæs underðeodd
flæsclicum lustum, and hwonlice hogode ymbe ða toweardan yrmða ðe hyre ða gyt bediglode wæron. Gif heo ðære
yrmðe forewittig wære, ne mihte heo mid orsorgum mode
ðære gesundfulnysse andweardes lifes brucan.

6   Drihten adræfde of ðam temple ða cypmen, þus cweðende, "Hit is awriten þæt min hus is gebedhus, and ge hit
habbað gedon sceaðum to screafe." Þæt tempel wæs Gode

the shameful miseries which befell the besieged Jews before they would yield. The greater part of those impious ones was destroyed by the shameful famine, and the Roman army killed the survivors of the famine and razed the city to the ground, so that there did not remain one stone upon another, as the savior had prophesied with weeping. Of boys who were less than sixteen years old, they sent ninety thousand to all nations in slavery, and in that land there remained nothing of the accursed people. The city was afterward built in another place and settled with Saracens.

The savior showed the reason why this dispersion of the 5 city happened when he said, "Because you did not know the time of your visitation." He visited the inhabitants in his humanity, but they were not mindful of him, neither by love nor by fear. Of that heedlessness the prophet spoke with lamenting voice, saying, "The stork and the swallow keep the time of their coming, and this people did not know the judgment of God." The Lord said to the city, "If you knew what is ahead for you, you would weep with me. Truly on this day you dwell in peace, but the coming miseries are hidden from your eyes." The inhabitants were dwelling in worldly peace while they were carelessly subservient to fleshly pleasures, and little thought of the miseries to come, which were still hidden from them. If they had foreseen that misery, they could not have enjoyed the prosperity of their present life with a carefree mind.

The Lord drove the merchants from the temple, saying, 6 "It is written that my house is a house of prayer, and you have made it a den of thieves." The temple was consecrated

gehalgod to his ðenungum and lofsangum, and to gebedum
ðam geleaffullum; ac ða gytsigendan ealdorbiscopas geðafedon þæt ðær cyping binnan gehæfd wære. Drihten, ða ða he
þæt unriht geseah, he worhte ane swipe of rapum and hi
ealle mid gebeate ut ascynde. Þeos todræfednys getacnode
ða toweardan toworpennysse ðurh þone Romaniscan here,
and se hryre gelamp swyðost þurh gyltas ðæra ealdorbiscopa, ðe binnan ðam temple wunigende, mid gehywedre
halignysse þæs folces lac underfengon, and ðæra manna
ehton ðe butan lace þæt tempel gesohton. Hwæt wæs þæt
tempel buton swylce sceaðena scræf, þa þa ða ealdorbiscopas mid swylcere gytsunge gefyllede wæron, and ða leaslican
ceapas binnan ðam Godes huse geðafedon? Hit is on oðrum
godspelle awriten þæt ðær sæton myneteras, and ðær wæron
gecype hryðeru, and scep, and culfran. On ðam dagum,
æfter gesetnysse ðære ealdan æ, man offrode hryðeru, and
scep, and culfran for getacnunge Cristes ðrowunge; ða tihte
seo gitsung þa sacerdas þæt man ðillic orf þær to ceape
hæfde, gif hwa feorran come and wolde his lac Gode offrian,
ðæt he on gehendnysse to bicgenne gearu hæfde. Drihten ða
adræfde ðillice cypan of ðam halgan temple, forðan ðe hit
næs to nanum ceape aræred, ac to gebedum.

7   "Him ða to genealæhton blinde and healte and he hi gehælde, and wæs lærende þæt folc dæghwomlice binnan ðam
temple." Se mildheorta Drihten, ðe læt scinan his sunnan
ofer ða rihtwisan and unrihtwisan gelice, and sent renas and
eorðlice wæstmas godum and yfelum, nolde ofteon his lare
þam ðwyrum Iudeiscum, forðan ðe manega wæron gode betwux þam yfelan, þe mid ðære lare gebeterode wæron, þeah
ðe ða þwyran hyre wiðcwædon. He eac mid wundrum ða lare
getrymde, þæt ða gecorenan ðy geleaffulran wæron and ða

to God for his rites and songs of praise, and the prayers of the faithful; but the greedy high priests allowed commerce to be transacted within. The Lord, when he saw that wrong, made a whip of ropes and drove them all out with blows. This expulsion signified the future destruction by the Roman army, and the ruin happened chiefly through the sins of the high priests who, dwelling within the temple, received the people's offerings with feigned holiness, and persecuted those who sought the temple without offerings. What was that temple but as it were a den of thieves, when the high priests were filled with such covetousness, and allowed false commerce within the house of God? It is written in another gospel that there sat money changers, and there were oxen for sale, and sheep, and doves. In those days, according to the decree of the old law, they offered oxen, sheep, and doves as a sign of Christ's passion; then greed drove the priests to have such animals there for sale, so if anyone came from afar and wanted to offer his gift to God, he might have it ready at hand to buy. The Lord then drove such merchants from the holy temple, because it was not raised for any commerce, but for prayers.

"Then the blind and lame drew near to him and he healed them, and was teaching the people daily within the temple." The merciful Lord, who lets his sun shine over the righteous and unrighteous alike, and sends rains and earthly fruits to the good and evil, would not withdraw his teaching from the perverse Jews, because there were many good among the evil, who were improved by that instruction, although the perverse opposed it. He also confirmed his teaching by miracles, so the chosen might be more believing and the 7

wiðercorenan nane beladunge nabbað, forðan ðe hi ne ðurh godcunde tacna ne þurh liflice lare þam soðfæstan hælende gelyfan noldon. Nu cwyð se eadiga Gregorius þæt heora to-worpennys hæfð sume gelicnysse to gehwilcum þwyrlicum mannum, þe blissiað on yfeldædum and on ðam wyrstan ðingum fægniað. Swilcera manna besargað se mildheorta Drihten dæghwomlice, se ðe ða þa losigendlican buruhware mid tearon bemænde. Ac gif hi oncneowon ða geniðerunge þe him onsihð, hi mihton hi sylfe mid sarigendre stemne heofian.

8   Soðlice ðære losigendlican sawle belimpð þes æfterfili-genda cwyde: "On ðysum dæge þu wunast on sibbe, ac seo towearde wracu is nu bediglod fram ðinum eagum." Witod-lice seo ðwyre sawul is on sibbe wunigende on hire dæge þonne heo on gewitendlicere tide blissað, and mid wurð-myntum bið upahafen, and on hwilwendlicum bricum bið ungefoh, and on flæsclicum lustum bið tolysed, and mid nanre fyrhte þæs toweardan wites ne bið geegsod, ac be-dygelað hire sylfre ða æfterfiligendan yrmða; forðan gif heo embe ða smeað, þonne bið seo woruldlice bliss mid þære smeagunge gedrefed. Heo hæfð ðonne sibbe on hire dæge ðonne heo nele ða andweardan myrhðe gewæcan mid nanre care þære toweardan ungesælðe, ac gæð mid beclysedum eagum to ðam witnigendlicum fyre. Seo sawul ðe on ðas wisan nu drohtnað heo is to geswencenne ðonne ða riht-wisan blissiað; and ealle ða ateorigendlican ðing þe heo nu to sibbe and blisse talað beoð hire ðonne to byternysse and to ceaste awende, forðan ðe heo micele sace wið hi sylfe hæfð hwi heo ða geniðerunge, ðe heo ðonne ðolað, nolde ær on life mid ænigre carfulnysse foresceawian. Be ðam is awriten, "Eadig bið se man þe symle bið forhtigende; and soðlice se

rejected would have no excuse, because they would not believe in the true savior either by divine signs or by living teaching. Now, the blessed Gregory says that their overthrow has some similarity to all perverse people, who rejoice in evil deeds and exult in the worst things. The merciful Lord, who then lamented the perishing inhabitants with tears, bewails such people daily. But if they knew the condemnation that hangs over them, they would themselves lament with sorrowing voice.

Truly this following sentence applies to the perishing 8 soul: "On this day you dwell in peace, but the coming vengeance is now hidden from your eyes." The perverse soul is indeed dwelling in peace in its day when in transitory time it rejoices, and is exalted with honors, and is immoderate in temporary enjoyments, and is dissipated in fleshly desires, and is not awed with any fear of future punishment, but hides from itself the miseries that follow; because if it reflected on them, then worldly joy would be troubled by that reflection. It has peace in its day when it will not afflict its present mirth with any care for future unhappiness, but goes with closed eyes to the punishing fire. The soul which now lives in this way will be afflicted when the righteous rejoice; and all the perishable things which it now considers peace and joy will then be turned to bitterness and strife, because it will have great debate within itself about why it would not earlier in life foresee with any carefulness the condemnation which it will then be suffering. About this it is written, "Blessed is the man who is ever fearing; and truly

heardmoda befylð on yfel." Eft on oðre stowe mynegað þæt halige gewrit, "On eallum ðinum weorcum beo ðu gemyndig þines endenextan dæges, and on ecnysse ðu ne syngast."

9 Seo halige ræding cwyð, "Se tyma cymð þæt ðine fynd ðe ymbsittað mid ymbtrymminge, and ðe on ælce healfe genyrwiað, and to eorðan þe astreccað and ðine bearn samod ðe on ðe sind." Þæra sawla fynd sind ða hellican gastas þe besittað þæs mannes forðsið, and his sawle, gif heo fyrenful bið, to ðære geferrædene heora agenre geniðerunge mid micelre angsumnysse lædan willað. Þa deoflu æteowiað þære synfullan sawle ægðer ge hyre yfelan geðohtas and ða derigendlican spræca and ða manfullan dæda, and hi mid mænigfealdum ðreatungum geangsumiað, þæt heo on ðam forðsiðe oncnawe mid hwilcum feondum heo ymbset bið, and ðeah nan utfær ne gemet hu heo ðam feondlicum gastum oðfleon mage. To eorðan heo bið astreht ðurh hire scylda oncnawennysse, ðonne se lichama þe heo on leofode to duste bið formolsnod. Hire bearn on deaðe hreosað ðonne ða unalifedlican geðohtas ðe heo nu acenð beoð on ðære endenextan wrace eallunga toworpene, swa swa se sealmsceop be ðam gyddigende sang, "Nelle ge getruwian on ealdormannum, ne on manna bearnum, on ðam nis nan hæl. Heora gast gewit, and hi to eorðan gehwyrfað, and on ðam dæge losiað ealle heora geðohtas."

10 Soðlice on ðam godspelle fyligð, "And hi ne forlætað on ðe stan ofer stane." Þæt ðwyre mod, þonne hit gehypð yfel ofer yfele, and þwyrnysse ofer þwyrnysse, hwæt deð hit buton swilce hit lecge stan ofer stane? Ac ðonne seo sawul bið to hire witnunge gelæd, ðonne bið eal seo getimbrung hire smeagunge toworpen, forðan ðe heo ne oncneow ða tid hire geneosunge. On manegum gemetum geneosað se ælmihtiga

the hard minded will fall into evil." Again in another place the holy scripture warns, "In all your works be mindful of your last day, and you will not sin in eternity."

The holy reading says, "The time is coming when your 9 enemies will surround you with fortifications, and oppress you on every side, and lay you out on the earth together with your children who are in you." The enemies of the soul are the hellish spirits which beset a person's departure, and with great tribulation will lead his soul, if it is sinful, to the fellowship of their own damnation. The devils show the sinful soul both its evil thoughts and its harmful speeches and wicked deeds, and they afflict it with manifold reproaches, that it may know on its departure by what foes it is beset, and yet find no way out by which it might flee from the hostile spirits. It will be laid out on the earth by a knowledge of its sins, when the body in which it lived will be crumbled to dust. Its children will fall in death when the forbidden thoughts to which it now gives birth will be entirely overthrown in the final vengeance, as the psalmist sang in chanting, "Do not trust in princes, nor in the children of men, in whom there is no health. Their spirit departs, and they return to earth, and in that day all their thoughts perish."

Truly in the gospel it follows, "And they will not leave in 10 you stone upon stone." The perverse mind, when it heaps evil upon evil, and perversity upon perversity, what does it do but as it were lay stone upon stone? But when the soul will be led to its punishment, then all the structure of its thinking will be overthrown, because it did not know the time of its visitation. The almighty God visits people's souls

God manna sawla: hwiltidum mid lare, hwilon mid wundrum, hwilon mit untrumnyssum; ac gif heo ðas geneosunga
forgymeleasað, ðam feondum heo bið betæht on hire geendunge to ecere witnunge, þam ðe heo ær on life mid healicum
leahtrum gehyrsumode. Þonne beoð ða hire witneras on
ðære hellican susle, ða ðe ær mid mislicum lustum hi to ðam
leahtrum forspeonon.

11   Drihten eode into ðam temple and mid swipe ða cypan
utadræfde. Þa cypmen binnon ðam temple getacnodon un-
rihtwise lareowas on Godes gelaðunge. Ðær wæron gecype
oxan, and scep, and culfran, and þær sæton myneteras. Oxa
teolað his hlaforde, and se lareow sylð oxan on Godes cyrcan
gif he begæð his Hlafordes teolunga—þæt is, gif he bodað
godspel his underðeoddum—for eorðlicum gestreonum
and na for godcundre lufe. Mid sceapum he mangað gif he
dysigra manna herunga cepð on arfæstum weorcum. Be
swylcum cwæð se hælend, "Hi underfengon edlean heora
weorca," þæt is se hlisa idelre herunge, ðe him gecweme
wæs.

12   Se lareow bið culfran cypa þe nele ða gife ðe him God
forgeaf butan his geearnungum oðrum mannum butan
sceattum nytte don; swa swa Crist sylf tæhte, "Butan ceape
ge underfengon ða gife; syllað hi oðrum butan ceape." Se ðe
mid gehywedre halignysse him sylfum teolað on Godes
gelaðunge, and nateshwon ne carað ymbe Cristes teolunge,
se bið untwylice mynetcypa getalod. Ac se hælend todræfð
swylce cypan of his huse ðonne he mid geniðerunge fram
geferrædene his gecorenra hi totwæmð.

13   "Min hus is gebedhus, and ge hit habbað gedon sceaðum
to scræfe." Hit getimað forwel oft þæt ða ðwyran becumað
to micclum hade on Godes gelaðunge, and hi ðonne gastlice

in many ways: sometimes with instruction, sometimes with miracles, sometimes with illnesses; but if it neglects these visitations, at its end it will be delivered for eternal punishment to the fiends whom it had obeyed in life with deadly sins. Then its torturers in hell's torment will be those who had previously enticed it to sins by various pleasures.

The Lord went into the temple and drove out the merchants with a whip. The merchants within the temple signified unrighteous teachers in God's Church. There were oxen for sale, and sheep, and doves, and money changers sat there. The ox toils for his master, and the teacher sells oxen in God's Church if he performs his Lord's toil—that is, if he preaches the gospel to those under his care—for earthly gains and not for divine love. He traffics with sheep if he buys the praises of foolish ones with pious works. Of such the savior said, "They have received the reward of their works," that is the fame of idle praise, which was pleasing to them. 11

The teacher is a seller of doves who will not give to others without money the gift which God has given him without any merit of his own; as Christ himself taught, "Without price you have received the gift; give it to others without price." He who with feigned holiness toils for himself in God's Church, and cares nothing for Christ's toil, will undoubtedly be accounted a money changer. But the savior will drive such merchants from his house when he will separate them with condemnation from the fellowship of his chosen. 12

"My house is a house of prayer, and you have made it a den of thieves." It happens too often that the perverse achieve great status in God's Church, and then with their 13

ofsleað mid heora yfelnysse heora underðeoddan, ða ðe hi sceoldon mid heora benum geliffæstan. Hwæt sind ðyllice buton sceaðan? Anes gehwilces geleaffulles mannes mod is Godes hus, swa swa se apostol cwæð, "Godes tempel is halig, þæt ge sind." Ac þæt mod ne bið na gebedhus, ac sceaðena scræf, gif hit forlysð unscæððignysse and bilewitnysse soðre halignysse, and mid ðwyrlicum geðohtum hogað oðrum dara.

14   "And he wæs tæcende dæghwomlice binnan ðam temple." Crist lærde ða þæt folc on his andweardnysse, and he lærð nu dæghwomlice geleaffulra manna mod mid godcundre lare smeaðancellice, þæt hi yfel forbugon and god gefremman. Ne bið na fulfremedlic þam gelyfedan þæt he yfeles geswice buton he god gefremme. Se eadiga Gregorius cwæð, "Mine gebroðru, ic wolde eow ane lytle race gereccan, seo mæig ðearle eower mod getimbrian, gif ge mid gymene hi gehyran wyllað. Sum æðelboren mann wæs on ðære scire Valeria se wæs gehaten Crisaurius, se wæs swa micclum mid leahtrum afylled swa micclum swa he wæs mid eorðlicum welum gewelgod. He wæs toðunden on modignysse, and his flæsclicum lustum underðeod, and mid ungefohre gytsunge ontend. Ac ða ða God gemynte his yfelnysse to geendigenne, ða wearð he geuntrumod, and to forðsiðe gebroht. Þa on ðære ylcan tide þe he geendian sceolde, ða beseah he up, and stodon him abutan swearte gastas, and mid micclum ðreate him onsigon þæt hi his sawle on ðam forðsiðe mid him to hellicum clysungum gegripon. He ongann ða bifian and blacian, and ungefohlice swætan, and mid micclum hreame fyrstes biddan, and his sunu Maximus, ðone ic geseah munuc syððan, mid gedrefedre stemne clypode, and cwæð, 'Min cild, Maxime, gehelp min! Onfoh me on ðinum geleafan;

evil spiritually kill those placed under their care, to whom they ought to give life with their prayers. What are such people but thieves? The mind of every believer is a house of God, as the apostle said, "The temple of God is holy, which you are." But the mind will be no house of prayer, but a den of thieves, if it loses the innocence and meekness of true holiness, and with perverse thoughts intends harm to others.

"And he was teaching daily within the temple." Then 14 Christ taught the people in his presence, and now he daily teaches the minds of the faithful with divine teaching most subtly, so that they might avoid evil and do good. It is not perfect for a believer to cease from evil unless he does good. The blessed Gregory said, "My brothers, I want to tell you a little story, which may greatly edify your minds, if you will hear it attentively. There was a certain nobleman in the province of Valeria who was called Chrysaurius, who was as much filled with sins as he was enriched with earthly riches. He was puffed up with pride, and enslaved to his fleshly de-sires, and inflamed with excessive covetousness. But when God intended to put an end to his wickedness, he became sick, and was brought to the point of death. At the very time that he should die, he looked up, and there stood around him dark spirits, and they descended on him in a great troop to carry off his soul at its departure with them to the prisons of hell. He began to tremble and grow pale, and to sweat ex-cessively, and with a great cry to beg for more time, and with troubled voice called his son Maximus, whom I afterward saw as a monk, and said, 'My child, Maximus, help me! Receive me in your faith; I have not been hurtful to you in

næs ic ðe derigende on ænigum ðingum.' Se sunu ða Maximus, mid micclum heofe gedrefed, him to com. He wand þa
swa swa wurm; ne mihte geðolian þa egeslican gesihðe ðæra
awyrgedra gasta. He wende hine to wage, ðær hi him æt-
wæron; he wende eft ongean, þær he hi funde. Þa ða he swa
swiðe geancsumod his sylfes orwene wæs, ða hrymde he mid
micelre stemne and ðus cwæð, 'Lætað me fyrst oð tomerigen, huruðinga fyrst oð tomerigen'; ac mid ðisum hreame ða
blacan fynd tugon ða sawle of ðam lichaman and aweg gelæddon." Be ðam is swutol þæt seo gesihð him wearð æteowod
for oðra manna beterunge, na for his agenre. La, hwæt fremode him, ðeah ðe he on forðsiðe þa sweartan gastas gesawe, ðonne he ne moste þæs fyrstes habban ðe he gewilnode? Ac uton we beon carfulle þæt ure tima mid ydelnysse
us ne losige, and we ðonne to weldædum gecyrran willan,
ðonne us se deað to forðsiðe geðreatað.

15   Þu, ælmihtiga Drihten, gemiltsa us synfullum, and urne
forðsið swa gefada þæt we, gebettum synnum, æfter ðisum
frecenfullum life, ðinum halgum geferlæhte beon moton. Sy
ðe lof and wuldor on ealra worulda woruld. Amen.

any way.' The son Maximus came to him, troubled with great sorrow. He was wriggling like a worm; he could not endure the dreadful sight of the cursed spirits. He turned himself to the wall, there they were present to him; he turned back again, he found them there. When, so greatly afflicted, he was despairing of himself, he cried with a loud voice and said, 'Give me time until tomorrow, at least time until tomorrow'; but with this cry the black fiends drew the soul from the body and led it away." It is clear from this that the vision was shown to him for the improvement of other people, not for his own. Alas, what did it profit him, though he saw dark spirits at his departure, when he might not have the time he desired? But let us be careful that our time not be lost to us in idleness, and then when we want to turn to good deeds, death impels us to our departure.

Almighty Lord, have mercy on us sinners, and so arrange 15 our departure that we, having atoned for our sins, may, after this perilous life, be united with your saints. To you be praise and glory for ever and ever. Amen.

29

IIII IDUS AUGUSTI

Passio beati Laurentii martyris

On Decies dæge, þæs wælhreowan caseres, wæs se halga biscop Sixtus on Romana byrig drohtnigende; ða færlice het he his gesihðum ðone biscop mid his preostum samod ge-andwerdian. Sixtus ða unforohtmod to his preostum cly-pode, "Mine gebroðra, ne beo ge afyrhte; cumað, and eower nan him ne ondræde ða scortan tintregunga. Þa halgan mar-tyras geðrowodon fela pinunga þæt hi orsorge becomon to wulderbeage þæs ecan lifes." Þa andwyrdon his twegen diaconas, Felicissimus and Agapitus, "Ðu, ure fæder, hwider fare we butan ðe?" On ðære nihte wearð se biscop mid his twam diaconum hrædlice to ðam reðum ehtere gebroht. Se casere Decius him cwæð to, "Geoffra ðine lac ðam undead-licum godum, and beo ðu þæra sacerda ealdor." Se eadiga Sixtus him andwyrde, "Ic symle geoffrode, and gyt offrige mine lac ðam ælmihtigan Gode, and his Suna hælendum Criste, and ðam Halgum Gaste, hluttre onsægednysse and ungewemmede." Decius cwæð, "Gebeorh ðe and ðinum preostum, and geoffra. Soðlice gif ðu ne dest, þu scealt beon eallum oðrum to bysne." Sixtus soðlice andwyrde, "Hwene ær ic ðe sæde þæt ic symle geoffrige ðam ælmihtigum Gode." Decius ða cwæð to his cempum, "Lædað hine to ðam temple Martis þæt he ðam gode Marti geoffrige: gif he nelle

29

Saint Lawrence

AUGUST 10

The Passion of Blessed Lawrence, Martyr

In the days of the cruel emperor Decius, the holy bishop Sixtus was living in the city of Rome; suddenly the emperor commanded the bishop and his priests to appear in his presence. Unafraid, Sixtus said to his priests, "My brothers, do not be afraid; come, and let none of you dread brief torments. The holy martyrs suffered many tortures so that they might come without sorrow to the glorious crown of eternal life." His two deacons, Felicissimus and Agapitus, answered, "Our father, where would we go without you?" On that night the bishop and his two deacons were quickly brought to the cruel tormentor. The emperor Decius said to him, "Offer your sacrifice to the immortal gods, and be the chief of the priests." The blessed Sixtus answered him, "I have always offered, and still offer, my sacrifice to the almighty God, and his Son the savior Christ, and the Holy Spirit, a pure and unblemished sacrifice." Decius said, "Save yourself and your priests, and offer sacrifice. If you do not, you will be an example to all the others." But Sixtus answered, "A little earlier I said that I will always sacrifice to the almighty God." Decius said to his soldiers, "Lead him to the temple of Mars so that he might sacrifice to the god Mars: if he will not offer

offrian, beclysað hine on ðam cwearterne Mamortini." Þa
cempan hine læddon to ðam deofolgylde and hine ðreato-
don þæt he ðære deadan anlicnysse his lac offrian sceolde.
Þa ða he ðæs caseres hæse forseah and ðam deofolgylde offrian nolde, ða gebrohton hi hine mid his twam diaconum
binnan ðam blindan cwearterne.

2   Þa betwux ðam com Laurentius, his ercediacon, and ðone
halgan biscop mid ðisum wordum gespræc: "Ðu min fæder,
hwider siðast ðu butan ðinum bearne? Þu halga sacerd,
hwider efst ðu butan ðinum diacone? Næs ðin gewuna þæt
ðu butan ðinum diacone Gode geoffrodest. Hwæt mislicode
ðe, min fæder, on me? Geswutela ðine mihte on ðinum
bearne, and geoffra Gode þone ðe ðu getuge, þæt þu ðy or-
sorglicor becume to ðam æðelan wulderbeage." Þa ða se
eadiga Laurentius mid þisum wordum and ma oðrum bemænde þæt he ne moste mid his lareowe ðrowian, ða andwyrde se biscop, "Min bearn, ne forlæte ic ðe, ac ðe gerist
mara campdom on ðinum gewinne. We underfoð, swa swa
ealde men, scortne ryne þæs leohtran gewinnes; soðlice þu
geonga underfehst miccle wulderfulran sige æt ðisum reðan
cyninge. Min cild, geswic ðines wopes: æfter ðrim dagum ðu
cymst sigefæst to me to ðam ecum life. Nim nu ure cyrcan
maðmas and dæl Cristenum mannum be ðan ðe ðe gewyrð."

3   Se ercediacon ða Laurentius, be ðæs biscopes hæse, ferde
and dælde þære cyrcan maðmas preostum, and ælðeodigum
ðearfum, and wudewum, ælcum be his neode. He com to
sumere wudewan hire nama wæs Quiriaca, seo hæfde behyd
on hire hame preostas and manega læwede Cristenan. Ða se
eadiga Laurentius ðwoh heora ealra fet and ða wudewan
fram hefigtimum heafodece gehælde. Eac sum ymesene man
mid wope his fet gesohte, biddende his hæle. Laurentius ða

sacrifice, lock him in the Mamertine prison." The soldiers led him to the pagan idol and urged him to offer his sacrifice to the dead image. When he scorned the emperor's command and would not offer to the idol, they took him and his two deacons to the dark prison.

Then his archdeacon Lawrence came among them, and spoke to the holy bishop in these words: "My father, where are you going without your child? Holy priest, where do you hasten without your deacon? It has not been your custom to offer to God without your deacon. What has displeased you in me, my father? Show your power in your child, and offer to God the one you have trained, that you might less sorrowfully attain the noble crown of glory." When the blessed Lawrence, with these words and others, had lamented that he might not suffer with his teacher, the bishop answered, "My child, I am not forsaking you, but a greater battle suits you in your conflict. We, like old men, will undergo the short course of a lighter conflict; truly you, a young man, will undergo a much more glorious triumph from this cruel king. My child, cease your weeping: after three days you will come to me triumphant in everlasting life. Take our church's treasures and distribute to Christians however it seems good to you." 2

The archdeacon Lawrence then went at the bishop's command and distributed the church's treasures to priests, and poor strangers, and widows, to each according to his need. He came to a certain widow whose name was Quiriaca, who had hidden priests and many lay Christians in her home. Then the blessed Lawrence washed the feet of them all and healed the widow of a burdensome headache. Also, a blind man sought his feet with weeping, praying for his cure. 3

mearcode rodetacen on ðæs blindan eagan, and he ðærrihte beorhtlice geseah. Se ercediacon ða gyt geaxode ma Cristenra manna gehwær, and hi ær his ðrowunge mid gastlicere sibbe and mid fotðweale geneosode.

4 Þa ða he ðanon gewende, ða wæs his lareow Sixtus mid his twam diaconum of ðam cwearterne gelædd ætforan ðam casere Decium. He wearð þa gehathyrt ongean ðone halgan biscop, ðus cweðende, "Witodlice we beorgað ðinre ylde: gehyrsuma urum bebodum, and geoffra ðam undeaðlicum godum." Se eadiga biscop him andwyrde, "Ðu earming, beorh ðe sylfum, and wyrc dædbote for ðæra halgena blode ðe ðu agute." Se wælhreowa cwellere mid gebolgenum mode cwæð to his heahgerefan Valeriane, "Gif ðes bealdwyrda biscop acweald ne bið, siððan ne bið ure ege ondrædendlic." Valerianus him andwyrde, "Beo he heafde becorfen. Hat hi eft to ðæs godes temple Martis gelædan, and gif hi nellað to him gebigedum cneowum gebiddan and heora lac offrian, underfon hi beheafdunge on ðære ylcan stowe." Þæs caseres cempan hine læddon to ðam deofolgylde mid his twam diaconum; ða beseah se biscop wið ðæs temples and ðus cwæð, "Þu dumba deofolgyld! Þurh ðe forleosað earme menn þæt ece lif. Towurpe ðe se ælmihtiga Godes Sunu." Þa mid þam worde tobærst sum dæl ðæs temples mid færlicum hryre. Laurentius ða clypode to ðam biscope, "Þu halga fæder, ne forlæt ðu me, forðan ðe ic aspende ðære cyrcan maðmas swa swa ðu me bebude." Hwæt ða cempan ða hine gelæhton, forðan ðe hi gehyrdon hine be ðam cyrclicum madmum sprecan. Sixtus ða soðlice underhnah swurdes ecge, and his twegen diaconas samod, Felicissimus and Agapitus, ætforan ðam temple, on ðam sixtan dæge þyses monðes.

Lawrence then made the sign of the cross on the blind man's eyes, and he immediately saw clearly. The archdeacon heard further of more Christians elsewhere, and before his suffering visited them with spiritual peace and with foot washing.

When he returned from there, his teacher Sixtus and his 4 two deacons were led from the prison before the emperor Decius. He became enraged against the holy bishop, saying, "Indeed we have consideration for your age: obey our commands, and offer sacrifice to the immortal gods." The blessed bishop answered him, "You wretch, have consideration for yourself, and do penance for the blood of the saints which you have shed." The bloodthirsty executioner with wrathful mind said to his chief reeve Valerianus, "If this impertinent bishop is not killed, then our terror will no longer be frightening." Valerianus answered him, "Let his head be cut off. Order them to be led back to the temple of the god Mars, and if they will not pray to him on bended knees and offer their sacrifices, let them suffer beheading in the same place." The emperor's soldiers led him to the pagan temple with his two deacons; then the bishop looked toward the temple and said, "You mute idol! Wretched men lose everlasting life because of you. May the almighty Son of God overthrow you." With that word, a part of the temple burst apart with a sudden collapse. Lawrence then cried to the bishop, "Holy father, do not forsake me, for I have distributed the church's treasures as you commanded." At once the soldiers seized him, for they had heard him speak of the church's treasures. Sixtus then sank under the sword's edge along with his two deacons, Felicissimus and Agapitus, before the temple, on the sixth day of this month.

5   Laurentius witodlice wearð siððan gebroht to ðam casere,
and se reða cwellere hine ða befran, "Hwær sind ðære cyrcan
madmas ðe ðe betæhte wæron?" Se eadiga Laurentius mid
nanum worde him ne geandwyrde. On ðam ylcan dæge
betæhte se Godes feond ðone halgan diacon his heahgerefan Valeriane mid ðysum bebode, "Ofgang ða madmas mid
geornfulnysse, and hine gebig to ðam undeadlicum godum."
Se gerefa ða hine betæhte his gingran, ðæs nama wæs Ypolitus, and he hine beclysde on cwearterne mid managum
oðrum. Þa gemette he on ðam cwearterne ænne hæðenne
man, se wæs ðurh micelne wop ablend. Ða cwæð he him
to, "Lucille, gif ðu gelyfst on hælend Crist, he onliht ðine
eagan." He andwyrde, "Æfre ic gewilnode þæt ic on Cristes
naman gefullod wære." Laurentius him to cwæð, "Gelyfst ðu
mid ealre heortan?" He andwyrde mid wope, "Ic gelyfe on
hælend Crist, and ðam leasum deofolgyldum wiðsace."
Ypolitus mid geðylde heora wordum heorcnode. Se gesæliga
Laurentius tæhte ða ðam blindan soðne geleafan ðære halgan Þrynnysse, and hine gefullode. Lucillus æfter ðam fulluhtbæðe mid beorhtre stemne clypode, "Sy gebletsod se
eca God, hælend Crist, ðe me ðurh his diacon onlihte. Ic
wæs blind bam eagum, nu ic beorhtlice leohtes bruce."
Witodlice ða fela oðre blinde mid wope comon to ðam eadigan diacone, and he asette his handa ofer heora eagan and hi
wurdon onlihte.

6   Se tungerefa Ypolitus cwæð ða to ðam diacone, "Geswutela me ðære cyrcan madmas." Laurentius cwæð, "Eala ðu
Ypolite, gif ðu gelyfst on God Fæder, and on his Sunu
hælend Crist, ic ðe geswutelige ða madmas, and þæt ece lif
behate." Ypolitus cwæð, "Gif ðu ðas word mid weorcum gefylst, ðonne do ic swa ðu me tihtst." Laurentius ða halgode

Later Lawrence was brought to the emperor, and the 5
fierce executioner asked him, "Where are the church's treasures which were entrusted to you?" The blessed Lawrence
answered him not a word. On the same day the enemy of
God handed over the holy deacon to his chief reeve Valerianus with this command, "Extort the treasures zealously,
and make him bow to the immortal gods." The reeve then
handed him over to his subordinate, whose name was Hippolytus, and he locked him in a prison with many others.
In the prison he found a heathen man, who was blinded
through great weeping. He said to him, "Lucillus, if you will
believe in the savior Christ, he will give light to your eyes."
He answered, "I have always wanted to be baptized in
Christ's name." Lawrence said to him, "Do you believe with
all your heart?" He answered with weeping, "I believe in the
savior Christ, and renounce false idols." Hippolytus listened
to their words with patience. The blessed Lawrence then
taught the blind man true belief in the holy Trinity, and baptized him. After the baptismal bath Lucillus cried with clear
voice, "Blessed be the eternal God, the savior Christ, who
has enlightened me through his deacon. I was blind in both
eyes, now I clearly enjoy the light." Then there came many
others blind with weeping to the blessed deacon, and he laid
his hands over their eyes and they were enlightened.

The town reeve Hippolytus said to the deacon, "Show me 6
the church's treasures." Lawrence said, "O Hippolytus, if
you will believe in God the Father, and in his Son the savior
Christ, I will show you the treasures, and promise you eternal life." Hippolytus said, "If you will fulfill those words with
deeds, I will do as you urge me." Lawrence then consecrated

fant and hine gefullode. Soðlice Ypolitus æfter ðam fulluhtbæðe wæs clypigende mid beorhtre stemne, "Ic geseah un-
scæððigra manna sawla on Gode blissigan." And he mid
tearum to ðam eadigan diacone cwæð, "Ic halsige ðe on ðæs
hælendes naman þæt eal min hiwræden gefullod wurðe."
Witodlice Laurentius mid bliðum mode him ðæs getiðode,
and nigontyne wera and wifa his hiwisces mid wuldre gefullode.

7   Æfter ðisum sende se heahgerefa and bebead Ypolite þæt
he Laurentium to ðæs cynges cafertune gelædde. Ypolitus
þæt bebod mid eadmodre spræce cydde ðam eadigan Laurentie. He cwæð, "Uton faran, forðan ðe me and ðe is wuldor
gegearcod." Hi ða hrædlice comon, and unforhte him ætforan stodon. Þa cwæð Valerianus to ðam halgan cyðere,
"Awurp nu ðine anwilnysse, and agif ða madmas." Se Godes
cyðere him andwyrde, "On Godes ðearfum ic hi aspende,
and hi sind ða ecan madmas ðe næfre ne beoð gewanode." Se
gerefa cwæð, "Hwæt fagettest ðu mid wordum? Geoffra
ðine lac urum godum, and forlæt ðone drycræft ðe ðu on ge-
truwast." Laurentius cwæð, "For hwilcum ðingum neadað se
deofol eow þæt ge Cristene men to his biggengum ðreat-
niað? Gif hit riht sy þæt we to deoflum us gebiddon swiðor
þonne to ðam ælmihtigan Gode, deme ge hwa þæs wurðmyntes wurðe sy, se ðe geworht is oððe se ðe ealle ðing gesceop?" Se casere ða andwyrde, "Hwæt is se ðe geworht is,
oððe hwæt is se ðe geworhte?" Godes cyðere cwæð, "Se ælmihtiga Fæder ures hælendes is scyppend ealra gesceafta,
and ðu cwyst þæt ic me gebiddan sceole to dumbum stanum, ða ðe sind agrafene ðurh manna handa." Hwæt se
casere ða hine gebealh, and het on his gesihðe ðone diacon
unscrydan and wælhreowlice swingan, and se casere sylf

a font and baptized him. After his baptismal bath, Hippolytus was crying with a clear voice, "I saw the souls of the innocent rejoicing in God." And with tears he said to the blessed deacon, "I beseech you in the name of the savior that all my household might be baptized." Lawrence granted him this with cheerful mind, and with glory baptized nineteen men and women of his family.

After this, the high reeve sent and commanded Hippolytus to lead Lawrence to the king's court. Hippolytus with humble speech made that command known to the blessed Lawrence. He said, "Let us go, for glory is prepared for me and for you." They went quickly, and stood fearless before him. Then Valerianus said to the holy martyr, "Cast away your willfulness, and give up the treasures." God's martyr answered him, "I have spent them on God's poor, and they are the eternal treasures which will never be diminished." The reeve said, "Why do you bandy words? Offer your sacrifice to our gods, and forsake the magic in which you trust." Lawrence said, "Why does the devil compel you to urge Christians to his worship? If it is right that we should pray to devils rather than to the almighty God, then judge who is worthy of that honor, he who is made or he who created all things?" The emperor answered, "Who is he who is made, or who is he who made?" God's martyr said, "The almighty Father of our savior is the maker of all creation, and you say that I should pray to mute stones, which are carved by human hands." At this the emperor grew angry, and commanded the deacon to be stripped in his sight and cruelly

7

clypode, "Ne hyrw ðu ure godas." Se eadiga Laurentius on ðam tintregum cwæð, "Witodlice ic ðancige minum Gode, þe me gemedemode to his halgum; and ðu, earming, eart ge-ancsumod on ðinre gewitleaste." Decius cwæð to ðam cwel-lerum, "Ræað hine upp, and æteowiað his gesihðum eal þæt witatol." Þa wurdon hrædlice forðaborene isene clutas, and isene clawa, and isen bedd, and leadene swipa and oðre gepilede swipa. Þa cwæð se casere, "Geoffra ðine lac urum godum, oððe þu bist mid eallum ðisum pinungtolum getin-tregod." Se eadiga diacon cwæð, "Þu ungesæliga, þas estmet-tas ic symle gewilnode; hi beoð me to wuldre, and ðe to wite." Se casere cwæð, "Geswutela us ealle ða manfullan ðine gelican, þæt ðeos burh beo geclænsod; and ðu sylf geof-fra urum godum, and ne truwa ðu nateshwon on ðinum goldhordum." Þa cwæð se halga martyr, "Soðlice ic truwige, and ic eom orsorh be minum hordum." Decius andwyrde, "Wenst ðu la þæt þu beo alysed mid ðinum hordum fram ðisum tintregum?" and het ða mid gramlicum mode þæt þa cwelleras mid stearcum saglum hine beoton. Witodlice Lau-rentius on ðam gebeate clypode, "Þu earming, undergyt huru nu þæt ic sigrige be Cristes madmum, and ic ðine tin-tregu naht ne gefrede." Decius cwæð, "Lecgað ða isenan clu-tas hate glowende to his sidan." Se eadiga martyr ða wæs biddende his Drihten, and cwæð, "Hælend Crist, God of Gode, gemiltsa þinum ðeowan; forðan ðe ic gewreged ðe ne wiðsoc; befrinen ic ðe geandette." Þa het se casere hine aræran, and cwæð, "Ic geseo þæt ðu, ðurh ðinne drycræft, ðas tintregan gebysmerast; ðeahhwæðere ne scealt ðu me gebysmrian. Ic swerige ðurh ealle godas and gydena þæt þu scealt geoffrian, oððe ic ðe mid mislicum pinungum acwelle." Laurentius ða bealdlice clypode, "Ic on mines

scourged, and the emperor himself cried, "Do not insult our gods." The blessed Lawrence in these torments said, "Truly I thank my God, who has deigned to accept me among his holy ones; and you, wretch, are afflicted in your foolishness." Decius said to the executioners, "Raise him up, and display in his sight all the instruments of torture." Then quickly were brought forth iron plates, iron claws, an iron bed, leaden whips, and other spiked whips. The emperor said, "Offer your sacrifice to our gods, or you will be tortured with all these instruments of torment." The blessed deacon said, "You unfortunate one, I have always desired these luxuries; they will be a glory to me, and a torment to you." The emperor said, "Reveal to us all the wicked like you, that this city may be cleansed; and you yourself make offerings to our gods, and do not trust at all in your hoards of gold." Then the holy martyr said, "Truly I trust, and I have no worry for my hoards." Decius answered, "Do you think then that you will be released from these torments by your hoards?" and then with an angry heart commanded the executioners to beat him with stout clubs. During the beating Lawrence cried, "You wretch, know at least that I triumph by Christ's treasures, and I do not feel your torments at all." Decius said, "Lay the glowing-hot iron plates on his side." The blessed martyr then was praying to his Lord, saying, "Savior Christ, God of God, have mercy on your servant; for accused, I did not deny you; questioned, I acknowledged you." Then the emperor ordered him to be raised up, and said, "I see that, through your magic, you mock these torments; nevertheless you shall not mock me. I swear by all the gods and goddesses that you will offer sacrifice, or I will kill you by various tortures." Lawrence then boldly cried, "In the

Drihtnes naman nateshwon ne forhtige for ðinum tintregum, ðe sind hwilwendlice; ne ablin ðu þæt ðu begunnen
hæfst."

8   Þa wearð se casere mid swyðlicere hatheortnysse geyrsod,
and het ðone halgan diacon mid leadenum swipum langlice
swingan. Laurentius ða clypode, "Hælend Crist, þu ðe ge-
medemodest þæt ðu to menniscum menn geboren wære,
and us fram deofles ðeowte alysdest, onfoh minne gast." On
ðære ylcan tide him com andswaru of heofonum, þus
cweðende, "Gyt ðu scealt fela gewinn habban on ðinum
martyrdome." Decius ða gehathyrt clypode, "Romanisce
weras, gehyrde ge ðæra deofla frofor on ðisum eawbræcum,
ðe ure godas geyrsode ne ondræt, ne ða asmeadan tintregan?
Astreccað hine, and mid gepiledum swipum swingende geangsumiað." Laurentius ða, astreht on ðære hengene, mid
hlihendum muðe ðancode his Drihtne: "Drihten God,
Fæder hælendes Cristes, sy ðu gebletsod, þe us forgeafe ðine
mildheortnysse; cyð nu ðine arfæstnysse, þæt ðas ymbstan-
dendan oncnawon þæt ðu gefrefrast ðine ðeowan." On ðære
tide gelyfde an ðæra cempena, ðæs nama wæs Romanus, and
cwæð to ðam Godes cyðere, "Laurentie, ic geseo Godes
engel standende ætforan ðe mid handclaðe, and wipað ðine
swatigan limu. Nu halsige ic ðe þurh God þæt þu me ne forlæte." Þa wearð Decius mid facne afylled, and cwæð to his
heahgerefan, "Me ðincð þæt we sind ðurh drycræft oferswiðde." And he het ða alysan ðone diacon of ðære hengene,
and betæcan ðam tungerefan Ypolite—and nyste ða gyt þæt
he Cristen wæs.

9   Þa betwux ðam brohte se gelyfeda cempa Romanus ceac-
fulne wæteres, and mid wope ðæs halgan Laurenties fet
gesohte, fulluhtes biddende. Laurentius ða hrædlice þæt

name of my Lord I do not at all fear your torments, which are transitory; do not cease from what you have begun."

Then the emperor was enraged with violent fury, and commanded the holy deacon to be scourged a long time with leaden whips. Lawrence then cried, "Savior Christ, you who deigned to be born a human being, and redeemed us from slavery to the devil, receive my spirit." At the same time an answer came to him from heaven, saying, "You will yet have much affliction in your martyrdom." Furious, Decius then cried, "Roman men, did you hear the comfort of the devils to this impious one, who does not fear our wrathful gods, nor the torments we have devised? Stretch him, and torture him by scourging with spiked whips." Then Lawrence, stretched out on the cross, with laughing mouth thanked his Lord: "Blessed be you, Lord God, Father of the savior Christ, who have given us your mercy; show now your compassion, that these bystanders may know that you comfort you servants." At that time one of the soldiers, whose name was Romanus, believed, and said to the martyr of God, "Lawrence, I see God's angel standing before you with a hand cloth, and he wipes your bleeding limbs. I now beseech you through God that you do not forsake me." Then Decius was filled with guile, and said to his high reeve, "It seems to me that we are overcome by magic." And he then ordered the holy deacon to be released from the cross, and delivered to the town reeve Hippolytus—he did not yet know that he was a Christian.

Meanwhile the believing soldier Romanus brought a jug of water, and fell at the feet of the holy Lawrence weeping, asking for baptism. Lawrence quickly consecrated the water

wæter gehalgode and ðone geleaffullan ðegen gefullode. Þa
ða Decius þæt geaxode, ða het he hine wædum bereafian
and mid stearcum stengum beatan. Romanus ða ungeaxod
clypode on ðæs caseres andwerdnysse, "Ic eom Cristen." On
ðære ylcan tide het se reða cwellere hine underhnigan
swurdes ecge. Eft on ðære ylcan nihte, æfter ðæs cempan
martyrdome, ferde Decius to ðam hatum baðum wið þæt
botl Salustii, and het ðone halgan Laurentium him to gefeccan. Þa ongann Ypolitus sarlice heofian, and cwæð, "Ic wylle
mid ðe siðian, and mid hluddre stemne hryman þæt ic Cristen eom, and mid þe licgan." Laurentius cwæð, "Ne wep ðu,
ac swiðor suwa and blissa, forðan ðe ic fare to Godes wuldre.
Eft æfter lytlum fyrste, ðonne ic ðe clypige, gehyr mine
stemne, and cum to me."

Decius ða het gearcian eal þæt pinungtol ætforan his
domsetle, and Laurentius him wearð to gelæd. Decius cwæð,
"Awurp ðone truwan ðines drycræftes, and gerece us ðine
mægðe." Se eadiga Laurentius andwyrde, "Æfter menniscum
gebyrde ic eom Hispanienscis, Romanisc fostorcild, and
Cristen fram cildcradole, getogen on ealre godcundre æ."
Decius andwyrde, "Soðlice is seo æ godcundlic ðe ðe swa gebylde þæt ðu nelt ure godas wurðian, ne ðu nanes cynnes
tintregan þe ne ondrætst." Laurentius cwæð, "On Cristes
naman ne forhtige ic for ðinum tintregum." Se wælhreowa
casere ða cwæð, "Gif ðu ne offrast urum godum, eall ðeos
niht sceal beon aspend on ðe mid mislicum pinungum." Laurentius cwæð, "Næfð min niht nane forsworcennysse, ac heo
mid beorhtum leohte scinð." Þa het se wælhreowa mid stanum ðæs halgan muð cnucian. Hwæt ða Laurentius wearð
gestrangod ðurh Godes gife, and mid hlihendum muðe
cwæð, "Sy ðe lof, Drihten, forðan ðe ðu eart ealra ðinga

and baptized the believing officer. When Decius learned of
that, he ordered him to be stripped of his garments and
beaten with stout staves. Romanus then cried in the emper-
or's presence without being asked, "I am a Christian." At the
same time the fierce executioner ordered him to fall under
the sword's edge. Later that same night, after the soldier's
martyrdom, Decius went to the hot baths opposite the
house of Sallust, and commanded the holy Lawrence to be
fetched to him. Then Hippolytus began sorely to lament,
and said, "I will go with you, and with loud voice cry that I
am a Christian, and fall with you." Lawrence said, "Do not
weep, but rather be silent and rejoice, for I am going to
God's glory. After a little time, when I call you, hear my
voice, and come to me."

Decius then ordered all the tools of torture to be pre- 10
pared before his seat of judgment, and Lawrence was led to
him. Decius said, "Cast aside trust in your magic, and tell us
about your family." The blessed Lawrence answered, "By human birth I am Spanish, a Roman foster child, and a Christian from my cradle, trained up in all divine law." Decius answered, "Truly the law is divine which has made you so bold
that you will not worship our gods, nor do you dread any
kind of torment." Lawrence said, "In Christ's name I do not
fear your torments." The cruel emperor then said, "If you do
not offer sacrifice to our gods, you will pass this whole night
in various tortures." Lawrence said, "My night has no darkness, but shines with bright light." Then the cruel one commanded that the mouth of the saint be struck with stones.
But lo, Lawrence was strengthened by the grace of God, and
said with a laughing mouth, "Praise to you, Lord, for you are

God." Decius cwæð to ðam cwellerum, "Ahebbað þæt isene
bed to ðam fyre, þæt se modiga Laurentius hine ðæron gereste." Hi ðærrihte hine wædon bereafodon and on ðam
heardan bedde astrehton, and mid byrnendum gledum þæt
bed undercrammodon, and hine ufan mid isenum geaflum
ðydon.

11 Decius cwæð ða to þam Godes cyðere, "Geoffra nu urum
godum." Laurentius andwyrde, "Ic offrige me sylfne ðam ælmihtigan Gode on bræðe wynsumnysse; forðan þe se ge-
drefeda gast is Gode andfenge onsægednys." Soðlice ða
cwelleras tugon ða gleda singallice under þæt bedd, and wiðufan mid heora forcum hine ðydon. Ða cwæð Laurentius,
"Eala ge ungesæligan, ne undergyte ge þæt eowre gleda nane
hætan minum lichaman ne gedoð, ac swiðor celinge?" He ða
eft mid þam wlitegostan nebbe cwæð, "Hælend Crist, ic
ðancige ðe þæt ðu me gestrangian wylt." He ða beseah wið
þæs caseres, þus cweðende, "Efne ðu, earming, bræddest
ænne dæl mines lichaman, wend nu þone oðerne and et." He
cwæð ða eft, "Hælend Crist, ic ðancige ðe mid inweardre
heortan þæt ic mot faran into ðinum rice." And mid þysum
worde he ageaf his gast, and mid swylcum martyrdome þæt
uplice rice geferde, on ðam he wunað mid Gode a on ecnysse. Þa forlet se wælhreowa casere ðone halgan lichaman
uppon ðam isenan hyrdle, and tengde mid his heahgerefan
to ðam botle Tyberianum.

12 Ypolitus ða bebyrigde ðone halgan lichaman mid micelre
arwurðnysse on ðære wudewan legerstowe Quiriace, on ðysum dægðerlicum dæge. Witodlice æt ðære byrgene wacode
micel menigu Cristenra manna mid swiðlicere heofunge. Se
halga sacerd Iustinus ða him eallum gemæssode and gehuslode. Æfter ðisum gecyrde Ypolitus to his hame, and mid

God of all things." Decius said to the executioners, "Raise the iron bed to the fire, that the proud Lawrence may rest on it." They immediately took away his garments and stretched him out on the hard bed, and filled underneath the bed with burning coals, and from above pierced him with iron forks.

Decius said to the martyr of God, "Offer sacrifice now to our gods." Lawrence answered, "I offer myself to the almighty God in the odor of pleasantness; for the afflicted spirit is an acceptable sacrifice to God." Truly the executioners kept pushing the burning coals under the bed, and pierced him with their forks from above. Then Lawrence said, "O you unblessed, do you not understand that your burning coals cause no heat to my body, but rather cooling?" He then again with the most beautiful countenance said, "Savior Christ, I thank you for strengthening me." He then looked toward the emperor, saying, "Look, wretch, you have roasted one side of my body, now turn the other and eat." He then said again, "Savior Christ, I thank you with inward heart that I may go into your kingdom." And with these words he gave up his spirit, and with such martyrdom went to the kingdom on high, in which he dwells with God through all eternity. The cruel emperor then left the holy body on the iron griddle, and hastened with his high reeve to the Tiberian palace. 11

Then on this present day Hippolytus buried the holy body with great reverence in the burial plot of the widow Quiriaca. Indeed, at the grave there kept watch a great many Christians with great lamentation. The holy priest Justin celebrated Mass and gave the Eucharist to them all. After this Hippolytus returned to his home, and with God's peace 12

Godes sibbe his hywan gecyste and hi ealle gehuslode. Þa
færlice, mid ðam ðe he gesæt, comon ðæs caseres cempan
and hine gelæhton, and to ðam cwellere gelæddon. Hine befran ða Decius mid smercigendum muðe, "Hwæt la, eart ðu
to dry awend, forðan ðe ðu bebyrigdest Laurentium?" He
andwyrde, "Þæt ic dyde na swa swa dry, ac swa swa Cristen."
Decius ða yrsigende het mid stanum his muð cnucian, and
hine unscrydan, and cwæð, "La hu, nære ðu geornful big-
genga ura goda? and nu ðu eart swa stunt geworden þæt
furðon þe ne sceamað ðinre næcednysse." Ypolitus andwyrde, "Ic wæs stunt, and ic eom nu wis and Cristen. Þurh
nytenysse ic gelyfde on þæt gedwyld þe ðu gelyfst." Decius
cwæð, "Geoffra ðam godum ðy læs ðe ðu þurh tintrega
forwurðe swa swa Laurentius." He andwyrde, "Eala gif
ic moste ðam eadigan Laurentium geefenlæcan!" Decius
cwæð, "Astreccað hine swa nacodne, and mid stiðum saglum
beataþ." Þa ða he langlice gebeaten wæs, þa ðancode he
Gode. Decius cwæð, "Ypolitus gebysmrað eowre stengas —
swingað hine mid gepiledum swipum." Hi ða swa dydon, oð
þæt hi ateorodon. Ypolitus clypode mid hluddre stemne,
"Ic eom Cristen." Eornostlice se reða casere, ða ða he ne
mihte mid nanum pinungum hine geweman fram Cristes geleafan, ða het he his heahgerefan þæt he mid wælhreawum
deaðe hine acwellan sceolde.

13   On ðam ylcan dæge asmeade Valerianus his æhta, and
gemette nygontyne wera and wifa his hiwisces ðe wæron æt
ðæs eadigan Laurenties handum gefullode. To ðam cwæð
Valerianus, "Sceawiað eowre ylde, and beorgað eowrum
feore, ðy læs ðe ge samod losian mid eowrum hlaforde Ypolite." Hi ða anmodlice andwyrdon, "We wilniað mid urum
hlaforde clænlice sweltan, swiðor ðonne unclænlice mid

kissed his family and gave them all the Eucharist. Then suddenly, while he was sitting, the emperor's soldiers came and seized him, and led him to the executioner. Decius then asked him with a smirking mouth, "What, are you turned into a magician, since you have buried Lawrence?" He answered, "I did that not as a magician, but as a Christian." Decius then angrily ordered his mouth struck with stones, and for him to be stripped, and said, "Lo, were you not a diligent worshipper of our gods? and now you have become so foolish that you are not even ashamed of your nakedness." Hippolytus answered, "I was foolish, and now I am wise and a Christian. Through ignorance I believed in the error you believe." Decius said, "Offer sacrifice to the gods, lest you perish by torments like Lawrence." He answered, "Oh, if I might imitate the blessed Lawrence!" Decius said, "Stretch him out naked, and beat him with strong clubs." When he had been beaten for a long time, he thanked God. Decius said, "Hippolytus mocks your cudgels—scourge him with spiked whips." They then did so, until they were worn out. Hippolytus cried with a loud voice, "I am a Christian." So the fierce emperor, when he could not lure him from faith in Christ by any torments, commanded his high reeve to kill him by a cruel death.

On the same day Valerianus looked into his property, and found nineteen men and women of his household who had been baptized at the hands of the blessed Lawrence. To them Valerianus said, "Consider your age, and have regard for your life, lest you perish together with your lord Hippolytus." They answered unanimously, "We want to die purely with our lord, rather than to live impurely with you." 13

eow lybban." Þa wearð Valerianus ðearle gehathyrt, and het lædan Ypolitum of ðære ceastre mid his hiwum. Ða se eadiga Ypolitus gehyrte his hired, and cwæð, "Mine gebroðra, ne beo ge dreorige ne afyrhte, forðan ðe ic and ge habbað ænne Hlaford, God ælmihtigne." Soðlice Valerianus het beheafdian on Ypolitus gesihðe ealle his hiwan, and hine sylfne het tigan be ðam fotum to ungetemedra horsa swuran, and swa teon geond ðornas and bremelas; and he ða mid þam tige his gast ageaf on ðam ðreotteoðan dæge þises monðes. On ðære ylcan nihte gegaderode se halga Iustinus heora ealra lic and bebyrigde.

14   Eornostlice æfter ðæra halgena ðrowunge ferde Decius on gyldenum cræte and Valerianus samod to heora hæðenum gylde, þæt hi ða Cristenan to heora manfullum offrungum geðreatodon. Þa wearð Decius færlice mid feondlicum gaste awed, and hrymde, "Eala ðu Ypolite, hwider tihst ðu me, gebundenne mid scearpum racenteagum?" Valerianus eac awed hrymde, "Eala ðu Laurentius, unsoftlice tihst ðu me, gebundenne mid byrnendum racenteagum!" And he ðærrihte swealt. Witodlice Decius egeslice awedde, and binnon ðrym dagum mid deoflicre stemne singallice hrymde, "Ic halsige ðe, Laurentius, ablin hwæthwega ðæra tintregena." Hwæt ða la asprang micel heofung and sarlic wop on ðam hame, and ðæs caseres wif het ut alædan ealle ða Cristenan ðe on cwearterne wæron, and Decius on ðam ðriddan dæge mid micclum tintregum gewat.

15   Soðlice seo cwen Triphonia gesohte ðæs halgan sacerdes fet Iustines mid biterum tearum, and hire dohtor Cyrilla samod, biddende þæs halgan fulluhtes. Iustinus ða mid micelre blisse hi underfeng, and him bebead seofon dagena fæsten, and hi syððan mid þam halgum fulluhtbæðe fram

528

Then Valerianus was greatly enraged, and ordered Hippolytus to be led from the city with his household. The blessed
Hippolytus then cheered his household, and said, "My
brothers, do not be sad or afraid, for I and you have one
Lord, God almighty." Truly Valerianus ordered all his household to be beheaded in the sight of Hippolytus, and himself
he ordered to be tied by the feet to the necks of wild horses,
and so dragged through thorns and brambles; with that
binding he gave up his spirit on the thirteenth day of this
month. On the same night the holy Justin gathered all their
bodies and buried them.

After the passion of those saints Decius went in a golden   14
chariot together with Valerianus to their heathen temple,
that they might force the Christians to their wicked offerings. Then Decius suddenly became mad with a devilish
spirit, and cried, "Alas, Hippolytus, where do you drag
me, bound with sharp chains?" Valerianus, also mad, cried,
"Alas, Lawrence, roughly you drag me, bound with burning
chains!" And he died right there. But Decius became horri-
bly mad, and for three days continually cried out with a
fiendish voice, "I beseech you, Lawrence, cease those torments a little." At this, great lamentation and painful weeping arose in his home, and the emperor's wife ordered all the
Christians who were in prison to be led out, and on the third
day, Decius in great torments departed.

Truly the queen Tryphonia, together with her daughter   15
Cyrilla, sought the feet of the holy priest Justin with bitter
tears, praying for holy baptism. Justin then with great joy
received them, and ordered them to fast for seven days, and
afterward washed them from all their sins by the holy bath

eallum heora mandædum aðwoh. Þa ða þæs caseres ðegnas gehyrdon þæt seo cwen Triphonia and Decius dohtor Cyrilla to Cristes geleafan and to ðam halwendum fulluhte gebogene wæron, hi ða mid heora wifum gesohton ðone halgan sacerd, and bædon miltsunge and fulluhtes. Se eadiga Iustinus, ðisum gewordenum, rædde wið þa Cristenan hwæne hi to bisceope ceosan woldon on Sixtes setle. Hi ða anmodlice sumne arwurðfulne wer gecuron ðæs nama wæs Dionisius, ðone gehadode se bisceop Maximus, of ðære byrig Ostiensis, to ðam Romaniscum bisceopsetle mid wurðmynte.

16   Uton nu biddan mid eadmodre stemne ðone halgan Godes cyðere Laurentium, þæs freolstid geswutelað þes andwerda dæg ealre geleaffulre gelaðunge þæt he us ðingige wið ðone heofenlican cyning, for ðæs naman he ðrowode mid cenum mode menigfealde tintregu, mid ðam he orsorhlice on ecnysse wuldrað. Amen.

30

XVIII KALENDAS SEPTEMBRIS

Assumptio sanctae Mariae virginis

Hieronimus se halga sacerd awrat ænne pistol be forðsiðe þære eadigan Marian, Godes cennestran, to sumum halgan mædene hyre nama wæs Eustochium, and to hyre meder

of baptism. When the emperor's officers heard that the queen Tryphonia and the daughter of Decius, Cyrilla, had submitted to the faith of Christ and to the saving baptism, they with their wives sought the holy priest, and prayed for mercy and baptism. When these things were done, the blessed Justin took counsel with the Christians whom they would choose for bishop in the chair of Sixtus. They then unanimously chose a venerable man whose name was Dionysius, whom the bishop Maximus, of the city of Ostia, consecrated to the Roman episcopal see with honor.

Let us now pray with humble voice to the holy martyr of God, Lawrence, whose feast day on this present day makes known to all the faithful Church that he might intercede for us with the heavenly king, for whose name he suffered with bold mind many torments, and with whom, free from care, he glories in eternity. Amen. 16

30

Assumption of Mary

AUGUST 15

The Assumption of the Blessed Virgin Mary

The holy priest Jerome wrote a letter on the death of the blessed Mary, mother of God, to a holy virgin named Eustochium and her mother Paula, who was a consecrated

Paulam, seo wæs gehalgod wydewe. To þysum twam wifmannum awrat se ylca Hieronimus menigfealde trahtbec,
forþan ðe hi wæron haliges lifes men, and swiðe gecneordlæ-
cende on boclicum smeagungum. Þes Hieronimus wæs halig
sacerd, and getogen on Hebreiscum gereorde and on Greciscum and on Ledenum fulfremedlice; and he awende ure
Bibliothecan of Hebreiscum bocum to Leden spræce. He is
se fyrmesta wealhstod betwux Hebreiscum, and Grecum,
and Ledenwarum. Twa and hundseofontig boca þære ealdan
æ and þære niwan he awende on Leden, to anre Bibliothecan, buton oðrum menigfealdum trahtbocum ðe he mid
gecneordum andgite deopþancollice asmeade. Ða æt nextan
he dihte þisne pistol to þære halgan wydewan Paulam and to
þam Godes mædene Eustochium, hyre dehter, and to eallum þam mædenlicum werode þe him mid drohtnigende
wæron, þus cweðende:

2   "Witodlice ge neadiað me þæt ic eow recce hu seo eadige
Maria on ðisum dæigþerlicum dæge to heofonlicere wununge genumen wæs, þæt eower mædenlica heap hæbbe þas
lac Ledenre spræce, hu ðes mæra freolsdæig geond æighwyl-
ces geares ymbrene beo aspend mid heofonlicum lofe and
mid gastlicere blisse gemærsode sy, þy læs ðe eow on hand
becume seo lease gesetnyss þe ðurh gedwolmannum wide
tosawen is, and ge ðonne þa gehiwedan leasunge for soðre
race underfoð.

3   "Soðlice fram anginne þæs halgan godspelles ge leorn-
odon hu se heahengel Gabrihel þam eadigan mædene Marian þæs heofonlican æþelinges acennednysse gecydde, and
þæs hælendes wundra, and þære gesæligan cennestran
þenunge, and hyre lifes dæda on þam feower godspellicum
bocum ge swutellice oncneowon. Iohannes se godspellere

widow. Jerome wrote several treatises to these two women, because they were people of holy life, and very diligent in the study of books. This Jerome was a holy priest, perfectly learned in the Hebrew language and in Greek and Latin; he translated our Bible from Hebrew books into the Latin language. He is the foremost interpreter among the Hebrews, Greeks, and Latins. He translated seventy-two books of the old and new law into Latin, into one Bible, apart from many other treatises that he profoundly devised with diligent understanding. Finally, he composed this letter to the holy widow Paula and the virgin of God Eustochium, her daughter, and to all the company of virgins who were living with them, saying:

"You have urged me to tell you how on this present day 2 the blessed Mary was taken to the heavenly dwelling, so that your company of virgins may have this gift in the Latin language, how this great feast day should be spent in heavenly praise and celebrated with spiritual joy in the course of every year, lest the false account which has been widely disseminated by heretics should fall into your hands, and you take those feigned lies for a true account.

"Truly from the beginning of the holy gospel you have 3 learned how the archangel Gabriel announced the birth of the heavenly prince to the blessed virgin Mary, and you have clearly known the miracles of the savior, and the blessed mother's services, and the deeds of her life, from the four books of the gospels. John the Evangelist wrote that at

awrat on Cristes þrowunge þæt he sylf and Maria stodon
mid dreorigum mode wið ðære halgan rode þe se hælend on
gefæstnod wæs. Ða cwæð he to his agenre meder, 'Þu
fæmne, efne her is þin sunu.' Eft he cwæð to Iohanne, 'Loca
nu, her stent þin modor.' Syððan, of ðam dæge, hæfde se
godspellere Iohannes gymene þære halgan Marian, and mid
carefulre þenunge swa swa agenre meder gehyrsumode.

4   "Drihten þurh his arfæstnysse betæhte þæt eadige
mæden his cennestran þam clænan men Iohanne, se ðe on
clænum mæigðhade symle wunode. And he forþy synderlice
þam Drihtne leof wæs, to þan swiðe þæt he him þone deorwurðan maðm, ealles middangeardes cwene, betæcan wolde;
gewislice þæt hire clænesta mæigðhad þam clænan men ge-
þeod wære mid gecwemre geferrædene on wynsumre drohtnunge. On him bam wæs an miht ansundes mæigðhades, ac
oþer intinga on Marian: on hire is wæstmbære mæigðhad,
swa swa on nanum oðrum. Nis on nanum oþrum men
mæigðhad gif þær bið wæstmbærnys, ne wæstmbærnys gif
þær bið ansund mæigðhad. Nu is forþi gehalgod æigðer ge
Marian mæigðhad ge hyre wæstmbærnys þurh ða godcundlican acennednysse, and heo ealle oðre oferstihð on mæigðhade and on wæstmbærnysse. Ðeahhwæþere, þeah heo
synderlice Iohannes gymene betæht wære, hwæþere heo
drohtnode gemænelice, æfter Cristes upstige, mid ðam
apostolicum werode, infarende and utfarende betwux him,
and hi ealle mid micelre arwurðnysse and lufe hire þenodon.
And heo him cuðlice ealle þing ymbe Cristes menniscnysse
gewissode, forþan ðe heo fram frymðe gewislice þurh ðone
Halgan Gast hi ealle geleornode, and mid agenre gesihðe geseah, þeah ðe þa apostoli þurh ðone ylcan Gast ealle þing
undergeaton, and on ealre soðfæstnysse gelærede wurdon.

Christ's passion he himself and Mary stood with sorrowing mind at the holy cross on which the savior was fastened. Then he said to his own mother, 'Woman, behold, here is your son.' Then he said to John, 'Look now, here stands your mother.' Afterward, from that day, the Evangelist John took care of the holy Mary, and with diligent service obeyed her like his own mother.

"The Lord in his compassion entrusted the blessed virgin 4
his mother to the chaste man John, who had always lived in chaste virginity. And for that reason he was especially dear to the Lord, so much so that he would entrust to him that precious treasure, the queen of the whole world; surely so that her most chaste virginity might be associated with that chaste man in befitting fellowship in a joyful way of life. In both of them was one virtue of unbroken virginity, but a second attribute in Mary: in her, as in no other, is fruitful virginity. In no other person is there virginity if there is fruitfulness, nor fruitfulness if there is perfect virginity. Therefore now both Mary's virginity and her fruitfulness are consecrated through the divine birth, and she excels all others in virginity and in fruitfulness. Nevertheless, though she was especially entrusted to John's care, yet after Christ's ascension she lived in common with the company of the apostles, going in and out among them, and they all served her with great piety and love. And she fully made known to them all things concerning Christ's humanity, for she had from the beginning truly learned them all through the Holy Spirit, and seen them with her own sight, though the apostles understood all things through the same Spirit, and were

Se heahengel Gabrihel hi ungewemmede geheold, and heo
wunode on Iohannes and on ealra þæra apostola gymene, on
þære heofenlican scole, embe Godes æ smeagende, oððæt
God on þysum dæge hi genam to þam heofonlican þrymsetle and hi ofer engla weredum geufrode.

5   "Nis geræd on nanre bec nan swutelre gewissung be hire
geendunge, buton þæt heo nu todæig wuldorfullice of þam
lichaman gewat. Hyre byrigen is swutol eallum onlociendum
oð þysne andweardan dæg, on middan þære dene Iosaphat.
Seo dene is betwux þære dune Sion and þam munte Olifeti,
and seo byrigen is æteowed open and emtig, and þær onup-
pon on hire wurðmynte is aræred mære cyrce, mid wunder-
licum stangeweorce. Nis nanum deadlicum men cuð hu
oððe on hwilcere tide hyre halga lichama þanon gebroden
wære, oððe hwider he ahafen sy, oððe hwæðer heo of deaðe
arise; cwædon þeah gehwylce lareowas þæt hyre Sunu, se þe
on þam ðriddan dæge mihtilice of deaðe aras, þæt he eac his
moder lichaman of deaðe arærde, and mid undeadlicum
wuldre on heofenan rice gelogode. Eac swa gelice forwel
menige lareowas on heora bocum setton be ðam geedcuce-
dum mannum þe mid Criste of deaðe arison, þæt hi ecelice
arærede sind. Witodlice hi andetton þæt ða aræredan menn
næron soðfæste gewitan Cristes æristes buton hi wæron
ecelice arærede. Ne wiðcweþe we be þære eadigan Marian
þa ecan æriste, þeah, for wærscipe gehealdenum geleafan, us
gedafenað þæt we hit wenon swiþor þonne we unrædlice hit
geseþan þæt ðe is uncuð buton ælcere fræcednysse.

6   "We rædað gehwær on bocum þæt forwel oft englas comon to godra manna forðsiþe, and mid gastlicum lofsangum
heora sawla to heofenum gelæddon. And, þæt gyt swutelicor
is, men gehyrdon on þam forðsiðe wæpmanna sang and

instructed in all truth. The archangel Gabriel kept her un-
corrupted, and she continued in the care of John and of all
the apostles in the heavenly company, meditating on God's
law, until on this day God took her to the heavenly throne
and exalted her above the hosts of angels.

"There is not read in any book any clearer information 5
about her end, except that on this day she gloriously departed from the body. Her tomb is visible to all onlookers to
this present day, in the middle of the valley of Jehoshaphat.
The valley is between Mount Sion and the Mount of Olives,
and the tomb appears open and empty, and above it a large
church is raised in her honor, with wondrous stonework. It
is not known to any mortal how or at what time her holy
body was brought there, or from where it has been brought,
or whether she arose from death; yet some teachers say that
her Son, who on the third day mightily arose from death,
also raised his mother's body from death, and placed it with
immortal glory in the kingdom of heaven. In the same way
very many teachers have put down in their books that the
revived people who arose from death with Christ are raised
eternally. Indeed, they profess that those raised people
would not have been true witnesses of Christ's resurrection
unless they had been raised eternally. We do not deny the
eternal resurrection of the blessed Mary, though as a cau-
tion, preserving our belief, it is fitting that we rather hope it
than that we rashly assert what is unknown without any
danger.

"We read in many places in books that very often angels 6
came at the departure of good people, and with spiritual
hymns led their souls to heaven. And, what is yet more certain, at their departure people have heard the song of men

wimmanna sang, mid micclum leohte and swetum breðe; on
þam is cuð þæt ða halgan menn þe to Godes rice þurh godum geearnungum becomon, þæt hi on oðra manna forðsiþe
heora sawla underfoð and mid micelre blisse to reste gelædað. Nu gif se hælend swilcne wurðmynt on his halgena
forðsiðe oft geswutelode, and heora gastas mid heofenlicum
lofsange to him gefeccan het, hu micele swiðor wenst ðu þæt
he nu todæig þæt heofonlice werod togeanes his agenre
meder sendan wolde, þæt hi mid ormætum leohte and unasecgendlicum lofsangum hi to þam þrymsetle gelæddon þe
hire gegearcod wæs fram frymðe middangeardes?

7   "Nis nan twynung þæt eall heofonlic þrym þa mid una-
secgendlicere blisse hire tocymes fæignian wolde. Soðlice
eac we gelyfað þæt Drihten sylf hire togeanes come, and
wynsumlice mid gefean to him on his þrymsetle hi gesette;
witodlice he wolde gefyllan þurh hine sylfne þæt he on his æ
bebead, þus cweþende, 'Arwurða ðinne fæder and þine
moder.' He is his agen gewita þæt he his Fæder gearwurþode,
swa swa he cwæð to þam Iudeiscum, 'Ic arwurðie minne
Fæder, and ge unarwurðiað me.' On his menniscnysse he
arwurðode his moder þa ða he wæs, swa swa þæt halige
godspel seigð, hire underþeod on his geogoðhade. Micele
swiþor is to gelyfenne þæt he his modor mid unasecgend-
licere arwurðnysse on his rice gewurþode, þa ða he wolde
æfter þære menniscnysse on ðysum life hyre gehyrsumian.

8   "Ðes symbeldæig oferstihð unwiðmetenlice ealra oþra
halgena mæssedagas, swa micclum swa þis halige mæden,
Godes modor, is unwiðmetenlic eallum oþrum mædenum.
Ðes freolsdæig is us gearlic, ac he is heofonwarum singallic.
Be þysre heofonlican cwene upstige wundrade se Halga
Gast on lofsangum, þus befrinende, 'Hwæt is þeos þe her

and women, with a great light and sweet odor; by this is known that those holy ones who have come to God's kingdom through good merits receive the souls of others at their departure and lead them to rest with great joy. Now, if the savior has often shown such honor at the death of his saints, and has commanded their souls to be brought to him with heavenly hymns, how much more do you think he would send the heavenly host to meet his own mother today, so that they might lead her with great light and inexpressible hymns to the throne which was prepared for her from the beginning of the world?

"There is no doubt that all the heavenly host would rejoice with inexpressible bliss at her coming. Truly we also believe that the Lord himself came to meet her, and joyously with delight placed her beside him on his throne; indeed, he would fulfill in himself what he had commanded in his law, saying, 'Honor your father and your mother.' He is his own witness that he honored his Father, as he said to the Jews, 'I honor my Father, and you dishonor me.' In his human state he honored his mother when he was obedient to her in his youth, as the holy gospel says. It is even more believable that he honored his mother with inexpressible veneration in his kingdom, when he would obey her in this life in his human nature. 7

"This festival incomparably exceeds the Mass days of all other saints, as much as this holy virgin, God's mother, is incomparable with all other virgins. This feast day is annual for us, but for the inhabitants of heaven it is perpetual. At the ascension of this heavenly queen, the Holy Spirit wondered in hymns, asking, 'What is this that here ascends like 8

astihð swilce arisende dæigrima, swa wlitig swa mona, swa
gecoren swa sunne, and swa egeslic swa fyrdtruma?' Se Halga
Gast wundrode, forþan ðe he dyde þæt eal heofonwaru wundrode þisre fæmnan upfæreldes. Maria is wlitigre þonne se
mona forðan þe heo scinð buton æteorunge hire beorhtnysse. Heo is gecoren swa swa sunne mid leoman healicra
mihta, forþan ðe Drihten, se ðe is rihtwisnysse sunne, hi geceas him to cennestran. Hire fær is wiðmeten fyrdlicum truman, forþan ðe heo wæs mid halgum mægnum ymbtrymed
and mid engla þreatum.

9   "Be þissere heofonlican cwene is gecweden gyt þurh þone
ylcan Godes Gast, he cwæð, 'Ic geseah þa wlitegan swilce
culfran astigende ofer streamlicum riðum, and unasecgendlic bræð stemde of hire gyrlum; and, swa swa on lengctenlicere tide, rosena blostman and lilian hi ymtrymedon.'
Ðæra rosena blostman getacniað mid heora readnysse martyrdom, and þa lilian mid heora hwitnysse getacniað þa
scinendan clænnysse ansundes mæigðhades. Ealle þa gecorenan þe Gode geþugon þurh martyrdom oððe þurh clænnysse, ealle hi gesiðodon mid þære eadigan cwene; forþan ðe
heo sylf is æigðer ge martyr ge mæden. Heo is swa wlitig swa
culfre, forþan ðe heo lufode þa bilewitnysse, þe se Halga
Gast getacnode þa ða he wæs gesewen on culfran gelicnysse
ofer Criste on his fulluhte. Oþre martyras on heora lichaman þrowodon martyrdom for Cristes geleafan, ac seo
eadige Maria næs na lichamlice gemartyrod, ac hire sawul
wæs swiðe geangsumod mid micelre þrowunge þa ða heo
stod dreorig foran ongean Cristes rode and hire leofe cild
geseah mid isenum næglum on heardum treowe gefæstnod.
Nu is heo mare þonne martyr, forþan ðe heo þrowade þone
martyrdom on hire sawle þe oþre martyras þrowodon on

the rising morning dew, as beautiful as the moon, as chosen as the sun, and as terrible as a martial troop?' The Holy Spirit wondered, for he made all heaven's inhabitants wonder at the ascension of this woman. Mary is more beautiful than the moon because she shines without decrease of her brightness. She is as chosen as the sun with beams of elevated virtues, because the Lord, who is the sun of righteousness, chose her for his mother. Her course is compared to a martial troop, for she was surrounded with heavenly powers and with companies of angels.

"Of this heavenly queen the same Spirit of God spoke 9 further when he said, 'I saw the beautiful one rising like a dove above the streaming rivers, and an inexpressible fragrance exhaled from her garments; and blossoms of roses and lilies surrounded her as in springtime.' The blossoms of roses signify by their redness martyrdom, and the lilies by their whiteness signify the shining purity of perfect virginity. All the chosen who have risen to God through martyrdom or through chastity journeyed with the blessed queen; for she herself is both martyr and virgin. She is as beautiful as a dove, for she loved meekness, which the Holy Spirit signified when he was seen in the likeness of a dove over Christ at his baptism. Other martyrs suffered martyrdom in their bodies for Christ's faith, but the blessed Mary was not bodily martyred, but her soul was sorely afflicted with great suffering when she stood sad before Christ's cross and saw her dear child fastened with iron nails on the hard tree. Now she is more than a martyr, for she suffered that martyrdom in her soul which other martyrs suffered in their

heora lichaman. Heo lufode Crist ofer ealle oþre men, and forþy wæs eac hire sarnys be him toforan oþra manna, and heo dyde his deað hire agenne deað, forþan ðe his þrowung swa swa swurd þurhferde hire sawle.

10 "Nis heo nanes haliges mæignes bedæled, ne nanes wlites, ne nanre beorhtnysse; and forðy heo wæs ymbtrymed mid rosam and lilian, þæt hyre mihta wæron mid mihtum underwriðode, and hyre fægernys mid clænnysse wlite wære geyht. Godes gecorenan scinað on heofonlicum wuldre ælc be his geþingcðum; nu is geleaflic ðæt seo eadige cwen mid swa micclum wuldre and beorhtnysse oðre oferstige, swa micclum swa hire geðincðu oðra halgena unwiðmetenlice sind. Drihten cwæð ær his upstige þæt on his Fæder huse sindon fela wununga; soðlice we gelyfað þæt he nu todæg þa wynsumestan wununge his leofan meder forgeafe. Godes gecorenra wuldor is gemetegod be heora geearnungum, and nis hwæðere nan ceorung ne anda on heora ænigum, ac hi ealle wuniað on soðre lufe and healicere sibbe, and ælc blissað on oðres geðincðum swa swa on his agenum.

11 "Ic bidde eow, blissiað on ðyssere freolstide. Witodlice nu todæg þæt wuldorfulle mæden heofonas astah, þæt heo, unasecgendlice mid Criste ahafen, on ecnysse rixige. Seo heofenlice cwen wearð todæg generod fram ðyssere manfullan worulde. Eft ic cweðe fægniað, forðan ðe heo becom orsorhlice to ðam heofonlicum botle. Blissige eal middangeard, forðan ðe nu todæg us eallum is ðurh hire geearnunga hæl geyht. Þurh ure ealdan modor Euan us wearð heofonan rices geat belocen, and eft ðurh Marian hit is us geopenod, þurh þæt heo sylf nu todæg wuldorfullice inn ferde.

12 "God ðurh his witegan us bebead þæt we sceolon hine herian and mærsian on his halgum, on ðam he is wundorlic.

542

bodies. She loved Christ above all others, and therefore her pain for him was also greater than others', and she made his death her own death, for his suffering pierced her soul like a sword.

"She is not lacking in any holy virtue, nor any beauty, nor any brightness; and therefore she was surrounded with roses and lilies, that her virtues might be supported by virtues, and her fairness might be increased by the beauty of chastity. God's chosen ones shine in heavenly glory, each according to his merits; it is therefore believable that the blessed queen with so much glory and brightness excels others, as much as her merits are incomparable with those of the other saints. The Lord said before his ascension that in his Father's house are many dwellings; truly we believe that today he has given his mother the most joyful dwelling. The glory of God's chosen is measured by their merits, and yet there is no murmuring or envy in any of them, but they all dwell in true love and profound peace, and each rejoices in another's honors as in his own. 10

"I pray you, rejoice in this feast day. Truly today that glorious virgin ascended to heaven, so that she, inexpressibly exalted with Christ, may reign forever. Today the heavenly queen was rescued from this wicked world. Again I say rejoice, for she has gone without sorrow to the heavenly mansion. Let all the earth be glad, for today, through her merits, salvation is increased to us all. Through our old mother Eve the gate of heaven's kingdom was closed against us, and through Mary it is opened to us again, through which she herself has this day gloriously entered. 11

"Through his prophets God has commanded us to praise and magnify him in his saints, in whom he is wonderful. It is 12

Micele swiðor gedafenað þæt we hine, on ðisre mæran freolstide his eadigan meder, mid lofsangum and wurðfullum
herungum wurðian sceolon, forðan ðe untwylice eal hire
wurðmynt is Godes herung. Uton nu forði mid ealre estful-
nysse ures modes ðas mæran freolstide wurðian, forðan ðe
þæt siðfæt ure hæle is on lofsangum ures Drihtnes. Þa ðe on
mæigðhade wuniað blission hi, forðan ðe hi geearnodon þæt
beon þæt hi heriað; habbon hi hoge þæt hi syn swilce þæt hi
wurðfullice herigan magon. Þa ðe on clænan wudewanhade
sind herion hi and arwurðion, forðan ðe swutol is þæt hi ne
magon beon clæne buton ðurh Cristes gife, seo ðe wæs fulfremedlice on Marian, ðe hi herigað. Herigan eac and
wurðian ða ðe on sinscipe wuniað, forðan ðe ðanon flewð
eallum mildheortnys and gifu þæt hi herigan magon. Gif
hwa synful sy, he andette, and nalæs herige, ðeah ðe ne beo
wlitig lof on ðæs synfullan muðe; hwæðere ne geswice he
ðære herunge, forðan ðe ðanon him is behaten forgyfenys."

13   Þes pistol is swiðe menigfeald us to gereccenne, and eow
swiðe deop to gehyrenne. Nu ne onhagað us na swiðor be
ðam to sprecenne, ac we wyllað sume oðre trimminge be
ðære mæran Godes meder gereccan, to eowre gebetrunge.
Soðlice Maria is se mæsta frofer and fultum Cristenra
manna, þæt is forwel oft geswutelod, swa swa we on bocum
rædað. Sum man wæs mid drycræfte bepæht swa þæt he
Criste wiðsoc, and wrat his handgewrit þam awyrgedan
deofle, and him mannrædene befæste. His nama wæs Theophilus. He ða eft syððan hine beðohte, and ða hellican pinunge on his mode weolc, and ferde ða to sumere cyrcan þe
wæs to lofe ðære eadigan Marian gehalgod, and ðær binnan
swa lange mid wope and fæstenum hire fultumes and ðingunge bæd oð þæt heo sylf mid micclum wuldre him to com,

even more fitting that on this great feast of his blessed
mother, we should honor him with hymns and honorable
praises, for undoubtedly all honor to her is praise of God.
Let us now, therefore, with all the devotion of our mind
honor this great feast day, for the path of our salvation is in
hymns to our Lord. Let those who dwell in virginity rejoice,
for they have attained to be that which they praise; let them
take care that they be such that they may praise worthily.
Let those who are in pure widowhood praise and honor her,
for it is clear that they cannot be pure except through
Christ's grace, which was perfect in Mary, whom they praise.
Let those who are in wedlock also praise and honor her, for
mercy and grace flow from there to all so that they may
praise her. If anyone is sinful, let him confess, and nonethe-
less praise, though praise is not beautiful in the mouth of
the sinful; yet let him not cease from praise, for from it forgiveness is promised to him."

This letter is very complex for us to explain, and very 13
deep for you to hear. It does not now seem good to us to
speak more about it, but we will relate for your improvement some other edifying matter concerning the great
mother of God. Truly Mary is the greatest comfort and support of Christians, which is very often shown, as we read in
books. A certain person was so deluded by magic that he
denied Christ, and wrote a contract with the accursed devil,
and entered into a pact with him. His name was Theophilus.
He afterward came to his senses, and turned over in his
mind the torment of hell, and went to a church that was
consecrated to the praise of the blessed Mary, and in there
prayed so long with weeping and fasts for her aid and intercession that she herself came to him with great glory, and

and cwæð þæt heo him geðingod hæfde wið þone heofenlican deman, hire agenne Sunu.

14   We wyllað eac eow gereccan be geendunge ðæs arleasan
Godes wiðersacan Iulianes. Sum halig biscop wæs Basilius
gehaten, se leornode on anre scole and se ylca Iulianus
samod. Þa gelamp hit swa þæt Basilius wearð to biscope
gecoren to anre byrig ðe is gehaten Cappadocia, and Iulianus to casere, ðeah ðe he æror to preoste bescoren wære.
Iulianus ða ongann to lufigenne hæðengyld, and his cristendome wiðsoc, and mid eallum mode hæðenscipe beeode,
and his leode to ðan ylcan genydde. Þa æt suman cyrre
tengde he to fyrde ongean Perscisne leodscipe, and gemette
ðone biscop, and cwæð him to, "Eala ðu Basili, nu ic hæbbe
ðe oferðogen on uðwitegunge." Se biscop him andwyrde,
"God forgeafe þæt ðu uðwitegunge beeodest," and he mid
þam worde him bead swylce lac swa he sylf breac, þæt wæron
ðry berene hlafas, for bletsunge. Þa het se wiðersaca onfon
ðæra hlafa, and agifan ðam biscope togeanes gærs, and
cwæð, "He bead us nytena fodan, underfo he gærs to leanes."
Basilius underfeng þæt gærs, ðus cweðende, "Eala ðu casere,
soðlice we budon ðe ðæs ðe we sylfe brucað, and ðu us seald-
est to edleane ungesceadwisra nytena andlyfene, na us to fodan ac to hospe." Se Godes wiðersaca hine ða gehathyrte
and cwæð, "Þonne ic fram fyrde gecyrre ic towurpe ðas burh
and hi gesmeðige, and to yrðlande awende, swa þæt heo
bið cornbære swiðor þonne mannbære. Nis me uncuð þin
dyrstignys and ðissere burhware—ðe ðurh ðine tihtinge ða
anlicnysse ðe ic arærde and me to gebæd, tobræcon and
towurpon." And he mid ðisum wordum ferde to Persciscum
earde.

15   Hwæt ða Basilius cydde his ceastergewarum ðæs reðan

546

said that she had interceded for him with the heavenly judge, her own Son.

We will also tell you about the end of the impious adversary of God, Julian. There was a certain holy bishop named Basil, who had studied in a school together with this same Julian. It happened that Basil was chosen to be bishop of a city called Cappadocia, and Julian to be emperor, though he earlier had been tonsured to be a priest. Julian then began to love idolatry, and renounced his Christianity, and practiced heathenism with all his mind, and compelled his people to do the same. Then, at a certain time he went on an expedition against the Persian nation, and met the bishop, and said to him, "O Basil, I have now exceeded you in philosophy." The bishop answered him, "Would that God has granted you to practice philosophy," and with that word he offered him such a gift as he partook of himself, that was three barley loaves, for a blessing. Then the apostate commanded the loaves to be seized, and to give grass to the bishop in return, and said, "He has offered us the food of beasts, let him receive grass in reward." Basil received the grass, saying, "O emperor, truly we have offered you what we ourselves partake of, and you have given us in return the food of irrational beasts, not for food but as an insult." The adversary of God then grew angry and said, "When I return from the expedition I will overthrow this city and level it, and turn it to farmland, so that it shall produce grain rather than people. Your audacity and that of these citizens is not unknown to me—at your urging they broke and cast down the image which I had raised and prayed to." With these words he went to the Persian territory.

At this Basil made known to his fellow citizens the cruel 15

caseres ðeowrace, and him selost rædbora wearð, þus
cweðende, "Mine gebroðra, bringað eowre sceattas, and
uton cunnian, gif we magon, ðone reðan wiðersacan on his
geancyrre gegladian." Hi ða mid glædum mode him to
brohton goldes, and seolfres, and deorwurðra gimma ungerime hypan. Se bisceop ða underfeng ða madmas, and bebead his preostum and eallum ðam folce þæt hi heora lac
geoffrodon binnon ðam temple ðe wæs to wurðmynte ðære
eadigan Marian gehalgod, and het hi ðær binnon andbidigan
mid ðreora daga fæstene, þæt se ælmihtiga wealdend, þurh
his moder ðingrædene, towurpe þæs unrihtwisan caseres
andgit. Þa on ðære ðriddan nihte ðæs fæstenes geseah se
bisceop micel heofenlic werod on ælce healfe ðæs temples,
and on middan ðam werode sæt seo heofenlice cwen Maria,
and cwæð to hire ætstandendum, "Gelangiað me ðone martyr Mercurium, þæt he gewende wið ðæs arleasan wiðersacan Iulianes and hine acwelle, se ðe mid toðundenum
mode God minne Sunu forsihð." Se halga cyðere Mercurius
gewæpnod hrædlice com and be hyre hæse ferde. Þa eode se
bisceop into ðære oðre cyrcan, þær se martyr inne læig, and
befran ðone cyrcweard hwær ðæs halgan wæpnu wæron. He
swor þæt he on æfnunge æt his heafde witodlice hi gesawe.
And he ðærrihte wende to Sancta Marian temple and ðam
folce gecydde his gesihðe, and ðæs wælhreowan forwyrd. Þa
eode he eft ongean to ðæs halgan martyres byrgenne and
funde his spere standan mid blode begleddod.

16   Þa æfter ðrim dagum com an þæs caseres ðegna, Libanius
hatte, and gesohte ðæs bisceopes fet, fulluhtes biddende,
and cydde him and ealre ðære buruhware þæs arleasan
Iulianes deað. Cwæð þæt seo fyrd wicode wið ða ea Eu-
fraten, and seofon weardsetl wacodon ofer ðone casere. Þa

emperor's threat, and was a most excellent counselor to them, saying, "My brothers, bring your treasures, and let us try, if we can, to appease the cruel apostate on his return." Then with glad mind they brought him gold, and silver, and precious gems in an immense heap. The bishop then took the treasures, and commanded his priests and all the people to offer their gifts within the temple that was consecrated to the honor of the blessed Mary, and ordered them to wait inside with a fast of three days so that the almighty ruler, through his mother's intercession, might overthrow the unrighteous emperor's intention. Then on the third night of the fast the bishop saw a great heavenly host on each side of the temple, and in the middle of the host sat the heavenly queen Mary, and she said to her attendants, "Bring me the martyr Mercurius, that he may go against the impious apostate Julian and slay him, who with a puffed-up mind despises God my Son." Quickly the holy martyr Mercurius came armed and went at her command. The bishop went into the other church, in which the martyr lay, and asked the church-warden where the saint's weapons were. He swore that he had certainly seen them at his head that evening. At once he returned to Saint Mary's temple and made known to the people his vision, and the destruction of the tyrant. He then went again to the holy martyr's tomb and found his spear standing, stained with blood.

Then after three days came one of the emperor's officers 16 called Libanius, and sought the bishop's feet, praying for baptism, and informed him and all the citizens of the death of the impious Julian. He said that the army was encamped on the river Euphrates, and seven sentinels watched over

com ðær stæppende sum uncuð cempa, and hine hetelice
ðurhðyde, and ðærrihte of hyra gesihðum fordwan; and
Iulianus ða mid anðræcum hreame forswealt. Swa wearð seo
burhwaru ahred þurh Sancta Marian wið ðone Godes wiðersacan. Þa bead se bisceop ðam ceastergewarum hyra sceattas, ac hi cwædon þæt hi uðon ðæra laca þam undeadlican
cyninge ðe hi swa mihtelice generede, micele bet ðonne ðam
deadlican cwellere. Se bisceop ðeah nydde þæt folc ðæt hi
ðone ðriddan dæl þæs feos underfengon, and he mid þam
twam dælum þæt mynster gegodode.

17   Gif hwa smeage hu ðis gewurde, þonne secge we þæt ðes
martyr his lif adreah on læwedum hade; ða wearð he ðurh
hæðenra manna ehtnysse for Cristes geleafan gemartyrod,
and Cristene men syððan his halgan lichaman binnon ðam
temple wurðfullice gelogedon, and his wæpna samod. Eft, ða
ða seo halige cwen hine asende swa swa we nu hwene ær sædon, þa ferde his gast swyftlice, and mid lichamlicum wæpne
ðone Godes feond ofstang his weardsetlum onlocigendum.

18   Mine gebroðra ða leofostan, uton clypigan mid singalum
benum to ðære halgan Godes meder, þæt heo us on urum
nydþearfnyssum to hire bearne geðingige. Hit is swiðe geleaflic þæt he hyre miceles ðinges tiðian wylle, se ðe hine
sylfne gemedemode þæt he ðurh hi for middangeardes
alysednysse to menniscum men acenned wurde, se ðe æfre is
God butan anginne, and nu ðurhwunað, on anum hade, soð
man and soð God, a on ecnysse. Swa swa gehwilc man wunað
on sawle and on lichaman an mann, swa is Crist, God and
mann, an hælend, se ðe leofað and rixað mid Fæder and
Halgum Gaste on ealra worulda woruld. Amen.

the emperor. Then an unknown warrior came walking there, violently pierced him through, and immediately vanished from their sight; and Julian then died with a horrible cry. So the citizens were saved through Saint Mary from the adversary of God. Then the bishop offered the citizens their treasures, but they said that they would much rather give those gifts to the immortal king who had so powerfully saved them than to the mortal murderer. The bishop nevertheless insisted that the people take a third part of the money, and with the two parts endowed the monastery.

If anyone wonders how this could happen, we say that 17 this martyr had spent his life as a layman; then for his faith in Christ he was martyred through the persecution of the heathens, and afterward Christians honorably placed his holy body within the temple, together with his weapons. Later, when the holy queen sent him as we said a little before, his spirit went swiftly, and with a physical weapon stabbed the enemy of God while his guards looked on.

My dearest brothers, let us call with constant prayers to 18 the holy mother of God, that she may intercede with her son for us in our need. It is very believable that he will grant much to her, who humbled himself to be born a human being through her for the redemption of the world, who is ever God without beginning, and now remains, in one person, true human and true God, forever in eternity. Just as every person exists in soul and body one person, so is Christ, God and human, one savior, who lives and reigns with the Father and the Holy Spirit for ever and ever. Amen.

31

Passio sancti Bartholomei apostoli

Wyrdwriteras secgað þæt ðry leodscipas sind gehatene
India. Seo forme India lið to ðæra Silhearwena rice, seo oðer
lið to Medas, seo ðridde to ðam micclum garsecge; þeos
ðridde India hæfð on anre sidan þeostru, and on oðere ðone
grimlican garsecg. To ðyssere becom Godes apostol Bartholomeus, and eode into ðam temple to ðam deofolgylde
Astaroð, and swa swa ælðeodig ðær wunade. On ðam deofolgylde wunade swilc deofol ðe to mannum þurh ða anlicnysse
spræc, and gehælde untruman, blinde and healte þa ðe he
sylf ær awyrde. He derode manna gesihðum and heora lichaman mid mislicum untrumnyssum awyrde, and andwyrde
him ðurh ða anlicnysse þæt hi him heora lac offrian sceoldon
and he hi gehælde; ac he him ne heolp mid nanre hæle, ac ða
ða hi to him bugon, ða geswac he ðære lichamlican gedreccednysse forðan ðe he ahte ða heora sawla. Þa wendon dy-
sige men þæt he hi gehælde ða ða he ðære dreccednysse
geswac.

2 Þa mid þam ðe se apostol into ðam temple eode, ða adumbode se deofol Astaroð and ne mihte nanum ðæra ðe he
awyrde gehelpan, for ðæs halgan Godes ðegnes neawiste. Þa
lagon ðær binnan ðam temple fela adligra manna, and dæghwomlice þam deofolgylde offrodon; ac þa ða hi gesawon

31

Saint Bartholomew

AUGUST 25

The Passion of Saint Bartholomew the Apostle

Historians say that there are three nations called India. The first India lies near the kingdom of the Ethiopians, the second near the Medes, and the third near the great ocean; this third India has darkness on one side, and the grim ocean on the other. To this one came God's apostle Bartholomew, and he went into the temple to the idol Astaroth, living there as a stranger. In that idol dwelled the kind of devil who spoke to people through the image, and healed the sick, blind, and lame whom he himself had afflicted. He injured people's sight and afflicted their bodies with various diseases, and answered them through the image that they should offer their sacrifices to him and he would cure them; but he did not help them with any cure, but when they bowed down to him, he stopped afflicting their bodies because he had possession of their souls. Then foolish people thought he had healed them when he stopped afflicting them.

When the apostle went into the temple, the devil Astaroth became mute and could not help any of those he had injured, because of the presence of the holy servant of God. Many sick people lay there in the temple, and daily they offered to the idol; but when they saw that he could not help

2

þæt he heora helpan ne mihte, ne nanum andwyrdan, þa ferdon hi to gehendre byrig þær ðær oðer deofol wæs gewurðod, þæs nama wæs Berið, and him offrodon, and befrunon hwi heora god him andwyrdan ne mihte. Se deofol ða Berið andwyrde and cwæð, "Eower god is swa fæste mid isenum racenteagum gewriðen þæt he ne gedyrstlæcð þæt he furðon orðige oððe sprece syððan se Godes apostol Bartholomeus binnan þæt tempel becom." Hi axodon, "Hwæt is se Bartholomeus?" Se deofol andwyrde, "He is freond þæs ælmihtigan Godes, and ði he com to ðyssere scire þæt he aidlige ealle ða hæðengyld þe ðas Indiscan wurðiað." Hi cwædon, "Sege us his nebwlite, þæt we hine oncnawan magon." Berið him andwyrde, "He is blæcfexede and cyrps, hwit on lichaman, and he hæfð steape eagan and medemlice nosu and side beardas, hwon harwencge, medemne wæstm, and is ymbscryd mid hwitum oferslype, and binnan six and twentig geara fæce. Næs his reaf horig ne tosigen, ne his scos forwerode. Hund siðon he bigð his cneowa on dæge and hund siðon on nihte, biddende his Drihten. His stemn is swylce ormæte byme, and him farað mid Godes englas, ðe ne geðafiað þæt him hunger derige oððe ænig ateorung. Æfre he bið anes modes and glæd þurhwunað. Ealle ðing he foresceawað and wat, and ealra ðeoda gereord he cann. Nu iu he wat hwæt ic sprece be him, forðan ðe Godes englas him ðeowiað and ealle ðing cyðað. Þonne ge hine secað, gif he sylf wyle, ge hine gemetað; gif he nele, soðlice ne finde ge hine. Ic bidde eow þæt ge hine geornlice biddon þæt he hider ne gewende, þelæs ðe Godes englas ðe him mid synd me gebeodon þæt hi minum geferan Astaroð gebudon." And se deofol mid þisum wordum suwode.

3   Hi gecyrdon ongean, and sceawodon ælces ælðeodiges

them, or answer anyone, they went to a nearby city where another devil was worshiped, whose name was Berith, and offered to him, and asked why their god could not answer them. The devil Berith answered, saying, "Your god is bound so firmly with iron chains that he dares not even breathe or speak since God's apostle Bartholomew came into the temple." They asked, "Who is this Bartholomew?" The devil answered, "He is a friend of the almighty God, and he has come to this province to profane all the idols that these Indians worship." They said, "Describe his appearance to us, so that we might recognize him." Berith answered them, "He has fair and curling hair, is white of body, and has deep eyes and a moderate-sized nose and a broad beard, a bit gray haired, of moderate stature, and is dressed in a white outer garment, and is under the age of twenty-six years. His clothing is not dirty or threadbare, nor his shoes worn out. He bends his knees a hundred times a day and a hundred times at night, praying to his Lord. His voice is like a great trumpet, and with him go God's angels, who do not allow hunger or any weakness to hurt him. He is always of one mind and continually happy. He foresees and knows all things, and he understands the languages of all nations. Long ago he knew what I am saying of him now, for God's angels serve him and reveal all things. When you seek him, if he himself wishes, you will find him; if he does not, truly you will not find him. I ask you to ask him earnestly not to come here, lest God's angels who are with him command me as they have commanded my companion Astaroth." And with these words the devil fell silent.

They turned back, and observed the face and garments of 3

mannes andwlitan and gyrlan, and hi nateshwon binnan twegra daga fæce hine ne gemetton. Þa betwux ðisum hrymde sum wod mann ðurh deofles gast and cwæð, "Eala ðu Godes apostol, Bartholomee, ðine gebedu geancsumiað me and ontendað." Se apostol ða cwæð, "Adumba, ðu unclæna deofol, and gewit of ðam menn." And ðærrihte wearð se mann geclænsod fram ðam fulan gaste and gewittiglice spræc, se ðe for manegum gearum awedde.

4   Þa geaxode se cyning Polimius be ðam witseocum menn, hu se apostol hine fram ðære wodnysse ahredde, and het hine to him gelangian, and cwæð, "Min dohtor is hreowlice awed: nu bidde ic ðe þæt þu hi on gewitte gebringe, swa swa ðu dydest Seustium, se ðe for manegum gearum mid egeslicere wodnysse gedreht wæs." Þa ða se apostol þæt mæden geseah mid heardum racenteagum gebunden — forðan ðe heo bat and totær ælcne ðe heo geræcan mihte, and hire nan man genealæcan ne dorste — ða het se apostol hi unbindan. Þa ðenas him andwyrdon, "Hwa dearr hi hreppan?" Bartholomeus andwyrde, "Ic hæbbe gebunden ðone feond þe hi drehte, and ge gyt hi ondrædað. Gað to and unbindað hi, and gereordigað, and on ærne merigen lædað hi to me." Hi ða dydon be ðæs apostoles hæse, and se awyrigeda gast ne mihte na leng hi dreccan.

5   Þa ðæs on merigen se cyning Polimius gesymde gold, and seolfor, and deorwurðe gymmas, and pællene gyrlan uppan olfendus and sohte ðone apostol, ac he hine nateshwon ne gemette. Eft ðæs on merigen com se apostol into ðæs cyninges bure beclysedre dura, and hine befran, "Hwi sohtest ðu me mid golde and mid seolfre and mid deorwurðum gymmum and gyrlum? Þas lac behofiað þa ðe eorðlice welan secað. Ic soðlice nanes eorðlices gestreones, ne flæsclices

every stranger, and during a space of two days they did not find him at all. Then in the meantime some insane person cried out through the devil's spirit and said, "O you apostle of God, Bartholomew, your prayers torment and inflame me." The apostle then said, "Be silent, unclean devil, and depart from this person." Immediately the person, who had been mad for many years, was cleansed from the foul spirit and spoke rationally.

Then the king Polymius heard how the apostle had saved 4 the insane person from that madness, and he commanded him to be fetched to him, and said, "My daughter is cruelly mad: now I beseech you to bring her to her wits, as you did Seustius, who had been afflicted for many years with terrible madness." When the apostle saw the maiden bound with hard chains—because she bit and tore everyone she could reach, and no one dared approach her—the apostle ordered her to be unbound. The servants answered him, "Who dares to touch her?" Bartholomew answered, "I have bound the fiend that tormented her, and you still fear her. Go to her and unbind her, and feed her, and early in the morning lead her to me." They did then as the apostle ordered, and the accursed spirit could no longer torment her.

Then in the morning the king Polymius loaded gold, sil- 5 ver, precious gems, and purple garments upon camels and sought the apostle, but he did not find him. Later in the morning the apostle came to the king's chamber with the door closed, and asked him, "Why did you seek me with gold and with silver and with precious gems and garments? These gifts are for those who seek earthly wealth. Truly I desire no earthly treasure or fleshly pleasure, but I want you

lustes ne gewilnige, ac ic wille þæt þu wite þæt ðæs ælmihtigan Godes Sunu gemedemode hine sylfne þæt he ðurh
mædenlicne innoð acenned wearð, se ðe geworhte heofonas
and eorðan and ealle gesceafta; and he hæfde anginn on
ðære menniscnysse, se ðe næfre ne ongann on godcundnysse, ac he sylf is anginn, and eallum gesceaftum ægðer
ge gesewenlicum ge ungesewenlicum anginn forgeaf. Þæt
mæden ðe hine gebær forhogode ælces weres gemanan, and
ðam ælmihtigan Gode hire mægðhad behet. Hire com to
Godes heahengel Gabriel and hire cydde þæs heofonlican
æðelinges tocyme on hire innoð, and heo his wordum gelyfde, and swa mid þam cilde wearð."

6   Se apostol ða þam cyninge bodade ealne Cristendom, and
middangeardes alysednysse ðurh ðæs hælendes tocyme, and
hu he ðone hellican deofol gewylde and him mancynnes
benæmde, and cwæð, "Drihten Crist, se ðe ðurh his unscyldigan deað þone deofol oferswiðde, sende us geond ealle
ðeoda þæt we todræfdon deofles ðenas, ða ðe on anlicnyssum wuniað, and þæt we ða hæðenan ðe hi wurðiað of heora
anwealde ætbrudon. Ac we ne underfoð gold ne seolfor, ac
forseoð, swa swa Crist forseah; forðan ðe we gewilniað þæt
we rice beon on his rice, on ðam næfð adl, ne untrumnyss, ne
unrotnyss, ne deað, nænne stede, ac þær is ece gesælð and
eadignys, gefea butan ende mid ecum welum. Forði ic ferde
to eowerum temple, and se deofol ðe eow ðurh ða anlicnysse
geandwyrde, ðurh Godes englas ðe me sende, is gehæft. And
gif ðu to fulluhte gebihst, ic do þæt þu ðone deofol gesihst
and gehyrst mid hwilcum cræfte he is geðuht þæt he untrumnysse gehæle. Se awyrigeda deofol, siððan he ðone
frumsceapenan mann beswac, syððan he hæfde anweald
on ungelyfedum mannum, on sumum maran, on sumum

to know that the Son of almighty God, who made heaven and earth and all creation, humbled himself to be born of a virgin's womb; he had a beginning in humanity who never began in his divinity, for he himself is the beginning, and gave beginning to all creatures both visible and invisible. The virgin who bore him shunned every man's fellowship, and dedicated her virginity to the almighty God. God's archangel Gabriel came to her and announced to her the advent of the heavenly prince into her womb, and she believed his words, and so became with child."

The apostle then preached all of Christianity to the king, 6 and the redemption of the world through the coming of the savior, how he overcame the hellish devil and deprived him of humankind, saying, "The lord Christ, who through his innocent death overpowered the devil, has sent us among all nations to drive out the devil's servants, who dwell in images, and to take away from their control the heathens who worship them. We do not receive gold or silver, but scorn them, as Christ scorned them; for we desire to be rich in his kingdom, in which neither sickness, nor infirmity, nor sadness, nor death, has any place, but there is eternal happiness and blessedness, joy without end with eternal riches. Therefore I came to your temple, and the devil who answered you through the image is made captive by the angels of God, who sent me. And if you will consent to be baptized, I will cause you to see the devil and to hear by what art he appears to heal sickness. Ever since he deceived the first-created human, the accursed devil has had power over unbelievers,

læssan: on ðam maran ðe swiðor syngað, on ðam læssan ðe hwonlicor syngað. Nu deð se deofol mid his lotwrencum þæt ða earman men geuntrumiað, and tiht hi þæt hi sceolon gelyfan on deofolgyld. Þonne geswicð he ðære gedreccednysse, and hæfð heora sawla on his anwealde þonne hi cweðað to ðære deofollican anlicnysse, 'Þu eart min god.' Ac ðes deofol ðe binnan eowrum temple wæs is gebunden, and ne mæg nateshwon andwyrdan þam ðe him to gebiddað. Gif ðu wylt afandian þæt ic soð secge, ic hate hine faran into ðære anlicnysse, and ic do þæt he andet þis ylce, þæt he is gewriðen and nane andsware syllan ne mæg."

7   Þa andwyrde se cyning, "Nu to merigen hæfð þis folc gemynt þæt hi heora lac him offrion; ðonne cume ic ðærto þæt ic geseo ðas wunderlican dæda." Witodlice on ðam oðrum dæge com se cyning mid þære burhware to ðam temple, and ða hrymde se deofol mid egeslicere stemne ðurh ða anlicnysse, and cwæð, "Geswicað, earme! Geswicað eowra offrunga, ðelæs ðe ge wyrsan pinunge ðrowion ðonne ic. Ic eom gebunden mid fyrenum racenteagum fram Cristes englum, ðone ðe ða Iudeiscan on rode ahengon; wendon þæt se deað hine gehæftan mihte. He soðlice ðone deað oferswyðde, and urne ealdor mid fyrenum bendum gewrað, and on ðam ðriddan dæge sigefæst aras, and sealde his rodetacen his apostolum and tosende hi geond ealle ðeoda. An ðæra is her, ðe me gebundenne hylt. Ic bidde eow þæt ge me to him geðingion, þæt ic mote faran to sumere oðre scire."

8   Þa cwæð se apostol Bartholomeus, "Þu unclæna deofol, andette hwa awyrde ðas untruman menn." Se unclæna gast andwyrde, "Ure ealdor, swa gebunden swa he is, sent us to mancynne, þæt we hi mid mislicum untrumnyssum awyrdon—ærest heora lichaman, forðan ðe we nabbað nænne

over some greater, some less: greater on those who sin more, less on those who sin less. Now, the devil by his tricks causes wretched people to fall sick, and encourages them to believe in an idol. Then he stops that affliction, and has their souls in his power when they say to the devilish image, 'You are my god.' But the devil who was in your temple is bound, and cannot answer those who pray to him in any way. If you want to test whether I speak truth, I will command him to go into the image, and I will make him confess the same, that he is bound and can give no answer."

Then the king answered, "Tomorrow these people intend 7 to offer him their sacrifices; then I will come there so that I may see these wonderful deeds." Indeed, on the next day the king came to the temple with the citizens, and then the devil cried with terrible voice through the image, saying, "Cease, wretches! Cease your offerings, lest you suffer worse torment than I. I am bound with fiery chains by the angels of Christ, whom the Jews hanged on a cross; they thought that death might hold him captive. He truly overcame death, and bound our prince with fiery chains, and on the third day rose triumphant, and gave the sign of his cross to his apostles and sent them throughout all nations. One of them is here, who keeps me bound. I pray that you intercede for me to him, that I may go to some other province."

Then the apostle Bartholomew said, "Unclean devil, con 8 fess who has afflicted these sick people." The unclean spirit answered, "Our prince, bound as he is, sent us to humankind, that we might afflict them with various infirmities — first their bodies, for we have no power over their souls

anweald on heora sawlum buton hi heora lac us geoffrion.
Ac ðonne hi for heora lichaman hælðe us offriað, þonne geswice we ðæs lichaman gedreccednysse, forðan ðe we habbað syððan heora sawla on urum gewealde. Þonne bið
geðuht swilce we hi gehælon ðonne we geswicað þæra
awyrdnyssa. And menn us wurðiað for godas þonne we
soðlice deoflu sind, þæs ealdres gingran ðe Crist, þæs
mædenes Sunu, gewrað. Fram ðam dæge þe his apostol Bartholomeus hider com, ic eom mid byrnendum racenteagum
ðearle fornumen, and forði ic sprece ðe he me het; elles ic ne
dorste on his andwerdnysse sprecan, ne furðon ure ealdor."

9   Þa cwæð se apostol, "Hwi nelt ðu gehælan ðas untruman,
swa swa ðin gewuna wæs?" Se sceocca andwyrde, "Þonne
we manna lichaman derigað, buton we ðære sawle derian
magon, ða lichaman þurhwuniað on heora awyrdnysse." Bartholomeus cwæð, "And hu become ge to ðære sawle awyrdnysse?" Se deofol andwyrde, "Þonne hi gelyfað þæt we godas
sind and us offriað, þonne forlæt se ælmihtiga God hi, and
we ðonne forlætað ðone lichaman ungebrocodne, and cepað
ðære sawle þe us to gebeah, and heo ðonne on ure anwealde
bið."

10   Þa cwæð se apostol to eallum ðam folce, "Efne nu ge habbað gehyred hwilc ðes god is ðe ge wendon þæt eow gehælde; ac gehyrað nu ðone soðan God eowerne scyppend,
þe on heofonum eardað, and ne gelyfe ge heononforð on
idele anlicnyssa. And gif ge willað þæt ic eow to Gode geðingige, and þæt ðas untruman hælðe underfon, towurpað
þonne ðas anlicnysse and tobrecað. Gif ge ðis doð, þonne
halgige ic ðis tempel on Cristes naman, and eow ðær onin-
nan mid his fulluhte fram eallum synnum aðwea." Þa het se
cyning ða anlicnysse towurpan. Hwæt þæt folc ða caflice

unless they offer us their sacrifices. But when they offer to us for their bodies' health, then we stop afflicting the body, because then we have their souls in our power. Then it seems as though we have healed them when we cease from those afflictions. People worship us as gods when we really are devils, disciples of the prince whom Christ, the virgin's Son, has bound. From the day his apostle Bartholomew came here, I have been severely tormented with burning chains, and therefore I speak as he has commanded me; otherwise neither I nor even our prince would dare to speak in his presence."

Then the apostle said, "Why will you not heal the sick, as 9 was your custom?" The demon answered, "When we injure people's bodies, unless we can injure the soul, the bodies continue in their affliction." Bartholomew said, "And how do you achieve the affliction of the soul?" The devil answered, "When they believe that we are gods and offer to sacrifices us, then the almighty God forsakes them, and then we leave the body unharmed, seeking the soul that has bowed to us, and then it is in our power."

The apostle said to all the people, "Now you have heard 10 what sort of god this is that you thought healed you; but hear now the true God your creator, who dwells in heaven, and do not believe in vain images anymore. And if you wish me to intercede for you with God, and for these sick to receive health, overthrow this image and shatter it. If you do this, then I will consecrate this temple in Christ's name, and within it I will wash you from all sins with his baptism." The king then commanded the image to be cast down. At this

mid rapum hi bewurpon, and mid stengum awegdon, ac hi
ne mihton for ðam deofle þa anlicnysse styrian.

11   Þa het se apostol tolysan ða rapas, and cwæð to ðam
awyrgedan gaste ðe hire on sticode, "Gyf ðu wylle þæt ic
ðe on niwelnysse ne asende, gewit of ðyssere anlicnysse, and
tobrec hi, and far to westene, þær nan fugel ne flyhð, ne
yrðling ne erað, ne mannes stemn ne swegð." He ðærrihte ut
gewat, and sticmælum tobræc ða anlicnysse, and ealle ða
græftas binnon ðam temple tobrytte. Þæt folc ða mid anre
stemne clypode, "An ælmihtig God is, ðone ðe Bartholomeus bodað." Se apostol ða astrehte his handa wið heofonas
weard, þus biddende, "Þu ælmihtiga God, on ðam ðe Abraham gelyfde, and Isaac, and Iacob, þu ðe asendest ðinne ancennedan Sunu þæt he us alysde mid his deorwurðan blode
fram deofles ðeowdome, and hæfð us geworht ðe to bearnum, þu eart unacenned Fæder, he is Sunu of ðe æfre
acenned, and se Halga Gast is æfre forðstæppende of ðe and
of ðinum Bearne, se forgeaf us on his naman ðas mihte þæt
we untrume gehælon, and blinde onlihton, hreoflige geclænsian, deoflu aflian, deade aræran, and cwæð to us, 'Soð
ic eow secge, swa hwæt swa ge biddað on minum naman æt
minum Fæder, hit bið eow getiðod.' Nu bidde ic on his naman þæt þeos untrume menigu sy gehæled, þæt hi ealle oncnawon þæt ðu eart ana God on heofonan, and on eorðan,
and on sæ, þu ðe hælðe geedstaðelast ðurh ðone ylcan urne
Drihten, se ðe mid ðe and mid þam Halgan Gaste leofað and
rixað on ealra worulda woruld." Mid þam ðe hi andwyrdon,
"Amen," þa wearð eall seo untrume menigu gehæled, and
ðær com ða fleogende Godes engel, scinende swa swa sunne,
and fleah geond ða feower hwemmas þæs temples, and agrof
mid his fingre rodetacn on ðam fyðerscytum stanum, and

the people quickly wrapped ropes around it, and pushed it with poles, but they could not move the idol because of the devil.

Then the apostle commanded the ropes to be loosened, and said to the accursed spirit that remained in it, "If you do not want me to send you into the abyss, depart from this image, break it, and go to the desert, where no bird flies, nor farmer plows, nor human voice sounds." He went out at once, and broke the image into pieces, and shattered all the carvings within the temple. The people then cried with one voice, "There is one almighty God, whom Bartholomew preaches." The apostle then stretched out his hand toward heaven, praying, "Almighty God, in whom Abraham believed, and Isaac, and Jacob, you who have sent your only-begotten Son to redeem us with his precious blood from slavery to the devil, and have made us your children, you are the unbegotten Father, he is the Son ever begotten of you, and the Holy Spirit is ever proceeding from you and your Son, who has given us this power to heal the sick in his name, and give light to the blind, cleanse lepers, drive out devils, raise the dead, and has said to us, 'Truly I say to you, whatever you ask of my Father in my name, it will be granted to you.' Now I pray in his name that this sick multitude be healed, that they all may know that you alone are God in heaven, and on earth, and on the sea, you who restore health through the same our Lord, who with you and with the Holy Spirit lives and reigns for ever and ever." As they answered "Amen," all the sick multitude was healed, and God's angel came flying there, shining like the sun, and flew over the four corners of the temple, and engraved the sign of the cross with his finger on the four-sided stones, saying, "The

cwæð, "Se God ðe me sende cwæð þæt swa swa ðas untruman synd gehælede fram eallum coðum, swa he geclænsode
þis templ fram þæs deofles fulnyssum ðone ðe se apostol het
to westene gewitan. And God bebead me þæt ic ðone deofol
eowrum gesihðum ær æteowige; ne beo ge afyrhte þurh his
gesihðe, ac mearciað rodetacen on eowrum foreheafdum,
and ælc yfel gewit fram eow."

12   And se engel ða æteowde þam folce ðone awyrigedan gast
on ðyssere gelicnysse: he wearð ða æteowod swylce ormæte
Silhearwa, mid scearpum nebbe, mid sidum bearde. His loc-
cas hangodon to ðam anccleowum, his eagan wæron fyrene
spearcan sprengende; him stod swæflen lig of ðam muðe, he
wæs egeslice gefiðerhamod, and his handa to his bæce gebundene. Þa cwæð se Godes engel to ðam atelican deofle,
"Forðan ðe ðu wære gehyrsum ðæs apostoles hæsum and tobræce þas deofellican anlicnysse, nu æfter his behate ic ðe
unbinde, þæt þu fare to westene þær ðær nanes mannes
drohtnung nis, and ðu þær wunige oð þone micclan dom."
And se engel hine ða unband, and he mid hreowlicere
wanunge aweg gewat, and nawar siððan ne æteowde. Se engel ða, him eallum onlocigendum, fleah to heofonum.

13   Hwæt ða se cyning Polimius, mid his wife and his twam
sunum and mid ealre his leode, gelyfde on ðone soðan God
and wearð gefullod, and awearp his cynehelm samod mid his
purpuran gyrlum, and nolde ðone Godes apostol forlætan.
Æfter ðisum gesamnodon gehwylce ðwyrlice wiðercoran,
and wrehton ðone cyning to his breðer Astrigem, se wæs cyning on oðrum leodscipe, and cwædon, "Þin broðer is geworden anes dryes folgere, se geagnað him ure tempel and
ure godas tobrycð." Þa wearð se cyning Astriges gehathyrt,
and sende ðusend gewæpnodra cempena þæt hi ðone

God who sends me said that just as these sick are healed from all diseases, so has he cleansed this temple from the foulness of the devil whom the apostle has commanded to depart to the desert. And God has commanded me that I first reveal the devil to your sight; do not be afraid at the sight of him, but mark the sign of the cross on your foreheads, and every evil will depart from you."

The angel then showed the people the accursed spirit in this likeness: he appeared as an enormous Ethiopian, with sharp visage, with broad beard. His locks hung to his ankles, his eyes were scattering fiery sparks; sulfurous flames came from his mouth, he was frightfully covered in feathers, and his hands were bound behind his back. Then God's angel said to the hideous devil, "Because you were obedient to the apostle's commands and broke the diabolical image, now according to his promise I will unbind you, so that you may go to the desert where no human life is, and remain there until the great judgment." And the angel unbound him, and with woeful lamentation he went away, and appeared nowhere afterward. The angel then flew to heaven, with all looking on. 12

At this the king Polymius, with his wife, his two sons, and all his people, believed in the true God and was baptized, and threw away his crown together with his purple garments, and did not want to leave God's apostle. After this all the perverse reprobates assembled, and accused the king to his brother Astryges, who was king in another country, and said, "Your brother has become the follower of a magician, who seizes our temples and shatters our gods." The king Astryges was enraged, and sent a thousand armed soldiers to 13

apostol gebundenne to him bringan sceoldon. Þa ða se apostol him to gelæd wæs, ða cwæð se cyning, "Hwi amyrdest ðu minne broðor mid þinum drycræfte?" Bartholomeus andwyrde, "Ne amyrde ic hine, ac ic hine awende fram hæðenum gylde to ðam soðan Gode." Se cyning him to cwæð, "Hwi towurpe ðu ure godas?" He andwyrde, "Ic sealde ða mihte ðam deoflum, ðe hi tocwysdon ða idelan anlicnysse þe hi on wunodon, þæt þæt mennisce folc fram heora gedwyldum gecyrde and on ðone ecan God gelyfde." Þa cwæð se cyning, "Swa swa ðu dydest minne broðor his god forlætan and on ðinne God gelyfan, swa do ic eac ðe forlætan ðinne God and on minne gelyfan." Þa andwyrde se apostol, "Ic æteowode þone god ðe ðin broðor wurðode him gebundenne, and ic het þæt he sylf his anlicnysse tobræce. Gif ðu miht ðis don minum Gode, þonne gebigst ðu me to ðines godes biggengum; gif ðu ðonne þis minum Gode don ne miht, ic tobryte ealle ðine godas, and ðu ðonne gelyf on ðone soðan God þe ic bodige."

14   Mid þam ðe hi ðis spræcon, þa cydde sum man þam cyninge þæt his mæsta god Baldað feolle and sticmælum toburste. Se cyning ða totær his purpuran reaf, and het mid stiðum saglum ðone apostol beatan and siððan beheafdian. And he ða on ðisum dæge swa gemartyrod to ðam ecan life gewat. Witodlice æfter ðisum com se broðor mid his folce and ðone halgan lichaman mid wulderfullum lofsangum aweg feredon, and getimbrodon mynster wundorlicere micelnysse, and on ðam his halgan reliquias arwurðlice gelogedon. Eornostlice on ðam þrittigoðan dæge se cyning Astriges, ðe ðone apostol ofslean het, wearð mid feondlicum gaste gegripen and egeslice awedde; swa eac ealle ða ðwyran hæðengyldan þe ðone apostol mid niðe to ðam cyninge

bring the apostle to him bound. When the apostle was led to him, the king said, "Why have you corrupted my brother with your magic?" Bartholomew answered, "I have not corrupted him, but I have turned him from the worship of idols to the true God." The king said to him, "Why have you cast down our gods?" He answered, "I gave that power to the devils, so they might crush the vain image in which they dwelled, and people might turn from their errors and believe in the eternal God." Then the king said, "Just as you have made my brother forsake his god and believe in your God, so too I will make you forsake your God and believe in mine." The apostle answered, "I showed your brother the god that he worshiped bound, and I commanded that he should break his image himself. If you can do this to my God, then you will convert me to the worship of your god; but if you cannot do this to my God, I will break all your gods, and then believe in the true God whom I preach."

While he was saying this, someone announced to the king that his greatest god Baldath had fallen and burst into pieces. The king then tore his purple robe, and commanded the apostle to be beaten with stiff clubs and afterward beheaded. And so martyred, on this day he departed to the eternal life. Indeed, after this the brother came with his people and bore away the holy body with glorious hymns, and built a church of wonderful greatness, and honorably placed his holy relics in it. Then on the thirtieth day the king Astryges, who had ordered the apostle to be killed, was seized with a demonic spirit and became dreadfully mad; so also all the perverse idolaters who had maliciously accused

14

gewregdon aweddon samod mid him, and urnon hi and he to
his byrgene, and ðær wedende swulton. Þa asprang micel
oga and gryre ofer ealle ða ungeleaffullan, and hi ða gelyfdon
and gefullode wurdon æt ðæra mæssepreosta handum ðe se
apostol ær gehadode. Þa onwreah se apostol Bartholomeus
be ðam geleaffullan cyninge Polimius þæt he biscophad underfenge, and ða Godes ðeowan and þæt geleaffulle folc
hine anmodlice to ðam hade gecuron. Hit gelamp ða, æfter
ðære hadunge, þæt he worhte fela tacna on Godes naman
ðurh his geleafan, and ðurhwunode twentig geara on ðam
biscopdome, and on goddre drohtnunge; and fulfremedum
geðincðum gewat to Drihtne, þam is wurðmynt and wuldor
a on worulde.

15   We magon niman bysne be ðære apostolican lare þæt nan
Cristen mann ne sceal his hæle gefeccan buton æt ðam ælmihtigan scyppende ðam ðe gehyrsumiað lif and deað, untrumnyss and gesundfulnys, se ðe cwæð on his godspelle þæt
an lytel fugel ne befylð on deað butan Godes dihte. He is swa
mihtig þæt he ealle ðing gediht and gefadað butan geswince;
ac he beswincgð mid untrumnyssum his gecorenan, swa swa
he sylf cwæð, "Þa ðe ic lufige, ða ic ðreage and beswinge."
For mislicum intingum beoð Cristene men geuntrumode:
hwilon for heora synnum, hwilon for fandunge, hwilon
for Godes wundrum, hwilon for gehealdsumnysse goddra
drohtnunga, þæt hi ðy eadmodran beon; ac on eallum ðisum
þingum is geðyld nydbehefe. Hwilon eac þurh Godes wrace
becymð þam arleasan menn swiðe egeslic yfel, swa þæt his
wite onginð on ðyssere worulde, and his sawul gewit to ðam
ecum witum for his wælhreawnysse, swa swa Herodes ðe ða
unscæððigan cild acwealde on Cristes acennednysse, and
manega oðre toeacan him. Gif se synfulla bið gebrocod for

the apostle to the king went mad together with him, and they and he ran to his grave, and there died raving. Then great fear and horror sprang up over all the unbelievers, and they believed and were baptized at the hands of the priests whom the apostle had ordained. Then the apostle Bartholomew revealed that the believing king, Polymius, should receive the rank of bishop, and the servants of God and the faithful people chose him to that office unanimously. It happened then, after the ordination, that he performed many signs in God's name through his faith, and continued twenty years in the episcopal office in a good course of life; and in full dignity he departed to the Lord, to whom is honor and glory for ever and ever.

We may take example by the apostolic teaching that no 15 Christian should procure his health except from the almighty creator whom life and death, sickness and health obey, who said in his gospel that a little bird does not fall in death without God's direction. He is so mighty that he directs and orders all things without effort; but he scourges his chosen ones with diseases, as he himself said, "Those whom I love I chastise and scourge." For various reasons Christians are afflicted with disease: sometimes for their sins, sometimes for trial, sometimes for God's miracles, sometimes for preservation of good ways of life, that they may be humbler; but in all these things patience is needed. Sometimes too, very dreadful evil comes to the impious through God's vengeance, so that his punishment begins in this world, and his soul departs to eternal punishments for his cruelty, like Herod, who slew the innocent children at Christ's birth, and many others in addition to him. If a sinful

his unrihtwisnysse, þonne gif he mid geðylde his Drihten
herað and his miltsunge bitt, he bið ðonne aðwogen fram his
synnum ðurh ða untrumnysse swa swa horig hrægl þurh sa-
pan. Gif he rihtwis bið, he hæfð þonne maran geðincðe þurh
his brocunge gif he geðyldig bið. Se ðe bið ungeþyldig and
mid gealgum mode ceorað ongean God on his untrumnysse,
he hæfð twyfealde geniðerunge, forðan ðe he geycð his
synna mid þære ceorunge, and ðrowað naðelæs.

16   God is se soða læce þe ðurh mislice swingla his folces
synna gehælð. Nis se woruldlæce wælhreow, ðeah ðe he þone
gewundodan mid bærnette oððe mid ceorfsexe gelacnige.
Se læce cyrfð oððe bærnð, and se untruma hrymð, þeahhwæðere ne miltsað he þæs oðres wanunge, forðan gif se
læce geswicð his cræftes þonne losað se forwundoda. Swa
eac God gelacnað his gecorenra gyltas mid mislicum bro-
cum; and þeah ðe hit hefigtyme sy ðam ðrowigendum, þeahhwæðere wyle se goda læce to ecere hælðe hine gelacnigan.
Witodlice se ðe nane brocunge for ðisum life ne ðrowað, he
færð to ðrowunge. For agenum synnum bið se mann geuntrumod, swa swa Drihten cwæð to sumum bedridan ðe him
to geboren wæs, "Min bearn, ðe synd þine synna forgifene;
aris nu, and ber ham ðin legerbed."

17   For fandunge beoð sume menn geuntrumode, swa swa
wæs se eadiga Iob, ða ða he wæs rihtwis and Gode gehyrsum. Þa bæd se deofol þæt he his fandigan moste, and he
ða anes dæges ealle his æhta amyrde, and eft hine sylfne
mid þam mæstan broce geuntrumode, swa þæt him weollon
maðan geond ealne ðone lichaman. Ac se geðyldiga Iob, on
eallum ðisum ungelimpum, ne syngode mid his muðe ne
nan ðing stuntlices ongean God ne spræc, ac cwæð, "God
me forgeaf ða æhta, and hi eft æt me genam; sy his nama

person falls sick for his unrighteousness, but he praises his Lord with patience and prays for his mercy, he will be washed from his sins by that sickness like a filthy garment by soap. If he is righteous, he will have greater honor through his illness if he is patient. He who is impatient and murmurs against God in his sickness with a gloomy mind will have a double condemnation, for he increases his sins by that murmuring, and suffers nevertheless.

God is the true physician, who by various afflictions heals 16 the sins of his people. The worldly physician is not cruel, though he might cure the wounded with burning or with the surgeon's knife. The physician cuts or burns, and the patient cries out, yet he has no mercy on the other's moaning, for if the physician ceases his craft, then the wounded will perish. So too God cures the sins of his chosen with various diseases; and though it might be wearisome to the sufferer, yet will the good physician cure him to everlasting health. Indeed, he who suffers no sickness in this life will go to suffering. A person is sickened for his own sins, as the Lord said to a certain bedridden person who was borne to him, "My child, your sins are forgiven you; arise now, and bear home your sickbed."

Some are afflicted with disease for trials, as was the 17 blessed Job, when he was righteous and obedient to God. Then the devil asked that he might test him, and he in one day destroyed all his possessions, and afterward afflicted him with the greatest disease, so that maggots swarmed over all his body. But the patient Job, in all these misfortunes, did not sin with his mouth nor say anything foolish against God, but said, "God gave me possessions, and then took them from me; blessed be his name." Then

gebletsod." God eac ða hine gehælde, and his æhta mid twyfealdum him forgeald. Sume menn beoð geuntrumode for Godes tacnum, swa swa Crist cwæð be sumum blindan men, ða ða his leorningcnihtas hine axodon for hwæs synnum se mann wurde swa blind acenned. Þa cwæð se hælend þæt he nære for his agenum synnum, ne for his maga, blind geboren, ac forði þæt Godes wundor þurh hine geswutelod wære. And he þærrihte mildheortlice hine gehælde, and geswutelode þæt he is soð scyppend, ðe ða ungesceapenan eahhringas mid his halwendan spatle geopenode.

18   For gehealdsumnysse soðre eadmodnysse beoð forwel oft Godes gecorenan geswencte, swa swa Paulus se apostol be him sylfum cwæð, "Me is geseald sticels mines lichaman, þæt se sceocca me gearplæt, þæt seo micelnys Godes onwrigenyssa me ne onhebbe. Forðan ic bæd þriwa minne Drihten þæt he afyrsode þæs sceoccan sticels fram me, ac he me andwyrde, 'Paule, ðe genihtsumað min gifu; soðlice mægen bið gefremod on untrumnysse.' Nu wuldrige ic lustlice on minum untrumnyssum, þæt Cristes miht on me wunige."

19   Se Cristena mann ðe on ænigre þissere gelicnysse bið gebrocod, and he ðonne his hælðe secan wyle æt unalyfedum tilungum, oððe æt wyrigedum galdrum, oððe æt ænigum wiccecræfte, ðonne bið he ðam hæðenum mannum gelic þe ðam deofolgylde geoffrodon for heora lichaman hælðe and swa heora sawla amyrdon. Se ðe geuntrumod beo bidde his hæle æt his Drihtne, and geðyldelice þa swingla forbere. Loc hu lange se soða læce hit foresceawige, and ne beceapige na ðurh ænigne deofles cræft mid his sawle ðæs lichaman gesundfulnysse; bidde eac goddra manna bletsunge, and æt halgum reliquium his hæle gesece. Nis nanum Cristenum menn alyfed þæt he his hæle gefecce æt nanum stane, ne æt

God also healed him, and restored his possessions to him twofold. Some are afflicted for the signs from God, as Christ said of a certain blind person, when his disciples asked him for whose sins the man had been born blind. The savior said that he was not born blind for his own sins, nor for those of his parents, but so that God's miracles might be manifested through him. And at once he mercifully healed him, revealing that he is the true creator, who opened the misshapen eye sockets with his healthful spittle.

For the preservation of true humility, God's chosen are very often afflicted, as Paul the apostle said of himself, "To me is given a thorn in my body, so that the devil buffets me, that the greatness of God's revelations might not exalt me. Three times I asked my Lord to remove the devil's thorn from me, but he answered me, 'Paul, my grace will be enough for you; truly power is perfected in weakness.' Now I glorify joyfully in my weaknesses, that the power of Christ may dwell in me." 18

The Christian who is afflicted in anything like this, and who then will seek his health in forbidden practices, or accursed enchantments, or any witchcraft, will be like those heathens who sacrificed to an idol for their bodies' health and so destroyed their souls. Let the one who is sick pray for his health to his Lord, and patiently endure the scourges. See how long the true physician ordains it, and do not buy the body's health with his soul through any devil's craft; let him also ask for the blessing of good people, and seek his health at holy relics. It is not allowed for any Christian to procure his health from any stone, nor from any tree, unless 19

nanum treowe, buton hit sy halig rodetacen, ne æt nanre
stowe buton hit sy halig Godes hus; se ðe elles deð he begæð
untwylice hæðengild. We habbað hwæðere þa bysne on halgum bocum þæt mot se ðe wile mid soðum læcecræfte his
lichaman getemprian, swa swa dyde se witega Isaias, þe
worhte ðam cyninge Ezechie cliðan to his dolge and hine
gelacnode.

20   Se wisa Augustinus cwæð þæt unpleolic sy þeah hwa læce-
wyrte ðicge, ac þæt he tælð to unalyfedlicere wiglunge gif
hwa ða wyrt on him becnitte, buton he hi to ðam dolge
gelecge. Þeahhwæðere ne sceole we urne hiht on læcewyr-
tum besettan, ac on ðone ælmihtigan scyppend þe ðam wyrtum ðone cræft forgeaf. Ne sceal nan man mid galdre wyrte
besingan, ac mid Godes wordum hi gebletsian, and swa ðic-
gan.

21   Wite ðeahhwæðere gehwa, þæt nan man butan earfoðnyssum ne becymð to ðære ecan reste, þa ða Crist sylf nolde
his agen rice butan micelre earfoðnysse astigan; swa eac his
apostoli and ða halgan martyras mid heora agenum feore
þæt heofonlice rice beceapodon. Syððan eac halige andet-
teras mid micelre drohtnunge on Godes ðeowdome, and
þurh miccle forhæfednyssa and clænnysse halige wurdon.
Hwæt wylle we, endemenn ðyssere worulde, gif we for urum
synnum gebrocode beoð, buton herian urne Drihten, and
eadmodlice biddan þæt he us þurh ða hwilwendlican swingla
to ðam ecan gefean gelæde? Sy him wuldor and lof on ealra
worulda woruld. Amen.

it is the holy sign of the cross, nor from any place except the holy house of God; he who does otherwise undoubtedly commits idolatry. We have, nevertheless, examples in holy books that he who wishes may cure his body with true medical practice, as the prophet Isaiah did, who made a poultice for the king Hezekiah's sore and cured him.

The wise Augustine said that it is not dangerous if anyone takes a medicinal herb, but he condemns as a forbidden sorcery if anyone binds those herbs on himself, unless he lays them on the sore. Nevertheless, we should not set our hope in medicinal herbs, but in the almighty creator who has given that virtue to those herbs. Nor should anyone sing over an herb with an incantation, but bless it with God's words, and so take it. [20]

Let everyone know, however, that no one comes to the eternal rest without tribulations, when Christ himself would not ascend to his own kingdom without great tribulation; likewise his apostles and the holy martyrs purchased the heavenly kingdom with their own lives. Later too holy confessors became holy with great perseverance in God's service, and through great abstinence and chastity. What should we do, people in the last age of this world, if we are afflicted with sickness for our sins, but praise our Lord, and humbly pray that through temporary scourges he may lead us to everlasting joy? To him be glory and praise for ever and ever. Amen. [21]

32

IIII KALENDAS SEPTEMBRIS

Decollatio sancti Iohannis baptistae

M̄isit Herodes et tenuit Iohannem, et reliqua.

2 Marcus se godspellere awrat on Cristes bec be ðam mæran Fulluhtere, Iohanne, þæt "se wælhreowa cyning Herodes
hine gehæfte and on cwearterne sette for his broðor wife
Herodiaden ða he genam of ðam breðer Philippe. Iohannes
hine ðreade and cwæð þæt hit manfullic wære þæt he his
broðor wife hæfde; and þæt wife Herodias syrwde embe
Iohanne, and wolde hine to deaðe gedon gif heo mihte.
Herodes soðlice hæfde micelne ege to ðam Fulluhtere; wiste
þæt he wæs rihtwis and halig, and hine geheold, and be his
lare fela ðing dyde, and to langere hwile him gehyrde. Þa become se dæg his acennednysse, and he gelaðode his ealdormenn and his witan to his gereorde. Þa eode his dohtor inn
mid hire mædenum and plegode ætforan ðam fæder, and
him ðearle gelicode hire plega, and eallum ðam gebeorum.
Þa cwæð se cyning to his dehter, 'Bide me loc hwæs ðu wylle,
and ðu bist tiða.' He swor ða mid miclum aðe þæt he hire
forgifan wolde ðeah ðe heo healfne dæl his rices bæde. Heo
ða befran ða modor hwæt heo biddan scolde; heo cwæð,
'Bide þæt he ðe forgife Iohannes heafod þæs Fulluhteres.' Þa
cwæð seo dohtor to ðam cyninge, 'Ic bidde þæt þu hate
nu rihte beran to me Iohannes heafod on anum disce.' Þa

32

The Beheading of John the Baptist

AUGUST 29

The Beheading of John the Baptist

Herod sent and arrested John, etc.

Mark the Evangelist wrote in Christ's book concerning   2
the great Baptist, John, that "the cruel king Herod bound
him and put him in prison for the sake of his brother's wife,
Herodias, whom he had taken from his brother Philip. John
rebuked him and said that it was sinful to have his brother's
wife; the wife Herodias plotted against John, and wanted to
put him to death if she could. But truly Herod had great fear
of the Baptist; he knew that he was righteous and holy, so he
kept him, and did many things according to his teaching,
and listened to him for a long while. Then came the day of
his birth, and he invited his ealdormen and counselors to his
feast. Then his daughter came in with her maidens and
danced before the father, and her dancing greatly pleased
him, and all the guests. The king said to his daughter, 'Ask
me for whatever you want, and you will receive it.' Then he
swore with a great oath that he would give it to her even if
she asked for half his kingdom. She asked her mother what
she should ask for; she said, 'Ask that he give you the head of
John the Baptist.' Then the daughter said to the king, 'I ask
that you command that the head of John be brought directly

579

wearð se cyning gedrefed for ðære bene, and nolde ðeah, for his aðe ne for ðam gebeorum, his word awægan, ne ða dohtor ahwænan; ac sende ðærrihte ænne cwellere and het his heafod bringan on anum disce. Se cwellere ða beheafdode ðone mæran witegan binnon ðam cwearterne, and þæt heafod þam cyninge brohte, and he hit ræhte his dehter, and seo dohtor þære meder. Comon ða syððan his folgeras and his lic bebyrigdon."

3   Þes Iohannes wæs se mærosta mann, swa swa Crist be him cyðnysse gecydde; he cwæð, "Betwux wifa bearnum ne aras nan mærra man þonne Iohannes se Fulluhtere." Nu hæbbe ge oft gehyred be his mæran drohtnunge and be his ðenunge; nu wylle we embe ðises godspelles trahtnunge sume swutelunge eow gereccan.

4   Þes Herodes, ðe Iohannem beheafdian het, and on ðæs hælendes ðrowunge Pilate ðam ealdormenn geðafode, and hine to his dome betæhte, wæs ðæs oðres Herodes sunu, ðe on ðam timan rixode ðe Crist geboren wæs; ac hit wæs swa gewunelic on ðam timan þæt rice menn sceopon heora bearnum naman be him sylfum, þæt hit wære geðuht þæs ðe mare gemynd þæs fæder ða ða se sunu his yrfenuma wæs geciged þæs fæder naman. Se wælhreowa fæder Herodes læfde fif suna: þry he het acwellan on his feorhadle, ærðan ðe he gewite; þa wearð he hreowlice and hrædlice dead æfter ðam ðe he ða cild acwealde for Cristes acennednysse. Þa feng Archelaus his sunu to rice; ða embe tyn geara fyrst wearð he ascofen of his cynesetle forðan þe þæt Iudeisce folc wrehton his modignysse to ðam casere, and he ða hine on wræcsið asende. Þa dælde se casere þæt Iudeisce rice on feower, and sette ðærto feower gebroðra: ða sind gecwedene æfter Greciscum gereorde *tetrarche,* þæt sind "fyðerrican."

to me on a platter.' The king was troubled by the request, and yet would not break his word for his oath and for his guests, nor displease the daughter; so he sent at once an executioner and commanded him to bring him his head on a platter. The executioner beheaded the great prophet in the prison, and brought the head to the king, and he gave it to his daughter, and the daughter to the mother. Afterward his followers came and buried his body."

This John was the greatest person, as Christ bore witness 3 concerning him; he said, "Among the children of women there has not arisen any greater one than John the Baptist." You have often heard of his famous way of life and of his ministry; now we will relate to you some explanation concerning the exposition of this gospel.

This Herod, who ordered John to be beheaded, and 4 agreed with the ealdorman Pilate in the savior's suffering, and delivered him to his judgment, was the son of the other Herod, who ruled at the time Christ was born; for it was the custom at that time for rich men to name their children after themselves, that it might seem a greater remembrance of the father when his son and heir was called by his father's name. The cruel father Herod left five sons: three he commanded to be slain while in his mortal illness, before he died; then he himself was dead, miserably and suddenly, after he had slain the children because of Christ's birth. Then Archelaus his son succeeded to the kingdom; after ten years he was driven from his throne because the Jewish people complained of his pride to the emperor, and he sent him into exile. The emperor then divided the Jewish kingdom into four parts, and placed four brothers over it: these are called, according to the Greek tongue, *tetrarch,* that is "ruler

Fyðerrica bið se ðe hæfð feorðan dæl rices. Þa wæs an ðyssera gebroðra Philippus gehaten, se gewifode on ðæs cyninges dehter Arethe, Arabiscre ðeode, seo hatte Herodias. Þa æfter sumum fyrste wurdon hi ungesome, Philippus and Arethe, and he genam ða dohtor of his aðumme, and forgeaf hi his breðer Herode forðan ðe he wæs furðor on hlisan and on mihte. Herodes ða awearp his riht æwe, and forligerlice manfulles sinscipes breac.

5   Þa on ðam timan bodade Iohannes se Fulluhtere Godes rihtwisnysse eallum Iudeiscum folce, and þreade ðone Herodem for ðam fulan sinscipe. *"Aecclesiastica historia" ita narrat:* Þa geseah Herodes þæt eal seo Iudeisce meniu arn to Iohannes lare and his mynegungum geornlice gehyrsumodon, þa wearð he afyrht, and wende þæt hi woldon for Iohannes lare his cynedom forseon; and wolde ða forhradian, and gebrohte hine on cwearterne on anre byrig þe is gecweden Macherunta. Hwæt ða Iohannes asende of ðam cwearterne twegen leorningcnihtas to Criste and hine befran, þus cweðende, "Eart ðu se ðe toweard is, oþþe we oðres andbidian sceolon?" Swilce he cwæde, "Geswutela me gyf ðu sylf wylle nyðerastigan to hellwarum for manna alysednysse, swa swa ðu woldest acenned beon for manna alysednysse; oððe gif ic sceole cyðan ðinne tocyme hellwarum, swa swa ic middangearde þe toweardne bodade, geswutela." Hwæt ða se hælend on ðære ylcan tide, swa swa Lucas se godspellere awrat, gehælde manega untruman fram mislicum coðum, and wodum mannum gewitt forgeaf, and blindum gesihðe; and cwæð syððan to Iohannes ærendracum, "Farað nu to Iohanne and cyðað him þa ðing þe ge gesawon and gehyrdon. Efne nu blinde geseoð, and ða healtan gað, and hreoflige men synd geclænsode; deafe gehyrað, and ða deadan arisað,

over a fourth." A tetrarch is one who has a fourth part of a kingdom. One of these brothers was called Philip, who married Herodias, the daughter of the king Arethe of the Arabian people. Then, after some time, Philip and Arethe were disunited, and he took the daughter from his son-in-law, giving her to his brother Herod because he was greater in fame and in power. Herod then cast off his lawful wife, and adulterously lived in a sinful marriage.

At that time John the Baptist preached God's righteousness to all the Jewish people, and rebuked Herod for that foul marriage. *The "Ecclesiastical History" tells it thus:* When Herod saw that all the Jewish multitude ran to John's teaching and eagerly obeyed his admonitions, he was afraid, and thought that through John's teaching they would despise his rule; he wanted to prevent that, and put him in prison in a town which is called Machaerus. Then John sent two disciples from the prison to Christ and asked him, saying, "Are you the one who is to come, or should we wait for another?" As though he had said, "Make known to me whether you yourself will descend to the inhabitants of hell for the redemption of humanity, just as you would be born for the redemption of humanity; or if I should announce your coming to the inhabitants of hell, just as I have preached to the world that you were to come, make that known." At the same time the savior, as the Evangelist Luke wrote, was healing many sick from various diseases, giving reason to the insane and sight to the blind; and afterward he said to John's messengers, "Go now to John and tell him the things you have seen and heard. Behold, the blind see, and the lame walk, and lepers are cleansed; the deaf hear, the dead arise, and ðearfan bodiað godspel, and se bið eadig þe on me ne bið geæswicod." Swylce he cwæde to Iohanne, "Þyllice wundra ic wyrce, ac swaðeah ic wylle deaðe sweltan for mancynnes alysednysse, and ðe sweltende æfterfyligan, and se bið gesælig þe mine wundra nu herað, gif he minne deað ne forsihð, and for ðam deaðe ne geortruwað þæt ic God eom." Þus onwreah se hælend Iohanne þæt he wolde hine sylfne gemedemian to deaðe, and syððan hellwara geneosian.

6   Þa betwux ðisum gelamp þæt Herodes, swa we ær cwædon, his witan gefeormode on ðam dæge þe he geboren wæs, forðan ðe hi hæfdon on ðam timan micele blisse on heora gebyrdtidum. Seo dohtor ða, swa swa we ær sædon, plegode mid hire mædenum on ðam gebeorscipe, him eallum to gecwemednysse, and se fæder ða mid aðe behet þæt he wolde hire forgyfan swa hwæs swa heo gewilnode. Þreo arleasa scylda we gehyrdon: ungesælige mærsunge his gebyrdtide, and ða unstæððigan hleapunge þæs mædenes, and ðæs fæder dyrstigan aðsware. Þam ðrim ðingum us gedafenað þæt we wiðcweðon on urum ðeawum. We ne moton ure gebyrdtide to nanum freolsdæge mid idelum mærsungum awendan, ne ure acennednysse on swilcum gemynde habban; ac we sceolon urne endenextan dæg mid behreowsunge and dædbote forhradian, swa swa hit awriten is, "On eallum ðingum beo ðu gemyndig þines endenextan dæges, and þu ne syngast on ecnysse." Ne us ne gedafenað þæt we urne lichaman, ðe Gode is gehalgod on ðam halwendan fulluhte, mid unþæslicum plegan and higleaste gescyndan, forðan ðe ure lichaman sind Godes lima, swa swa Paulus cwæð, "And he bebead þæt we sceolon gearcian ure lichaman liflice onsægednysse and halige, and Gode andfenge." Se lichama bið liflic onsægednys ðe wið heafodleahtras bið gescyld, and ðurh halige

the poor preach the gospel, and blessed is he who will not be offended in me." As though he had said to John, "I work such wonders, and yet I will perish by death for the redemption of humankind, and dying follow after you, and blessed will be he who now praises my wonders, if he does not despise my death, and on account of that death does not doubt that I am God." In this way the savior revealed to John that he would humble himself to die, and afterward visit the inhabitants of hell.

Meanwhile it happened that Herod, as we said before, 6 feasted with his counselors on the day that he was born, for at that time they had great rejoicing on their birthdays. The daughter then, as we have said, danced with her maidens at the feast, pleasing them all, and the father then promised with an oath that he would give her whatever she desired. We have heard three impious sins: the unfortunate celebration of his birthday, and the giddy dancing of the maiden, and the father's rash oath. It is fitting that we oppose these three things in our conduct. We may not turn our birthday into any holiday with vain celebrations, nor keep our birth in such remembrance; rather we should anticipate our last day with repentance and penance, just as it is written, "In all things be mindful of your last day, and you will never sin." It is not fitting for us to put our body, which is consecrated to God in saving baptism, to shame with indecent and foolish play, for our bodies are God's limbs, as Paul said, "And he commanded that we should prepare our bodies as a living and holy sacrifice, and acceptable to God." The body is a living sacrifice which is shielded against deadly sins, and

mægnu Gode bið andfenge and halig. God sylf forbyt ælcne
að Cristenum mannum, þus cweðende, "Ne swera ðu þurh
heofenan, forðan ðe heo is Godes þrymsetl; ne swera ðu
þurh eorðan, forðan ðe heo is Godes fotsceamol; ne swera
þu ðurh ðin agen heafod, forðan ðe ðu ne miht wyrcan an
hær þines feaxes hwit oððe blacc. Ic secge eow, ne swerige ge
þurh nan ðing, ac beo eower spræc ðus geendod: 'Hit is swa
ic secge, oþþe hit nis swa.' Swa hwæt swa ðær mare bið þurh
að, þæt bið of ðam yfelan."

7   Crist sylf gefæstnode his spræce þa ða he spræc to anum
Samaritaniscan wife mid ðisum worde, "*Crede mihi*," þæt is
"Gelyf me." Þeahhwæðere gif we hwær unwærlice swerion,
and se að us geneadige to wyrsan dæde, þonne bið us rædli-
cor þæt we ðone maran gylt forbugon and ðone að wið God
gebetan. Witodlice Dauid swor þurh God þæt he wolde
þone stuntan wer Nabal ofslean and ealle his ðing adylegian;
ac æt ðære forman þingunge þæs snoteran wifes Abigail he
awende his swurd into ðære sceaðe, and herode ðæs wifes
snoternysse, ðe him forwyrnde þone pleolican mannsliht.
Herodes swor þurh stuntnysse þæt he wolde ðære hleapen-
dan dehter forgyfan swa hwæt swa heo bæde; þa, forðam ðe
he nolde fram his gebeorum beon gecweden manswara,
ðone beorscipe mid blode gemencgde, and ðæs mæran witegan deað þære lyðran hoppystran hire gliges to mede forgeaf.
Micele selre him wære þæt he ðone að tobræce þonne he
swylcne witegan acwellan hete.

8   On eallum ðingum we sceolon carfullice hogian gif we
awar, þurh deofles syrwunge, on twam frecednyssum samod
befeallað, þæt we symle ðone maran gylt forfleon þurh ut-
fære þæs læssan, swa swa deð se ðe his feondum ofer sumne
weall ætfleon wile—ðonne cepð he hwær se weall unhehst

through holy virtues is acceptable to God and holy. God himself forbids any oath to Christians, saying, "Do not swear by heaven, for it is God's throne; do not swear by earth, for it is God's footstool; do not swear by your own head, for you cannot make one hair of your locks white or black. I say to you, do not swear by anything, but let your speech be thus ended: 'It is as I say, or it is not so.' Whatever more there is by oath, that is of evil."

Christ himself confirmed his speech when he spoke to a Samaritan woman with these words, *"Believe me,"* that is, "Believe me." Yet if we heedlessly swear anywhere, and the oath compels us to a worse deed, then it will be more advisable for us to avoid the greater guilt and atone to God for the oath. Indeed, David swore by God that he would kill the foolish man Nabal and destroy all his things; but at the first intercession of the prudent woman Abigail he returned his sword to its sheath, and praised the woman's prudence, who forbade him that dangerous murder. Herod swore foolishly that he would give the dancing daughter whatever she might ask for; then, because he would not be called a perjurer by his guests, he stained the feast with blood, and gave the death of the great prophet to the lewd dancer as a reward for her play. It would have been much better for him to have broken the oath than to have commanded such a prophet to be slain. 7

In all things we should carefully consider that if we ever fall into two dangers at once through the devil's schemes, we should always flee from the greater guilt by the outlet of the lesser, just as someone does who wants to flee from his enemies over a wall—he looks where the wall is lowest, and 8

sy, and ðær oferscyt. Witodlice Herodes, ða ðe he nolde, þurh Iohannes mynegunge, þone unclænan sinscipe awendan, ða wearð he to manslihte befeallen; and wæs seo læsse synn intinga þære maran, þæt he for his fulan forligre, ðe he georne wiste þæt Gode andsæte wæs, ðæs witegan blod ageat, þe he wiste þæt Gode gecweme wæs. Þis is se cwyde þæs godcundlican domes, be ðam þe is gecweden, "Se ðe derað, derige he gyt swyðor; and se ðe on fulnyssum wunað, befyle hine gyt swyðor." Þes cwyde gelamp þam wælhreowan Herode. Nu is oðer cwyde be godum mannum sceortlice gecweden: "Se ðe halig is, beo he gyt swyðor gehalgod." Þis gelamp þam Fulluhtere Iohanne, se ðe wæs halig þurh menigfealde geearnunga, and he wæs gyt swyðor gehalgod ða ða he ðurh soðfæstnysse bodunge becom to sigefæstum martyrdome.

9   Herodes hiwode hine sylfne unrotne þa seo dohtor hine þæs heafdes bæd; ac he blissode on his digelnyssum, forðan ðe heo þæs mannes deað bæd ðe he ær acwellan wolde, gif he intingan hæfde. Witodlice gif þæt cild bæde þæs wifes heafod, mid micclum graman he wolde hire wiðcweðan. Næs Iohannes mid ehtnysse geneadod þæt he Criste wiðsoce, ac ðeah he sealde his lif for Criste ða ða he wæs for soðfæstnysse gemartyrod. Crist sylf cwæð, "Ic eom soðfæstnys." Iohannes wæs Cristes forrynel on his acennednysse and on his bodunge, on fulluhte, on ðrowunge, and hine to hellwarum mid deorwurðum deaðe forestop. Þa ða he beheafdod wæs, ða comon his leorningcnihtas and his halige lic ferodon to anre byrig seo is gecweden Sebaste, and hi ðær hine geledon. Þæt halige heafod wearð on Hierusalem bebyrged.

jumps over there. Indeed Herod, when he would not turn away from his unclean marriage through John's remonstrance, fell into murder; and the lesser sin was the cause of the greater, so that for his foul adultery, which he well knew was hateful to God, he shed the prophet's blood, who he knew was acceptable to God. This is the sentence of the divine judgment, by which it is said, "He who injures, let him injure still more; and he who lives in foulness, let him defile himself still more." This sentence befell the cruel Herod. Now there is another sentence briefly said concerning good people: "He who is holy, let him be still more hallowed." This befell the Baptist, John, who was holy through many merits, and he was yet more hallowed when he came to triumphant martyrdom through the preaching of truth.

Herod pretended to be sad when the daughter asked him for the head; but he secretly rejoiced, because she asked for the death of that man whom he would have slain earlier, if he had had any cause. Indeed, if the child had asked for the woman's head, he would have refused her with great anger. John was not compelled to deny Christ by persecution, yet he gave his life for Christ when he was martyred for truth. Christ himself said, "I am truth." John was Christ's forerunner in his birth and in his preaching, in baptism, in suffering, and with his precious death preceded him among the inhabitants of hell. When he was beheaded, his disciples came and took his holy body to a city called Sebaste, and they laid him there. The holy head was buried at Jerusalem. 9

10 Sume gedwolmenn cwædon þæt þæt heafod sceolde abla-
wan ðæs cyninges wif Herodiaden, ðe he fore acweald wæs,
swa þæt heo ferde mid windum geond ealle woruld; ac hi
dwelodon mid þære segene, forðan ðe heo leofode hire lif oð
ende æfter Iohannes slege. Soðlice Iohannes heafod wearð
syððan geswutelod twam easternum munecum, þe mid
gebedum ða burh geneosodon, and hi ðanon þone deorwurðan maðm feredon to sumere byrig þe is Edissa gehaten;
and se ælmihtiga God þurh þæt heafod ungerime wundra
geswutelode. His ban æfter langum fyrste wurdon gebrohte
to ðære mæran byrig Alexandria, and þær mid micclum
wurðmynte gelogode.

11 Nu is to besceawigenne humeta se ælmihtiga God be his
gecorenan and ða gelufedan ðenas, þa ðe he to ðam ecan life
forestihte, geðafað þæt hi mid swa micclum witum beon fornumene and tobrytte on ðisum andweardan life. Ac se apostol Paulus andwyrde be ðisum, and cwæð þæt "God þreað
and beswingð ælcne ðe he underfehð to his rice, and swa he
forsewenlicor bið gewitnod for Godes naman, swa his wuldor bið mare for Gode." Eft cwæð se ylca apostol on oðre
stowe, "Ne sind na to wiðmetenne ða þrowunga þyssere tide
ðam toweardan wuldre þe bið on us geswutelod."

12 Nu cwyð se trahtnere þæt nan wilde deor, ne on fyðerfotum ne on creopendum, nis to wiðmetenne yfelum wife.
Hwæt is betwux fyðerfotum reðre þonne leo? oððe hwæt is
wælhreowre betwux næddercynne ðonne draca? Ac se wisa
Salomon cwæð þæt selre wære to wunigenne mid leon and
dracan þonne mid yfelan wife and oferspræcum. Witodlice
Iohannes on westene wunade betwux eallum deorcynne
ungederod, and betwux dracum, and aspidum, and eallum
wyrmcynne, and hi hine ondredon. Soðlice seo awyrigede

Some heretics have said that the head blew on the king's   10
wife Herodias, who was responsible for his death, so that
she went with the winds over all the world; but they erred in
saying that, because she lived her life to its end after the
slaying of John. But John's head was afterward revealed to
two eastern monks, who visited that city with prayers, and
they carried the precious treasure from there to a city called
Edessa; and through that head the almighty God manifested
countless miracles. After a long time his bones were brought
to the great city of Alexandria, and deposited there with
great honor.

Now we ought to consider why the almighty God allows   11
his chosen and his beloved servants, whom he has predes-
tined to eternal life, to be destroyed and broken with so
many tortures in this present life. But the apostle Paul has
answered concerning this, and said that "God corrects and
scourges every one he receives into his kingdom, and the
more contemptibly he is tortured for the name of God, so
much greater will his glory be before God." Again, the same
apostle said in another place, "The sufferings of this life are
not to be compared with the future glory which will be manifested in us."

Now, the commentator says that no wild beast, neither   12
four footed nor crawling, is to be compared to an evil
woman. What among the four-footed beasts is fiercer than a
lion? or what among the serpent kind is crueler than a
dragon? But the wise Solomon said that it would be better
to dwell with a lion and a dragon than with an evil and garrulous woman. Indeed, John had lived in the desert unharmed among all kinds of beasts, and among dragons, asps,
and all kinds of serpents, and they feared him. But the

Herodias mid beheafdunge hine acwealde, and swa mæres
mannes dead to gife hire dehter hleapunge underfeng. Danihel se witega læg seofan niht betwux seofan leonum on
anum seade ungewemmed, ac þæt awyrigede wif Gezabel
beswac done rihtwisan Naboþ to his feore þurh lease gewitnysse. Se witega Ionas wæs gehealden unformolten on dæs
hwæles innode dreo niht, and seo swicole Dalila þone strangan Samson mid olæcunge bepæhte and, besceorenum fexe,
his feondum belæwde. Eornostlice nis nan wyrmcynn ne
wilddeora cynn on yfelnysse gelic yfelum wife.

13   Se wyrdwritere Iosephus awrat on dære cyrclican gereccednysse þæt se wælhreowa Herodes lytle hwile æfter Iohannes deade rices weolde, ac weard for his mandædum
ærest his here on gefeohte ofslegen, and he sylf siddan of his
cynerice ascofen and on wræcsid asend swide rihtwisum
dome; da da he nolde hlystan Iohannes lare to dam ecan life,
þæt he eac hrædlice his hwilwendan cynedom mid hospe
forlure. Augustinus se wisa us manad mid þisum wordum,
and cwyd, "Besceawiad, ic bidde eow, mine gebrodra, mid
gleawnysse hu wræcfull dis andwyrde lif is, and deah ge on-
drædad eow þæt ge hit to hrædlice forlæton. Ge lufiad þis lif
on dam þe ge mid geswince wuniad: du hogast embe dine
neode; du yrnst and byst geancsumod; þu erast, and sæwst,
and eft gegaderast; þu grinst and bæcst; þu wyfst and wæda
tylast, and earfodlice wast ealra dinra neoda getel, ægder ge
on sæ ge on lande, and scealt ealle þas foresædan ding, and
eac din agen lif, mid earfodnysse geendian. Leorniad nu fordi
þæt ge cunnon þæt ece lif geearnian, on dam de ge nan dys-
sera geswinca ne drowiad, ac on ecnysse mid Gode rixiad."

14   On disum life we ateoriad gif we us mid bigleofan ne

cursed Herodias killed him by beheading, and received the death of such a great man as a gift for her daughter's dancing. Daniel the prophet lay seven nights uninjured in a den among seven lions, but the accursed woman Jezebel betrayed the righteous Naboth to his death by false witness. The prophet Jonah was kept undigested in the belly of the whale for three nights, and the treacherous Delilah deceived the strong Samson with flattery and, when his locks were cut off, betrayed him to his enemies. Indeed, there is no kind of serpent or wild beast equal in evilness to an evil woman.

The historian Josephus wrote in the ecclesiastical history 13 that the cruel Herod ruled his kingdom a little while after the death of John, but first for his wicked deeds his army was slain in battle, and he himself afterward was driven from his kingdom and sent into exile by a very righteous judgment; when he would not, for eternal life, listen to John's teachings, then he should also suddenly lose his transitory kingdom in disgrace. The wise Augustine exhorts us with these words, and says, "I pray you, my brothers, consider with understanding how wretched this present life is, and yet you fear that you will leave it too quickly. You love this life in which you dwell with toil: you worry about your need; you run and are anxious; you plow, and sow, and then gather; you grind and bake; you weave and prepare garments, and hardly know the number of all your needs, both on sea and on land, and all these aforesaid things, and even your own life, will end with tribulation. Learn now, therefore, how you may know how to merit eternal life, in which you will suffer none of these toils, but will reign with God for eternity."

In this life we grow weak if we do not sustain ourselves 14

ferciað; gif we ne drincað, we beoð mid þurste fornumene; gif we to lange waciað, we ateoriað; gif we lange standað, we beoð gewæhte, and þonne sittað; eft gif we to lange sittað, us slapað ða lyma. Sceawiað eac æfter ðisum, þæt nan stede nis ures lichaman: cildhad gewit to cnihthade, and cnihthad to geðungenum wæstme; se fulfremeda wæstm gebyhð to ylde, and seo yld bið mid deaðe geendod. Witodlice ne stent ure yld on nanre staþolfæstnesse, ac swa micclum swa se lichama wext, swa micclum beoð his dagas gewanode. Gehwær is on urum life ateorung and werignyss and brosnung ðæs lichaman, and ðeahhwæðere wilnað gehwa þæt he lange lybbe. Hwæt is lange lybban buton lange swincan? Feawum mannum gelimpð on ðisum dagum þæt he gesundfull lybbe hundeahtatig geara, and swa hwæt swa he ofer ðam leofað hit bið him geswinc and sarnyss, swa swa se witega cwæð, "Yfele sind ure dagas"—and ðæs þe wyrsan þe we hi lufiað. Swa olæcð þes middangeard forwel menige þæt hi nellað heora wræcfulle lif geendian. Soð lif and gesælig þæt is þonne we arisað of deaðe and mid Criste rixiað. On ðam life beoð gode dagas, na swaðeah manega dagas, ac an, se nat nænne upspring ne nane geendunge, ðam ne fyligð merigenlic dæg forðan ðe him ne forestop se gysternlica; ac se an dæg bið ece æfre ungeendod butan ælcere nihte, butan gedreccednyssum, butan eallum geswincum þe we hwene ær on ðyssere rædinge tealdon. Þes dæg and þis lif is behaten rihtwisum Cristenum; to ðam us gelæde se mildheorta Drihten, se ðe leofað and rixað mid Fæder and mid Halgum Gaste a butan ende. Amen.

with food; if we do not drink, we are destroyed by thirst; if we stay awake too long, we grow weak; if we stand long, we are tired, and then sit; and then if we sit too long, our limbs fall asleep. Consider also this, that there is no stability in our body: childhood passes to youth, and youth to full growth; full growth bends to age, and age is ended by death. Indeed, our age stands on no stability, but as much as the body grows, by so much are its days diminished. Everywhere in our life are faintness and weariness and decay of the body, and yet everyone desires that he might live long. What is to live long but to toil long? It happens to few in these days that they live eighty years in health, and whatever one lives beyond that is toil and pain to him, as the prophet said, "Evil are our days"—and what is worse, we love them. This world so flatters very many that they are unwilling to end their life of exile. A true and blessed life it will be when we arise from death and reign with Christ. In that life will be good days, yet not many days, but one, which knows no rising nor ending, which no tomorrow follows because no yesterday preceded it; but the one day will forever be unending without any night, without afflictions, without all the toils which we recounted a little before in this reading. This day and this life are promised to righteous Christians; may the merciful Lord lead us to them, he who lives and reigns with the Father and the Holy Spirit ever without end. Amen.

33

Dominica XVII *post Pentecosten*

I̲bat Iesus in civitatem quae vocatur Naim, et reliqua.

2 "Ure Drihten ferde to sumere byrig seo is gehaten Naim, and his gingran samod and genihtsum menigu. Þa ða he genealæhte þam portgeate, þa ferede man anes cnihtes lic to byrgene. His modor wæs wudewe, and mid wope ðam lice folgode, forðan ðe heo wæs wereleas and hire ancennedan suna benæmed. Efne ða se hælend beseah wið hire and wearð mid mildheortnysse astyred, and hire to cwæð, 'Ne wep ðu.' He ða genealæhte and hrepode ða bære, and ða bærmen þærrihte ætstodon. Se hælend cwæð, 'Þu cniht, ic secge ðe aris,' and he ðærrihte gesæt and sprecende wæs. Drihten ða hine betæhte þære meder and hire gefrefrode. Hwæt ða micel oga asprang on eallum ðam folce, and hi mærsodon God þus cweðende, 'Eala, mære witega aras betwux us, and God geneosode his folc.'"

3 Beda se trahtnere cwæð þæt seo burh *Naim* is gereht "yðung" oððe "styrung." Se deada cniht ðe on manegra manna gesihðe wæs geferod getacnað gehwylcne synfulne mannan þe bið mid healicum leahtrum on ðam inran menn adydd, and bið his yfelnys mannum cuð. Se cniht wæs ancenned sunu his meder, swa bið eac gehwilc Cristen man gastlice ðære halgan gelaðunge sunu, seo is ure ealra modor and ðeahhwæðere ungewemmed mæden; forðan ðe hire

33

Seventeenth Sunday after Pentecost

Seventeenth Sunday after Pentecost

*J*esus *went into a city called Naim, etc.*

"Our Lord went to a city called Naim with his disciples ₂
and a sizable crowd. As he neared the city gate, a young
man's body was being carried out to be buried. His mother
was a widow, and followed the body with weeping, because
she was without a husband and deprived of her only-
begotten son. Then the savior looked at her and was moved
with pity, and said to her, 'Do not weep.' He approached and
touched the bier, and the pallbearers immediately stopped.
The savior said, 'Young man, I say to you, arise,' and at once
he sat up and was speaking. The Lord then entrusted him to
his mother and comforted her. At this, a great fear sprang up
among all the people, and they glorified God, saying, 'Lo, a
great prophet has arisen among us, and God has visited his
people.'"

The commentator Bede said that the city of *Naim* is in- ₃
terpreted "inundation" or "agitation." The dead youth who
was carried in sight of many signifies every sinful person
whose inner self is destroyed by deadly sins, and whose evil
is known to others. The youth was the only-begotten son of
his mother, as every Christian is also spiritually a son of the
holy Church, which is the mother of us all and nevertheless
an undefiled virgin; for her offspring is not physical but

team nis na lichamlic ac gastlic. Gehwilc Godes ðeow, þonne he leornað, he bið bearn gecweden; eft, þonne he oðerne lærð, he bið modor, swa swa se apostol Paulus be ðam aslidenum mannum cwæð, "Ge synd mine bearn, ða ðe ic nu oðre siðe geeacnige, oðþæt Crist beo on eow geedniwod." Þæt portgeat getacnað sum lichamlic andgit þe menn ðurh syngiað. Se mann ðe tosæwð ungeþwærnysse betwux Cristenum mannum, oððe se ðe sprecð unrihtwisnysse on heannysse ðurh his muðes geat, he bið dead gefered. Se ðe behylt wimman mid galre gesihðe and fulum luste ðurh his eagena geat, he geswutelað his sawle deað. Se ðe idele spellunge oððe tallice word lustlice gehyrð þonne macað he his eare him sylfum to deaðes geate. Swa is eac be ðam oðrum andgitum to understandenne.

4   Se hælend wearð astyred mid mildheortnysse ofer ðære meder þæt he us bysene sealde his arfæstnysse, and he ðone deadan syððan arærde þæt he us to his geleafan getrymede. He genealæhte and hrepode þa bære, and þa bærmenn ætstodon. Seo bær ðe þone deadan ferode is þæt orsorge ingehyd þæs orwenan synfullan. Soðlice ða byrðeras ðe hine to byrgenne feredon synd olæcunga lyffetyndra geferena, þe mid olæcunge and geættredum swæsnyssum þone synfullan tihtað and heriað, swa swa se witega cwæð, "Se synfulla bið geherod on his lustum, and se unrihtwisa bið gebletsod"; þonne he bið mid idelum hlisan and lyffetungum befangen, þonne bið hit swylce he sy mid sumere moldhypan ofhroren. Be swylcum cwæð se hælend to anum his gecorenan ða ða he wolde his fæder lic bebyrian, he cwæð, "Geðafa þæt ða deadan bebyrion heora deadan. Far ðu, and boda Godes rice." Witodlice ða deadan bebyriað oðre deadan þonne gehwilce synfulle menn oðre heora gelican mid derigendlicere

spiritual. Every servant of God, when he is learning, is called a child; later, when he teaches another, he is a mother, as the apostle Paul said of the fallen, "You are my children, whom I now conceive a second time, until Christ is renewed in you." The gate signifies the bodily sense through which people sin. The person who sows dissension among Christians, or who speaks unrighteousness in high places through the gate of his mouth, is carried dead. He who beholds a woman with lecherous sight and foul lust through the gate of his eyes, he reveals his soul's death. He who hears with delight idle speech or backbiting words makes his ear a gate of his own death. We should understand the same of the other senses as well.

The savior was moved to pity for the mother so that he might give us an example of his piety, and later he raised the dead so that he might strengthen our faith in him. He approached and touched the bier, and the pallbearers stood still. The bier which carried the dead person is the heedless mind of the hopeless sinner. Truly the bearers who carried him to the grave are the blandishments of flattering companions, who with blandishment and poisoned sweetness incite and praise the sinful, as the prophet said, "The sinful is praised for his lusts, and the unrighteous is blessed"; when he is surrounded by empty fame and flatteries, then is it as if he were overwhelmed by a heap of dust. Of such people the savior said to one of his chosen when he wanted to bury his father's body, "Let the dead bury their dead. Go, and preach God's kingdom." Indeed, the dead bury other dead when sinful people entice others like them with harmful praise

herunge geolæcað and mid gegaderodum hefe þære wyrstan
lyffetunge ofðriccað. Be swylcum is gecweden on oðre
stowe, "Lyffetyndra tungan gewriðað manna sawla on synnum."

5   Mid þam ðe Drihten hrepode ða bære, ða ætstodon þa
bærmenn. Swa eac gif ðæs synfullan ingehyd bið gehrepod
mid fyrhte þæs upplican domes, þonne wiðhæfð he ðam
unlustum and ðam leasum lyffeterum, and clypigendum
Drihtne to ðam ecan life caflice geandwyrt, swylce he of
deaðe arise. "Drihten cwæð to ðam cnihte, 'Ic secge ðe, aris,'
and he ðærrihte gesæt and spræc, and se hælend betæhte
hine his meder." Se geedcucoda sitt þonne se synfulla mid
godcundre onbryrdnysse cucað. He sprecð þonne he mid
Godes herungum his muð gebysgað and mid soðre andetnysse Godes mildheortnysse secþ. He bið his meder betæht
þonne he bið þurh sacerda ealdordom gemænscipe ðære
halgan gelaðunge geferlæht. Þæt folc wearð mid micclum
ege ablicged; forðan swa swa mann fram marum synnum gecyrð to Godes mildheortnysse, and his ðeawas æfter Godes
bebodum gerihtlæcð, swa ma manna beoð gecyrrede ðurh
his gebysnunge to Godes herunge.

6   "Þæt folc cwæð þæt mære witega aras betwux us, and þæt
God his folc geneosode." Soð hi sædon be Criste þæt he
mære witega is, ac he is witegena witega, and heora ealra witegung; forðan ðe ealle be him witegodon, and he ðurh his
tocyme heora ealra witegunge gefylde. We cweðað nu mid
maran geleafan þæt he is mære witega, forðan ðe he wat
ealle ðing, and eac fela witegode, and he is soð God of soðum
Gode, ælmihtig Sunu of ðam ælmihtigan Fæder, se ðe his
folc geneosode þurh his menniscnysse and fram deofles
ðeowte alysde.

and oppress them with the accumulated weight of the worst flattery. Of such it is said in another place, "The tongues of flatterers bind souls in sins."

When the Lord touched the bier, the pallbearers stood 5 still. So too if the mind of the sinner is touched by fear of the judgment on high, then he refrains from evil lusts and false flatteries, and promptly answers the Lord calling to eternal life, as if he were arising from death. "The Lord said to the youth, 'I say to you, arise,' and he immediately sat up and spoke, and the savior entrusted him to his mother." The revived person sits up when a sinner quickens with divine compunction. He speaks when he busies his mouth with praises of God and seeks God's mercy with true confession. He is entrusted to his mother when through the priest's authority he is joined to the fellowship of the holy Church. The people were astonished with great awe; for just as a person turns from great sins to God's mercy, and corrects his conduct after God's commandments, so more people will be turned to the praise of God through his example.

"The people said that a great prophet has arisen among 6 us, and that God has visited his people." Truly they said of Christ that he is a great prophet, for he is a prophet of prophets, and the prophecy of them all; for they all prophesied about him, and by his coming he fulfilled the prophecy of them all. We say now with great faith that he is a great prophet, for he knows all things, and also prophesied many things, and he is true God of true God, almighty Son of the almighty Father, who visited his people through his incarnation and released them from enslavement to the devil.

7   We rædað gehwær on bocum þæt se hælend fela deade to
life arærde, ac ðeahhwæðere nis nan godspell gesett be
heora nanum buton ðrim anum. An is þes cniht þe we nu
embe spræcon, oðer wæs anes ealdormannes dohtor, þridde
wæs Lazarus, Marthan broðer and Marian. Þyssera ðreora
manna ærist getacnað þæt ðryfealde ærist synfullra sawla.
Þære sawle deað is þreora cynna: an is yfel geðafung, oðer is
yfel weorc, ðridda is yfel gewuna. Ðæs ealdormannes dohtor
læig æt forðsiðe, and se fæder gelaðode ðone hælend þærto,
forðan ðe he wæs on ðam timan þær on neawiste. Heo ða
forðferde ærðan ðe he hire to come; þa ða he com, ða genam
he hi be ðære handa and cwæð, "Þu mæden, ic secge ðe,
aris." And heo ðærrihte aras and metes bæd.

8   Þis mæden, ðe inne læg on deaðe geswefod, getacnað
þære synfullan sawle deað ðe gelustfullað on yfelum lustum
digellice, and ne bið gyt mannum cuð þæt heo þurh synna
dead is; ac Crist geswutelode þæt he wolde swa synfulle
sawle geliffæstan gif he mid geornfullum gebedum to gelaðod bið, þa ða he arærde þæt mæden binnan ðam huse,
swa swa digelne leahter on menniscre heortan lutigende.
Nu syndon oðre synfulle þe gelustfulliað on derigendlicum
lustum mid geðafunge, and eac heora yfelnysse mid weorcum cyðað; swilce getacnode se deada cniht ðe wæs on þæs
folces gesihðe geferod. Swilce synfulle arærð Crist gif hi
heora synna behreowsiað, and betæcð hi heora meder, þæt
is, þæt he hi geferlæcð on annysse his gelaðunge.

9   Sume synfulle men geðafiað heora lustum, and ðurh yfele
dæda mannum cyðað heora synna, and eac gewunelice syngigende hi sylfe gewemmað; þyllice getacnode Lazarus, þe læg
on byrgene feower niht fule stincende. Witodlice Godes
nama is ælmihtig, forðan ðe he mæg ealle ðing gefremman.

We read in many places in books that the savior raised 7
many dead persons to life, yet there is no gospel composed
about any of them except for three only. One is this youth
we have just spoken about, the second was an ealdorman's
daughter, the third was Lazarus, the brother of Martha and
Mary. The resurrection of these three people signifies the
threefold resurrection of sinful souls. The soul's death is of
three kinds: one is evil consent, the second is evil deeds, the
third is evil habit. The ealdorman's daughter lay at the point
of death, and the father called the savior to her, because he
was there in the neighborhood at that time. She departed
before he could come to her; when he came, he took her by
the hand, and said, "Maiden, I say to you, arise." And she
arose at once and asked for food.

This maiden, who lay inside asleep in death, signifies the 8
death of the sinful soul which secretly delights in evil pleasures, and people do not yet know that it is dead through
sins; but Christ revealed that he would give life to so sinful a
soul if he is called to it with fervent prayers, when he raised
the maiden within the house, like a secret sin lurking in the
human heart. Now there are other sinners who delight in
harmful lusts by consent, and also manifest their evil by
deeds; the dead youth who was carried in sight of the people
signified this. Christ raises such sinners if they repent of
their sins, and delivers them to their mother, that is, he
unites them in the unity of his Church.

Some sinful people consent to their desires, and show 9
their sins to others by evil deeds, and also defile themselves
by habitually sinning; these are signified by Lazarus, who lay
four days foully stinking in the tomb. Indeed, God's name is
almighty, for he can accomplish all things. He can give life to

He mæg ða synfullan sawle ðurh his gife geliffæstan, ðeah ðe
heo on gewunelicum synnum fule stince, gif heo mid car-
fulre drohtnunge Godes mildheortnysse secð; ac swa mare
wund swa heo maran læcedomes behofað. Þæt geswutelode
se hælend þa þa he mid leohtlicere stemne þæt mæden
arærde on feawra manna gesihðe, forðan ðe he ne geðafode
þæt ðæra ma manna inne wære buton se fæder, and seo
modor, and his ðry leorningcnihtas: and he cwæð ða, "Þu
mæden, aris."

10   Swa bið eac se digla deað ðære sawle eaþelicor to
arærenne ðe on geðafunge digelice syngað þonne synd ða
openan leahtras to gehælenne. Þone cniht he arærde on
ealles folces gesihðe, and mid þysum wordum getrymede,
"Þu cniht, ic secge ðe, aris." Þa diglan gyltas man sceal digelice betan, and ða openan openlice, þæt ða beon getimbrode
þurh his behreowsunge ðe ær wæron þurh his mandæda
geæswicode.

11   Drihten, ða ða he Lazarum stincendne arærde, ða ge-
drefde he hine sylfne and tearas ageat, and mid micelre
stemne clypode, "Lazare, ga forð"; ða he geswutelode þæt se
ðe swiðe langlice and gewunelice syngode, þæt he eac mid
micelre behreowsunge and wope sceal his yfelan gewunan to
Godes rihtwisnysse geweman. Nis nan synn swa micel þæt
man ne mæge gebetan, gif he mid inneweardre heortan be
ðæs gyltes mæðe on soðre dædbote þurhwunað. Is þeahhwæðere micel smeagung be anum worde þe Crist cwæð: he
cwæð, "Ælc synn and tal bið forgifen behreowsigendum
mannum, ac þæs Halgan Gastes tal ne bið næfre forgifen.
Þeah ðe hwa cweðe tallic word ongean me, him bið forgyfen
gif he deð dædbote; soðlice se ðe cweð word ongan ðone
Halgan Gast ne bið hit him forgifen on ðyssere worulde ne

the sinful soul through his grace, though it foully stinks in habitual sins, if it seeks God's mercy with careful conduct; but the more wounded it is, the more medicine it requires. The savior revealed that when with a clear voice he raised the maiden in the sight of a few persons, because he did not allow more people to be within than the father, the mother, and his three disciples: he then said, "Maiden, arise."

So too it is easier to raise the secret death of the soul 10 which sins secretly by consent than it is to heal open vices. He raised the youth in the sight of all the people, and confirmed it by these words, "Youth, I say to you, arise." Secret sins should be atoned for secretly, and open ones openly, that those who had formerly been seduced by his sins may be edified by his repentance.

The Lord, when he raised the stinking Lazarus, was trou- 11 bled and shed tears, and cried out with a loud voice, "Lazarus, go forth"; by this he revealed that he who has sinned very long and habitually should also turn from his evil habits to God's righteousness with great repentance and weeping. There is no sin so great that one cannot atone for it, if with inward heart he continues in true penitence according to the degree of the sin. There is, however, great speculation concerning one sentence which Christ said: he said, "Every sin and blasphemy will be forgiven to those repenting, but blasphemy against the Holy Spirit will never be forgiven. Though someone speak a blasphemous word against me, he will be forgiven if he does penance; but he who says a word against the Holy Spirit will not be forgiven in this world or

on ðære towerdan." Nis nan synne forgifenys buton ðurh ðone Halgan Gast. An ælmihtig Fæder is, se gestrynde ænne Sunu of him sylfum. Nis se Fæder gehæfd gemænelice Fæder fram ðam Suna and þam Halgan Gaste, forðan ðe he nis heora begra fæder. And se Sunu nis na gemænelice Sunu fram þam Fæder and þam Halgan Gaste, forðan ðe he nis hera begra sunu. Se Halga Gast soðlice is gemænelice ge-hæfd fram ðam Fæder and þam Suna, forðan ðe he is heora begra Gast, þæt is heora begra lufu and willa, þurh ðone beoð synna forgyfene. Witodlice ðære Halgan Ðrynnysse weorc is æfre untodæledlic, þeahhwæðere belimpð ælc for-gifenyss to ðam Halgan Gaste, swa swa seo acennednys be-limpð to Criste anum.

12   Hi ne magon beon togædere genemnede, Fæder, and Sunu, and Halig Gast, ac hi ne beoð mid ænigum fæce fram him sylfum awar totwæmede. On eallum weorcum hi beoð togædere, þeah ðe to ðam Fæder synderlice belimpe þæt he bearn gestrynde, and to ðam Suna belimpe seo acennednys, and to þam Halgan Gaste seo forðstæppung. Se Sunu is ðæs Fæder wisdom æfre of þam Fæder acenned; se Halga Gast nis na acenned, forðan ðe he nis na sunu, ac he is heora begra lufu and willa, æfre of him bam forðstæppende, þurh ðone we habbað synna forgyfenysse, swa swa we habbað þurh Crist alysednysse; and þeahhwæðere on ægðrum weorce is seo Halige Ðrynnyss wyrcende untodæledlice. Se cwyð tal ongean ðone Halgan Gast se ðe mid unbehreowsigendre heortan þurhwunað on mandædum, and forsihð þa forgyfe-nysse ðe stent on ðæs Halgan Gastes gife; þonne bið his scyld unalysendlic, forðan ðe he sylf him belicð þære forgife-nysse weg mid his heardheortnysse. Behreowsigendum bið forgifen, forseondum næfre.

the one to come." There is no forgiveness of sins except through the Holy Spirit. There is one almighty Father, who produced one Son of himself. The Father is not held in common as Father between the Son and the Holy Spirit, for he is not the father of them both. And the Son is not held in common as Son between the Father and the Holy Spirit, because he is not the son of them both. But the Holy Spirit is held in common between the Father and the Son, for he is the Spirit of them both, that is the love and will of them both, through whom sins are forgiven. Truly the work of the Holy Trinity is ever indivisible, yet all forgiveness belongs to the Holy Spirit, just as birth belongs to Christ alone.

They cannot be named together, Father, and Son, and 12 Holy Spirit, but they are not separated from themselves by any space anywhere. They are together in all works, though to the Father exclusively belongs his begetting of a son, and to the Son belongs birth, and to the Holy Spirit procession. The Son is the wisdom of the Father ever begotten of the Father; the Holy Spirit is not begotten, because he is not a son, but is the love and will of them both, ever proceeding from them both, through whom we have forgiveness of sins, just as we have redemption through Christ; and yet in either work the Holy Trinity is working indivisibly. He speaks blasphemy against the Holy Spirit who persists in wicked deeds with an unrepentant heart, and despises the forgiveness which is in the grace of the Holy Spirit; then his guilt will be unredeemable, for he himself closes the way of forgiveness with his hardheartedness. The repenting shall be forgiven, the despising never.

13 Uton we biddan þone ælmihtigan Fæder, se ðe us þurh
his wisdom geworhte, and þurh his Halgan Gast geliffæste,
þæt he ðurh ðone ylcan Gast us do ure synna forgyfenysse,
swa swa he us ðurh his ænne ancennedan Sunu fram deofles
ðeowte alysde. Sy lof and wuldor þam ecan Fæder se ðe
næfre ne ongann, and his anum bearne se ðe æfre of him is,
and þam Halgan Gaste se ðe æfre is of him bam, hi ðry an
ælmihtig God, untodæledlic, a on ecnysse rixigende. Amen.

34

III KALENDAS OCTOBRIS

*Dedicatio ecclesiae sancti
Michaelis archangeli*

Manegum mannum is cuð seo halige stow Sancte Mi-
chaheles, on þære dune þe is gehaten Garganus. Seo dun
stent on Campania landes gemæron, wið þa Sæ Adriaticum,
twelf mila on upstige fram anre byrig þe is gehaten Sepon-
tina. Of ðære stowe wearð aræred þises dæges freols geond
geleaffulle gelaðunge. Þær eardode sum þurhspedig mann
Garganus gehaten; of his gelimpe wearð seo dun swa

Let us pray to the almighty Father, who has made us 13 through his wisdom, and given us life through his Holy Spirit, that through the same Spirit he may grant us forgiveness of our sins, just as through his only-begotten Son he has freed us from servitude to the devil. Praise and glory be to the eternal Father who never began, and to his only Son who is ever of him, and to the Holy Spirit who is ever of them both, these three one almighty God, indivisible, reigning forever in eternity. Amen.

34

Dedication of the Church of Saint Michael the Archangel

SEPTEMBER 29

*Dedication of the Church of
Saint Michael the Archangel*

Many people know the holy place of Saint Michael, on the mountain called Gargano. The mountain is on the border of Campania, by the Adriatic Sea, twelve miles up from a city called Siponto. Today's feast day was established in that place throughout the faithful Church. A prosperous man named Garganus lived there; the mountain was named after

geciged. Hit gelamp þa þa seo ormæte micelnyss his orfes on ðære dune læswede, þæt sum modig fearr wearð angencga and þære heordedrafe oferhogode. Hwæt se hlaford þa Garganus gegaderode micele menigu his incnihta and ðone fearr gehwær on ðam westene sohte, and æt nextan hine gemette standan uppon ðam cnolle þære healican dune, æt anes scræfes inngange; and he ða mid graman wearð astyred hwi se fearr angenga his heorde forsawe, and gebende his bogan and mid geættrode flan hine ofsceotan wolde. Ac seo geættrode fla wende ongeann swilce mid windes blæde aðrawen, and þone ðe hi sceat þærrihte ofsloh.

2   His magas ða and nehgeburas wurdon þearle þurh ða dæde ablicgede, and heora nan ne dorste ðam fearre genealæcan. Hi ða heora biscop rædes befrunon hwæt him be ðam to donne wære. Se biscop ða funde him to ræde þæt hi mid þreora daga fæstene swutelunge þæs wundres æt Gode bædon. Þa on ðære ðriddan nihte þæs fæstenes æteowde se heahengel Michahel hine sylfne þam biscope on gastlicere gesihðe, þus cweðende, "Wislice ge dydon þæt ge to Gode sohton þæt þæt mannum digle wæs. Wite ðu gewislice þæt se mann ðe mid his agenre flan ofscoten wæs, þæt hit is mid minum willan gedon. Ic eom Michahel se heahengel Godes ælmihtiges, and ic symle on his gesihðe wunige. Ic secge ðe þæt ic ða stowe þe se fearr geealgode synderlice lufige, and ic wolde mid þære gebicnunge geswutelian þæt ic eom ðære stowe hyrde; and ealra ðæra tacna ðe ðær gelimpað, ic eom sceawere and gymend." And se heahengel mid þisum wordum to heofonum gewat.

3   Se biscop rehte his gesihðe þam burhwarum, and hi ða syððan gewunelice þider sohton, and þone lifigendan God and his heahengel Michahel geornlice bædon. Twa dura hi

what happened to him. It happened that when the great multitude of his cattle was grazing on the mountain, a proud bull wandered by alone and scorned the herd. At this, the lord Garganus gathered a great many of his household servants and went looking for the bull everywhere in the wilderness, and finally found him standing on the ridge of the high mountain, at the entrance to a cave; he was moved with anger because the solitary bull had scorned his herd, so he bent his bow and intended to shoot him with a poisoned arrow. But the poisoned arrow turned back as if blown by a gust of wind, and instantly killed the one who shot it.

His kinsmen and neighbors were greatly astonished by 2
that deed, and none of them dared approach the bull. They asked their bishop for advice as to what they should do about it. The bishop then found it advisable that they should ask God for an explanation of the miracle with a fast of three days. On the third night of the fast the archangel Michael revealed himself to the bishop in a spiritual vision, saying, "You did wisely to seek from God what was hidden to humans. Know certainly that the man who was shot with his own arrow, that it was done by my will. I am Michael the archangel of God almighty, and I dwell always in his sight. I say to you that I particularly love the place which the bull defended, and by that sign I wanted to reveal that I am the guardian of the place; and I am the observer and guardian of all the signs that happen there." And with these words the archangel departed to heaven.

The bishop recounted his vision to the citizens, and they 3
afterward frequently sought out that place, fervently praying to the living God and his archangel Michael. They saw

gesawon on ðære cyrcan, and wæs seo suþ duru sume dæle
mare, fram ðære lagon stapas to ðam westdæle; ac hi ne dorston þæt halige hus mid ingange geneosian, ac dæghwomlice
geornlice æt ðære dura hi gebædon.

4   Þa on ðære ylcan tide Neapolite, þe wæron ða gyt on hæðenscipe wunigende, cwædon gefeoht togeanes þære burhware Sepontiniscre ceastre, þe þa halgan stowe wurðodon,
and togeanes Beneventanos. Hi ða, mid heora biscopes
mynegungum gelærde, bædon þreora daga fæc, þæt hi binnon þam ðrim dagum mid fæstene þæs heahengles Micha-
heles fultum bædon. Þa hæðenan eac swilce mid lacum and
offrungum heora leasra goda gecneordlice munde and gescyldnysse bædon.

5   Efne ða, on ðære nihte þe þæt gefeoht on merigen
toweard wæs, æteowde se heahengel Michahel hine sylfne
ðam biscope, and cwæð þæt he heora bena gehyrde, and his
fultum him behet, and het þæt hi ane tid ofer undern hi ge-
trymedon ongean heora fynd. Hi ða on merigen, bliðe and
orsorge þurh ðæs engles behat and mid truwan his fultumes,
ferdon togeanes ðam hæðenum. Þa sona on anginne þæs ge-
feohtes wæs se munt Garganus bifigende mid ormætre cwa-
cunge, and micel liget fleah of ðære dune swilce flan wið þæs
hæðenan folces, and þæs muntes cnoll mid þeosterlicum ge-
nipum eal oferhangen wæs. Hwæt ða hæðenan ða forht-
mode fleames cepton, and gelice hi wurdon mid þam fyrenum flanum ofscotene, gelice mid þæra Cristenra wæpnum
hindan ofsette, oð þæt hi heora burh Neapolim samcuce
gesohton. Soðlice ða ðe ða frecednyssa ætflugon oncneowon
þæt Godes engel ðam Cristenum to fultume becom, and hi
ðærrihte heora swuran Criste underþeoddon and mid his

two doors in the church, and the south door was somewhat larger, from which steps led to the west part; but they dared not approach to enter the holy house, but daily prayed fervently at the door.

Then at the same time the Neapolitans, who were still heathens, declared war against the inhabitants of the city of Siponto, who honored the holy place, and against the Beneventans. Instructed by the admonitions of their bishop, they then prayed for a space of three days, so that they might within those three days ask for the help of the archangel Michael with their fasting. The heathen likewise diligently implored the protection and defense of their false gods with sacrifices and offerings.

And then, on the night before the morning when the fight was to take place, the archangel Michael himself appeared to the bishop, and said that he had heard their prayers, and promised them his support, and commanded them to array themselves against their enemies one hour after midmorning. Then in the morning, happy and free from care because of the angel's promise and with confidence in his support, they advanced against the heathen. At the very beginning of the fight Mount Gargano was trembling with immense quaking, and great lightning flew from the mountain like arrows against the heathen people, and the peak of the mountain was all overhung with dark clouds. At this the frightened heathens took to flight, and they were equally being shot with fiery arrows and beset from behind by the weapons of the Christians, until they sought their city Naples, half dead. Those who escaped from those perils acknowledged that God's angel came to the aid of the Christians, and they immediately submitted their necks to Christ

geleafan gewæpnode wurdon. Witodlice þæs wæles wæs
geteald six hund manna mid þam fyrenum flanum ofsceo-
tene. Þa Cristenan ða sigefæste mid micelre bylde and blisse
ham gecyrdon, and ðam ælmihtigan Gode and his heahengle
Michahele heora behat to ðam temple gebrohton. Þa gesawon hi ætforan ðære cyrcan norðdura on þam marmanstane
swilce mannes fotlæsta fæstlice on ðam stane geðyde, and hi
ða undergeaton þæt se heahengel Michahel þæt tacen his
andwerdnysse geswutelian wolde. Hi ða sona ðærofer cyrcan
arærdon and weofod, þam heahengle to lofe ðe him on þam
stede fylstende stod.

6   Þa wearð micel twynung betwux ðære burhware be ðære
cyrcan, hwæðer hi inn eodon oððe hi halgian sceoldon.
Hwæt hi ða on þam eastdæle ðære stowe cyrcan arærdon,
and þam apostole Petre to wurðmynte gehalgodon, and þær
binnan Sancte Marian and Iohanne ðam Fulluhtere weofod
asetton. Þa æt nextan sende se biscop to ðam papan, and
hine befran hu him embe þæs heahengles getimbrunge to
donne wære. Se papa þisum ærende ðus geandwyrde: "Gif
mannum alyfed is þæt hi ða cyrcan ðe se heahengel sylf getimbrode halgian moton, þonne gebyrað seo halgung on
ðam dæge þe he eow sige forgeaf þurh unnan ðæs ælmihtigan. Gif ðonne hwæt elles þam heahengle gelicige, axiað
his willan on þam ylcan dæge." Þa ða ðeos andswaru þam biscope gecydd wæs, þa bead he his ceastergewarum þreora
daga fæsten, and bædon þa halgan Þrynnysse þæt him wurde
geswutelod sum gewiss beacn embe heora twynunge. Se
heahengel ða Michahel, on ðære ðriddan nihte þæs fæstenes,
cwæð to ðam biscope on swefne, "Nis eow nan neod þæt ge
ða cyrcan halgion þe ic getimbrode; ic sylf hi getimbrode
and gehalgode. Ac gað eow into ðære cyrcan unforhtlice,

and became armed with his faith. Truly in that slaughter was counted six hundred people shot with the fiery arrows. The Christians then returned home victorious, with great confidence and joy, and brought to the temple their promise to almighty God and his archangel Michael. On the marble stone before the north door of the church they saw something like a person's footsteps firmly impressed on the stone, and then they understood that the archangel Michael wanted to reveal that sign of his presence. At once they raised a church and an altar over it, in praise of the archangel who had stood in that place supporting them.

Then there was great doubt among the citizens about 6 whether they should go in or consecrate that church. Lo, then they raised a church in the east part of the place, consecrated it to the honor of the apostle Peter, and there within placed an altar to Saint Mary and John the Baptist. Then finally the bishop sent to the pope, asking him what they should do about the archangel's building. The pope answered the letter thus: "If humans are allowed to consecrate the church which the archangel himself constructed, then the consecration ought to be on the day on which he gave you victory through the gift of the almighty. But if anything else should please the archangel, ask his will on the same day." When this answer was announced to the bishop, he asked his fellow citizens for a fast of three days, and prayed to the holy Trinity that some clear sign might be revealed to him concerning their doubt. Then on the third night of the fast the archangel Michael said to the bishop in a dream, "There is no need for you to consecrate the church I have built; I myself built and consecrated it. But go into the

and me ætstandendum geneosiað þa stowe æfter gewunan mid gebedum; and þu þær to merigen mæssan gesing, and þæt folc æfter godcundum ðeawe to husle gange, and ic þonne geswutelige hu ic ða stowe ðurh me sylfne gehalgode."

7   Hi ða sona þæs on merigen ðider mid heora offrungum bliðe comon, and mid micelre anrædnysse heora bena on ðam suþdæle inn eodon. Efne ða hi gesawon an lang portic on ðam norðdæle astreht fornean to ðam marmanstane þe se engel onstandende his fotlæste æteowde. On ðam east-dæle wæs gesewen micel cyrce to ðære hi stæpmælum asti-gon. Seo cyrce mid hire portice mihte fif hund manna eaðe-lice befon on hire rymette; and þær stod, gesett wið middan þæs suðwages, arwurðe weofod mid readum pælle gescrydd. Næs þæt hus æfter manna gewunan getimbrod, ac mid mis-licum torrum gehwemmed, to gelicnysse sumes scræfes. Se hrof eac swylce hæfde mislice heahnysse—on sumere stowe hine man mihte mid heafde geræcan, on sumere mid handa earfoðlice. Ic gelyfe þæt se heahengel mid þam geswutelode þæt he micele swiðor sohte and lufode þære heortan clæn-nysse þonne ðæra stana frætwunge. Þæs muntes cnoll wiðu-tan is sticmælum mid wuda oferwexen, and eft sticmælum mid grenum felda oferbræded.

8   Soðlice æfter ðære mæssan and ðam halgan huselgange gecyrde gehwa mid micclum gefean to his agenum. Se biscop ða ðær Godes ðeowas gelogode, sangeras, and ræderas, and sacerdas, þæt hi dæghwomlice ðær Godes þenunge mid þæslicere endebyrdnysse gefyldon, and him ðær mynsterlic botl timbrian het. Nis þeahhwæðere nan mann to ðam dyrstig þæt he on nihtlicere tide binnan ðære cyrcan cuman durre, ac on dægrede, þa Godes þeowas þær binnan Godes lof singað. Of ðam hrofstane on norþdæle þæs halgan

church fearlessly, and in my presence approach the place with prayers according to custom; and sing Mass there tomorrow, and let the people go to Communion according to the divine rites, and then I will reveal how I consecrated the place through myself."

The next morning they went there joyfully with their offerings, and with great steadfastness in their prayers went into the south part. At once they saw a long portico on the north part stretching very near to the marble stone where the angel, standing, had revealed his footprint. On the east part a great church was seen, to which they ascended step-by-step. The church with its portico could easily hold five hundred people in its space; and there stood, placed against the middle of the south wall, a venerable altar covered with a red pall. That house was not built after human fashion, but was pointed with many projections of stone like a cave. The roof also was of various heights—in one place a person might touch it with his head, in another hardly with his hand. I believe that by this the archangel revealed that he sought and loved purity of heart much more than ornaments of stones. The mountain's peak outside is partly overgrown with wood, and partly overspread with a green field.

After the Mass and holy Communion everyone returned with great joy to his own home. The bishop then placed God's servants there, cantors, and lectors, and priests, that they might daily perform God's service there in suitable order, and commanded a monastic house to be built there for them. Yet there is no one so daring that he dares to come within the church in the nighttime, but only at dawn, when God's servants are singing God's praise within. From the roof stone on the north part of the holy altar there runs

weofodes yrnð dropmælum swiðe hluttor wæter and wered,
þæt gecigdon ða ðe on þære stowe wunodon *stillam,* þæt
is "dropa." Þær is ahangen sum glæsen fæt mid sylfrenne
racenteage, and þæs wynsuman wætan onfehð. Þæs folces
gewuna is þæt hi æfter þam halgan huselgange stæpmælum
to ðam fæte astigað and þæs heofonlican wætan onbyriað.
Se wæta is swiðe wynsum on swæcce, and swiðe halwende
on hrepunge. Witodlice forwel menige æfter langsumum
fefere and mislicum mettrumnyssum, þurh ðises wætan
þigene, hrædlice heora hæle brucað. Eac swilce on oðrum
gemete, ungerime untruman þær beoð oft and gelome gehælede, and menigfealde wundra þurh ðæs heahengles
mihte ðær beoð gefremode, and ðeah swiðost on þysum
dæge, ðonne þæt folc of gehwilcum leodscipe þa stowe geneosiað, and þæs engles andwerdnyss mid sumum gemete
ðær swiðost bið, þæt ðæs apostoles cwyde beo lichamlice
gefylled, þæt þæt he gastlice gecwæð: he cwæð þæt "englas
beoð to ðeninggastum fram Gode hider on worulde asende,
þæt hi beon on fultume his gecorenum, þæt hi ðone ecan
eðel onfon mid him."

Evangelium

9 *Accesserunt ad Iesum discipuli, dicentes, "Quis putas maior est in
regno caelorum," et reliqua.*

10 Þis dægþerlice godspell cwyð þæt "Drihtnes leorningcnihtas to him genealæhton, þus cweðende, 'La leof,
hwa is fyrmest manna on heofenan rice?' Se hælend him ða
to clypode sum gehwæde cild, and het hit standan him to-
middes, and cwæð, 'Soð ic eow secge, ne fare ge into heofenan rice buton ge beon awende and gewordene swa swa cild.

water, drop by drop, very pure and sweet, which those who dwelt in the place called *stilla,* that is, "drop." There a glass vessel, hung with a silver chain, receives the pleasant liquid. It is the people's custom after holy Communion to go up step-by-step to the vessel and taste the heavenly liquid. The liquid is very pleasant in taste, and very health giving to the touch. Indeed, by drinking this liquid very many speedily recover their health after a lengthy fever and various sicknesses. Also in another manner, countless sick people are often and frequently healed there, and many miracles are performed there through the archangel's power, most especially on this day, when the people from every nation visit the place, and the angel's presence is in some manner strongest there, so that the words of the apostle which he spoke spiritually may be fulfilled physically: he said that "angels will be sent as ministering spirits from God here into the world, that they may be a support to his chosen ones, that they may receive the eternal country with him."

Gospel

The disciples came to Jesus, saying, "Who do you think is greater in the kingdom of heaven," etc. 9

This day's gospel says that "The Lord's disciples approached him, saying, 'Sir, who is first in the kingdom of heaven?' The savior then called a little child to him, and told him to stand in their midst, and said, 'Truly I say to you, you will not go to the kingdom of heaven unless you are changed and become like a child. Indeed, he who humbles himself 10

Witodlice se ðe hine sylfne geeadmet swa swa ðis cild, he
bið mære on heofonen rice, and se ðe underfehð ænne
swilcne lyttling on minum naman, he underfehð me sylfne.
Se ðe geæswicað anum þyssera lyttlinga ðæra þe on me gelyfað, selre him wære þæt his swura wære getiged to anum
cwyrnstane and he swa wurde besenct on deopre sæ. Wa
middangearde for æswicungum! Neod is þæt æswicunga cumon, þeah wa ðam men ðe æswicunga ofcumað. Gif ðin
hand oþþe ðin fot ðe æswicige, aceorf of þæt lim and wurp
fram ðe. Betere ðe bið þæt þu wannhal oððe healt fare to
ðam ecan life þonne þu mid eallum limum beo asend to
ecum fyre. Gif ðin eage þe æswicige, hola hit ut and wurp
fram ðe. Selre þe bið anegede faran to heofonan rice ðonne
mid twam eagum beon aworpen on ece susle. Behealdað þæt
ge ne forseon ænne þyssera lytlinga; ic secge eow þæt heora
englas symle geseoð mines Fæder ansyne se ðe on heofonum
is.'"

Hægmon trahtnað þis godspell, and segð hu ðæs caseres
tolleras axodon Petrus ðone apostol, ða ða hi geond ealne
middangeard ðam casere toll gegaderodon; hi cwædon,
"Wyle eower lareow Crist ænig toll syllan?" Þa cwæð Petrus
þæt he wolde. Þa mid þam ðe Petrus wolde befrinan þone
hælend, þa forsceat se hælend hine, ðe ealle ðing wat, þus
cweðende, "Hwæt ðincð þe, Petrus, æt hwam nimað eorðlice cynegas gafol oððe toll—æt heora gesiblingum, oþþe æt
ælfremedum?" Petrus cwæð, "Æt ælfremedum." Se hælend
cwæð, "Hwæt la synd heora siblingas frige? Þe læs ðe we hi
æswicion, ga to ðære sæ and wurpe ut ðinne angel, and þone
fisc ðe hine hraðost forswelhð, geopena his muð; þonne
fintst þu ðæron ænne gyldenne wecg—nim ðone, and syle to
tolle for me and for ðe."

like this child will be great in the kingdom of heaven, and he who receives one such little one in my name receives me. He who offends one of these little ones who believe in me, it would be better for him if his neck were tied to a millstone and he were sunk in the deep sea. Woe to the earth for offenses! It is necessary that offenses come, but woe to the one from whom offenses come. If your hand or foot offends you, cut off that limb and cast it away from you. It is better for you to go maimed or limping into eternal life than for you to be sent with all your limbs to eternal fire. If your eye offends you, pluck it out and cast it from you. It is better for you to travel one eyed to heaven than to be thrown with two eyes into eternal torment. Take care that you do not despise one of these little ones; I say to you that their angels always see the face of my Father who is in heaven.'"

Haymo expounds this gospel, and tells how the emperor's tax collectors, when they were gathering taxes for the emperor over all the world, asked the apostle Peter, "Will your teacher Christ pay any tax?" Peter said that he would. Then, when Peter wanted to ask the savior, the savior, who knows all things, prevented him, saying, "What do you think, Peter, from whom do earthly kings take tribute or tax—from their own relatives, or from strangers?" Peter said, "From strangers." The savior said, "What, are their relatives free? Lest we should offend them, go to the sea and cast out your hook, and open the mouth of the fish which most quickly swallows it; then you will find inside a golden coin—take it, and give the tax for me and for you."

11

12   Þa for ðam intingan þe he cwæð, "Syle for me and for ðe,"
wendon þa apostolas þæt Petrus wære fyrmest, and axodon
ða ðone hælend hwa wære fyrmest manna on heofonan rice.
Þa wolde se hælend heora dwollican geþohtas mid soðre
eadmodnysse gehælan, and cwæð þæt hi ne mihton becuman to heofonan rice buton hi wæron swa eadmode and
swa unscæððige swa þæt cild wæs ðe he him to clypode.
Bilewite cild ne gewilnað oðra manna æhta, ne wlitiges
wifes; þeah ðe hit beo gegremod, hit ne hylt langsume ungeþwærnysse to ðam ðe him derode, ne hit ne hiwað mid
wordum þæt hit oðer ðence and oðer sprece. Swa eac sceolon Godes folgeras, þæt synd þa Cristenan, habban þa unscæððignysse on heora mode þe cild hæfð on ylde.

13   Se hælend cwæð, "Soð ic eow secge, ne becume ge to heofonan rice buton ge beon awende and gewordene swa swa
lyttlingas." Ne bebead he his gingrum þæt hi on lichaman
cild wæron, ac þæt hi heoldon bilewitra cildra unscæððignysse on heora þeawum. On sumere stowe he cwæð, þa ða
him man to bær cild to bletsigenne and his gingran þæt be-
mændon, "Geðafiað þæt ðas cild to me cumon; swilcera is
soðlice heofonan rice." Be ðisum manode se apostol Paulus
his underðeoddan, and cwæð, "Ne beo ge cild on andgite, ac
on yfelnyssum; beoð on andgite fulfremede." Se hælend
cwæð, "Swa hwa swa hine sylfne geeadmet swa swa ðis cild,
he bið fyrmest on heofonan rice." Uton habban ða soðan
eadmodnysse on urum life, gif we willað habban ða healican
geðincðe on Godes rice; swa swa se hælend cwæð, "Ælc ðæra
ðe hine onhefð bið geeadmet, and se ðe hine geeadmet, he
bið ahafen." Se hæfð bilewites cildes unscæððignysse þe him
sylfum mislicað to ði þæt he Gode gelicige; and he bið
swa micele wlitegra ætforan Godes gesihðe swa he swiðor

Then because he said "Give for me and for you," the apos-   12
tles thought that Peter was first, and asked the savior who
was the first in the kingdom of heaven. The savior then
wanted to heal their erring thoughts with true humility, and
said that they could not come to the kingdom of heaven unless they were as humble and as innocent as the child whom
he called to himself. A gentle child does not desire the possessions of others, nor a beautiful woman; though it might
be annoyed, it holds no lasting hostility toward the one who
have injured it, nor does it feign with words so that it thinks
one thing and says another. So too should God's followers,
that is, Christians, have the innocence in their mind that a
child has in its age.

The savior said, "Truly I say to you, you will not come to   13
the kingdom of heaven unless you are changed and become
like children." He did not command his disciples that they
should be children physically, but that they should maintain
the innocence of gentle children in their conduct. In one
place he said, when someone brought a child to him to be
blessed and his disciples complained about it, "Let these
children come to me; truly of such is the kingdom of
heaven." The apostle Paul admonished his followers about
this, saying, "Do not be children in understanding, but in
evils; in understanding, be perfect." The savior said, "Whoever humbles himself like this child will be first in the kingdom of heaven." Let us have true humility in our lives, if we
want to have high dignity in God's kingdom; as the savior
said, "Every person who exalts himself will be humbled, and
he who humbles himself will be exalted." He who is displeas-
ing to himself so that he may be pleasing to God has the innocence of a gentle child; and the humbler he will be before

ætforan him sylfum eadmodra bið. "Se ðe underfehð ænne swilcne lyttling on minum naman, he underfehð me sylfne." Eallum Godes ðearfum man sceall weldæda þenian, ac ðeah swiðost þam eadmodum and liðum, þe mid heora lifes ðeawum Cristes bebodum geþwæriað; forðam him bið geðenod mid his ðearfena þenunge, and he sylf bið underfangen on heora anfenge.

14 He cwæð eac on oðre stowe, "Se ðe witegan underfehð, he hæfð witegan mede; se ðe rihtwisne underfehð, he hæfð rihtwises mannes edlean." Þæt is, se ðe witegan oððe sumne rihtwisne Godes ðeow underfehð, and him for Godes lufon bigwiste foresceawað, þonne hæfð he swa micele mede his cystignysse æt Gode swilce he him sylf witega wære oþþe rihtwiss Godes þeow. "Se ðe geæswicað anum ðyssera lyttlinga ðe on me gelyfað, selre him wære þæt him wære getiged an ormæte cwyrnstan to his swuran, and he swa wurde on deoppre sæ besenced." Se æswicað oðrum þe hine on Godes dæle beswicð, þæt his sawul forloren beo. Se cwyrnstan, þe tyrnð singallice and nænne færeld ne ðurhtihð, getacnað woruldlufe, ðe on gedwyldum hwyrftlað and nænne stæpe on Godes wege ne gefæstnað. Be swylcum cwæð se witega, "Þa arleasan turniað on ymbhwyrfte." Se ðe genealæhð halgum hade on Godes gelaðunge, and siððan mid yfelre tihtinge oþþe mid leahterfullre drohtnunge oðrum yfele bysnað, and heora ingehyd towyrpð, þonne wære him selre þæt he on woruldlicere drohtnunge ana losode, þonne he on halgum hiwe oðre mid him þurh his ðwyrlican þeawas to forwyrde getuge.

15 "Wa middangearde for æswicungum." Middangeard is her gecweden þa ðe þisne ateorigendlican middangeard lufiað swiðor þonne þæt ece lif, and mid mislicum swicdomum

himself, the fairer he will be in the sight of God. "He who receives one such little one in my name, receives me." We should minister to all God's poor with good deeds, but above all to the humble and weak, who in their life's conduct conform to Christ's commandments; for he will be served by serving his poor, and he himself will be received by receiving them.

He also said in another place, "He who receives a prophet will have a prophet's reward; he who receives a righteous person will have a righteous person's recompense." That is, he who receives a prophet or a righteous servant of God, and provides sustenance for him for love of God, will have as great a reward from God for his generosity as if he himself were a prophet or a righteous servant of God. "He who offends one of these little ones who believe in me, it would be better for him if a great millstone were tied to his neck, and he were sunk in the deep sea." He who deceives another on the part of God offends him, so that his soul is lost. The millstone, which turns continually yet completes no course, signifies love of the world, which revolves in errors and takes no step on the way to God. Of such the prophet said, "The wicked turn in a circle." He who enters into a holy order in God's Church, and afterward by evil instigation or by sinful life gives an evil example to others, and perverts their understanding, then it would be better for him that he alone perished in his worldly way of life, than that he in holy guise should draw others with him to destruction through his depraved morals.

"Woe to the world for offenses." The world is here called those who love this perishable world more than eternal life, 15

625

hi sylfe and oðre forþæraŏ. "Neod is þæt æswicunga cumon,
ðeahhwæðere wa ðam menn ðe hi of cumað." Þeos woruld is
swa mid gedwyldum afylled þæt heo ne mæg beon butan
æswicungum, and þeah wa ðam menn ðe oðerne æt his
æhtum oððe æt his feore beswicð, and ðam bið wyrs þe mid
yfelum tihtingum oþres mannes sawle to ecum forwyrdum
beswicð. "Gif ðin hand oððe ðin fot þe æswicige, ceorf of
þæt lim and awurp fram ðe." Þis is gecweden æfter gastlicere
getacnunge, na æfter lichamlicere gesetnysse; ne bebead
God nanum menn þæt he his lima awyrde. Seo hand getacnað urne nydbehefan freond, þe us dæghwomlice mid
weorce and fultume ure neode deð; ac ðeah, gif swilc freond
us fram Godes wege gewemð, þonne bið us selre þæt we his
flæsclican lufe fram us aceorfon, and mid twæminge awurpon, þonne we, ðurh his yfelan tihtinge, samod mid him on
ece forwyrd befeallon. Ealswa is be ðam fet and be ðam
eagan. Gif hwilc sibling þe bið swa deorwurðe swa ðin eage,
and oðer swa behefe swa ðin hand, and sum swa geðensum
swilce ðin agen fot, gif hi ðonne þe þwyrlice tihtað to ðinre
sawle forwyrde, þonne bið þe selre þæt þu heora geðeodræ-
dene forbuge þonne hi ðe forð mid him to ðam ecan forwyrde gelædon. "Behealdað þæt ge ne forseon ænne of
þysum lytlingum." Se ðe bepæhð ænne Godes þeowena, he
geæbiligð ðone Hlaford, swa swa he sylf þurh his witegan
cwæð, "Se ðe eow hrepað, hit bið me swa egle swilce he
hreppe mines eagan seo."

16   "Ic secge eow þæt heora englas symle geseoð mines Fæder
ansyne se ðe on heofonum is." Mid þisum wordum is geswutelod þæt ælcum geleaffullum men is engel to hyrde geset, þe hine wið deofles syrwunge gescylt and on halgum
mægnum gefultumað, swa swa se sealmscop be gehwilcum

and with various offenses destroy themselves and others. "It is necessary that offenses come, yet woe to the one from whom they come." This world is so filled with errors that it cannot be without offenses, and yet woe to the one who deceives another in his property or in his life, and it will be worse for the one who with evil enticement deceives another's soul to eternal destruction. "If your hand or your foot offend you, cut off that limb and cast it from you." This is said in its spiritual signification, not as a physical precept; God did not command anyone to destroy his limbs. The hand signifies our needful friend, who supplies our needs every day with work and support; but yet, if such a friend lures us from the way of God, then it will be better for us that we cut off his fleshly love from us, and by separating from it cast it away, than that we, through his evil instigation, should fall into eternal destruction along with him. So is it also with the foot and the eye. Even if a relation is as dear to you as your eye, and another as useful to you as your hand, and one as serviceable as your own foot, if they perversely entice you to the destruction of your soul, it will be better for you to turn away from their fellowship than that they lead you forth with them to eternal destruction. "Be careful that you do not despise any of these little ones." He who deceives one of God's servants angers the Lord, as he himself said through his prophet, "He who touches you, it will be as painful to me as if he touched the sight of my eye."

"I say to you that their angels always see the face of my Father who is in heaven." These words reveal that over every believer an angel is set as a guardian, who shields him against the devil's schemes and who supports him in holy virtues, as the psalmist said of every righteous person,

rihtwisum cwæð, "God bebead his englum be ðe, þæt hi ðe healdon and on heora handum hebban, þe læs ðe ðu æt stane þinne fot ætspurne." Micel wurðscipe is Cristenra manna þæt gehwilc hæbbe fram his acennednysse him betæhtne engel to hyrdrædene, swa swa be ðam apostole Petre awriten is, þa ða se engel hine of ðam cwearterne gelædde and he to his geferum becom, and cnucigende inganges bæd. Þa cwædon þa geleaffullan, "Nis hit na Petrus þæt ðær cnucað, ac is his engel." Þa englas soðlice ðe God gesette to hyrdum his gecorenum, hi ne gewitað næfre fram his andweardnysse; forðan ðe God is æghwær, and swa hwider swa ða englas fleoð, æfre hi beoð binnan his andwerdnysse, and his wuldres brucað. Hi bodiað ure weorc and gebedu þam ælmihtigan, þeah ðe him nan ðing digle ne sy, swa swa se heahengel Raphahel cwæð to ðam Godes menn, Tobian, "Þa ða ge eow gebædon, ic offrode eower gebedu ætforan Gode."

17 Seo ealde æ us sægð þæt heahenglas sind gesette ofer gehwilce leodscipas, þæt hi ðæs folces gymon, ofer ða oðre englas, swa swa Moyses, on ðære fiftan bec ðære ealdan æ, þysum wordum geswutelode: "Þa ða se healica God todælde and tostencte Adames ofspring, þa sette he ðeoda gemæru æfter getele his engla." Þisum andgite geþwærlæcð se witega Danihel on his witegunge. Sum Godes engel spræc to Danihele embe ðone heahengel þe Perscisce ðeode bewiste, and cwæð, "Me com to se heahengel, Greciscre þeode ealdor, and nis heora nan min gefylsta buton Michahel, Ebreisces folces ealdor. Efne nu Michahel, an ðæra fyrmestra ealdra, com me to fultume, and ic wunode ðær wið þone cyning Persciscre ðeode." Mid þisum wordum is geswutelod hu micele care ða heahenglas habbað heora ealdordomes ofer mancynn, ða ða he cwæð þæt Michahel him come to fultume.

"God has commanded his angels concerning you, that they may preserve you and raise you up in their hands, lest you dash your foot against a stone." It is a great honor for Christians that everyone from his birth has an angel assigned to him for watchful care, just as it is written of the apostle Peter, when the angel led him from the prison and he came to his companions and, knocking, asked for admission. Then the faithful said, "It is not Peter who knocks there, but his angel." Truly those angels whom God has set as guardians over his chosen ones never depart from his presence; for God is everywhere, and wherever the angels fly, they are always in his presence, and share in his glory. They announce our works and prayers to the almighty, though nothing is hidden to him, as the archangel Raphael said to the man of God, Tobias, "When you prayed, I offered your prayers before God."

The old law tells us that, above the other angels, archangels are set over every nation to take care of the people, as Moses, in the fifth book of the old law, made clear in these words: "When God on high divided and scattered Adam's offspring, he set the boundaries of nations according to the number of his angels." The prophet Daniel agrees with this sense in his prophecy. An angel of God spoke to Daniel concerning the archangel who directed the Persian people, and said, "The archangel, the prince of the Greek people, came to me, and none of these is my supporter except Michael, the prince of the Hebrew people. Lo, Michael, one of the foremost princes, came to me in support, and I dwelled there with the king of the Persian nation." These words reveal how much care the archangels have of their authority over humanity, when he said that Michael came to his support.

18 Is nu geleaflic þæt se heahengel Michahel hæbbe gymene Cristenra manna, se ðe wæs ðæs Ebreiscan folces ealdor þa hwile ðe hi on God belyfdon; and þæt he geswutelode þa ða he him sylfum cyrcan getimbrode betwux geleaffulre ðeode on ðam munte Gargano, swa swa we hwene ær ræddon. Þæt is gedon be Godes fadunge, þæt se mæra heofonlica engel beo singallice Cristenra manna gefylsta on eorðan, and þin-gere on heofonum to ðam ælmihtigan Gode, se ðe leofað and rixað a on ecnysse. Amen.

35

Dominica xxi *post Pentecosten*

*L*oquebatur Iesus cum discipulis suis in parabolis, dicens, et reli-
qua.

2 Drihten wæs sprecende on sumere tide to his apostolum mid bigspellum, þus cweðende, "Heofonan rice is gelic su-mum cyninge þe worhte his suna gyfte. Þa sende he his bydelas to gelaðigenne his underðeoddan to þam giftum, ac hi noldon cuman. Þa sende he eft oðre bydelas and cwæð, 'Secgað þam gelaðodum, efne ic gearcode mine god; ic ofsloh mine fearras and gemæste fugelas, and ealle mine þing eow gearcode. Cumað to þam gyftum.' Hi soðlice hit forgymeleasodon and ferdon sume to heora tunum, sume to

It is now credible that the archangel Michael, who was 18
prince of the Hebrew people while they believed in God,
has care of Christians; and he revealed that when he himself
built a church among the faithful people on Mount Gargano, as we have read a little earlier. That is done by God's
dispensation, that the great heavenly angel should be the
perpetual supporter of Christians on earth, and their intercessor in heaven with almighty God, who lives and reigns
forever in eternity. Amen.

35

Twenty-First Sunday after Pentecost

Twenty-First Sunday after Pentecost

J esus was speaking to his disciples in parables, saying, etc.

The Lord was speaking at a certain time to his apostles in 2
parables, saying, "The kingdom of heaven is like a certain
king who had a wedding feast for his son. He sent his messengers to invite his subjects to the wedding, but they would
not come. Then he sent other messengers and said, 'Say to
those invited, look, I have prepared my provisions; I have
slaughtered my oxen and fatted fowls, and all my things are
ready for you. Come to the wedding feast.' But they ignored
him and set out, some to their farms, some to their

heora ceape; sume eac gelæhton þa ærendracan and mid teonan hi gewæhton and ofslogon. Hwæt se cyning ða swiðlice yrsode ða ða he þæt geaxode, and sende his here to and þa manslagan fordyde, and heora burh forbærnde. Syððan eft he cwæð to his ðegnum, 'Þas gifta sind gearwe, ac ða ðe ic ðærto geladode næron his wyrðe. Farað nu to wegena utscytum, and swa hwilce swa ge gemetað, laðiað to þisum gyftum.' Hi ða ferdon geond wegas and gegaderodon ealle ða ðe hi gemetton, yfele and gode, and gesetton þa giftu endemes. Þa com se cyning inn and sceawode ða gebeoras, and geseah þær ænne mannan þe næs mid giftlicum reafe gescrydd, and cwæð him to, 'Þu freond, humeta dorstest ðu inngan betwux þisum gebeorum buton giftlicum reafe?' He ða adumbode. Þa cwæð se cyning to his ðeningmannum, 'Bindað hine handum and fotum, and wurpað on ða yttran þeostru, þær bið wop and toða gebitt. Fela sind geladode, and feawa gecorene.'"

3   We folgiað þæs papan Gregories trahtnunge on þyssere rædinge.

4   Mine gebroðra þa leofostan, gelomlice ic eow sæde þæt gehwær on halgum godspelle þeos andwerde gelaðung is gehaten heofenan rice; witodlice rihtwisra manna gegaderung is gecweden heofonan rice. God cwæð þurh his witegan, "Heofon is min setl." Salomon cwæð, "Rihtwises mannes sawul is wisdomes setl." Paulus se apostol cwæð þæt "Crist is Godes miht and Godes wisdom." Swutelice we magon understandan þæt gehwilces rihtwises mannes sawul is heofon, þonne Crist is Godes wisdom, and rihtwises mannes sawul is þæs wisdomes setl, and seo heofen is his setl. Be þisum cwæð se sealmscop, "Heofonas cyðað Godes wuldor." Godes

merchandise; some also seized the messengers and afflicted them with injury and killed them. When the king heard this, he grew very angry, and sent his army and destroyed the murderers, and burned down their city. After this he said to his servants, 'The wedding feasts are ready, but those I invited to it were not worthy of it. Go now to the outlets of the highways, and invite whomever you meet to this wedding.' They then went out along the highways and gathered all they met, evil and good, and completely filled the wedding feast. Then the king came in and looked at the guests, and saw a person who was not dressed in a wedding garment, and said to him, 'Friend, how did you dare to come in among these guests without a wedding garment?' He was silent. Then the king said to his servants, 'Bind him hand and foot, and cast him into the outer darkness, where there will be weeping and gnashing of teeth. Many are called, and few chosen.'"

We follow the exposition of Pope Gregory on this reading. 3

My dearest brothers, I have frequently told you that in 4 many places in the holy gospel this present Church is called the kingdom of heaven; indeed a gathering of righteous people is called the kingdom of heaven. God said through his prophet, "Heaven is my seat." Solomon said, "The soul of the righteous is the seat of wisdom." Paul the apostle said that "Christ is God's might and God's wisdom." Clearly we may understand that the soul of every righteous person is heaven, when Christ is God's wisdom, and the soul of a righteous person is the seat of wisdom, and heaven is his seat. Concerning this the psalmist said, "The heavens declare the glory of God." He calls God's messengers the heavens.

bydelas he het heofonas. Eornostlice haligra manna gelaðung is heofonan rice, forðan ðe heora heortan ne beoð begripene on eorðlicum gewilnungum, ac hi geomriað to ðam upplican; and God nu iu rixað on him, swa swa on heofenlicum wunungum.

5   Se cyning ðe worhte his suna gifta is God Fæder, þe ða halgan gelaðunge geðeodde his Bearne ðurh geryno his flæsclicnysse. Seo halige gelaðung is Cristes bryd, þurh ða he gestrynð dæghwomlice gastlice bearn, and heo is ealra Cristenra manna modor, and ðeahhwæðere ungewemmed mæden. Þurh geleafan and fulluht we beoð Gode gestrynde, and him to gastlicum bearnum gewiscede þurh Cristes menniscnysse and þurh gife þæs Halgan Gastes.

6   God sende his ærendracan þæt he gehwilce to ðisum giftum gelaðode. Æne he sende and eft, forðan ðe he sende his witegan, þe cyddon his Suna menniscnysse towearde, and he sende eft siððan his apostolas, þe cyddon his tocyme gefremmedne, swa swa ða witegan hit ær gewitegodon. Þa ða hi noldon cuman to ðam giftum, ða sende he eft, þus cweðende, "Secgað ðam gelaðodum, 'Efne, ic gegearcode mine god, ic ofsloh mine fearras and mine gemæstan fugelas, and ealle mine ðing ic gearcode: cumað to þam giftum.'"

7   Þa fearras getacniað ða heahfæderas ðære ealdan æ, þe moston ða, be leafe ðære ealdan æ, on fearres wisan heora fynd ofslean. Hit is þus awriten on þære ealdan æ, "Lufa ðinne freond, and hata ðinne feond." Þus wæs alyfed þam ealdum mannum, þæt hi moston Godes wiðerwinnan and heora agene fynd mid stranglicere mihte ofsittan and mid wæpne acwellan. Ac se ylca God þe þas leafe sealde þurh Moyses gesetnysse ær his tocyme, se ylca eft, ða ða he þurh menniscnysse to middangearde com awende ðone cwyde,

Therefore the congregation of holy ones is the kingdom of heaven, because their hearts are not possessed by earthly desires, but they sigh for what is above; and God has reigned in them for a long time, as in the heavenly dwellings.

The king who made a wedding feast for his son is God the 5 Father, who united the holy Church with his Son through the mystery of his incarnation. The holy Church is Christ's bride, by which he daily begets spiritual children, and she is the mother of all Christians, and yet an undefiled virgin. Through faith and baptism we are begotten of God, adopted as his spiritual children through Christ's humanity and through the grace of the Holy Spirit.

God sent his messengers to invite everyone to this wed- 6 ding feast. He sent once and again, for he sent his prophets, who announced his Son's humanity beforehand, and afterward he sent his apostles, who announced his advent fulfilled, just as the prophets had prophesied it. When they would not come to the wedding feast, he sent again, saying, "Say to those who are invited, 'Look, I have prepared my provisions, I have slaughtered my oxen and my fatted fowls, and have prepared all my things: come to the wedding feast.'"

The oxen signify the patriarchs of the old law, who were 7 allowed by permission of the old law to slay their enemies in the manner of an ox. It is thus written in the old law, "Love your friend, and hate your enemy." People of old were allowed to oppress with strong might and slay with weapons the adversaries of God and their own enemies. But the same God who gave this permission through the law of Moses before his advent later changed the decree when he came to the world in human nature, saying, "I command

þus cweðende, "Ic bebeode eow, lufiað eowre fynd, and doþ tela þam ðe eow hatiað, and gebiddað for eowre ehteras, þæt ge beon bearn þæs heofonlican Fæder, se ðe læt his sunnan scinan ofer gode and yfele, and he sylð renscuras and wæstmas rihtwisum and unrihtwisum." Hwæt getacniað þa fearras buton fæderas ðære ealdan æ? Hwæt wæron hi buton fearra gelican, þa ða hi, mid leafe þære ealdan æ, heora fynd mid horne lichamlicere mihte potedon?

8   Þa gemæstan fugelas getacniað þa halgan lareowas þære Niwan Gecyðnysse. Þa sind gemæste mid gife þæs Halgan Gastes to ðam swiðe þæt hi wilniað þæs upplican færeldes mid fyðerum gastlicere drohtnunge. Hwæt is þæt man besette his geðanc on nyðerlicum þingum buton swilce modes hlænnys? Se þe mid fodan þære upplican lufe bið gefylled he bið swilce he sy mid rumlicum mettum gemæst. Mid þyssere fætnysse wolde se sealmwyrhta beon gemæst ða ða he cwæð, "Beo min sawul gefylled swa swa mid rysle and mid ungele." Hwæt is, "Mine fearras sind ofslagene, and mine gemæstan fugelas," buton swilce he cwæde, "Behealdað ðæra eald-fædera drohtnunga, and understandað þæra witegena gyddunge and þæra apostola bodunge embe mines Bearnes menniscnysse, and cumað to ðam giftum"? Þæt is, cumað mid geleafan, and geðeodað eow to ðære halgan gelaðunge, ðe is his bryd and eower modor.

9   "Hi hit forgymeleasodon and ferdon, sume to heora tunum, sume to heora ceape." Se færð to his tune and forsihð Godes gearcunge se ðe ungemetlice eorðlice teolunge begæð to ðan swiðe þæt he his Godes dæl forgymeleasað. Se færð embe his mangunge, se ðe mid gytsunge woruldlicra gestreona cepð swiðor þonne ðæs ecan lifes welan. Eornostlice þonne hi sume mid eorðlicum teolungum ungefohlice hi

you, love your enemies, and do good to those who hate you, and pray for your persecutors, that you may be children of the heavenly Father, who lets his sun shine over the good and evil, and gives rain showers and fruits to the righteous and the unrighteous." What do the oxen signify but the fathers of the old law? What were they if not like oxen, when, by permission of the old law, they struck their enemies with the horn of bodily might?

The fatted fowls signify the holy teachers of the New Testament. These are so fattened with the grace of the Holy Spirit that they long for the heavenly journey with the wings of spiritual life. What is it for one to set his thoughts on lower things but a sort of leanness of mind? One who is filled with the food of exalted love is, as it were, fattened with generous food. With this fatness the psalmist wished to be fattened when he said, "Let my soul be filled as with fat and with tallow." What is, "My oxen are slain, and my fatted fowls," but as though he had said, "Behold the lives of the old fathers, and understand the singing of the prophets and the preaching of the apostles about my Son's humanity, and come to the wedding feast"? That is, come with faith, and join yourselves to the holy Church, which is his bride and your mother. 8

"They ignored it and set out, some to their farms, some to their merchandise." He goes to his farm and neglects God's preparation who attends to earthly concerns so immoderately that he ignores God's portion. He goes about his commerce who with covetousness strives for worldly gains more than the riches of eternal life. Consequently, when some busy themselves excessively with earthly pur- 9

gebysgiað, and sume mid woruldlicum hordum, þonne ne
magon hi for ðære bysga smeagan embe þæs hælendes menniscnysse, and eac him bið swiðe hefigtyme geðuht þæt hi
heora þeawas be his regole geemnetton. Sume eac beoð swa
ðwyrlice gemodode þæt hi ne magon Godes bodunge gehyran, ac mid ehtnysse Godes bydelas geswencað, swa swa þæt
godspel her bæftan cwæð, "Sume hi gelæhton þa bydelas
and mid teonan gewæhton and ofslogon. Ac se cyning, ða ða
he þis geaxode, sende his here to and þa manslagan fordyde
and heora burh forbærnde."

10   Þa manslagan he fordyde forðan ðe he ða arleasan ehteras
hreowlice acwealde, swa swa we gehwær on martyra þrowun-
gum rædað. Nero, se wælhreowa casere, het ahon Petrum
and Paulum beheafdian, ac he wearð færlice of his rice afly-
med, and hine wulfas totæron. Herodes beheafdode þone
apostol Iacob, and Petrum gebrohte on cwearterne; ac God
hine ahredde of his hæftnede, and þa ða se cyning smeade
hu he of ðam cwearterne come, þa æfter þan him com to
Godes engel and hine to deaðe gesloh. Astriges, se Indisca
cyning þe Bartholomeum ofsloh, awedde, and on þam
wodan dreame gewat. Ealswa Egeas, þe Andream ahencg,
þærrihte on wodan dreame geendode. Langsum bið us to gereccenne ealra þæra arleasra ehtera geendunga, hu gramlice
se ælmihtiga God his halgena þrowunga on him gewræc.
Ðæt godspel cwyð þæt he heora burh forbærnde, forþan þe
hi beoð ægðer ge mid sawle ge mid lichaman on ecere susle
forbærnde. "He sende his here to," forþan ðe he þurh his
englas þa manfullan fordeð; hwæt sind þæra engla werod buton here þæs heofonlican cyninges? He is gehaten *Dominus
Sabaoð*, þæt is "heres Hlaford" oððe "weroda Drihten."

11   Se cyning cwæð ða to his þegnum, "Ðas gyfta sind

suits, and some with worldly treasures, then because of that busyness they cannot contemplate the savior's humanity, and it seems very burdensome to them to adjust their conduct to his rule. Some also are so perversely minded that they cannot hear God's preaching, but attack God's messengers with persecution, as the gospel says hereafter, "Some seized the messengers and afflicted them with injury and killed them. But the king, when he heard of this, sent his army and destroyed the murderers and burned down their city."

He destroyed the murderers, because he fiercely killed the impious persecutors, as we read everywhere in the passions of the martyrs. Nero, the cruel emperor, commanded Peter to be crucified and Paul beheaded, but he was suddenly driven from his realm, and wolves tore him to pieces. Herod beheaded the apostle James, and put Peter into prison; but God rescued him from his captivity, and when the king inquired how he had come out of the prison, God's angel came to him afterward and struck him dead. Astryges, the Indian king who killed Bartholomew, went mad, and departed in a fit of madness. Likewise Egeas, who crucified Andrew, ended suddenly in a fit of madness. It would take too long to recount the ends of all the impious persecutors, how sternly almighty God avenged the sufferings of his saints on them. The gospel says that he burned down their city, because they will be burned in eternal torment both in soul and in body. "He sent his army," because through his angels he destroys the wicked; what are the hosts of angels but the army of the heavenly king? He is called *Dominus Sabaoth*, that is, "Lord of an army" or "Lord of hosts."

The king then said to his servants, "The wedding feasts 11

gearowe, ac þa ðe ic þærto gelaðode næron his wyrðe. Farað
nu to wega utscytum, and swa hwylce swa ge gemetað, laþiað
to þam gyftum." Wegas sind mislice manna dæda. Utscytas
þæra wega sind ateorung woruldlicra weorca; and þa forwel
oft becumað to Gode þe on eorðlicum weorcum hwonlice
speowð. "Hwæt ða ðæs cyninges ærendracan ferdon geond
wegas, gadrigende ealle þa ðe hi gemetton, ægðer ge yfele ge
gode, and gesetton þa gifta endemes." On þyssere andwerdan gelaðunge sind gemengde yfele and gode swa swa clæne
corn mid fulum coccele; ac on ende þyssere worulde se soða
dema hæt his englas gadrian þone coccel byrþenmælum and
awurpan into ðam unadwæscendlicum fyre. Byrþenmælum
hi gadriað þa synfullan fram þam rihtwisum; þonne ða manslagan beoð togædere getigede innon þam hellicum fyre,
and sceaþan mid sceaþum, gytseras mid gytserum, forliras
mid forlirum, and swa gehwylce manfulle geferan on þam
ecum tintregum samod gewriþene cwylmiað. And se clæna
hwæte bið gebroht on Godes berne, þæt is, þæt ða rihtwisan
beoð gebrohte to þam ecan life, þær ne cymð storm ne nan
unweder þæt ðam corne derie. Ðonne ne beoð þa godan
nahwar buton on heofenum, and þa yfelan nahwar buton on
helle.

12   Mine gebroþra, gif ge gode sind, þonne sceole ge emlice
wiþercorenra manna yfelnysse forberan swa lange swa ge on
þisum andweardan life wuniað. Ne bið se god se þe yfelne
forberan nele. Be þisum cwæð Godes stemn to þam witegan
Ezechiel, "Ðu mannes bearn, ungeleaffulle and yfel tihtende
sind mid þe, and þu wunast mid þam wyrstan wyrmcynne."
Eft Paulus se apostol geleaffulra manna lif herode and getrymde, þus tihtende, "Ge wuniað betwux þwyrum mancynne; scinað betwux þam swa swa steorran, lifes word heal-
dende."

are ready, but those I invited to them were not worthy of it. Go now to the outlets of the highways, and invite whomever you meet to the wedding." Highways are the various deeds of people. The outlets of ways are the failure of worldly works; very often people come to God who prosper but little in earthly works. "At this the king's messengers went through the highways, gathering all they found, both evil and good, and completely filled the wedding feast." In this present Church evil and good are mingled like clean grain with foul cockles; but at the end of this world the true judge will command his angels to gather the cockles in sheaves and cast them into the unquenchable fire. They will gather in sheaves the sinful from the righteous; then murderers will be tied together in the hellish fire, and robbers with robbers, the greedy with the greedy, adulterers with adulterers, and so all wicked companions will suffer, bound together in everlasting torments. Then the clean wheat will be brought into God's barn, that is, the righteous will be brought to eternal life, where there comes no storm or tempest that might damage the grain. Then the good will be nowhere but in heaven, and the evil nowhere but in hell.

My brothers, if you are good, then you should bear patiently the evil of reprobates, as long as you remain in this present life. The person who will not bear with evil is not good. About this the voice of God said to the prophet Ezekiel, "You child of man, unbelievers and instigators to evil are with you, and you dwell with the worst race of serpents." Again, Paul the apostle praised and confirmed the lives of believers, thus encouraging them, "You dwell among perverse people; shine among them like stars, holding the word of life." 12

₁₃ "Se cyning eode inn and gesceawode þa gebeoras; þa ge-
seah he þær ænne mann þe næs gescryd mid gyftlicum
reafe." Þæt giftlice reaf getacnað þa soþan lufe Godes and
manna. Þa lufe ure scyppend us geswutelode þurh hine
sylfne þa ða he gemedemode þæt he us fram þam ecan deaþe
mid his deorwurþan blode alysde; swa swa Iohannes se godspellere cwæð, "Swa swiþe lufode God þysne middaneard
þæt he his ancennedan Sunu sealde for us." Se Godes Sunu,
þe ðurh lufe to mannum becom, gebicnode on þam godspelle þæt ðæt giftlice reaf getacnode—þa soðan lufe. Ælc
þæra þe mid geleafan and fulluhte to Gode gebihð he cymð
to þam gyftum; ac he ne cymð na mid gyftlicum reafe gif he
þa soþan lufe ne hylt. Witodlice ge geseoð þæt gehwam
sceamað, gif he gelaðod bið to woruldlicum gyftum, þæt he
waclice gescryd cume to þære scortan blisse; ac micele mare
sceamu bið þam ðe mid horium reafe cymð to Godes
gyftum, þæt he for his fulum gyrelan fram þære ecan blisse
ascofen beo into ecum þeostrum. Swa swa reaf wlitegað
þone man lichamlice, swa eac seo soðe lufu wlitegað ure
sawle mid gastlicere fægernysse. Ðeah se mann hæbbe fullne
geleafan, and ælmessan wyrce, and fela to gode gedo, eal him
bið ydel, swa hwæt swa he deð, buton he hæbbe soþe lufe to
Gode and to eallum Cristenum mannum. Seo is soð lufu þæt
gehwa his freond lufie on gode, and his feond for gode.
Dæghwamlice gæð se heofonlica cyning into þam gyftum,
þæt is, into his gelaðunge, and sceawað hwæðer we beon
mid þam gyftlicum reafe innan gescrydde; and swa hwylcne
swa he gemet butan soþre lufe, ðæne he befrinð mid graman,
þus cweþende, "Ðu freond, humeta dorstest ðu gan to minre
gearcunge buton gyftlicum reafe?" Freond he hine het, and
þeah awearp fram his gebeorum. Freond he wæs ðurh

"The king went in and beheld the guests; then he saw 13
there a person who was not dressed in a wedding garment."
The wedding garment signifies the true love of God and humanity. Our creator manifested that love to us in himself
when he deigned to redeem us from eternal death with his
precious blood; as John the Evangelist said, "God so greatly
loved this world that he gave his only-begotten Son for us."
The Son of God, who came to humanity through love, indicated in the gospel what the wedding garment signified—
true love. Each of those who turn to God with faith and
baptism comes to the wedding; but he does not come with a
wedding garment if he does not have true love. Indeed, you
see that everyone is ashamed, if he is invited to a worldly
wedding, to come poorly dressed to that brief pleasure; but
it will be a much greater shame for one who comes to God's
wedding with a filthy garment, so that for his foul clothing
he will be cast out from eternal bliss into eternal darkness.
Just as a garment adorns one physically, so true love adorns
our soul with spiritual beauty. Though one might have full
faith, and give alms, and do much good, whatever he does
will all be in vain unless he has true love for God and for
all Christians. It is true love that everyone should love his
friend in good, and his enemy for his good. The heavenly
king goes daily to the wedding feast, that is, into his Church,
and looks whether we are inwardly clad in the wedding garment; and he angrily questions anyone he finds without true
love, saying, "Friend, how did you dare come to my preparation without a wedding garment?" He called him friend, and
yet cast him out from his guests. He was a friend through

geleafan, and wiþercora þurh weorc. He þærrihte adumbode, forþan þe æt Godes dome ne bið nan beladung ne
wiþertalu; ac se dema þe wiðutan þreað is gewita his inge-
hides wiðinnan. Ðeah ðe hwa þa soþan lufe gyt fulfremedlice
næbbe, ne sceal he ðeah his sylfes geortruwian, forþan ðe se
witega be swylcum cwæð to Gode, "Min Drihten, þine eagan gesawon mine unfulfremednysse, and on þinre bec ealle
sind awritene."

14   Se cyning cwæð to his ðegnum, "Bindað þone misscryd-
dan handum and fotum, and wurpað into ðam yttrum þeostrum, þær bið wop and toða gebitt." Þa handa and þa fet þe
nu ne beoð gebundene mid Godes ege fram þwyrlicum
weorcum, hi beoð þonne þurh strecnysse Godes domes
fæste gewriðene. Þa fet ðe nellað untrumne geneosian, and
ða handa þe nan ðing þearfum ne syllað, þa beoð þonne mid
wite gebundene, forðan þe hi synd nu sylfwilles fram godum
weorcum gewriðene. Se misscrydda wæs aworpen on ða
yttran þeostru. Þa inran þeostru sind þære heortan blind-
nys, þa yttran þeostru is seo swearte niht þære ecan geniðerunge. Se fordemda þonne þrowað on þam yttrum þeostrum
neadunge, forðan ðe he nu sylfwilles his lif adrihð on blindnysse his heortan, and næfð nan gemynd þæs soðan leohtes,
þæt is, Crist, þe be him sylfum cwæð, "Ic eom middangeardes leoht; se ðe me fyligð, ne gæð he on þeostrum, ac he
hæfð lifes leoht." On ðam yttrum þeostrum bið wop and
toða gebit. Þær wepað ða eagan on ðam hellican lige, þe nu
ðurh unalyfedlice gewilnunga goretende hwearftliað; and þa
teð, þe nu on oferæte blissiað, sceolon þær cearcian on þam
unasecgendlicum pinungum þe Godes wiðerwinnum gegearcod is. Þa eagan soðlice for swiðlicum smice tyrað, and
þa teð for micclum cyle cwaciað; forðan ðe ða wiðercoran

faith, and a reprobate in works. He at once fell silent, because at God's judgment there will be no excuse or defense;
for the judge who convicts without is aware of the mind
within. Though someone may not yet have true love perfectly, he should not despair of himself, for of such people
the prophet spoke to God, "My Lord, your eyes have seen
my imperfections, and all are written in your book."

The king said to his servants, "Bind the badly dressed one 14
hand and foot, and cast him into outer darkness, where
there will be weeping and gnashing of teeth." The hands and
the feet, which are not now bound from perverse works by
fear of God, shall then be fast bound through the sternness
of God's judgment. The feet which will not visit the sick,
and the hands which give nothing to the poor, will then be
bound in torment, because they are now restrained from
good works by their own will. The one badly dressed was
cast into outer darkness. The inner darkness is the blindness
of the heart, the outer darkness is the black night of eternal
condemnation. The condemned will then suffer by necessity in outer darkness, because he now voluntarily passes his
life in blindness of heart, and has no remembrance of the
true light, that is, Christ, who said of himself, "I am the light
of the world; he who follows me does not go in darkness, but
has the light of life." In the outer darkness will be weeping
and gnashing of teeth. There the eyes, which now dart
around, wandering with illicit desires, will weep in the hellish flame; and the teeth which now rejoice in gluttony will
grind in the unspeakable torments which are prepared for
God's adversaries. Truly the eyes will fill with tears from the
powerful smoke, and the teeth chatter with the great chill;

unacumendlice hætu þrowiað and unasecgendlicne cyle. Witodlice þæt hellice fyr hæfð unasecgendlice hætan and nan leoht, ac ecelice byrnð on sweartum ðeostrum.

15   Gif hwam twynige be æriste, þonne mæg he understandan on þisum godspelle þæt þær bið soð ærist þær ðær beoð eagan and teð. Eagan sind flæscene, and teð bænene; forðan þe we sceolon, wylle we nelle we, arisan on ende þyssere worulde mid flæsce and mid bane, and onfon edlean ealra ura dæda, oððe wununge mid Gode for godum geearnungum, oþþe hellewite mid deofle for mandædum. Be þisum cwæð se eadiga Iob, "Ic gelyfe þæt min alysend leofað, and ic sceal on þam endenextan dæge of eorðan arisan, and eft ic beo mid minum felle befangen, and on minum flæsce ic geseo God—ic sylf, and na oðer." Þæt is, na oðer hiw þurh me, ac ic sylf hine geseo.

16   Þises godspelles geendung is swiðe egefull: "Fela sind gecigede, and feawa gecorene." Efne nu ure ealra stemn clypað Crist, ac ure ealra lif ne clypað; forðan þe manega wiðcweðað on heora ðeawum þæt þæt hi mid heora stemne geandettað. Sume menn habbað god anginn sume hwile, ac hi geendiað on yfele. Sume habbað yfel anginn, and wel geendiað þurh soðe dædbote. Sume onginnað wel and bet geendiað. Nu sceal gehwa hine sylfne micclum ondrædan, þeah ðe he gode drohtnunge hæbbe, and nateshwon be him sylfum gedyrstlæcan; forðan þe he nat hwæðer he wurðe is into þam ecan rice. Ne he ne sceal be oðrum geortruwian, þeah ðe he on leahtras befealle; forðan ðe he nat þa menigfealdan welan Godes mildheortnysse.

17   Cwyð nu Sanctus Gregorius þæt sum broðor gecyrde to anum mynstre þe he sylf gestaðelode, and æfter regollicere fandunge munuchad underfeng. Þam filigde sum flæsclic

for the reprobates will suffer intolerable heat and unspeakable chill. Indeed, the fire of hell has unspeakable heat and no light, but burns eternally in black darkness.

If anyone should doubt the resurrection, he may understand in this gospel that there will be a true resurrection where there are eyes and teeth. Eyes are of flesh, and teeth of bone; for whether we want it or not, we will arise at the end of this world with flesh and bone, and receive the reward of all our deeds, either a dwelling with God for good deserts, or torments of hell with the devil for evil deeds. Of this the blessed Job said, "I believe that my redeemer lives, and I will arise from earth on the last day, and I will again be enclosed in my flesh, and in my flesh I will see God—I myself, and no other." That is, no other form through me, but I myself will see him. 15

The ending of this gospel is very terrifying: "Many are called, and few chosen." Behold, now all our voices call Christ, but all our lives do not call him; for many deny in their habits that which they profess with their voice. Some have a good beginning for a while, but they end in evil. Some have an evil beginning, and end well through true penitence. Some begin well and end better. Now everyone should greatly fear, even though he might lead a good life, and not presume on himself; for he does not know whether he is worthy of the eternal kingdom. Nor should one despair for another, though he might fall into vices; for he does not know the manifold abundance of God's mercy. 16

Saint Gregory now says that a certain brother entered into a monastery which he himself had founded, and after probation in the rule received the monastic habit. A fleshly 17

broðor to mynstre, na for gecnyrdnysse goddre drohtnunge
ac for flæsclicere lufe. Se gastlica broðor eallum þam myn-
stermunecum þearle ðurh gode drohtnunge gelicode, and
his flæsclica broðor micclum his lifes ðeawum mid þwyrnysse wiðcwæð. He leofode on mynstre for neode swiðor
þonne for beterunge. He wæs gegafspræce, and þwyr on dædum, wel besewen on reafe, and yfele on ðeawum. He nahte
geðyld gif hine hwa to goddre drohtnunge tihte. Wearð ða
his lif swiðe hefigtyme ðam gebroðrum, ac hi hit emlice for-
bæron for his broðer godnysse. He ne mihte nan ðing to
gode gedon, ne he nolde nan god gehyran. Þa wearð he
færlice mid sumere coðe gestanden and to deaðe gebroht.
Þa ða he to forðsiðe ahafen wæs, ða comon þa gebroðra to ði
þæt hi his sawle becwædon. He læg acealdod on nyþewear-
dum limum; on ðam breoste anum orðode ða gyt se gast. Þa
gebroðra ða swa micel geornfullicor for hine gebædon, swa
micclum swa hi gesawon þæt he hrædlice gewitan sceolde.
He ða færlice hrymde, þus cweðende, "Gewitað fram me!
Efne her is cumen an draca þe me sceal forswelgan, ac he ne
mæg for eower andwerdnysse. Min heafod he hæfð mid his
ceaflum befangen. Rymað him, þæt he me leng ne swence.
Gif ic þisum dracan to forswelgenne geseald eom, hwi sceal
ic elcunge þrowian for eowerum oferstealle?"

18   Þa gebroðra him cwædon to, "Hwi sprecst þu mid swa
micelre orwennysse? Mearca ðe sylfne mid tacne þære halgan rode." He andwyrde be his mihte, "Ic wolde lustbære
mid tacne þære halgan rode me bletsian, ac ic næbbe ða
mihte, forðan þe se draca me ðearle ofþryhð." Hwæt ða
munecas ða hi astrehton mid wope to eorðan, and ongunnon geornlicor for his hreddinge þone wealdendan God
biddan. Efne ða færlice awyrpte se adliga cniht, and mid

brother followed him to the monastery, not for desire of a good life but for fleshly love. The spiritual brother exceedingly pleased the monks of the monastery by his good life, but his fleshly brother, with perverseness, greatly contradicted the practices of his life. He lived in the monastery more from necessity than for his betterment. He was inclined to idle talk, and perverse in deeds, flashy in clothing, and evil in morals. He had no patience if anyone exhorted him to a good course of life. His life became very burdensome to the brothers, but they endured it calmly for the sake of his brother's goodness. He could do nothing good, and would not hear any good. Then he was suddenly seized with some disease and brought to the point of death. When he was lifted up for his departure, the brothers came in to pray for his soul. He lay chilled in his lower limbs; in his breast alone the spirit still breathed. The more the brothers saw that he would quickly depart, the more fervently they prayed for him. He then suddenly cried out, saying, "Depart from me! Lo, here has come a dragon that will swallow me, but he cannot because of your presence. He has seized my head in his jaws. Give him room, that he may afflict me no longer. If I am given to this dragon to be swallowed, why should I suffer delay through your presence?"

The brothers said to him, "Why do you speak with such 18 great despair? Mark yourself with the sign of the holy cross." He answered as he was able, "I would joyfully bless myself with the sign of the holy cross, but I do not have the strength, for the dragon fiercely oppresses me." At this the monks prostrated themselves to the earth with weeping, and began more fervently to pray to the ruling God for his salvation. Just then the sick young man suddenly regained

blissigendre stemne cwæð, "Ic þancige Gode! Efne nu se
draca þe me forswelgan wolde is afliged for eowerum benum. He is fram me ascofen and standan ne mihte ongean
eowre þingunge. Beoð nu mine ðingeras, biddende for
minum synnum; forðan ðe ic eom gearo to gecyrrenne to
munuclicere drohtnunge, and woruldlice ðeawas ealle forlætan." His cealdan limu þa geedcucodon, and he mid ealre
heortan to Gode gecyrde, and mid langsumum broce on his
gecyrrednysse wearð gerihtlæced, and æt nextan on þære ylcan untrumnysse gewat; ac he ne geseah þone dracan on his
forðsiðe, forðan ðe he hine oferswiðde mid gecyrrednysse
his heortan.

19   Ne sceole we beon ormode, þeah ðe on þyssere andweardan gelaðunge fela syndon yfele and feawa gode; forðan þe
Noes arc on yþum ðæs micclan Flodes hæfde getacnunge
þyssere gelaðunge, and he wæs on nyðeweardan wid and on
ufeweardan nearo. On ðære nyðemystan bytminge wunodon þa reðan deor and creopende wurmas. On oþre fleringe
wunodon fugelas and clæne nytenu. On þære ðriddan fleringe wunode Noe mid his wife, and his ðry suna mid heora
þrim wifum. On ðære bytminge wæs se arc rum, þær ða
reðan deor wunedon, and wiðufan genyrwed, þær ðæra
manna wunung wæs; forðan ðe seo halige gelaðung on flæsclicum mannum is swiðe brad and on gastlicum nearo. Heo
tospræt hire bosm þær ðær þa reðan wuniað on nytenlicum
ðeawum, and heo is genyrwed on þone ende þe þa gescead-
wisan wuniað, on gastlicum ðeawum drohtnigende; forðan
swa hi haligran beoð on þyssere andwerdan gelaðunge, swa
heora læs bið. Micele ma is þæra manna þe lybbað be
agenum lustum þonne ðæra sy þe heora lifes ðeawas æfter
Godes bebodum gerihtlæcað; þeahhwæðere symle bið

his health, and with exulting voice said, "I thank God! Behold now the dragon which wanted to swallow me is put to flight through your prayers. He is driven away from me and could not stand against your intercession. Be now my intercessors, praying for my sins; for I am ready to turn to the monastic life, and to completely forsake worldly practices." His cold limbs then revived, and he turned to God with all his heart, and by long sickness was justified in his conversion, and at length died of the same disease; but he did not see the dragon at his departure, for he had overcome him by the conversion of his heart.

We should not despair, though in this present Church 19 many are evil and few good; for Noah's ark on the waves of the great Flood was a symbol of this Church, and it was wide in the lower part and narrow in the upper. In the lowest bottom level dwelt the fierce beasts and creeping serpents. On the second floor dwelt birds and clean animals. On the third floor dwelt Noah with his wife, and his three sons with their three wives. The ark was roomy at the bottom, where the fierce beasts dwelt, and grew narrower above, where the dwelling of humans was; for the holy Church is very broad in fleshly people and narrow in spiritual ones. She spreads her bosom where the fierce dwell in beastly habits, and she is narrowed at the end which the reasonable dwell, living in spiritual practices; for the holier they are in this present Church, the fewer of them there are. There are many more of those who live for their own pleasures than there are of those who regulate their life's actions after God's commandments; yet the number of holy ones is ever increased

haligra manna getel geeacnod þurh arleasra manna wanunge. Nis þæt getel Godes gecorenra lytel, swa swa Crist on oðre stowe cwæð, "Manega cumað fram eastdæle and fram west-dæle, and sittað mid þam heahfædere Abrahame, and Isaace, and Iacobe on heofonan rice." Eft se sealmwyrhta be Godes gecorenum cwæð, "Ic hi getealde, and heora getel is mare ðonne sandceosol." On ðisum andweardan life sind þa ge-corenan feawa geðuhte ongean getel þæra wiðercorenra, ac þonne hi to ðam ecan life gegaderode beoð, heora tel bið swa menigfeald þæt hit oferstihð, be ðæs witegan cwyde, sandceosles gerim.

20   Læd us, ælmihtig God, to getele ðinra gecorenra halgena, inn to þære ecan blisse ðines rices, þe þu gearcodest fram frymðe middangeardes þe lufigendum, þu ðe leofast and rixast mid þam ecan Fæder and Halgum Gaste on ealra worulda woruld. Amen.

36

KALENDAS NOVEMBRIS

Natale omnium sanctorum

Halige lareowas ræddon þæt seo geleaffulle gelaðung þisne dæg eallum halgum to wurþmynte wurðige and arwurðlice freolsige, forðan þe hi ne mihton heora ælcum

through the decrease of the impious. The number of God's chosen is not small, as Christ said in another place, "Many shall come from the east and from the west, and sit with the patriarch Abraham, and Isaac, and Jacob in the kingdom of heaven." Again, the psalmist said of God's chosen, "I counted them, and their number is greater than the grains of sand." In this present life, the chosen seem few in comparison with the number of the reprobates, but when they will be gathered to the eternal life, their number will be so great that it will exceed, as the prophet said, the number of grains of sand.

Lead us, almighty God, to the number of your chosen 20 saints, into the everlasting bliss of your kingdom, which you have prepared from the beginning of the world for those who love you, you who live and reign with the eternal Father and the Holy Spirit for ever and ever. Amen.

36

All Saints

NOVEMBER I

The Feast of All Saints

Holy teachers have advised that the faithful Church should celebrate and piously solemnize this day in honor of all saints, because they could not establish a feast day for

synderlice freolstide gesettan, ne nanum menn on andweardum life nis heora eallra nama cuð, swa swa Iohannes se godspellere on his gastlican gesihðe awrat, þus cweðende, "Ic
geseah swa micele menigu swa nan man geryman ne mæg, of
eallum ðeodum and of ælcere mægðe, standende ætforan
Godes þrymsetle, ealle mid hwitum gyrlum gescrydde, heal-
dende palmtwigu on heora handum; and sungon mid hluddre stemne, 'Sy hælu urum Gode þe sitt ofer his þrymsetle.'
And ealle englas stodon on ymbhwyrfte his ðrymsetles, and
aluton to Gode, þus cweðende, 'Sy urum Gode bletsung and
beorhtnys, wisdom and þancung, wurðmynt and strengð, on
ealra worulda woruld, amen.'"

2   Godes halgan sind englas and menn. Englas sind gastas
butan lichaman. Þa gesceop se ælmihtiga wealdend on
micelre fægernysse, him sylfum to lofe and to wuldre and
wurðmynte his mægenðrymme on ecnysse. Be þam we
forhtiað fela to sprecenne, forðan ðe Gode anum is to gewitenne hu heora ungesewenlice gecynd butan ælcere be-
smitennysse oþþe wanunge on ecere hluttornysse þurhwunað. Þeahhwæðere we oncnawað on halgum gewritum þæt
nigon engla werod sind wunigende on heofonlicum þrymme,
þe næfre nane synne ne gefremedon. Þæt teoðe werod þurh
modignesse losode, and to awyrgedum gastum behwyrfede
wurdon, and ascofene of heofonlicere myrhðe inn to hel-
licere susle.

3   Soþlice sume ðæra haligra gasta þe mid heora scyppende
þurhwunodon to us asende cumað and towearde ðing cyðað.
Sume hi wyrcað, be Godes dihte, tacna and gelomlice wundra on middangearde. Sume hi synd ealdras gesette þam
oðrum englum to gefyllenne þa godcundlican gerynu. Þurh
sume gesett God and toscæt his domas. Sume hi sind swa

each of them separately, nor are the names of all of them known to anyone in the present life, as John the Evangelist wrote in his spiritual vision, saying, "I saw a multitude so great that no one can count it, of all nations and of every tribe, standing before the throne of God, all clad in white garments, holding palm branches in their hands; and they sang with a loud voice, 'Salvation be to our God who sits on his glorious throne.' And all the angels stood around his throne, and bowed down to God, saying, 'Blessing and brightness be to our God, wisdom and thanksgiving, honor and strength, for ever and ever, amen.'"

God's saints are angels and humans. Angels are spirits 2 without body. The almighty ruler created these in great beauty, for his own praise and to the glory and honor of his majesty in eternity. We are afraid to say much about them, because it is for God alone to know how their invisible nature dwells in eternal purity without any pollution or decay. Nevertheless, we know from holy writings that there are nine hosts of angels dwelling in heavenly majesty, who never committed any sin. The tenth host perished through pride, and were turned into accursed spirits, and driven from heavenly joy into the torment of hell.

Truly, some of those holy spirits who remained with their 3 creator are sent to us to come and announce future things. Some of them, by God's direction, frequently work signs and miracles in the world. Some of them are chiefs set over the other angels for the fulfillment of the divine mysteries. Through some God establishes and decides his judgments.

micclum to Gode geðeodde þæt nane oðre him betwynan ne synd, and hi ðonne on swa micclan maran lufe byrnende beoð swa micclum swa hi Godes beorhtnysse scearplicor sceawiað. Nu is þes dæg þisum englum arwurðlice gehalgod, and eac þam halgum mannum þe þurh miccle geðincða fram frymðe middangeardes Gode geþugon. Of þisum wæron ærest heahfæderas, eawfæste and wuldorfulle weras on heora life, witegena fæderas, þæra gemynd ne bið forgiten, and heora nama þurhwunað on ecnysse forðan ðe hi wæron Gode gecweme þurh geleafan, and rihtwisnysse, and gehyrsumnysse. Þisum fyligð þæra witegena gecorennys: hi wæron Godes gesprecan, and þam he æteowde his digelnysse, and hi onlihte mid gife þæs Halgan Gastes swa þæt hi wiston þa towerdan ðing and mid witigendlicere gyddunge bododon. Witodlice þa gecorenan witegan mid manegum tacnum and forebicnungum on heora life scinende wæron. Hi gehældon manna untrumnysse, and deaddra manna lic to life arærdon. Hi eac for folces þwyrnysse heofonan scuras oftugon, and eft miltsigende getiþodon. Hi heofodon folces synna, and heora wrace on him sylfum forscytton. Cristes mennisc-nysse, and his ðrowunge, and ærist, and upstige, and ðone micclan dom, þurh ðone Halgan Gast gelærede, hi witego-don. On ðære Nywan Gecyðnysse forðstop Iohannes se Ful-luhtere, se ðe mid witegunge Cristes tocyme bododce, and eac mid his fingre hine gebicnode. "Betwux wifa bearnum ne aras nan mærra mann þonne is Iohannes se Fulluhtere."

4   Þisum Godes cempan geþwærlæcð þæt twelffealde getel Cristes apostola, þe he sylf geceas him to leorningcnihtum, and hi mid rihtum geleafan and soðre lare geteah and eallum

Some of them are so greatly joined to God that no others are between them, and then the more clearly they behold the brightness of God, the more greatly are they burning in love. Now, this day is piously consecrated to these angels, and also to those holy persons who through great excellences have attained to God from the beginning of the world. Of these, the patriarchs were first, religious and glorious men in their lives, the fathers of the prophets, whose memory will not be forgotten, and their names will last forever because they were acceptable to God through faith, righteousness, and obedience. These are followed by the chosen company of prophets: they spoke with God, and to them he revealed his secrets, and enlightened them with the grace of the Holy Spirit so that they knew the things to come and announced them in prophetic song. Truly the chosen prophets were illustrious in their lives by many signs and foreshadowings. They healed people's sickness, and raised the bodies of the dead to life. They also, for the people's perversity, withheld the showers of heaven, and then in mercy permitted them. They bewailed the people's sins, and by themselves prevented their punishment. Instructed by the Holy Spirit, they prophesied Christ's incarnation, his passion, resurrection, ascension, and the great judgment. In the New Testament, John the Baptist went forth, who preached the coming of Christ with prophecy, and also pointed him out with his finger. "Among the children of women there has arisen no greater one than John the Baptist."

To these warriors of God is joined the twelvefold number 4 of Christ's apostles, whom he himself chose for his disciples, and he instructed them in right belief and true doctrine and

ðeodum to lareowum gesette, swa þæt se sweg heora bodunge ferde geond ealle eorðan, and heora word becomon to
gemærum ealles ymbhwyrftes. To ðisum twelf apostolum
cwæð se ælmihtiga hælend, "Ge sind middangeardes leoht;
scine eower leoht swa ætforan mannum, þæt hi geseon
eowre godan weorc, and wuldrian eowerne Fæder þe on
heofonum is." "Ge sind mine frynd, and ic cyðe eow swa
hwæt swa ic æt minum Fæder gehyrde." Eornostlice Drihten forgeaf þa mihte his twelf apostolum þæt hi ða ylcan
wundra worhton þe he sylf on middangearde gefremode.
And swa hwæt swa hi bindað ofer eorðan, þæt bið on heofonum gebunden, and swa hwæt swa hi unbindað ofer
eorðan, þæt bið unbunden on heofonum. Eac he him behet
mid soðfæstum behate þæt hi on ðam micclum dome ofer
twelf domsetl sittende beoð, to demenne eallum mannum
þe æfre on lichaman lif underfengon.

5   Æfter þam apostolican werode we wurðiað þone ge-
fæstan heap Godes cyðera, þe ðurh mislice tintrega Cristes
ðrowunge werlice geefenlæhton, and ðurh martyrdom þæt
upplice rice geferdon. Sume hi wæron mid wæpnum ofslagene, sume on lige forswælede, oðre mid swipum ofbeatene,
oþre mid stengum þurhðyde, sume on hengene gecwylmede,
sume on widdre sæ besencte, oðre cuce behylde, oðre mid
isenum clawum totorene, sume mid stanum ofhrorene,
sume mid winterlicum cyle geswencte, sume mid hungre
gecwylmede, sume handum and fotum forcorfene, folce to
wæfersyne for geleafan and halgum naman hælendes Cristes. Þas sind þa sigefæstan Godes frynd, þe ðæra forscyld-
godra ealdormanna hæsa forsawon, and nu hi sind gewuldor-
beagode mid sige heora þrowunga on ecere myrhðe. Hi
mihton beon lichamlice acwealde, ac hi ne mihton fram

set them as teachers to all nations, so that the sound of their preaching went out over all the earth, and their words came to the boundaries of the whole world. To these twelve apostles the almighty savior said, "You are the light of the world; let your light so shine before people, that they may see your good works, and glorify your Father who is in heaven." "You are my friends, and I make known to you whatever I have heard from my Father." Indeed, the Lord gave power to his twelve apostles to work the same wonders he himself performed on earth. And whatever they bind on earth will be bound in heaven, and whatever they unbind on earth will be unbound in heaven. He also promised them with a true promise that at the great judgment they will be sitting on twelve judgment seats, to judge all who have ever received life in the body.

After the apostolic company, we honor the steadfast 5 troop of God's martyrs, who through various torments courageously imitated the passion of Christ, and through martyrdom went to the realm on high. Some of them were slain with weapons, some burned in flame, others beaten with whips, others pierced with stakes, some slain on the cross, some sunk in the wide sea, others flayed alive, others torn with iron claws, some overwhelmed with stones, some afflicted with winter's cold, some slain by hunger, some with hands and feet cut off, as a spectacle to people for their faith and the holy name of the savior Christ. These are the triumphant friends of God, who despised the commands of those criminal ealdormen, and now they are crowned with glory in the triumph of their sufferings in eternal joy. They might be slain in the body, but they could not be turned away from

Gode þurh nane tintregunga beon gebigede. Heora hiht wæs mid undeadlicnysse afylled, þeah ðe hi ætforan mannum getintregode wæron. Hi wæron sceortlice gedrehte, and langlice gefrefrode, forðan ðe God heora afandode swa swa gold on ofne, and he afunde hi him wyrðe, and swa swa halige offrunga hi underfeng to his heofonlican rice.

6 Æfter ablunnenre ehtnysse reðra cynega and ealdormanna, on siblicere drohtnunge Godes gelaðunge, wæron halige sacerdas Gode ðeonde þa mid soðre lare and mid halgum gebysnungum folces menn to Gode symle gebigdon. Heora mod wæs hluttor and mid clænnysse afylled, and hi mid clænum handum Gode ælmihtigum æt his weofode ðenodon, mærsigende þa halgan gerynu Cristes lichaman and his blodes. Eac hi offrodon hi sylfe Gode liflice onsægednysse butan womme oþþe gemencgednysse þwyrlices weorces. Hi befæston Godes lare heora underþeoddum to unateorigendlicum gafele, and heora mod mid þreatunge, and bene, and micelre gymene to lifes wege gebigdon, and for nanum woruldlicum ege Godes riht ne forsuwodon; and ðeah ðe hi swurdes ecge ne gefreddon, þeah ðurh heora lifes geearnunga hi ne beoð martyrdomes bedælede, forðan þe martyrdom bið gefremmed na on blodes gyte anum, ac eac swylce on synna forhæfednysse and on biggenge Godes beboda.

. 7 Þysum fyligð ancersetlena drohtnung and synderlic ingehyd. Þa on westenum wunigende woruldlice estas and gælsan mid strecum mode and stiðum life fortrædon. Hi forflugon woruldmanna gesihðe and herunge and, on waclicum screafum oððe hulcum lutigende deorum geferlæhte, to engelicum spræcum gewunode, on micclum wundrum scinende wæron. Blindum hi forgeafon gesihðe, healtum

God by any torments. Their hope was filled with immortality, though they were tormented before people. They were afflicted for a short time, and comforted for a long time, for God tried them like gold in a furnace, and he found them worthy of him, and received them like holy offerings into his heavenly kingdom.

After the end of the persecution by the cruel kings and ealdormen, in the peaceful life of God's Church, there were holy priests aspiring to God who with true doctrine and holy examples ever inclined the common people to God. Their minds were pure and filled with chastity, and with clean hands they served God almighty at his altar, celebrating the holy mystery of Christ's body and blood. They likewise offered themselves as a living sacrifice to God without blemish or mingling of perverse work. They delivered God's doctrine to their followers as an imperishable tribute, and with chastisement, prayer, and great care turned their minds to the way of life, and did not keep silent about God's law for any fear of the world; and though they did not feel the sword's edge, yet through the merits of their lives they are not deprived of martyrdom, for martyrdom is not carried out by bloodshed alone, but also by abstinence from sin and by the observance of God's commandments. 6

Following these is the life and special resolve of anchorites. Dwelling in the wilderness, these trampled on worldly delicacies and luxuries with stern minds and strict life. They fled from the sight and praise of worldly people and, crouching in meager caves or huts alongside wild beasts, accustomed to the speeches of angels, they were shining in great wonders. To the blind they gave sight, to the lame motion, 7

færeld, deafum hlyst, dumbum spræce. Deoflu hi ofer-
swyðdon and afligdon, and ða deadan þurh Godes mihte
arærdon. Seo boc þe is gehaten *Vitae patrum* sprecð menigfealdlice embe þyssera ancersetlena, and eac gemænelicra
muneca drohtnunge, and cwyð þæt heora wæs fela ðusenda
gehwær on westenum and on mynstrum wundorlice drohtnigende, ac swaþeah swyðost on Egypta lande. Sume hi
leofodon be ofete and wyrtum, sume be agenum geswince,
sumum ðenodon englas, sumum fugelas, oðþæt englas eft on
eaðelicum forðsiðe hi to Gode feredon.

8   Eala ðu eadige Godes cennestre, symle mæden Maria,
tempel ðæs Halgan Gastes, mæden ær geeacnunge, mæden
on geeacnunge, mæden æfter geeacnunge, micel is ðin mærð
on ðisum freolsdæge betwux þam foresædum halgum,
forðan ðe ðurh þine clænan cenninge him eallum becom
halignyss and ða heofonlican geðincðu. We sprecað be
ðære heofonlican cwene endebyrdlice æfter wifhade, þeahhwæðere eal seo geleaffulle gelaðung getreowfullice be hire
singð þæt heo is geuferod and ahafen ofer engla werod to
þam wuldorfullan heahsetle. Nis be nanum oðrum halgan
gecweden þæt heora ænig ofer engla werod ahafen sy, buton
be Marian anre. Heo æteowde mid hire gebysnungum þæt
heofonlice lif on eorðan, forðan þe mægðhad is ealra mægna
cwen and gefera heofonlicra engla. Ðyses mædenes gebysnungum and fotswaðum fyligde ungerim heap mægðhades
manna—on clænnysse þurhwunigende, forlætenum giftum,
to ðam heofonlicum brydguman Criste geþeodende mid anrædum mode and haligre drohtnunge and sidefullum gyrlan,
to þan swiðe þæt heora forwel menige for mæigðhade martyrdom geðrowodon, and swa mid twyfealdum sige to heofonlicum eardungstowum wuldorfulle becomon.

to the deaf hearing, to the mute speech. They overcame devils and put them to flight, and through God's might they raised the dead. The book called *Vitae patrum* tells many things about the lives of these anchorites, and also of communal monks, saying that there were many thousands of them living wonderfully everywhere in the wilderness and in monasteries, but most especially in the land of Egypt. Some of them lived on fruit and herbs, some by their own labor, some were served by angels, some by birds, until angels afterward bore them by an easy death to God.

O blessed mother of God, ever-virgin Mary, temple of the Holy Spirit, virgin before conception, virgin in conception, virgin after conception, great is your glory on this feast day among the saints mentioned above, because through your pure childbirth holiness and heavenly honors came to them all. We speak of the heavenly queen in due order according to her womanhood, yet all the faithful Church confidently sings of her that she is exalted and raised above the hosts of angels to the glorious throne. It is not said of any of the other saints that any of them is raised above the hosts of angels, but of Mary alone. By her example she showed the heavenly life on earth, for virginity is queen of all virtues and the companion of the heavenly angels. A countless troop of persons in virginity followed the example and footsteps of this virgin—living in chastity, renouncing marriage, joining themselves to the heavenly bridegroom Christ with steadfast mind and holy life and modest dress, so much so that very many of them suffered martyrdom for virginity, and so with twofold victory gloriously came to the heavenly dwelling places.

8

9   Eallum ðisum foresædum halgum, þæt is, englum and
Godes gecorenum mannum, is þyses dæges wurðmynt
gemærsod on geleaffulre gelaðunge him to wurðmynte and
us to fultume, þæt we ðurh heora þingrædene him geferlæhte beon moton. Þæs us getiðige se mildheorta Drihten,
þe hi ealle and us mid his deorwurðan blode fram deofles
hæftnedum alysde. We sceolon on ðyssere mærlican freolstide mid halgum gebedum and lofsangum us geinnian swa
hwæt swa we on oðrum freolsdagum ealles geares ymbrynes,
þurh mennisce tyddernysse hwonlicor gefyldon, and carfullice hogian þæt we to ðære ecan freolstide becumon.

Evangelium

10   *Videns Iesus turbas ascendit in montem, et reliqua.*

11   Ðæt halige godspel þe nu lytle ær ætforan eow gerædd
wæs micclum geþwærlæcð þyssere freolstide, forðan þe hit
geendebyrt þa eahta eadignyssa ðe ða halgan to heofonlicum
geðincðum gebrohton.

12   Matheus awrat on þysum dægþerlican godspelle þæt se
hælend on sumere tide gesawe micele menigu him fyligende;
þa astah he upp on ane dune. Þa ða he gesæt, þa genealæhton his leorningcnihtas him to, and he undyde his muð and
hi lærde, þus cweðende, "Eadige beoð þa gastlican ðearfan,
forðan þe heora is heofonan rice. Eadige beoð þa liðan,
forðan þe he geagniað þæt land. Eadige beoð ða þe heofiað,
forðan ðe hi beoð gefrefrode. Eadige beoð þa ðe sind ofhingrode and ofþyrste æfter rihtwisnysse, forðan ðe hi beoð gefyllede. Eadige beoð þa mildheortan, forðam þe hi bigytað
mildheortnysse. Eadige beoð þa clænheortan, forðan ðe hi
geseoð God sylfne. Eadige beoð þa gesibsuman, forðan ðe hi

To all these saints mentioned before, that is, angels and 9
God's chosen ones, the honor of this day is celebrated in the
faithful Church for their honor and our aid, that through
their intercession we may be united with them. May the
merciful Lord grant us this, who with his precious blood redeemed them all and us from the captivity of the devil. On
this great festival we should complete with holy prayers and
hymns whatever we have, through human weakness, inade-
quately performed on other festivals during the course of
the whole year, and carefully consider how we may come to
the eternal festival.

Gospel

Jesus, seeing the crowd, went up to the mountain, etc. 10

The holy gospel that was read before you a little while 11
ago accords greatly with this feast day, for it sets forth in order the eight beatitudes which have brought the saints to
heavenly honors.

Matthew wrote in this day's gospel that the savior at a 12
certain time saw a great crowd following him; then he went
up on a mountain. When he sat, his disciples approached
him, and he opened his mouth and taught them, saying,
"Blessed are the poor in spirit, for theirs is the kingdom of
heaven. Blessed are the meek, for they will possess the land.
Blessed are those who mourn, for they will be comforted.
Blessed are those who hunger and thirst for righteousness,
for they will be filled. Blessed are the merciful, for they will
receive mercy. Blessed are the pure of heart, for they will see
God himself. Blessed are the peaceful, for they will be called

beoð Godes bearn gecigede. Eadige beoð þa ðe þoliað ehtnysse for rihtwisnysse, forðan ðe heora is heofonan rice. Ge
beoð eadige þonne eow man wyrigð and eower eht, and ælc
yfel ongean eow sprecð leogende for me; blissiað and fægniað, forðan þe eower med is menigfeald on heofonum."

13   Se wisa Augustinus trahtnode þis godspel, and sæde þæt
seo dun þe se hælend astah getacnað ða healican bebodu
soðre rihtwisnysse: þa læssan beboda wæron gesette ðam
Iudeiscan folce. An God þeahhwæðere gesette, þurh his
halgan witegan, þa læssan bebodu Iudeiscre ðeode, þe mid
ogan ða gyt gebunden wæs, and he gesette þurh his agenne
Sunu þa maran bebodu Cristenum folce, þa ðe he mid soðre
lufe to alysenne com. Sittende he tæhte; þæt belimpð to
wurðscipe lareowdomes. Him to genealæhton his discipuli,
þæt hi gehendran wæron lichamlice, þa ðe mid mode his bebodum genealæhton. Se hælend geopenode his muð: witodlice se geopenode his muð to þære godspellican lare, se ðe
on ðære ealdan æ gewunelice openode þæra witegena muð;
þeahhwæðere his muðes geopenung getacnað þa deoplican
spræce ðe he ða forð ateah. He cwæð, "Eadige beoð þa gastlican ðearfan, forðan þe heora is heofonan rice." Hwæt sind
ða gastlican ðearfan buton ða eadmodan, þe Godes ege habbað and nane toðundennysse nabbað? Godes ege is wisdomes angynn, and modignyss is ælcere synne anginn. Fela
sind ðearfan þurh hafenleaste and na on heora gaste, forðan
ðe hi gewilniað fela to hæbbenne. Sind eac oðre ðearfan, na
ðurh hafenleaste ac on gaste, forðan þe hi synd, æfter þæs
apostolican cwyde, "Swa swa naht hæbbende and ealle ðing
geagnigende." On þas wisan wæs Abraham ðearfa, and Iacob, and Dauid, se ðe, on his cynesetle ahafen, hine sylfne
geswutelode þearfan on gaste, þus cweðende, "Ic soðlice

children of God. Blessed are those who suffer persecution for righteousness, for theirs is the kingdom of heaven. Blessed are you when they curse you and persecute you and, lying, speak every evil against you because of me; rejoice and be glad, for your reward is abundant in heaven."

The wise Augustine expounded this gospel, and said that 13 the mountain which the savior ascended signifies the high commandments of true righteousness: the lesser commandments were appointed for the Jewish people. Yet one God, through his holy prophets, appointed the lesser commandments for the Jewish nation, which was still bound by fear, and through his own Son he established the greater commandments for Christian people, whom he came to redeem with true love. He taught sitting down; that befits the dignity of teaching. His disciples approached him, so they who approached his commandments with their minds might be nearer him physically. The savior opened his mouth: indeed, he who in the old law usually opened the mouths of the prophets opened his mouth to the gospel teaching; yet the opening of his mouth signifies the deep speech which he then drew forth. He said, "Blessed are the poor in spirit, for theirs is the kingdom of heaven." Who are the poor in spirit but the humble, who have fear of God and have no arrogance? Fear of God is the beginning of wisdom, and pride is the beginning of every sin. Many are poor through indigence and not in their spirit, because they desire to have much. There are also other poor, not through indigence but in spirit, because they are, according to the apostolic saying, "As if having nothing and possessing all things." In this way Abraham was poor, and Jacob, and David, who showed himself poor in spirit while raised on his throne, saying, "I truly

eom wædla and þearfa." Þa modigan rican ne beoð þearfan
ne þurh hafenleaste ne on gaste, forðan ðe hi synd gewelgode mid æhtum and toðundenne on mode. Þurh hafenleaste and on gaste synd þearfan ða fullfremedan munecas
þe for Gode ealle ðing forlætað to ðan swiðe þæt hi nellað
habban heora agenne lichaman on heora anwealde, ac lybbað be heora gastlican lareowas wissunge; and forði swa
micclum swa hi her for Gode on hafenleaste wuniað, swa
micclum hi beoð eft on ðam toweardan wuldre gewelgode.

14 "Eadige beoð þa liðan, forðan þe hi þæt land geagniað."
Þa synd liðe and gedefe þa ðe ne wiðstandað yfelum, ac ofer-
swyðað mid heora goodnysse þone yfelan. Hi habbað þæt
land þe se sealmsceop embe spræc: "Drihten, þu eart min
hiht; beo min dæl on þæra lybbendra eorðan." Þæra lybbendra eorðe is seo staðelfæstnyss þæs ecan eardes, on ðam gerest seo sawul swa swa se lichama on eorðan. Se eard is rest
and lif gecorenra halgena.

15 "Eadige beoð ða þe heofiað, forðan ðe hi beoð gefrefrode." Ne beoð þa eadige þe for hynðum oððe lirum hwil-
wendlicra hynða heofiað; ac ða beoð eadige ðe heora synna
bewepað, forðan þe se Halga Gast hi gefrefrað, se ðe deð
forgyfenysse ealra synna, se is gehaten *Paraclitus,* þæt is, "frefrigend," forðan ðe he frefrað þæra behreowsigendra heortan þurh his gife.

16 "Eadige beoð þa þe sind ofhingrode and ofþyrste æfter
rihtwisnysse, forðan ðe hi beoð gefyllede." Se bið ofhingrod
and ofðyrst æfter rihtwisnysse se ðe Godes beboda lustlice
gehyrð, and lustlicor mid weorcum gefylð; se bið þonne mid
þam mete gefylled ðe Drihten embe spræc, "Min mete is
þæt ic wyrce mines Fæder willan, þæt is, rihtwisnys." Þonne
mæg he cweðan mid þam sealmsceope, "Drihten, ic beo

am poor and needy." The proud rich are needy neither through poverty nor in spirit, for they are enriched with possessions and arrogant in mind. Poor through poverty and in spirit are those perfect monks who so completely forsake all things for God that they will not have their own bodies under their control, but live by direction of their spiritual teacher; and therefore, as greatly as they dwell here in poverty for God, so greatly will they be later enriched in the glory to come.

"Blessed are the meek, for they will possess the land." They are meek and gentle who do not withstand evil, but overcome the evil with their goodness. They will have the land of which the psalmist spoke: "Lord, you are my hope; be my portion in the country of the living." The country of the living is the stability of the eternal land, in which the soul rests as the body does on earth. That land is the rest and life of the chosen saints. 14

"Blessed are those who mourn, for they shall be comforted." They are not blessed who mourn for injuries or losses of transitory comforts; but they are blessed who weep for their sins, for the Holy Spirit will comfort them, who grants forgiveness of all sins, who is called *Paraclete,* that is, "comforter," because he comforts the hearts of the penitent by his grace. 15

"Blessed are those who hunger and thirst after righteousness, for they will be filled." He is hungry and thirsty after righteousness who joyfully hears God's commandments, and more joyfully fulfills them by works; he will then be filled with the food of which the Lord said, "My food is that I work my Father's will, that is, righteousness." Then he can say with the psalmist, "Lord, I will appear with righteous- 16

æteowed mid rihtwisnysse on ðinre gesihðe, and ic beo gefylled þonne ðin wuldor geswutelod bið."

17 "Eadige beoð þa mildheortan, forðan þe hi begytað
mildheortnysse." Eadige beoð þa ðe earmra manna þurh
mildheortnysse gehelpað, forðan ðe him bið swa geleanod
þæt hi sylfe beoð fram yrmðe alysede.

18 "Eadige beoð þa clænheortan, forðan ðe hi geseoð God
sylfne." Stunte synd þa ðe gewilniað God to geseonne mid
flæsclicum eagum, þonne he bið mid þære heortan gesewen;
ac heo is to clænsigenne fram leahtrum þæt heo God geseon
mage. Swa swa eorðlic leoht ne mæg beon gesewen buton
mid clænum eagum, swa eac ne bið God gesewen buton mid
clænre heortan.

19 "Eadige beoð þa gesibsuman, forðan ðe hi beoð Godes
bearn gecigede." On sibbe is fulfremednyss þær ðær nan
ðing ne þwyrað; forði synd þa gesibsuman Godes bearn,
forðan ðe nan ðing on him ne wiðerað ongean God. Gesib-
sume sind þa on him sylfum ðe ealle heora modes styrunga
mid gesceade gelogiað, and heora flæsclican gewilnunga
gewyldað swa þæt hi sylfe beoð Godes rice. Ðeos is seo sib
ðe is forgyfen on eorðan þam mannum þe beoð godes willan.
God ure Fæder is gesibsum; witodlice forði gedafenað þam
bearnum þæt hi heora Fæder geefenlæcon.

20 "Eadige beoð ða ðe þoliað ehtnysse for rihtwisnysse,
forðan ðe heora is heofonan rice." Fela sind ða ðe ehtnysse
ðoliað for mislicum intingum, swa swa doð mannslagan, and
sceaðan, and gehwilce fyrnfulle; ac seo ehtnys him ne becymð to nanre eadignysse. Ac seo ehtnys ana þe bið for
rihtwisnysse geðolod becymð to ecere eadignysse. Nis to
ondrædenne ðwyrra manna ehtnys, ac ma to forðyldigenne,
swa swa Drihten to his leorningcnihtum cwæð, "Ne

ness in your sight, and I will be filled when your glory is revealed."

"Blessed are the merciful, for they will receive mercy." 17
Blessed are those who help wretched people through mercy, for they shall be so rewarded that they themselves will be redeemed from misery.

"Blessed are the pure of heart, for they will see God himself." Those who desire to see God with fleshly eyes are foolish, because he is seen with the heart; but it must be cleansed from sins so that it may see God. Just as earthly light cannot be seen except with pure eyes, so also God cannot be seen except with a pure heart.

"Blessed are the peaceful, for they will be called children 19
of God." In peace there is perfection where nothing is in conflict; therefore the peaceful are children of God, because nothing in them is in opposition to God. They are peaceful in themselves who order all the disturbances of their mind with reason, and govern their fleshly desires so that they themselves are God's kingdom. This is the peace which is given on earth to those who are of good will. God our Father is peaceful; therefore it is fitting that the children imitate their Father.

"Blessed are those who suffer persecution for righteous- 20
ness, for theirs is the kingdom of heaven." There are many who suffer persecution for various causes, as murderers do, and thieves, and all criminals; but persecution does not lead them to any blessedness. Only the persecution which is suffered for righteousness leads to everlasting blessedness. The persecution from perverse men is not to be feared, but rather to be patiently endured, as the Lord said to his

ondræde ge eow ða ðe eowerne lichaman ofsleað, forðan ðe
hi ne magon eowre sawle ofslean; ac ondrædað God, ðe mæg
ægðer ge sawle ge lichaman on helle susle fordon." Ne sceole
we ðeah þa ðwyran to ure ehtnysse gremian, ac swiðor, gif hi
astyrede beoð, mid rihtwisnysse gestillan. Gif hi ðonne þære
ehtnysse geswycan nellað, selre us bið þæt we ehtnysse
ðolion þonne we riht forlæton.

21 Eahta eadignyssa synd on þisum godspelle geendebyrde;
is ðeah gyt an cwyde bæftan, ðe is geðuht swilce he sy se
nygoða stæpe, ac he soðlice belimpð to ðære eahteoðan
eadignysse, forðan ðe hi butu sprecað be ehtnysse for rihtwisnysse and for Criste. Þa eahta eadignyssa belimpað to
eallum geleaffullum mannum, and se æftemysta cwyde, þeah
ðe he synderlice to þam apostolum gecweden wære, belimpð
eac to eallum Cristes limum, forðan ðe he nis nygoða, ac
fyligð þære eahteoðan eadignysse, swa swa we ær sædon. Se
hælend cwæð, "Eadige ge beoð þonne man eow wyrigð and
eower eht, and ælc yfel ongean eow sprecð leogende for me."
Se bið eadig and gesælig þe for Criste ðolað wyriunge and
hospas fram leasum licceterum, forðan ðe seo lease wyriung
becymð þam rihtwisum to eadigre bletsunge.

22 "Blissiað and fægniað, forðan ðe eower med is menigfeald
on heofonum." Geleaffullum gedafenað þæt hi wuldrion on
gedrefednyssum, forðan ðe seo gedrefednys wyrcð geðyld,
and þæt geðyld afandunge, and seo afandung hiht. Se hiht
soðlice ne bið næfre gescynd, forðan þe Godes lufu is agoten
on urum heortum þurh ðone Halgan Gast se ðe us is forgifen. Be þisum cwæð se apostol Iacobus, "Eala ge mine gebroðra, wenað eow ælcere blisse þonne ge beoð on mislicum
costnungum, forðan þe seo afandung eowres geleafan is
miccle deorwurðre þonne gold þe bið ðurh fyr afandod." Eft

disciples, "Do not fear those who slay your body, for they cannot slay your soul; but fear God, who can destroy both soul and body in the torment of hell." Yet we should not provoke the perverse to persecute us, but rather, if they are provoked, quiet them with righteousness. If they will not then cease from persecution, it will be better for us to suffer persecution than to forsake the right.

Eight beatitudes are set forth in this gospel; there is yet 21 one sentence remaining, which seems as though it were the ninth step, but it truly belongs to the eighth beatitude, for they both speak of persecution for righteousness and for Christ. The eight beatitudes belong to all believers, and the last sentence, though it was said specifically to the apostles, belongs also to all members of Christ, for it is not the ninth, but follows the eighth beatitude, as we have said. The savior said, "Blessed are you when they curse you and persecute you and, lying, speak every evil against you because of me." He will be blessed and happy who suffers cursing and insults for Christ from false hypocrites, because false curses become a blessed benediction to the righteous.

"Rejoice and be glad, for your reward is abundant in 22 heaven." It is fitting for the faithful to glory in tribulations, for tribulation produces patience, and patience trial, and trial hope. This hope is never put to shame, because God's love is poured into our hearts by the Holy Spirit, who is given to us. Of this the apostle James said, "O my brothers, expect every joy for yourselves when you are in various temptations, for the trial of your faith is much more precious than gold which has been tried by fire." Again, the

cwyð þæt halige gewrit, "Læmene fatu beoð on ofne afandode, and rihtwise menn on gedrefednysse heora costnunge." Be þisum cwæð eac se hælend on oðre stowe to
his leorningcnihtum, "Gif ðes middangeard eow hatað, wite
ge þæt he me hatode ær eow; and gif hi min ehton, þonne
ehtað hi eac eower." Crist sylf wæs fram arleasum mannum
acweald, and swa eac his leorningcnihtas and martyras; and
ealle ða ðe gewilniað arfæstlice to drohtnigenne on geleaffulre gelaðunge hi sceolon ehtnysse ðolian, oððe fram ungesewenlicum deofle oððe fram gesewenlicum arleasum
deofles limum. Ac þas hwilwendlican ehtnyssa oþþe gedre-
fednyssa we sceolon mid gefean for Cristes naman geðafian,
forðan ðe he þus behet eallum geðyldigum, "Blissiað and
fægniað, efne eower med is menigfeald on heofonum."

23   We mihton ðas halgan rædinge menigfealdlicor trahtnian
æfter Augustines smeagunge, ac us twynað hwæðer ge magon maran deopnysse ðæron þearflice tocnawan; ac uton
biddan mid inweardre heortan þone ælmihtigan wealdend,
se ðe us mid menigfealdre mærsunge ealra his halgena nu
todæg geblissode, þæt he us getiðige genihtsumnysse his
miltsunge þurh heora menigfealdan þingrædena, þæt we on
ecere gesihðe mid him blission, swa swa we nu mid hwil-
wendlicere þenunge hi wurðiað. Sy wuldor and lof hælendum Criste, se ðe is anginn and ende, scyppend and alysend
ealra halgena, mid Fæder and mid Halgum Gaste, a on
ecnysse. Amen.

holy scripture says, "Vessels of clay are tried in a furnace, and the righteous in the affliction of their temptation." Of this the savior also said in another place to his disciples, "If this world hates you, know that it hated me before you; and if they persecuted me, then they will also persecute you." Christ himself was slain by impious persons, and likewise his disciples and martyrs; and all those who desire to live piously in the faithful Church will suffer persecution, either from the invisible devil or from visible impious members of the devil. But we should endure these transitory persecutions or tribulations with joy for Christ's name, because he has promised to all the patient, "Rejoice and be glad, for your reward is abundant in heaven."

We might more abundantly expound this holy text according to the interpretation of Augustine, but we doubt whether you can usefully understand the greater deepness of it; but let us pray with inward heart to the almighty ruler, who has gladdened us today with the abundant celebration of all his saints, that he may grant us abundance of his mercy through their manifold intercessions, so that in their eternal presence we may rejoice with them, as we now with transitory service honor them. Glory and praise be to the savior Christ, who is the beginning and end, creator and redeemer of all saints, with the Father and the Holy Spirit, forever in eternity. Amen.

37

IX KALENDAS DECEMBRIS

Natale sancti Clementis martyris

Menn ða leofostan, eower geleafa bið þe trumra gif ge gehyrað be Godes halgum, hu hi þæt heofonlice rice geearnodon; and ge magon ðe cuðlicor to him clypian gif heora lifes drohtnunga eow þurh lareowa bodunge cuðe beoð.

2 Þes halga wer Clemens, þe we on ðisum andweardan freolsdæge wurðiað, wæs þæs eadigan Petres apostoles leorningcniht. Þa wæs he ðeonde on gastlicere lare and gecneordnysse to ðan swiðe þæt se apostol Petrus hine geceas to papan Romaniscre ðeode æfter his dæge, and ær his ðrowunge hine to papan gehadode and on his biscopsetle gesette, to ði þæt he ðæra Cristenra manna gymene hæfde. He gehadode twegen biscopas ær ðan, Linum et Cletum, ac he ne sette na hi on his setle, swa swa he dyde þisne halgan wer þe we todæg wurðiað. Hwæt ða, Clemens æfter Petres ðrowunge geðeah on fægernysse goddra ðeawa, swa þæt he gecweme wæs Iudeiscum, and hæðenum, and Cristenum samod. Þam hæðenum leodum he gelicode forðan ðe he mid hospe heora godas ne gebysmrode, ac mid boclicum gesceade him geswutelode hwæt hi wæron, and hwær acennede þa ðe hi him to godum wurðodon, and heora drohtnunge and geendunge mid swutelum seðungum gewissode; and cwæð þæt hi sylfe eaðelice mihton to Godes miltsunge

37

Saint Clement

NOVEMBER 23

Feast of Saint Clement, Martyr

Most beloved people, your faith will be firmer if you hear how God's saints merited the heavenly kingdom; and you may call to them more certainly if the course of their lives is known to you through the preaching of teachers.

This holy man Clement, whom we honor on this present 2 feast day, was a disciple of the blessed apostle Peter. Then he was thriving so greatly in spiritual learning and devotion that the apostle Peter chose him for pope of the Roman people after his day, and before his passion ordained him pope and placed him in his episcopal seat, so that he might take care of the Christians. He had ordained two bishops before this, Linus and Cletus, but he did not place them in his seat, as he did this holy man whom we honor today. After Peter's passion, Clement flourished in the beauty of good customs, so that he was acceptable to Jews, and heathens, and Christians alike. He pleased the heathen people because he did not contemptuously insult their gods, but used scholarly reasoning to reveal to them what they were, and where those whom they honored as their gods were born, and showed their lives and ends to them with clear proofs; and said that they themselves might easily attain to God's

becuman gif hi fram heora dwollicum biggengum eallunga gecyrdon. Iudeiscre ðeode hylde he begeat forþan þe he soðlice geseðde þæt heora forðfæderas Godes frynd gecigede wæron, and him God halige æ sette to heora lifes rihtinge; and cwæð þæt hi fyrmeste on Godes gecorennysse wæron gif hi mid geleafan his bebodum gehyrsumodon. Fram Cristenum he wæs swiðost gelufod forðan ðe he gehwilce eardas namcuðlice on gemynde hæfde, and þa wanspedigan Cristenan þæra earda ne geðafode þæt hi openre wædlunge underðeodde wurdon, ac mid dæghwomlicere bodunge he gemanode þa rican and þa spedigan þæt hi ðæra Cristenra wædlunge mid heora spedum gefrefrodon, þe læs ðe hi ðurh hæðenra manna gifa besmitene wurdon.

3   And Dionisius, Godes cyðere, se ðe þurh Paules apostoles lare and tacna to Cristes geleafan mid haligre drohtnunge gecyrde, gewende on ðam timan fram Greclande to ðam halgan papan Clementem, Petres æftergencga, and he hine mid micclum wurðmynte underfeng, and for arwurðnysse his halgan lifes him cuðlice tolet, and mid lufe geheold. Eft æfter fyrste cwæð se eadiga Clemens to ðam halgan were Dionisium, "Si ðe forgyfen miht to gebindenne and to alysenne, swa swa me is; and þu far to ðæra Francena rice, and boda him godspel and heofonan rices wuldor." Dionisius þa wearð his hæsum gehyrsum, and mid geferum ferde to Franclande, Cristendom bodigende mid micclum wundrum to ðan swiðe þæt þa reðan hæðenan, swa hraðe swa hi hine gesawon, oððe hi feallende his fet gesohton, him and Gode gehyrsumigende, oððe gif heora hwylc ðwyrode, þonne wearð se mid swa micelre fyrhte fornumen þæt he ðærrihte his andweardnysse forfleah. Wearð ða gebiged eal Francena rice to Godes geleafan þurh bodunge and wundra þæs

mercy if they would completely turn away from their mistaken rituals. He won the favor of the Jewish people because he truly proved that their ancestors were called friends of God, and that God gave them a holy law to direct their lives; he said that they would have been foremost among God's chosen if they had obeyed his commandments with faith. By the Christians he was most beloved because he held the names of all countries in his memory, and did not allow the indigent Christians of those countries to be reduced to public begging, but by daily preaching he exhorted the rich and prosperous to alleviate the poverty of the Christians with their prosperity, lest they should be corrupted by the gifts of heathens.

And Dionysius, God's martyr, who had turned to faith in   3
Christ with a holy life through the teaching and miracles of Paul the apostle, returned at that time from Greece to the holy pope Clement, Peter's successor, who received him with great honor, and in veneration openly entrusted his holy life to him, and held him with love. Then after a time the blessed Clement said to the holy man Dionysius, "Let power be given to you to bind and to loose, as there is to me; go to the kingdom of the Franks, and preach to them the gospel and the glory of heaven's kingdom." Dionysius was obedient to his commands, and went with his companions to the land of the Franks, preaching Christianity with great miracles so effectively that the fierce heathens, as soon as they saw him, either falling down sought his feet, obeying him and God, or if any of them was hostile, he was seized with such great fear that he immediately fled from his presence. Then all the realm of the Franks was inclined to God's faith through the preaching and miracles of the blessed man

eadigan weres Dionisii; and he eac sume his geferan to Is-
panian gesende þæt hi ðan leodscipe lifes word gecyddon.

4   Hwæt ða, Clemens Romana papa wearð gewreht to ðam
casere Traianum for ðam micclan Cristendome þe he gehwær on his rice arærde. Þa sende se casere Traianus gewritu
ongean þæt se halga papa Clemens to hæðengylde gebugan
sceolde oððe hine mann asende ofer sæ on wræcsið to sumum westene, on þam þe Cristene menn for geleafan fordemde wræcsiðedon. Þæs caseres hæs wearð þa forðgencge,
and swa micele gife foresceawode se ælmihtiga God Clem-
ente þæt se hæðena dema his sið mid wope bemænde, þus
cweðende, "Se God þe ðu wurðast gefrefrige ðe and ful-
tumige on ðinum wræcsiðe." And het ða hine to scipe lædan,
and ealle his neoda foresceawian þe he to bigwiste habban
mihte. Wearð ða þæt scip gefylled mid Cristenum mannum
þe þone halgan papan forlætan noldon.

5   Þa ða he to ðam westene becom, þa gemette he ðær ma
þonne twa ðusend Cristenra manna þe mid langsumere
genyðerunge to marmstan gedelfe gesette wæron, þe his
tocymes micclum fægnodon, mid anre stemne cweðende,
"Efne her is ure hyrde; efne her is se frefrigend ures
geswinces and weorces." Þa ða he mid tihtendlicum wordum
heora gewæhtan mod getrymde and gefrefrode, ða geaxode
he þæt hi dæghwomlice ofer six mila him wæter on heora
exlum gefetton. Ða cwæð se eadiga biscop, "Uton biddan
mid fæstum geleafan Drihten hælend, þæt he us his andet-
terum ða æddran his wyllspringes gehendor geopenige, þæt
we on his weldædum blission." Þa ða ðis gebed gefylled wæs,
þa beheold se biscop on ælce healfe, and geseah ða on þa
swiðran healfe an hwit lamb standan, þe bicnode mid his
swyðran fet swilce hit þa wæteræddran geswutelian wolde.

Dionysius; he also sent some of his companions to Spain to proclaim the word of life to that nation.

After this, Clement, the Romans' pope, was denounced 4 to the emperor Trajan for the great Christianity which he had raised up everywhere in his kingdom. The emperor Trajan sent letters back saying that the holy pope Clement should bow to heathenism or he would be sent over the sea in exile to a wilderness where Christians who were condemned for their belief were exiled. The emperor's command was carried out, and almighty God provided so much grace to Clement that the heathen judge bewailed his journey with weeping, saying, "May the God whom you worship comfort and support you in your exile." He then ordered him to be led to a ship, and all his needs to be provided for so that he might have sustenance. The ship was filled with Christians who would not abandon the holy pope.

When he came to the wilderness, he found there more 5 than two thousand Christians who by a lengthy sentence were set to quarrying marble, and who greatly rejoiced at his coming, saying with one voice, "Behold here is our shepherd; behold here is the comforter of our tribulation and toil." When he had confirmed and comforted their afflicted minds with persuasive words, he learned that every day they fetched water for themselves on their shoulders more than six miles. Then the blessed bishop said, "Let us pray to the Lord savior with firm faith, that he might open the streams of his wellsprings nearer at hand for us his confessors, that we may rejoice in his benefits." When this prayer was ended, the bishop looked on both sides, and saw a white lamb standing on the right side, which beckoned with his right foot as if it wanted to reveal the spring. Clement understood

Ða undergeat Clemens þæs lambes gebicnunge and cwæð, "Geopeniað þas eorðan on þyssere stowe þær ðær þæt lamb togebicnode." His geferan ða his hæse gefyldon, and þærrihte æt ðam forman gedelfe swegde ut ormæte wyllspring and mid micclum streame forðyrnende wæs. Hwæt hi ealle ða micclum blissodon, and Gode ðancodon heora geswinces lisse. Þa wæs se cwyde gefylled, þe hi on ðæs biscopes tocyme gecwædon: "Efne her is ure hyrde; efne her is se frefrigend ures geswinces."

6 Ðis wundor ða asprang geond þa gehendan scira, and hi ealle þone halgan biscop mid arwurðnysse geneosodon, biddende þæt he hi mid his lare getrymde. He ða hi ealle to Godes geleafan gebigde, and binnan feawum dagum þær fif hund manna gefullode; and wurdon ða fela cyrcan gehwær aærede and deofolgild toworpene, swa þæt binnan anes geares fyrste næs gemet hæðengild geond hundteontig mila neawiste.

7 Þa gelamp hit þæt sume ða hæðenan wurdon mid andan getyrigde, and heora ærende to ðam casere asendon and him cyddon þæt his folc eall endemes astyred wære and eallunga fram his biggencgum gecyrred þurh Clementem, ðæra Cristenra biscop. Þa wearð se hæþena casere Traianus mycclum astyred, and asende ænne wælhreowne heretogan his nama wæs Aufidianus, se mid mislicum witum fela Cristenra manna acwealde, þæt he ðone halgan biscop mid þam geleaffullan folce adylegian sceolde. Se arleasa cwellere ða Aufidianus, ða ða he ne mihte mid nanum þeowracan ða Cristenan geegsian—forðan ðe hi ealle samod blissigende to martyrdome onetton—þa forlet he þæt folc and ðone biscop ænne to þam hæðengylde genydde; ac ða ða he geseah þæt he nateshwon hine gebigan ne mihte, þa cwæð he to his

the lamb's beckoning and said, "Open the earth in this place where the lamb beckoned." His companions carried out his command, and at the very first digging an immense spring roared out and began running forth in a great stream. They all greatly rejoiced at this, and thanked God for relief from their tribulation. Then the saying which they said at the bishop's coming was fulfilled: "Behold, here is our shepherd; behold, here is the comforter of our tribulation."

This miracle then became known through the neighboring provinces, and they all approached the holy bishop with reverence, praying that he would confirm them with his teaching. He converted them all to God's faith, and within a few days baptized five hundred people there; many churches were raised everywhere and idols overthrown, so that within the space of one year idolatry was not found throughout a neighborhood of a hundred miles. 6

It happened then that some of the heathens were provoked by envy, and sent their message to the emperor to let him know that his people were all completely stirred up and wholly turned from his worship through Clement, the Christians' bishop. The heathen emperor Trajan was greatly upset, and sent a cruel commander named Aufidianus, who had killed many Christians with various torments, to destroy the holy bishop along with the faithful people. Then the impious murderer Aufidianus, when he could not terrify the Christians by any threats—for they all hastened together to martyrdom rejoicing—left the people alone and tried to force only the bishop to idolatry; but when he saw that he could not convert him by any means, he said to his 7

underðeoddum, "Lædað hine to middere sæ, and getigað
ænne ancran to his swuran, and ascufað hine ut on middan
þære dypan." Hit wearð þa gedon be hæse þæs wælhreowan
cwelleres, and micel menigu þæra Cristenra stod on þære sæ
strande, wepende and biddende þone Ælmihtigan þe sæ and
eorðan gesceop, þæt hi moston his halige lic mid heora
ðenungum behwurfan.

8   Þa cwædon his twegen leorningcnihtas, Febus and Cornelius, "Eala ge gebroðra, uton anmodlice biddan urne
Drihten þæt he us geswutelige ða arwurðfullan andweardnysse his halgan cyðeres." Hwæt ða seo sæ, ðurh Godes hæse
utflowende, him gerymde þreora mila dries færeldes, swa
þæt þa Cristenan bealdlice inn eodon, and gemetton niwe
ðruh of marmanstane on cyrcan wison gesceapene, and þæs
halgan cyðeres lic ðærbinnan ðurh engla ðenunge gelogod,
and þone ancran wið his sidan licgende. Þa wearð him
geswutelod þæt he æt Gode abæde þæt on ælces geares
ymbryne, ymbe his ðrowungtide, seo sæ seofan dagas drigne
grund þam folce gegearcige, þæt hi binnan ðam fyrste his
halgan lichaman gesecan magon. Þæt belimpð to lofe and
herunge ures hælendes, se ðe his halgan cyðere ða arwurðan
byrgene gegearcode. Þa ðurh ðis tacn wurdon ealle þa ungeleaffullan Cristene, swa þæt nateshwon næs gemet on ðam
earde naðor ne hæðen ne Iudeisc ðe nære gebiged to Cristenum geleafan. Soðlice æt þære halgan þryh sind getiðode
heofonlice lacnunga adlium lichaman, þurh ðingunge ðæs
halgan cyðeres. Swa hwa swa on his freolstide untrum his
byrgene gesehð, he gewent blissigende and gesundful ongean. Þær beoð blinde onlihte, and deofolseoce gewittige,
and gehwilce gedrehte þær beoð geblissode; and ealle geleaffulle his weldæda brucað, and mid wurþmynte Godes gerynu
ðær beoð gefyllede.

subordinates, "Lead him to the middle of the sea, and tie an anchor to his neck, and push him overboard into the middle of the deep." It was then done by the command of the cruel murderer, and a great multitude of Christians stood on the seashore, weeping and praying to the Almighty who made sea and earth, that they might tend his holy body with their services.

Then his two disciples, Phoebus and Cornelius, said, "O you brothers, let us resolutely pray to our Lord that he may show us the venerable presence of his holy martyr." At this the sea, flowing out at God's command, cleared three miles of dry passage for them, so that the Christians boldly went in, and found a new coffin of marble made in the shape of a church, with the holy martyr's body placed inside through the ministry of angels, and the anchor lying by his side. Then it was revealed to them that they should ask God that, in the course of every year, at the time of his passion, the sea should provide dry ground for the people for seven days, so that during that time they might seek out his holy body. This happens to the praise and honor of our savior, who provided that honorable burial place for his holy martyr. Through this sign all the unbelievers became Christians, so that there was not found either heathen or Jew in that country who was not converted to the Christian faith. Truly, at the holy coffin heavenly cures are permitted for diseased bodies, through the intercession of the holy martyr. Whatever sick person seeks his burial place on his feast day returns rejoicing and healthy. There the blind are given light, and those possessed with devils restored to reason, and all afflicted are made joyful there; and all the faithful enjoy his benefits, and God's mysteries are fulfilled there with reverence.

9   Hit gelamp ða on sumum geare on his freolstide þæt sum wif mid hire nywerenan cylde betwux oðrum mannum þone halgan wer geneosode. Þa geendodum dagum þære freolstide, com seo sæ færlice swegende and þæt folc swiðlice aweg efste, and þæt wif ðurh ða færlican styrunge ne gymde hire cildes ærðan þe heo to lande becom. Heo ða sarig þa twelf monað adreah, and eft embe ðæs geares ymbryne, on þære ylcan freolstide, forarn ðam folce and genealæhte to þære byrgene mid wope, þus biddende, "Þu Drihten hælend, þe ðære wydewan ancennedan sunu to life arærdest, beseoh me to miltse, þæt ic, ðurh ðingunge þines halgan þe her gerest, beo ðæs tiðe þe ic geornlice bidde." Þa mid þyssere bene beseah heo to ðære stowe ðær heo þæt cild ær forlet, and gemette hit swa slapende swa heo hit ær gelede. Heo ða mid micelre blisse hit awehte, and wepende cossode. Þa befran heo þæt cild, betwux ðam cossum, hu hit macode on eallum ðam fyrste þæs geares ymbrynes. Þæt cild þære meder geandwyrde, "Modor min, nyste ic hu ðyses geares ymryne geendode, forðan ðe ic softum slæpe me gereste, swa swa ðu me forlete, oð þæt þu eft me nu awrehtest." Þæt geleaffulle folc ða micclum blissigende herode and bletsode þone ælmihtigan hælend, se ðe his halgan mid tacnum and wundrum gewurðað, and swa heora geearnunga geswutelað.

10   Oft hwonlice gelyfede menn smeagað, mid heora stuntan gesceade, hwi se ælmihtiga God æfre geðafian wolde þæt þa hæðenan his halgan mid gehwilcum tintregum acwellan moston; ac we wyllað nu eow gereccan sume geswutelunge of ðære ealdan æ and eac of ðære niwan, hu mihtiglice se wealdenda Drihten his halgan wið hæðenne here oþþe wælhreowe ehteras gelome ahredde, and heora wiðerwinnan bysmorlice gescynde.

It happened in a certain year on his feast day that a 9
woman with her young child visited the holy man, along
with other people. When the days of the feast were ended,
the sea came suddenly roaring back and the people hurried
away, and because of the sudden commotion the woman did
not take notice of her child before she came to land. She
then passed the twelve months in sorrow, and again after the
course of the year, on the same feast day, ran before the people and approached the tomb with weeping, praying, "You
Lord savior, who raised the widow's only son to life, look on
me with mercy, so that through the intercession of your holy
one who rests here, I may obtain what I fervently pray for."
Then, with this prayer she looked to the place where she
had left the child, and found it sleeping just as she had laid it
before. She awakened it with great joy and, weeping, kissed
it. In between her kisses she asked the child how it had fared
in all that time for a whole year. The child answered the
mother, "My mother, I do not know how this whole year has
passed, for I was resting in soft sleep, just as you left me,
until you have now awakened me again." Then the believing
folk, greatly rejoicing, praised and blessed the almighty savior, who honors his saints with signs and wonders, and so
reveals their merits.

People of little faith, with their foolish understanding, 10
often wonder why the almighty God would ever allow the
heathen to kill his saints with all kinds of torments; but we
will now tell you some revelations from the old law and also
from the new, how mightily the ruling Lord has frequently
saved his holy ones from heathen armies or from cruel persecutors, and shamefully confounded their adversaries.

11   Hit gelamp on ðam feowerteoðan geare Ezechian cynedomes, Iudeisces cyninges, þæt Sennacherib, Syria cyning,
manega leoda mid micclum cræfte to his anwealde gebigde,
and swa wolde eac þone gelyfedan cyning Ezechiam, and
asende his heretogan Rapsacen to þære byrig Hierusalem
mid micclum ðrymme, and mid ærendgewritum þæs ælmihtigan Godes mihte gehyrwde, þus cweðende to ðam ymbset-
tan folce, "Ne bepæce Ezechias eow mid leasum hopan þæt
God eow wið me ahredde. Ic gewyllde and oferwann fela
ðeoda, and heora godas ne mihton hi gescyldan wið minne
ðrymm. Hwæt is se god þe mage ðas burh wið minne here
bewerian?" Hwæt ða se cyning Ezechias awearp his purpuran reaf, and dyde hæran to his lice, and bær ða gewritu
into Godes temple, and astrehtum limum hine gebæd, þus
cweðende, "Drihten weroda God, þu ðe gesitst ofer engla
ðrymm, þu eart ana God ealra ðeoda; þu geworhtest heofonas and eorðan and ealle gesceafta. Ahyld ðin eare and gehyr,
geopena ðine eagan and geseoh ðas word þe Sennacherib
asende to hospe and to tale ðe and þinum folce. Soðlice he
towende þa hæðenan godas and hi forbærnde, forðan ðe hi
næron godas, ac wæron manna handgeweorc treowene and
stænene, and he hi forði tobrytte. Alys us nu, Drihten, fram
his gebeote and mihte, þæt ealle ðeoda tocnawon þæt þu
ana eart ælmihtig God."

12   Ezechïas eac asende his witan mid hæran gescrydde to
ðam witegan Isaiam, þus cweðende, "Ahefe ðine gebedu for
Israhela ðeode, þæt se ælmihtiga God gehyre þa talu ðe
Syria cyning asende to hospe and to edwite his micclan mæ-
genðrymme." Þa andwyrde se witega Isaias þam bodum,
"Secgað eowrum hlaforde þæt he unforht sy. God ælmihtig

It happened in the fourteenth year of the reign of the 11
Jewish king Hezekiah that Sennacherib, king of Assyria, had
subdued many nations to his power with great skill, and he
wanted to do the same to the faithful king Hezekiah; Sennacherib sent his general Rabshakeh to the city of Jerusalem
with a great host, and scorned the power of the almighty
God with letters, saying to the beleaguered people, "Do not
let Hezekiah deceive you with the false hope that God will
save you from me. I have conquered and overcome many nations, and their gods could not shield them against my host.
Who is the god that can defend this city against my army?"
At this the king Hezekiah cast off his purple robe, put haircloth on his body, took the letters into God's temple, and
prayed with outstretched limbs, saying, "Lord God of hosts,
you who sit above the company of angels, you alone are God
of all nations; you made the heavens and earth and all creatures. Incline your ear and hear, open your eyes and see
these words which Sennacherib has sent in scorn and reproach to you and your people. Truly he overthrew the heathen gods and burned them, for they were not gods, but
were human handiwork of wood and of stone, and so he
smashed them to pieces. Rescue us now, Lord, from his
threats and his might, that all nations may know that you
alone are almighty God."

Hezekiah also sent his counselors clad in haircloth to the 12
prophet Isaiah, saying, "Raise your prayers for the people of
Israel, that the almighty God may hear the insults which the
king of Assyria has sent in scorn and reproach of his great
majesty." Then the prophet Isaiah answered the messengers,
"Say to your lord that he should be fearless. God almighty

cwyð: ne ascytt Sennacherib flan into ðære byrig Hierusalem, ne mid his scylde hi ne gewylt; ac ic geslea ænne wriðan
on his nosu and ænne bridel on his weleras, and ic hine
gelæde ongean to his leode, and ic do þæt he fylð under
swurdes ecge on his agenum eðele; and ic ða burh gescylde
for me and for minum ðeowan Dauid." Þa on ðære nihte
ferde Godes engel and ofsloh ðæs Syrian cyninges here an
hund þusend manna, and fif and hundeahtatig þusenda. Þæs
on merigen aras Sennacherib, and geseah ða deadan lic, and
gecyrde mid micelre sceame ongean to þære byrig Niniue.
Hit gelamp ða þæt he hine gebæd to his deofolgylde, and his
twegen suna hine mid swurde acwealdon, swa swa se witega
þurh Godes Gast gewitegode.

13   Eft siððan Nabochodonossor, se Chaldeisca cyning, het
gebindan handum and fotum þa ðry gelyfedan cnihtas, Annanias, Azarias, Missael, and into anum byrnendum ofne
awurpan, forþan ðe hi noldon hi gebiddan to his deofolgilde.
Ac se ælmihtiga God, þe hi anrædlice on belyfdon, asende
his engel into ðam ofne mid þam cnihtum, and he ða tosceoc
þone lig of ðam ofne swa þæt þæt fyr ne mihte him derigan,
ac sloh ut of ðam ofne nigan and feowertig fæþma and
forswælde þa cwelleras þe þæt fyr onældon. Þa sceawode se
cyning þæra ðreora cnihta feax and lichaman, þus cweðende,
"Sy gebletsod eower God, se ðe asende his engel, and swa
mihtelice his ðeowan of þam byrnendan ofne alysde."

14   Eac syððan, on Cyres dagum cyninges, wrehton ða Babi-
loniscan þone witegan Daniel forðan ðe he towearp heora
deofolgyld, and cwædon anmodlice to ðam foresædan cyninge Cyrum, "Betæc us Daniel, ðe urne god Bel towearp
and þone dracan acwealde þe we on belyfdon. Gif ðu hine
forstenst, we fordylegiað þe and ðinne hyred." Þa geseah se

says: Sennacherib will not shoot arrows into the city of Jerusalem, nor overpower it with his shield; but I will cast a hook into his nose and a bridle on his lips, and I will lead him back to his people, and I will make him fall under the sword's edge in his own country; and I will protect the city for myself and for my servant David." Then on that night God's angel went and slew a hundred eighty-five thousand people in the Assyrian king's army. In the morning Sennacherib arose, saw the dead bodies, and turned with great shame back to the city of Nineveh. It happened then that he was praying to his idol, and his two sons killed him with a sword, as the prophet had prophesied through the Spirit of God.

Later, Nebuchadnezzar, the Chaldean king, commanded 13 that the three faithful youths, Hananiah, Azariah, and Mishael, be bound hand and foot and cast into a burning oven, because they would not pray to his idol. But the almighty God, in whom they steadfastly believed, sent his angel into the oven with the youths, and he scattered the flame from the oven so the fire could not hurt them, but struck out of the oven forty-nine fathoms and burned up the executioners who had kindled the fire. Then the king beheld the hair and bodies of the three youths, saying, "Blessed be your God, who has sent his angel, and so mightily released his servants from the burning oven."

Afterward, in the days of King Cyrus, the Babylonians ac- 14 cused the prophet Daniel because he had cast down their idol, and said unanimously to the aforesaid King Cyrus, "Deliver Daniel to us, who has cast down our god Bel and slain the dragon which we believed in. If you protect him, we will destroy you and your household." The king saw that

cyning þæt hi anmode wæron, and neadunga þone witegan him to handum asceaf. Hi ða hine awurpon into anum seaðe on þam wæron seofan leon, þam mann sealde dæghwomlice twa hryðeru and twa scep, ac him wæs ða oftogen ælces fodan six dagas þæt hi ðone Godes mann abitan sceoldon.

15   On þære tide wæs sum oðer witega on Iudea lande his nama wæs Abacuc, se bær his ryfterum mete to æcere. Þa com him to Godes engel and cwæð, "Abacuc, bær ðone mete to Babilone, and syle Daniele, se ðe sitt on ðæra leona seaðe." Abacuc andwyrde þam engle, "La leof, ne geseah ic næfre ða burh, ne ic ðone seað nat." Þa se engel gelæhte hine be ðam fexe and hine bær to Babilone, and hine sette bufan ðam seaðe. Ða clypode se Abacuc, "Þu Godes ðeowa, Daniel, nim ðas lac ðe þe God sende." Daniel cwæð, "Min Drihten hælend, sy ðe lof and wurðmynt þæt þu me gemundest." And he ða ðære sande breac. Witodlice Godes engel þærrihte mid swyftum flihte gebrohte ðone discðen Abacuc þær he hine ær genam. Se cyning ða Cyrus on ðam seofoðan dæge eode dreorig to ðæra leona seaðe, and inn beseah, and efne ða Daniel sittende wæs gesundful on middan þam leonum. Þa clypode se cyning mid micelre stemne, "Mære is se God þe Daniel on belyfð." And he ða mid þam worde hine ateah of ðam scræfe, and het inn awurpan ða þe hine ær fordon woldon. Þæs cyninges hæs wearð hrædlice gefremmed, and þæs witegan ehteras wurdon asceofene betwux ða leon, and hi ðærrihte mid grædigum ceaflum hi ealle totæron. Þa cwæð se cyning, "Forhtion and ondrædon ealle eorðbuende Danieles God, forðan ðe he is alysend and hælend, wyrcende tacna and wundra on heofonan and on eorðan."

they were unanimous, and unwillingly delivered the prophet into their hands. They then cast him into a pit in which were seven lions, which were given two oxen and two sheep every day, but then all food had been withheld from them for six days so that they might devour the man of God.

At that time there was another prophet in the land of Ju- 15 dah whose name was Habakkuk, who bore food to the field for his reapers. Then the angel of God came to him and said, "Habakkuk, bear the food to Babylon, and give it to Daniel, who sits in the lions' pit." Habakkuk answered the angel, "Sir, I never saw the city, nor do I know the pit." Then the angel seized him by the hair and carried him to Babylon, and set him above the pit. Then Habakkuk cried, "You servant of God, Daniel, take this gift which God has sent you." Daniel said, "My Lord savior, praise and honor be to you because you have remembered me." And he ate of the dish. And God's angel at once, with swift flight, brought the dish bearer Habakkuk to the place from which he had taken him. Then the king Cyrus on the seventh day went, sad minded, to the lions' pit, and looked in, and behold, there was Daniel sitting unhurt in the midst of the lions. Then the king cried with a loud voice, "Great is the God in whom Daniel believes." With that word he pulled him from the pit, and ordered those who wanted to destroy him to be cast in. The king's command was quickly carried out, and the prophet's persecutors were thrown among the lions, and they immediately tore them all to pieces with greedy jaws. Then the king said, "Let all dwellers on earth fear and dread the God of Daniel, for he is the redeemer and savior, working signs and wonders in heaven and on earth."

16 On ðære Niwan Gecyðnysse, æfter Cristes ðrowunge and his æriste and upstige to heofonum, wurdon ða Iudeiscan mid andan afyllede ongean his apostolas, and gebrohton hi on cwearterne. On ðære ylcan nihte Godes engel undyde þa locu ðæs cwearternes and hi ut alædde, þus cweðende, "Gað to ðam temple, and bodiað þam folce lifes word." And hi swa dydon. Hwæt ða Iudeiscan þæs on merien ðeahtodon embe ðæra apostola forwyrd, and sendon to ðam cwearterne þæt hi man gefette. Þa cwelleras ða geopenodon þæt cweartern and nænne ne gemetton. Hi ða cyddon heora ealdrum, "Þæt cweartern we fundon fæste beclysed, and ða weardas wiðutan standende, ac we ne gemetton nænne wiðinnan."

17 Eft siððan Herodes, Iudea cyning, sette ðone apostol Petrum on cwearterne mid twam racenteagum gebundenne, and weardas wiðinnan and wiðutan gesette; ac on ðære nihte þe se arleasa cyning hine on merigen acwellan wolde, com Godes engel scinende of heofonum and gelædde hine ut ðurh ða isenan gatu, and stod eft on merigen þæt cweartern fæste belocen.

18 Domicianus, se hæðena casere, het awurpan þone godspellere Iohannem on weallendne ele, ac he, þurh Godes gescyldnysse, swa gesundfull ut eode swa he inn aworpen wæs. Þam ylcan Iohanne sealde sum hæðengylda attor drincan, ac he, æfter ðam drence, ansund and ungederod ðurhwunode.

19 Paulus se apostol awrat be him sylfum, and cwæð þæt he ænne dæg and ane niht on sægrunde adruge. Eft, æt sumum sæle hine gelæhte an næddre be ðam fingre, ac he ascoc hi into byrnendum fyre, and he ðæs ættres nan ðing ne gefredde.

20 Ne mæg nan eorðlic mann mid gewritum cyðan, ne mid

In the New Testament, after Christ's passion and resur- 16
rection and ascension into heaven, the Jews were filled with
anger toward his apostles, and put them in prison. On that
same night God's angel undid the locks of the prison and led
them out, saying, "Go to the temple, and preach the word of
life to the people." And they did so. Then in the morning
the Jews deliberated on the destruction of the apostles, and
sent to the prison to fetch them. The executioners opened
the prison and found no one. They announced to their elders, "We found the prison fast closed, and the guards standing outside, but we found no one within."

After that Herod, king of Judea, put the apostle Peter in 17
prison, bound with two chains, and set guards within and
without; but on the night before the morning when the impious king would kill him, God's angel came shining from
heaven and led him out through the iron gates, though in
the morning the prison again remained locked fast.

Domitian, the heathen emperor, commanded the Evan- 18
gelist John to be thrown into boiling oil, but through God's
protection he came out as unhurt as when he was cast in. An
idol worshipper gave the same John poison to drink, but after the drink he remained sound and uninjured.

Paul the apostle wrote about himself, saying that he 19
passed one day and one night at the bottom of the sea.
Again, at a certain time a serpent seized him by the finger,
but he shook it into the burning fire, and he felt nothing of
the poison.

No earthly person can make known by writings, nor 20

tungan gereccan, hu oft se ælmihtiga wealdend his gecorenan fram mislicum frecednyssum ahredde, to lofe and to
wurðmynte his mægenþrymnysse. Ac he geðafað forwel oft
þæt ða arleasan his halgan ðearle geswencað, hwilon mid he-
figtymre ehtnysse, hwilon mid slege, þæt seo reðe ehtnyss
becume ðam rihtwisan to ecere reste, and ðam cwellerum to
ecum wite. Se sealmscop cwæð, "Fela sind þæra rihtwisra gedreccednyssa, ac Drihten fram eallum ðysum hi alyst." On
twa wisan alyst God his gecorenan, openlice and digellice.
Openlice hi beoð alysede þonne hi on manna gesihðe beoð
ahredde, swa swa we nu eow rehton. Digellice hi beoð alysede þonne hi ðurh martyrdom becumað to heofonlicum
geðincðum. Gif hi for soðum geleafan oððe for rihtwisnysse
þrowiað, hi beoð þonne martyras. Gif hi ðonne unscyldige
gecwylmede beoð, heora unscæððignyss hi gelæt to Godes
halgena geferrædene; forðan þe unscæððignyss æfre orsorh
wunað. Gif hwa ðonne for synnum ehtnysse ðolað, and
hine sylfne oncnæwð, swa þæt he Godes mildheortnysse
inweardlice bidde, þonne forscyt þæt hwilwendlice wite ða
ecan geniðerunge. For mandædum wæron þa twegen
sceaðan gewitnode ðe mid Criste hangodon, ac heora oðer
mid micclum geleafan gebæd hine to Criste, þus cweðende,
"Drihten, geðenc min þonne ðu to þinum rice becymst."
Crist him andwyrde, "Soð ic þe secge, nu todæg þu byst mid
me on Neorxnawanges myrhðe." Unwilles we magon forleosan ða hwilwendlican god, ac we ne forleosað næfre unwilles
ða ecan god. Þeah se reða reafere us æt æhtum bereafige,
oððe feores benæme, he ne mæg us ætbredan urne geleafan
ne þæt ece lif, gif we us sylfe mid agenum willan ne forpærað.
Se soða Drihten us ahredde fram eallum frecednyssum, and
to ðam ecan life gelæde, se ðe leofað and rixað a butan ende.
Amen.

relate with tongue, how often the almighty ruler has saved his chosen ones from various perils, to the praise and honor of his majesty. But very often he allows the impious to afflict his saints severely, sometimes with painful persecution, sometimes with blows, so that fierce persecution might lead the righteous to eternal rest, and the murderers to eternal torment. The psalmist said, "Many are the tribulations of the righteous, but the Lord will release them from all these." God releases his chosen in two ways, openly and secretly. Openly they are released when they are saved in the sight of people, as we have now recounted to you. Secretly they are released when they achieve heavenly honors through martyrdom. If they suffer for true faith or for righteousness, they will be martyrs. If they are slain guiltless, their innocence will lead them to the fellowship of God's saints; for innocence ever remains secure. But if anyone suffers persecution for sins, and knows himself enough to pray inwardly for God's mercy, then the temporary punishment will prevent eternal damnation. The two thieves who were crucified with Christ were punished for crimes, but one of them prayed to Christ with great faith, saying, "Lord, think of me when you come to your kingdom." Christ answered him, "Truly I say to you, now today you will be with me in the joy of Paradise." We may lose transitory goods against our will, but we will never against our will lose the eternal good. Though a fierce robber might steal our property from us, or deprive us of life, he cannot take our faith from us or eternal life, if we do not destroy ourselves of our own will. May the true Lord save us from all dangers, and lead us to everlasting life, who lives and reigns forever without end. Amen.

38

I KALENDAS DECEMBRIS

Natale sancti Andreae apostoli

A mbulans Iesus iuxta mare Galilee, et reliqua.

2 "Crist on sumere tide ferde wið þære Galileiscan Sæ, and
geseah twegen gebroðra, Simonem, se wæs geciged Petrus,
and his broðor Andream, wurpende heora net on sæ; hi
wæron soðlice fisceras. Þa cwæð se hælend him to, 'Fyligað
me, and ic do þæt ge beoð manna fisceras.' Hi ðærrihte
forleton heora net and him fyligdon. Se hælend ða þanon
stæppende gemette oðre twegen gebroðra, Iacobum and
Iohannem, on scipe mid heora fæder Zebedeo, remigende
heora nett, and he hi to him clypode. Hi eac ðærrihte forleton heora fæder and net and Criste fyligdon."

3 Mine gebroðra, oft ge gehyrdon þæt seo sæ getacnað þas
andwerdan woruld, þe mid mislicum gelimpum ðære sæ
swangetunge geefenlæcð. Se hælend clypode his leorningcnihtas of ðære yðigendan sæ forðan ðe he hi ateah fram
woruldlicum stirungum to þære gastlican stilnysse, and to
heofonlicum drohtnungem.

4 Se hælend cwæð, "Cumað æfter me, and ic do þæt ge
beoð mann fisceras." Swa swa hi ær mid nette fixodon on
sælicum yðum, swa dyde Crist þæt hi siððan mid his heofonlican lare manna sawla gefixodon; forðan ðe hi ætbrudon folces menn fram flæsclicum lustum and fram woruldlicum

38

Saint Andrew

NOVEMBER 30

Feast of Saint Andrew the Apostle

Jesus was walking along the Sea of Galilee, etc.

"At a certain time Christ went along the Sea of Galilee, 2
and saw two brothers, Simon, who was called Peter, and his
brother Andrew, casting their nets into the sea; they were
fishermen. The savior said to them, 'Follow me, and I will
make you fishers of people.' At once they abandoned their
nets and followed him. The savior then proceeding on met
two other brothers, James and John, in a boat with their father Zebedee, arranging their nets, and he called them to
him. They also at once abandoned their father and their
nets and followed Christ."

My brothers, you have often heard that the sea signifies 3
this present world, which with its various accidents is like
the fluctuation of the sea. The savior called his disciples
from the wave-tossed sea because he drew them from
worldly disturbances to spiritual stillness, and to a heavenly
way of life.

The savior said, "Come after me, and I will make you fish- 4
ers of people." Just as they had once fished on the sea's waves
with a net, so Christ caused them afterward to fish for
human souls with his heavenly teaching; for they drew people away from fleshly pleasures and worldly errors to the

gedwyldum to staðolfæstnysse lybbendra eorðan, þæt is to
ðam ecan eðle be ðam cwæð se witega, þurh Godes Gast, "Ic
asende mine fisceras, and hi gefixiað hi; mine huntan, and hi
huntiað hi of ælcere dune and of ælcere hylle." Fisceras and
ungetogene menn geceas Drihten him to leorningcnihtum,
and hi swa geteah þæt heora lar oferstah ealne woruldwisdom, and hi mid heora bodunge caseras and cyningas to
soðum geleafan gebigdon. Gif se hælend gecure æt fruman
getinge lareowas, and woruldlice uðwitan and ðyllice to
bodigenne sende, þonne wære geðuht swilce se soða geleafa
ne asprunge ðurh Godes mihte, ac of woruldlicere getingnysse. He geceas fisceras ærðan ðe he cure caseras, forðan ðe
betere is þæt se casere, þonne he to Romebyrig becymð, þæt
he wurpe his cynehelm and gecneowige æt ðæs fisceres gemynde, þonne se fiscere cneowige æt þæs caseres gemynde.
Caseras he geceas, ac ðeah he geendebyrde þone unspedigan
fiscere ætforan ðam rican casere. Eft siððan he geceas ða
welegan; ac him wære geðuht swilce hi gecorene wæron for
heora æhtum gif he ær ne gecure þearfan. He geceas siððan
woruldlice uðwitan, ac hi modegodon gif he ær ne gecure þa
ungetogenan fisceras.

5   Smeagað nu hu Drihten mancynne ætbræd wuldor, þæt
he him wuldor forgeafe. He ætbræd us ure wuldor, þæt he us
his forgeafe. He ætbræd ure idele wuldor, þæt he us þæt ece
forgeafe. Ne scealt ðu on ðe silfum wuldrian, ac, swa swa se
apostol cwæð, "Se ðe wuldrige, wuldrige on Gode."

6   Petrus and Andreas, be Cristes hæse, ðærrihte forleton
heora net and him fyligdon. Ne gesawon hi ða gyt hine ænige

stability of the land of the living, that is, to the eternal country, of which the prophet, through God's Spirit, said, "I will send my fishermen, and they will fish for them; my hunters, and they will hunt them from every mountain and from every hill." The Lord chose fishermen and uneducated people for his disciples, and so instructed them that their teaching excelled all worldly wisdom, and they converted emperors and kings to the true faith by their preaching. If the savior had chosen eloquent teachers at the beginning, and sent worldly philosophers and the like to preach, then it might have seemed as though the true faith had sprung up not through God's might, but from worldly eloquence. He chose fishermen before he chose emperors, because it is better that the emperor, when he comes to Rome, should cast aside his crown and kneel at the fisherman's memorial, than that the fisherman should kneel at the emperor's memorial. He chose emperors, but he ranked the poor fisherman before the rich emperor. Later he chose the wealthy; but it would have appeared as though they had been chosen for their possessions if he had not previously chosen the needy. He later chose worldly philosophers, but they might have grown proud had he not first chosen the uneducated fishermen.

Consider now how the Lord took glory away from hu- 5
mankind, so that he might give them glory. He took our glory from us, so that he might give us his. He took away our empty glory, so that he might give us the eternal. You shall not glory in yourself, but, as the apostle said, "He who glories, let him glory in God."

At Christ's command Peter and Andrew at once left their 6
nets and followed him. They had not yet seen him work any

wundra wyrcan, ne hi naht ne gehyrdon ða gyt æt his muðe be mede þæs ecan edleanes, and hi ðeah, æfter stemne anre hæse, þæt þæt hi hæfdon forgeaton. Fela Godes wundra we habbað gehyred and eac gesewene; mid manegum swinge- lum gelome we sind geswencte, and mid menigfealdum ðeo- wracena teartnyssum gebregede, and swaðeah we forseoð Godes hæse, and him to lifes wege fylian nellað. Nu he sitt on heofonum, mid þære menniscnysse gescrydd þe he on ðisum life gefette, and mynegað us be ure gecyrrednysse, þæt we ure ðeawas fram leahtrum symle clænsion and be his bebodum gerihtlæcon. Eallunga he underðeodde ðeoda swuran his geoce, he astrehte middangeardes wuldor, and mid gelomlæcendum hryrum nealæcunge his strecan domes geswutelað, and swaðeah ure modige mod nele sylfwilles for- lætan þæt þæt hit dæghwomlice forlyst neadunge. Mine ge- broðra, hwilcere tale mage we brucan on his dome, nu we nellað bugan fram ðyssere andweardan woruldlufe þurh his beboda, ne we ne synd þurh his swingla gerihtlæhte?

7   Wen is þæt eower sum cweðe to him sylfum on stillum geðohtum, hwæt forleton þas gebroðru, Petrus and An- dreas, þe fornean nan ðing næfdon? Ac we sceolon on þisum ðinge heora gewilnunge swiðor asmeagan þonne heora gestreon. Micel forlæt se ðe him sylfum nan ðing ne gehylt. Witodlice we healdað ure æhta mid micelre lufe, and ða ðing þe we nabbað we secað mid ormætre gewilnunge. Micel forlet Petrus and Andreas ða ða heora ægðer þone willan to hæbbenne eallunga forlet, and agenum lustum wiðsoc. Cwyð nu sum mann, ic wolde geefenlæcan þam apostolum, þe ealle woruldðing forsawon, ac ic næbbe nane æhta to forlætenne. Ac God sceawað þæs mannes heortan, and na his æhta. Ne he ne telð hu miccle speda we on his lacum

wonders, nor had they yet heard from his mouth of the recompense of eternal reward, and yet, after the utterance of one command, they forgot whatever they had. We have heard of, and also seen, many of God's miracles; by many scourges we are often afflicted, and terrified by the various sharpness of threats, and yet we scorn God's command, and will not follow him to the way of life. Now he sits in heaven, clothed with the humanity which he brought from this life, and reminds us of our conversion, that we should always cleanse our actions from sins and direct them by his commandments. He has wholly subjected the necks of nations to his yoke, he has prostrated the glory of the world, and by frequent destructions reveals the approach of his strict judgment, and yet our proud mind will not voluntarily let go of that which it daily is forced to lose. My brothers, what excuse can we use at his judgment, when we will not turn from love of this present world through his commandments, nor are we corrected by his scourges?

I expect that one of you might say to himself in his quiet 7 thoughts, what did these brothers, Peter and Andrew, give up, who had almost nothing? But in this case we should consider their desire rather than their wealth. He gives up much who holds nothing for himself. Indeed we hold our possessions with great love, and the things we do not have, we seek with excessive desire. Peter and Andrew gave up much when both of them entirely gave up the will to have, and renounced their own desires. Someone will now say, I would imitate the apostles, who scorned all worldly things, but I have no possessions to give up. But God sees one's heart, not one's possessions. He does not count what great riches we spend on gifts to him, but observes with how much

aspendon, ac cepð mid hu micelre gewilnunge we ða lac him geoffrion. Efne nu þas halgan cypan, Petrus and Andreas, mid heora nettum and scipe him þæt ece lif geceapodon.

8 Næfð Godes rice nanes wurðes lofunge, ac bið gelofod be ðæs mannes hæfene. Heofonan rice wæs alæten þisum foresædum gebroðrum for heora nette and scipe, and eft syððan ðam rican Zacheo to healfum dæle his æhta, and sumere wudewan to anum feorðlinge, and sumum menn to anum wæteres drence. Ic wene þæt þas word ne sind eow full cuðe gif we hi openlicor eow ne onwreoð. Zacheus wæs sum rice mann, and cepte þæs hælendes fær and wolde ge-seon hwilc he wære; ac he ne mihte for ðære menigu ðe him mid ferde, forðan ðe he wæs scort on wæstme. Þa forarn he ðam hælende and stah uppon an treow þæt he hine geseon mihte. Crist ða beseah upp wið þæs rican and cwæð, "Zachee, stih ardlice adun, forðan þe me gedafenað þæt ic nu todæg þe gecyrre." Zacheus ða swyftlice of ðam treowe alihte, and hine blissigende underfeng. Þa ða Zacheus Crist gelaðod hæfde, ða astod he ætforan him, and him anmodlice to cwæð, "Drihten, efne ic todæle healfne dæl minra goda ðearfum, and swa hwæt swa ic mid facne berypte þæt ic wylle be feowerfealdum forgyldan." Drihten him to cwæð, "Nu todæg is ðisum hirede hæl gefremmed, forðan ðe he is Abrahames ofspring. Ic com to secenne and to gehælenne þæt þe on mancynne losode." Þa hæfde Zacheus beceapod heofonan rice mid healfum dæle his æhta: ðone oþerne dæl he heold to ðy þæt he wolde þam be feowerfealdum forgyl-dan þe he ær unrihtlice bereafode.

9 Eft, "Æt sumum sæle gesæt se hælend binnan ðam temple on Hierusalem, ætforan ðam maðmhuse, and beheold hu þæt folc heora ælmyssan wurpon into ðam maðmhuse, and

desire we offer our gifts to him. Indeed, these holy merchants, Peter and Andrew, with their nets and ship purchased for themselves everlasting life.

God's kingdom has no fixed price, but is priced according 8 to a person's property. The kingdom of heaven was given to these aforementioned brothers for their net and ship, and later to the rich Zacchaeus for half his possessions, and to a certain widow for one farthing, and to a certain person for a drink of water. I imagine these words will not be entirely clear to you if we do not explain them more openly. Zacchaeus was a rich man, and had watched the savior's path and wanted to see who he was; but he could not see because of the crowd that went with him, because he was short of stature. He then ran before the savior and climbed a tree so that he might see him. Christ then looked up toward the rich man and said, "Zacchaeus, come down quickly, for it is fitting that I should come home with you today." Zacchaeus then quickly alighted from the tree and received him, rejoicing. When Zacchaeus had invited Christ, he stood before him, and said to him resolutely, "Lord, behold, I will distribute half my goods to the poor, and whatever I have robbed by fraud I will repay fourfold." The Lord said to him, "Now today salvation is fulfilled in this household, for he is Abraham's offspring. I have come to seek and to save that which was lost among humankind." So Zacchaeus had purchased the kingdom of heaven with half of his possessions: the other half he held back so that he could repay fourfold those whom he had unjustly robbed.

Again, "At a certain time the savior sat within the temple 9 at Jerusalem, before the treasury, and saw how the people put their alms into the treasury, and many rich brought great

ða fela rican brohton micele ðing. Þa com ðær an earm
wudewe, and geoffrode Gode ænne feorðling. Drihten ða
cwæð to his leorningcnihtum, 'Ic secge eow to soðan þæt
þeos earme wydewe brohte maran lac þonne ænig ðyssera
riccra manna. Hi ealle sealdon þone dæl heora speda þe him
geðuhte, ac ðeos wydewe ealne hire bigleofan mid estfullum
mode geoffrode.'" Þa hæfde seo earme wudewe mid lytlum
feo, þæt is, mid anum feorðlinge, þæt ece lif geceapod.

10   Se hælend cwæð on sumere stowe to his apostolum, "Soð
ic eow secge, swa hwa swa sylð ceald wæter drincan anum
þurstigan menn ðæra ðe on me gelyfað, ne bið his med forloren." Mine gebroðra, scrutniað nu ða mid hu waclicum
wurðe Godes rice bið geboht, and hu deorwurðe hit is to
geagenne. Se ceap ne mæg wið nanum sceatte beon geeht, ac
he bið ælcum men gelofod be his agenre hæfene.

11   We rædað on Cristes acennednysse þæt heofonlice englas
wæron gesewene bufan ðam acennedan cilde, and hi ðisne
lofsang mid micclum dreame gesungon: *Gloria in excelsis Deo,
et in terra pax hominibus bonae voluntatis,* þæt is on urum gereorde, "Sy wuldor Gode on heannyssum, and on eorðan
sibb ðam mannum ðe synd godes willan." Ne bið nan lac
Gode swa gecweme swa se goda willa. Gif hwa ne mage
ðurhteon þa speda þæt he gesewenlice lac Gode offrige, he
offrige ða ungesewenlican, þæt is, se goda willa, þe ða eorðlican sceattas unwiðmetenlice oferstihð. Hwæt is god willa
buton godnys, þæt he oðres mannes ungelimp besargige and
on his gesundfulnysse fægnige; his freond na for middangearde, ac for Gode lufige; his feond mid lufe forberan,
nanum gebeodan þæt him sylfum ne licige, his nextan neode
be his mihte gehelpan, and ofer his mihte wyllan? Hwæt is
ænig lac wið þisum willan, ðonne seo sawul hi sylfe Gode

things. Then a poor widow came there and offered to God one farthing. The Lord said to his disciples, 'I say to you in truth that this poor widow has brought a greater gift than any of these rich men. They all gave the portion of their goods which suited them, but this widow has offered all her substance with a devout mind.'" Thus the poor widow purchased eternal life with a little money, that is, with one farthing.

The savior said in a certain place to his apostles, "Truly I say to you, whoever gives a drink of cold water to one thirsty person of those who believe in me, his reward shall not be lost." My brothers, consider now with what trifling value God's kingdom is bought, and how precious it is to possess. The purchase cannot be increased for any sum of money, but it will be priced to everyone according to his own possessions. 10

We read that at Christ's birth heavenly angels were seen above the newborn child, and they sang this hymn with great joy: *Glory to God in the highest, and on earth peace to people of good will,* that is, in our language, "Glory be to God in the highest, and on earth peace to people who are of good will." No gift is as acceptable to God as good will. If anyone cannot obtain the means to offer a visible gift to God, let him offer an invisible one, that is, good will, which incomparably excels earthly treasures. What is good will but goodness, so that he grieves for another's misfortune and rejoices in his prosperity; loves his friend not for the world, but for God; to bear with his enemy with love, to command to no one that which would not please himself, to help his neighbor's need according to his power, and to be willing beyond his power? What is any gift in comparison with this will, when 11

geoffrað on weofode hire heortan? Be ðisum cwæð se sealmscop, "*In me sunt, Deus, vota tua, quae reddam laudationes tibi;*
God ælmihtig, on me synd þine behat, þa ic ðe forgylde ðurh
herunga." Swilce he openlice cwæde, "Þeah ðe ic næbbe ða
uttran lac ðe to offrigenne, ic gemete swaþeah on me sylfum
hwæt ic lecge on weofode þinre herunge, forðan ða þu ne
leofast be ure sylene, ac ðu bist swiðor gegladod on offrunge
ure heortan." Ne mæg ðeos offrung beon on ðære heortan
ðe mid gytsunge oððe andan gebysgod bið, forðan ðe hi
ðwyriað wið þone godan willan, and swa hraðe swa hi þæt
mod hreppað, swa gewit se goda willa. Forði noldon þa halgan bydelas nan ðing on ðyssere worulde mid gitsunge gewilnian, ne nane synderlice æhta habban, to ðy þæt hi
mihton butan andan inweardlice him betwynan lufian.

12   Witodlice ðas apostolas geseah se witega Isaias towearde
ða ða he þurh Godes Gast cwæð, "Hwæt sind þas þe her
fleogað swa swa wolcnu, and swa swa culfran to heora ehðyrlum?" Se witega hi geseah ða eorðlican hæfene forseon,
and mid heora mode heofonum genealæcan, and on lifes
wordum genihtsumian, on wundrum scinan, and gecigde hi
culfran and fleogende wolcnu. Ure ehðyrla sind ure eagan,
þurh ða besceawað ure sawul swa hwæt swa heo wiðutan
gewilnað. Culfre is bilewite nyten, and fram geallan biternysse ælfremed. Soðlice ða halgan apostolas wæron swilce
culfran æt heora ehðyrlum ða ða hi nan ðing on þisum
middangearde ne gewilnodon, ac hi ealle ðing bilewitlice
sceawodon, and næron mid gecnyrdnysse æniges reaflaces
getogene to ðam ðe hi wiðutan sceawodon. Se ðe þurh reaf-
lac gewilnað ða ðing þe he mid his eagum wiðutan sceawað,
se is glida, na culfre æt his ehðyrlum.

13   We habbað nu ðyses godspelles traht be dæle oferurnen;

the soul offers itself to God on the altar of its heart? Of this the psalmist said, "*In me, God, are your promises, which I will repay to you through praise;* God almighty, your promises are in me, which I will repay to you through praise." As if he had openly said, "Though I have no outward gifts to offer you, yet will I find in myself something to lay on the altar of your praise, for you do not live by our gift, but are more pleased by the offering of our hearts." This offering cannot be in a heart occupied with covetousness or envy, for they are opposed to good will, and as soon as they touch the mind, the good will departs. Therefore the holy messengers would not desire anything in this world with covetousness, nor have any separate possessions, so that they might inwardly love each other without envy.

Indeed, the prophet Isaiah saw the future apostles when he said through the Spirit of God, "Who are these that here fly like clouds, and like doves to their windows?" The prophet saw them scorning earthly possessions, and with their minds approaching heaven, and abounding in the words of life, shining in wonders, and called them doves and flying clouds. Our windows are our eyes, through which our soul beholds whatever it desires without. A dove is a gentle animal, and a stranger to the bitterness of gall. Truly the holy apostles were like doves at their windows when they desired nothing in this world, but they meekly beheld all things, and were not drawn to what they beheld outside by desire of any robbery. He who by robbery desires the things that he beholds outside with his eyes is a kite, not a dove at his windows. 12

We have now partly run through the exposition of this 13

nu wylle we eow secgan ða getacnunge ðæra feowera apostola namena þe Crist æt fruman geceas. Eornostlice *Simon* is
gereht "gehyrsum," and *Petrus* "oncnawende," *Andreas* "ðegenlic," *Iacob* is gecweden "forscrencend," and *Iohannes*
"Godes gifu"; þas getacnunge sceal gehwilc Cristen mann on
his drohtnunge eallunga healdan. Petrus wæs geciged *Simon*
ær his gecyrrednysse, ac Crist hine gehet *Petrus,* þæt getacnað "oncnawende," forðan ðe he oncneow Crist mid soðum
geleafan þa ða he cwæð, "þu eart Crist, ðæs lifigendan Godes
Sunu." Untwylice se ðe God rihtlice oncnæwð and him gehyrsumað, he hylt on his drohtnunge þyssera twegra namena
getacnunge. Gif he ðegenlice for Godes naman earfoðnysse
forberð, and werlice deofles costnungum wiðstent, ðonne
gefylð he on his ðeawum *Andrees* getacnunge, ðe is gereht
"ðegenlic." *Iacob* is gecweden "forscrencend," and se bið un-
leas forscrencend þe mid gleawnysse his flæsclican leahtras
and deofles tihtinge forscrencð. *Iohannes* is gecweden
"Godes gifu." Se bið gelimplice Godes gifu geciged þe ðurh
gode geearnunga Godes gife begyt, to ði þæt he his beboda
geornlice gefylle.

Passio eiusdem

14 Se apostol Andreas, æfter Cristes ðrowunge, ferde to ðam
lande þe is gehaten Achaia, and ðær bodade Drihtnes geleafan and middangeardes alysednysse ðurh his ðrowunge.
Þa wolde Egeas, sum wælhreow dema, his bodunge adwæscan and ða Cristenan geneadian to ðam deofellicum biggengum. Andreas him cwæð to, "Þe gedafenode, nu ðu
manna dema eart, þæt þu oncneowe ðinne deman ðe on
heofonum is, and hine wurðodest, se ðe is soð God, and ðin

gospel; now we will tell you the signification of the names of those four apostles whom Christ first chose. Indeed, *Simon* is interpreted "obedient," and *Peter* "acknowledging," *Andrew* "brave," *James* is interpreted "overcoming," and *John* "God's grace"; every Christian should certainly hold these significations in his conduct. Peter was called *Simon* before his conversion, but Christ called him *Peter,* which signifies "acknowledging," because he acknowledged Christ with true faith when he said, "You are Christ, Son of the living God." Undoubtedly, he who rightly acknowledges God and obeys him holds in his conduct the signification of these two names. If he bravely endures hardship for God's name, and manfully withstands the devil's temptations, then he fulfills in his conduct the signification of *Andrew,* which is interpreted "brave." *James* is called "overcoming," and he is truly overcoming who with prudence overcomes his fleshly vices and the urges of the devil. *John* is interpreted "God's grace." He is suitably called God's grace who obtains the grace of God through good merits, so that he may zealously fulfill his commandments.

Passion of the Same

The apostle Andrew, after Christ's passion, went to the land called Achaia, and there preached the faith of the Lord and the redemption of the world through his passion. Then Aegeus, a cruel judge, wanted to suppress his preaching and force the Christians to idolatrous worship. Andrew said to him, "It would be fitting, since you are a judge of people, that you should know your judge who is in heaven, and worship him, who is the true God, and turn your mind away

14

mod awendest fram ðam leasum godum." Egeas him andwyrde, "Eart ðu Andreas, þe towyrpst ura goda tempel, and
tihtst ðis mennisce to ðære ydelan lare ðe Romanisce ealdras awurpon and adwæscan heton?" Andreas him andwyrde, "Romanisce ealdras gyt ne oncneowon Godes soðfæstnysse, hu Godes Sunu to mannum com, and tæhte þæt
þas deofolgyld þe ge begað ne synd na godas, ac synd ða
wyrstan deoflu, manncynna fynd, ðe þæt mannum tæcað hu
hi ðone ælmihtigan God gremion, and he hi ðonne forlæt,
and se deofol hi gebysmrað swa lange oðþæt hi gewitað of
heora lichaman scyldige and nacode, naht mid him ferigende buton synna anum." Egeas cwæð, "Þas synd ydele
word; witodlice ða eower hælend ðas word bodade, þa gefæstnodon Iudei hine on rode gealgan." Andreas him andwyrde, "Eala gif ðu witan woldest þære halgan rode gerynu,
mid hu sceadwisre lufe manncynna ealdor for ure edstaðe-
lunge þære rode gealgan underfeng, na geneadod, ac sylfwilles." Egeas sæde, "Humeta segst ðu 'sylfwilles,' ða ða he
wæs belæwed, and be ðæra Iudeiscra bene þurh ðæs ealdormannes cempan ahangen?" Andreas andwyrde, "Forði ic
cwæð 'sylfwilles,' forðan ðe ic wæs samod mid him ða ða he
fram his leorningcnihte belæwed wæs, and he on ær his
ðrowunge us foresæde, and þæt he wolde on ðam þriddan
dæge of deaðe arisan: cwæð þæt he hæfde mihte his sawle to
syllenne, and mihte hi eft to onfonne." Egeas cwæð, "Ic
wundrige ðe snoterne wer, þæt ðu ðyssere lare fylian wylt;
swa hu swa hit gewurde, sylfwilles oððe neadunge, þæt he on
rode gefæstnod wære." Andreas him andwyrde, "Micel is
ðære rode gerynu, ða ic ðe geopenige, gif ðu me gehyran
wylt." Egeas sæde, "Hit ne mæg soðlice beon gesæd gerynu,
ac wite." Andreas cwæð, "Þæt sylfe wite þu ongytst beon

from false gods." Aegeus answered him, "Are you Andrew, who casts down the temples of our gods, and urges this people to the vain doctrine which the Roman elders have rejected and ordered to be suppressed?" Andrew answered him, "The Roman elders do not yet know God's truth, how the Son of God came to humanity, and taught that these idols you worship are not gods, but are the worst devils, enemies of humanity, who teach people how they may provoke the almighty God, so he then forsakes them, and the devil deludes them for a long time until they depart from their bodies guilty and naked, bearing nothing with them but sins alone." Aegeus said, "These are idle words; indeed, when your savior preached these words, the Jews fastened him on a gallows cross." Andrew answered him, "If only you would know the mystery of the holy cross, with what discerning love the prince of humanity accepted the cross for our restoration, not compelled, but voluntarily." Aegeus said, "How do you say 'voluntarily,' when he was betrayed, and at the request of the Jews was crucified by the soldiers of the governor?" Andrew answered, "I said 'voluntarily' because I was with him when he was betrayed by his disciple, and he had earlier foretold his passion to us, and that he would arise from death on the third day: he said that he had power to give his soul, and power to take it up again." Aegeus said, "I wonder that you, a wise man, would follow this doctrine; however it might have happened, voluntarily or by compulsion, he was fastened on a cross." Andrew answered him, "Great is the mystery of the cross, which I will disclose to you, if you will hear me." Aegeus said, "It cannot truly be called a mystery, but a punishment." Andrew said, "If you will hear me patiently, you will understand that that same

gerynu mancynnes edniwunge, gif ðu geðyldelice me gehyran wylt." Egeas andwyrde, "Ic ðe geðyldelice gehyre, ac gif ðu me ne gehyrsumast, ðu scealt onfon ðære ylcan rode gerynu on ðe sylfum." Andreas him andwyrde, "Gif ic me ondrede þære rode gealgan, þonne nolde ic ðære rode wuldor bodian." Egeas sæde, "Þin gewitlease spræc bodað rode wite to wuldre, forðan ðe ðu þurh dyrstignysse þe ne ondrætst deaðes wite." Andreas andwyrde, "Na ðurh dyrstignysse, ac ðurh geleafan ic me ne ondræde deaðes wite. Rihtwisra manna deað is deorwyrðe, and synfulra manna deað is forcuð." Egeas sæde, "Buton ðu offrige lac urum ælmihtigum godum, on ðære ylcan rode ðe ðu herast ic ðe hate gewæhtne afæstnian." Andreas him cwæð to, "Dæghwomlice ic offrige mine lac ðam ælmihtigan Gode, se ðe ana is soð God. Na hlowendra fearra flæsc, oððe buccena blod, ac ic offrige dæghwomlice on weofode þære halgan rode þæt ungewemmede lamb, and hit ðurhwunað ansund and cucu syððan eal folc his flæsc et and his blod drincð." Egeas befran, "Hu mæg þæt swa gewurðan?" Andreas him andwyrde, "Gif ðu leornian wille hu þæt gewurðan mæge, þonne undernim ðu leorningcnihtes hiw, þæt þu ðas gerynu leornian mæge." Egeas sæde, "Ic wille mid tintregum æt ðe ofgan ðises ðinges insiht." Se halga apostol andwyrde, "Ic wundrige ðearle ðin, humeta þu sy to swa micelre stuntnysse gehworfen þæt ðu wenst me for tintregum ðe geopenian ða godcundan gerynu. Þu gehyrdest ðære halgan rode gerynu; þu gehyrdest þære halgan offrunge gerynu; nu, gif ðu gelyfst þæt Crist, Godes Sunu, se ðe wæs on rode ahangen, sy soð God, þonne geopenige ic ðe hu þæt lamb on his rice ðurhwunað ansund and ungewemmed syððan hit geoffrod bið, and his flæsc geeten and his blod gedruncen. Gif ðu ðonne

punishment is the mystery of the renewing of humanity." Aegeus answered, "I will hear you patiently, but if you do not obey me, you will receive the same mystery of the cross for yourself." Andrew answered him, "If I feared the gallows cross, then I would not preach the glory of the cross." Aegeus said, "Your senseless speech preaches the punishment of the cross as a glory, because in your audacity you do not dread the punishment of death." Andrew answered, "Not through audacity, but through faith I do not dread the punishment of death. The death of the righteous one is precious, and the death of the sinful one is disgraceful." Aegeus said, "Unless you offer sacrifices to our almighty gods, I will order you to be fastened, tortured, on the same cross which you praise." Andrew said to him, "Daily I offer my sacrifice to the almighty God, who alone is the true God. Not the flesh of lowing oxen, or blood of goats, but I offer daily on the altar of the holy cross the undefiled lamb, and it remains sound and living after all people have eaten its flesh and drunk its blood." Aegeus asked, "How can that be so?" Andrew answered him, "If you want to learn how that can be, take on the role of a disciple, that you may learn this mystery." Aegeus said, "I will extort an insight into this matter from you with torments." The holy apostle answered, "I wonder greatly at you, how you have turned to such great folly that you imagine I will disclose the divine mystery to you because of torments. You have heard the mystery of the holy cross; you have heard the mystery of the holy offering; now, if you believe that Christ, the Son of God, who was hanged on a cross, is true God, then I will reveal to you how the lamb remains sound and undefiled in its kingdom after it is offered, and its flesh eaten and its blood drunk. But if you

gelyfan nelt, ne becymst ðu næfre to insihte þyssere soðfæstnysse."

15   Hwæt ða Egeas hine gebealh, and het sceofan þone apostol on sweartum cwearterne. Þær com ða micel menigu ealre
ðære scire to ðam cwearterne, and woldon Egeam acwellan
and alædan ðone apostol of ðam cwearterne. Ða cwæð Andreas to ealre ðære menigu, "Mine gebroðra, ne astyrige ge
ðone stillan Drihten to ænigre yrsunge mid eowerum anginne. Ure hælend wæs belæwed, and he hæfde geðyld; he
ne flat ne ne hrymde, ne nan mann his stemne on strætum
ne gehyrde. Habbað eow nu stilnysse and sibbe, and ne
hremmað minne martyrdom, ac swiðor gearciað eow sylfe
swa swa Godes cempan, þæt ge mid unforhtum mode ealle
ðeowracan and lichamlice wita ðurh geðyld oferswyðon. Gif
ænig oga is to ondrædenne, þonne is se to ondrædenne þe
nænne ende næfð. Witodlice mannes ege is smice gelic, and
hrædlice þonne he astyred bið fordwinð. Þa sarnyssa on ðyssere worulde oððe hi sind leohte and acumenlice, oððe hi
sind swære and hrædlice ða sawle ut adræfað. Þa sarnyssa ðe
on ðære towerdan worulde yfelum gegearcode synd þa beoð
ece; ðær bið dæghwomlice wop, and wanung, and heofung,
and endeleas cwylming, to ðam onet Egeas unforwandod-
lice. Beoð swyðor gearwe, to ðam þæt ge ðurh hwilwendlice
gedreccednysse becumon to ðam ecum gefean, þær ge symle
blissiað, blowende and mid Criste rixigende."

16   Þa ða se apostol ðyllice word þam folce geond ealle þa
niht lærde, ða on dægrede sende Egeas to ðam cwearterne
and het him lædan to þone halgan apostol, and cwæð, "Ic
wende þæt þu on nihtlicere smeagunge sceoldest ðin mod
fram dwæsnysse awendan and geswican ðære herunge þines
Cristes, þæt ðu mihtest mid us lifes gefean brucan. Dyslic

716

will not believe, you will never come to an insight into this truth."

At this Aegeus grew angry, and ordered the apostle to be 15 thrown into a dark prison. There came a great multitude from all over the province to the prison, and they wanted to kill Aegeus and lead the apostle out of the prison. Then Andrew said to all the multitude, "My brothers, do not stir up the peaceful Lord to any anger with your plan. Our savior was betrayed, and he had patience; he neither struggled nor cried out, nor did anyone hear his voice in the streets. Be now quiet and peaceful, and do not hinder my martyrdom, but rather prepare yourselves as God's soldiers, that you may overcome all threats and bodily torments by patience with fearless mind. If any terror is to be dreaded, then you should dread that which has no end. Indeed, fear of a person is like smoke, and quickly vanishes when it is stirred up. The pains in this world are either light and bearable, or they are heavy and quickly drive out the soul. The pains in the world to come which are prepared for the evil will be eternal; there will be daily weeping, and wailing, and groaning, and endless torment, to which Aegeus hastens without delay. Instead, be ready, that through transitory tribulation you may come to eternal joy, where you will rejoice forever, blossoming and reigning with Christ."

When the apostle had taught the people all night in such 16 words, Aegeus sent to the prison at dawn and ordered the holy apostle to be led to him, and said, "I hoped that in contemplation overnight you would turn your mind from foolishness and cease from the praise of your Christ, that you might enjoy the pleasures of life with us. It is foolish that a

bið þæt man sylfwilles to rode gealgan efste and hine sylfne to tintregum asende." Andreas andwyrde, "Blisse ic mæg mid þe habban gif ðu on Crist gelyfst and ðine deofolgild forlætst. Crist me sende to ðyssere scire, on ðære ic him gestrynde unlytel folc." Egeas cwæð, "Forði ic ðreatige ðe to ura goda offrunge, þæt ðis folc ðe ðu bepæhtest forleton ða idelnysse ðinre lare, þæt hi urum godum geoffrian magon ðancwurðe onsægednysse. Ne belaf nan ceaster on eallum ðisum earde on ðære þe næron ure goda templa forlætene, and nu sceal eft beon geedstaðelod ura goda biggeng ðurh ðe, þæt hi magon beon ðe gegladode and ðu on urum freondscipe beon mage. Gif ðu þis nelt, ðonne scealt ðu, for ware ura goda, mislice wita ðrowian, and syððan on rode gealgan, ðe ðu herodest, hangigende ateorian." Se apostol him andwyrde, "Þu deaðes bearn, gehyr me, and ðu ceaf, ecum ontendnyssum gegearcod, gehyr me, Godes ðeowan, and hælendes Cristes apostol. Oð þis ic spræc ðe liðelice to, þæt þu mid gesceade ðone soðan geleafan oncneowe; ac nu ðu ðurhwunast on ðinre sceamleaste and wenst þæt ic sceole for ðinum ðeowracum forhtian. Swa hwæt swa ðe is geðuht gyt mare on tintregum, asmea; swa micclum ic beo andfengra minum cyninge, swa micclum swa ic for his naman on tintregum mid andetnysse þurhwunige."

17   Þa het se reða cwellere hine astreccan and hine seofon siðon beswingan; het hine syððan aræran, and cwæð him to, "Andreas, gehyr me, and awend þinne ræd for agotennysse þines blodes. Gif ðu swa ne dest, ic do þæt þu losast on rode gealgan." Se apostol andwyrde, "Ic eom Cristes ðeowa, and ic sceal his rode sigor swiðor wiscan ðonne ondrædan. Þu soðlice miht ætberstan þam ecum cwylmingum þe ðe synd

person should hurry voluntarily to the gallows cross and send himself to torments." Andrew answered, "I can have joy with you if you will believe in Christ and abandon your idolatry. Christ sent me to this province, in which I have gained for him no small number of people." Aegeus said, "Therefore I will force you to offer to our gods, that this people you have deceived may forsake the vanity of your teaching, and they may offer a grateful sacrifice to our gods. Not a city has remained in all this country in which the temples of our gods have not been forsaken, and now the worship of our gods shall be restored through you, that they may be pleased with you and you may be in our friendship. If you will not do this, then for the security of our gods you will suffer various torments, and then perish, hanging on the gallows cross you have praised." The apostle answered him, "You child of death, hear me, and you chaff, prepared for everlasting kindling, hear me, God's servant, and apostle of the savior Christ. Until now I have spoken to you kindly, so that you might with reason acknowledge the true faith; but now you persist in your shamelessness and think that I should be afraid because of your threats. Whatever torments seem even worse to you, devise them; the more I endure torments for his name with profession, the more acceptable I will be to my king."

Then the cruel executioner ordered him to be stretched 17
out and scourged seven times; he afterward ordered him to be raised, and said to him, "Andrew, hear me, and give up your plan for shedding your blood. If you do not do so, I will make you perish on the gallows cross." The apostle answered, "I am Christ's servant, and I will rather wish than fear the triumph of his cross. Truly you might escape the

gemynte gif ðu on Crist gelyfst syððan ðu mine anrædnysse afandast. Ic me ondræde þin forwyrd, and ic for minre ðrowunge ne eom gedrefed. Min ðrowung geendað on anum dæge, oððe on twam, oððe be ðam mæstan on þrim; soðlice ðin cwylming ne mæg binnon ðusend geara to ende gecuman. Forði, earming, ne geyc ðu swiðor þine yrmða, and ne onæl ðu ðe sylfum þæt ece fyr."

18   Hwæt ða Egeas geæbyligd het hine ahon on rodehencgene, and bebead ðam cwellerum þæt hi hine mid wiððum handum and fotum on þære rode gebundon, þæt he langlice ðrowian sceolde. Þa arn þæt Cristene folc togeanes ðam cwellerum ðe hine to þære rode læddon, clypigende and cweðende, "Hwæt hæfð þes rihtwisa mann and Godes freond gefremod, þæt he rodehengene wyrðe sy?" Andreas soðlice bæd þæt folc þæt hi his ðrowunge ne geletton. Eode him mid bliðum mode fægnigende and þæt folc lærende. He ofseah ða feorran ða rode þe him gegearcod wæs, and clypode mid micelre stemne, ðus cweðende, "Hal sy ðu, rod, þe on Cristes lichaman gehalgod wære, and mid his limum gefrætwod swa swa mid meregrotum. Þu hæfdest eorðlicne ege ærðan ðe ure Drihten þe astige; nu ðu hæfst heofonlice lufe, and byst astigen for behate. Orsorh and blissigende ic cume to ðe, swa þæt ðu me blissigende underfo, ðæs leorningcniht ðe on ðe hangode, forðan þe ic ðe symle lufode, and ic gewilnode ðe to ymbclyppenne. Eala ðu gode rod, þe wlite and fægernysse of Drihtnes lymum underfenge, ðu wære gefyrn gewilnod and carfullice gelufod, butan toforlætennysse gesoht, and nu æt nextan minum wilnigendum mode gegearcod. Onfoh me fram mannum, and agif me minum lareowe, þæt he ðurh ðe me underfo, se ðe þurh ðe me alysde."

eternal torments that are intended for you if you will believe in Christ after you have tested my steadfastness. I dread your destruction, and I am not troubled for my suffering. My suffering will end in one day, or two, or at most in three; truly your torment cannot come to an end within a thousand years. Therefore, wretch, do not increase your miseries any further, and do not kindle for yourself the everlasting fire."

At this Aegeus, provoked, ordered him to be hanged on a cross, and commanded the executioners to bind him hand and foot on the cross with willow branches, so he might suffer slowly. Then the Christian people ran toward the executioners who led him to the cross, crying and saying, "What has this righteous man and friend of God done, that he is worthy of hanging on a cross?" But Andrew asked the people not to hinder his suffering. He went with them rejoicing with a happy mind and instructing the people. Then he saw from afar the cross which was prepared for him, and cried with a loud voice, saying, "Hail to you, cross, which was consecrated by the body of Christ, and adorned with his limbs as with pearls. You had earthly fear before our Lord ascended you; now you have heavenly love, and are ascended because of a vow. I come to you carefree and rejoicing, that you, rejoicing, may receive me, the disciple of him who hung on you, for I have ever loved you, and I have longed to embrace you. O good cross, which received beauty and fairness from the limbs of the Lord, you have been desired and diligently loved from long ago, sought without pause, and now at last prepared for my longing mind. Receive me from humanity, and give me to my teacher, that he who has redeemed me through you might receive me through you." 18

19 Æfter ðisum wordum he hine unscrydde, and þam cwellerum his gewæda betæhte. Hi ða genealæhton, and hine on
ðære rode ahofon, and ealne his lichaman mid stearcum
wiððum, swa swa him beboden wæs, gewriðon. Þær stodon
ða ma þonne twentig ðusend manna mid Egeas breðer,
samod clypigende, "Unrihtwis dom, þæt se halga wer swa
ðrowode." Se halga Andreas soðlice of ðære rode gehyrte
ðæra geleaffulra manna mod, tihtende to hwilwendlicum
geðylde, secgende þæt þeos sceorte þrowung nis to wiðmetenne þam ecan edleane.

20 Þa betwux ðisum eode eall þæt folc to Egeas botle, ealle
samod clypigende and cweðende þæt swa halig wer hangian
ne sceolde; sidefull mann, and mid þeawum gefrætwod,
æðele lareow, arfæst and gedefe, gesceadwis and syfre, ne
sceolde swa ðrowian, ac sceolde beon alysed lybbende of
ðære rode, forðan ðe he ne geswicð soð to bodigenne, nu
twegen dagas cucu hangigende. Hwæt ða Egeas him ondred
ða menigu, and behet þæt he wolde hine alysan swa swa hi
gewilnodon, and eode forð mid. Þa befran se apostol, mid
þam ðe he hine geseah, "Hwæt nu, Egeas, hwi come ðu to
us? Gif ðu wylt gelyfan gyt on ðone hælend, þe bið gemiltsod, swa swa ic ðe behet. Gif ðu to ði come þæt þu me alyse,
nelle ic beon alysed lybbende heonon. Nu ic geare geseo
minne soðan cyning; ic stande on his gesihðe to him me ge-
biddende. Ðin me ofhrywð and þinre yrmðe, forðan ðe þin
andbidað þæt ece forwyrd. Efst nu, earming, þa hwile ðe ðu
ænig ðing miht, ðelæs ðe ðu wille þonne ðe forwyrned bið."
Þa woldon hi hine alysan, ac heora handa astifedon swa hwa
swa hreopode þa rode mid handum. Þa clypode se apostol to
hælendum Criste mid ormætre stemne, þus biddende, "Min
goda lareow, ne læt ðu me alysan buton þu underfo ær minne
gast."

After these words he unclothed himself, and gave his gar- 19
ments to the executioners. They approached, raised him
on the cross, and bound all his body with strong willow
branches, as they had been commanded. There stood more
than twenty thousand people with Aegeus's brother, together crying, "Unjust judgment, that the holy man should
suffer so." But from the cross the holy Andrew cheered the
minds of those faithful people, urging them to temporary
patience, saying that this short suffering is not to be compared with the eternal reward.

Then in the meanwhile all the people went to the house 20
of Aegeus, all crying together and saying that so holy a man
ought not to hang; a modest man, adorned with pure morals, a noble teacher, pious and meek, discreet and sober,
ought not to suffer so, but should be released from the cross
alive, for he does not cease from preaching truth, hanging
alive for two days now. At this Aegeus feared the multitude,
and promised that he would release him as they desired, and
went forth with them. Then the apostle, when he saw him,
asked, "How now, Aegeus, why do you come to us? If you will
yet believe in the savior, you will receive mercy, as I promised you. If you come to release me, I will not be released
from here living. Now I already see my true king; I stand in
his sight praying to him. I grieve for you and your misery, for
eternal destruction awaits you. Hasten now, wretch, while
you still can do something, lest it be forbidden to you when
you want it." They wanted to release him, but the hands of
anyone who touched the cross with his hands grew stiff.
Then the apostle cried out with a great voice to the savior
Christ, praying, "My good teacher, let me not be released
unless you first receive my spirit."

21 Æfter ðisum wordum wearð gesewen leoht micel of heofonum færlice cumende to ðam apostole, and hine ealne
ymbscean, swa þæt mennisce eagan hine ne mihton geseon
for ðam heofonlican leohte ðe hine befeng. Þæt leoht ðurhwunode swa fornean ane tide, and Andreas ageaf his gast on
ðam leohte, and ferde to Criste samod mid þam leoman,
þam is a wuldor geond ealle woruld.

22 Egeas wearð gelæht fram atelicum deofle hamwerd be
wege, ærðan ðe he to huse come, and he ðearle awedde,
aworpen to eorðan on manna gesihðe þe him mid eodon. He
gewat ða of worulde wælhreow to helle, and his broðor
heold þæs halgan Andreas lic mid micelre arwurðnysse, þæt
he ætwindan moste. Swa micel oga asprang ofer eallum ðam
mennisce þæt ðær nan ne belaf ðe ne gelyfde on God.

23 Þas ðrowunge awriton þære ðeode preostas and ða ylcan
diaconas ðe hit eal gesawon, ðylæs þe hwam twynige þyssere
gereccednysse. Uton nu biddan ðone ælmihtigan wealdend
þæt his eadiga apostol ure ðingere beo, swa swa he wunode
his gelaðunge bydel. Sy ðam metodan Drihtne wurþmynt
and lof a on ecnysse. Amen we cweðað.

After these words a great light was seen suddenly coming 21
from heaven to the apostle, and shone all around him, so
that human eyes might not see him for the heavenly light
that surrounded him. The light continued nearly an hour,
and Andrew gave up his spirit in that light, and went together with that beam to Christ, to whom is glory forever
throughout all the world.

Aegeus was seized by a horrible devil on the way home, 22
before he came to his house, and he went severely mad,
thrown down to the earth in the sight of those who went
with him. He then departed, bloodthirsty, from the world
into hell, and his brother kept the body of the holy Andrew
with great reverence, that he might avoid that. Such great
awe sprang up over all the people that not one remained
there who did not believe in God.

The priests of that nation and the same deacons who saw 23
it all recorded this passion, lest anyone should have doubt
about this narrative. Let us now pray to the almighty ruler
that his blessed apostle may be our intercessor, as he had
been the herald of his Church. To the Lord creator be honor
and praise forever in eternity. Amen, we say.

39

Dominica prima in adventum Domini

Þyses dæges þenung and ðyssere tide mærð sprecað embe
Godes tocyme. Þeos tid oð midne winter is gecweden *Ad-
ventus Domini,* þæt is "Drihtnes tocyme." His tocyme is his
menniscnys. He com to us ða ða he genam ure gecynd to his
ælmihtigan godcundnysse, to ði þæt he us fram deofles anwealde alysde.

2   Nu stent se gewuna on Godes gelaðunge þæt ealle Godes
ðeowan on cyrclicum ðenungum, ægðer ge on halgum ræ-
dingum ge on gedremum lofsangum, ðæra witegena gyd-
dunga singallice on þyssere tide reccað. Þa witegan, þurh
Godes Gast, witegodon Cristes tocyme ðurh menniscnysse,
and be ðam manega bec setton, ða ðe we nu oferrædað æt
Godes ðeowdome ætforan his gebyrdtide, him to wurðmynte, þæt he us swa mildheortlice geneosian wolde. Crist
com on ðam timan to mancynne gesewenlice, ac he bið æfre
ungesewenlice mid his gecorenum þeowum, swa swa he sylf
behet, þus cweðende, "Efne ic beo mid eow eallum dagum,
oð þissere worulde gefyllednysse." Mid ðisum wordum he
geswutelode þæt æfre beoð, oð middangeardes geendunge,
him gecorene menn, ðe þæs wyrðe beoð þæt hi Godes
wununge mid him habban moton.

3   Þa halgan witegan witegodon ægðer ge ðone ærran tocyme on ðære acennednysse and eac ðone æftran æt ðam

39

First Sunday in Advent

First Sunday of the Lord's Advent

The service of this day and the celebration of this time speak of God's advent. This time until midwinter is called *Advent of the Lord,* that is, "the Lord's advent." His advent is his incarnation. He came to us when he took our nature to his almighty divinity, so that he might release us from the power of the devil.

The custom now stands in God's Church that at this time [2] all God's servants in the church services, both in holy readings and in harmonious hymns, constantly recite the songs of the prophets. The prophets, through the Spirit of God, prophesied Christ's advent through his incarnation, and composed many books about it, which we now read through at God's service in his honor before the time of his birth, when he so mercifully would visit us. Christ came to humanity visibly at that time, but invisibly he is always with his chosen servants, as he himself promised, saying, "Lo, I will be with you all days, until the consummation of this world." By these words he revealed that until the ending of the world there will always be people chosen by him, who will be worthy that they may have a dwelling in God with him.

The holy prophets prophesied both the first advent at [3] the birth and also the second at the great judgment. We,

micclum dome. We eac, Godes ðeowas, getrymmað urne geleafan mid þyssere tide þenungum, forðan ðe we on urum
lofsangum geandettað ure alysednysse þurh his ærran tocyme, and we us sylfe maniað þæt we on his æftran tocyme
gearwe beon, þæt we moton fram ðam dome him folgian to
ðam ecan life, swa swa he us behet. Be ðyssere tide mærsunge spræc se apostol Paulus on ðyssere pistolrædinge, to
Romaniscum leodum and eac to eallum geleaffullum mannum, þus manigende, "Mine gebroðra, wite ge þæt nu is
tima us of slæpe to arisenne; ure hæl is gehendre þonne we
gelyfdon. Seo niht gewat, and se dæg genealæhte. Uton
awurpan ðeostra weorc, and beon ymbscrydde mid leohtes
wæpnum, swa þæt we on dæge arwurðlice faron; na on oferætum and druncennyssum, na on forligerbeddum and unclænnyssum, na on geflite and andan, ac beoð ymbscrydde
þurh Drihten hælend Crist."

4   Se apostol us awrehte þæt we of slæpe ure asolcennysse
and ungeleaffulnysse æt sumon sæle arison, swa swa ge on
ðyssere andwerdan rædinge gehyrdon. "Mine gebroðra, wite
ge þæt nu is tima us of slæpe to arisenne." Witodlice ne
gedafenað us þæt we symle hnesce beon on urum geleafan
swa swa ðas merwan cild, ac we sceolon onettan to fulfreme-
dre geðincðe þurh gehealdsumnysse Godes beboda. We
sceolon asceacan ðone sleacan slæp us fram, and deofles
weorc forlætan, and gan on leohte, þæt is, on godum weorcum. Gefyrn scean leoht ingehydes geond eorðan ymbhwyrft, and forwel menige scinað on soðfæstnysse wege, þa
ðe farað ðurh godspellic siðfæt to ðæs ecan lifes gefean. Efne
nu "ure hæl is gehendre þonne we gelyfdon." Þurh ðeonde
ingehyd and godne willan, anum gehwilcum is hæl gehendre
ðonne him wære ða ða he æt fruman gelyfde, and forði he

God's servants, also confirm our faith with the services of this time, because in our hymns we confess our redemption through his first advent, and we admonish ourselves to be ready for his second advent, that we may follow him from that judgment to eternal life, as he promised us. The apostle Paul spoke of the celebration of this time in this epistle reading to the Roman people and also to all believers, admonishing, "My brothers, know that now is the time for us to arise from sleep; our salvation is nearer than we believed. The night has departed, and the day has approached. Let us cast off works of darkness, and be clothed around with the weapons of light, so that we may go honorably by day; not in gluttony and drunkenness, not in adulteries and uncleanness, not in strife and envy, but be clothed by the Lord savior Christ."

The apostle has roused us to rise at a certain time from the sleep of our sluggishness and unbelief, as you have heard in this present lesson. "My brothers, know that it is now time for us to arise from sleep." Indeed it does not suit us to be always delicate in our faith like a tender child, but we should hasten to perfect excellence through the observance of God's commandments. We should shake sluggish sleep from ourselves, and forsake the devil's works, and go in the light, that is, in good works. Long ago the light of knowledge shone across the whole sphere of the earth, and very many who travel the gospel path to the joy of everlasting life shine in the way of truth. Lo, now "our salvation is nearer than we believed." Through increasing knowledge and good will, salvation is nearer to everyone than it was when he first

sceal symle geðeon on dæghwomlicere gecnyrdnysse, swa swa se sealmscop cwæð be Godes gecorenum, "Þa halgan farað fram mihte to mihte."

5   Eac is gehwilcum men his endenexta dæg near and near, and se gemænelica dom dæghwomlice genealæhð, on ðam underfehð anra gehwilc be ðam ðe he geearnode on lichaman, swa god swa yfel. Uton forði ælc yfel forfleon and god be ure mihte gefremman, þylæs ðe we ðonne willon ðonne we ne magon, and we ðonne fyrstes biddon ðonne us se deað to forðsiðe geneadað. "Seo niht gewat, and se dæg genealæhte." Her asette se apostol niht for ðære ealdan nytennysse ðe rixode geond ealne middangeard ær Cristes tocyme; ac he toscoc ða dwollican nytennysse ðurh onlihtinge his andwerdnysse, swa swa se beorhta dæg todræfð þa dimlican þeostru ðære sweartan nihte. Deofol is eac niht gecweden, and Crist dæg, se ðe us mildheortlice fram deofles ðeostrum alysde, and us forgeaf leoht ingehydes and soðfæstnysse. "Uton awurpan þeostra weorc, and beon ymbscrydde mid leohtes wæpnum, swa þæt we on dæge arwurðlice faron." Uton awurpan ðurh andetnysse and behreowsunge þa forðgewitenan yfelu, and uton heononforð stranglice wiðstandan deofles tihtingum, swa swa se ylca apostol on oðre stowe his underðeoddan manode, "Wiðstandað þam deofle, and he flihð fram eow; genealæcað Gode, and he genealæhð to eow." Leohtes wæpna synd rihtwisnysse weorc and soðfæstnysse. Mid ðam wæpnum we sceolon beon ymbscrydde swa þæt we on dæge arwurðlice faron. Swa swa dæges leoht forwyrnð gehwilcne to gefremmenne þæt þæt seo niht geðafað, swa eac soðfæstnysse ingehyd— þæt is, geðoht ures Drihtnes willan—us ne geðafað mandæda to gefremmenne.

believed, and therefore he should always increase in daily diligence, as the psalmist said of God's chosen, "The holy go from strength to strength."

Everyone's last day is also nearer and nearer, and the universal judgment approaches daily, at which everyone will receive as he has merited in body, whether good or evil. Let us then flee from every evil and do good according to our power, lest when we want to we cannot, and then we pray for a respite when death compels us to depart. "The night has departed, and the day has approached." Here the apostle has placed night for the old ignorance which reigned through all the world before Christ's advent; but he scattered the false ignorance by the illumination of his presence, as the bright day drives away the dim darkness of the black night. The devil is also called night, and Christ day, who has mercifully released us from the devil's darkness, and given us the light of knowledge and truth. "Let us cast away works of darkness, and be clothed around with weapons of light, so that we may go honorably by day." Let us cast away past evils by confession and repentance, and let us henceforth strongly withstand the urgings of the devil, as the same apostle in another place exhorted his followers, "Withstand the devil, and he will flee from you; draw near to God, and he will draw near to you." The weapons of light are works of righteousness and truth. We should be clothed with those weapons so that we may go honorably by day. Just as the light of day prevents everyone from doing that which is fitting to the night, so also the knowledge of truth—that is, the thought of our Lord's will—is not fitting for performing wicked deeds.

6   Symle we beoð fram Gode gesewene, ægðer ge wiðutan
ge wiðinnan; þi sceal eac gehwa se ðe fordemed beon nele
eallunga warnian þæt he Godes beboda ne forgæge, na on
oferætum and druncennyssum. We sceolon habban gastlice
gereordunge, swa swa se ylca apostol ðisum wordum tæhte:
"Þonne ge eow to gereorde gaderiað, hæbbe eower gehwilc
halwende lare on muðe and sealmboc on handa." Druncennys is cwylmbære ðing and galnysse antimber. Salomon
cwæð, "Ne bið nan ðing digle þær ðær druncennys rixað."
On oðre stowe beweop se ylca apostol ungemetegodra
manna lif, ðus cweðende, "Heora wamb is heora God, and
heora ende is forwyrd, and heora wuldor on gescyndnysse."
"Na on forligerbeddum and on unclænnyssum," ac beo ar-
wyrðe sinscipe betwux gelyfedum mannum, swa þæt furðon
nan forliger ne unclænnyss ne sy genemned on Godes
gelaðunge. "Na on geflite and andan": Crist cwæð be gesib-
sumum mannum þæt hi sind Godes bearn gecigede, and
witodlice ða geflitfullan sind deofles lyma. Se yfela secð
symle ceaste, and wælhreaw engel bið asend togeanes him.
Anda is derigendlic leahter, and æfre bið se niðfulla wunigende on gedrefednysse, forðan ðe se anda ablent his mod
and ælcere gastlicere blisse benæmð. Þurh andan bepæhte
se deofol þone frumsceapenan mann, and se niðfulla is þæra
deofla dælnimend. Seo soðe sibb afligð ungeðwærnysse and
ðæs modes digelnysse onliht, and witodlice se anda gemenigfylt yrsunge.

7   Se apostol beleac þisne pistol mid þisum wordum: "Ac
beoð ymbscrydde ðurh Drihten hælend Crist." Ealle ða ðe
on Criste beoð gefullode, hi beoð mid Criste ymbscrydde gif
hi ðone Cristendom mid rihtwisnysse weorcum geglengað.
Ðas gewædu awrat se ylca apostol swutellicor on oðre stowe,

We are always seen by God, both without and within;   6
therefore everyone who does not want to be condemned
should especially take care that he not transgress God's
commandments, either by gluttony or drunkenness. We
should have a spiritual meal, as the same apostle taught in
these words: "When you gather yourselves to meals, let each
of you have salutary teaching in the mouth and a psalter in
the hand." Drunkenness is a deadly thing and the cause of
lechery. Solomon said, "Nothing is secret where drunkenness reigns." In another place the same apostle bewailed the
life of intemperate people, saying, "Their belly is their God,
and their end is destruction, and their glory in pollution."
"Not in adulteries and uncleanness," but let there be honorable marriage between believers, so that at least no fornication or uncleanness be named in God's Church. "Not in
strife and envy": Christ said of peaceful persons that they
are called children of God, and indeed the quarrelsome are
limbs of the devil. The evil one always seeks contention, and
a fierce angel will be sent against him. Envy is a harmful vice,
and the envious will always be dwelling in affliction, because
envy blinds his mind and deprives it of every spiritual bliss.
Through envy the devil deceived the first-created human,
and the envious person is a sharer with devils. True peace
drives away discord and enlightens the mind's darkness, and
indeed envy multiplies anger.

The apostle closed this epistle with these words: "But be   7
clothed around with the Lord savior Christ." All those who
are baptized in Christ are clothed with Christ if they adorn
their Christianity with works of righteousness. The same
apostle wrote more plainly of these garments in another

ðus cweðende, "Ymbscrydað eow, swa swa Godes gecorenan, mid mildheortnysse and mid welwillendnysse, mid eadmodnysse, mid gemetfæstnysse, mid geðylde, and habbað
eow toforan eallum ðingum þa soðan lufe, seo ðe is bend
ealra fulfremednyssa; and Cristes sib blissige on eowrum
heortum, on ðære ge sind gecigede on anum lichaman. Beoð
þancfulle, and Godes word wunige betwux eow genihtsumlice, on eallum wisdome tæcende and tihtende eow betwynan, on sealmsangum and gastlicum lofsangum, singende
mid gife Godes on eowrum heortum. Swa hwæt swa ge doð
on worde oððe on weorce, doð symle on Drihtnes naman,
þancigende ðam ælmihtigan Fæder ðurh his Bearn, þe mid
him symle on annysse þæs Halgan Gastes wunað."

8   Uton forði us gearcian mid þisum foresædum reafum be
ðæs apostoles mynegunge, þæt we to ðære wundorlican gebyrdtide ures Drihtnes mid freolslicere ðenunge becumon,
þam sy wuldor and lof a on ecnysse. Amen.

40

Dominica II in adventum Domini

*E*runt signa in sole et luna et stellis, et reliqua.

2   Se godspellere Lucas awrat on ðisum dægðerlican godspelle þæt ure Drihten wæs sprecende þisum wordum to his
leorningcnihtum be ðam tacnum ðe ær þyssere worulde

place, saying, "Clothe yourselves, as God's chosen, with mercy and with benevolence, with humility, with moderation, with patience, and have before all things true love, which is the bond of all perfections; and let Christ's peace rejoice in your hearts, in which you are called in one body. Be thankful, and let God's word dwell among you abundantly, in all wisdom teaching and encouraging one another, in psalms and spiritual hymns, singing with God's grace in your hearts. Whatever you do in word or in work, do it always in the name of the Lord, thanking the almighty Father through his Son, who always dwells with him in the unity of the Holy Spirit."

Let us therefore prepare ourselves with these aforesaid 8 garments according to the apostle's admonition, that we may come to the wonderful time of our Lord's birth with the service appropriate to this feast, to whom be glory and praise forever in eternity. Amen.

40

Second Sunday in Advent

Second Sunday of the Lord's Advent

T here will be signs in the sun and moon and stars, etc.

The Evangelist Luke wrote in this day's gospel that our 2 Lord was speaking in these words to his disciples about the signs which will occur before the ending of this world. The

geendunge gelimpað. Drihten cwæð, "Tacna gewurðað on sunnan, and on monan, and on steorrum, and on eorðan bið þeoda ofðryccednyss for gemengednysse sælicra yða and sweges. Menn forseariað for ðam micclan ogan and andbidunge þæra ðinga ðe becumað ofer ealne ymhwyrft. Soðlice heofonan mihta beoð astyrode, and ðonne hi geseoð mannes Bearn cumende on wolcnum mid micclum mægenðrymme and mihte. Þonne ðas wundra onginnað, ahebbað þonne eowre heafdu and behealdað, forðan ðe eower alysednyss genealæhð." He sæde ða ðis bigspel: "Behealdað þas fictreowa and ealle oðra treowa; þonne hi spryttað þonne wite ge þæt hit sumerlæcð. Swa eac ge magon witan, ðonne ge ðas foresædan tacna geseoð, þæt Godes rice genealæhð. Soð ic eow secge, ne gewit ðeos mæigð oðþæt ealle ðas ðing gewurðað. Heofon and eorðe gewitað, and mine word næfre ne gewitað."

3   Se halga Gregorius us trahtnode þyses godspelles digelnysse, þus undergynnende: Drihten ure alysend us gewilnað gearwe gemetan, and forþi cydde ða yfelnyssa ðe folgiað þam ealdigendan middangearde þæt he us fram his lufe gestilde. He geswutelode hu fela ðrowunga forestæppað þyssere worulde geendunge, gif we God on smyltnysse ondrædan nellað, þæt we huru his genealæcendan dom mid mislicum swinglum afærede ondrædon. Her wiðufan on þyssere rædinge cwæð se hælend, "Ðeod arist ongean ðeode, and rice ongean rice, and micele eorðstyrunga beoð gehwær, and cwealm, and hunger." And syððan betwux ðam þus cwæð, "Tacna beoð on sunnan, and on monan, and on steorrum, and on eorðan ðeoda ofðriccednys, for gemencgednysse sælicra yða and sweges."

4   Sume ðas tacna we gesawon gefremmede, sume we on-

Lord said, "There will be signs in the sun, and in the moon, and in the stars, and on earth there will be affliction of nations for the confusion and roaring of the waves of the sea. People will shrink for the great fear and expectation of the things that will come upon the whole world. Truly the powers of heaven will be moved, and then they will see the Son of man coming in the clouds with great majesty and power. When these wonders begin, lift up your heads and look, because your redemption approaches." He then told this parable: "Look at the fig tree and all other trees; when they bring forth fruit then you know that summer is near. So too, when you see these aforesaid signs you may know that the kingdom of God is near. Truly I say to you, this generation will not pass away until all these things come to pass. Heaven and earth will pass away, and my words will never pass away."

The holy Gregory has expounded the mystery of this gospel for us, thus beginning: The Lord our redeemer desires to find us ready, and therefore revealed the evils which follow the decaying world so that he might restrain us from love of it. He showed how much suffering will precede the end of this world so that, if we will not fear God in untroubled times, we may at least fear his coming judgment when we are terrified by various scourges. Here before this reading the savior said, "Nation will rise against nation, and kingdom against kingdom, and there will be great earthquakes everywhere, and pestilence, and hunger." And then within it he said, "There will be signs in the sun, and in the moon, and in the stars, and on earth affliction of nations for the confusion and roaring of the waves of the sea."

Some of these signs we have seen fulfilled, some we fear 4

737

drædað us towearde. Witodlice on ðisum niwum dagum arison ðeoda ongean ðeoda, and heora ofþriccednyss on eorðan
gelamp swiðor þonne we on ealdum bocum rædað. Oft
eorðstyrung gehwær fela burhga ofhreas, swa swa gelamp on
Tyberies dæge þæs caseres, þæt ðreottyne byrig ðurh eorð-
styrunge afeollon. Mid cwealme and mid hungre we sind gelome geswencte, ac we nateshwon gyta swutele tacna on
sunnan, and on monan, and on steorrum ne gesawon. We
rædað on tungelcræfte þæt seo sunne bið hwiltidum þurh
ðæs monelican trendles underscyte aðystrod, and eac se
fulla mona færlice fagettað þonne he ðæs sunlican leohtes
bedæled bið ðurh ðære eorðan sceadwunge. Sind eac sume
steorran leohtbeamede, færlice arisende and hrædlice gewitende, and hi symle sum ðing niwes mid heora upspringe
gebicniað; ac ne mænde Drihten ðas tacna on ðære godspellican witegunge, ac ða egefullan tacna þe ðam micclan
dæge forestæppað. Matheus se godspellere awrat swutelicor
þas tacna, þus cweðende, "Þærrihte æfter ðære micclan gedrefednysse bið seo sunne aðystrod, and se mona ne sylð nan
leoht, and steorran feallað of heofonum, and heofonan
mihta beoð astyrode, and ðonne bið æteowed Cristes rodetacn on heofonum, and ealle eorðlice mægða heofiað." Ðære
sæ gemengednyss and ðæra yða sweg ungewunelice gyt ne
asprungon, ac ðonne fela ðæra foresædra tacna gefyllede
sind, nis nan twynung þæt þa feawa ðe þær to lafe sind
witodlice gefyllede beon.

5   Mine gebroðra, þas ðing sind awritene þæt ure mod ðurh
wærscipe wacole beon, þæt hi ðurh orsorhnysse ne asleacion
ne ðurh nytennysse geadlion; ac þæt symle se oga hi gebys-
gige, and seo embhydignys on godum weorcum getrymme.
Drihten cwæð, "Menn forseariað for ogan and andbidunge

are to come. Indeed, in these recent days nations have arisen against nations, and their affliction on earth has happened worse than we have read in old books. Earthquakes in many places have often overthrown many cities, as happened in the days of the emperor Tiberius, when thirteen cities fell through an earthquake. We are frequently afflicted with pestilence and hunger, but we have not yet seen clear signs in the sun, and in the moon, and in the stars. We read in astronomy that the sun is sometimes darkened by the intervention of the lunar orb, and also the full moon suddenly grows dim when it is deprived of the sun's light by the shadow of the earth. There are also some stars beaming light, suddenly rising and quickly departing, and by their rising they always indicate some new thing; but the Lord did not mean these signs in the gospel prophecy, but rather the awful signs which will precede the great day. Matthew the Evangelist wrote more plainly of these signs, saying, "Right after the great tribulation the sun will be darkened, and the moon will give no light, and stars will fall from heaven, and the powers of heaven will be moved, and then the sign of Christ's cross will appear in the heavens, and all earthly powers will lament." The churning of the sea and the sound of the waves have not yet occurred in any unusual way, but when many of the aforesaid signs have been fulfilled, there is no doubt that the few which remain will also be fulfilled.

My brothers, these things are written so that our minds 5 may be vigilant through heedfulness, that they not slacken from carelessness nor languish through ignorance; but that fear should always occupy them, and attention to good works confirm them. The Lord said, "People will shrink for the terror and expectation of the things that will come upon

ðæra ðinga þe becumað ofer ealne middangeard. Witodlice heofonan mihta beoð astyrode." Heofonan mihta sind englas and heahenglas, þrymsetl, ealdorscipas, hlafordscipas and anwealdu. Þas engla werod beoð æteowde gesewenlice urum gesihðum on tocyme ðæs strecan deman, þæt hi stiðlice æt us ofgan þæt þæt se ungesewenlica scyppend emlice forberð. Þonne we geseoð mannes Bearn cumende on wolcnum mid micelre mihte and mægenðrymme. Drihten gecigde hine sylfne mannes Bearn gelomlicor ðonne Godes Bearn, for eadmodnysse þære underfangenan menniscnysse, þæt he us mynegige mid þam gecynde þe he for us underfeng. He is soðlice mannes Bearn, and ne manna Bearn, and nis nan oðer anes mannes bearn buton Crist ana. He bið on mihte and on mægenðrymme geswutelod þam ðe hine on eadmodnysse wunigende gehyran noldon, þæt hi ðonne gefredon his mihte swa miccle stiðlicor, swa micclum swa hi nu heora swuran to his geðylde nellað gebigan. Þas word sind gecwedene be ðam wiðercorenum, ac her fyliað þa word ðe ða gecorenan frefriað. Se hælend cwæð, "Þonne ðas wundra ongynnað, ahebbað þonne eowre heafda and behealdað, forðan ðe eower alysednyss genealæhð." Swilce he swutellice his gecorenan manode, "Þonne middangeardes wita gelomlæcað, þonne se oga ðæs micclan domes bið æteowod, ahebbað þonne eowre heafda, þæt is, gladiað on eowrum mode, forði ðonne þes middangeard bið geendod þe ge ne lufodon; þonne bið gehende seo alysednyss ðe ge sohton." On halgum gewrite bið gelomlice heafod gesett for þæs mannes mode, forðan ðe þæt heafod gewissað þam oðrum limum swa swa þæt mod gediht ða geðohtas. We ahebbað ure heafda þonne we ure mod arærað to gefean þæs heofonlican eðles. Þa ðe

the whole world. Indeed the powers of heaven will be moved." The powers of heaven are angels and archangels, thrones, principalities, lordships, and dominions. These hosts of angels will appear visible to our sight at the coming of the severe judge, to sternly exact from us that which the invisible creator patiently forbears. Then we will see the Son of man coming in the clouds with great might and majesty. The Lord called himself the Son of man more often than the Son of God, from the humility of his assumed humanity, in order to admonish us with the nature he received for us. He is truly Son of man, and not Son of men, and there is no other son of one person but Christ alone. He will be revealed in might and in majesty to those who would not obey him while he dwelled in humility, so that the more they will not bow their necks to his patience now, the more severely they will feel his might then. These words are said of the reprobates, but here follow the words which comfort the chosen. The savior said, "When these wonders begin, lift up your heads and look, for your redemption approaches." As if he had clearly exhorted his chosen ones, "When the torments of the world grow more frequent, when the terror of the great judgment appears, then raise your heads, that is, be glad in your minds, for then this world which you did not love will be ended; then the redemption you sought will be at hand." In holy writings the head is very frequently put for the human mind, because the head directs the other limbs as the mind devises the thoughts. We lift up our heads when we raise our minds to the joy of the heavenly homeland.

God lufiað, hi sind gemanode þæt hi gladion on middangeardes geendunge, forðan þonne he gewit ðe hi ne lufodon,
ðonne witodlice hi gemetað þone ðe hi lufodon.

6   Ne gewurðe hit la þæt ænig geleafful se ðe gewilnað God
to geseonne, þæt he heofige for middangeardes hryrum! Hit
is soðlice awriten, "Swa hwa swa wile beon freond þyssere
worulde, he bið Godes feond geteald." Witodlice se ðe ne
blissað on nealæcunge middangeardes geendunge se geswutelað þæt he his freond wæs, and bið þonne oferstæled þæt
he Godes feond is. Ac gewite þises middangeardes freondscipe fram geleaffulra manna heortan, and gewite fram ðam
ðe þæt oðer lif gelyfað toweard and hit ðurh weorc lufiað. Þa
sceolon heofian for middangeardes toworpennysse þa ðe
heora heortan wyrtruman on his lufe aplantodon, þa ðe þæt
towearde lif ne secað, ne his furðon ne gelyfað; we soðlice,
ðe þæs heofonlican eðles gefean eallunga oncneowon, sceolon anmodlice to ðam onettan. Us is to gewiscenne þæt we
hrædlice to ðam faron and þurh ðone scyrtran weg becumon, forðan ðe ðes middangeard is mid menigfealdum un-
rotnyssum geðread, and mid ðwyrnyssum geangsumod.

7   Hwæt is ðis deadlice lif buton weg? Understandað nu
hwilc sy on weges geswince to ateorigenne, and ðeah nelle
þone weg geendigan. Drihten cwæð, "Behealdað þæs fictreowa and ealle oðre treowa, þonne hi spryttað ðonne wite
ge þæt hit sumorlæhð. Swa eac ge magon witan, ðonne ge
ðas foresædan tacna geseoð, þæt Godes rice genealæhð."
Soðlice mid þisum wordum is geswutelod þæt ðises middangeardes wæstm is hryre. To ðam he wext þæt he fealle; to ðy
he sprytt þæt he mid cwyldum fornyme swa hwæt swa he ær
sprytte. Þes middangeard is ðam ealdigendan menn gelic:
on iugoðe bið se lichama þeonde on strangum breoste, on

Those whom God loves are exhorted to be glad for the ending of the world, for when that which they did not love passes away, then certainly they will find what they loved.

Oh let it not be that any believer who desires to see God 6 should mourn for the fall of the world! Truly it is written, "Whoever would be a friend of this world will be accounted an enemy of God." Indeed, he who does not rejoice at the approach of the ending of the world reveals that he was its friend, and will then be convicted as God's enemy. But let friendship for this world depart from the hearts of believers, and depart from those who believe in the other life to come and love it with their deeds. They should mourn for the destruction of the world who have planted the root of their heart in its love, who do not seek the life to come, nor even believe in it; but truly we, who well know the joys of the heavenly country, should resolutely hasten to it. We ought to wish that we might go to it quickly and arrive by the shorter way, for this world is afflicted with many tribulations, and tormented with depravity.

What is this mortal life but a way? Understand now what 7 it would be to grow weak through the toil of the way, and yet not to desire the way to end. The Lord said, "Behold these fig trees and all other trees, when they bring forth fruit then you know that summer is near. So too you may know, when you see these aforesaid signs, that God's kingdom is near." Truly by these words it is revealed that the fruit of this world is destruction. It grows so that it may fall; it sprouts that it may destroy with diseases whatever it had sprouted before. This world is like an aging person: in youth the body is thriving with strong breast, with full and healthy limbs, but in

fullum limum and halum, witodlice on ealdlicum gearum bið
· þæs mannes wæstm gebiged, his swura aslacod, his neb geri-
fod, and his lyma ealle gewæhte; his breost bið mid sicetun-
gum geðread, and betwux wordum his orðung ateorað. Þeah
ðe him adl on ne sitte, þeah forwel oft his hæl him bið adl.
Swa is ðisum middangearde: æt fruman he wæs ðeonde
swylce on geogoðhade, he wæs on lichamlicere hælðe
growende, and on speda genihtsumnysse fætt, langsum on
life, stille on langsumere sibbe. Ac he is nu mid ylde ofsett,
swylce mid gelomlæcendum hefigtymnyssum to deaðe
geðread. Mine gebroðra, ne lufige ge þisne middangeard þe
ge geseoð þæt lange wunian ne mæg. Be ðisum cwæð se
apostol, "Ne lufige ge middangeard, ne ða ðing ðe him on
wuniað, forðan swa hwa swa middangeard lufað næfð he
Godes lufe on him." Wel is Godes rice sumerlicere tide
wiðmeten, forði ðonne gewitað þa genipu ure dreorignysse,
and lifes dagas ðurh beorhtnysse þære ecan sunnan scinað.

8   Ealle ðas foresædan ðing sind mid micelre gewissunge
getrymde þurh ðisne æfterfyligendan cwyde: "Soð ic eow
secge, ne gewit ðeos mægð oðþæt ealle ðas ðing gewurðað."
Þas word spræc Drihten to Iudeiscre mægðe, and heora
cynn ne gewit þurh ateorunge ærðan ðe þes middangeard
geendað. Be ðisum andgite cwæð se apostol Paulus þæt
"Drihten sylf astihð of heofonum on stemne þæs heahengles
and mid Godes byman, and ða deadan ærest arisað; syððan
we ðe lybbað and on lichaman beoð gemette beoð gelæhte
forð mid þam oðrum on wolcnum togeanes Criste, and we
swa symle syððan mid Gode beoð. Frefriað eow mid þisum
wordum." Eac on ðisum andgite geðwærlæhð se godspellere
Matheus þisum wordum: "Drihten asent his englas mid byman and micelre stemne, and hi gaderiað his gecorenan fram

older years one's stature is bowed, his neck slackened, his face wrinkled, and his limbs all afflicted; his breast is tormented with sighs, and between his words his breath fails. Even if disease does not sit on him, yet very often his health is itself a disease to him. So it is with this world: in the beginning it was thriving as in youth, it was growing in bodily health, and fat in abundance of good things, long in life, quiet in longer peace. But now it is oppressed with age, as if with frequent tribulations afflicted to death. My brothers, do not love this world which as you see cannot long endure. Of this the apostle said, "Do not love the world, nor anything that dwells in it, for whoever loves the world does not have God's love in him." Well is the kingdom of God compared with the summer season, for then the clouds of our dreariness pass away, and the days of life shine through the brightness of the eternal sun.

All these aforesaid things are confirmed with great certainty by this following statement: "Truly I say unto you, this generation will not pass away until all these things take place." The Lord spoke these words to the Jewish people, and their tribe will not pass away through decay before this world ends. Of this knowledge the apostle Paul said that "the Lord himself will descend from heaven with the voice of the archangel and with the trumpet of God, and the dead will first arise; afterward we who live and are found in the body will be caught forth with the others in clouds to Christ, and so we will forever after be with God. Comfort yourselves with these words." The Evangelist Matthew agrees with this knowledge in these words: "The Lord will send his angels with trumpet and loud voice, and they will gather his

8

feower windum, of eallum eorðlicum gemærum oð ða healican heofonan."

9   Se apostol cwæð, "we ðe lybbað." Ne mænde he hine sylfne mid þam worde, ac ða ðe on life þurhwuniað oþ geendunge þyssere worulde. Mid þam is eac geswutelod þæt mancynn mid ealle ne ateorað ær ðære geendunge, ac hi habbað hwæðere sceortne deað, þa ðe þonne on life gemette beoð; forðan ðe heofonlic fyr ofergæð ealne middangeard mid anum bryne, and ða deadan arisað of heora byrgenum mid ðam fyre, and ða lybbendan beoð acwealde þurh ðæs fyres hætan, and ðærrihte eft geedcucode to ecum ðingum. Ne derað þæt fyr nan ðing þam rihtwisum ðe ær fram synnum geclænsode wæron; ac swa hwa swa ungeclænsod bið he gefret þæs fyres æðm, and we ðonne ealle to ðam dome becumað. Ne bið se dom on nanum eorðlicum felda gedemed, ac bið swa swa se apostol her wiðufan on þyssere rædinge cwæð, þæt we beoð gegripene on wolcnum togeanes Criste, geond þas lyft; and þær bið seo twæming rihtwisra manna and arleasra. Þa rihtwisan nahwar syððan ne wuniað buton mid Gode on heofonan rice, and ða arleasan nahwar buton mid deofle on helle suslum.

10   Se Hælend beleac þis godspel mid þisum wordum: "Heofen and eorðe gewitað, and mine word næfre ne gewitað." Ne awendað heofon and eorðe to nahte, ac hi beoð awende of ðam hiwe ðe hi nu on wuniað to beteran hiwe, swa swa Iohannes se godspellere cwæð, "Þonne bið niwe heofon and niwe eorðe." Ne beoð witodlice oðre gesceapene, ac ðas beoð geedniwode. Heofon and eorðe gewitað, and ðeah ðurhwuniað, forðan ðe hi beoð fram ðam hiwe ðe hi nu habbað þurh fyr geclænsode, and swaðeah symle on heora gecynde standað. Þonne bið seo sunne be seofonfealdum

chosen from the four winds, from all the borders of the earth to the high heavens."

The apostle said, "we who live." He did not mean himself 9 by those words, but those who continue in life until the ending of this world. By that it is also revealed that humanity will not wholly perish before the ending, but that those who will then be found alive will nevertheless have a short death; for heavenly fire will pass over all the world with one burning, and the dead will rise from their graves with that fire, and the living will be killed by the fire's heat, and at once revived for eternity. The fire will in no way harm the righteous who had been cleansed from sins beforehand; but whoever is uncleansed will feel the fire's breath, and then we will all come to judgment. The judgment will not be judged on any earthly field, but will be as the apostle said in this reading above, that we will be seized up in the clouds to Christ, through the air; and there will be the separation of the righteous and impious. The righteous will afterward dwell nowhere but with God in the kingdom of heaven, and the impious nowhere but with the devil in the torments of hell.

The savior concluded this gospel with these words: 10 "Heaven and earth will pass away, but my words will never pass away." Heaven and earth will not turn to nothing, but they will be changed from the form in which they now exist to a better form, as John the Evangelist said, "Then there will be a new heaven and a new earth." Others will not be created, but these will be renewed. Heaven and earth will pass away, but yet will continue, for they will be cleansed by fire from the form which they now have, and will yet stand forever in their own nature. Then the sun will be seven times

beorhtre þonne heo nu sy, and se mona hæfð þære sunnan leoht.

11 Dauid soðlice be Cristes tocyme þisum wordum witegode: "God cymð swutellice, and he ne suwað. Fyr byrnð on his gesihðe, and on his ymbhwyrfte bið swiðlic storm." Se storm aðwyhð swa hwæt swa þæt fyr forswælð. Be ðam dæge cwæð se witega Sofonias, "Se miccla Godes dæg is swiðe gehende, and ðearle swift. Biter bið þæs dæges stemn; þær bið se stranga gedrefed. Se dæg is yrres dæg, and gedrefednysse dæg and angsumnysse, yrmðe dæg and wanunge, þeostra dæg and dimnysse, byman dæg and cyrmes."

12 Mine gebroðra, settað þises dæges gemynd ætforan eowrum eagum, and swa hwæt swa bið nu hefigtyme geðuht, eal hit bið on his wiðmetennysse geliðegod. Gerihtlæcað eower lif and awendað eowre ðeawas, witniað mid wope eowre yfelan dæda, wiðstandað deofles costnungum; bugað fram yfele and doð god, and ge beoð swa micclum orsorgran on tocyme þæs ecan deman, swa micclum swa ge nu his strecnysse mid ege forhradiað. Se witega cwæð þæt se miccla Godes dæg is swiðe gehende and þearle swyft. Þeah ðe gyt wære oðer þusend geara to ðam dæge, nære hit langsum; forðan swa hwæt swa geendað þæt bið sceort and hræd, and bið swilce hit næfre ne gewurde, þonne hit geendod bið. Hwæt þeah hit langsum wære to ðam dæge, swa hit nis, þeah ne bið ure tima langsum, and on ure geendunge us bið gedemed hwæðer we on reste oþþe on wite ðone gemænelican dom anbidian sceolon. Uton forþi brucan þæs fyrstes þe us God forgeaf, and geearnian þæt ece lif mid him se þe leofað and rixað on ealra worulda woruld. Amen.

EXPLICIT HIC LIBER

brighter than it is now, and the moon will have the light of the sun.

Truly David prophesied Christ's coming in these words: "God will come clearly, and he will not be silent. Fire will burn in his sight, and around him will be a mighty storm." The storm will wash whatever the fire burns. Of that day the prophet Zephaniah said, "The great day of God is very near at hand, and exceedingly swift. Bitter will be the voice of that day; there the strong will be afflicted. That day is a day of wrath, and a day of affliction and anxiety, a day of misery and wailing, a day of darkness and dimness, a day of the trumpet and of outcry." 11

My brothers, set the remembrance of this day before your eyes, and whatever now appears troublesome, it shall all be diminished by comparison with it. Correct your lives and change your conduct, punish your evil deeds with weeping, withstand the temptations of the devil; turn from evil and do good, and the more you now anticipate his severity with fear, the more secure you will be at the coming of the eternal judge. The prophet said that the great day of God is very near at hand and very swift. Even if there were yet another thousand years to that day, it would not be long; for whatever ends is short and quick, and when it is ended it will be as if it had never been. Lo, though it might be long to that day, as it is not, yet our time will not be long, and at our ending it will be determined whether we should await the universal judgment in rest or in torment. Let us therefore use the time which God has given us, and merit the eternal life with him who lives and reigns for ever and ever. Amen. 12

HERE ENDS THIS BOOK

Abbreviations

For manuscript sigla, see the Note on the Text.

ASE = *Anglo-Saxon England*

ASMMF = Anglo-Saxon Manuscripts in Microfiche Facsimile

Bede, *Homiliae* = Bede, *Homiliae evangelii,* ed. David Hurst, *Homiliarum evangelii libri* II, in *Opera homiletica; Opera rhythmica,* ed. David Hurst and J. Fraipont, CCSL 122 (Turnhout, 1955)

CCCM = Corpus Christianorum Continuatio Mediaevalis

CCSL = Corpus Christianorum Series Latina

CH 1 = Ælfric's *Catholic Homilies,* First Series

CH 2 = Ælfric's *Catholic Homilies,* Second Series

Clemoes, *First Series* = *Ælfric's Catholic Homilies: The First Series,* ed. Peter Clemoes, EETS s.s. 17 (Oxford, 1997)

CSASE = Cambridge Studies in Anglo-Saxon England

EEMF = Early English Manuscripts in Facsimile

EETS = Early English Text Society: o.s. = original series; s.s. = supplementary series

G/L = Helmut Gneuss and Michael Lapidge, *Anglo-Saxon Manuscripts: A Bibliographical Handlist of Manuscript and Manuscript Fragments Written or Owned in England up to 1100* (Toronto, 2014)

Godden, *Introduction* = Malcolm Godden, *Ælfric's Catholic Homilies: Introduction, Commentary, and Glossary,* EETS s.s. 18 (Oxford, 2000)

Godden, *Second Series* = *Ælfric's Catholic Homilies: The Second Series,* ed. Malcolm Godden, EETS s.s. 5 (Oxford, 1979)

Gregory, *Homiliae in evangelia* = Gregory the Great, *Homiliae in evangelia,* ed. Raymond Étaix, CCSL 141 (Turnhout, 1999)

JEGP = Journal of English and Germanic Philology

Ker, *Catalogue* = N. R. Ker, *Catalogue of Manuscripts Containing Anglo-Saxon* (Oxford, 1957)

Lives of Saints = Ælfric, *Old English Lives of Saints,* ed. and trans. Mary Clayton and Juliet Mullins, 3 vols., DOML 58–60 (Cambridge, MA, 2019)

Mombritius, *Sanctuarium* = Boninus Mombritius, ed., *Sanctuarium seu vitae sanctorum,* 2nd ed. (Paris, 1910; repr., Hildesheim and New York, 1978)

MRTS = Medieval and Renaissance Texts and Studies

PL = *Patrologia Latina,* ed. J.-P. Migne, 221 vols. (Paris, 1844–1865)

Pope, *Homilies* = John C. Pope, ed., *Homilies of Ælfric: A Supplementary Collection,* 2 vols. EETS o.s. 259 and 260 (Oxford, 1967–1968)

RES = Review of English Studies

Note on the Text

The *Catholic Homilies* survive in whole or part in more than two dozen manuscripts and fragments, which represent various stages in the composition, publication, dissemination, and fragmentation of the collection. For a comprehensive look at this complex history, see Clemoes, *First Series,* 64–168. After composing the *Catholic Homilies* Ælfric revised and rethought them throughout his writing career. As copies were made, scribes introduced further changes and errors, adding additional layers to the complexity of the work's textual history. The manuscripts are referred to here by the letters (called *sigla*) that are commonly used in Ælfric studies. These are most thoroughly laid out in Clemoes, *First Series,* and Aaron J. Kleist, *The Chronology and Canon of Ælfric of Eynsham,* Anglo-Saxon Studies 37 (Cambridge, 2019).

In addition to their notices in Ker, *Catalogue,* and G/L, most of the manuscripts discussed below are given full descriptions in ASMMF, and in Orietta Da Rold, Takako Kato, Mary Swan, and Elaine M. Treharne, eds., *The Production and Use of English Manuscripts 1060 to 1220* (Leicester, 2010–2013), online at https://www.le.ac.uk/english/em1060to1220/index .html; individual detailed descriptions can be found by searching that site. A few manuscripts containing only fragmentary texts or small excerpts are not listed here.

A = London, British Library, Royal 7 c.xii (Ker, *Catalogue* 257, G/L 472; last decade of the tenth century, Cerne Abbas, Dorset)

Manuscript A is one of only four manuscripts of the complete series of CH 1 (the others are H, K, and Q). It represents a first composition, possibly made from Ælfric's own unbound texts; shortly after its completion it received over a thousand authorial revisions, some of which are probably in Ælfric's own hand. Manuscript A is the basis of Clemoes's edition and is generally considered to be the best evidence for the work's original composition. It has been reproduced in facsimile and described in Norman Eliason and Peter Clemoes, eds., *Ælfric's First Series of Catholic Homilies, British Museum Royal 7. C. xii, Fols. 4–218,* EEMF 13 (Copenhagen, 1965), and see the description in Jonathan Wilcox, ed., *ASMMF 17: Homilies by Ælfric and other Homilies* (Tempe, AZ, 2008), 37–52.

B = Oxford, Bodleian Library, Bodley 343 (Ker, *Catalogue* 310, not in G/L; second half of the twelfth century, West Midlands, probably Worcester or Hereford)

Manuscript B is a collection of homilies by Ælfric and others. Material from CH 1 and CH 2 is generally separate from other homilies but sometimes mixed and reorganized, and partially ordered into a yearly cycle of *temporale* and *sanctorale* homilies from Advent to the Common of the Saints. The manuscript appears to be in several self-contained sections and may have been copied from different exemplars.

Though it is a late manuscript with a great many idiosyncra-
sies, some of its readings appear to go back to early stages of
Ælfric's composition. Susan Irvine, ed., *Old English Homi-
lies from MS Bodley 343,* EETS o.s. 302 (Oxford, 1993), edits
seven non-Ælfrician texts unique to this manuscript and
provides a detailed description. See also the description in
Wilcox, *ASMMF* 17, pp. 69–100, and the discussion in Aidan
Conti, "The Circulation of the Old English Homily in the
Twelfth Century: New Evidence from Oxford, Bodleian Li-
brary, MS. Bodley 343," in *The Old English Homily: Precedent,
Practice, and Appropriation,* ed. Aaron J. Kleist, Studies in the
Early Middle Ages 17 (Turnhout, 2007), 365–402.

C = Cambridge, Corpus Christi College 303 (Ker, *Catalogue* 57, not in
G/L; first half of the twelfth century, probably Rochester)

Manuscript C contains a collection of homilies, mostly by
Ælfric, rearranged in an incomplete sequence for the *temporale* (in two sections, pp. 1–75 and 211–90) and *sanctorale*
(pp. 76–202), along with other miscellaneous items by Ælfric. The manuscript combines Ælfric's homilies from CH 1
and 2 and his *Lives of Saints,* along with shorter works by
Ælfric and anonymous works. The manuscript is described
in Timothy Graham, Raymond J. S. Grant, Peter J. Lucas,
and Elaine M. Treharne, *ASMMF* 11, *Corpus Christi College,
Cambridge I,* MRTS 265 (Tempe, AZ, 2000), 55–66. The texts
from CH 1 in C are related to those in the second volume of
D (Oxford, Bodleian Library, Bodley 340 and 342), another
manuscript possibly from Rochester; some items are related
to F (Cambridge, Corpus Christi College 162), probably from
Canterbury; see Godden, *Second Series,* xxxii–xxxvii.

D = Oxford, Bodleian Library, Bodley 340 and 342 (Ker, *Catalogue* 309, G/L 569; beginning of the eleventh century, Canterbury or Rochester)

Manuscript D is a large collection, now split into two volumes, containing CH 1 and 2, along with some additional material, combined into a single sequence for the full liturgical year from Christmas to Advent; for more on this practice of combining homilies from CH 1 and 2, see the description of O below. The manuscript is mainly in one hand and has been heavily corrected and altered in hands ranging from the eleventh century to the fourteenth. The contents are very similar to E. Manuscript D has been described in Jonathan Wilcox, *ASMMF* 17, pp. 53–69. A detailed discussion is found in Kenneth Sisam, "MSS. Bodley 340 and 342: Ælfric's *Catholic Homilies*," *RES* 7 (1931): 7–27; reprinted in *Studies in the History of Old English Literature,* by Kenneth Sisam (Oxford, 1953), 148–98. See also Clemoes, *First Series,* 7–10.

E = Cambridge, Corpus Christi College 198 (Ker, *Catalogue* 48, G/L 64; second half of the eleventh century, later additions from Worcester)

Manuscript E is described by Clemoes, *First Series,* as "an orderly set of homilies for Sundays and festivals" (11). Homilies are by Ælfric and others; material from CH 1 is roughly in sequence, but interspersed with homilies from CH 2 and others by anonymous authors. The series runs from Christmas to the feast of Saint Paul (June 30), and is supplemented with material on separate quires, added at the appropriate points in the Church year. Some of these additions are contemporary with the main hands in the manuscript. Manuscript E is described by Peter J. Lucas, *ASMMF* 25, *Corpus Christi College, Cambridge, II* (Tempe, AZ, 2016), 73–98. See also Clemoes, *First Series,* 10–13. Generally speaking, E appears to be a reorganized but incomplete version of the homiliary found in D, with nearly the same contents in the same order; see Godden, *Second Series,* xxviii–xxxi.

F = Cambridge, Corpus Christi College 162, pp. 1–138 and 161–564 (Ker, *Catalogue* 38, G/L 50 and 54; beginning of the eleventh century, southeast, possibly Saint Augustine's Abbey in Canterbury)

Manuscript F contains homilies from CH 1 and 2, along with other homilies by Ælfric and others, rearranged mostly in the order of the *temporale* for the liturgical year, from the second Sunday after Epiphany to the second Sunday in Advent. It is textually close to D and E; the three manuscripts DEF represent an early stage of the circulation of CH 1, possibly deriving from a copy sent to Archbishop Sigeric in Canterbury, with numerous small alterations and additions not necessarily authorized by Ælfric (Clemoes, *First Series,* 67–68). Manuscript F has been described by Lucas, *ASMMF* 25, pp. 19–40, and see also Donald G. Scragg, "Cambridge Corpus Christi College 162," in *Anglo-Saxon Manuscripts and Their Heritage,* ed. Philip Pulsiano and Elaine M. Treharne (Aldershot, 1998), 71–83.

G = London, British Library, Cotton Vespasian D.xiv (Ker, *Catalogue* 209, G/L 392; middle of the twelfth century, Canterbury or Rochester)

Manuscript G is a collection of homiletic and hagiographical works, containing fifty-three texts. About half of these are works by Ælfric, mostly from CH 1 and 2; many of these are extracts rather than whole texts. The manuscript is mainly in one hand, but the general lack of any clear organizing principle gives it the feel of a commonplace book or collection rather than a carefully constructed volume. Items from CH 1 and 2 are textually related to DEF. Manuscript G has been described in Jonathan Wilcox, *ASMMF* 8, *Wulfstan Texts and Other Homiletic Materials* (Tempe, AZ, 2000), 53–64.

H = London, British Library, Cotton Vitellius C.v (Ker, *Catalogue* 220, G/L 403; late tenth or early eleventh century)

Manuscript H was badly damaged by fire in 1731 but originally contained a full set of CH 1 homilies, in order. These were supplemented by other homilies by Ælfric, including some from CH 2, with some added at the end of CH 1, and others interpolated between CH 1 homilies at the appropriate points in the liturgical year. The manuscript is one of only four copies of the complete First Series (the others are A, K, and Q). It is described in Wilcox, *ASMMF* 17, pp. 21–36.

J = London, British Library, Cotton Cleopatra B.xiii, fols. 1–58, and London, Lambeth Palace 489 (Ker, *Catalogue* 144 and 283, G/L 322/323 and 520; third quarter of the eleventh century, Exeter)

The *siglum* J designates two manuscripts, once together but now separated. They contain what may once have been a full set of homilies, with material and extracts mostly from CH 1, along with some anonymous homilies and teaching texts. Cotton Cleopatra B.xiii was rearranged, probably in the sixteenth century, and is not in its original order; a description can be found in Wilcox, *ASMMF* 8, pp. 23–29. Lambeth 489 contains eight homilies, five of which are from CH 1; a description can be found in Wilcox, *ASMMF* 8, pp. 79–82, and see Clemoes, *First Series,* 21–24.

K = Cambridge, University Library Gg. 3. 28 (Ker, *Catalogue* 15, G/L 11; end of the tenth century, possibly Cerne Abbas, Dorset, and later in Durham)

Manuscript K, the base text for this edition, contains a complete set of CH 1 and 2, in order (with a few pages missing), along with Latin and English prefaces and a few other short Latin texts all by Ælfric, including the *Ammonitio* (a warning against drunkenness, before CH 2.1), *De sancta Maria* (explaining why he is reluctant to write about the origins of Mary, after CH 2.31), *Excusatio dictantis* (explaining why he does not include a passion of Thomas, after CH 2.34), a formulaic closing, or *explicit,* to CH 2, and an *oratio* (after the *explicit*) in which Ælfric explains that the homilies are to teach the unlearned, says (prematurely, as it turned out) that he is through with such work, and urges scribes to make accurate copies. After CH 2 are other works by Ælfric, including *De temporibus anni,* a collection of prayers in English, and the pastoral letter for Bishop Wulfsige of Sherborne. For *De temporibus anni,* see Martin Blake, ed., *Ælfric's "De temporibus anni,"* Anglo-Saxon Texts 6 (Cambridge, 2009); for the prayers, see Donald G. Bzydl, "The Sources of Ælfric's Prayers in Cambridge University Library MS. Gg. 3. 28," *Notes and Queries* 24 (1977): 98–102; for the letter, Dorothy Whitelock, Martin Brett, and Christopher N. L. Brooke, eds., *Councils and Synods, with Other Documents Relating to the English Church I, A.D. 871–1204; I. 871–1066* (Oxford, 1981), 196–226.

This is the only manuscript of Ælfric's work to contain all of both series of *Catholic Homilies* in order, the only manuscript of the full Second Series of homilies, and the only copy of the prefaces to CH 1 and CH 2. The remarkable degree of completeness and organization in the manuscript, along with the fidelity of the text and the fact that its contents are all by Ælfric, led Clemoes to characterize it as representing "the standard product of Ælfric's scriptorium" (*First Series,* 161). Robert K. Upchurch, "Shepherding the Shepherds in the Ways of Pastoral Care: Ælfric and Cambridge University Library, MS Gg.3.28," in *Saints and Scholars: New Perspectives on Anglo-Saxon Literature and Culture in Honour of Hugh Magennis,* ed. Stuart McWilliams (Cambridge, 2012), 54–74 (at 55), states that "no other Ælfrician manuscript contains so comprehensive a set of texts assembled for the clergy's use or furnishes so complete an overview of pastoral preaching, preparation and practice as Ælfric imagined ought to be between 995 and 1000." We do not know whether K was written at Cerne Abbas, or at Ælfric's alma mater at Winchester, or perhaps as a faithful copy, made in Canterbury, of the book Ælfric sent to Sigeric, but its source is undoubtedly close to Ælfric himself. It was sent to Durham at some point before the twelfth century, where it appears in a catalog of Durham Cathedral Priory as *Omeliaria vetera duo,* "two old books of homilies." The manuscript is described in Wilcox, *ASMMF* 17, pp. 1–20.

L = Cambridge, University Library Ii. 1. 33 (Ker, *Catalogue* 18, not in G/L; second half of the twelfth century, Rochester or Christ Church Canterbury, later Ely)

Manuscript L is a collection of saints' lives and homilies, mostly by Ælfric, along with penitential material and Ælfric's translation of Genesis. Texts from CH 1 and 2, mainly the hagiographical homilies, are mixed with material from

Ælfric's *Lives of Saints.* The manuscript was "possibly assembled over time"; Orietta Da Rold, "Cambridge, University Library, Ii. 1. 33," in Da Rold, Kato, Swan, and Treharne, *The Production and Use of English Manuscripts 1060 to 1220.* Material from CH 1 and 2 is textually similar to the versions found in K. Manuscript L is described in Rolf H. Bremmer and Kees Dekker, *ASMMF 21, Saints' Lives and Homilies* (Tempe, AZ, 2013), 1–20, and in William Schipper, "A Composite Old English Homiliary from Ely: Cambr. Univ. Lib. MS Ii.1.33," *Transactions of the Cambridge Bibliographical Society* 8 (1983): 285–98. See also Oliver Traxel, *Language Change, Writing and Textual Interference in Post-Conquest Old English Manuscripts: The Evidence of Cambridge, University Library, Ii.1.33* (Frankfurt am Main, 2004).

M = Cambridge, University Library Ii. 4. 6 (Ker, *Catalogue* 21, G/L 18; middle of the eleventh century, New Minster in Winchester)

Manuscript M contains homilies for the *temporale,* including Sundays and feast days, organized according to the Church year, from the Second Sunday of Epiphany to the Sunday after Pentecost. It may once have contained a complete set of *temporale* homilies. Two homilies for Rogationtide are displaced to the end of the set. All homilies (except for two Rogationtide homilies in the main sequence) are by Ælfric, and combine material from CH 1 and 2. Some homilies are composite texts from various sources, but may have authorial text that is not found in A or K; on these, see Malcolm Godden, "Old English Composite Homilies from Winchester," *ASE* 4 (1975): 57–65. The manuscript is closely related to N and O. The manuscript is described by Bremmer and Dekker, *ASMMF 21,* pp. 21–34, and see Loredana Teresi, "Ælfric's or Not? The Making of a *Temporale* Collection in Late Anglo-Saxon England," in Kleist, *The Old English Homily: Precedent, Practice and Appropriation*, 284–310.

N = London, British Library, Cotton Faustina A.ix (Ker, *Catalogue* 153, not in G/L; first half of the twelfth century, possibly southeastern)

Manuscript N contains homilies for the *temporale*, including Sundays and feast days from Epiphany to Pentecost. It may once have contained a complete set of *temporale* homilies. Ælfrician material from CH 1, CH 2, and other homilies, some of them excerpted, appears alongside anonymous homilies from other sources to cover Sundays for which Ælfric did not write homilies. The manuscript is closely related to M and O; see Godden, *Second Series,* xlvii–l. The manuscript is described in Bremmer and Dekker, *ASMMF 21,* pp. 75–88, and in Elaine M. Treharne, "The Dates and Origins of Three Twelfth-Century Old English Manuscripts," in Pulsiano and Treharne, *Anglo-Saxon Manuscripts and Their Heritage,* 227–53.

O = Cambridge, Corpus Christi College 302 (Ker, *Catalogue* 56, G/L 86; end of the eleventh century)

Manuscript O is a *temporale* collection with homilies, mainly by Ælfric, organized according to the Church year. The manuscript is incomplete, containing texts for occasions from Advent to Rogationtide, but may originally have contained a complete *temporale* sequence. Texts from CH 1 and 2 are mixed with texts from Ælfric's *Lives of Saints* and other homilies, as well as a homily by Wulfstan and some anonymous texts. It is closely related to M and (especially) N; see Godden, *Second Series,* l–li. The manuscript is described by Graham, Grant, Lucas, and Treharne, *ASMMF* 11, pp. 48–54.

All three manuscripts—M, N, and O—appear to reflect concerted efforts to compile selected homilies from CH 1 and 2 into a full-year collection for the *temporale* (all the annual feasts of the Church apart from the saints' days). Whether this was done by Ælfric himself or by others is not clear. There are features of MNO that suggest revision by Ælfric himself, and Clemoes has argued that these three manuscripts represent a late stage in his development of the *Catholic Homilies;* see Clemoes *First Series,* 78–83. Expanded texts for some homilies (see the Notes to the Translation for CH 1.8, CH 1.17, and CH 1.18) appear to be by Ælfric, and may indicate that he himself was responsible for reorganizing his two series of homilies into a full *temporale* cycle. But the presence of authorial additions or alterations does not necessarily mean that Ælfric himself supervised these collections, only that the compilers had access to later copies of CH 1 that had Ælfric's revisions in them. Teresi suggests instead that the *temporale* series represented by M and NO was assembled independently and without Ælfric's supervision: "anyone who had access to Ælfric's material (the two series of *Catholic Homilies,* his *Lives of Saints,* and the few supplementary items needed to fill the gaps) would have been able to make a similar collection" ("Ælfric's or Not?," 298).

P = Oxford, Bodleian Library, Hatton 115; one leaf survives in Lawrence, KS, Kenneth Spencer Research Library, Pryce C2:2 (Ker, *Catalogue* 332, G/L 639; second half of the eleventh century, probably southeastern, later in Worcester)

Manuscript P is a collection of booklets containing some thirty works by Ælfric, along with some anonymous texts and a partial Wulfstan homily. The Ælfrician works are from CH 1 and 2, in short sequences mixed with other works, and from *Lives of Saints* and other works. The main hand is the same as London, British Library, Cotton Faustina A.x. The manuscript is textually related to G (Godden, *Second Series,* lxviii). It is described by Christine Franzen, *ASMMF* 6, *Worcester Manuscripts* (Tempe, AZ, 1998), 44–54; see also Treharne, "Dates and Origins."

Q = Cambridge, Corpus Christi College 188 (Ker, *Catalogue* 43, G/L 58; second quarter of the eleventh century)

Manuscript Q contains a nearly complete series of the homilies in CH 1 (it is lacking CH 1.1 and CH 1.21), in order, augmented with some other homilies by Ælfric. CH 1.17 includes a long continuation based on Ezekiel 34:2–16; CH 1.39 has an authorial addition adapted from the English Preface to CH 1. These are printed in Clemoes, *First Series,* 535–42 (Appendix B.3) and 175–76, respectively. Manuscript Q appears to represent a late stage in Ælfric's revisions of the homilies. Other copies reflecting this late stage are R, S, and T. It is described by Lucas, *ASMMF* 25, pp. 59–72.

R = Cambridge, Corpus Christi College 178, pp. 1–270, and Cambridge, Corpus Christi College 162, pp. 139–60 (Ker, *Catalogue* 41a, G/L 54; first half of the eleventh century, Worcester)

Manuscript R is a collection of homilies and texts, all probably by Ælfric. The leaves now in Cambridge, Corpus Christi College 162 were probably moved there by Archbishop Matthew Parker in the late sixteenth century. The first part of the manuscript contains homilies for general occasions; the second part reorganizes some homilies from CH 1 and 2 into a sequence for the *temporale* and *sanctorale* from Christmas to Pentecost. Ælfrician material from CH 1 is related textually to Q and derives from Worcester (Clemoes, *First Series*, 156). The manuscript is described by Lucas, *ASMMF* 25, pp. 19–58.

S = Oxford, Bodleian Library, Hatton 116 (Ker, *Catalogue* 333, not in G/L; first half of the twelfth century, probably Worcester)

Manuscript S is a collection of homilies, mainly for saints' days, from the early or mid twelfth century. Most texts are by Ælfric, drawn from the hagiographical homilies in CH 1. Texts in the second part of the manuscript are various works by Ælfric and are closely related to those in R. It is described by Wilcox, *ASMMF* 17, pp. 101–10, and see also Clemoes, *First Series*, 40–41.

T = Oxford, Bodleian Library, Hatton 113 and 114, and Junius 121 (Ker, *Catalogue* 338 and 331, G/L 637, 638, 644; third quarter of the eleventh century, Worcester)

Manuscript T consists of a two-volume collection of homilies, Hatton 113 and 114, which were originally one volume, and which form a continuation of the episcopal material in Junius 121, a copy of Archbishop Wulfstan's "Commonplace Book." Most of the material in Hatton 113 is by Wulfstan, but excerpts from CH 1 and CH 2 appear at the end of the manuscript. Most of the homilies in Hatton 114 are by Ælfric, mixing CH 1 and CH 2 homilies roughly in the order of the liturgical year, with a number of homilies for saint's feasts. Junius 121 contains material by or related to Wulfstan

and has only two homilies from CH 1 (for Advent), plus
the English Preface adapted as a homily (as in P) and one
from CH 2. Manuscript T is described by Franzen, *ASMMF*
6, pp. 26–44 and 56–69; see also Hans Sauer, "The Trans-
mission and Structure of Archbishop Wulfstan's 'Commonplace Book,'" in *Old English Prose: Basic Readings,* ed. Paul E.
Szarmach (New York, 2000), 339–93.

U = Cambridge, Trinity College B.15.34 (Ker, *Catalogue* 86, G/L 177;
middle of the eleventh century, probably Christ Church, Canterbury)

Manuscript U is an ordered collection of homilies for the
temporale, with twenty-five homilies by Ælfric for Sundays
and festivals from Easter to the Eleventh Sunday after Pentecost. The collection is imperfect and may have been longer.
Texts are in an order similar to that in M; homilies from CH
1 and 2 are mixed together along with other homilies by Ælfric, other texts by Ælfric, and a few anonymous homilies. It
is textually similar to H (Godden, *Second Series,* lxx–lxxi).
The manuscript is described by Jonathan Wilcox in Peter
Lucas and Jonathan Wilcox, *ASMMF* 16, *Manuscripts Relating to Dunstan, Ælfric, and Wulfstan; the "Eadwine Psalter"
Group* (Tempe, AZ, 1997), 17–26.

V = Cambridge, Corpus Christi College 419 and 421 (Ker, *Catalogue*
68 and 69, G/L 108 and 109; first half of the eleventh century, possibly
Canterbury; additions from the third quarter of the eleventh century,
Exeter)

Manuscript V is a collection of homilies supplemented by
the addition of other material; the added material was written in Exeter. Cambridge, Corpus Christi College 419 con-

tains material mostly by Wulfstan and anonymous authors, with some material by Ælfric, including his homilies for Rogationtide and Ascension (CH 1.18–21). The first part of Cambridge, Corpus Christi College 421, added to the manuscript in Exeter in the later eleventh century, contains material by Ælfric, mixing material for general occasions from CH 1 and 2. Parts of these additions are by the scribe of J. There is a description in Wilcox, *ASMMF* 8, pp. 7–13, and in Erika Corradini, "The Composite Nature of Eleventh-Century Homiliaries: Cambridge, Corpus Christi College 421," in *Textual Cultures: Cultural Texts, Essays and Studies,* ed. Orietta Da Rold and Elaine M. Treharne (Woodbridge, 2010), 5–19.

X^g = London, British Library, Cotton Vespasian A.xxii, fols. 54–59 (not in Ker, *Catalogue* or G/L; beginning of the thirteenth century, Rochester)

A small collection of very late Old English material, which forms the third part of a manuscript otherwise containing a Latin miscellany. Material by Ælfric includes versions of CH 1.1 ("On the Origin of the Created World") and CH 1.24 ("Fourth Sunday after Pentecost"), both adapted and abridged and accompanied by other anonymous texts. The quire is, unusually, ruled for two columns; see Mary Swan, "Preaching Past the Conquest: Lambeth Palace 487 and Cotton Vespasian A.xxii," in Kleist, *The Old English Homily: Precedent, Practice, and Appropriation,* 403–23 (at 414). Clemoes, *First Series,* 136, argues that the two Ælfrician pieces were copied from D. Its Ælfric texts are not collated here. There is a description of the manuscript in Wilcox, *ASMMF* 8, pp. 46–52, and Mary Richards, "MS Cotton Vespasian A. XXII: The Vespasian Homilies," *Manuscripta* 22 (1978): 97–103.

X^i = London, Lambeth Palace 487 (not in Ker, *Catalogue* or G/L; late twelfth or early thirteenth century, West Midlands, probably Worcestershire)

A small manuscript in early Middle English, X^i contains homilies and devotional texts. Many of its items are post-Conquest, but five homiletic texts reuse Old English works, some by Ælfric, including excerpts from two homilies in CH 1. These have been reshaped by the manuscript's compiler. The manuscript was "not the high-quality formal production of a prestigious scriptorium, or of a highly trained scribe" (Swan, "Preaching Past the Conquest," 413). Its Ælfrician texts are not collated here. It is described by Wilcox, *ASMMF* 8, pp. 72–78; by Swan, "Preaching Past the Conquest"; and by Celia Sisam, "The Scribal Tradition of the *Lambeth Homilies*," *RES* n.s. 2 (1951): 105–13.

THIS EDITION

As noted, A, H, K, and Q are the only surviving complete copies of the First Series of homilies. While A represents the earliest phase of composition, K represents the text as released for publication, "the definitive type of the homiletic products of Ælfric's scriptorium" (Clemoes, *First Series,* 69). The manuscript is in one main hand of the end of the tenth century or beginning of the eleventh; it was probably produced at Cerne Abbas, but was in Durham Cathedral Priory from at least the twelfth century, and was given to Cambridge University Library in 1574.

The text here is based on K, newly transcribed from the manuscript; where leaves are missing, the gaps have been supplied from A. Manuscript K was previously edited and translated by Benjamin Thorpe in 1844; Thorpe's transcription is incomplete (he left out many Old English passages providing gospel translations at the beginnings of homilies) but reasonably accurate. Both Thorpe's edition and the magnificent EETS edition of manuscript A by Clemoes (1997) were consulted in compiling the text, as were the editions of the English and Latin prefaces by Jonathan Wilcox, *Ælfric's Prefaces,* Durham Medieval Texts 9 (Durham, 1994). Following the editorial practices of the Dumbarton Oaks Medieval Library, the Old English text is presented in an accessible format, with modern paragraphing, punctuation, and capitalization added, Latin text set in italics, and abbreviations silently expanded; manuscript foliation and layout are not recorded. In the translation and notes, Latin orthography has been regularized, and names of people and places have been modernized.

In many places the main scribe of K makes corrections as he copies, adding a short word or missed letter above a word with a comma-like caret indicating where it belongs, as in CH 1.1.6, *Nast þu \na/,* or CH 1.1.11, *ne onbyri\g/de.* He corrects single letters in a word by putting a dot (called a *punctus*) under the letter and writing the correction above it, as in CH 1.2.13, *totwæman* corrected to *totwæm\o/n.* These are recorded in the Notes to the Text. Longer omissions, probably caused when the scribe's eye skipped from one line to another, are noted and supplied from A.

CH 1 survives in a large number of manuscripts with a vast range of textual variations; the list of variants recorded in the Notes to the Text is by no means complete. Differences between A (the basis for Clemoes's edition of CH 1) and K are recorded, but readings found in only one other manuscript are omitted, except for a few cases where a long passage was added to another manuscript. Variation in spelling and minor differences in word order and inflection, even where these may bear witness to Ælfric's evolving thinking on English grammar and style, are not recorded. For a complete list of variants and a thorough study of the relations between manuscripts, see the EETS editions of Clemoes and Godden.

The following symbols are used in the Notes to the Text:

\ / = addition to the manuscript by the scribe

<.> = erased characters

Notes to the Text

Manuscripts: The Latin Preface is found only in K, fols. 1r–1v; the English Preface is found in its entirety only in K, fols. 1v–3r, but the section on Antichrist (CH 1.0.6–10, *Men behofiað . . . for swylcum bebodum*) is adapted as a separate text in P, R, and T, and incorporated into CH 1.39 in Q.

1	Haegmonem: *last letter lost*
2	persuadentes: *last letters blurred*
	sive: *nearly illegible*
	speramus: *two letters blurred*
6	menn behofiað: PQRT *begin here*
	swiðost: and swiðost nu QRT
7	swa swa ure hælend . . . on anum hade: he bið begyten mid forlire of were and of wife; and he biþ mid deofles gaste afylled QRT
9	gehiwige: Be þam cwæþ se apostol Paulus þæt se Antecrist wyrcð mid bedydrunge and gedwymore þas wundra, swa þeah on Godes geþafunge for þam Iudeiscum þe noldon underfon Crist þe is soðfæstnys him to alysednysse, þæt hi underfon þone leasan Antecrist and hi his gedwyldum gelyfan him sylfum to forwyrde *added* QRT
10	bebodum: we secgað eow þas lare þæt ge æfre gelyfon on þone ælmihtigan God se þe ealle gesceafta gesceop þurh his mihte; þam sy wuldor and lof a to woruld. AMEN *added* PQRT, *which end here*
11	habere: \h/abere K

1. On the Origin of the Created World

Manuscripts: CH 1.1 is found in K, fols. 3r–7r. It is also found in A (with some text lost), B, D, E, F, G (an extract), H, J, R, X^g, and two fragments.

title	*varies in different manuscripts*
1	and ealle eorðe he belicð on his handa: *omitted* K
3	don: *omitted* BG
5	gelogode: Ac he wearð þurh deofles swicdome ut adræfd *added* G *(which ends here)*
6	Nast þu: Nast þu \na/ FK
7	genamode: nemde R; genemnode B
11	onbyrigde: onbyri\g/de K
	ealles: eal\les/ K
14	gehref: ge\h/ref K
	symble: sym\b/le K
15	adrenct: adren\c/t K
17	sume of treowe: sume eac of treowe BF; eac sume of treowe R
18	forneah: fornean *with* h *written above second* n K
19	Gabrihel: *found only in* FK; *not in other manuscripts*
20	getingnysse: \spæce/ *added above in a different hand* K
22	astah: ast\a/h K
23	ecnysse: ecnys\s/e K
	rixað: leofað and rixað a buton ende DF; rixaþ aa worulde E

2. The Nativity of the Lord

Manuscripts: CH 1.2 is found in K, fols. 7r–10r. It is also found in A, B, H, J, L, O, Q, and R.

title	*varies in different manuscripts*
1	se ðe æfre buton angynne of ðam ælmightigan Fæder acennyd wæs: *omitted* BK
4	us God æteowde: geworden is and God us geswutelode BOQ
5	foresende: foresende \ær/ K
6	geciged: gehaten BL
8	gehaten: geciged AHJL

Crist, se soða hlaf, acenned, ðe be him sylfum cwæð, "Ic eom se
liflica hlaf": acenned Crist se soða hlaf BOQR

11   næfre ne geendað: næfre \ne/ geendað K
      waclicum: wlaclicum K; wacum O
12   singendra: singend\r/a K
      Gloria in excelsis Deo, et in terra pax hominibus bonae volunta-
      tis; þæt is on urum gereorde: *omitted* K
13   totwæmon: *altered from* totwæman K; totwæman *other manu-
      scripts*
15   scyppende: Gode þe is scyppend ealra þinga O *and added to* J

3. SAINT STEPHEN

Manuscripts: CH 1.3 is found in K, fols. 10r–13r, and in A, D, E, H, L, M (an
extract), O, Q, T, and two fragments.

title *varies in different manuscripts*
2   ðurh hine spræc: he ymbe spræc DET
4   of ðære byrig: of ðære \byrig/ K *(with* byrig *in a different hand)*; of
       þære stowe L
       leasan gewitan: leas\an/ gewitan K *(with* an *in a different hand)*;
       leasan gewitan O; leasgewitan *other manuscripts*
       oftorfian: oftorfian<ne> *erased* K; torfienne OT; to oftorfienne
       other manuscripts
       onfoh: \vel under/ *written above* K; underfoh ADEHOQT
5   mannes Bearn standende: KL; mannes Bearn standan ADE
       HOQT
8   and Saulus wearð alysed; se arfæsta wæs gehyred: *omitted* DET
       gladað: \is/ gegladod T *(with* is *in a different hand)*; \his/ gegladod
       D *(with* his *in a different hand)*; wearð gegladod E
       Iudeiscra: iudeiscra manna DEHOQT
       oferwreah: ofeswyðde O; oferswað Q
       welwillende: we willendlice O; welwyllendlice Q; welwillendum T
       gebæd, and þærtoeacan: \ge/bæd, and þærtoe\a/can K
9   Gif ge forgyfað: Eft he cwyð. Gyf ge forgyfað M *(which begins
       here)*
       eower fæder: eower heofenlica fæder ADEHOQT

godspellere: god\s/pellere K

10   Godes freond; and na þæt an þæt ðu his freond sy, ac eac swilce
þu bist: *omitted* EO

on heofenum is: Þeah se mann habbe fullne geleafa and ælmyssan wyrce, and fela to gode gedo, eall him byð wel swa hwæt
swa he deþ buton he habbe soðe lufe to Gode and to eallum
Cristenum mannum. Seo soðe lufe is þæt gehwa his freond lufige on Gode and his feond for Gode *added* M

12   unrihtwisnysse: M *ends here*

4. Assumption of John the Evangelist

Manuscripts: CH 1.4 is found in K, fols. 13r–17r, and in A, D, E, H (with
some text lost), L, O, Q, T, and one fragment.

title	*varies in different manuscripts*
1	sunu: *altered from* suna K
	wearð ateorod: ateorode A
	gelufod: leof E; leof and gelufod O; \leof and/ gelufod T *(with* leof and *in a different hand)*
2	het bescufon: besceofon A
3	cystigum: cristenum D *(altered from* godum*)* ET
4	deorwurðan gymstanas: HKLQ; deorwurðan gimmas O; deor-wurðan stanas ADET
5	Þa heofenlican æhta sind us eallum gemæne: *omitted* OQ
	nacode we wæron acennede, and nacode we gewitað: *omitted* DET
	cyrcan duru: cyrcan DET
6	ða bær: ða bær \<man\> K
	þa wydewan: *omitted* LO
	ðæra: *altered from* ðære K
	and mid brastligendum ligum, mid unasecgendlicum witum af-yllede: *omitted* DT
8	menniscnysse: mennisc *written on erasure* K
	dyrstignesse: dyrsti\g/nesse K
	ealre þære godspellican gesetnysse: ealre \þære/ godspellican ge-setnys\se/ K

menniscnysse: mennis\c/nysse K
9 þe þa gyt ungeleaffulle: þe þa gytsunge geleaffulle D; þe þære
gytsunge geleaffulle E; þa þe þa gytsunge leaffulle O
clypiað ealle: KL; clypiað ADEHOQT
10 ðines Godes naman: ðines drihtnes naman DET
11 gerihta: HKL; lare T; riht ADEOQ
gesang: \ge/sang K
wæter: fæder DET
12 ðingunge: ðenunge ET
and Halgum Gaste: and mid Halgum Gaste T; and mid þam Halgan Gaste DO; and mid sune and mid Halgum Gaste E

5. The Feast of the Holy Innocents

Manuscripts: CH 1.5 is found in K, fols. 17v–20r, and in A, D, E, H, L, Q, T,
and a fragment.

title *varies in different manuscripts*
6 langsume fær: langsume \fær/ *(with* fær *in a different hand)* K
dægþerlicum: *omitted* DELT
7 cynecenne: cynne ET; \cyne/cynne *(with* cyne *in a different
hand)* D
8 æniges oðres: ænig oðer þing DT
9 fremian swa micclum swa: fremian swa DET
forste: *omitted* DT
forsodene: forsmorede DT
ðrowunge: \vel passionis/ *added above* K
10 gefrefrod: \ge/frefrod K
bewypð: beweop DET
11 innoð: lichaman DET
12 ricene: hraðe HQ
heofenlican æþelinges: æþelinges DET
13 þe is gehaten: *omitted* DET
forwurdon: for ðan þe Archelaus Herodes sunu ofsloh æfter his
fæder forðsiðe nigon þusenda þæra iudeiscra þegna *added* Q
14 ælmihtigum: *altered from* ælmihtigam K; Gode *added* DET

6. CIRCUMCISION

Manuscripts: CH 1.6 is found in K, fols. 20r–22v, and in A, B (with many passages abridged or omitted), D, E, H, Q, R, and T.

title	*varies in different manuscripts*
3	to þan swiðe þæt God behet eallum mancynne bletsunge: *omitted* BDET
5	tacen: tac\e/n K
	þære halgan æ: þære ealdan æ DT
	gehælð: gehealde A
6	mannum: *omitted* DE
7	lease Cristene: gehaten *added* DT
8	Cristes: drihtnes DET
	geares ymbryne: geares angin BQ
9	lengctenlicere: len\g/ctenlicere K
10	ælmihtiga: God *added* DET
	for his micclum: for miclum DET
11	sume: \sume/ K
	gedwæsmenn: gedwolmen BD

7. EPIPHANY

Manuscripts: CH 1.7 is found in K, fols. 22v–26v, and in A, D, E, H, Q, and T.

title	*varies in different manuscripts*
6	gescynd þa ða seo heofonlice healicnyss wearð: *omitted* DET
7	geswutelunge: \ge/swutelunge K
8	eallum: *altered from* eallam K
10	heora gedwylde: *omitted* DET
	wunað: leofað DET
11	stuntra: stun\t/ra K
	his agen: \cyre/ *added in a different hand* K; \agene cyre/ *added in a different hand* T
12	ðeah wære: þeahhwæðere DET
13	and eac ðæra modigra gasta and arleasra manna: *omitted* DET
	forwurðað: ne forwurðað DET

17   nateshwon: \na/teshwon K
        gedwolan: gedwolmen HQ

8. THIRD SUNDAY AFTER EPIPHANY

Manuscripts: CH 1.8 is found in K, fols. 26v–29v, and in A, B, C, D, E, F, H, M, N, and Q.

title   *varies in different manuscripts*
1   cum: cum autem BNQ
2   nanum menn: *omitted* CF
3   se lareow Hægmon: se lareow \awrat and/ E; se lareow þe þis
        godspel getrahtnode N
4   swiðe halwende: halwende CF
5   begripen: gegripæn C; gegripen D; gewri<.>en E; begriwen A;
        begrowen B
        swa eac he alysde: swa alysde he A
8   oðre: men *added* CDEF
        unðeawas: \un/ðeawas K
10   mid þam de: mid þam worde ðe CDEF
        godcundnysse: his godcundnysse CDEF
        sume for leofra: sume for heora leofra DEF; sume for heora.
        sume for heora leofra C
14   to gehyrenne: \to/ gehyrenne K
15   se dæg: Mine gebroðra, understandað þis—manega cumað fram
        eastdæle and westdæle and gerestað hi mid Abrahame and
        Isaace and Iacobe on heofonan rice. Ne mæg nan eorðlic cyning
        cynelic lybban buton he hæbbe ðegenas, and swa gelogodne
        hired swa his cynescipe gerisan mæge. Hwæt wenst ðu la, nele
        se ælmihtiga cyning þe gesceop heofonas and eorðan habban
        ormætne hired þe him mid rixie? Fela he wile habban of man-
        ncynne to his heofonlican hirede, and gehwa hæft ðær þone
        weorðscipe be ðam ðe he her on worulde geearnode. *added* NQ
16   rican bearn: rican CF
17   wiðutan; ða inran þeostru sind þæs modes blindnyssa: *omitted* BN
        fire: bryne CF
18   wearð: wea\r/ð K
        se bedreda: se \bedreda/ cniht A *(with* bedreda *in a different hand)*

mægena: \mæ/gena K

angynne and ende: angynne, se ðe leofað and rixað a buton ælcum ende C; angynne, se ðe leofað and rixað on ealra worulda
woruld a buton ende F

9. Purification

Manuscripts: CH 1.9 is found in K, fols. 29v–33r, and in A, B, D, E, H, Q, R,
and T.

title	*varies in different manuscripts*
1	Postquam . . . reliqua: *omitted* DE; Postquam impleti T
	purificationis: purgationis *other manuscripts*
2	cennynge: cenninge *with* y *written above* i K
4	wæs getiðod: wæs DE
5	Godes: *omitted* K
	þa lytlan: þa lytlan men BQRT
	Hwæt synd ða lytlan . . . to his rice: *omitted* RT
6	sceoldon: *altered from* sceoldan K
	him offrian: him of\f/rian K
7	geoffrode: geof\f/rode K
	sceole: s\c/eole K
	þæt sind þa fugelas, þe wæron wannspedigra manna lac: *omit-ted* DE
8	bringenne: *altered from* bringanne K
9	geoffrað: geof\f/rað K
13	witegunge: word DE
	lybbende: libbe ælc wuduwe E; \scolde/ libbe ælc wuduwe D *(with* scolde *in a different hand)*
14	þrittigfealde: þritti\g/fealde K
15	he wæs Godes Sunu: he \wæs/ Godes Sunu K
	deadlic: *three or four characters erased* K

10. Quinquagesima (Sunday before Ash Wednesday)

Manuscripts: CH 1.10 is found in K, fols. 33r–36r, and in A, B, C, D, E, F, G
(a short extract), H, M, N (with some text lost at the end), O, Q, and T.

title	*varies in different manuscripts*
1	suos: secreto et ait illis *added* BNO
	et reliqua: *omitted* DEF
2	nu: *omitted* BDE
	we sceolon: we nu sceolon A
	ferdon: eodon A
3	Cristes segene: þa segene NO
	mid wundrum: \mid/ wundrum K; mid wordum NO
	þæs werodes: þæs folces C; þæs werodes \vel folces/ D
4	þa wearð mancyn onliht and gesihðe underfeng: *omitted* B; *omitted, then added* F
	Crist cwæð: Se hælend cwæð G *(which begins here)*
8	sawle: *altered from* sawla K
	lichama: licha\ma/ K
9	geseon mihte: ge\se/on mihte K
	teah: ahnode BCDEF
10	woldon on rode ahon: ahengon NO
11	halige ðing: ðing BCDEFM
	dysig: dyrstig BCE; dyrstig \vel disig/ *(added in a different hand)* D; dyrstig *altered to* dysig F
	þe hine mislæt: *omitted* NO
	softnysse: soþfestnessæ B; soðfæstnysse *altered to* softnysse F
12	wundor: *omitted* BCDEF

11. First Sunday in Lent

Manuscripts: CH 1.11 is found in K, fols. 36r–39r, and in A, C, E, F, H, J (an extract), M, N (with some text lost), O, Q, and T.

title	*varies in different manuscripts*
1	a Spiritu: *omitted* OQT
3	se costnere: se ealde costnere CF
	furðon: forðon *altered to* furðon Q; furðon *altered to* forðon ACT; furþor *altered to* furþon E; forðon *other manuscripts*
4	ure: *altered from* ura K
5	na: \na/ K
6	on handum: on heora handum H; mid heora handum O

7	heagan: *omitted* OQT

7 heagan: *omitted* OQT
ne sceal man: ne sceal nan man NO

8 awearp ða into helle. And eac no his dyrstignys hine: *omitted* CNO

oþþe ðurh leasunge: *omitted* JM

ðurh oðre leahtras: ðurh unrihthæmed, oððe þurh mansliht, oððe þurh mane aðas, oððe þurh lease gewitnysse, oððe þurh oðe mislice synna J

9 Quidam dicunt. . . epistola: *found in* EKM; *not in other manuscripts*

10 þingunga: *altered from* þingunge K

11 eaðmodnys: mildheortnes and his geþoht NO

12 ðreo: oþre NQ

13 he wæs oferswiðed: hi wæron oferswiðede NO
ge beoð: \ge/ beoð K

15 se heretoga: se mæra heretoga NO

16 teoðingdagas: t\e/oðingdagas K

17 þenas: þenas and his þegenas NO
sibbe: soðræ sibbe CF

18 on ecnysse: *omitted* A; on ecnysse we cweðað M

12. MID-LENT SUNDAY

Manuscripts: CH 1.12 is found in K, fols. 39r–41r, and in A, C, F, H, M, N, O, Q, and T.

title *varies in different manuscripts*

2 mycel mennisc: micel manigu C; micel folc F
ðisum folce: ðisum mannum NO
gelice eac: gelice he NO
wilian: fulle *added* NO

3 to ðisre worulde on menniscnyyse, and ðis life oferferde; he com: *omitted* NO
swa is: swa is eac HNO
nu bliðe and: unbliðe N; hwilon bliðe and O

4 micel mennisc: mycel mænigu CF
mihton: *altered from* mihtan K

5 ungewunelic: ungesewenlic C; ungesewenlic \wunelic/ F *(with*
  wunelic *in a different hand)*
  besawen: *altered from* besawon K
6 sceawige: herie NO
7 þæron nan gastlic andgit: þær nan andgit on NO
  folce: mannum NO
  eallum Cristenum folce: A *contains a long canceled passage (see the*
  Notes to the Translation) and the marginal comment, probably in Æl-
  fric's own handwriting, Ðeos racu is fullicor on ðære oðre bec,
  and we hi forbudon on ðyssere þy læs þe hig æþryt þince gif
  heo on ægðre bec beo.
8 Alii evangeliste. . . turbis: *found in* KM; *not in other manuscripts*
  gastlice: *omitted* NO
9 gereordað: gewurðað NO
11 gereordiað: geweorðiað NO
12 habban: \h/abban K
14 witegena witega: witegena witegung NOQT
  þæt he is: þæt \he/ is K

13. ANNUNCIATION

Manuscripts: CH 1.13 is found in K, fols. 41r–44r, and in A, B, C, D, E, G
(an extract), H, Q, R, and T.

title *varies in different manuscripts*
1 Missus est Gabrihel angelus, et reliqua: *omitted* BDE; *omitted*
  then added H; a deo *added* AC
1 Ure se: Men þa leofestan, ure se CT
3 halgum gewritum: halgum bocum RT
  witegunga: witegena QRT; witegunga *altered to* witega H
  on ecnysse: o\n/ ecnysse K
  and mæden æfter ðære cenninge: *omitted* R; *omitted then added* T
4 of Dauides cynne: of þan æþelan cynecynne Abrahames and of
  Dauides cynne C
  beweddod þam rihtwisan Iosepe: betæht and beweddod þam
  ealdum geþungenum and rihtwisan Iosepe to þam þæt he wære
  hire gewita þæt heo æfre þurhwunode on clænum mægðhade C

hæfst: hæf\s/t K

mage: \vel mæge/ *added* K

5 derigendlican: dægþerlican RT

6 þa wearð he dreorig: þa wearð he swiðe dreorig and afæred, and mycclum afyrht C

ðreora: ðr\e/ora K

Ioseph ða: dyde *added* BDE

8 gehyrte: gegrette RT

he is: he is soðlice RT

hi ealle: hi RT

9 Hu wæs heo ofersceadewod: *omitted* RT

12 engles bodungum: bodungum BE

and grette his wife: G *begins here with* Sum æwfest Godes þeign wæs gehaten Zacharias. His gebedde wæs gecegd Elizabeth. Þeos Elizabeth wæs on hyre ellde bearnechnynde. To þyssere huse becom seo eadige Maria and grette

13 awearp: awea\r/þ K

15 lufiað swiðor: swiðor lufedon oððe gyt lufiað BDE

heofonlican: Crist eac sæde þæt mæ mihte eðteon ænne olfend þurh anre nædle eage þonne man mæge þone rice man bringan to heofona rice for his ofermodignesse and his micclan welan *added* C

17 þæt eadige and þæt gesælige mæden Marian: þæt eadige mæden and þæt swiðe gesælige mæden Marian, Cristes modor C

hælende Criste: and ure alesende hælendum Criste þæt he us gemiltsige C

14. Palm Sunday

Manuscripts: CH 1.14 is found in K, fols. 44v–47v, and in A, B, C, H, M, N (with some text lost), O, Q, R (an extract), T (an extract), and two fragments.

title *varies in different manuscripts*

1 et venisset Bethfage ad montem Oliveti: *found in* KM; *not in other manuscripts*

3 sungon: sungon Osanna filio David; benedictus qui venit in nomine Domini rex Israel; þæt is C

4	symle: *omitted* MNO
5	unclæne: unclæne nyten CH

Se getemeda assa hæfde getacnunge þæs Iudeiscan folces, þe
wæs getemed under þære ealdan æ: *omitted* NO

| 6 | þwyrlice: *omitted* NO |

to Gode: to Godes lare CH

þone ælmihtigan: þone ælmihtigan God BCNO

| 7 | and ðus cwæð: Discite a me, quia mitis sum et humilis corde,
and invenietis requiem animabus vestris *added* C |
| 9 | bið mid: *omitted* NO; \þurh/ O |

apostol cwæð: Empti enim estis precio magno; glorificate and
portate Deum in corpore vestro *added* C

gewemð: amerð NO

10	gehalgod: gehadod M; gelaþod N
11	adrencte: adruncene NO
14	oð deað, and mancunn alysan from ðam ecan deaðe: *omitted* NO

tithe: nydde NO

| 16 | Frige æfen: æfen NO |

gelyfede men: belyfede men NO; þegenas M

ac uton nu . . . wurðmynte: Ðam si wuldor and lof a to worulde,
Amen. RT *(which end here)*

| 17 | offringsange: lofsang NO |

generode: geneosode NO

| 19 | on ecnysse: *found in* KM; *not in other manuscripts* |

Circlice ðeawas. . . swigdagum: *in* BHKQ; *added* A; *omitted other
manuscripts*

15. Easter Sunday

Manuscripts: CH 1.15 is found in K, fols. 47v–50r, and in A (with some text
lost), B, C, D, E, H, J, M, N, Q, R, T, U, and one fragment.

title	*varies in different manuscripts*
1	Maria Magdalene et Maria Iacobi, et reliqua: *not in* K; *appears
here in other manuscripts, and in* M *before 1.15.3*
5	and hi gefrefrode. Þa æt nextan com se hælend to his leorning-
cnihtum: *omitted* BC

ne beo ge na: ne beo \ge/ na K

he ða him forgeaf andgit þæt: he heom þa forgeaf andgit M; he þa hi man forgeaf þæt andgit N; he ða forgeaf him andgyt U; *omitted* C

7   gecneordnysse: gecyðnysse N; eadmodnysse U

ðeos dæd: þes dæg BJ

Se engel awylte . . . faran of middangearde: *omitted* A *(originally on a separate slip, now lost)*

beclysedne: beclysed\n/e K

byrgenne: byrgen\n/e K

hand: healfe JN

9   of ðisum life: *omitted* RT

11   tobræc: oferswiðde NQRTU; ofercome B

12   Þa manfullan he let bæftan to ðam ecum witum: *added in a different hand* A

13   Eorðe oncneow: Eorðe oncneow hine C; Eorðe oncneow Crist N

16. First Sunday after Easter

Manuscripts: CH 1.16 is found in K, fols. 50r–52r, and in A, D, E, F, H, M, N, Q, R, T, and U.

title *varies in different manuscripts*

1   Cum esset sero die illo una sabbatorum, et reliqua: *omitted* DE; et fores essent clause *added* F

2   synna: *altered from* synne K

4   on Cristes: o\n/ Cristes K

9   sceal don synna forgifenysse: sceal don forgifenysse FM

lið: bið AFN

11   of eowrum heafde: *a long passage by Ælfric is added in* NQRTHU, *but is not found in* ADEFK *(see the Notes to the Translation for more details)*

syððan synna: syððan nane synne DEF

17. Second Sunday after Easter

Manuscripts: CH 1.17 is found in K, fols. 52r–53v, and in A, B (with some text missing), D, E, F, H, J, M, N, O (with some text missing), Q, U, and a fragment.

title   *varies in different manuscripts*

1   Dixit Iesus discipulis suis, "Ego sum pastor bonus," et reliqua:
            omitted DE; ego sum pastor bonus, et reliqua A; bonus pastor
            animam suam ponit pro ovibus suis *added* BHJMNQU

3   bebead: be\be/ad K

4   untruman: unstrangan N; unstrangan *altered to* untruman E
            gewissað: and him wel bysnað *added* MNQU
            his agenum: æhtum *added* MNQU

5   he flyhð: *omitted* EF
            geseh unrihtwisnysse and suwade. He flyhð þe he: *omitted* JN
            fræcednyssa: gerecednesse NO

6–7   Be ðisum awrat. . . he bysnað: *omitted* MNOQU

7   be him: sylfum *added* FHJNOQU

8   lande; ðær wæs an eowd of ðam mannum: lande. \Þan folce/ þe
            þær wæs æteowed of ðam mannum D *(with* þan folce *in a differ-*
            ent hand); lande. Ðær wæs æteowod on ðam mannum E; lande.
            Þær he wæs æteowod <of> þam mannum F
            Manega sind hyrdas. . . ecnysse. Amen: *a long passage by Ælfric is*
            substituted in MNOQU

18. On the Greater Litany (Rogationtide)

Manuscripts: CH 1.18 is found in K, fols. 53v–56v, and in A, B, C (with some
text omitted), D, G (a short extract), H, J (an extract), M (extracted), O, Q,
T (extracts), U, and V. This homily is heavily extracted and adapted in different manuscripts; not all contain the whole text.

title   *varies in different manuscripts*

3   fyrenful: fyrnful H; syrnful Q; synfull *other manuscripts*
            læg and slep: læg slep K

4   bodode: þær *added* GD   ·

5   amicum: et ibit ad illum media nocte *added other manuscripts*
            syndon: *omitted* CD

6   Ðrynnysse: ðrymnysse BC

7   eow bið forgifen: eow bið geseald MO

8   næddran: næ\d/dran K
            and soðe lufe to Gode: *omitted* C; *omitted then added* H
            bið a on ecnysse: a on ecnysse þurhwunað CD

forðan ðe we geseoð þonne þæt we nu gelyfað. Ure hiht bið eac
    geended: *omitted* BM

9   ateorigendlice; þa ðe we ne geseoð, and us sind behatene, hi
    sind: *omitted* CD

       we nu sceolon: we \nu/ sceolon K

11   gecweden: \for þæt/ *added in different hand* K

12   mancgere: man BO; man<gere> U

       brosnigendlicum feo: brosnigendlicum \his/ feo (*his added in a
    different hand*) K

       æmtigne pusan: \scættod/ *added in a different hand* K

       æhtum: anum *added* OQUV

13   earman: þearfan CD

       wyrtruma: lareow and wyrttruma UV

       se apostol Paulus: \for þi/ *added in a different hand* K

19. Tuesday, On the Lord's Prayer

Manuscripts: CH 1.19 is found in K, fols. 56v–60r, and in A, B, D, F, G (a
short extract), H, J (extracts), M (with some text lost), O, P, Q, R, T, U, V,
and two fragments.

title   *varies in different manuscripts*

1   menniscnysse: menniscny\s/se K

       Pater noster: *added to* K; *omitted* T; Pater Noster qui es in celis
    other manuscripts

       Þæt is on Englisc: *not in other manuscripts*

1–3   sy þin nama . . . and min sweoster: *omitted* J

3   and min modor: *omitted* DR; *omitted then added* F

       ge unæðelborene: *omitted* OQRTUV

4   cwyð: *altered from* cwæð K

       swa micel bið: bið JP

5   nane gebedu: na\ne/ gebedu K

6   mines Fæder: to mines Fæder DFO; *omitted* J; mines Fæder
    bearn T

       his agenum Fæder: his Fæder *other manuscripts*

7   gemete: mægene UV

8   gereorde: geþeode FTV; geþeode *altered to* gereorde R

8–10   urne dæghwamlican hlaf. . . we ne abreoðon: *omitted* M

8   ær gebete: ær geandette and bete T; \geandette and/ ær gebete F
       (with geandette and *in a different hand)*; ær \geandette and/ bete
       R *(with* geandette and *in a different hand)*; ær \geandette his
       scriftan and/ gebete U *(with* geandette his scriftan and *in a dif-
       ferent hand)*; ær geandette his scriftan and gebete V

10   nan man ne cymð: Ne becymð nan mann G *(which begins here)*

10–12 to Gode gecyrre. . . gebedu belimpað: *omitted* M
       on hellewite: G *ends here*

12   bletsiað: blissiað OQRTUV

14   behreowsian: \and his scriftan hy geandettan/ *added in a different
       hand* U; and his scriftan hy geandettan V
       sawul: \sa/wul K
       winnað: *altered from* wynnað K
       godnysse: godcundnysse DF
       us ealle ðing: \us/ ealle ðing K

15   gesette: \ge/sette K
       Godes: Cristes RT
       adune: þæradune A; *omitted* O

17   woruld: a buton ende *added* BDFH
       on ecnysse: *omitted* A; a on ecnysse O

20. WEDNESDAY, ON THE CATHOLIC FAITH

Manuscripts: CH 1.20 is found in K, fols. 60r–64r, and in A (with some
text lost), B, D, F, G (extracts), H, N, O (with some text lost), P, Q (a short
extract), U, V, and two fragments.

title *varies in different manuscripts*

2   Menn he gesceop mid gaste and mid lichaman: *omitted* NOUV;
       omitted then added P

3   wuniað: syndon NO
       He wæs æfre . . . ælmihtig God: *omitted* NO

3–4   Forði ælc edwist. . . anre godcundnysse: *omitted* NO

4–10   Nu habbað ge. . . ac is Ðrynnys: *omitted* G

5   nanum oðrum: men *added* NO

6   þy bet: *omitted* NO

beorhtnys: beorh\t/nys K

Nis na... of ðam fyre: *omitted* NO

ðe heo of cymð: *omitted* UV

7   be him: *omitted* NO

8   se ðe is heora... se Halga Gast: *omitted* NO

9–10   Seo sunne... totwæmede: *omitted* A (*originally on a separate slip, now lost*)

Se leoma is æfre... mid hire: *omitted* UV

12   mægenðrynnysse: mægenðrymnysse BDHNP

13   ealre his fare: Nu se man þe ne mage þas deopnysse asmeagan [understandan N] gelyfe on þone ælmightigan God þe ealle þing gesceop heofenas and eorðan, and he bið gehealden *added* NUV

15   upasprincð: upasprin\c/ð K

16   togædere wyrcende: G *ends*

18   gedwolman: \gedwolman/ K

he wære: wære D; *omitted* N; *omitted then added* U

wære Halig Gast: Halig Gast N; \he wære/ Halig Gast U (*with* he wære *in a different hand*); he wære Halig Gast V

21. Ascension

Manuscripts: CH 1.21 is found in K, fols. 64r–67v, and in A, B, C, D, E, H, M, N, R, T, U, and V (with some text lost).

title   *varies in different manuscripts*

1   Primum quidem sermonem feci: *omitted* ABCDEH; de omnibus, o Theophile, et reliqua *added* N

2   ðisre pistolrædinge: þe man nu on Þunresdæg rædde *added* RT

gecweden: gehaten *other manuscripts*

3   Æðele: heofonlica DE

5   ricum and reðum: ricum kiningum and reþum kaserum RT

9   Nu todæg: On Þunresdæg þe nu wæs on þissere wucan nu todæg RT

10   Recumbentibus undecim discipulis, et reliqua: *found in* HK; *not in other manuscripts*

teala: sona sel UV

11	nan lif: lif CDE
12	forhtiað: *in* K; biuiað \vel forhtiað/ A *(with* vel forhtiað *in a different hand)*; aforhtigað B; biuiað *other manuscripts*
	in quodam tractu... similis est: *not in other manuscripts*
14	deofles: ær his fulluhte *added* CDE
15	gode men: gode NRTUV
16	yfemystan: *altered from* yfemæstan K
17	Heliam: \H/eliam K
	cræte: Criste EN
20	lande: *omitted* UV
	Scithia: Chithia lande UV; Achaia CDE; \achagia/ *added in a different hand* K

22. Pentecost

Manuscripts: CH 1.22 is found in K, fols. 67v–71r, and in A, B, C, D, E, F, H, M, N, Q (with much text lost), R, (with some text lost), T, U, and V.

title	*varies in different manuscripts*
1	fyrde: *altered from* ferde K; and wolde hi ofslean oððe habban to his þeowte *added* RT
3	Cristes upstige: upstige ures drihtnes CD
	gecweden: gehaten BFH
4	hwæt ðis: wundor *added* RT
9	æteowod: *altered from* æteowed K
10	wæs gesewen: \wæs/ gesewen K
	flæsclice: flæs\c/lice K
11	butan bilewitnysse: butan heo hæbbe bilewitnysse RTU
	butan rihtwisnysse: butan heo hæbbe rihtwisnysse RTU
12	he wæs æteowod: *omitted* CD
	se ylca Godes gast: se halga Godes gast Q; þe Halga Gast B
	geceas: \ge/ceas K
13	wissað: symle *added* QTU
14	Crist ableow ðone Halgan Gast upon ða apostolas: *omitted* CDEF
	geleaffullan: heofonlican CD
	ylcan Gast: Halgan Gaste CDEF
16	gefullude men: geleaffullum mannum CDEF

23. SECOND SUNDAY AFTER PENTECOST

Manuscripts: CH 1.23 is found in K, fols. 71r–73v, and in A (with some text lost), B, C, D, E, F, H, Q, and U.

title	*varies in different manuscripts*
1	dives: et induebatur purpura *added* ACDEFH; et induebatur purpura et bisso *added* BQ
2	betwux us: and eow *added* CE
	heorcnian: hlystan CDEF
4	forðan ðe him is cuð: hwi? For ðam þe him is cuð CD forðon ðe he geseah: forðon ðe he gese\a/h K
5	on helle: on hellewite A
	to mundboran: to mundboran and to helpe CDEF
	drypan: mid wætere drypan CDEF
6	men ða leofostan: *omitted* CDEF
	tallice hwæt: tallice hwæt littles CDEF
	gehwæde: ge\h/wæde K
7	mod: *omitted* CDE; \gemynd/ *added* F *in a different hand*
10	wið ðone ælmihtigan: to Gode E; wið ðone ælmihtigan Gode CDFBU
11	Yrnað, yrnað: yrnað swiðe C; Yrnað earma ADE; yrnað earma \yrnað/ F *(with second* yrnað *in a different hand)*
12	rixað: leofað and rixað CDEF

24. FOURTH SUNDAY AFTER PENTECOST

Manuscripts: CH 1.24 is found in K, fols. 73v–76v, and in A (with some text lost), B, C, D, F, H, Q, R, and U.

title	*varies in different manuscripts*
1	ad Iesum: publican et peccatorii *added* BH
3	syngigende: syngi\g/ende K
5	gesewenlice: \ge/sewenlice K
	ungesewenlican: þing *added* CDF
6	teoðe wearð: teoðe werod wearð CDF

8 arfæstnysse: fæstnysse CD; \soð/fæstnysse F *(with* soð *in a differ-*
   ent hand); earfoðnysse U
  se ælmihtiga: se ælmihtiga God BCD
11 siðan: siððan BCDFU
14 wununga: *altered from* wununge K
15 begæð unrihtwisnysse: begæð on unrihtnysse C; he gæð on \un/
   rihtnysse D *(with* un *in a different hand)*
  nanra: *altered from* nanre K
16 menniscum Gode: mænniscu CD
  worulda woruld: a buton ende *added* CDFH

25. The Nativity of John the Baptist

Manuscripts: CH 1.25 is found in K, fols. 76v–79v, and in A, B, C, D, E, G
(extract), H, Q, S, and T.

title *varies in different manuscripts*
2 cynnestre: Elizabeth *added* CG
  be ðam ðuhte: be ðam geþuhte and ræhton him græf and wex-
   bred on to writenne þæs cildes naman C
  gewidmærsod: ge\wid/mærsod K; gemærsod C
  ðigene: þing G *(which ends here)*
4 ferde: ferde þa eft C; ferde þa DE
  He bodade: Johannes cwæð to þan Iudeisce folce be Criste,
   "Æfter me cymð strængre se þe ær me wæs, and æfre bið. Ic ne
   eam for þam wyrðe þæt ic his scoþwang uncnytte. Ic eow ful-
   lige on wætere; he eow fullað on Haligum Gaste, and sylð synna
   forgifennesse." Iohannes bodade C
5 cynnestran: \vel e/ *written above* y, \vel y/ *written above* e K
12 unscyldig: unscæððig BQS
14 werlice: \vel viriliter/ *added* K; wærlice ABCDEHT
  gecneordlice: geornfullice C; \vel geornlice/ *added* E *in a different*
   hand
  forluron: and swa to awyrgedum deoflum wurdon awænde, and
   to egeslicum hellewitum besceofene *added* C
16 þurh ongyte: \per infusionem/ *added* K
16–18 þurh ongyte ... deopnyssa: *omitted* DE

26. THE PASSION OF THE APOSTLES PETER AND PAUL

Manuscripts: CH 1.26 is found in K, fols. 79v–84r, and in A, B, C, D, E, G (a short extract), H (with some text lost), L (extract), Q, S, T, and three fragments.

title   *varies in different manuscripts*

2   geciged: gehaten *other manuscripts*
     bintst: bin\t/st K

4   geunnen: genumen E; genumen \vel unnan/ D *(with* vel unnan *in a different hand)*
     se gehyrsuma: \se/ gehyrsuma K
     ðeoda: *altered from* ðeode K
     sume on fyr: sume on wætere, sume on treowum, sume on stanum *added* C
     lif forgeaf: \lif/ forgeaf K
     ðrym: *omitted* DE

5   sunu: bearn ES
     flæsclice: flæs\c/lice K

6   ofer ðone geleafan: ofer me sylfne, mid ðam geleafan BQST
     andetst: nu be me cyddest BQST
     weorc: þæt is of ðam rihtan geleafan, hit *added* DE
     lyre: hryre BQS

7   Manega: Mane\ga/ K

8   se anweald þe him Crist forgeaf: se micle mære anweald þe him Crist on þisum halige dæge forgeaf C
     infær: Drihten cwæð to Petre *added* C; swa swa Crist sylf him to cwæð *added* QST

10   DE PASSIONE APOSTOLORUM: *varies or omitted in other manuscripts*
     We wyllað . . . geendebyrd: Men þa leofestan, eower geleafa bið þe trumra gif ge gehyrað be Godes halgum, hu hi þæt heofenlice rice geearnodon, and ge magon þe cuðlicor to h\eo/m\e/ clypian gif heora lifes drohtnunga eow þurh lareowa bodiunge cuðe beoð. We wyllað eow gereccan þara apostola drohtnunge and geendunge Petrus and Paulus mid scortre race, for þan þe heora þrowung ys gehwær on ængliscum gereorde fullice geendebyrð, þus cweþende. L *(which begins here); see CH 1.37.1*

11	gehaten: KLB; genemned *other manuscripts*
	ormætum: micclum \vel ormætum/ H *(with* vel ormætum *in a different hand)*
13	biddende: cweðende DE
14	wæs: \w/æs K
	ormætne: *omitted* BQST
15	tomerigen: tomer\i/gen K
16	Non passus... reversus est: *found in* KL; *not in other manuscripts*
	neawiste: Paulus eac arærde ænne cniht of deaþe to life þurh Godes mihte, se was Patroclus gehaten, þæs caseres beorle *added* C
18	caseres eare: *in* KL; cyninges eare *other manuscripts*
	he ða cwæð: Petrus cwæð þa C; he ða Petrus cwæð DET
21	hellican: healican DE
23	gestilde: gespræc DE
	earfoðnysse: carfullnysse DE
24	Igitur Hieronimus... sunt: *found in* KL; *not in other manuscripts*
	heora: *altered from* heara K
25	ðeaht: \ðeaht/ K
	on ðam holte: *omitted* A
26	lichaman, and: gastice clypung þæt man wolde þa halgan leoht-fatu of Romana rice gelædon *added* C
	ðeodscipas: leodscipum DE; leodscypas HS
	tiðe, ðam sy wuldor and lof a: gyfe. Uton biddan ealle eadmod-lice þas haligan apostolas þæt hi for heora mæron geearnungon us geþingian to þan mildheortan hælende, þæt he us gemiltsie, and sylle forgifenesse ealre ure synna þe we siððe oððe ær ge-worhtan oððe geþohtan ongean his leofan willan, and þæt he geunnon us gesundfulnesse on þisre woruld, and forgife us soþe sibbe on þise læne life, and on þan toweardan ece reste on heof-onan rice mid his eadigan apostolan þe we nu todæg wurþiað, and mid eallon his halgan, se þe leofað and rixað a buton ende C

27. SAINT PAUL

Manuscripts: CH 1.27 is found in K, fols. 84r–87v, and in A, B, C, D, E, G (extract), H (with some text lost), L (extract), Q, S, T, and two fragments.

title   *varies in different manuscripts*

1   Godes gelaðung: Dixit Simon Petrus ad Iesum ecce nos reliqui-
        mus omnia, et reliqua. *added* A

5   geleaffullum ðe he ær tæhte: geleaffullum mannum þe he he ær
        tæhte and lærde to drihtnes geleafum C
        lifes wege: and ofte fela manna of deaðe to life arærde *added* C

6   We willað . . . hæbbende sy: Men þa leofestan C

7   arfæstne: arfæst\n/e K
        arfæstne Paulum: þæt is on urum gereorde lamb gecweðen *added*
        C
        hine man: hi\ne/ man K *(with* ne *in a different hand)*
        merigen: mer\i/gen K
        Mid his handcræfte . . . neode foresceawode: *omitted* C
        heora: *altered from* heara K

8   Evangelium. Dixit Simon . . . reliqua: *not in other manuscripts*; L
        ends here

13   ge gebletsode: \ge/ gebletsode K
        beeodon: b\e/eodon K
        cwyde: þe ðus cwyð *added* QST

14   Þæt godspell cwyð forð gyt: Soð is to secgene, þa þa wyreceð on
        Godes wille, þa becumeð on myrhðe. Ðæt godspell cwyð G
        (which begins here)
        magon: ne magon EG

15–17   Se ðe betwux munecum . . . habban moton. Amen: Men þa leof-
        estan, beon we carfulle þæt ure time mid idelnesse us ne losie,
        and we þonne to weldædum gecerran willan, þonne us se deað
        to forðsiðe geþreatað. Ðu ælmihtiga drihten, gemiltsa us syn-
        fullum, and urne forsið swa gefada þæt we gebettum synnum
        æfter þisum fræcenfullum life þinum halgum geferlæhte beon
        moton. Sy þe lof and wuldor on ealra worulda woruld. C
        rice mann: mære mann DEG

28. Eleventh Sunday after Pentecost

Manuscripts: CH 1.28 is found in K, fols. 87v–90v, and in A, B, C, D, F, G,
H (with some text missing), Q, U (with some text missing), and two fragments.

title	*varies in different manuscripts*
1	Hierusalem: videns civitatem *added* AB
	et reliqua: *omitted* ABQU
3	ðære byrig: Hierusalem ðære byrig CDFG
4	oferwinnenne: oferwinnen\n/e K
	manna: \vel in cronica sic habetur/ *added in a different hand* K
	hrædlice: \h/rædlice K
	ymbsettum Iudeiscum: æfter Cristes þrowunge *added* CDFG
6	wunigende: wæren *added* C; wæron and *added* F
	hryðeru: gode hryðeru *other manuscripts*
8	wunast: \wu/nast K
	woruldlice bliss: woruldlice sib A
	hwi heo: Swyce beoð CDFG
	nolde: for ði ðe heo nolde CDFG
	mid: hi mid CDFG
9	agenre: *omitted* BQU
10	geneosunga: *altered from* geneosunge K
11	Ðær wæron: alswa we ær sædan *added* C; ealswa we ær cwædon *added* DFG
12	teolunge: gelaðunge CDF
13	sceaðan: sceaðum gelice CDFG
	and bilewitnysse soðre halignysse: soðre halignysse CDF; *omitted* G
	oðrum dara: oðrum hearm QU
14	abutan: \a/butan K
	fyrst oð tomerigen: *omitted* CG; *deleted* D
15	ealra: ea\l/ra K

29. SAINT LAWRENCE

Manuscripts: CH 1.29 is found in K, fols. 90v–94v, and in A, B, C, E, H (with some text lost), L, Q (with some text lost), S, and three fragments.

title	*varies in different manuscripts*
1	deadan: deadlican AEH
3	ymesene: blind CL; bysene E
6	geswutelige: g\es/wutelige K
	tihtst: lærdest C; tæcst E

sawla: *omitted, then added in a different hand* K
7 gebiddon: *altered from* gebiddan K
11 and et: forþon ne awændst þu næfre min geþanc ne minne geleafan fram Criste middaneardes hælende *added* C
hyrdle: bedde CS
12 sibbe: blisse AEH
15 gehadode: gehalgode AEH

30. ASSUMPTION OF MARY

Manuscripts: CH 1.30 is found in K with some text lost, the extant portion
appearing on fols. 97v–98v (two leaves have been lost between fols. 94 and
97), and in A, B, G, H, Q (with some text lost), S, T, and two fragments.

title K *is missing two folios at this point; text is supplied from* A
varies in different manuscripts
3 godspellere: Marian swuster sunu *added* S; Cristes moddrian sunu
added T
carefulre: car\e/fulre A
gehyrsumode: \ge/hyrsumode A
4 Iohanne: \uterque sexus virgo dicitur/ *added in a different hand* A
cwene: cwen\e/ A
Cristes menniscnysse: Cris\tes/ menniscnysse A
5 munte: mun\te/ A
6 wimmanna: wim\man/na A
micelre: mice\l/re A; swylcere GST; swyþlicere H
gastas: gast\as/ A
9 riðum: *altered from* ryðum A
blostman: blo\s/tman A
gesiðodon: \ge/siðodon A; syndon S
foran ongean: forn angean A
þe oþre martyras: þ\e/ oþre martyras A
10 cwen mid: K *resumes*
11 becom: be\c/om K
heofonan rices: heofonan ABG
13 to sumere cyrcan: \to/ sumere cyrcan K *(with* to *in a different
hand)*

14   uðwitegunge: þæt is on wisdome *added* QS; and mid wisdom
        added T
        uncuð: na uncuð S; no uncuð T
18   benum: gebeden GS

31. SAINT BARTHOLEMEW

Manuscripts: CH 1.31 is found in K, fols. 98v–103v, and in A, B, E (with some text omitted), H, L, Q, S, T, and two fragments.

title	*varies in different manuscripts*
1	swilc: swi\l/c K
2	fæce: *omitted* AH; *omitted then added* E
3	unclæna: unclæne *with a written over* e K
4	se apostol: he ABHQST
5	Godes sunu: sunu BQST; \Godes/ *added in a different hand* T
	ælces weres: ælces <mannes> weres K
7	bendum gewrað: racenteagum geband ST
	hylt. Ic bidde: hæft. Nu bidde ic ST
9	se ælmihtiga God: God ST
10	tempel: temp\e/l K
	eallum: *omitted* QST
11	mannes stemn: nan stemn BQST
	feower: *omitted* ST
13	ealre his leode: eallum his leodscipum E; ealle his þeoda S
	sceoldon: *altered from* sceolden K
14	feredon: *altered from* ferodon K
	wedende: wepende BST
	goddre: go\d/dre K
	a on worulde: AMEN *added* E *(which ends here)* LT
18	se apostol: *omitted* A
20	hiht: hi\h/t K *(with second* h *in a different hand)*

32. THE BEHEADING OF JOHN THE BAPTIST

Manuscripts: CH 1.32 is found in K, fols. 103v–6v, and in A, C, G, H, L (a brief extract), Q, and S.

title	*varies in different manuscripts*
5	Aecclesiastica historia ita narrat: *not in other manuscripts*
	Hwæt ða Iohannes . . . se hælend Iohanne: *added in a different* *hand with* Hælend þa mid diglum wordum onwreah *erased* A
	Eart ðu: \Gregorius sic tractavit/ *in margin* K
	ic God eom: ic \God/ eom K
6	gehyrdon: nu her *added* QS
7	herode ðæs wifes snoternysse, ðe him forwyrnde þone pleolican mannsliht: *omitted with* \and herode þæs wifes snotornysse/ *added then erased and* \and herode þæs wifes/ \snotornysse þe him forwyrnde þone pleolica mansliht/ *added in two different hands* A
8	se ðe his feondum: \se ðe/ his feondum K
12	Nu cwyð se trahtnere þæt: Se wisa eft cwæð þæt L *(which begins here)*
	betwux seofan leonum: \betwux seofan leonum/ K
13	ðinra: *altered from* ðinga K
14	fornumene: gewæhte *other manuscripts*
	forwel menige: men *added* CQS
	gysternlica: gyster\n/lica K; dæg *added* C

33. Seventeenth Sunday after Pentecost

Manuscripts: CH 1.33 is found in K, fols. 106v–8r, and in A, B, C, D, F, H, and Q.

title	*varies in different manuscripts*
2	wereleas: *corrected from* weres *by a different hand* K; weres AHQ
3	gecweden: geciged ACDFH
	ungeþwærnysse: mid leasungum *added* CDF
5	godcundre: incundre *other manuscripts*
6	mære witega: mære CD
11	geweman: gewænian CD; gewenian F
	Þeah ðe hwa . . . deð dædbote: *omitted* CDF
	Fæder. And se Sunu nis na gemænelice Sunu fram þam Fæder and þam Halgan Gaste, forðan ðe he nis hera begra: *omitted* K *(supplied from A)*

12   ægðrum: æg\ð/rum K
13   lof and wuldor: lof \and/ wuldor K
        næfre: Se forsihð þe næfre nele yfeles geswican ac æfre oð his
            lifes ende on þan fulan adlan ligð fule besylod *added* C; *added in
            margin* D
        ænne: *found in* BK; *not in other manuscripts*
        sunu: *found in* BKQ; *not in other manuscripts*

34. DEDICATION OF THE CHURCH OF SAINT MICHAEL THE ARCHANGEL

Manuscripts: CH 1.34 is found in K, fols. 108v–12v, and in A, B, C, E, G (an extract), H, Q, S, T, and two fragments.

title   *varies in different manuscripts*
1   manegum mannum: manegum *other manuscripts*
        sæ: se K
2   þreora: þr\e/ora K
5   to fultume: tu fultume K
6   þam heahengle: þam engle *other manuscripts*
8   hrædlice: *omitted* BCQST
9   Evangelium: *omitted* BCEQST
        Accesserunt ad Iesum . . . reliqua: *omitted* BCQST
10   gehwæde: lytel GT
11   Hægmon: Eac mon EG; Her mon T
        fintst: fin\t/st K
12   þa apostolas: ða oðre apostolas *other manuscripts*
15   feore: life C; feore \vel life/ T
16   wurðscipe is: wurðscipe K

35. TWENTY-FIRST SUNDAY AFTER PENTECOST

Manuscripts: CH 1.35 is found in K with some text lost, fols. 112v–16v (a leaf is lost between fols. 113 and 115), and in A, B, C, D, F, H, Q, and one fragment.

title   *varies in different manuscripts*
1   et reliqua: *omitted* ABHQ

2	gearwe: gegearcode CD; gearcode F
4	rihtwisra manna: rihtwisra *other manuscripts*
	Salomon cwæð . . . wisdomes setl: *omitted* K *(supplied from* A*)*
	iu rixað: gerixað CD; rixað F
6	siððan: \siððan/ K
7	Hwæt wæron hi buton fearra gelican, þa ða hi, mid leafe þære ealdan æ: *om.* CDF
9	swiðor þonne: swiþor þises lifes myrhðe þonne CDF
	her bæftan: herberforan CDF
10–13	het ahon Petrum . . . and on þinre bec ealle: *missing in* K *(supplied from* A*)*
10	bið us to gereccenne: bið \us/ to gereccenne A
	forþan þe: forþa\n/ þe A
11	gearowe: gegearwode CD; gegearcode F
	dæda: \dæda/ A
	yfele ge gode: yfele \ge/ gode A
12	swa ge: swa we *corrected to* swa ge A
	apostol: aposto A
13	gesceawode: \ge/sceawode A
	becom: \be/com A
	gebicnode: gebicnod\e/ A
	giftlice: gif\t/lice A
	gebihð: \ge/bihð A
	into his gelaðunge: \in/to his gelaðunge A
	ðæne: \ðæne/ A
	unfulfremednysse: \un/fulfremednysse A
	sind awritene: K *resumes*
16	hine sylfne: hine *other manuscripts*
20	ælmihtig: metoda A
	woruld: a on ecenysse *added* CDF

36. All Saints

Manuscripts: CH 1.36 is found in K, fols. 116v–20r, and in A, B, C, D, G (3.10–23 only), H, J (3.0–9 only), Q, S, T, and one fragment.

title	*varies in different manuscripts*
1	wurðige: \vel mærsige/ *added* K; mærsie *other manuscripts*

2	hellicere: helle CDH
4	Godes cempan: cempan CD
	gefremode: worhte BS
6	swurdes ecge: swurdes ehtnysse ACDGHJ
8	mæden on geeacnunge, mæden æfter geeacnunge: *omitted* CD
9	fyligde: *omitted* CD
	becumon: J *ends here*; AMEN *added* DH
10	Evangelium . . . reliqua: *title and Latin verse vary in different manuscripts*
12	Matheus: þe godspellere *added* BT
13	to alysenne: mancynn to alysenne CDG
14	sealmsceop: sealmsc\e/op K
15	hynða: hyðða ABDQST; æhten G; hyþþa \eahte/ *(with* eahte *in a different hand)* H
20	forlæton: forlætan oððe forsuwian CDG

37. SAINT CLEMENT

Manuscripts: CH 1.37 is found in K, fols. 120r–24r, and in A, C, D, G (an extract), H, L (extracts), Q, S, and two fragments.

title	*varies in different manuscripts*
1	Menn ða leofostan . . . cude beoð: *in* L *this sentence also introduces the Passion of Peter and Paul in 1.26.10*
2	apostoles: *omitted* A
	ðeode: leode A
	and hæðenum: *omitted* A
	wurdon: wæron CD
3	And Dionisius . . . word gecyddon: *omitted* L
5	westene: wætere CD
	gedelfe: \g/edelfe K
	eadiga biscop: halga biscop ABCDH
7	getyrigde: gestyrede D; ge\s/tyridge *(with* s *in a different hand)* S; gefylled L
8	geswutelod þæt he: geswutelod þæt hi ne moston his lic þanon styrigan and þæt he QS
	his weldæda: KL; þæs halgan weldæda *other manuscripts*
9	awehte: *altered from* awrehte K

geswutelað: geswuteliað. Sy him wuldor and wurðmynt a to wo-
rolde. AMEN L *(which ends here)*

11   cynedomes: *added* KQS; *omitted other manuscripts*
    hæðenan godas: hæþenan CDG

12   talu: *altered from* tale K
    merigen: mer\i/gen K
    mid micelre sceame: *omitted* A

14–15   cwædon anmodlice . . . hi ealle totæron: Se cyng hine heom
    betæhte, and heo hine awurpen into anen seaðe on þan wæron
    seofen hungrie leon. Ac God hine beah þæt heo him forbæren
    oð ðet on morgen þæt he wæs hal and gesund up atogen. Se
    cyng þa swyðe eadmodlice herede and þancode Danieles God,
    and let besufen in þone seað þæt witegan ehteres, and þa leone
    heo sone totæren G

38. SAINT ANDREW

Manuscripts: CH 1.38 is found in K, fols. 124r–28v, and in A, B (38.0–13
only), C, D (with some text lost), H, L (38.14–23 only), Q, S, and one fragment.

title   *varies in different manuscripts*

2   gemette: geseah *other manuscripts*

4   lybbendra: \i. viventium/ *added* K

5   wuldor þæt he us his forgeafe. He ætbræd ure: *omitted* CK *(sup-*
    plied from A)

9   heora speda: *omitted* BCQS

10   scrutniað: smeagað C; geðencað D; gecnawaþ scrutniaþ S
    geeht: ge\e/ht K

11   for Gode: \for/ Gode K
    nanum gebeodan: and nanum beode B; and nanum ne gebeodan
    C; nanum ne beode D; þæt he nanum men ne gebeode S
    sylfum: *omitted* CQS

13   gefylle: and healde þurh ðone þe leofað and rixað a buton ænde.
    AMEN *added* D; Beo wuldor and lof hælende Criste a on alræ
    woruldæ woruld a buton end. AMEN *added* B *(which ends here)*;
    We hæbbeð nu gesæd þis godspell sceortlice. Nu wille we eow

secgan hu se apostol Andreas, þe we nu todæg wurþiað, his
agen life sealde for Cristes geleafan for þære lare þe he bodode
soþan lare *added* CQS

Passio eiusdem: *varies in different manuscripts*

14 rode gerynu; þu gehyrdest þære halgan: *omitted* HKL *(supplied from* A)

15 Beoð swyðor: Eornostlice beoð swiþor A

18 handum and fotum on þære rode gebunden, þæt he langlice
ðrowian sceolde: fæste gebundon handum handum and fotum
to þære rode C; fæste gebundon handum and fotum to þere
rode gealgan D
astigen: \i. suspenderis/ *added* K

19 unrihtwisdom: þæt hit wæro unrihtwisdom CD

20 he ne geswicð: he \ne/ geswicð K

23 metodan: ælmihtigan HQS
we cweðað: *omitted* CL; Hit wære gelimplic, gif þises dæges
scortnys us geþafian wolde, þæt we eow þæs halgan apostoles
Andrees þrowunge gerehton, ac we wyllað on oðrum sæle gif
we gesundfulle beoð eow gelæstan, gif we hwæt lytles hwonlicor gefyldon. Uton nu eadmodlice gebiddan þæs ælmihtigan
Godes mægenþrum þæt his eadiga apostol Andreas beo ure ece
þingere to him, swa swa he wæs soð bydel his halgan gelaþunge.
Sy wuldor and lofe þam ælmihtigan scyppende a on ecynsse.
Amen. *added and deleted* A

39. FIRST SUNDAY IN ADVENT

Manuscripts: CH 1.39 is found in K, fols. 128v–30r, and in A, B, D, F, H, O,
Q, T. An extract from the English Preface is found as part of Q; the same
passage appears as a separate item in R and T.

title *varies in different manuscripts*

2 gedremum: \ge/dremum K; *omitted* O

4 symle: *omitted* BQT

5 to eow: \to/ eow K

7 Ymbscrydað: Ymbsc\r/ydað K
gife Godes: gife Gode K

8   þam sy wuldor and lof a on ecnysse. Amen: *omitted* T; *a long
     passage from the English Preface (1.0.6* menn behofiað . . . *1.0.10
     For swylcum bebodum) added here* Q

40. SECOND SUNDAY IN ADVENT

Manuscripts: CH 1.40 is found in K, fols. 130r–32v (with a leaf missing after fol. 132), and in A, B, D, F, G, H, O, Q, and T.

title   *varies in different manuscripts*
1   Erunt signa . . . reliqua: *omitted* BT
2   heofenan: \id est celorum/ *added* K
4   ealdum: eallum DO
         sweg ungewunelice: swegunge \unge/wunelice *(with* unge *in a
            different hand)* F; swegung gewunelice GT; swegunge wundelice
            OQ
         mihta: *altered from* mihte K
5   mihta: *altered from* mihte K
         swutellice: cwæde *added and canceled* K
         gewit ðe hi ne lufodon: gewit\neð/ <þa> ðe hine \ne/ lufedon
            (with the word ne *added in a different hand)* F; gewitt, þonne
            murneð þa þe hi ne lufedan G
6   his freond: \h/is freond K
         feond is: freond nis DFGO
         becumon: to ðam ecan life *added* DFGO
7   deaðe: ðeaðe K
8   Godes byman: byman DFGO
         Eac on ðisum andgite geðwærlæhð se godspellere Matheus,
            þisum wordum: *omitted* GT
10   heofon: *altered from* heofen K
11   angsumnysse: dæg *added* GO
         wanunge: dæg *added* GT
12   eower lif, and awendað eowre ðeawas, witniað mid wope: *omitted*
            DFGO
         hræd: \h/ræd K
         anbidian sceolon . . . Explicit hic liber: K *is missing a folio here; text
            is supplied from* A
         Explicit hic liber: *omitted* FGOBQT

Notes to the Translation

rubric   *Here begins the preface of this book*: The Prefaces are found only in manuscript K (the base manuscript for this edition, Cambridge, University Library Gg. 3. 28; see the Note on the Text for a comprehensive list of manuscripts and their sigla), though parts of the English Preface are excerpted in other manuscripts. In the Latin Preface, addressed to Archbishop Sigeric, Ælfric describes his translation method, lists his main sources, and explains the scope of his work; in the English Preface, introduced with a large initial and the title *Praefatio,* he laments the poor state of preaching in his day, worries about the coming of Antichrist, and insists on the necessity of preaching true doctrine to save souls. Both prefaces show a characteristic concern with orthodoxy and authority—not only that of his sources, but his own earned authority as a pastor, a scholar, and a thoughtful and painstaking writer.

1   *Æthelwold*: Bishop of Winchester, 963–984, a leader of the monastic reform.

       Sigeric: Archbishop of Canterbury, 990–994.

       We have not translated word for word throughout, but sense by sense: Ælfric's distinction is borrowed from Jerome's *Letter to Pammachius,* where he discusses the method used in his translation of the Bible.

       Augustine of Hippo . . . sometimes Haymo: Ælfric's sources are discussed in the Introduction.

2   *another book in composition*: This undoubtedly refers to CH 2.

3 *deign to correct them*: We do not have direct evidence for Sigeric's reaction to Ælfric's work, but in the Latin Preface to CH 2 he writes that the Archbishop has "overly praised our work, graciously receiving that translation" (CH 2.0.1).

English Preface

5 *Æthelred*: King of England, 978–1016. The expression "in King Æthelred's day" does not imply that Æthelred is dead when Ælfric writes this.

Ælfheah: Bishop of Winchester, 984–1006.

Æthelmær: Son of Ealdorman Æthelweard and later ealdorman himself, and founder of the monastery at Cerne Abbas, Dorset, where Ælfric resided.

translate this book: For the nature and scope of Ælfric's translation process, see the Introduction.

great error in many English books: A number of vernacular homilies and saints' lives survive from tenth-century England, and some of these do indeed include theologically questionable or erroneous teachings. See Malcolm Godden, "Ælfric and the Vernacular Prose Tradition," in *The Old English Homily and Its Backgrounds*, ed. Paul E. Szarmach and Bernard F. Huppé (Albany, 1978), 99–117.

Alfred: King of England, 871–899, and patron or translator of a number of works from Latin into English, including Gregory the Great's *Pastoral Care* and *Dialogues*, Boethius's *Consolation of Philosophy*, and (as Ælfric assumed, though modern scholarship rejects this attribution) Bede's *Ecclesiastical History*.

6 *which is the ending of this world*: The idea that the world was near its end was a common one in early medieval thought. Bede, following Augustine, divided the world into six ages, defined by biblical events; see Peter Darby, *Bede and the End of Time* (London, 2016). Other writers such as Gregory the Great favored a less rigorous, threefold division of time (which Ælfric describes in CH 1.22.2). But whether there were three or six ages, the present age was by general agreement the last, and the

present time its tail end, though the actual date of the end of the world was not knowable. In CH 1.40 Ælfric elaborates on the signs of the coming end and compares the world to an aging old man.

Then there will . . . shorten those days: The quotation is a combination of several verses from Matthew 24, including verses 21, 5, 24, and 22.

7–9   *Then the Antichrist . . . great misery*: This section on the Antichrist appears as a separate homily in manuscripts P, R, and T, and as a supplement to CH 1.39 in manuscript Q; this was apparently Ælfric's own adaptation (Godden, *Introduction,* 4). It was also used by Wulfstan as a source for two homilies (Dorothy Bethurum, *Homilies of Wulfstan* [Oxford, 1957], nos. 4 and 5). "Antichrist" is mentioned by name in the Bible only in 1 and 2 John; the idea was developed in some detail by later writers. See Richard K. Emmerson, *Antichrist in the Middle Ages: A Study of Medieval Apocalypticism, Art, and Literature* (Manchester, 1981).

8   *heals no one from . . . previously injured*: In CH 1.31.1 Ælfric repeats this idea that the devil inflicts diseases, then removes them so they will appear to have been cured.

three and a half years: The length of Antichrist's activity is taken from Revelation 11:3 (where it is given as 1,260 days) and 13:5 (given as forty-two months).

To tempt Job: The fire from heaven is mentioned in Job 1:16; Ælfric discusses the story in CH 2.30.6.

9   *If you do not . . . in his unrighteousness*: Ezekiel 3:18–19.

Cry out and . . . Jacob their sins: Isaiah 58:1.

10   *We are God's assistants*: 1 Corinthians 3:9.

11   *if anyone wants to transcribe this book*: Ælfric makes a similar plea in the Preface to his *Lives of Saints*. Not all the scribes of Ælfric's works were as careful as he hoped they would be.

What need is there . . . in his book: The Latin note is found only in K. Given how worried Ælfric was about his work being mixed with that of other, less orthodox writers, it is likely he left this note to explain the existence of a variant version of CH 1 with

more than the specified forty homilies. Æthelweard's copy of
CH I with forty-four homilies has not survived.

1. On the Origin of the Created World

title   This first homily offers a whirlwind tour of the most important
moments in Christian history, from the creation and fall of the
angels to the death and resurrection of Jesus. Its focus is on
Old Testament material and includes brief accounts of the creation and fall of the angels, Adam and Eve, Noah and the
Flood, the Tower of Babel, the rise of the Hebrews, the Annunciation, the ministry of Jesus, the Crucifixion, Resurrection,
and Ascension. The homily is not designated for any particular
occasion, but its form and content are catechetical, designed
for simple or newly baptized Christians. Its general content
and structure may owe something to Martin of Braga's *De correctione rusticorum,* ed. C. W. Barlow, in *Martini episcopi Braca-
rensis opera omnia* (New Haven, 1950), 183–203.

1   *He weighs all the mountains . . . in his hands*: An allusion that combines Isaiah 40:12 and Psalms 94(95):4.

2   *ten hosts of angels*: The idea of a hierarchy of angels is most fully
expressed in pseudo–Dionysius the Areopagite's *De caelesti hie-
rarchia,* but Ælfric probably knew it from Gregory the Great's
Homiliae in evangelia 34, ed. Raymond Étaix, CCSL 141 (Turnhout, 1999), the source for his later comments on the topic in
CH 1.24.6–8.

    the leader of this tenth host: Much of the narrative of Lucifer's re-
bellion and fall comes from Isaiah 14:12–15: "How you are fallen
from heaven, O Lucifer, who rose in the morning! How you are
fallen to the earth, that wounded the nations! You said in your
heart, I will ascend into heaven; I will raise my throne above
the stars of God, and I will sit in the mountain of the covenant,
in the sides of the north. I will ascend above the height of the
clouds; I will be like the Most High. But you will be brought
down to hell, into the depth of the pit." The narrative was
much embellished in both theological and popular discourse in
the Middle Ages.

5–9   The account of the creation of the world and of humankind is ultimately from Genesis 2.

7   *Later Adam gave her another name*: Genesis 3:20, "And Adam called the name of his wife Eve, because she is the mother of all living."

8   *God created and made all creation*: Much of what follows is a very loose paraphrase of Genesis 1.

     their blood is their life: The idea that the life of animals resides not in the soul but in the blood is found in several sources, including Cassiodorus, *De anima;* its ultimate source is Leviticus 17:14.

9   *Heretics*: It is not clear whom Ælfric is referring to here; it may be a popular error rather than a fully formed heresy. Ælfric repeats the assertion that the devil has not created any creature in CH 1.6.11.

10   The account of the Fall of humankind is derived from Genesis 3.

     you will be like angels: The reading of Genesis 3:5 in all manuscripts and commentaries is "you will be like gods"; Ælfric translates this as "angels" here, in CH 1.11, and in his portion of Genesis in the *Old English Heptateuch* (Richard Marsden, ed., *The Old English Heptateuch and Ælfric's Libellus de Veteri Testament et Novo*, vol. 1, EETS 330 [Oxford, 2008]).

10–11   *Because you were obedient . . . clothed with the skins*: A close paraphrase of Genesis 3:17–21.

12   *God had endowed . . . eternal dwelling*: This passage, ultimately from Alcuin's *De animae ratione*, is closely similar to a Latin sermon found in Boulogne-sur-Mer, Bibliothèque municipale MS 63, which may be by Ælfric himself. See T. H. Leinbaugh, "The Liturgical Homilies in *Ælfric's Lives of Saints*" (PhD diss., Harvard University, 1980); and Malcolm Godden, "Anglo-Saxons on the Mind," in *Learning and Literature in Anglo-Saxon England: Studies Presented to Peter Clemoes on the Occasion of His Sixty-Fifth Birthday*, ed. Michael Lapidge and Helmut Gneuss (Cambridge, 1985), 271–98.

     nine hundred thirty years: Genesis 5:5.

14–15   The account of the Flood is taken from Genesis 6–9.

16   The account of the Tower of Babel is in Genesis 11:1–9.

18   The lineage of Shem is listed in Genesis 11:10–32. The idea that
God favored the Hebrews because he would choose Mary from
among them is apparently Ælfric's own. Arphaxad is mentioned in Genesis 11:10 and in the long genealogy of Joseph in
Luke 3:23–38, at verse 36.

20   *he performed . . . thirty years*: A number of apocryphal legends of
the young Christ fill in the gaps in the canonical gospel story;
they recount how the child Jesus performed various small and
large miracles. Ælfric may have been aware of these, and eager
to discount their claims.

22   *during that time . . . after his passion*: The idea that Jesus descended
into hell and rescued the faithful from the devil's clutches—an
event traditionally known as the "harrowing of hell"—has little
biblical support but was widely believed in the early Church as
early as the Apostle's Creed. It is found in the apocryphal *Gospel of Nicodemus*, which was translated into Old English; see J. E.
Cross and D. Brearley, *Two Old English Apocrypha and Their
Manuscript Source: "The Gospel of Nichodemus" and "The Avenging
of the Saviour"* (Cambridge, 1996). Ælfric similarly claims in
CH 1.15.10 and 1.30.5 that the dead who were raised at the Crucifixion were taken bodily into heaven. The source of this
claim appears to be a tract by Paschasius Radbertus, *De assumptione sanctae Mariae virginis,* lines 83–86, which circulated as if it
were a letter from Jerome; this text is the source for most of
CH 1.30.

2. THE NATIVITY OF THE LORD

rubric   *December 25*: Ælfric uses the Roman system of dating, counting
forward inclusively to the Kalends (the first day of the month),
Nones (fifth, seventh, or eighth day of the month), and Ides
(fifteenth day of the month). December 25, being eight days
before January 1, is *VIII Kalendas Januarii,* the "eighth Kalends
of January." These dates have been translated into their modern equivalents throughout.

title   This is one of several homilies by Ælfric for the nativity (see also

CH 2.1 and *Lives of Saints* 1). The ultimate source is Luke 2:1–20, most of which was read at the first Mass on Christmas Day, but Ælfric seems also to have drawn many details from Bede's two homilies for Christmas, *Homiliae* 1.6 and 1.7 (Bede, *Homiliae evangelii,* ed. David Hurst, *Homiliarum evangelii libri ii,* in *Opera homiletica; Opera rhythmica,* ed. David Hurst and J. Fraipont, CCSL 122 [Turnhout, 1955]), both of which were available in the homiliary of Paul the Deacon, as well as from other homilies in that collection, such as Gregory the Great's *Homiliae in evangelia* 8 on the same gospel text. As usual in his homilies, Ælfric rarely follows one source in detail for more than a few lines, but freely edits, abridges, combines, and adds his own thoughts and interpretations. As is also usual, Ælfric is less interested in historical explanation than in allegorical interpretation. For a close study of this homily, see Hiroshi Ogawa, "Language for *cristes digelnysse*: Ælfric's Linguistic Theology in His First Nativity Homily," *JEGP* 117 (2018): 419–42.

2–4   A close translation of Luke 2:1–20.

2   *Christ's book*: This is the gospels; Ælfric uses *godspel* (gospel) as well as *Cristes boc* (Christ's book), and the distinction has been preserved.

   Octavian: The biblical text reads "Caesar Augustus." Ælfric may have substituted the name here because "Caesar" had become a generic name for any Roman emperor. He elaborates on the emperor's name "Augustus" in paragraph 6 below.

5   *uncommon peace . . . to him alone*: The *Pax Romana* or *Pax Augusta* (Roman Peace or Augustan Peace) was a period of two hundred years beginning somewhere around 30 BCE, during which the world was said to be at relative peace. The idea was promoted by writers such as Seneca the Younger to flatter the Roman emperors. Ælfric's statement that Christ's birth was appropriate at this time comes from his source, Bede's *Homilia* 1.6.

6   *as great a number of humankind*: Ælfric makes this point again in CH 1.24.7; his source is Gregory the Great, *Homiliae in evangelia* 34.

7   *Cyrinus is interpreted "heir"*: Most of Ælfric's etymologies derive

ultimately from Jerome's *Liber interpretationis Hebraicorum nominum,* ed. P. de Lagarde, in *S. Hieronymi presbyteri opera,* part 1.1, CCSL 72 (Turnhout, 1959); for Cyrinus, see *Liber interpretationis* 64.9. Etymological interpretation was a widespread mode of understanding in early medieval England; see Joyce Hill, "Ælfric's Use of Etymologies," *ASE* 17 (1988): 35–44, and more generally, Fred Robinson, "The Significance of Names in Old English Literature," *Anglia* 86 (1968): 14–58.

8   *You, Bethlehem . . . the people of Israel:* The original biblical prophecy is in Micah 5:2, quoted in Matthew 2:6.

           I am the bread . . . all eternity: A conflation of John 6:41 and 6:50.

12–13   *Indeed, humanity had discord . . . human for you:* This recounting of the enmity and subsequent concord between humans and angels is closely based on Gregory the Great, *Homiliae in evangelia* 8.

13   *See that you . . . God alone:* Revelation 22:9.

14   *In the beginning . . . the word was God:* John 1:1.

           We might give you a little example: This analogy is not in Ælfric's sources and appears to be original to him.

15   *Mary was betrothed, by God's direction:* Ælfric discusses the legal necessity of Mary's marriage to Joseph in CH 1.13.6.

           That is eternal life . . . the savior Christ: John 17:3.

16   *The ox knows . . . his lord's manger:* Isaiah 1:3.

17   *The memory of these three shepherds:* The village of Beit Sahur southeast of Bethlehem contains two rival sites that claim to be the location of the shepherd's memorial; at least one of them dates to the fourth century, when it was seen by the pilgrim Egeria. Ælfric's knowledge of the site undoubtedly comes from Bede's *Homilia* 1.7, as does most of the second half of the homily.

3. Saint Stephen

title   The story of the death of Stephen, the first martyr, is told in Acts 6:8–11 and 7:53–60. Ælfric adapts and expands on this text and turns it to a discussion of love and forgiveness. His primary source is a homily once attributed to Augustine (as he notes in paragraph 5) but now thought to be by Caesarius of Arles (*Sermo* 219). This and his other sources were available to Ælfric in the homiliary of Paul the Deacon.

1–2   A paraphrase of Acts 6:5–15.

3   *chief priest*: Here and elsewhere Ælfric uses Old English *ealdor-bisceop* (chief bishop) to describe the priests of the Jewish religion.

    He began to explain . . . great temple to God: This is a very concise summary of Acts 7:2–50.

    You resist . . . have not held it: A loose translation of Acts 7:51–53.

4   A paraphrase of Acts 7:54–59.

5   *The wise Augustine*: As noted above, the homily is now attributed to Caesarius of Arles.

    But it was fitting: In CH 1.40 and CH 2.7, Ælfric returns to the idea that Christ is properly called the "Son of man" because he is the child of only one human parent.

6   *The death . . . in God's sight*: A reference to Psalms 115:5 (116:15).

8   *with bended knees . . . to redeem Saul*: Not in the biblical account; Ælfric may have taken this detail from Augustine, *Sermo* 382.

9   *If you forgive those . . . forgive your sins*: Matthew 6:14–15.

    Though I spend . . . of no benefit to me: 1 Corinthians 13:3.

    He who does not love his brother remains in death: 1 John 3:14.

    Anyone who hates his brother is a murderer: 1 John 3:15.

    If you offer your gift . . . then offer your gift: Matthew 5:23–24.

10   *Love your enemies . . . Father who is in heaven*: Matthew 5:44–45.

11–12   These two paragraphs are a reworking of passages in *Sermo* 3 of Fulgentius.

4. Assumption of John the Evangelist

title   This homily does not address the gospel usually read on this day (John 21:2–13) but instead tells the story of the saint's life and death. Ælfric's primary source is Bede's *Homilia* 1.9 for the opening section, and some version of the pseudo-Mellitus *Passio Iohannis apostoli* for the rest, including the long depiction of the backsliding young philosophers. The pseudo-Mellitus *Passio Iohannis* can be found in Mombritius, *Sanctuarium,* vol. 2, pp. 55–61. On some manuscript variants of this text, see Patrick H. Zettel, "Ælfric's Hagiographical Sources and the Latin Legendary Preserved in B. L. MS Cotton Nero E.i + CCCC MS 9 and Other Manuscripts" (DPhil diss., Oxford University, 1979), and Malcolm Godden, "Experiments in Genre: The Saints' Lives in Ælfric's *Catholic Homilies,*" in *Holy Men and Holy Women: Old English Prose Saints' Lives and Their Contexts,* ed. Paul E. Szarmach (Albany, 1996), 261–87, particularly at 266–69. Most of the stories told by Ælfric are found in the apocryphal *Acts of John,* ed. and trans. Wilhelm Schneemelcher and R. McL. Wilson, in *New Testament Apocrypha: Writings Related to the Apostles, Apocalypses and Related Subjects,* rev. ed. (Louisville, KY, 1991–1992), vol. 2, pp. 152–212.

1   *Christ was invited to his wedding*: The story of the wedding feast at Cana is told in John 2:1–12. The identification of the groom with John the Evangelist himself was traditional and is found in Haymo of Auxerre's *Homiliae de tempore* 18. The tradition that John's mother was Mary's sister is a favorite of Ælfric's; see Pope, *Homilies,* 217–18.

2   *a cruel emperor . . . after Nero*: In fact, a number of emperors ruled between Nero and Domitian, including Galba, Otho, Vitellius, Vespasian, and Titus. Ælfric is either condensing or misunderstanding his source (the pseudo-Mellitus *Passio Iohannis*) here; the source actually says that Domitian was the next great persecutor of Christians after Nero, not the next emperor.

    Blessed is he who comes in God's name: From the liturgical canticle *Sanctus,* recited at every Mass.

4   *the philosopher Graton*: In his source the philosopher's name is Craton, possibly a remembrance of the Cynic philosopher Crates (around 300 BCE); Ælfric's spelling *Graton* suggests a variant manuscript tradition.

    and throw it in the sea: Ælfric describes the same practice in CH 1.27.10, where he ascribes it to Socrates.

    he should sell all his wealth: Paraphrasing Matthew 19:16–21.

5   *In vain every person . . . for whom he gathers*: A paraphrase of Psalms
       38:7 (39:6).

8   *In the beginning . . . nothing is created* John 1:1–2.

11   *through water and the Holy Spirit*: That is, through the sacrament
       of baptism.

5. The Feast of the Holy Innocents

title   This homily is a largely historical exposition of the gospel read-
          ing for the day, Matthew 2:1–23. The same material is treated
          more allegorically in the homily for Epiphany, CH 1.7. Ælfric
          draws on many sources for the homily, most of which were
          found in the homiliary of Paul the Deacon; see J. E. Cross, "Æl-
          fric: Mainly on Memory and Creative Method in Two Catholic
          Homilies," *Studia Neophilologica* 41 (1969): 135–55, particularly
          137–47. For the historical sections he primarily uses Haymo of
          Auxerre's *Homiliae de tempore* 12 and 15, for this feast and the
          Epiphany. For more on sources, see Joyce Hill, "Ælfric's Hom-
          ily on the Holy Innocents: The Sources Reviewed," in *Alfred
          the Wise: Studies in Honour of Janet Bately on the Occasion of her
          Sixty-Fifth Birthday,* ed. Jane Roberts, Janet L. Nelson, and Mal-
          colm Godden (Cambridge, 1997), 89–98.

2–4   A fairly close translation of Matthew 2:1–15.

2   *three astrologers*: These are the "Three Wise Men." The Old Eng-
          lish word *tungelwitega* (literally, "star scholar") means "astrono-
          mer," but the context of the story suggests that "astrologer" is
          a better term. In medieval culture little distinction was made
          between astronomical observation of the heavens and astro-
          logical speculation into celestial influence on earthly affairs.

          O Bethlehem . . . the people of Israel: Micah 5:2.

5   *saw that he . . . because they are no more*: Translating Matthew
          2:16–18.

          A voice is heard . . . they are no more: Jeremiah 31:15.

7   *the royal line . . . Christ himself came*: A paraphrase of Genesis
          49:10.

          No wisdom or counsel is of any value against God: Proverbs 21:30.

9   *they will arise . . . in full growth*: This is Ælfric's own addition to his sources, and he mentions it several times in the homilies, including CH 1.16.12. The idea probably reached him through Julian of Toledo's *Prognosticon futuri saeculi* 3.20.20–23, a work that Ælfric himself adapted and abridged; see Milton McC. Gatch, *Preaching and Theology in Anglo-Saxon England: Ælfric and Wulfstan* (Toronto, 1977), 129–46.

11   The elaborately graphic description of Herod's illness is from Rufinus's *Historia ecclesiastica*.

13   Translating Matthew 2:19–23.

6. CIRCUMCISION

title   Ælfric translates the brief gospel for the day (Luke 2:21), then gives the Old Testament background on the practice of circumcision (Genesis 17) and explains its spiritual significance. He follows this with a lengthy warning against the use of divination and prognostics, a number of which were associated with New Year's Day. Prognostics are found in many monastic manuscripts from the eleventh century, so Ælfric's warnings were apparently timely but not very effective; for Ælfric's views, see Audrey Meaney, "Ælfric and Idolatry," *Journal of Religious History* 13 (1984): 119–35, particularly 123–26. The primary sources for this homily are Bede's *Homilia* 1.11, on the Circumcision, and Haymo of Auxerre's *Homiliae de tempore* 14, on the same occasion. The warning against prognostics is partly from Martin of Braga's *De correctione rusticorum* (see CH 1.1); the accompanying science of lunar influence is from Bede's *De temporum ratione* 28–29, trans. Faith Wallis, *Bede: The Reckoning of Time* (Liverpool, 1999), 80–85.

1   *After the eight days . . . in the womb*: Luke 2:21.

     Jesus, that is, 'savior': As is usual in Old English, Ælfric almost universally translates the name *Jesus* by the etymological translation *hælend*, "savior" (literally, "healer"). He generally does this without comment or explanation; in the few cases where the name is explicitly mentioned, he calls attention to the translation. For more on this see Damian Fleming, "*Jesus, that is hælend*: Hebrew names and the Vernacular Savior in Anglo-Saxon England," *JEGP* 112 (2013): 26–47.

2   A paraphrase of Genesis 17:1–19.

3   *Abraham was a hundred years old*: This detail is found in Genesis 17:17.

5   *Unless someone . . . kingdom of heaven*: John 3:5.
     Whatever male child . . . disregarded my covenant: Genesis 17:14.
     he did not come . . . but to fulfill it: Matthew 5:17.

6   *The person did not . . . has become like them*: Psalms 48:13 (49:12).

7   *God will call his servants by another name*: Isaiah 65:15.
     You will be called . . . has named: Isaiah 62:2.
     If you are Christ's . . . according to the promise: Galatians 3:29.
     As Sarah obeyed . . . fearing any affliction: 1 Peter 3:6.

8   *The stone truly was Christ*: 1 Corinthians 10:4.

9   This discussion of the beginning of the year is from Martin of Braga's *De correctione rusticorum* with additional details probably from Bede, *De temporum ratione* 36; the preference for beginning the year on March 21 (coincidentally also the feast of Saint Benedict) is also found in Bede's *De temporum ratione* 6. See Malcolm Godden, "New Year's Day in Late Anglo-Saxon England," *Notes and Queries* 237 (1992): 148–50. It is worth noting that no surviving early medieval English calendar or computistical work begins the year on March 21; Ælfric was in a decided minority in this opinion.
     This month is . . . of the year: Exodus 12:2.

10   *which you call "Hlyda"*: Bede, *De temporum ratione* 15, states that the English name for the month corresponding to March is *Hreþmonaþ*. Ælfric gives the alternate name *Hlyda*.
     The almighty established all the heavenly bodies: A paraphrase of Genesis 1:14.

11   *various divinations*: Prognostics for health, weather, etc., based on the day of the week, or on the weekday on which January 1 falls (often called the *Revelatio Esdrae*), as well as lunar calendars for childbirth, illness, bloodletting, journeys, and other activities, are found in a number of eleventh-century man-

uscripts. These include London, British Library, Cotton Tiberius A.iii, from Christ Church Canterbury and probably belonging to the archbishop of Canterbury, edited in Roy M. Liuzza, *Anglo-Saxon Prognostics: Studies and Texts from London, British Library, MS Cotton Tiberius A.iii* (Woodbridge, 2010); and London, British Library, Titus D.xxvi–xxvii, the personal prayer book of Ælfwine, abbot of Winchester, edited in Beate Günzel, *Ælfwine's Prayerbook (London, British Library, Cotton Titus D.xxvi + xxvii),* Henry Bradshaw Society 108 (Woodbridge, 1993). Both manuscripts are about a generation later than Ælfric, but their texts circulated widely and were apparently popular in monastic establishments, appearing in psalters, calendars, and works of computus, the early medieval science of the calendar and celestial observation.

will not let their blood on Monday: A text listing three critical Mondays on which it is not good to let blood (or take medicine, eat gooseflesh, or be born) is found in a number of manuscripts from before and after Ælfric's time; see L. S. Chardonnens, *Anglo-Saxon Prognostics, 900–1100: Studies and Texts,* Brill's Studies in Intellectual History 153 (Leiden, 2007), 336–44. It is not clear why Ælfric relates this to the allegedly widespread belief that Monday is the first day of the week, for which there is little evidence.

Some kinds of animals which one should not bless: Ælfric alludes to the belief that some animals are created by the devil in CH 1.1.9

12   *Whatever you do . . . through his Son*: Colossians 3:17.

I believe that . . . with vain divinations: Galatians 4:10–11.

13   The belief that plants and animals are stronger during the waxing than the waning moon is found, among other places, in Bede's *De temporum ratione* 28–29.

four points: In early medieval reckoning a "point," or *punctus,* was one quarter of an hour. This information on the tides is from Bede, *De temporum ratione* 29.

14   *has established . . . and in weight*: Wisdom 11:21. This was a favorite quotation for those who worked on the computus.

7. EPIPHANY

title   This homily is an exegesis of the gospel for the day, Matthew
2:1–12. The same text was the basis for CH 1.5, but this interpretation is more allegorical and figurative; for example, it interprets the three gifts of the Magi as representing the triple
nature of Christ as human, king, and God. A mention of the
star of Bethlehem prompts a discussion of fate, predestination, and free will. As usual Ælfric draws on several sources for
his work, most prominently on Gregory the Great's *Homiliae in
evangelia* 10 for the occasion.

1   *a few days ago*: In CH 1.5, for December 28, the feast of the Holy
Innocents.

2–3   A translation of Matthew 2:1–12, identical to that given in CH
1.5.

    three astrologers: See note to CH 1.5.2 above.

4   *This is my beloved Son . . . obey him*: Matthew 3:17.

5   *Truly the psalmist wrote*: A reference to Psalms 117(118):22.

    At his coming the savior . . . enmity in himself: A paraphrase of Ephe-
sians 2:15–17.

8   *All creatures acknowledged*: Ælfric repeats this idea, in almost the
same words, in CH 1.15.13.

    until the ninth hour: Ancient and medieval people divided the day
into two unequal portions, one of daylight and one of darkness,
each subdivided into twelve hours. In the summer the daylight
hours were long and the night hours short, in winter vice versa.
The first hour of the day was sunrise, the twelfth sunset; the
"ninth hour" is the middle of the afternoon, usually around
3 p.m.

10   *Indeed holy scripture says*: Referring to Romans 9:12–13 rather
than the story in Genesis. Interestingly, Ælfric adds that Jacob
and Esau were differently loved "for their different merits,"
but Paul's epistle makes the opposite point: "Not because of
works, but because of him who calls, it was said to her, 'The elder shall serve the younger'" (Romans 9:12).

11   *Now foolish people often say*: The long discussion of predestina-

tion and free will that follows, though based on Augustine, is largely Ælfric's own invention; see Lynne Grundy, *Books and Grace: Aelfric's Theology* (London, 1991), 115–47.

14   *Through God's grace we are held in faith*: Ephesians 2:8.

        I test people's hearts . . . his own behavior: Jeremiah 17:10.

18   *A desirable treasure lies in the mouth of the wise*: Proverbs 21:20.

        Lord, let my prayer . . . in your sight: Psalms 140(141):2.

        My hands dripped myrrh: Song of Songs 5:5.

        The beasts rotted in their dung: Joel 1:17.

8. THIRD SUNDAY AFTER EPIPHANY

title   This homily is an exposition of the gospel reading for the day, divided into two parts, the healing of a leper (Matthew 8:1–4) and the healing of a centurion's servant (Matthew 8:5–13). Its main source, very freely adapted, is Haymo of Auxerre's *Homiliae de tempore* 19. Ælfric cites this source, but draws on several others as well.

2   A close translation of Matthew 8:1–4.

3   *The teacher Haymo*: Haymo of Auxerre (d. ca. 865) was a prolific Carolingian writer of homilies and biblical commentaries. These were widely circulated and had some influence on Ælfric's work. See further Introduction, "Sources."

4   *He spoke . . . and they were created*: Psalms 32(33):9.

5   *A leper's body*: Paraphrasing Leviticus 13:2.

        Truly, he himself . . . bore our pains: Isaiah 53:4.

7   *The old law commanded*: See Leviticus 13 and 14.

        Go into the city . . . ought to do: Acts 9:7.

8   *Remove the evil one . . . infect the whole flock*: 1 Corinthians 5:13, combined with a remark from Benedict's *Rule* 28.8.

9   Ælfric continues with a translation of Matthew 8:5–13.

        centurion: Ælfric uses the literal Old English equivalent *hundredes ealdor* (leader of a hundred).

        The rich children: For unknown reasons Ælfric translates the Latin *filii regni* (children of the kingdom) as *ða rican bearn* (the rich children), using the association between the Old English adjective *rice* (rich) and noun *rice* (kingdom). The Old English version of the gospels translate the phrase as *þises rices bearn* (children of this kingdom), which is more correct.

11 *John the evangelist*: Ælfric recounts a similar miracle told in John 4:46–53.

12 *The exalted Lord ... knows from afar*: Psalms 137(138):6.

14 *Mary and Martha*: Sisters of Lazarus, whom Jesus raised from the dead; their words are from John 11:21.

15 *the day ends*: Two manuscripts (N and Q) add a passage that is probably by Ælfric: "My brothers, understand this—many will come from the east and the west and rest with Abraham and Isaac and Jacob in the kingdom of heaven. No earthly king can live royally unless he has servants and a household arranged as befits his kingship. Lo, do you not suppose that the almighty king who made heaven and earth would have an immense household that would reign with him? He would have much of humanity in his heavenly household, and each there will have the honor that he merited here in the world."

16 *The rich children*: Ælfric continues to translate *filii regni* (children of the kingdom) as *þa rican bearn* (the rich children). The mention of Zacchaeus in a list of "rich" men makes it clear that *rice* means "wealthy" and not "powerful" (another possible meaning). It is clear from this paragraph that he is doing this deliberately; this interpretation is not in any of his sources, and his reasons are not clear.

17 *There their worm ... fire be quenched*: Mark 9:43.

18 *without it no one can be pleasing to God*: Hebrews 11:6.

the righteous lives by his faith: Habakkuk 2:4.

9. PURIFICATION

title This feast goes by several names, including Candlemas and the Presentation in the Temple; liturgical practices on this day are discussed by M. Bradford Bedingfield, "Reinventing the Gospel: Ælfric and the Liturgy," *Medium Aevum* 68 (1999): 13–31, at 15–23. Ælfric's homily is a paraphrased explanation of the gospel for the day, Luke 2:22–32, extended to include Luke 2:33–40. This homily and Vercelli 17 are the only two Old English homilies for this feast day; a discussion of the Vercelli homily is found in Samantha Zacher, "Rereading the Style and Rhetoric of the Vercelli Homilies," in *The Old English Homily: Precedent, Practice, and Appropriation*, ed. Aaron Kleist, Studies in the Early Middle Ages 17 (Turnhout, 2007), 173–207. Ælfric's text is drawn from Bede's *Homilia* 1.18 on the occasion and his *Commentarius in Lucam*, as well as from Haymo of Auxerre's *Homiliae de tempore* 13 and 14. See Mary Clayton, *The Cult of the Virgin Mary in Anglo-Saxon England*, Cambridge Studies in Anglo-Saxon England 2 (Cambridge, 1990), for more on this homily's sources.

2   *in the old law*: Specifically Leviticus 12:2–6.

      nor into bed with her husband: This is not in Leviticus, but is found in the homily by Bede that Ælfric uses as a source. In Bede's *Ecclesiastical History* 1.23, Gregory the Great writes to Augustine of Canterbury that the prohibition against intercourse still applied, but a woman was no longer barred from the church after giving birth.

3   This paragraph paraphrases Luke 2:22–32.

      My Lord, you let me . . . your people Israel: Luke 2:29–32. This prayer, called the *Nunc dimittis*, was said at every monastic office of Compline, the last service of the day.

4–5   These two paragraphs are derived from Augustine's *Sermo* 370.

6   *In the old law*: Exodus 13:2 and Numbers 18:15–16.

      we should repent of our wickedness with our five senses: In Bede's homily this is clearer; he says we should repent *pro singulis . . . sensibus*, "on behalf of our senses" which have sinned.

9   *You will be sad . . . to eternal joy*: John 16:20.

      Blessed are those . . . will be comforted: Matthew 5:5.

10   *I am the light of all the world . . . of life*: John 8:12.

11–12   A translation and exposition of Luke 2:33–34.

11   *and it will be contradicted*: For Latin *contradicetur* Ælfric uses Old English *wiðcweden* (denied, spoken against).

13   A translation and exposition of Luke 2:36–38.

The widow who lives . . . but is dead: 1 Timothy 5:6.

14   *There are three states*: Ælfric's exposition of the three states of chastity, widowhood, and marriage, and their association with the parable of the sower (Matthew 13:3–9), is found elsewhere in his work, including CH 2.4 and CH 2.6. It is partly paralleled in Augustine, *Sermo* 370, used elsewhere as a source for this homily.

Let those . . . though they had none: 1 Corinthians 7:29.

15   A translation and exposition of Luke 2:39–40.

and in him dwells all fullness of divinity: Colossians 2:9.

16   Ælfric offers a description of the liturgical ceremony of Candlemas. The details here are different from those given in Ælfric's *Letter to the Monks of Eynsham* 25, ed. and trans. Christopher A. Jones, Cambridge Studies in Anglo-Saxon England 24 (Cambridge, 1998), and the *Regularis concordia* 54, ed. and trans. Dom Thomas Symons, *Regularis concordia Anglicae nationis monachorum sanctimonialiumque: The Monastic Agreement of the Monks and Nuns of the English Nation* (London, 1953). In those works, the descriptions suggest that only monks are involved in the procession; here the laity are clearly part of the ceremony, and the language suggests that they process from church to church rather than within one church. For more on this ritual see M. Bradford Bedingfield, *The Dramatic Liturgy of Anglo-Saxon England* (Woodbridge, 2002), chapter 3.

10. QUINQUAGESIMA (SUNDAY BEFORE ASH WEDNESDAY)

title   The Sundays before Lent were counted backward from Easter, beginning with *Septuagesima* (the ninth Sunday before Easter, or seventy days, more or less) and *Sexagesima* (the eighth Sunday before Easter, roughly sixty days). *Quinquagesima,* the seventh Sunday before Easter (fifty days), is also the Sunday before Lent begins. This homily translates and allegorically interprets the gospel of the day, Luke 18:31–43, about the healing of a blind person on the road to Jericho. Its main source is Gregory the Great's *Homiliae in evangelia* 2, with some parts of

Haymo of Auxerre's *Homiliae de tempore* 23, which is also based in part on Gregory's reading of the text. An anonymous homily on the same text, Blickling 2, ed. R. Morris, *The Blickling Homilies of the Tenth Century*, EETS o.s. 58, 63, 73 (Oxford, 1874–1880), 15–25, agrees with Ælfric in some details, but this appears to be because the two authors were using the same sources. This homily and those that follow are discussed by Robert K. Upchurch, "Catechetic Homiletics: Ælfric's Preaching and Teaching During Lent," in *A Companion to Ælfric*, ed. Hugh Magennis and Mary Swan (Leiden, 2009), 216–46.

2   A paraphrase of Luke 18:31–43.

4   The interpretation of Jericho as "moon" is found in Haymo of Auxerre's *Homiliae de tempore* 23, which served as one of Ælfric's sources.

      I am the way, and truth, and life: John 14:6.

6   *Your heavenly Father . . . him for anything*: Matthew 6:8.

9   *He who will serve me, let him follow me*: John 12:26.

      The beasts have holes . . . lay down my head: Matthew 8:20.

10   A paraphrase of John 6:15–19.

      Whoever will be . . . enemy of God: James 4:4.

11   *The way is very narrow . . . torment of hell*: Matthew 7:13–14.

      Christ suffered for us . . . follow his footsteps: 1 Peter 2:21.

11. FIRST SUNDAY IN LENT

title   This homily translates the gospel for this Mass, Matthew 4:1–11, the story of Christ's temptation in the wilderness. Its main sources are Gregory the Great's *Homiliae in evangelia* 16 and Haymo of Auxerre's *Homiliae de tempore* 28, which is also based on Gregory's homily. An anonymous Old English homily on the same gospel passage, surviving only in the twelfth-century manuscript B (Oxford, Bodleian Library, Bodley 343) and edited by Susan Irvine, *Old English Homilies from MS Bodley 343*, EETS o.s. 302 (Oxford, 1993), 115–22, is often close to Ælfric's text, but (as with CH 1.10) this may be because both homilies are drawing from the same sources.

2   *I fear that you cannot understand*: Ælfric's warning about the diffi-

culty of this text is unusual; he may have been concerned about his listeners leaping to false conclusions about the nature of evil or the relationship between God and the devil.

3   A translation of Matthew 4:1–11.

4   *he would be tempted there . . . would not dare test Christ*: Ælfric is careful to distinguish between tempting (Old English *costnung*) and testing (Old English *fandung*); the former is evil—we are tempted to sin—and the latter is morally neutral—we are tested to discover our true nature. The distinction is apparently Ælfric's own; neither the Latin Vulgate nor the commentaries on this passage make this distinction, using *temptationes* for both senses of the word, and other Old English translations use *costnung* only. Ælfric discusses the distinction further in CH 1.19.10.

5   The devil's doubts about the nature of Christ are discussed by Jerome, *Commentarii in evangelium Matthaei* 1.342–45, as well as in other authors known to Ælfric.

6   *it is commanded . . . against a stone*: The citation is Psalms 90(91):11–12, "For he has given his angels charge over you, to keep you in all your ways; they shall bear you up in their hands, lest you dash your foot against a stone." As Ælfric points out, the devil's interpretation is unorthodox.

he has set his angels over us as guardians: Ælfric expands on the idea of guardian angels in CH 1.34, using this same scriptural passage.

8   *The earth and all . . . are God's possessions*: Psalms 23(24):1.

Christ said . . . should be driven out: John 12:31, "Now the prince of this world is cast out."

9   *Some say that the savior . . . writes in a letter*: The Latin note is unusual and somewhat confusing; it discusses the textual variants *vade* (go), which is the standard Vulgate reading, *vade retro* (go behind), a common variant in Insular manuscripts, including the Old English version of the gospels, and *vade retro me* (go behind me), found in some Latin manuscripts of the gospel. The reference to a letter of Jerome may be to his *Commentarii in evangelium Matthaei* (1.378–85), used elsewhere in the homily.

10 *Do not do it . . . pray to God alone*: Revelation 22:9.

825

13   *You will be . . . of that tree*: Genesis 3:5, which actually says, "You will be like gods"; Ælfric, as he does in CH 1.1.10 and in his translation of Genesis, silently translates Latin *dii* (gods) as "angels."

15   *Moses . . . and forty nights*: Exodus 34:28.

           The prophet Elijah also fasted just as long: 1 Kings 19:8.

17   *according to the apostle's teaching*: 2 Corinthians 6:3–7.

           And do as God taught . . . do not despise your own flesh: Referring to Isaiah 58:17, "Share your bread with the hungry, bring the needy and the homeless into your house; when you see someone naked, clothe them, and do not despise your own flesh."

           Woe to you . . . mourn and weep: Luke 6:25.

           Blessed are they . . . be comforted: Matthew 5:5.

12. MID-LENT SUNDAY

title   This homily translates and offers an allegorical interpretation of the gospel of the day, John 6:1–14, the parable of the loaves and fishes. Its primary source is a homily of Augustine, *In Iohannis evangelium tractatus* 24, sometimes filtered through the readings of Bede's *Homilia* 2.2 or Haymo of Auxerre's *Homiliae de tempore* 49, also derived from Augustine.

2   Translates John 6:1–14.

3   Ælfric's image of the mutability of the sea, and his comparison to the vicissitudes of life, is partly from Haymo's exposition of this passage, but partly too his own contribution.

5–6   The idea of "everyday miracles" and that of the need to understand God's miracles, not merely marvel at them, are from Augustine.

6   *Often someone sees fair letters written*: This analogy, though it is found in Augustine, may owe something to a letter of Gregory the Great; see R. Gameson, "Ælfric and the Perception of Script and Picture in Anglo-Saxon England," *Anglo-Saxon Studies in Archaeology and History* 5 (1992): 85–101, at 90.

7   *to all Christian people*: Manuscript A, the manuscript closest to Ælfric's original composition, originally had a long passage giv-

ing a rudimentary account of Moses and the ten commandments:

> If anyone inquires who this Moses was, then we say that he
> was the man whom God spoke to frequently, and he was the
> leader of the people whom God led from the land of Egypt
> with great miracles. And they went over the Red Sea with dry
> feet, and afterward God fed them forty winters with heavenly
> food. And there were in the people six hundred thousand,
> five hundred fifty fighting men. And every day heavenly food
> came to them; they did not plow or till, nor was their clothing
> worn out, during that forty years. Then God imposed a law
> on the people and commanded that Moses write five peerless
> books for the people, and he was with God and set down in
> the five books, by God's dictation, how God made the heav-
> ens and the earth and all creation, and he also wrote in his
> account that no one should bow down to any idolatry, and
> all should pray to God alone, who alone is true God. Nor
> should anyone speak God's name in any idleness, and every-
> one should observe Sunday with honor, and should honor his
> father and his mother, and whoever curses or offends father
> and mother is condemned to death. He also said, "Do not
> fornicate unrightly; do not kill anyone; do not steal or be a
> false witness; do not desire another man's wife, nor another
> person's possessions." These words are said openly, but in
> each of the words is some hidden thing that requires consid-
> eration.

Ælfric canceled the passage and wrote a note (which survives
in A in his own hand) saying, "This matter is fuller in the other
book, and we forbid it in this one, lest it seem tiresome if it
were in the other book." The very basic knowledge conveyed
by this paragraph suggests that Ælfric originally conceived of
his audience as lay people having "a remarkably lower standard of understanding" than his monastic or clerical colleagues
(Godden, *Introduction*, 98).

8   *Other Evangelists report . . . the crowd*: Ælfric's Latin note, com-

paring a detail of the narrative to the parallel accounts in other gospels, is found in Bede's *Homilia* 2.2.

10   *All flesh is grass ... the blooming of plants*: Isaiah 40:6.

11   *Be watchful ... and be bold*: 1 Corinthians 16:13.

13   *Blessed are they ... proclaim my miracles*: A paraphrase of John 20:29.

13. ANNUNCIATION

title   This homily is a translation and exposition of the gospel of the day, Luke 1:26–38, along with the biblical story of the Visitation, Luke 1:39–55. Its main sources are two homilies by Bede (*Homiliae* 1.3 and 1.4) on the Annunciation and Visitation, freely adapted here.

2   Ælfric's treatment of the Fall and redemption of humanity is similar to CH 1.1.

3   *Behold, a virgin ... be called Emmanuel*: Isaiah 7:14.

    This gate shall not ... shut for eternity: Ezekiel 44:2.

4   *When the fullness ... redemption of humankind*: A paraphrase of Galatians 4:4–5.

    God's archangel Gabriel ... from her sight: A paraphrase and translation of Luke 1:26–38.

5   *the devil sent another devil*: The idea that the serpent in the garden of Eden was not Satan but some subordinate demon is not in Ælfric's sources, but it is found in the Old English poem *Genesis B*. Elsewhere in his writings Ælfric does not appear to insist on this point; he may be presenting it here to highlight the contrast between God sending an angel and Satan sending a subordinate devil.

    The Lord is strong and mighty in battle: Psalms 23(24):8.

6   *Joseph understood that Mary was with child*: Very freely paraphrased from Matthew 1:19–20.

8   *Israel is interpreted ... "supplanter"*: As elsewhere, Ælfric gets his etymologies ultimately from Jerome's *Liber interpretationis Hebraicorum nominum* 61.27, where *Iacobus* is interpreted *subplantator vel subplantans* (supplanter or supplanting). The Old English

word *forscrencend,* translated "supplanter" here, occurs only in Ælfric and only as a gloss on the name Jacob; it is presumably derived from the verb *forscrencan* (overthrow, undermine).

9 *She was so overshadowed that she was purified*: Ælfric, like Bede, asserts that Mary became sinless at the Annunciation; the view that Mary was sinless from birth (the "Immaculate Conception") later prevailed to become Catholic Christian doctrine.

10 *conceived in unrighteousness and born in sins*: A paraphrase of Psalms 50:7 (51:5).

   When you are great . . . reward with God: Sirach 3:20.

12 A translation of Luke 1:40–45.

13 *My soul magnifies . . . his offspring forever*: Luke 1:46–55. This canticle, called the *Magnificat,* was, as Ælfric points out, sung every evening at Vespers in the Divine Office.

14 *Everyone who exalts himself . . . will be exalted*: Luke 14:11.

15 *Blessed are those . . . filled with righteousness*: Matthew 5:6.

   The rich man's wealth is his soul's redemption: Proverbs 13:8.

16 *Truly, if you are Christians . . . to the promise*: Galatians 3:29.

14. Palm Sunday

title This homily does not address the gospel of the day, usually Matthew 26:2–27:66 (for this, see CH 2.14), but rather provides an allegorical reading of the story of Christ's entry into Jerusalem, told in all four gospels. This story, in the version either of John 12:9–13 or Matthew 21:1–9, was read at the Palm Sunday procession. Its major sources are Bede's *Homilia* 2.3 (on Matthew 21:1–9) and *Opus imperfectum in Matthaeum* homily 37, falsely attributed to John Chrysostom and found in the homiliary of Paul the Deacon.

3 This account weaves together material from Matthew 21:1–5, Luke 19:30–38, and John 12:9–13.

   The prophet Isaiah . . . riding on an ass: Zechariah 9:9. In CH 2.1.9 Ælfric attributes the quotation to Ezekiel.

4 *Every person is bound with the ropes of his sins*: Proverbs 5:22.

5 *Go out over . . . have taught you*: Matthew 28:19–20.

7   *Learn from me . . . for your souls*: Matthew 11:29.

9   *Lord, your priests are clothed with righteousness*: Psalms 131(132):9.

     You are bought . . . in your bodies: 1 Corinthians 6:20.

     He who defiles . . . will destroy him: 1 Corinthians 3:17.

10   *We will tell you a parable*: Ælfric's observation on kingship and power closely follows a passage in one of his sources, the pseudo-Chrysostom *Opus imperfectum* homily 37. It is not likely that he is commenting on specifically English ideas about kingship, though we may assume that he expected his listeners to understand and agree with his point.

12   *We believe that . . . as they are*: Acts 15:11.

13   *That all heavenly . . . reestablished in Christ*: Ephesians 1:10.

14   *The savior was staying in the temple*: Loosely based on Luke 19:47–48.

15   *as it does to a greedy fish*: This striking image is from Gregory the Great's *Homiliae in evangelia* 25, for Easter.

16   *his divinity was in hell during that time*: Ælfric discusses the harrowing of hell in CH 1.1.22.

17   *The custom exists in God's Church*: Ælfric's description of Palm Sunday is similar to that found in *Regularis concordia* 36, ed. and trans. Symons, pp. 34–36, and in Ælfric's own *Letter to the Monks of Eynsham* 32, but Ælfric explains the significance of the ceremony in greater detail here. Presumably the ceremony would take place in the church right after this sermon.

18   *Then the righteous . . . their Father's kingdom*: Matthew 13:14.

19   *Church customs . . . silent days*: This note also appears in three other manuscripts (BHQ), and is added to A (see Notes to the Text); it appears again in CH 2.14. The practice of observing silence in the days before Easter may have been a monastic custom at Winchester, but was apparently not a widespread practice; both the Latin homiliaries from which Ælfric drew most of his sources and other English collections of homilies provide readings for the three so-called "silent days." Ælfric may have been trying to encourage the spread of the custom; see Joyce Hill, "Ælfric's 'Silent Days'," *Leeds Studies in English* 16 (1985): 118–25.

15. Easter Sunday

title This homily offers an expanded translation and commentary on the gospel reading for Easter Sunday, Mark 16:1–7, interwoven with details from parallel passages in other gospels. Its main source, as Ælfric states, is Gregory the Great's homily on this passage (*Homiliae in evangelia* 21), with, as is usual for Ælfric, details from other homilies such as Bede's *Homilia* 2.7.

2 A loose translation of Matthew 27:62–66.

3 This paragraph combines paraphrases and translations of Luke 23:55–56, Mark 16:1–4, and Matthew 28:2–8, reconciling their inconsistencies and adding details of his own. No other source specifies that Mary the mother of Jesus was among the women who went to the tomb; Ælfric seems to have invented this detail.

4 A translation of Matthew 28:9–15.

 became known throughout all the land of Judea: Most commentaries understand this verse (Matthew 28:15) to mean that the false story told by the bribed guards was current in Judea; Ælfric interprets it, unusually, to mean that the story of their bribery, and Christ's resurrection, became known throughout Judea.

5 A translation of Luke 24:36–47.

7 *The angel rolled the lid*: This detail, taken from Bede's *Homilia* 2.7 for Easter rather than Gregory's homily that is Ælfric's named source, was apparently written on a separate slip in manuscript A, which is close to Ælfric's original; the slip is lost, but the passage appears in all other copies of the text. It may represent an afterthought or early revision by Ælfric.

8 *His countenance was . . . white as snow*: Ælfric takes this detail from Matthew 28:3.

10 *The Evangelist Matthew wrote*: Matthew 27:52. The idea that the dead raised at the Crucifixion were eternally raised, and are thus evidence for the doctrine of the resurrection of the body, is also found in CH 1.30, and in Christine Rauer, ed., *The Old English Martyrology: Edition, Translation, and Commentary* (Woodbridge, 2013), text for March 25.

11   *If he is the king . . . believe in him*: Matthew 27:42.

12   This story of Samson is told in the biblical book of Judges, chapter 16. The analogy is from Gregory's homily that is Ælfric's source.

        Christ broke . . . and Eve: Another reference to the harrowing of hell.

        He left behind the wicked to eternal torments: This is added in a different hand in manuscript A; it is not in Gregory's homily and may be another afterthought or early revision by Ælfric.

13   *All creatures acknowledged their creator*: Ælfric refers to this idea, in virtually the same words, in CH 1.7.8.

16. First Sunday after Easter

title   The homily is an exposition of the gospel for the day, John 20:19–31. Its main sources are Gregory the Great's *Homiliae in evangelia* 26, Julian of Toledo's *Prognosticon futuri saeculi,* and Haymo of Auxerre's *Homiliae de tempore* 81, also based on Gregory.

2–4   A translation of John 20:19–31.

6   *We read in the book called* Acts of the Apostles: The story is told in Acts 5:17–23.

8   *Christ blew . . . does not see physically*: Ælfric repeats this passage, taken from Gregory's homily, almost word for word in CH 1.22.14.

        He who does not . . . does not see physically: 1 John 4:20.

9   *Release his bonds, that he may go*: John 11:44.

10   *He who professes . . . by those works*: A paraphrase of Titus 1:16, "They profess to know God, but deny him by their actions."

        Faith without good works is dead: James 2:26.

11   *Not one hair of your head shall be lost to you*: Luke 21:18.

12   *The apostle Paul said*: Ephesians 4:13 says that the body of Christ will be built up "until we all attain to the unity of faith and of the knowledge of the Son of God, to a perfect man, to the measure of the age of the fullness of Christ," which was interpreted to mean that bodies would rise from death at Christ's age of

thirty-three. This section is based on Ælfric's reading of Julian of Toledo's *Prognosticon futuri saeculi;* see Milton McC. Gatch, "MS Boulogne-sur-Mer 63 and Ælfric's First Series of Catholic Homilies," *JEGP* 65 (1966): 482–90, particularly at 486–88.

13   *No man will marry . . . dwell with angels*: Luke 20:35–6.

forever in eternity. Amen: In some manuscripts (HNQRTU; see Notes to the Text) an additional passage appears here, apparently added by Ælfric at some time after he composed the original homily, explaining the resurrection in terms of the regrowth of plants after winter, the metamorphosis of silkworms, the rebirth of the phoenix, and other things.

17. SECOND SUNDAY AFTER EASTER

title   This brief homily is an exposition of the gospel for the day, John 10:11–16. Its source is Haymo of Auxerre's *Homiliae de tempore* 83, a revision of Gregory the Great's *Homiliae in evangelia* 14 on the gospel; for his exposition of Ezekiel he uses Augustine's *Sermo* 46 or an abridged version (Godden, *Introduction,* 137).

2   A translation of John 10:11–16.

6–7   *The prophet Ezekiel . . . according to his example*: In some manuscripts (MNOQU) this passage is omitted and a long passage is added at the end of the homily (see 8 below).

6   *You shepherds . . . and in righteousness*: Paraphrasing Ezekiel 34:5–16.

7   *If the teacher . . . according to his example*: A paraphrase of Matthew 23:3.

8   In manuscripts MNOQU an added passage appears, by Ælfric, in his later rhythmical prose style, expounding further on the passage from Ezekiel, translating Ezekiel 34:2–16, and warning against the dangers of corrupt clergy and secular leaders.

18. ON THE GREATER LITANY (ROGATIONTIDE)

title   The three days preceding Ascension Thursday were called Litanies (later, Rogationtide or Rogation Days). They were days of fasting, prayer, and procession in early medieval England and were a major occasion for preaching; see J. Bazire and J. E. Cross, eds., *Eleven Old English Rogationtide Homilies,* Toronto Old English Series 7 (Toronto, 1982). Ælfric provides homilies for all three days in both CH 1 and CH 2. This homily for the Monday of Rogationtide explains the origins of the feast and expounds the gospel of the day, Luke 11:5–13. His sources for this homily are various, and include Haymo of Auxerre's *Homiliae de tempore* 90 and 92, and Augustine's *Sermones* 61 and 105 (PL 38, cols. 409–14 and 618–25). For more on the Rogation liturgies, see Stephen J. Harris, "The Liturgical Context of Ælfric's Homilies for Rogation," in Kleist, *The Old English Homily: Precedent, Practice, and Appropriation,* 143–68.

2   Ælfric's account of the origins of Rogationtide is taken from the *Liber officialis* of Amalarius of Metz (1.37.18–32). Vienne is a city in southwestern France, south of Lyon; its bishop Mamertus died around 475. Notably, Amalarius later retracted the view Ælfric reports here and stated instead that the fast had been instituted by Gregory the Great in Rome.

3–4   A quick summary of the biblical book of Jonah. For stylistic considerations, see Paul E. Szarmach, "Three Versions of the Jonah Story: An Investigation of Narrative Technique in Old English Homilies," *ASE* 1 (1972): 183–92.

3   *They took the example of the fast:* Few of Ælfric's sources connect the Rogationtide fast to the people of Nineveh; the connection is found in the Old English Vercelli Homily 19 and may have been a common tradition in Ælfric's time.

5   *follow our relics out and in:* Procession with relics was common practice in early medieval England; see Bazire and Cross, *Eleven Old English Rogationtide Homilies,* xvi and following.

The savior said to his disciples . . . those who ask him: A translation of Luke 11:5–13.

the serpent that is called scorpion: Old English *ðone wyrm ðe is gehaten ðrowend.* The Latin Vulgate has only *scorpionem* (scorpion) here; the Old English version of the gospels explains this as *þæt is an wyrmcynn* (that is, a type of serpent). Old English *wyrm,* which usually means "serpent," can also mean "reptile" more generally.

6   *Saint Augustine commented*: Augustine's *Sermo* 105, but Ælfric follows this only somewhat loosely.

8   *its nature is that the more the waves toss it*: Ælfric derives this bit of natural history from Haymo of Auxerre's *Homiliae de tempore* 92.

9   *The things we see . . . are eternal*: A paraphrase of 2 Corinthians 4:18.

       I will praise my Lord at all times: Psalms 33:2 (34:1).

11   *No one is good but God alone*: Luke 18:19.

       Lord, heal me . . . I will be saved: Jeremiah 17:14.

12   *He distributed his things . . . remains forever*: Psalms 111(112):9.

       We brought nothing . . . from it: 1 Timothy 6:7.

13   *Covetousness is the root . . . into damnation*: 1 Timothy 6:9–10.

       Warn the rich . . . for love of him: 1 Timothy 6:17–19.

14   *Whatever you do . . . you do for me*: Matthew 25:40.

19. TUESDAY, ON THE LORD'S PRAYER

title   This homily for the Tuesday in Rogationtide does not have an immediate source. It deals with the importance of the Lord's Prayer (the *Paternoster,* or "Our Father"), one of two prayers, along with the Creed, that all Christians were supposed to know. Some of his ideas are drawn from Augustine, *De sermone Domini in monte,* ed. A. Mutzenbecher, CCSL 35 (Turnhout, 1967).

1   The text of the prayer follows the version in Matthew 6:9–13 rather than the parallel Luke 11.

3   *He who does . . . and my sister*: Matthew 12:50.

4   *I fill heaven and earth with myself*: Jeremiah 23:24.

       Heaven is his throne . . . his footstool: Matthew 5:34–35.

       We turn eastward when we pray because heaven rises from there: Most early churches were oriented with their sanctuaries facing east; various scriptural authorities were given for this, including Ezekiel 43:4, "And the majesty of the Lord went into the temple by way of the gate that looked to the east," and Matthew 24:27, "For as lightning comes out of the east and appears even in the west, so shall the coming of the Son of man

NOTES TO THE TRANSLATION

be." The practice continues in the Orthodox Church to the present day. In ancient and medieval cosmology, the sun, planets, and all the heavens revolved around the earth, so the east is "where heaven rises."

6   *Come, you blessed . . . of the world*: Matthew 25:34.
    When he delivers the kingdom to his Father: 1 Corinthians 15:24.

9   *When you stand . . . the last farthing*: A combination of Mark 11:25–26 and Matthew 5:25–26.

10   *Temptation is one thing, trial is another*: Ælfric's distinction between temptation *(costnung)* and testing or trial *(fandung)*, drawn from Augustine, is also found in CH 1.11 and elsewhere in his writings.

20. WEDNESDAY, ON THE CATHOLIC FAITH

title   This homily for the Wednesday in Rogationtide is an exposition of the Creed, the other prayer all Christians were supposed to know. The Creed expounded here is a combination of the Nicene and Athanasian Creeds. Ælfric's primary focus is on one of his favorite topics, the nature of the Trinity, and he does not really address much of the Creed beyond that; evidence for several revisions in early copies suggests that Ælfric struggled to present this difficult topic in ways that his listeners would understand. Ælfric draws on a number of sources, none of them closely; the general ideas and some of the images and analogies are found in Augustine's sermons and in *De Trinitate*.

1   *the wise Augustine commented on the holy Trinity*: Ælfric may be referring to Augustine's *De Trinitate,* a source for much of what follows.

2   *There is one creator of all things visible and invisible*: Based on the beginning of the Nicene Creed, "I believe in one God, the Father Almighty, maker of heaven and earth, of all that is seen and unseen."

4   *God dwells in indivisible Trinity*: Based on the Athanasian Creed, verses 5–6 and 13–14, "For there is one Person of the Father; another of the Son; and another of the Holy Ghost. But the Godhead of the Father, of the Son, and of the Holy Ghost is

all one; the glory equal, the majesty coeternal . . . So likewise the Father is almighty; the Son almighty; and the Holy Ghost almighty. And yet they are not three Almighties; but one Almighty."

6 *Unless you believe it, you cannot understand it*: Isaiah 7:9.

7 *The Spirit of God . . . of every speech*: Wisdom 1:7.
 The Spirit of comfort . . . witness about me: John 15:26.
 he is the life-giving God, who proceeds from the Father and the Son: From the Nicene Creed, verse 5, "I believe in the Holy Spirit, the Lord, the giver of life, who proceeds from the Father and the Son."

9–10 *The sun which shines over us . . . nowhere separated*: This passage was apparently added by Ælfric after his first draft of the homily in manuscript A was complete; it was added on a loose slip that is now lost, but appears in all other copies of the text. It is also found in a revised form in Ælfric's *Lives of Saints* 1.1.9.
 There is no one . . . from his heat: Psalms 18:7 (19:6).

10 *The Father is God*: From the Athanasian Creed, verses 15–16: "So the Father is God; the Son is God; and the Holy Spirit is God. And yet they are not three Gods; but one God."

11 *No one of them is greater than the other*: From the Athanasian Creed, verses 25–26: "And in this Trinity none is before or after another; none is greater or less than another. But the whole three persons are coeternal, and coequal."

12 *Christ was born of the pure virgin Mary*: From the Nicene Creed, verse 4: "By the power of the Holy Spirit he was born of the virgin Mary."

13 *Look with wisdom at the sun*: A cross before this passage in manuscript A suggests that it was added by Ælfric, or was otherwise singled out for revision. At the end of this paragraph some manuscripts (NUV) have an added sentence in Ælfric's later rhythmical style: "Now the person who cannot understand this complexity, let him believe in the almighty God who made all things in heaven and earth, and he will be saved." This statement seems to be acknowledging the difficulty of his subject and the impossibility of explaining adequately the mystery of the Trinity.

14   *he disposed . . . and in weight*: Isaiah 40:12. See CH 1.6.14.

15   *The spirit of God tests the hearts of all people*: Ælfric repeats this sentence in CH 2.32. Its ultimate sources is Jeremiah 17:10: "I, the Lord, search the heart, I test the mind, to give to each person according to his ways, according to the results of his deeds."

16   *Let us make a human in our own likeness*: Genesis 1:26.

    The human soul has . . . memory, and understanding, and will: This argument that the threefold nature of the human soul is a reflection of the Trinity ultimately comes from Augustine, *De Trinitate* 10.11.18, but Ælfric took it from Alcuin's *De animae ratione* (see note to CH 1.1.12). He returns to this theme in the first homily in his *Lives of Saints*.

17   *There was a heretic called Arius*: Ælfric presumably draws his account of the heresies of Arius and Sabellius from Haymo of Auxerre's *Historiae sacrae epitome* (PL 118, cols. 863A–67A). Despite repeated condemnations of it in the early Church, Arianism was a fairly successful heresy whose influence did not end with its founder's frankly suspicious death in Constantinople in 336; Arianism was popular among the Germanic-speaking peoples inside and outside the Roman Empire, and several Roman emperors embraced Arius's views of the Trinity.

20   *God does not work these miracles at any Jewish tombs*: Ælfric makes the same argument at the end of his *Life of Saint Edmund* (*Lives of Saints* 32). A useful study of Ælfric's attitude toward the Jewish people—theoretical and ideological, since there were no actual Jews in England in his day—can be found in Andrew Scheil's *The Footsteps of Israel: Understanding Jews in Anglo-Saxon England* (Ann Arbor, 2004), esp. pp. 285–330.

21   *no one may be baptized twice*: Presumably a response to the Nicene Creed, verse 5: "I confess one baptism for the forgiveness of sins."

21. ASCENSION

title   This homily incorporates the epistle text of the day, Acts 1:3–15, along with Luke 24:50–53, and the day's gospel reading, Mark 16:14–20. It has several sources, including Bede's commentary on Acts, ed. M. Laistner, *Expositio Actuum apostolorum,* CCSL 121 (Turnhout, 1983), 3–99, his homily on Luke 24:36–47 (Bede, *Homiliae* 2.9), and Gregory the Great's *Homiliae in evangelia* 29 on Mark. For more on sources, see J. E. Cross, "More Sources for Two of Ælfric's Catholic Homilies," *Anglia* 86 (1968): 135–55.

2 A translation of Acts 1:3–9.

  by many reproofs: The text of the Latin Vulgate has *in multis argumentis* (by many proofs). The Old English word *þrafung* (reproof, rebuke) is an odd translation.

  And he led them out of the city: From Luke 24:50–51.

3 A translation of Acts 1:10–15.

5 *When he comes . . . said to you*: A paraphrase of John 14:26.

6 *No one knows . . . save God alone*: Matthew 24:36.

8 *With his ascension the writ of our condemnation is canceled*: For "writ" Ælfric uses the Old English word *cyrographum,* translating the Latin *chirographum* in Gregory's *Homiliae in evangelia* 29. A chirograph was a document written in duplicate with the Latin word *chirographum* (from Greek, meaning "handwritten") written across the middle; the document was cut through across the word, usually along a wavy or serrated line, so that the two halves could be verified when the document was reassembled. This is a rare word in Old English, however, and here it may just refer to any written document.

9 *You are earth . . . turn to dust*: Genesis 3:19; Ælfric quotes both the Old Latin version of this verse (*terra es,* "you are earth"), found in Gregory's *Homiliae in evangelia* 29, and the Vulgate version (*pulvis es,* "you are dust").

  Let the wicked . . . from the impious: Isaiah 26:10. Ælfric quotes this verse in its Old Latin version, as does Bede's *Expositio Actuum apostolorum* 1.108.

10 A translation of Mark 16:14–20.

11 *according to the exposition of Gregory*: Ælfric's follows Gregory, *Homiliae in evangelia* 29, for most of the rest of this homily.

12 *He who says . . . is a liar*: 1 John 2:4.

  The faith which . . . works is dead: James 2:17.

  What does it . . . but they fear: James 2:14, 2:19.

You are the Son . . . to destroy us: Luke 4:34.

In a certain tract . . . like a demon: Ælfric's Latin note, probably a marginal addition that in manuscript K was copied here as part of the text, is from the pseudo-Hilarius commentary on the Epistle of James, ed. R. E. McNally, *Tractatus in septem epistolas*, CCSL 108B (Turnhout, 1973), 53–124, a text he does not use elsewhere.

15   *I say to you . . . you unrighteous workers*: Matthew 7:22–23.

16   *Enoch and Elijah*: The brief story of Enoch (not the son of Cain) is recounted in Genesis 5:21–24, which says that Enoch "walked with God, and was no more, for God took him," interpreted by early commentators to mean that he entered heaven alive. The story of Elijah is told in 1 and 2 Kings; in 2 Kings 2:11 it is said that Elijah went up to heaven by a whirlwind in a fiery chariot. Naturally two such dramatic departures gave rise to much speculation; Elijah's return is still awaited every year in the Jewish celebration of Passover. Ælfric focuses on their means of ascension into heaven as it corresponds to their degree of chastity.

18   *He who comes . . . hate his wife*: Luke 14:26.

19   *the commentator*: Gregory the Great, *Homiliae in evangelia* 29; see CH 1.3.5, the homily for Saint Stephen, where the same passage is used, though attributed to Augustine, and the same distinction is made between sitting and standing.

20   *Andrew in Scythia*: Ælfric's sources (probably Rufinus's *Historia ecclesiastica* 3.1 or Haymo of Auxerre's *Epitome* 3.2) give Andrew's province as Scythia; Achaia is mentioned in Gregory the Great's *Homiliae in evangelia* 17. Some manuscripts (CDE) have "Achaia," and that word is added to K in a different hand.
       You can do nothing without me: John 15:5.
       I will be . . . of this world: Matthew 28:20.

22. PENTECOST

title   The gospel read for this day was John 13:23–31; Ælfric does not discuss the gospel directly, but talks in more general terms about the Old Testament origins of Pentecost and the coming of the Holy Spirit. He does translate the epistle for the day, Acts 2:1–11, as well as some passages from elsewhere in Acts 2. The source for this homily is Gregory the Great's *Homiliae in evangelia* 30 for Pentecost.

1   The account of the first Pentecost is found in Exodus 12–14 and 19–22. The parallels between the Jewish festival and the Christian feast were traditional.

mark the sign of a cross: Ælfric repeats this idea, which may be his own, in CH 2.3 and CH 2.15. The account in Exodus and the commentaries on that text do not specify the shape of the mark on the doors.

2   *There are three ages in this world*: This idea had become a commonplace by Ælfric's time; he repeats it elsewhere. See also the English Preface, CH 1.0.6.

3–4   A translation of Acts 2:1–11 and a looser paraphrase of Acts 2:12–45.

5   A translation of Acts 4:4 and 4:32–35.

6   *Then God worked . . . received the Holy Spirit*: A paraphrase of Acts 5:12, 5:15–16, 8:17.

There was an officer . . . who heard of it: The story of Ananias and Sapphira is a paraphrase of Acts 5:1–11.

7   *from that example*: The idea that the communal life of the first disciples was the model for later monastic life is not found in Ælfric's sources.

8   *It happened after Noah's Flood*: The story of the tower of Babel is found in Genesis 11.

9   *We read in books about this type of bird*: Ælfric does not say what kind of books these are; they may be a Physiologus (a collection of moralized descriptions of creatures) or a bestiary.

he did not come to judge . . . but to save it: John 12:47.

He did not cry out: A paraphrase of Matthew 12:19, "He will not contend, nor cry out, nor shall anyone hear his voice in the streets."

11   *as it is said . . . gentle and righteous*: Job 1:1.

God is, as Paul said, a consuming fire: Hebrews 12:29.

I have come that . . . want it to burn: Luke 12:49.

13   *I said, 'You are gods . . . the Most High'*: Psalms 81(82):6, quoted by
Jesus in John 10:34.

14   *He who does not . . . not physically see*: 1 John 4:20.

15   *sevenfold gift*: The seven gifts of the Holy Spirit, a common
Christian theme, are ultimately derived from Isaiah 11:2–3.

16   *like one who practices idolatry*: Colossians 3:5.

23. SECOND SUNDAY AFTER PENTECOST

title   The homily expounds the gospel for the day, Luke 16:19–31, the
story of the rich man and Lazarus. The story was often read as
an allegory of the Jews and the Gentiles, but Ælfric keeps to
the literal level as he expounds the story; he also avoids some
of the thornier theological problems posed by the story's depiction of the afterlife. His source is Gregory the Great, *Homiliae in evangelia* 39 and 40.

2   A loose translation of Luke 16:19–31.

he was a leper: The biblical text says only that Lazarus was *ulceri-
bus plenus* (full of sores), and Gregory and other sources available to Ælfric do not specify that Lazarus suffered from leprosy. He came to be associated with leprosy (a term describing
a range of diseases) in later medieval tradition, but it is not
clear why Ælfric made this connection. See further Saul Na-
thaniel Brody, *The Disease of the Soul: Leprosy in Medieval Literature* (Ithaca, NY, 1974).

3   *The holy gospel . . . pride in his wealth*: Ælfric directly quotes Gregory's *Homiliae in evangelia* 40.

he was clothed with camel's hair: Ælfric takes this detail from
Gregory, who takes it from Matthew 3:4.

4   *through his choice . . . through their rejection*: Ælfric's Latin source
reads *per approbationem . . . per iudicium reprobationis* (through
approval . . . through the judgment of rejection); the sense is
that the poor are known by God because he approves of them,
and the rich are not known because they have been judged and

rejected. Ælfric's Old English translation *ðurh gecorennysse . . . ðurh heora aworpennysse* does not convey this sense very well and adds a note of Calvinist predestination to the passage.

the licking of a dog heals wounds: Ælfric again takes this detail from Gregory; there is no evidence for this belief in early English medical lore.

10   *Gain friends for yourself . . . eternal dwelling places*: A paraphrase of Luke 16:9.

I was hungry . . . you clothed me: Matthew 25:35–36.

11   *the holy Gregory says*: The story of Martyrius and the leper is found in Gregory the Great, *Homiliae in evangelia* 39.

24. Fourth Sunday after Pentecost

title   This homily expounds the gospel for the day, Luke 15:1–7, the parable of the lost sheep, and the following passage, the parable of the lost coins (Luke 15:8–10). Ælfric uses these texts as an occasion to discuss the nine orders of angels; the homily is "the first extensive discussion of the angelic orders in English" (Godden, *Introduction,* 192). The homily's source is Gregory the Great's *Homiliae in evangelia* 34.

2   A loose translation of Luke 15:1–7. Ælfric uses the term *gerefan* ("overseers" or, literally, "reeves") for Latin *publicani* (publicans); most translations in Old English simply call them "sinful."

6   An allusion to Luke 15:8–10.

8   *I will set you . . . Pharaoh's god*: Exodus 7:1.

9   *True love is the fulfillment of God's law*: Romans 13:10.

10   *Woe to the soul . . . the holy virtues*: Ælfric quotes Gregory the Great, *Homiliae in evangelia* 34.

11   *A thousand thousand . . . dwelt with him*: Daniel 7:10.

12   *Lord, you who sit . . . manifest yourself*: Psalms 79:2 (80:1).

14   *In my Father's house are many dwellings*: John 14:2.

15   *If the righteous . . . any of his sins*: A paraphrase of Ezekiel 33:12–16.

Behold, now you . . . worse befall you: John 5:14.

25. The Nativity of Saint John the Baptist

title   This homily describes the life and significance of John the Baptist. It draws on the biblical accounts in Luke 1:5–17 and 1:57–68, and also Luke 3:1–6, the first two of which were read at the vigil of the feast and the feast itself. The homily covers a lot of ground, but its common theme is the unique position of John the Baptist as precursor of Christ and exemplar of asceticism. Its sources are indirect but may include Bede's *Homiliae* 2.19 and 2.20, Gregory the Great's *Homiliae in evangelia* 7 and 20, and homilies by or attributed to Saint Augustine.

1   A fairly free translation of Luke 1:5–24.

any of the liquors by which people become drunk: A somewhat roundabout translation of Latin *sicera* (strong drink). Other Old English translations of the word render it simply as *beor* (beer). Ælfric uses the same expression in CH 2.2.3.

2   A translation and paraphrase of Luke 1:57–68. The intervening verses 25–56 are translated and discussed in CH 1.13.

3   A paraphrase that includes passages from Luke 1:80 and Matthew 3:4.

Fruit fed him: Ælfric presumably takes Latin *locustae* ("locusts," Matthew 3:4) as "locust beans." Other Old English translations render the word *gærstapan* (grasshoppers).

4   *In the fifteenth . . . prophecy of Isaiah*: A paraphrase of Luke 3:1–4.

7   *The old law . . . coming of John*: Luke 16:16.

9   *Among the children . . . John the Baptist*: Matthew 11:11.

11   *It is fitting . . . should be waning*: John 3:30.

12   *Look now, behold . . . of the world*: John 1:29.

In the beginning . . . word was God: John 1:1.

13   *From the days . . . violent seize it*: Matthew 11:12.

It is known to every wise person . . . in his presence is another: This is Ælfric's own contribution to his source.

14   *manfully*: The Latin source, *Sermo* 196 ascribed to Augustine, has *sensum viriliter revocare* (to manfully restrain one's senses). Most manuscripts of the text have *wærlice* (cautiously) here, but three, K, Q, and S, have *werlice* (bravely, manfully), which is

undoubtedly the correct reading. Manuscript K has the added Latin gloss *viriliter* (manfully), written in the main hand of the manuscript, which emphasizes this meaning.

15   *the voice of . . . and sharpness made smooth*: Isaiah 40:3, quoted in Luke 3:4–5.

16   *He who loves . . . dwell with him*: John 14:23.
        Everyone who exalts . . . will be exalted: Luke 14:11.
        In whom does . . . in the humble: Probably Isaiah 57:15.

17   *after his suffering . . . inhabitants of hell*: The idea that John preached to the inhabitants of hell before Christ's descent into that region is not in Ælfric's sources; it presumably comes from the *Gospel of Nicodemus* or a related text (see Cross and Brearley, *Two Old English Apocrypha,* 204).

26. THE PASSION OF THE APOSTLES PETER AND PAUL

title   In this homily Ælfric combines an exposition of the day's gospel, Matthew 16:13–19, with an account of the life and death of Peter and Paul, focusing on the opposition of Peter and Simon Magus. Such two-part homilies are found elsewhere in Ælfric (including, in this collection, CH 1.27 on Paul, CH 1.34 on Michael, and CH 1.38 on Andrew), and seem to be his own innovation in the homiletic tradition; see Hiroshi Ogawa, "Hagiography in Homily—Theme and Style in Ælfric's Two-Part Homily on SS Peter and Paul," *RES* 61 (2010): 167–87. The main source for the gospel exposition is Bede's *Homilia* 1.20; the account of the preaching and martyrdom of Peter and Paul is taken from various sources, most notably an anonymous *Passio sanctorum apostolorum Petri et Pauli*, ed. R. A. Lipsius and M. Bonnet, *Acta apostolorum apocrypha* (Leipzig, 1891–1908), vol. 1, pp. 119–77. In two Latin notes Ælfric insists that Peter and Paul were martyred on the same day; other homilies report that Paul was killed separately (see Zettel, "Ælfric's Hagiographical Sources," 94–97 and 177–78).

1   A translation of Matthew 16:13–19.
        Simon son of a dove: Ælfric interprets the Vulgate *Simon bar Jona*.

you are made of rock: Ælfric uses the etymological meaning of the Latin name *Petrus*. In CH 1.38.13 he interprets *Petrus* as "acknowledging."

4   *The idols of . . . body without life*: Psalms 113:12–15 (115:4–7).

6   *who is called "stone" by the apostle Paul*: In 1 Corinthians 10:4, "The rock was Christ."

8   *Receive the Holy Spirit . . . forgiveness will be withdrawn*: John 20:22–23.

10   *their passion is fully set forth in many places*: Blickling Homily 15, ed. Morris, *The Blickling Homilies,* 171–93, recounts the legend of Peter and Paul; Ælfric may be referring to this.

16   *Paul did not suffer . . . of his own accord*: Ælfric adds a Latin note here to clarify some chronological contradictions in the different accounts of the deaths of Peter and Paul.

21   *The four pieces adhered . . . this present day*: This detail is taken from Ælfric's source, the anonymous *Passio Petri et Pauli*. A church was later built on the site, now replaced by the church of Santa Francesca Romana; this church preserves a marble stone with two dents in it, though these are now said to have been made by Saint Peter when he kneeled to pray for Simon's demise.

24   *Thus Jerome . . . on the same day*: Not all versions of the martyrdom of the two saints relate that they were martyred on the same day, so Ælfric declares his authority for his account, presumably Jerome's *De viris inlustribus* 5, ed. Ernst Cushing Richardson, Texte und Untersuchungen zur Geschichte der altchristlichen Literatur 14 (Leipzig, 1896), pp. 9–100, especially p. 10, lines 21–23.

27. Saint Paul

title   The conversion of Saint Paul is narrated in Acts 9:1–19 and was read as the epistle for this day's feast, which follows the feast of Saints Peter and Paul in the Church calendar. Ælfric draws on and expands upon this text for his homily and includes an exposition of the gospel for the day, Matthew 19:27–29, which he uses as an occasion to praise the monastic life. The sources for this homily are complex, but they may include Smaragdus, *Col-*

lectiones in evangelia et epistolas (PL 102, cols. 395–99), Augustine's *Sermo* 279, and Bede's *Homilia* 1.13.

1   *It is not read . . . his own hands*: This disclaimer is not in any of Ælfric's sources and seems to be his own contribution.

2–4   A paraphrase of Acts 9:1–27.

4   *Some time later . . . chosen them*: A paraphrase of Acts 13:2–3.

6   *Paul persecuted Christians, not with malice*: Ælfric again insists on minimizing Paul's culpability for his actions before his conversion; this is not found in his sources.

     He who touches . . . of my eye: Zechariah 2:8.

7   *not because . . . for Christ's faith*: Again Ælfric departs from his sources in taking pains to defend Paul from any possible criticism.

     He was led to heaven as far as the third level: From 2 Corinthians 12:2–4.

8–9   The gospel exposition translates Matthew 19:27–29.

10   *Socrates*: This detail comes from Jerome's *Commentarii in evangelium Matthaei* 3.922–24. Jerome apparently related the story of the Stoic philosopher Crates; most manuscripts of his work, however, name the philosopher "Socrates." Ælfric also mentions this philosophical practice in CH 1.4.4.

11   *He called the universal resurrection "regeneration"*: This interpretation is in Ælfric's source, Smaragdus, *Collectiones in evangelia et epistolas;* Ælfric adds the parallel to our two other births, at our physical birth and at baptism.

13   *There will be four hosts . . . his accursed spirits*: This section appears to derive from Julian of Toledo's *Prognosticon futuri saeculi,* and particularly from the epitome of that work made by Ælfric himself (see Gatch, "MS Boulogne-sur-Mer 63," 483–86).

     Come to me . . . of the world: Matthew 25:34.

     Those who have . . . without any law: Romans 2:12.

     Depart from me . . . his accursed spirits: Matthew 25:41.

15   *He who, living among monks*: Ælfric's complaints about monks holding their own property is not in his sources; his concern may reflect contemporary monastic conditions in the generation after the Benedictine Reform (see Christopher A. Jones, "Ælfric and the Limits of 'Benedictine Reform,'" in Magennis

and Swan, *A Companion to Ælfric*, 93–95). The story of Gehazi (Giezi), the greedy servant of Elisha, is found in 2 Kings 5; the story of Ananias and Sapphira is found in Acts 5:1–11, and it is also told by Ælfric in CH 1.22.6.

28. Eleventh Sunday after Pentecost

title This homily translates and expounds the gospel for the day, Luke 19:41–7. Ælfric offers both historical and allegorical readings of the passage. Its main source is Gregory the Great, *Homiliae in evangelia* 39, with some material from Haymo of Auxerre's *Homiliae de tempore* 122 (also based on Gregory), and with the closing exemplum drawn from Gregory's *Homiliae in evangelia* 12.

2 Paraphrase of Luke 19:41–47.

 Then the blind and lame: This last detail is drawn from the parallel gospel account in Matthew 21:14.

3 Some of Ælfric's details on the siege of Jerusalem are drawn from Rufinus's Latin version of Eusebius's *Historia ecclesiastica*, 3.5–7.

4 *six hundred thousand people*: Manuscript K adds a note, "This is what the chronicle says," though it is not clear which chronicle Ælfric is referring to. Rufinus, Ælfric's source for much of this passage, says the number was three million.

 and settled with Saracens: This is Ælfric's own addition.

5 *The stork and . . . judgment of God*: A paraphrase of Jeremiah 8:7.

6 *It is written in another gospel*: John 2:14, "And he found in the temple those selling oxen and sheep and doves, and money changers sitting."

7 *who lets his sun shine*: An allusion to Matthew 5:45, "Your Father in heaven . . . makes his sun rise upon the good and bad, and rain upon the just and the unjust."

8 *Blessed is the man . . . fall into evil*: Proverbs 28:14.

 In all your works . . . sin in eternity: Sirach 7:40.

9 *Do not trust . . . their thoughts perish*: Psalms 145(146):3–4.

12 *Without price you . . . others without price*: Matthew 10:8.

13 *The temple of God is holy, which you are*: 1 Corinthians 3:17.

14 *The blessed Gregory said*: The story of Chrysaurius is found in Gregory the Great, *Homiliae in evangelia* 12.

  the province of Valeria: The late Roman province of Valeria Suburbicara is in central Italy, present-day L'Aquila-Reiti-Tivoli.

29. SAINT LAWRENCE

title Lawrence was widely venerated in early medieval England; the story of his life and martyrdom, mostly legendary, was told in an anonymous *Passio Polochronii, Parmenii, Abdon et Sennen, Xysti, Felicissimi et Agapiti et Laurentii et aliorum sanctorum*, ed. H. Delehaye, "Recherces sur le légendier romain," *Analecta Bollandiana* 51 (1933): 34–98, particularly at 72–98, which is the source for this homily.

1 *the cruel emperor Decius*: The cruel, persecuting Roman emperor is something of a stock figure in hagiography, but the actual emperor Decius, who reigned from 249 to 251 CE, was indeed responsible for the systematic persecution of Christians.

  the holy bishop Sixtus: Presumably Pope Sixtus II, who reigned from 257 to 258 CE.

4 *chief reeve Valerianus*: Presumably based on the emperor Valerian, who reigned from 253 to 260 CE. In the Latin source Valerianus is described as a *praefectus* (prefect), a title of indeterminate but generally high rank.

6 *town reeve Hippolytus*: In the Latin source Hippolytus is described as a *vicarius* (deputy).

7 *I have spent them on God's poor*: In the Latin source Lawrence gathers a crowd of poor and sick people and dramatically presents them to Decius, saying that in fact these are God's treasures.

15 *whose name was Dionysius*: Dionysius was pope from 259 to 268 CE.

30. ASSUMPTION OF MARY

title This homily is a cautious account of the death and assumption of Mary, probably written to counter what Ælfric regarded as the erroneous accounts found in other collections, such as the Blickling Homilies. Interestingly, he bases much of his argument on probability and plausibility rather than authority, and ends with a pair of miracles of the Virgin, indicating her power as an intercessor and protector. The homily is based, highly selectively, on a letter attributed to Jerome but probably by Paschasius Radbertus, *De assumptione sanctae Mariae virginis*, ed. A. Ripberger, CCCM 56C (Turnhout, 1985), 109–62; he also makes use of this source in CH I.I.22. He begins with a fairly close translation but quickly moves to a looser paraphrase. For the miracles of the virgin at the end of the homily, Ælfric probably drew on an anonymous *Certamen sancti martyris Mercurii*, ed. L. Surius, *De probatis sanctorum historiis* (Cologne, 1576–1581), vol. 6, pp. 569–72, and an anonymous *Vita Basilii*, ed. Surius, *De probatis sanctorum historiis*, vol. 1, pp. 4–19. For more on Ælfric's sources and treatment, see Clayton, *The Cult of the Virgin Mary in Anglo-Saxon England*.

1   *The holy priest Jerome*: The text on which Ælfric draws was generally attributed to Jerome.

2   *lest the false account*: This warning against heterodox versions of the story, which might seem to apply to other homilies circulating in Ælfric's day, is in fact found in Ælfric's source.

3   *Then he said . . . stands your mother*: John 19:26–27.

4   *the chaste man John*: A Latin note in manuscript A, presumably by Ælfric, says that "either sex can be called a virgin." He makes the same point in CH I.9.18.

5   *her tomb is visible*: The present church on the site, the Church of the Sepulchre of Saint Mary in Kidron Valley, is from the twelfth century, but there is evidence for earlier churches on the same site. Other traditions locate the tomb of Mary in Jerusalem, or Ephesus, or several other places.

We do not deny: This cautious note is found in Ælfric's source, Paschasius.

7   *Honor your father and your mother*: Matthew 15:4.

I honor my Father, and you dishonor me: John 8:49.

8   *What is this . . . as a martial troop*: Song of Songs 6:9.

9   *I saw the beautiful . . . lilies surrounded her*: The quotation (taken from Ælfric's source) is not from the Bible, but from the Office for the Assumption.

11   *I pray you, rejoice . . . gloriously entered*: A collection of quotations, also in Ælfric's source, drawn from the Office for the Assumption.

12   *in his saints, in whom he is wonderful*: An echo of Psalms 67:36 (68:35), "God is wonderful in his saints."

14   *Basil*: Basil the Great (330–379 CE) was bishop of Caesarea in Cappadocia. His student days with the future emperor Julian "the Apostate" may be historical, as is the emperor's early interest in philosophy and religion. The story of the emperor's death at the spectral hands of the deceased saint Mercurius is certainly exaggerated, however; most historians believe Julian died of a wound received in battle with the Sassanids in Persia.

17   *If anyone wonders how this could happen*: Ælfric takes pains to explain why a martyr would be buried in a church with his weapons, and how the saint's spirit could have wielded a physical weapon.

31. Saint Bartholomew

title   This homily is largely a vivid retelling of the martyrdom of Saint Bartholomew in India, a story apparently widely known in early medieval England; it concludes with some discussion of disease, healing, and medical practice. The source of the homily is an anonymous *Passio Bartholomaei* found in several versions (see Mombritius, *Sanctuarium*, vol. 1, pp. 140–44).

1   *Historians say that there are three nations called India*: This statement is in Ælfric's source. Many legends of Saint Bartholomew locate his missionary activity in Armenia, but Ælfric's source, following an older tradition, places it in India. For ancient confusion over the location of India, see Pierre Schneider, "The So-Called Confusion between India and Ethiopia: The Eastern and Southern Edges of the World from the Greco-Roman Perspective," in *Brill's Companion to Ancient Geography*, ed.

Serena Bianchetti, Michele Cataudella, and Hans-Joachim Gehrke (Leiden, 2016), 184–202.

darkness on one side: Ælfric is translating his source here, but the meaning is not clear. In his introduction to cosmology, *De temporibus anni*, he describes a spherical earth around which the sun revolves and shines on all parts, and places India near the equator.

2   *He has fair and curling hair . . . twenty-six years*: This remarkable physical description of the powerful but unprepossessing saint is matched later in the homily by a description of a horrifying but impotent demon.

4   *the king Polymius*: As far as can be known, this is a completely legendary figure. In other versions of the story he is said to be king of Armenia.

11   *the Holy Spirit . . . and your Son*: Ælfric alters the language of his source here (*unus Spiritus Sanctus qui ex Patre procedit*, "one Holy Spirit which proceeds from the Father") to make it conform to contemporary theological thought on the nature of the Trinity, where the Holy Spirit is believed to proceed from both the Father and the Son.

      Truly I say . . . granted to you: John 16:23.

12   *an enormous Ethiopian*: Ælfric's source says that the demon's form is *ingentem Egyptium nigriorem* (an enormous, black Egyptian); Ælfric's "Ethiopian" (*Silhearwa* in Old English) draws on an old racialized tradition linking Ethiopians and demons. He does the same thing in his account of the martyrdom of Simon and Jude in CH 2.33.12.

13   *Astryges*: This figure, like his brother Polymius, is entirely legendary.

15   *a little bird does not fall in death without God's direction*: See Matthew 10:29, "Are not two sparrows sold for a penny? And yet not one of them falls to the ground apart from your Father."

      Those whom I love, I chastise and scourge: Revelation 3:19.

      Herod, who slew the innocent children: Herod's afflictions are vividly described in CH 1.5.11–12.

16   *My child, your sins . . . your sickbed*: A paraphrase of Mark 2:5 and 2:11.

17   *God gave me possessions . . . blessed be his name*: A paraphrase of Job 1:21.

        a certain blind person: This story is recounted in John 9:1–6.

        he was not born blind . . . manifested through him: A close paraphrase of John 9:3.

18   *To me is given . . . dwell in me*: 2 Corinthians 12:7–9.

19   *seek his health in forbidden practices*: Ælfric expresses concern about lingering non-Christian practices in popular medicine. It was no doubt sometimes difficult to distinguish permissible medical practice—which included making the sign of the cross over a wound, praying over medicinal plants, and giving offerings at the shrines of the saints—from the unauthorized or forbidden pre-Christian practices of popular religion. See Audrey Meaney, "Ælfric and Idolatry," 119–35.

        as the prophet Isaiah did: Isaiah 38:21, "Isaiah ordered that they should take a lump of figs, and lay it as a plaster upon the wound, and he should be healed."

20   *The wise Augustine*: In *De doctrina Christiana* 2.29.9–13.

        Nor should anyone sing over an herb . . . and so take it: The *Pseudo-Egbert Penitential* (ed. J. Raith, *Die altenglische Version des Halitgar'shen Bussbuches [sog. Poenitentiale Pseudo-Ecgbertî]*, Bibliothek der angelsächsischen Prosa 13, Hamburg, 1933) 2.23 recommends saying the Pater Noster and the Creed over medicinal plants before picking them.

32. THE BEHEADING OF JOHN THE BAPTIST

title   The gospel reading for the feast of the "decollation" (beheading) of John the Baptist is given as Mark 6:17–29 in the Old English version of the gospels, and that is the reading Ælfric translates and explains here, mostly in historical terms. Ælfric includes an account from Luke 7 of John the Baptist in prison. The parallel gospel text is Matthew 14:1–12, and Ælfric's main source is

Bede's homily on that text, *Homilia* 2.23, along with Gregory the Great's *Homiliae in evangelia* 6 and Rufinus's *Historia ecclesiastica*.

2   A loose translation of Mark 6:17–29.

3   *Among the children . . . John the Baptist*: Matthew 11:11.

you have often heard of his famous way of life: Ælfric devotes CH 1.25 to John's life and ministry.

4   *for it was the custom at that time*: This is Ælfric's own speculation, not found in his sources.

three he commanded to be slain: This detail comes from Rufinus's *Historia ecclesiastica* and is mentioned by Ælfric in CH 1.5.

5   *The "Ecclesiastical History" tells it thus*: This Latin note appears only in manuscript K. Ælfric is presumably referring to the *Historia ecclesiastica* of Rufinus, his source for some of these historical details.

Then John sent two disciples . . . the savior revealed to John: This whole passage is added in a different hand in manuscript A, which is close to Ælfric's original draft of the homilies; originally that manuscript read, "The savior then with secret words revealed," and suggests that Ælfric's original intention may have been to pass over this difficult passage without comment.

Are you the one . . . wait for another: Luke 7:19, paralleled in Matthew 11:2–3. A Latin note in the margin of K, not found in other manuscripts, says, "Gregory has explained it thus," presumably referring to Gregory the Great, *Homiliae in evangelia* 6, which offers this explanation for the disciples' question.

As the Evangelist Luke wrote: In Luke 7:21–23.

Go now to . . . offended in me: Translating Luke 7:22–23.

the poor preach the gospel: Luke 7:22 reads *pauperes evangelizantur*, which means "the poor are preached to." The Old English version of the gospels also translates the verb as active, *þearfan bodiað* (the poor preach), and this interpretation is found in some commentaries on this passage, including Haymo of Auxerre and Smaragdus.

6   *for at that time . . . on their birthdays*: Ælfric seems alone in his belief that birthday celebrations are a thing of the past.

In all things . . . you will never sin: Sirach 7:40.

our bodies are God's limbs: From 1 Corinthians 6:15, "Do you not know that your bodies are Christ's members?"

And he commanded . . . acceptable to God: Romans 12:1.

Do not swear . . . that is of evil: Matthew 5:34–37.

7   *Believe me*: John 4:21.

David swore . . . dangerous murder: The story of David and Abigail, found in Ælfric's source Bede, *Homiliae* 2.23, is told in 1 Samuel 25.

8   *He who injures . . . himself still more*: Revelation 22:11.

He who is holy, let him be still more hallowed: Revelation 22:11.

9   *I am truth*: John 14:6.

10   *Some heretics . . . king's wife Herodias*: It is not known where Ælfric might have heard the strange story of John the Baptist's head blowing Herodias all over the world. It is not in his sources, nor in the *Old English Martyrology*, and is generally not found in England until the later Middle Ages, in the *South English Legendary* 1.243. It is notable that he questions the story's orthodoxy, not its physical plausibility.

11   *God corrects and . . . be before God*: Hebrews 12:6.

The sufferings of . . . manifested in us: Romans 8:18.

12   *Now, the commentator says*: Ælfric's complaint against women is from a homily attributed to John Chrysostom found in Paul the Deacon's homiliary (pseudo-Chrysostom, Homily 50, PL 95, cols. 1508–14).

better to dwell . . . and garrulous woman: Sirach 25:23.

13   *The historian Josephus*: Ælfric is still following Rufinus, *Historia ecclesiastica*, who cites Josephus's *History of the Jews* here.

I pray you . . . God for eternity: Paraphrased from, or quoting a variant version of, Augustine's *Sermo* 84 (PL 38, cols. 519–20). See also R. Demeulenaere, "Le sermon 84 de saint Augustin sur l'invitation de Jésus au jeune homme riche: Édition critique," in *Aevum inter utrumque: Mélanges offerts à Gabriel Sanders, professeur émérite à l'Université de Gand*, ed. M. Van Uytfanghe and R. Demeulenaure, Instrumenta Patristica 32 (Steenbrugge, 1991), 67–73.

14   *In this life we grow weak . . . our limbs fall asleep*: These are Ælfric's
own words, apparently not from any Augustinian source.

         as the prophet said, "Evil are our days": Ælfric is still quoting Au-
gustine here, though the quotation may come from Ephesians
5:16.

33. SEVENTEENTH SUNDAY AFTER PENTECOST

title   This homily contains an allegorical exposition of the gospel for
the day, Luke 7:11–16. Its sources are not clear but probably include Bede's *Commentarius in Lucam* and Heiric (Hericus) of
Auxerre, *Homiliae in circulum anni* 2.37. Both were found in the
homiliary of Paul the Deacon. For a different view, see Joyce
Hill, "Ælfric and Smaragdus," *ASE* 21 (1992): 203–37, particularly at 211–15.

2   Paraphrased translation of Luke 7:11–16.

3   *The commentator Bede*: In fact, this detail about the meaning of
the word *Naim* is in Ælfric's other source, Heiric of Auxerre.

         You are my . . . renewed in you: Galatians 4:19.

4   *The sinful is . . . is blessed*: Though Ælfric attributes this to "the
prophet," the quotation is from Psalms 9:24 (10:3).

         Let the dead . . . preach God's kingdom: Matthew 8:22.

         The tongues of . . . souls in sins: The quotation is not biblical, but is
from Gregory the Great's *Dialogi*, 1.4.127–28.

6   *Truly they said of Christ that he is a great prophet*: Ælfric makes this
point elsewhere, in CH 1.12.13–14.

7   *except for three only*: The story of the ealdorman's daughter is
found in Luke 8 (where he has the name Jairus); the story of
Lazarus is in John 11. The linking of these three resurrection
passages is in Ælfric's source Heiric of Auxerre.

9   *who lay four days foully stinking in the tomb*: The detail is from John
11:17.

         Maiden, arise: Luke 8:54.

11   *Lazarus, go forth*: John 11:43.

         Every sin and . . . one to come: Matthew 12:31–32. Ælfric's discus-
sion of the sin against the Holy Spirit is not in his sources, nor
is his discussion of the nature of the Trinity.

34. DEDICATION OF THE CHURCH OF
SAINT MICHAEL THE ARCHANGEL

title   The homily tells of the dedication of a church to Saint Michael on Mount Gargano in southeastern Italy; the dedication was elsewhere celebrated on May 8, but September 29 is the date given in other homilies known in early medieval England. Ælfric also translates and expounds the gospel for the day, Matthew 18:1–10. The sources for the homily include an anonymous *Relatio de dedicatione ecclesiae sancti Michaelis* (see Mombritius, *Sanctuarium,* vol. 1, pp. 389–91) and, for the exposition of the gospels, Haymo of Auxerre's *Homilia in festo sancti Michaelis* (PL 95, cols. 1525–30), both found in Paul the Deacon's homiliary. Smaragdus's *Collectiones* (PL 102, cols. 477–80) is another source. The homily is similar in its broad outlines and sometimes in close detail to the anonymous Blickling Homily 16, ed. Morris, *The Blickling Homilies,* 197–211, though this may be because both texts draw on a common source. See further Richard F. Johnson, *Saint Michael the Archangel in Medieval English Legend* (Woodbridge, 2005), 57–63.

1   *Many people know the holy place of Saint Michael*: The grotto church of Saint Michael on Monte Gargano was apparently established somewhere between the sixth and eighth centuries; it is one of a number of mountain shrines associated with the archangel Michael, such as Mont Saint-Michel in France and Saint Michael's Mount in Cornwall. Ælfric's abrupt opening sentence suggests that he thought his audience would already be familiar with the church and its feast.

    The mountain is on the border of Campania: Mount Gargano is in fact in Puglia (Apulia) near the Adriatic coast, some distance from Campania.

    twelve miles up from a city called Siponto: Siponto (*Sepontina,* in Ælfric's Old English) was a port city on the Adriatic Sea; its bishop Laurence of Siponto is the bishop mentioned in the following paragraph who had a vision of Saint Michael.

4   *Then at the same time the Neapolitans*: While the apparition of Saint Michael to the bishop of Siponto may be dated around

490, the attack of the Neapolitans appears in Paul the Deacon's *History of the Lombards* in the year 663.

8 *angels will be ... country with him*: Hebrews 1:14.

10 Fairly close translation of Matthew 18:1–10.

Woe to the earth for offenses: Ælfric uses the Old English word *æswicung* and the verb *æswician* to translate Latin *scandalum* and *scandalizare*. Modern biblical translations use "offense" and "offend," but Ælfric's choice of words suggests some element of deceit, disloyalty, or failure.

11 *Haymo expounds this gospel*: Here Ælfric acknowledges his source, Haymo's *Homilia in festo sancti Michaelis*.

how the emperor's tax collectors ... and for you: Paraphrase of Matthew 17:24–26.

13 *Let these children ... kingdom of heaven*: Matthew 19:14.

Do not be ... be perfect: 1 Corinthians 14:20.

Every person who ... will be exalted: A paraphrase of Luke 14:11.

14 *He who receives ... righteous person's recompense*: Matthew 10:41.

The wicked turn in a circle: Psalms 11:9 (12:8).

15 *He who touches you ... of my eye*: Zechariah 2:8.

16 *God has commanded ... against a stone*: Psalms 90(91):11–12.

It is not Peter who knocks there, but his angel: The story is told in Acts 12:6–15.

When you prayed ... prayers before God: Tobit 12:12.

17 *The old law tells us*: Here Ælfric departs from his sources to offer a discussion of guardian angels as national patrons.

When God on high ... of his angels: A common variant form of Deuteronomy 32:8.

The archangel ... the Persian nation: A paraphrase of Daniel 10:13 and 10:20–21.

18 *It is now credible*: The idea that Saint Michael has transferred his protection from Jews to Christians is apparently Ælfric's own.

35. Twenty-First Sunday after Pentecost

title The homily offers a translation and allegorical reading of the gospel for the day, Matthew 22:1–14, the parable of the wedding feast. Its main source is Gregory the Great, *Homiliae in evange-lia* 19 and 38.

2   A translation of Matthew 22:1–14.

4   *Heaven is my seat*: Isaiah 66:1.

    The soul of the righteous is the seat of wisdom: Not actually a biblical quotation, but may owe something to Wisdom 7:27, "(Wisdom) passes into holy souls."

    Christ is God's might and God's wisdom: 1 Corinthians 1:24.

    The heavens declare the glory of God: Psalms 18:2 (19:1).

7   *Love your friend, and hate your enemy*: Not actually in the Old Testament, but forms part of Jesus's summary of the old law in Matthew 5:43.

    I command you . . . and the unrighteous: Matthew 5:44–45.

8   *Let my soul . . . and with tallow*: Psalms 62:6 (63:5).

10   *Peter to be crucified and Paul beheaded*: The martyrdom of Peter and Paul is told in CH 1.26.

    Astryges . . . who killed Bartholomew: The story of Bartholomew is told in CH 1.31.

    Egeas, who crucified Andrew: Andrew's martyrdom is related in CH 1.38.

11   *mingled like clean grain with foul cockles*: The parable of the wheat and the tares (cockles) is found in Matthew 13:24–43.

12   *You child of man . . . race of serpents*: Ezekiel 2:6.

    You dwell among perverse . . . word of life: Philippians 2:15–16.

13   *God so greatly . . . Son for us*: John 3:16.

    Though one might have full faith . . . all Christians: A paraphrase of 1 Corinthians 13:2–3, "If I have all faith, so that I could move mountains, and I do not have love, I am nothing; and if I should give all my goods to the poor, and if I should give over my body to be burned, and do not have love, I gain nothing."

    My Lord, your eyes . . . written in your book: Psalms 138(139):16.

14   *I am the light . . . light of life*: John 8:12.

15   Ælfric takes the opportunity to return to one of his favorite themes, the resurrection of the dead.

    I believe that . . . and no other: Job 19:25–27.

17   *Saint Gregory now says*: Ælfric takes this story from Gregory's

Homiliae in evangelia 38, who says that it happened in his own monastery. The story is also told in Gregory's *Dialogues* 4.40, and some of Ælfric's details, such as calling the monk a *cniht* (young man) in 18, may come from this version rather than the homily.

19   The description of Noah's ark is in Gregory's *Homiliae in evangelia* 38, but Ælfric departs from Gregory in some details.

Many shall come . . . kingdom of heaven: Matthew 8:11.

I counted them . . . grains of sand: Psalms 138(139):18.

20   *almighty God*: Manuscript A has *metoda God,* using the poetic word *metod* (maker, creator), which is unusual for Ælfric—he elsewhere uses the word only in his rhythmical and alliterative prose in CH 2. Other manuscripts read *ælmihtig* (almighty), which is probably Ælfric's revision.

36. All Saints

title   The homily expounds the gospel for the day, Matthew 5:1–12, on the Beatitudes, and describes the different kinds of saints (angels, patriarchs, prophets, John the Baptist, apostles, martyrs, confessors, anchorites, and virgins, above all the Virgin Mary). The source of the first part is an anonymous homily (attributed to Bede) beginning *Legimus in ecclesiasticis historiis;* see J. E. Cross, *"Legimus in ecclesiasticis historiis'*: A Sermon for All Saints, and Its Use in Old English Prose," *Traditio* 33 (1977): 101–35. The second part is based primarily on Augustine, *De sermone Domini in monte.*

1   *I saw a multitude so great . . . ever and ever, amen*: Revelation 7:9–12.

3   *Truly, some of those . . . burning in love*: Ælfric gives a similar account of the nine orders of angels in CH 1.24.

Among the children . . . John the Baptist: Matthew 11:11.

4   *You are the light . . . who is in heaven*: Matthew 5:14 and 5:16.

You are my friends . . . from my Father: John 15:15.

And whatever they bind . . . unbound in heaven: Matthew 18:18.

they will be sitting . . . life in the body: A paraphrase of Matthew 19:28.

7   *The book called* Vita Patrum: The *Vita Patrum* (Lives of the Fathers) was a collection of stories about the Desert Fathers and Mothers who lived with great ascetic fervor in Egypt in the fourth century CE.

8   *in due order according to her womanhood*: It was apparently felt to be appropriate to speak of male saints before female ones, despite Mary's elevated status in the hierarchy of saints. Presumably the troop of virgins following in her footsteps are imagined to be female as well, though Ælfric elsewhere makes it clear that both chaste men and chaste women can be called virgins.

12   A translation of Matthew 5:1–12.

13   *The wise Augustine*: In his *De sermone Domini in monte*, Ælfric's main source for this section.

         Fear of God is the beginning of wisdom: Sirach 1:16.

         pride is the beginning of every sin: Sirach 10:16.

         As if having nothing and possessing all things: 2 Corinthians 6:10.

         I truly am poor and needy: Psalms 39:18 (40:17).

14   *Lord, you are . . . of the living*: Psalms 141:6 (142:5).

16   *My food is . . . that is, righteousness*: John 4:34.

         Lord, I will . . . glory is revealed: Psalms 16(17):15.

19   *This is the peace . . . of good will*: A reference to Luke 2:14.

20   *Do not fear . . . torment of hell*: Matthew 10:28. The quotation is not in Ælfric's sources.

22   *It is fitting . . . who is given to us*: A paraphrase of Romans 5:3–5.

         O my brothers . . . tried by fire: A paraphrase of James 1:2–3 and 1 Peter 1:6–7.

         Vessels of clay . . . of their temptation: Sirach 27:6.

         If this world . . . also persecute you: Paraphrasing John 15:18–20.

37. SAINT CLEMENT

title   Clement was bishop of Rome from around 92 to 101 CE and widely honored in early medieval England. Ælfric's homily is a retelling of the story of Clement's preaching and martyrdom. Its source is an anonymous *Passio Clementis;* see F. X. Funk and

F. Diekamp, eds., *Patres apostolici* (Tübingen, 1901–1913), vol. 2, pp. 51–81. To this Ælfric attaches a long series of biblical and hagiographical examples showing that—contrary to the many stories of martyrdom told here and elsewhere—God does sometimes rescue his saints from persecution. This seems to be Ælfric's own work, and no source has been found for it.

2   *Peter chose him for pope*: Ælfric suggests that Clement was Peter's immediate successor; there was apparently some controversy over this, though most sources agree that Clement was in fact the fourth pope, after Peter, Linus, and Cletus.

3   *Dionysius, God's martyr*: The reference to Dionysius is not in Ælfric's sources. He later writes a homily, *Lives of Saints* 29, about the saint's life and martyrdom.

9   This story of a miracle at Clement's underwater tomb is told in Gregory of Tours, *Miraculum eiusdem* (in Mombritius, *Sanctuarium*, vol. 1, pp. 344–46), and accompanies the *Passio Clementis* in some manuscripts.

11   The story of Hezekiah and Sennacherib is found in Isaiah 36–37.
    Do not let . . . against my army: Paraphrase of Isaiah 36:14–20.
    Lord God of hosts . . . are almighty God: Paraphrase of Isaiah 37:16–20.

13   The story of Hananiah, Azariah, and Mishael is found in Daniel 3.

14–15   The story of Daniel and Habakkuk is found in Daniel 14:27–41.

16   *Go to the . . . to the people*: Acts 5:20.
    We found the prison . . . no one within: Acts 5:23.

17   The story of Peter in chains is found in Acts 12:3–10.

18   Ælfric tells these stories of the persecution of John in CH 1.4.

19   *he passed one day . . . of the sea*: 2 Corinthians 11:25.
    a serpent seized him by the finger: The story is told in Acts 28:3–5.

20   *Many are the . . . from all these*: Psalms 33:20 (34:19).
    Lord, think of me . . . joy of Paradise: Luke 23:42–43.

38. SAINT ANDREW

title   A lively and dramatic account of Andrew's apocryphal adventures among the cannibals of Myrmidonia is found in the Old

English poem *Andreas;* this homily is an altogether more sober and restrained piece of work. Ælfric's original intention appears to have been to offer only an exposition of the gospel of the day, Matthew 4:18–22; a note (later canceled) at the end of the homily in manuscript A explains that he will tell the story of Andrew's martyrdom elsewhere; see the note to paragraph 23. In every surviving manuscript, however, Ælfric then offers an account of the saint's passion and death. Occasional passages in Ælfric's later rhythmical and alliterative style suggest that this second part of the homily may be a later addition, as this style does not really appear in its full form until the Second Series of homilies. The main sources of the homily are Gregory the Great's *Homiliae in evangelia* 5 for the gospel exposition, and an anonymous *Passio Andreae* (in Lipsius and Bonnet, eds., *Acta apostolorum apocrypha,* vol. 2, pp. 1–37) for the hagiographical section. See further Frederick M. Biggs, "Ælfric's Andrew and the Apocrypha," *JEGP* 104 (2005): 473–94.

2   A translation of Matthew 4:18–22.

3   The comparison of the world to the sea is a commonplace; Ælfric uses it elsewhere in CH 1.12 and other homilies.

4   *I will send . . . from every hill:* Jeremiah 16:16.

5   *He who glories, let him glory in God:* 1 Corinthians 1:31.

8   *I imagine these words:* Ælfric expands on his source, Gregory, by giving fuller accounts of the stories to which Gregory only alludes.

    Zacchaeus was a . . . among humankind: Luke 19:2–10.

9   *At a certain time . . . a devout mind:* Mark 12:41–44.

10   *Truly I say . . . not be lost:* Matthew 10:42.

11   *Glory to God . . . of good will:* Luke 2:14.

    In me, God . . . through praise: Psalms 55(56):12.

12   *Who are these . . . to their windows:* Isaiah 60:8.

13   *now we will tell you:* This section on the names of the disciples appears to depend on Heiric of Auxerre, *Homiliae in circulum anni* 2.46.

    You are Christ, Son of the living God: Matthew 16:16.

14   *the land called Achaia:* In CH 1.21.20 Ælfric notes that Andrew went to Scythia, but he does not mention this here. Achaia is a

province of Greece in the northwestern part of the Peloponnese peninsula.

Aegeus, a cruel judge: In the *Passio Andreae* Aegeus is described as proconsul, or governor, of the province of Achaia. The historical Aegeates was governor of Achaia around 70 CE, but not much is known about him.

gallows cross: The translation tries to preserve the distinction in the Old English text between *rod* (cross) and *rode gealgean* (gallows cross).

he said that he had power . . . take it up again: John 10:18.

15   *he neither struggled . . . in the streets*: Matthew 12:19.

22–23   Godden, *Introduction*, 329, notes that these final two paragraphs are written in a rhythmical and quasi-alliterative style, suggesting a later date of composition. The poetic word *metod* (creator) in 23 suggests the same; Ælfric rarely uses it in his non-rhythmical writing (it is found elsewhere in the First Series only at CH 1.35.20).

23   *Amen we say*: Manuscript A, which is close to Ælfric's original draft of CH 1, contains a passage here that is canceled in the manuscript: "It would be suitable, if the shortness of this day would allow us, that we recount to you the passion of the holy apostle Andrew, but we will do this for you at another time, if we are well, if we could fulfill it to some small extent. Let us now humbly ask the majesty of almighty God that his blessed apostle Andrew might be our eternal intercessor with him, just as he was a true herald of his holy church. Glory and praise be to the almighty Creator forever in eternity. Amen." This was apparently the original conclusion of the homily, before the story of Andrew's martyrdom (paragraphs 14–23) was added.

39. FIRST SUNDAY IN ADVENT

title   In this brief homily Ælfric chooses not to expound the gospel of the day (Matthew 21:1–9), which he discussed in CH 1.14 (the homily for Palm Sunday); instead he discusses the day's epistle, Romans 13:11–17, and the traditional Advent theme of preparing for the coming of Christ. In manuscript Q the homily is lengthened by the addition of a passage on Antichrist; see the note to paragraph 8 below. The sources of the homily are not clear but may include Haymo of Auxerre's *Expositio in Pauli epistolas* and Pelagius's *Expositions of Thirteen Epistles of Saint Paul*, which circulated under the name of Saint Jerome.

2   *The custom now stands in God's Church*: Readings from the Old Testament prophets, mainly Isaiah, were found in the monastic office, not the daily Mass. Ælfric expects "all God's servants" to read these; he urged secular priests as well as monks to pray the daily office.

Lo, I will be . . . of this world: Matthew 28:20.

3   *My brothers, know . . . Lord savior Christ*: Romans 13:11–14.

4   *The holy go from strength to strength*: Psalms 83:8 (84:7).

5   *the universal judgment . . . good or evil*: A paraphrase of 2 Corinthians 5:10.

Withstand the devil . . . near to you: Not in Paul's writings, but found in James 4:7–8. See Sarah Larratt Keefer, "An Interesting Error in Ælfric's *Dominica I in adventu Domini*," *Neophilologus* 60 (1976): 138–39.

6   *When you gather . . . in the hand*: 1 Corinthians 14:26.

Nothing is secret where drunkenness reigns: Proverbs 31:4.

Their belly is . . . glory in pollution: Philemon 3:19.

Christ said of . . . children of God: Matthew 5:9.

7   *Clothe yourselves . . . of the Holy Spirit*: Colossians 3:12–17.

8   *to whom be glory and praise forever in eternity. Amen*: Manuscript Q adds a long passage here from the English Preface, CH 1.0.6–10, on the coming of Antichrist. This is probably a late adaptation by Ælfric himself (Clemoes, *First Series*, 133).

40. Second Sunday in Advent

title   For the final homily in the First Series, Ælfric offers a discussion of the signs of the last days, expounding on the gospel of the day, Luke 21:25–33. In it he strikes a careful balance between emphasizing the urgency of the coming tribulations in the last days and avoiding any claim that these days are, in fact, at hand. Its main source is Gregory the Great's *Homiliae in evangelia* 1; see Hill, "Ælfric and Smaragdus," 215–16, for the suggestion that he also used Smaragdus.

2 A translation of Luke 21:25–33.

3 *Nation will rise . . . and hunger*: Luke 21:10.

4 *in the days of the emperor Tiberius*: No report of this sign (hardly a recent one) is found in Ælfric's sources for this homily; it may come from the *Chronicon* of Jerome, ed. R. Helm, *Die Chronik des Hieronymus*, vol. 7 of *Eusebius Werke*, Die Griechischen Christlichen Schriftsteller der ersten drei Jahrhunderte 47, 3rd ed. (Berlin, 1984)—though this work is not otherwise used by Ælfric.

  We read in astronomy: Ælfric is careful to distinguish between natural occurrences like eclipses and comets and the supernatural signs of the end of the world. He describes eclipses as natural phenomena in *De temporibus anni* 3.15–16, ed. Martin Blake, *Ælfric's De temporibus anni*, Anglo-Saxon Texts 6 (Cambridge, 2009), and comets in the same work, at 9.13; both are taken from Bede's *De natura rerum*.

  Right after the . . . powers will lament: Matthew 24:29–30.

5 *He is truly Son of man, and not Son of men*: Ælfric makes the same point in CH 1.3.

6 *Whoever would be . . . enemy of God*: James 4:4.

7 *This world is like an aging person*: Ælfric returns to this theme, found in his source Gregory, in his *Life of Saint Maurice* (*Lives of Saints* 28); see also J. E. Cross, "Gregory, *Blickling Homily X*, and Ælfric's *Passio s. Mauricii* on the World's Youth and Age," *Neuphilologische Mitteilungen* 66 (1965): 327–30.

  Do not love . . . God's love in him: 1 John 2:15.

8–9 *Of this knowledge . . . revived for eternity*: This passage, which owes some of its language to the *Prognosticon futuri saeculi* of Julian of Toledo, is not in Ælfric's sources. He is apparently concerned with the problem of what will happen to those who are still living when the day of judgment comes. His concern with the cleansing fires and the aerial judgment, both of which were discussed by Bede in *De temporum ratione* 70, suggests that the physics of doomsday was as puzzlingly complex as the theology.

8   *the Lord himself . . . with these words*: 1 Thessalonians 4:16–18.
       The Lord will . . . to the high heavens: Matthew 24:31.

10   *Then there will be a new heaven and a new earth*: Revelation 21:1.
       Then the sun will be . . . of the sun: From Isaiah 30:26.

11   *God will come clearly . . . a mighty storm*: Psalms 49(50):3.
       The great day . . . and of outcry: Zephaniah 1:14–16.

12   *turn from evil and do good*: Psalms 36(37):27.

Bibliography

Editions and Translations

Clemoes, Peter, ed. *Ælfric's Catholic Homilies: The First Series, Text.* EETS s.s. 17. Oxford, 1997.

Eliason, Norman, and Peter Clemoes, eds. *Ælfric's First Series of Catholic Homilies, British Museum Royal 7. C. xii, Fols. 4–218.* EEMF 13. Copenhagen, 1965.

Thorpe, Benjamin, ed. *The Sermones Catholici, or Homilies of Ælfric: In the Original Anglo-Saxon, with an English Version.* 2 vols. London, 1844–1846.

Wilcox, Jonathan, ed. *Ælfric's Prefaces.* Durham Medieval Texts 9. Durham, 1994.

Further Reading

Ælfric. *Ælfric's Catholic Homilies: The Second Series, Text.* Edited by Malcolm Godden. EETS s.s. 5. Oxford, 1979.

———. *Homilies of Ælfric: A Supplementary Collection.* Edited by John C. Pope. 2 vols. EETS o.s. 259 and 260. Oxford, 1967–1968.

———. *Old English Lives of Saints.* Edited by Mary Clayton and Juliet Mullins. 3 vols. Dumbarton Oaks Medieval Library 58, 59, 60. Cambridge, MA, 2019.

Clayton, Mary. "Homiliaries and Preaching in Anglo-Saxon England." *Peritia* 4 (1985): 207–42. Reprinted with corrections in *Old English Prose: Basic Readings,* edited by Paul Szarmach, 151–98. New York, 2000.

Clemoes, Peter. "The Chronology of Ælfric's Works." In *The Anglo-Saxons: Studies in Some Aspects of Their History and Culture Presented to Bruce Dickins,* edited by P. Clemoes, 212–47. London, 1959.

Gatch, Milton McC. *Preaching and Theology in Anglo-Saxon England: Ælfric and Wulfstan.* Toronto, 1977.

Godden, Malcolm. *Ælfric's Catholic Homilies: Introduction, Commentary, and Glossary.* EETS s.s. 18. Oxford, 2000.

Grundy, Lynne. *Books and Grace: Ælfric's Theology.* King's College Medieval Studies. London, 1991.

Hill, Joyce. "Authority and Intertextuality in the Works of Ælfric: The Sir Israel Gollancz Memorial Lecture for 2004." *Proceedings of the British Academy* 131 (2005): 157–81.

Kleist, Aaron J. *The Chronology and Canon of Ælfric of Eynsham.* Anglo-Saxon Studies 37. Cambridge, 2019.

——, ed., *The Old English Homily: Precedent, Practice, and Appropriation.* Studies in the Early Middle Ages 17. Turnhout, 2007.

Magennis, Hugh, and Mary Swan, eds. *A Companion to Ælfric.* Brill's Companions to the Christian Tradition 18. Leiden, 2009.

Szarmach, Paul E., and Bernard Huppé, eds. *The Old English Homily and Its Backgrounds.* Albany, 1978.

Tinti, Francesca, ed. *Pastoral Care in Late Anglo-Saxon England.* Woodbridge, 2005.

Index

Abigail, 32.7

Abraham (patriarch), 3.3, 6.2–4, 6.7,
    8.9, 8.14, 8.16, 13.16, 23.2, 23.5,
    31.11, 35.19, 36.13

Achaia (Greece), 38.14

Acts of the Apostles, 16.6, 22.3

Adam, 1.5–13, 1.22, 7.12, 7.14–15, 9.11,
    10.3, 11.13, 14.16, 15.12, 16.11, 18.9,
    18.11, 20.16, 21.9, 24.3, 34.17

Adriatic Sea, 34.1

Aegeus (judge), 38.14–20, 38.22

Ælfheah (bishop of Winchester),
    0.5

Æthelmær (ealdorman), 0.5

Æthelred (king of England), 0.5

Æthelweard (ealdorman), 0.11

Æthelwold (bishop of Win-
    chester), 0.1, 0.5

Agapitus (deacon), 29.1, 29.4

Agrippa (officer of Nero), 26.22

Agrippina, 26.16

Alexander (bishop), 20.17

Alexander (brother-in-law of King
    Herod), 5.12

Alexandria (Egypt), 32.10

Alfred (king of England), 0.5

Amos (prophet), 22.12

Ananias (disciple), 22.6, 27.15

Ananias (friend of Paul), 8.7, 27.3,
    27.7

Andrew (apostle), 12.2, 12.4, 21.3,
    21.20, 35.10, 38.2, 38.6–7, 38.13–22

angel(s), 1.1–3, 2.3, 2.10–13, 4.6, 4.8,
    5.13, 6.5, 7.5, 7.11, 11.3, 11.6, 11.10–
    11, 15.3, 15.7–8, 16.6, 16.13, 18.6–7,
    21.3, 21.8–9, 22.1, 23.5, 24.4, 24.6–
    8, 24.11, 24.13, 26.20, 30.6, 30.8,
    31.11–12, 34.16–17, 36.1–3, 36.7–8,
    37.8, 37.11, 37.15, 37.17, 38.11, 40.5

Anna, 9.13–14

Antichrist, 0.7–9, 21.16, 25.11

Antipater (son of King Herod), 5.12

Apocalypse, 4.2

Arabia, 32.4

Archelaus (son of King Herod),
    5.13, 32.4

Arethe (king of Arabia), 32.4

Aristomedus, 4.10

Arius (heretic), 20.17

Arphaxad (son of Shem), 1.18

Asia, 4.8, 21.20, 26.11

Assyria, 37.11–12

Astaroth (demon), 31.1–2
astrologers (Magi), 5.2–8, 7.2–7, 7.9,
    7.16, 7.19
Astryges (king), 31.13–14, 35.10
Atticus (follower of Graton), 4.4–7
Aufidianus, 37.7
Augustine of Hippo, 0.1, 3.5, 18.6,
    31.20, 32.13, 36.13, 36.23
Augustus (emperor), 2.6
Azariah, 37.13

Babel, 22.8
Babylon, 37.15; Babylonians, 37.14
Baldath (demon), 31.14
Barnabas (friend of Paul), 27.4–5
Bartholomew, 21.3, 21.20, 31.1–5,
    31.8–11, 31.13–14
Basil (bishop), 30.14–15
Bede, 0.1, 6.10, 26.3, 33.3
Bel (god), 37.14
Benedict, 6.10
Beneventans, 34.4
Berith (demon), 31.2
Bethlehem, 2.2, 2.4, 2.8, 2.14, 2.16–
    17, 5.2, 5.4, 7.2
Bethphage, 14.1
Bithynia (Turkey), 26.11

Caesarea Philippi, 26.2–3
Campania (Italy), 34.1
Caparnaum, 8.9
Cappodocia (Turkey), 26.11, 30.14
Catacombs (Rome), 26.26
centurion, 8.9–10, 8.12–13, 8.18
Cerne Abbas (Dorset), 0.5
Chaldea, 37.13
Chrysaurius (nobleman), 28.14

Clement (pope and martyr), 37.2–9
Cletus (pope), 37.2
Cornelius, 37.8
Cyrilla (daughter of Decius), 29.15
Cyrus (king), 37.14–15

Damascus, 27.2
Daniel (prophet), 24.11, 32.12, 34.17,
    37.14–15
David (king of Israel), 2.2–3, 2.11,
    3.3, 8.16, 10.2, 10.4, 13.4, 13.8,
    14.3, 14.12–13, 22.4, 22.12, 25.12,
    32.7, 36.13, 37.12, 40.11
Decius (emperor), 29.1, 29.4–5,
    29.7–14
Delilah, 32.12
devils/demons, 1.2, 1.20, 4.6, 6.11,
    7.9, 7.11, 10.5, 21.10, 21.12, 22.6,
    24.6, 26.21, 27.13, 28.9, 28.14, 31.1,
    31.3–4, 31.6–9, 31.11–13, 36.2. See
    also Satan
Dionysius (martyr), 37.3
Dionysius (pope), 29.15
Domitian (emperor), 4.2, 37.18
dove(s), 7.4, 22.9, 22.11–12, 26.5,
    28.6, 28.11–12, 30.9, 38.12. See also
    turtledove(s)
Drusiana (widow), 4.3, 4.6

Eber (son of Salah), 1.18
Edessa (Turkey), 32.10
Egeas, 35.10
Egypt, 5.4, 5.13, 22.1, 36.8;
    Egyptian(s), 6.9, 22.1, 22.8
Elijah (prophet), 11.15, 21.16–18,
    25.1, 25.11, 26.2, 26.4
Elisha (prophet), 27.15–16

Elizabeth, 13.4, 13.12, 25.1–2

Enoch, 21.16–18

Ephesus, 4.3

Esau (brother of Jacob), 7.10

Ethiopia, 21.20; Ethiopian(s), 31.1, 31.12

Eugenius (follower of Graton), 4.4–7

Euphrates, 30.16

Eustochium, 30.1

Eve, 1.7, 1.10, 1.22, 7.12, 7.15, 13.5, 14.16, 15.12, 30.11

Ezekiel (prophet), 0.9, 13.3, 17.6–7, 35.12

Felicissimus (deacon), 29.1, 29.4

Franks, 37.3

Gabriel (archangel), 1.19, 13.1, 13.4–5, 13.7–12, 25.1, 25.5, 30.3–4, 31.5

Galatia (Anatolia), 26.11

Galilee, 2.2, 5.13, 13.4, 15.3, 15.9, 21.3, 22.4

Galilee, Sea of, 12.1–2, 38.2

Gargano (mountain), 34.1, 34.5, 34.18

Garganus, 34.1

Gaza, 15.12

Gehazi (servant of Elisha), 27.15, 27.16

Graton (philosopher), 4.4

Greek (language), 30.1

Greeks (people), 6.9, 22.8, 26.26, 34.17

Gregory (pope), 0.1, 15.6, 15.11, 16.5, 21.11, 23.3, 23.11, 24.3, 24.10, 28.3, 28.7, 28.14, 35.3, 35.17, 40.3

Habbakuk (prophet), 37.15

Ham (son of Noah), 1.14

Hananiah, 37.13

Haymo, 0.1, 8.3, 34.11

Hebrew (language), 30.1

Hebrews (people), 1.18, 6.9–10, 22.8, 34.17–18. See also Israel; Jewish people

Herod (king of Judea), 5.1–8, 5.11–13, 7.2, 7.6, 7.9, 7.19, 31.15, 32.4

Herod (son of Herod), 32.2, 32.4, 32.6–9, 32.13, 35.10, 37.17

Herodias (wife of King Herod), 32.2, 32.4, 32.10, 32.12

Hezekiah (king), 31.19, 37.11–12

Hilarius (saint), 21.12

Hippolytus (servant of Decius), 29.5–8, 29.12–14

Illyricum, 26.19

India, 21.20, 31.1–2

Isaac (patriarch), 6.2, 7.10, 8.14, 31.11, 35.19

Isaiah (prophet), 0.9, 6.7, 8.5, 13.3, 14.3, 25.4, 25.15, 31.19, 37.12, 38.12

Israel (nation/people), 5.13, 6.3, 8.9, 8.13, 13.8, 13.13, 13.16, 14.3, 15.11, 22.1, 25.1, 25.2, 25.10, 27.9, 27.11, 27.12, 37.12. See also Hebrews; Jewish people; Judah

Italy, 26.11

Jacob (patriarch), 5.10, 7.10, 8.14, 13.4, 13.8, 31.11, 35.19, 36.13

James the Just (apostle), 21.3, 21.12, 22.7, 28.3, 36.22

James the Less (apostle), 21.3, 28.3, 35.10, 38.2, 38.13

Japeth (son of Noah), 1.14

Jehosaphat (valley), 30.4

Jeremiah (prophet), 5.4, 26.2, 26.4

Jericho, 10.2, 10.4

Jerome, 0.1, 11.9, 26.24, 30.1

Jerusalem, 10.2, 14.2–3, 14.8, 20.15, 21.2–3, 22.3, 26.19, 27.2, 27.4, 28.2, 28.4, 32.9, 37.11, 38.9

Jewish people, 1.21, 3.2, 3.4–5, 3.7, 5.12–13, 7.2, 7.5, 7.7–8, 8.16, 12.7, 13.6, 14.4–5, 14.14–17, 15.11, 15.13, 16.2, 16.8, 20.19, 20.20, 21.7, 22.12, 24.2–3, 27.6–7, 30.7, 32.4–5, 36.13, 37.2, 40.8. See also Hebrews; Israel; Judah

Jezebel, 32.12

Job, 31.17, 35.15

Joel (prophet), 22.4, 25.4

John (evangelist), 2.13, 3.9, 4.1–12, 8.11, 11.10, 14.3, 16.4, 16.8, 21.3, 21.12, 21.20, 25.12, 30.3–4, 35.13, 36.1, 37.18, 38.2, 38.13, 40.10

John the Baptist, 9.14, 13.12, 21.2, 23.3, 25.1–7, 25.9–11, 25.13, 25.15, 25.17–18, 26.2, 26.4, 32.2–3, 32.5, 32.8–10, 32.12–13, 34.6, 36.3

Jonah (prophet), 18.3, 32.12

Jordan (river), 5.11, 28.3

Joseph (foster father of Jesus), 2.2, 2.4, 2.15, 5.4, 5.13, 9.11, 9.15, 13.4, 13.6

Joseph of Arimathea, 14.16

Josephus, 32.13

Joshua, 2.13

Judah (Israel), 2.8, 25.12, 37.15. See also Hebrews; Israel; Jewish people

Judas (apostle), 21.3

Judas (betrayer of Jesus), 1.21, 21.15, 27.15

Judea, 5.4, 7.2, 7.6–7, 15.4, 17.8, 21.20

Julian (emperor), 30.14–16

Justin (priest), 29.13, 29.15

lamb(s), 9.7–8, 22.1–2, 25.12, 27.7, 37.5, 38.14

Latin (language), 30.1–2

Lawrence (martyr), 29.2–3, 29.5–16

Lazarus (brother of Martha and Mary), 14.3, 16.9, 33.7, 33.9, 33.11

Lazarus (poor leper), 23.2, 23.4–5, 23.7, 23.9–10

lepers, 8.2, 8.4–5, 8.7–8, 23.2, 23.11–12, 27.15–16, 32.5

Libanius (officer), 30.16

Linus (pope), 37.2

Livia (imperial consort), 26.16

Lot, 2.13

Lucillus (blind Roman), 29.5

Luke (evangelist), 2.1, 4.8, 6.1, 21.2, 21.10, 22.3, 25.1, 32.5, 40.2

Lycaonia (Turkey), 23.11

Machaerus, 32.5

Magi. See astrologers

Mamertine prison (Rome), 29.1

Mamertus (bishop), 18.2

Mark (evangelist), 4.8, 21.10, 21.19, 32.1

Mars, temple of, 29.1, 29.4

Martha (sister of Lazarus), 8.14, 33.7

Martyrius (monk), 23.11

Mary (mother of James the Less), 15.3

Mary (mother of Jesus), 1.19, 2.2, 2.4–5, 2.9, 2.15–16, 4.1, 4.8, 5.3, 7.3, 7.16, 9.1, 9.3, 9.5, 9.7, 9.11–12, 9.15, 13.3–7, 13.9–13, 13.16–17, 14.13, 15.3, 16.5, 19.3, 20.12, 21.3, 25.5–7, 25.9, 30.1–18, 31.5, 34.6, 36.8

Mary (sister of Lazarus), 8.14, 33.7

Mary Magdalene, 15.1, 15.3

Matthew (evangelist), 4.8, 5.1, 7.2, 8.2, 8.9, 15.10, 21.3, 21.20, 22.12, 26.1, 36.12, 40.4, 40.8

Maximus (bishop of Ostia), 29.15

Maximus (son of Chrysaurius), 28.14

Medes (people), 31.1

Mercurius (saint), 30.15

Micah (prophet), 5.2, 7.2

Michael (archangel), 34.1–7, 34.17, 34.18

Mishael, 37.13

Moses, 2.15, 3.2–3, 3.7, 6.3, 6.9, 8.2–3, 9.2, 11.15, 12.7, 22.1–2, 23.2, 23.9, 24.8, 34.17, 35.7

Naaman, 27.15–16

Nabal, 32.7

Naboth, 32.12

Naim, 33.2–3

Nazareth, 2.2, 5.13, 9.15, 13.4

Neapolitans, 34.4–5

Nebuchadnezzar, 37.13

Nero (emperor), 4.2, 26.15, 26.17–20, 26.22, 26.25, 35.10

Nerva (emperor), 4.2

Nicanor (deacon), 3.1

Nicodemus, 14.16

Nicolas (deacon), 3.1

Ninevah, 18.3–4, 37.12

Noah, 1.14–15, 6.2, 22.8, 35.19

Octavian (emperor), 2.2, 2.6

Olives, Mount of, 14.3, 21.2, 30.5

Ostia (Italy), 29.15

ox(en), 2.16, 27.6, 28.6, 28.11, 35.2, 35.6–8, 37.14, 38.14

Parmenas (deacon), 3.1

Patmos (island), 4.2

Paul, 0.9, 3.8–11, 6.7, 6.12, 7.5, 8.7–8, 9.13–14, 13.4, 13.16, 14.13, 16.12, 17.3, 18.12–13, 21.20, 22.11–12, 26.6, 26.15–16, 26.19, 26.21–22, 26.24, 27.1, 27.4–7, 31.18, 32.6, 32.11, 34.13, 35.4, 35.10, 35.12, 37.3, 37.19, 39.3, 40.8. See also Saul

Paula (mother of Eustochium), 30.1

Pergamon (Turkey), 4.5

Persian(s), 34.17

Peter (apostle), 6.7, 10.11, 12.2, 15.5, 17.3, 21.3, 21.20, 22.4, 22.6, 22.12, 26.2–6, 26.8–19, 26.21–24, 27.9–11, 34.6, 34.11–12, 34.16, 35.10, 37.2–3, 37.17, 38.2, 38.6–7, 38.13

Pharaoh, 22.1, 24.8

Pharisees, 24.2

Philip (apostle), 12.2, 12.4, 12.9, 21.3

Philip (deacon), 3.1

Philip (tetrarch), 26.3, 32.2, 32.4

Philistines, 15.12

Phoebus, 37.8

pigeon(s), 9.7–9

Pilate (governor), 15.2, 32.4

Polymius (king), 31.4–5, 31.7, 31.10, 31.13–14

Prochorus (deacon), 3.1

Quiriaca (widow), 29.3, 29.12

Quirinus (governor), 2.2, 2.7

Rabshakeh (general), 37.11

Rachel, 5.4, 5.10

Raphael (angel), 34.16

Rebekah (wife of Isaac), 7.10

Red Sea, 3.3, 22.1, 22.2

Revelation. See Apocalypse

Romanus (soldier), 29.8–9

Rome (city), 5.5, 20.15, 26.11, 26.14–16, 29.1, 38.4; emperor, 2.2, 5.5; empire, 2.6; episcopal see, 29.15; kingdom of, 4.2; Roman(s), 6.9, 22.8, 26.26, 28.3–4, 28.6, 29.8, 29.10, 37.2, 37.4, 38.14, 39.3

Sabellius (heretic), 20.18

Salah (son of Arphaxad), 1.18

Sallust, house of, 29.9

Salome (sister of King Herod), 5.12

Samaritans, 32.7

Samson, 15.12, 32.12

Sapphira (wife of the disciple Ananias), 22.6, 27.15

Saracens, 28.4

Sarah (wife of Abraham), 6.2–3, 6.7

Satan, 11.3, 11.9; the devil, 1.2, 1.4, 1.9–12, 1.21–23, 7.12, 7.14, 7.19, 9.5, 11.3–9, 11.11–14, 13.2, 13.5, 14.4–5, 14.9–10, 14.14–16, 17.4–5, 18.9, 19.3–4, 19.10–11, 19.14, 22.6, 23.12, 26.12, 31.6, 31.8, 31.17, 32.8, 38.13, 39.5, 40.9. *See also* devils/ demons

Saul (later Paul), 3.4, 3.8, 27.2–3, 27.6–7. *See* Paul

scorpion, 18.5, 18.8–10

Scythia, 21.20

Sebaste (city), 32.9

Sennacherib (king), 37.11–12

Seustius, 31.4

sheep, 17.2–3, 17.5–8, 24.2–4, 27.7, 28.6, 28.11

Shem (son of Noah), 1.14, 1.18

Sigeric (archbishop of Canterbury), 0.1, 0.3

Simeon (bishop), 22.7

Simeon (priest), 9.3, 9.5, 9.10–13

Simon (apostle), 21.3

Simon (later Peter). *See* Peter

Simon (sorcerer), 26.11–15, 26.17–18, 26.20–22

Sinai (mountain), 22.1

Sion, 14.8, 30.5

Siponto (Italy), 34.1

Sixtus (pope), 29.1–2, 29.4, 29.15

Smaragdus, 0.1

Socrates, 27.10

Solomon (king), 3.3, 7.18, 32.12, 35.4, 39.6

Spain, 29.10, 37.3

Stacteus, 4.6, 4.7

Stephen (protomartyr), 3.1–6, 3.8, 3.11–12, 21.19, 27.1, 28.3

Syria, 27.15

Theophilus, 30.13

Thomas (apostle), 16.3, 16.10, 21.3

Tiberius (emperor), 25.4, 26.3, 40.4; Tiberian palace, 29.11

Timothy (deacon), 3.1

Titus (son of Vespasian), 28.4

Tobias, 34.16

Trajan (emperor), 37.3, 37.7

Trinity, 1.1, 8.18, 9.15, 13.6, 13.11, 15.13, 18.6, 20.4–5, 20.10–12, 20.16, 20.20, 22.13, 22.15, 26.4, 29.5, 33.11–12, 34.6

Tryphonia (wife of Decius), 29.15

turtledove(s), 9.7–9. *See also* dove(s)

Valeria (Italy), 28.14

Valerianus (reeve of Decius), 29.4–5, 29.7, 29.13–14

Vespasian (emperor), 28.4

Vienne (France), 18.2

Vitae patrum, 36.7

wolf, 2.10, 6.11, 17.2, 17.4–6, 18.2, 26.14, 26.25, 27.7, 35.10

Zacchaeus, 8.16, 38.8

Zebedee, 38.2

Zechariah, 9.14, 13.12, 25.1–2, 25.5, 25.8

Zephaniah (prophet), 40.11